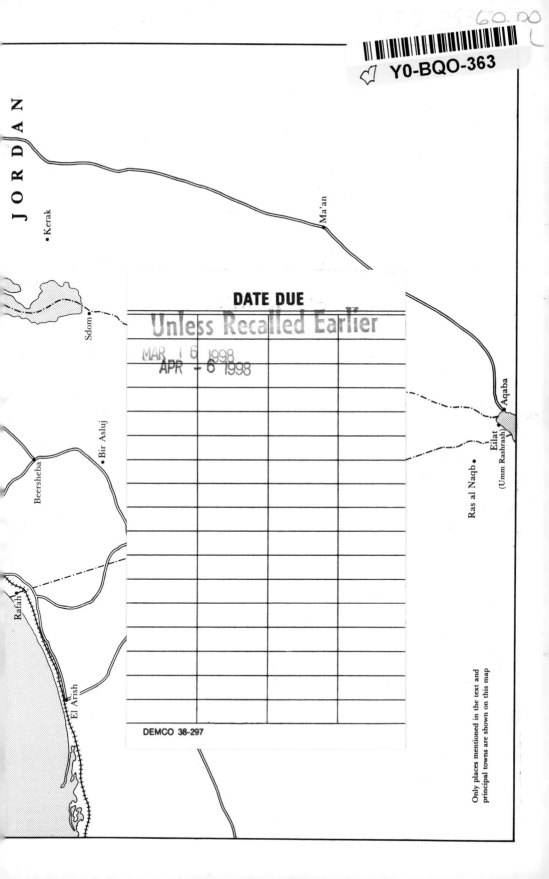

J O R D A N

Kerak

Ma'an

Sdom

Beersheba

Bir Asluj

Rafah

El Arish

Ras al Naqb

Eilat
(Umm Rashrash)

Aqaba

Only places mentioned in the text and
principal towns are shown on this map

COLLUSION ACROSS THE JORDAN

COLLUSION ACROSS THE JORDAN

*King Abdullah,
the Zionist Movement, and the
Partition of Palestine*

AVI SHLAIM

NEW YORK
COLUMBIA UNIVERSITY PRESS
1988

Library of Congress Cataloging in Publication Data
Shlaim, Avi.
*Collusion across the Jordan: King Abdullah, the Zionist movement,
and the partition of Palestine / Avi Shlaim.*
p.   cm.
Bibliography: p.
Includes index.
ISBN 0–231–66838–7
*1. Israel—Foreign relations—Jordan.   2. Jordan—Foreign
relations—Israel.   3. Abdallāh, King of Jordan, 1882–1951.
4. Palestine—History—Partition, 1947.   I. Title.*
DS119.8.J67S55   1988   327.569405695—dc19   87–32920

Printed in Great Britain

To Gwyn

ACKNOWLEDGEMENTS

Photographs appearing on the jacket of this book are of David Ben-Gurion and King Abdullah of Jordan. The photograph of King Abdullah first appeared in *O Jerusalem* by Larry Collins and Dominique Lapierre (Pocket Books, 1972). Every effort has been made to trace the copyright owners of these two photographs, but with no success. If notified, the author would be pleased to make acknowledgement in any future editions.

The author gratefully acknowledges permission to use previously published material in the preparation of maps for this volume, as follows: The base used in compiling the general map of Palestine is from a volume published by the Israel State Archives and Central Zionist Archives, *Political and Diplomatic Documents, December 1947–May 1948* (Jerusalem, 1979). Maps 1, 3, and 15 are reproduced with permission from Wm. Roger Louis and Robert W. Stookey (eds.), *The End of the Palestine Mandate* (London: I. B. Tauris, 1986). Map 2 is taken from the Peel Commission report. Map 4 has been redrawn on the basis of Meir Pail's, 'The Problem of Arab Sovereignty in Palestine, 1947–1949' (Heb.), *Zionism* 3 (1973). Maps 5, 6, 7, 8, 9, 11, 13, and 14 are based on maps which originally appeared in Sir John Bagot Glubb's *A Soldier with the Arabs* (London: Hodder and Stoughton, 1957). Maps 10 and 12 are reproduced with permission from the Israel State Archives' *Documents on the Foreign Policy of Israel*, vol. iii, *Armistice Negotiations with the Arab States, December 1948–July 1949* (Jerusalem, 1983).

PREFACE

This book is the result of a decade of grappling with the complexities of the Arab–Israeli conflict. In 1980 I embarked on a study of domestic politics and the management of national security in Israel. But several years of burrowing in British, American, and Israeli archives dampened my enthusiasm for 'scientific' explanations of Israel's foreign policy and re-directed my attention to the historical roots of the Arab–Israeli conflict. Accordingly, I planned a historical study of Israel and the Arab world in the period 1948 to 1956, from the Palestine War to the Suez War. But this again proved too vast a subject to treat adequately in one volume, so I decided to concentrate on Israeli–Jordanian relations up to King Abdullah's assassination in July 1951. My intention was to write an extended essay of about a hundred pages. The present volume is the actual outcome. It briefly traces the emergence and development of the special relationship between the amir of Transjordan and the Zionist movement but focuses mainly on the late 1940s when Palestine was partitioned and the State of Israel was created.

A detailed study of Hashemite–Zionist relations during this critical period became possible following the release of the official documents for research in British, American, and Israeli archives. This is an extremely valuable addition to the massive secondary literature available on the Arab–Israeli conflict in general as well as the diaries, private papers, and published memoirs of individuals who participated in the dramatic events of this period. Israel, which has adopted the British thirty-year rule for the declassification of official documents, offers the richest new sources. The Central Zionist Archives are immensely useful on the contacts with Abdullah in the period prior to independence, and the relevant Foreign Ministry papers and reports on most of the post-independence meetings with Abdullah and his emissaries are available in the Israel State Archives. Ben-Gurion's diary is likewise now accessible in the Ben-Gurion Archive in Sde Boker, while the Labour Party Archive in Kfar Saba contains protocols of relevant debates on Israel's Arab policy. Considerable use is also made in this study of interviews with Israeli politicians, officials, soldiers and intelligence operators who were involved in one way or another in the conduct of relations with Jordan. Details, little-known facts, insights, and reflections were culled from all these sources, but it was undoubtedly the State Archives that provided the most crucial documentary record for uncovering the clandestine exchanges that took place between the Hashemite and the Zionist sides prior to the 1948 Arab–Israeli war, during the war, in the course of the armistice talks, and during the protracted negotiations that culminated in the initialling of a formal Jordanian–Israeli peace treaty.

The writing of history is a perpetual dialogue between the historian and his sources. It should therefore come as no surprise that new sources lead to new conclusions, especially when these sources are as rich and revealing as those now open to researchers in Israeli archives. My own research has steered me towards a novel and no doubt controversial interpretation of the events surrounding the partition of Palestine. So let it be stated at the outset that this is a revisionist history which differs very sharply, and on many important points, from the pro-Zionist as well as the pro-Arab histories on this subject. I did not set out with the intention of writing a revisionist history. It was the official documents I came across in the various archives that led me to explore the historical roots of the Palestine question, drew my attention to the role of Transjordan, and led me to re-examine some of my own assumptions as well as the claims of previous historians.

It is striking to observe how great is the contrast between accounts of this period written without access to the official documents and an account such as this one, based on documentary evidence. One explanation is that much of the existing literature was written by Zionists and consciously or unconsciously incorporates the numerous legends that have come to surround the end of the Palestine mandate and the birth of the State of Israel. I have not come forward to redress the balance in favour of the Arabs and thus substitute one kind of partisanship for another, nor do I particularly relish the slaughtering of sacred cows. But the opportunity now exists to submit the claims of all the protagonists in the Palestine dispute to serious historical scrutiny and to discard those notions which, however deeply cherished, cannot stand up to such scrutiny.

At various stages on the long journey that ended with the publication of this book I have received generous support from institutions and individuals which it is my pleasure to acknowledge. My research was initiated with the help of a grant from the Social Science Research Council, now the Economic and Social Research Council. Some of the preparatory work was carried out while I was a Fellow at the Woodrow Wilson International Center for Scholars in Washington DC in 1980–1. A grant from the Ford Foundation enabled me to spend the 1981–2 academic year in Israel gathering primary data. On a subsequent visit, in the summer of 1983, the Harry S. Truman Institute for the

Advancement of Peace of the Hebrew University of Jerusalem provided both a home and excellent research facilities. To all these bodies I am immensely grateful.

Librarians and archivists in the following institutions facilitated access to a large body of primary and secondary sources: The University of Reading; the Middle East Centre of St Antony's College, Oxford; the Library and Press Library of the Royal Institute of International Affairs; the Public Record Office in London; the Wilson Centre; the Library of Congress; the National Archives in Washington DC; the David Ben-Gurion Archive in Sde Boker; the IDF Archive in Givatayim; the Labour Party Archive in Kfar Saba; the Central Zionist Archives in Jerusalem; and the Israel State Archives in Jerusalem. I was particularly fortunate to have the guidance and help of Yehoshua Freundlich while working at the State Archives.

A number of Israeli friends were extremely generous in sharing with me their own ideas and research materials, and in helping me to tap various additional sources of information. They include Dov Tsamir (who deserves special thanks for opening so many doors to the Israeli establishment despite his scepticism about some of my views), Varda Schiffer, Mordechai Bar-On, Yehoshafat Harkabi, Benjamin Geist, Edy Kaufman, Dan Horowitz, Ilan Pappé, Uri Bar-Joseph, and Yoram Nimrod. Many other individuals in Israel and elsewhere gave unselfishly of their time; some are mentioned by name in the Bibliography, in the list of persons interviewed, but I should like to extend my thanks to all of them.

All the writing was done while I was teaching in the Politics Department at the University of Reading—a most congenial environment for both teaching and research. I am grateful to all my former colleagues, and especially to Peter Campbell, Barry Holden, Roy Gregory, and Keith Sainsbury, for all their encouragement and support. Two of my research students at Reading rendered invaluable assistance: Mouayad al-Windawi helped with the Arabic sources and put at my disposal his entire collection of Iraqi and British documents; Anne Deighton read the complete manuscript with great care and made many constructive suggestions. I also wish to record my appreciation to Marjorie McNamara, Pamela Tyler, and Sheila Baxter who typed what must have looked like an interminable manuscript with exemplary patience, skill, and good cheer.

My thanks also go to the staff at the Oxford University Press: to Henry Hardy for his wise editorial direction and co-operation and understanding at all stages; to Nina Curtis for being so helpful in so many different ways; and to Connie Wilsack for the speed and meticulous attention with which she edited the massive typescript.

Finally I wish to thank my daughter Tamar, who was conceived at about the same time as this book and grew up with it, for the lively interest she has shown in the main characters, for her suggestion that we publish the story together as a children's book, and for her delightful company. My wife Gwyn, as always, was the source of many good ideas and gave me continuous encouragement in my scholarly meanderings round the Palestine tragedy. It is to her that this book is warmly dedicated.

All the above institutions and individuals deserve a share of the credit for this book, if any credit is due. For the errors, faults, and shortcomings that remain, I alone am responsible.

A.S.

Oxford
September 1987

CONTENTS

LIST OF APPENDICES

MAPS AND FIGURE

Maps

Figure

ABBREVIATIONS

AHC	Arab Higher Committee
BMEO	British Middle East Office
CAB	Cabinet Papers
CZA	Central Zionist Archives
DFPI	*Documents on the Foreign Policy of Israel*
Documents	Israel State Archives and Central Zionist Archives, *Political and Diplomatic Documents, December 1947–May 1948* (Jerusalem, 1979)
FRUS	*Foreign Relations of the United States* (Washington, DC: Government Printing Office, various years)
IDF	Israel Defence Forces
ISA	Israel State Archives
MAC	Mixed Armistice Commission
NA	National Archives, Washington
PCC	Palestine Conciliation Commission
PRO	Public Records Office
UNTSO	United Nations Truce Supervisory Organization

To study history one must know in advance that one is attempting something fundamentally impossible, yet necessary and highly important. To study history means submitting to chaos and nevertheless retaining faith in order and meaning. It is a very serious task, young man, and possibly a tragic one.

Hermann Hesse, *Magister Ludi*

INTRODUCTION

Seeds of conflict

This book tells the story of the unusual and highly secret relationship between Abdullah, the Hashemite ruler of Jordan, and the Zionist movement. Spanning three eventful decades, from the appointment of Abdullah as amir of Transjordan in 1921 to his assassination in 1951, it focuses in particular on the clandestine diplomacy that led to the partition of Palestine between the two sides and left the Palestine Arabs without a homeland. The central thesis is that in 1947 an explicit agreement was reached between the Hashemites and the Zionists on the carving up of Palestine following the termination of the British mandate, and that this agreement laid the foundation for mutual restraint during 1948 and for continuing collaboration in the aftermath of war. A subsidiary thesis is that, by secretly endorsing Abdullah's plan to enlarge his kingdom, Britian became an accomplice in the Hashemite–Zionist collusion to frustrate the United Nations partition resolution of 29 November 1947 and to prevent the establishment of a Palestinian Arab state.

The relationship between the Hashemites and the Zionists is only one thread in the complex web that makes up the Arab–Israeli conflict but its importance and significance cannot be overestimated. For while the relations between Arabs and Jews in Palestine over the last century have been characterized by conflict, the relations between the Hashemites and the Jews have been characterized by a much higher degree of mutual understanding and even support, by collaboration as well as conflict, by compromise no less than confrontation. The term 'alliance' is too strong to describe this relationship because of its informality and non-committal character, because of the ambiguities pervading it, and because of the limits and constraints that impeded its development. The term 'unholy alliance' is superficially attractive because this relationship did involve ideological deviation from the precepts of pan-Arabism, a breach of the Arab consensus to keep Palestine Arab, and, worst of all, collaboration with the Zionist enemy. But once again this term would be misleading because it focuses only on one aspect of Hashemite–Zionist relations and ignores the other, describing only collaboration and not conflict. To convey the essence of this unusual relationship, with all its many facets and contradictions, 'adversary partnership' or 'tacit alliance' would be more appropriate.

However one chooses to describe the bilateral relationship between the Hashemites of Transjordan and the Zionist movement, it remains one of the most fascinating and vital strands in the generally tragic encounter between Arab and Jewish nationalism. While studies of the Arab–Israeli conflict are legion, this particular strand of it has received surprisingly little attention. The present book sets out to fill this gap. It is based on the conviction that no proper understanding of the Arab–Israeli conflict or of the fate of Palestine is possible without due regard being paid to the role of King Abdullah and to his illicit contacts and collaboration with the Zionist movement. A study of these contacts will also enrich our knowledge of Zionist strategy and tactics in relation to the Arabs.

From the outset Palestine lay at the heart of the Arab–Jewish confrontation. It was both the main prize and the principal battlefield in the unfolding conflict between the two national movements. One of the commonest distortions lies in presenting this conflict as a symmetrical one between two monolithic political groups and failing to allow for the diversity and divisions that make up the Arab side. By focusing on the role of King Abdullah it becomes possible to highlight the opposing interests and divergent attitudes that weakened the Arabs in the struggle against the Jews and played a major part in the eventual loss of Palestine. In short, a detailed historical reconstruction of the tacit partnership between King Abdullah and the Zionist movement is not just interesting in and of itself; it is also essential for the light it sheds on one of the most complex and protracted international conflicts of modern times.

Unlike most international conflicts, the conflict over Palestine has an easily identifiable starting point: the year 1897. In that year the first World Zionist Congress convened in Basle, Switzerland, on the initiative of Theodor Herzl, the visionary of the Jewish state. The Congress declared as its objective the establishment of a Jewish national home in Palestine and set up the World Zionist Organization with Herzl as its president to work for the realization of the objective which was simply a euphemism for a Jewish state. At the time of the Basle Congress, Palestine was under the control of the Ottoman Turks. It was inhabited by nearly half a million Arabs and some 50,000 Jews. The Arabs, who made up 90 per cent of the population, also owned 99 per cent of the land. But, in keeping with the spirit of the age of European imperialism, the Jews did not allow these local realities to stand in the way of their own national aspirations.

To the Arabs, on the other hand, the programme proclaimed in Basle for a Jewish state in Palestine seemed absurd and monstrously unjust. Walid Khalidi, the eminent Palestinian historian, has depicted it as the root of all evil: 'Behind the seemingly labyrinthine complexities of the so-called Arab–Israeli conflict and the baffling maze of claims and counter-claims', writes Khalidi, 'there lies a continuous and continuing dual process. On the one hand, Zionist determination to implement, consolidate and expand the Basle "vision", irrespective of the Arab character and patrimony in Palestine and its hinterland; on the other, a corresponding development of Arab resistance to Zionist encroachment and self-fulfilment at Arab expense. This is the essence of the Palestine tragedy. All else is derivative.'[1]

If the resolution of the World Zionist Congress in 1897 marked the beginning of the Arab–Israeli conflict, the Balfour Declaration of 1917 marks the first major watershed in the development of this conflict. Having encountered opposition from the Arab inhabitants of Palestine and a polite refusal from the Ottoman Turks, the Zionists turned to Britain to sponsor their project for a national home in Palestine. Their most persuasive spokesman in Britain was Dr Chaim Weizmann. His efforts were crowned with success when, on 2 November 1917, Foreign Secretary Arthur J. Balfour issued a statement which said:

His Majesty's Government view with favour the establishment in Palestine of a national home for the Jewish people, and will use their best endeavours to facilitate the achievement of this object, it being clearly understood that nothing shall be done which may prejudice the civil and religious rights of existing non-Jewish communities in Palestine, or the rights and political status enjoyed by the Jews in any other country.

The declaration was endorsed by Britain's allies at the San Remo conference of April 1920 and incorporated in the terms of the mandate over Palestine conferred upon Britain by the League of Nations on 24 July 1922 (see Map 1). This mandate recognized the 'historical connection of the Jewish people with Palestine' and called on Britain to assist in the establishment of a Jewish national home and to prepare the country for self-government while safeguarding the civil and religious rights of all the inhabitants of Palestine. At the time when the Balfour Declaration was issued, the Jewish population of Palestine numbered some 56,000 as against an Arab population of 600,000, or less than 10 per cent. Small wonder, therefore, that the declaration was regarded as a major victory for Zionist diplomacy. Arab nationalists condemned the declaration on the ground that Britain was promising the Jews a land that not only belonged to the Arabs by right but had also been promised to them by Britain herself in her effort to win them over to her side during the First World War.

---

[1] *From Haven to Conquest: Readings in Zionism and the Palestine Problem until 1948*, edited with an introduction by Walid Khalidi (Beirut: Institute for Palestine Studies, 1971), p. xxii.

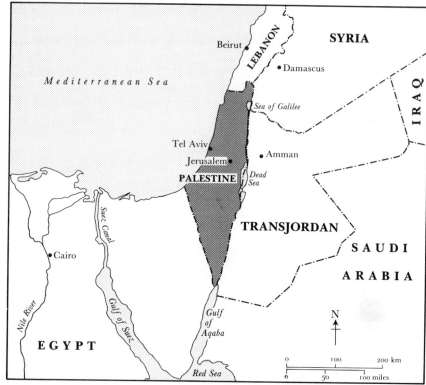

MAP I   Palestine: the regional setting under the British mandate (before May 1948)

The Arab case was clear and compelling. Palestine belonged to the people living in it, and the overwhelming majority were Arab. In language and culture as well as land ownership, the country had been Arab for centuries. Geographical proximity, historical ties, and religious affinity made Palestine an integral part of the Arab world. It was entitled to immediate independence. Jewish immigration and settlement could not take place without the consent of the country's Arab owners, and this consent was emphatically denied. Neither Britain nor the League of Nations had the right to promise a land that was not theirs so their promise was null and void.

The first stirrings of a national awakening among the politically minded urban middle class combined with the Islamic sentiments of the masses to fuel Palestinian Arab opposition to foreign domination and to Zionist encroachment. Visions of independence and pan-Arab union left no room for a Jewish Palestine. The possibility of coexistence and compromise were denied. If there were moderates among the

Palestinian Arab politicians, they were inhibited from giving public expression to their views; they did not command much popular following and they certainly failed to attain the highest positions of power and responsibility within their community. Resistance to the Balfour Declaration and to the Zionist enterprise was a cardinal tenet in the platforms of all the organizations and parties.

The Zionist counter-arguments—that the Jewish people had a right to the land that had been the cradle of the Jewish heritage; that they were entitled to reconstruct their national life on the land of their ancestors after nearly two thousand years of living in exile; that the rights of the Arab majority should be measured not in relation to the Jews already in the country but the whole Jewish people; that the economic development of the country would benefit both peoples; and that no Arab would be expelled as a result of the growth of the Jewish national home—all these claims fell on deaf ears.

The British mandate

With such a wide gulf separating the two local communities in Palestine, the British administration was bound to run into difficulties. Arab resistance to Zionism steadily escalated, with occasional outbursts of violence in 1920, 1921, and 1929, culminating in a full-scale Arab Revolt in 1936–9. During this period the Yishuv—the Jewish community in Palestine—began to organize itself more effectively behind the protective shield offered by the British, and the fledgling Jewish national home went from strength to strength. The foundations for self-government and self-defence had been laid with the establishment of the Jewish Agency in 1929, and important strides were made in forging political parties, a labour movement, new forms of settlement, a Hebrew education system, a national press, and so on. In the crucial field of numbers, however, the pace of growth fell far short of the Zionist leaders' expectations of a Jewish majority. From about 56,000 at the time of the Balfour Declaration, the Jewish population increased to an estimated 475,000 at the end of 1939, partly due to natural growth but largely due to immigration from Europe, especially after Hitler's rise to power in Germany. The Arab population during the same period increased from 600,000 to over a million as a result of a higher rate of natural growth. None the less, the Jewish population grew more than eightfold and, as a proportion of the total population, it grew from less than one-tenth to nearly one-half. By the end of 1939 the Jews owned about 5 per cent of the total land area of Palestine and about one-ninth of the cultivable land: over a quarter of a million cultivable acres, or twice the area owned by Jews in 1920.

The political life of the Palestinian Arabs under the mandate revolved round the land-owning and the clerical families. Two families in particular, the Husaynis and the Nashashibis, dominated the scene. The Husaynis gained the upper hand in 1922 with the appointment of the mufti of Jerusalem, Hajj Amin al-Husayni, to the presidency of the Supreme Muslim Council. The Muslim Council, like the Arab Executive set up in 1920, was torn by factional struggles between the nationalist followers of the Husayni clan and the opposition led by the Nashashibi clan. By the mid-1930s several distinct political parties emerged out of the factional splits and mergers. The Palestine Arab Party was dominated by Hajj Amin al-Husayni, though formally headed by his cousin, Jamal al-Husayni. The National Defence Party headed by Ragheb Nashashibi constituted the main opposition. Smaller groups included the *Istiqlal* or Independence Party led by Awni Abd al-Hadi and the Reform Party led by Dr Hussein Khalidi.

The Arab notables boycotted all the representative institutions proposed by the mandatory authorities. The programmes of the parties they formed all advocated the preservation of the Arab character of Palestine, resistance to the establishment of the Jewish national home and the improvement of the social, economic, and political conditions of the Arabs of Palestine. Though highly fragmented as a political community, the Palestine Arabs were united in their refusal to recognize the legality or authority of the British mandate and by their fear of Zionist intrusion.

Doubting that Jewish immigration flowed from a spontaneous desire to return to the Orient, the Palestine Arabs saw it as a Western bridgehead established under the spurious guise of international legality. They therefore tended to view Britain and the Zionist movement not as distinct enemies but as allies in a conspiracy to deprive them of their national patrimony. Even though the British commitment to a Jewish national home in Palestine did not necessarily imply support for eventual Jewish sovereignty, and even though the Zionists took some trouble to conceal that this was indeed their long-term goal, the Palestine Arabs were in no doubt about the nature and scale of the challenge they were facing. Accordingly, their opposition to the Zionist enterprise was deep, vociferous, and unequivocal.

The Arab Executive served as a forum for co-ordinating policy and disseminating propaganda against the Zionist and the mandatory regime. The Nashashibis were less extreme than their Husayni rivals in the public posture they adopted towards the Zionists and the British. But their moderation had its limits: they were more willing to negotiate over specific issues; they were not willing to sacrifice basic Arab interests. Moreover, although the Nashashibis had a very wide following in the country, Hajj Amin remained the dominant figure on the Arab Executive as well as becoming the chairman of the Arab Higher Committee formed in April 1936 to represent the six political parties then active in Palestine. But his ascendancy did not continue for much longer. In October 1937 the British authorities dismissed him from his position as the president of the Supreme Muslim Council for his part in inciting the Arab riots and rebellion against British rule.

The Council was disbanded, the Arab Higher Committee was outlawed, and Hajj Amin was banished into exile. Although Hajj Amin's power base was broken, he continued to exert his influence from abroad. In Iraq he was close to Rashid Ali al-Kilani and his circle of pro-Axis army officers, and after the collapse of Rashid Ali's revolt against British rule in 1941 Hajj Amin escaped to Germany where he spent the war collaborating with the Nazis, working to mobilize Muslim public opinion and recruit Muslim volunteers for the Nazi war effort.

In and out of the country, Hajj Amin had a decisive influence over the direction of the Palestine Arab community in its encounter with the British authorities and their Jewish protegés. Nationalist sentiment and religious fervour blended with his belief in the absolute moral justice of his own cause to produce a rigid and intransigent posture that was in no small part responsible for the disasters that befell the Arabs of Palestine. The view of the conflict between the Palestinian and Jewish national movements that he held and vigorously propagated might in today's jargon be called a zero-sum game, that is to say a game in which every gain by one party is necessarily at the expense of the other party. Historically, the emergence of the Palestinian national movement as a response and a reaction to the advent of Jewish nationalism was conducive to such a view. But it was Hajj Amin who more than any other individual moulded it into an ideology of total and unremitting opposition to Jewish aspirations in Palestine. This ideology, by denying the possibility of compromise or a *modus vivendi*, placed the Palestinian national movement on a collision course with the Jewish national movement and its backers. It was a high-risk strategy that ended in defeat because until the mid-1930s, the British prevented the Palestine Arabs from using their superior power to try and liquidate physically the Jewish national home, and subsequently the Jews became the stronger of the two local parties and were capable of looking after themselves.

If until the outbreak of the Arab Revolt in 1936 Britain could have reneged on her commitment to the Jewish national home but saw no reason to do so, thereafter she was tempted to retreat but her freedom of choice was considerably reduced. Spurred on by the Hitlerite persecution in Europe, the Zionists stepped up the pace of immigration to Palestine and expanded their capacity for self-defence. A policy reversal would not only have been difficult to justify on moral grounds but would have required as much force to implement as the suppression of the Arab Revolt. Britain was caught between her commitment to the Jews and her need to retain Arab goodwill in the struggle against the Axis powers. This dependence enabled the neighbouring Arab states to exert pressure on behalf of the Palestine Arabs. Having displayed a sympathetic and protective attitude to the Jews at the beginning of the mandate, and having gradually shifted towards a more evenhanded position, the British now came under growing pressure to subordinate their Palestine policy to their regional, European, and global strategic needs. Having had to adjudicate between rival moral and legal claims without making much headway, Britain now resorted to political expediency to safeguard her own interests.

The most expedient solution, whatever the moral rights and wrongs, was to partition Palestine into an Arab state, a Jewish state, and a British enclave, and this was the solution proposed by the Peel Commission in 1937. After reaching the conclusion that the mandate was no longer workable, the Peel Commission went on to recommend the partition of the country between the two warring communities. The Zionist leadership accepted the principle of partition and prepared for assiduous bargaining over the details. The Arab leadership, on the other hand, vehemently refused to consider partition and reasserted the Arab claim to the whole of Palestine. In February 1939 Britain convened a round-table conference in London to which Jewish, Palestinian, and Arab representatives were invited to discuss a solution to the Palestine dispute. The Arabs refused to sit down with the Jews and the British had to meet the two groups separately. No agreement was reached, and Britain reverted to rule by decree. A White Paper was issued in May 1939 that came close to reversing the Balfour Declaration by placing limits on Jewish immigration and Jewish land purchase and outlining a plan for an independent state of Palestine with an Arab majority after a transitional period of ten years. It was now the Jews' turn to embark on a course of resistance to British rule.

Jewish resistance to the policy of the White Paper took the form of illegal immigration and land purchases, supplemented towards the end of the Second World War by terrorist actions and physical harrassment of British personnel. After the war the British pursued a two-pronged strategy of cracking down on the Jewish terrorists while seeking a political solution, but after two years of abortive efforts the British government decided to hand over the task of finding a solution to the United Nations.

On 29 November 1947, the United Nations, like the Peel Commission before it, came out in favour of partition, thereby suggesting that the logic of partition had become inescapable. The Zionist leadership accepted both the logic and the plan, but once again the Arab leadership categorically denied the justice of partition and vehemently rejected the United Nations plan. To frustrate partition, the Palestine Arabs resorted to arms and won sufficiently impressive victories in the ensuing civil war as to make the Great Powers consider a retreat from partition in favour of a United Nations trusteeship over Palestine. But while the United Nations was deliberating, the Jews turned the tables on their opponents and gained control of most of the areas allocated to them by the United Nations partition plan. On 15 May 1948, the last day of the British mandate, the Jews proclaimed the establishment of their state, Israel. The armies of the neighbouring Arab states immediately crossed the borders of Palestine in another attempt to nullify the partition of Palestine by force. A clash between the Arab and Jewish communities over Palestine thus turned into a contest between the Arab states and the State of Israel. A new phase in the struggle for Palestine had begun.[2]

The British mandate during the three decades ending in 1948 thus had a profound effect on the development of the Palestinian and Jewish national movements and on the course and outcome of the conflict between them. Much of the complexity of this conflict derived from the fact that it was not a straightforward clash between two parties but a three-cornered contest involving two local communities and an outside power, with shifting roles and alignments and an endlessly fluctuating level of conflict and collaboration between them. In his history of Israel, Noah Lucas gives an admirably concise summary of the three distinct phases in this triangular conflict that corresponded to the three decades of the British mandate:

The first decade of the mandatory administration, in which the Jews were relatively weak, was characterized specifically by Arab–Jewish conflict which, after a lull following the riots of 1920 and 1921, erupted in a crescendo of violence in 1929. During this period an early step towards the modification of British policy was discernible in a growing tendency of the administration to interpret its function primarily as arbiter of Arab–Jewish conflict rather than as sponsor of Zionist aspirations. Hajj Amin had succeeded in driving a wedge between the British and the Zionists. The second decade of the regime, in which the Jews were stronger but still dependent on British protection, was marked by Arab–British conflict. A recurrence of violence in 1933 and a full-

---

[2] In the foregoing account of the final stages of the British mandate I have relied in particular on Nadav Safran, *From War to War: The Arab–Israeli Confrontation, 1948–1967* (Indianapolis: Pegasus, 1969), 21–8.

fledged rebellion in 1936 took a toll in Jewish life but were mainly aimed at British rule. As the Arab–Jewish conflict thus became overlaid by direct Arab–British struggle a disposition to appease Arab demands gradually swung the administration from the posture of arbiter to that of protector and finally sponsor of the Arab interest. However, this occurred only after the vigorous suppression of the Arab revolt and decimation of the Arab political leadership. The third and last decade of British rule, in which the Arabs were now relatively much weaker, was marked by Jewish–Arab and Jewish–British conflict and the collapse of British control. The conflict of the 'forties explicitly assumed the aspect of a struggle for the succession to British rule, all parties including the British having by then irrevocably abandoned the theory of the mandate and the national home. The Arabs had brought about the collapse of the national home policy, whereupon the Zionists proceeded to bring about the collapse of British rule.[3]

Zionism and the Arab question

When one looks at the behaviour of the two main protagonists during the period under discussion, an interesting pattern emerges. The Palestinian Arab leadership was inflexible both strategically and tactically: it wanted to keep Palestine in Arab hands and to turn it if possible into an independent and unitary Arab state, and it totally rejected the idea of a Jewish national home. The Zionist leadership, on the other hand, was inflexible strategically but flexible tactically: its aim from the very start was a Jewish state in Palestine but it tried to project an image of reasonableness and moderation and proposed numerous compromise plans for the settlement of the dispute with the Palestine Arabs. The methods it employed to achieve its end varied with changing historical circumstances and included not just flexible diplomacy but also bribery, deception, coercion, and physical force. During the half century that elapsed between the First Zionist Congress in Basle in 1897 and the establishment of the State of Israel, the emphasis gradually shifted from persuasion to coercion, from the peaceful to the violent end of the spectrum.

Notwithstanding its tactical flexibility, there is a sense therefore in which violence was implicit in Zionism from the outset. This is the theme of David Hirst's powerfully anti-Zionist book on the roots of violence in the Middle East. By quoting from the diaries of Theodor Herzl, Hirst tries to show that the prophet of Zionism foresaw that coercion and physical force were inevitable, that military power was an essential component of his strategy, that, ideally, he wanted the Zionists to acquire the land of their choice by armed conquest, but that

[3] Noah Lucas, *The Modern History of Israel* (London: Weidenfeld and Nicolson, 1974), 118.

he also contemplated more discreet and circumspect means for removing the native population and expropriating its land. The French
saying, 'Qui veut la fin, veut les moyens'—he who desires the end
desires the means—was cited by Herzl with approval. 'But in proposing such an end—a Jewish state in Palestine—and such means', argues
Hirst, 'he was proposing a great deception, and laying open his whole
movement to the subsequent charge that in any true historical perspective the Zionists were the original aggressors in the Middle East, the
real pioneers of violence, and that Arab violence, however cruel and
fanatical it might eventually become, was an inevitable reaction to
theirs.'[4]

Whether or not one accepts this contention that the Zionists alone
were responsible for the initiation of the cycle of violence in the Middle
East, there is no denying that their diplomacy was more subtle and
more supple than that of their opponents. Pre-independence Zionist
diplomacy was also more resourceful, more imaginative, and in many
ways more effective than post-independence Zionist diplomacy. Military capability is the key factor in accounting for this curious difference
in performance. In its formative years, the Zionist movement had to
compensate for its military impotence by mobilizing all its political and
intellectual resources and drawing on the traditional Jewish skills in
advocacy and persuasion to attain its goals. With the massive increase
in military power that accompanied the achievement of independence,
these skills were no longer at such a high premium. If diplomacy did not
yield the desired results, the State of Israel could always fall back on its
superior armed forces to protect its basic interests. In short, military
weakness stimulated diplomatic perseverance and ingenuity whereas
military power tended to downgrade the role of diplomacy as an
instrument of statecraft.

The leading diplomat of the Yishuv and the best exponent of its
diplomatic tradition of moderation was Moshe Sharett (formerly
Shertok) who was destined to become the first foreign minister of the
State of Israel. Born in Russia in 1894, he emigrated to Palestine with
his parents in 1906 and lived in an Arab village, becoming fluent in
Arabic, building up an impressive knowledge of Arab history, culture,
and politics, developing an empathy with the Arabs as a people that
was to remain with him for the rest of his life. Sharett studied law in
Turkey and served in the Turkish army during the First World War.
After a brief spell in Labour Zionist politics as a member of Ahdut
Haavodah, Sharett went to study at the London School of Economics
where he was also active in the Zionist Federation and fell under the

[4] David Hirst, *The Gun and the Olive Branch: The Roots of Violence in the Middle East* (London: Faber
and Faber, 1977), 18 f.

spell of the veteran Zionist leader, Dr Chaim Weizmann. In 1925 Sharett joined the editorial board of *Davar*, the daily newspaper of the Histadrut, a position he held until 1931 when he was appointed secretary of the Political Department of the Jewish Agency. One of his first assignments was to conduct the negotiations with Amir Abdullah on Jewish settlement in Transjordan. After the assassination of Dr Chaim Arlozoroff in 1933, Sharett was appointed head of the Political Department and quickly established himself as a spokesman for the Yishuv in relation to the British and the Arabs with whom he held numerous meetings in search for a peaceful solution to the Palestine problem.

Serving under Sharett in the Arab Section of the Political Department was a group of highly talented Jewish Arabists including Aharon Cohen, Eliahu Elath, Yaacov Shimoni, Reuven Shiloah, and Elias Sasson. Together they built up an apparatus for gathering information: channels of communication and an astonishingly diversified network of contacts not only with the Arabs of Palestine but with the political leaders of the neighbouring Arab states. These contacts were not confined to ministers, prime ministers, presidents, and the ruling élite but extended to political activists, opposition parties, business interests, the media, and pressure groups.

The outstanding figure among the Jewish Agency's Arab experts was Elias Sasson, originally from Damascus, who was placed by Sharett at the head of the Arab Section in 1937. A polyglot, a skilful diplomat, and a dedicated man of peace, Sasson had a wide circle of Arab friends and acquaintances inside and outside Palestine. In his official capacity as spokesman for the Jewish Agency he was a frequent visitor to Arab capitals where he held hundreds of talks with politicians of every ilk and complexion. A published selection of his letters and reports to the Jewish Agency on conversations with Arab leaders spanning the years from 1934 to 1948 gives an idea of the scale and intensity of Jewish–Arab contacts during this period as well as being a testimony to Sasson's own commitment to the cause of Jewish–Arab understanding.[5] Sasson occupies a unique position in the history of Zionist diplomacy as the only Oriental Jew who reached a position of some responsibility and influence; all the others were European Jews. For the story that follows, Sasson is doubly important: he was one of the most articulate exponents of Sharett's general philosophy of moderation towards the Arabs, and one of the chief architects of the Zionist–Hashemite connection.

While the Jewish Agency deserves credit for the resourceful, versatile, and assiduous diplomacy it conducted in search of peaceful coexistence with the Arabs, no amount of tactical flexibility should

[5] Eliahu Sasson, *On the Road to Peace* (Heb.) (Tel Aviv: Am Oved, 1978).

obscure the fact that the basic aim of the Zionist movement—a Jewish state in Palestine—in itself rendered the conflict with the Palestinian national movement ultimately inescapable. Diplomacy could attenuate the conflict; it could not remove its root cause. Fundamentally, the aspirations of the Jewish and Palestinian national movements were incompatible, and in this sense the conflict between them was inevitable.

Ben-Gurion and the Palestine Arabs

No single individual on the Jewish side understood or personified more clearly the truth of this assertion than David Ben-Gurion (formerly Green), the builder of the Yishuv's military power and the founder of the State of Israel. Born in 1886 in Plonsk, Poland, he arrived in Palestine in 1906, where he spent several years as an agricultural labourer and became active in the Socialist Zionist Poale Zion party, the forerunner of Mapai. From 1910 he served as editor of Poale Zion's organ, *Ahduth* (Unity), signing his first article with his new name Ben-Gurion, which had been the name of one of the last defenders of Jerusalem against the Roman legions. As a law student in Istanbul he advocated an Ottoman orientation for the Yishuv after the revolution of the Young Turks in 1908 but he was then expelled from Turkey at the beginning of the First World War. He spent the war in America, helping to establish *Hehalutz* (The Pioneer) movement, and returned to Palestine in early 1918 as a Jewish Legion volunteer. The idea behind the Jewish Legion was to make a contribution to the British war effort in order to accelerate the establishment of a Jewish national home in Palestine. Ben-Gurion also advocated the creation of an independent centre of Jewish strength in Palestine which would assist Jewish settlement and serve as the nucleus for 'the state in the making'. This nucleus was the General Federation of Labour in Palestine, the Histadrut, which was founded in 1920 with Ben-Gurion as its secretary-general. In 1935 Ben-Gurion was elected chairman of the Zionist Executive and the Jewish Agency, assuming direct responsibility for the Jewish defence forces in the struggle against the local Arabs and the British administration.

Throughout his political career Ben-Gurion grappled with what Zionists used to call 'the Arab question'. The early Zionists combined profound ignorance with an astonishing lack of curiosity about the social, economic, and demographic realities of the land of their devotions. The presence of half a million Arabs with centuries-old roots and deep attachment to the land was usually ignored, and its implications for the Zionist enterprise were not examined except in the most facile manner. The early Zionists rarely perceived and never conceded that

Arab opposition was grounded in principle, that it was only to be expected, and that it amounted to a root and branch rejection of the entire Zionist enterprise. It was more comforting to think that Arab hostility was the manifestation of specific grievances and that it could be overcome by gestures of conciliation, well-timed compromises, and economic rewards. And it was just as well, for had the Zionists paused to consider the reality facing them, they would have probably lost heart and recoiled from pursuing the Zionist idea to its ultimate fulfilment. What distinguished Ben-Gurion's approach to the Arab problem was deep intellectual insight and unflinching realism even in the face of the most unpalatable facts, and the formulation of policies that were based on those facts rather than on pious self-righteousness or wishful thinking.

A wide gulf separated Ben-Gurion's public utterances on the Arab question from his real convictions. There was also a certain development in his thinking on the subject, reflecting the lessons he distilled from practical experience. The romantic phase in his thinking did not last long. As early as 1910 he recognized that a conflict existed between Arab and Jewish aspirations and spoke openly of the hatred felt by the former for the latter. The decade from 1918 to 1929 was the socialist phase in the development of his thinking. During this period he denied the existence of the conflict, spoke of class solidarity between Jewish and Arab workers, and predicted that the coming social revolution would usher in peace and harmony. From 1929 to 1936 he conceded publicly again that the Jews and the Arabs were at cross-purposes but maintained that these differences could be resolved through negotiations. After 1936 Ben-Gurion admitted that the Arab–Jewish conflict was fundamentally political and as such not susceptible to peaceful resolution. Underlying these shifting public positions there were two unchanging convictions: that the support of a world power was more crucial for the Zionist movement than agreement with the Arabs, and that the Arab acceptance of Zionist presence in Palestine would only ensue from an appraisal of Zionist power. A careful comparison of Ben-Gurion's public and private positions leads to the conclusion that the twenty-year denial of the nature of the conflict was dictated not by genuine conviction but by the tactical need to gain time and to retain British support for the Zionist project.[6]

After his rise to the leadership of the Zionist movement, Ben-Gurion concentrated his formidable energies on the acceleration of Jewish immigration to Palestine but, recognizing that his movement faced a strong Arab national movement, he initiated talks with Arab leaders to see if a common platform for the aspirations of the two national

---

[6] Shabtai Teveth, *Ben-Gurion and the Palestinian Arabs: From Peace to War* (Oxford: Oxford University Press, 1985), pp. ix, 198 f.

movements could be found. Since a Jewish majority in Palestine was axiomatic to his thinking he was drawn to the idea of an Arab federation in which Palestine would be one of several component units. The federal idea was advocated as a possible solution to the intractable Palestine problem not just by Zionists but also by some British public figures and even a few Arabs. While differing on the scope and details, most protagonists tended to assume, firstly, that the inclusion of Palestine in a broader Arab federation would help to allay the fears that the Palestine Arabs felt as a result of the growth of Jewish settlement in Palestine, and, secondly, that the fulfilment of the goal of Arab unity would counterbalance the partial loss of Arab national rights in Palestine.[7]

The idea of an Arab Federation formed the basis for the talks that Ben-Gurion initiated with Arab leaders in the period 1933–6. Ben-Gurion was prepared to meet his arch-opponent, the mufti Hajj Amin al-Husayni, and even put out some feelers, but the mufti was evasive. With the Nashashibi leaders of the opposition, on the other hand, Ben-Gurion was not prepared to meet, since he regarded them as insignificant, corrupt, and unreliable. As partners in the talks he looked for Arab nationalists who were not moved by blind hatred of the Jews and who could not be bought with money or favours.

As his first interlocutor Ben-Gurion chose Musa Alami, a wealthy, Cambridge-educated, and widely respected Arab who served as assistant attorney-general for the mandatory government. At their first meeting Alami shattered the assumption prevalent among Zionists at the time that their arrival constituted a blessing to the Arabs of the country and that the latter therefore had no reason to oppose them. Musa Alami said he would prefer the land to remain poor and desolate even for another hundred years until the Arabs themselves were capable of developing it, and Ben-Gurion felt that as a patriotic Arab Alami had every right to this view. Ben-Gurion enquired whether there was any possibility at all of reaching an understanding with regard to the establishment of a Jewish state in Palestine, including Transjordan. Alami replied with a question: 'Why should the Arabs agree?' Ben-Gurion answered that in return the Zionists would lend their support for an Arab federation that would include Palestine so that the Arabs of Palestine, even if they constituted a minority in that country, would be linked with millions of Arabs in the neighbouring countries. Alami did not reject the idea out of hand but subsequent talks floundered on the issues of a Jewish majority in Palestine and a Jewish state which were unacceptable even to the moderates on the Arab side. Some years later Alami told Sharett that Ben-Gurion was incorrigibly intransigent:

[7] Yehoshua Porath, *In Search of Arab Unity: 1930–1945* (London: Frank Cass, 1986), 58.

while anxious to reach agreement with the Arabs, he insisted that they accept his Zionist programme *in toto* and failed to appreciate that an agreement necessarily involved give and take and could not be based on the consent of one side to all the demands and aspirations of the other.

Ben-Gurion's other interlocutors included Awni Abd al-Hadi, the leader of the pan-Arab Istiqlal Party in Palestine, Riad al-Sulh, the Lebanese pan-Arab activist, Amin Shakib Arslan and Ihsan al-Jabri, the Syrian nationalist leaders, and George Antonius, the theoretician of pan-Arabism. These talks finally convinced Ben-Gurion that the gulf separating the positions of the two national movements could not be bridged. He knew intuitively that his full-blooded Zionist programme had no chance of being accepted by any Arab nationalist, but its public rejection by Arslan and Jabri as arrogant and fantastic dashed any lingering hope there might have been of reaching agreement on the fundamental issue.[8]

The simple truth was that there were two peoples and one country, and both wanted it for themselves. In May 1936, after his talk with Antonius, Ben-Gurion conceded in public for the first time that the goals of the two peoples could not be reconciled. 'There is a conflict, a great conflict', he told the Jewish Agency directorate. 'We and they want the same thing: we both want Palestine. And that is the fundamental conflict.'[9] While some of his colleagues in the Jewish Agency continued to believe that a compromise solution might be possible, Ben-Gurion grasped that the essential structure of the conflict left no room for compromise and that this would entail the settlement of Zionist claims by violent means.

Reluctant to embark overtly on a collision course when the balance of power between Jews and Arabs in Palestine could not guarantee the desired outcome, Ben-Gurion developed a gradualist long-term strategy whose starting point was the acceptance of the principle of partition. A final point, a final goal, a final destination did not exist. In Ben-Gurion's thinking, as his biographer points out, every objective, every goal, was just a stage in the march of history and every goal, once attained, became a staging post for the attainment of the next goal. The partition lines were of secondary importance in Ben-Gurion's eyes because he intended to change them in any case; they were not the end but only the beginning.[10]

[8] David Ben-Gurion, *My Talks with Arab Leaders* (Jerusalem: Keter Books, 1972), 14–85.

[9] Quoted in Teveth, *Ben-Gurion and the Palestine Arabs*, 166.

[10] Michael Bar-Zohar, *Ben-Gurion: A Political Biography* (Heb.) 3 vols. (Tel Aviv: Am Oved, 1975), i. 356–8. On the development of Ben-Gurion's views towards the Arabs before and after independence and for a comparison with Sharett, see also Michael Brecher, *The Foreign Policy System of Israel: Setting Images, Process* (London: Oxford University Press, 1972), ch. 12; Uri Bialer, 'David Ben-Gurion and Moshe Sharett: The Shaping of Two Political Conceptions in the Arab–

The nature and extent of Ben-Gurion's territorial expansionism were revealed with startling frankness in a letter to his son Amos in October 1937. Power politics rather than morality was the theme of Ben-Gurion's analysis: 'There is no room in politics for sentimental considerations. The only thing we must weigh up is: what is desirable and good for us, what is the path that leads to the goal, what policy will strengthen us and what policy will weaken us.' The key question was: would the formation of a Jewish state help to turn the country into a Jewish one or would it hamper this? Ben-Gurion professed himself to be an enthusiastic advocate of a Jewish state, even if it involved the partitioning of Palestine, because he worked on the assumption that a partial Jewish state would not be the end but only the beginning. The acquisition of land was important not only for its own sake but because it would increase the strength of the Jews and help them to acquire the whole country. The formation of a state could accelerate this process and constitute 'a powerful lever in our historic effort to redeem the country in its entirety'. The plan was to bring into this state all the Jews it could possibly hold, to build a Jewish economy, to organize a first-class army, and then 'I am certain we will be able to settle in all the other parts of the country, whether through agreement and mutual understanding with our Arab neighbours or in another way'.

With a state, continued Ben-Gurion, the Jews would be able to penetrate deeper into the country. They would be stronger *vis-à-vis* the Arabs, and as the Jews grew in strength the Arabs would realize that it would be impossible to oppose them and that it would be best to work together and to allow them to settle in all parts of the country. If the Arabs were to act from 'sterile national feelings' and say 'We don't want your honey or your sting. We would rather the Negev remained desert than that it should be settled by Jews', it would be necessary 'to speak to them in another language. And we will have another language then— which we should not have without a State.' Both his mind and his heart told Ben-Gurion: 'Establish a Jewish State at once, even if it is not in the whole land. The rest will come in the course of time. It must come.'[11]

The Hashemite connection

The irreconcilable conflict between the Jewish and the Arab national movements in Palestine provided the setting for the emergence of the

Israeli Conflict' (Heb.), *Medina ve-Memshal* 1/2 (1971), 71–84; Gabriel Sheffer, 'Resolution *vs.* Management of the Middle East Conflict: A Re-examination of the Confrontation Between Moshe Sharett and David Ben-Gurion', *Jerusalem Papers on Peace Problems* no. 32 (Jerusalem: The Magness Press, 1980); Avi Shlaim, 'Conflicting Approaches to Israel's Relations with the Arabs: Ben-Gurion and Sharett, 1953–1956', *The Middle East Journal* 37/2 (1983), 180–201.

[11] David Ben-Gurion, *Letters to Paula* (London: Valentine, Mitchell, 1971), 153–7.

special relations between the Jewish Agency and Abdullah, the amir of Transjordan. Frustration in the quest of an understanding with the Palestine Arabs led Ben-Gurion to base Zionist policy on force to counter force and the threat of force. Other leaders with responsibility for Zionist diplomacy, notably Moshe Sharett, sought a counterweight to Palestinian Arab hostility in better relations with the neighbouring Arab countries. Indeed, the attempt to bypass the Palestine Arabs and forge direct links with rulers of the Arab states became a constant feature of Zionist diplomacy in the 1930s and 1940s.

Transjordan's special significance in this context stemmed from four main factors. First, there was the physical proximity and particularly close links between Transjordan and the branch of the Arab national movement that was on a collision course with the Zionist movement— the Palestine Arabs. With the growing recognition that no compromise with the Palestine Arabs could be reached, Amman emerged as a central point of reference in Zionist calculations and Zionist diplomatic activities relating to the future of Palestine. Secondly, there was the convergence of interests, arising out of these close links, between the Zionist movement and this particular Arab potentate. Thirdly, there was Abdullah's outstanding political realism and willingness to give expression to these convergent interests in a strategic partnership with the Jewish Agency and the State of Israel. Finally, there was Transjordan's key position from the military and strategic point of view during the struggle for Palestine in the late 1940s.[12]

The present study combines a general account of the origins and evolution of the special relationship between King Abdullah and the Zionist movement with a more detailed account of the period from 1947 to 1951. The aim is to identify the political and strategic rationale behind this relationship, to examine the factors that constrained the development of this relationship into a formal and open alliance, and to relate this relationship to the broader context of Arab–Jewish conflict over Palestine. The late 1940s are singled out for in-depth treatment because this was the most critical period in the history of Palestine, and one that saw the partition of that country and the emergence of the State of Israel. More than any other period the 1940s highlight the forces at play, the role of all the principal actors in the struggle for Palestine, and the scope, modalities, and limits of collaboration between the Hashemites and the Zionists.

Two significant conclusions follow from re-examining the history of the Arab–Israeli conflict in the late 1940s from the perspective of Hashemite–Zionist connection. The first and most important casualty is the view that from the moment of its birth, the State of Israel had to

[12] Dan Schueftan, *A Jordanian Option* (Heb.) (Yad Tabenkin: Hakibbutz Hameuhad, 1986), 15.

confront a monolithic Arab world that was implacable in its hostility and fanatical in its determination to wipe it off the Middle East map. This study tries to go beyond such self-serving claims and counter-claims and to uncover the more complex forces that have shaped the course of Arab–Israeli relations. It is not the first book to argue that the Arabs are not a monolithic bloc dedicated to overthrowing Israel but it does advance new arguments and new evidence to refute this view. It shows that far from being monolithic, the Arab rulers were divided all along in the strategy they advocated for dealing with the Zionist challenge and that one of these rulers—King Abdullah—favoured accommodation rather than confrontation. It also shows that the existence of a common enemy, in the form of unyielding Palestinian nationalism under the leadership of the mufti, helped to cement the unholy alliance between the Hashemites and the Zionists. And it exposes the gap between Abdullah's verbal commitment to the Arab cause and his operational strategy of collaborating with the Zionists in order to make himself the master of Arab Palestine.

A second major casualty is the notion of Arab unity which is so dear to the hearts of all Arab nationalists. In a very real sense this book is a case-study in inter-Arab conflict, rivalry, intrigue, and deception. It exposes the stark reality of national selfishness behind the rhetoric of commitment to the cause of the Palestine Arabs. It shows the Arab leaders to have been incapable of co-ordinating their diplomatic moves or their military strategy in face of the common enemy. When one looks at the military operations of the 1948 war, as dozens of historians have done, one gets the familiar picture of a broad and united Arab coalition in confrontation with Israel for possession of the whole of Palestine. But the politics underlying this war give a very different picture of a tacit understanding between Abdullah and the Zionists, with limited ter-ritorial objectives on both sides, and with common interests which Abdullah did not share with his official comrades-in-arms. In short, the Hashemite–Zionist connection is one of the keys to understanding how Palestine came to be partitioned, and why the Palestinian national movement suffered such a catastrophic defeat while the Jewish national movement realized its ambition of establishing an independent Jewish state over a substantial part of Palestine.

A FALCON TRAPPED IN A CANARY'S CAGE

The Hashemites and the Arab Revolt

A profound faith that the Hashemites were destined to rule over the entire Arab world inspired Abdullah throughout a long and eventful political career which carried him from his ancestral home in the Hijaz in western Arabia, to become amir of Transjordan and later king of Jordan. Second son of Husayn Ibn Ali, the grand sharif of Mecca, Abdullah belonged to.a noble Arab family which traced its descent from the Prophet's daughter Fatima, whose husband Ali was fourth of the caliphs and head of the house of Hashem. It was this ancestry, being thirty-seventh in the line of descent from Muhammad, that made the sharif the guardian of the Holy Places in the Hijaz and fostered his ambition for an independent Arab kingdom and for the caliphate. And it was knowledge of these pretensions that led the suspicious Ottoman rulers to 'invite' Husayn to Constantinople as the guest of the sultan where they could keep him under direct supervision. Husayn took with him to Constantinople his four sons, Ali, Abdullah, Faisal, and Zeid, and it was only after the Young Turks revolution in 1908 that he was allowed to return to the Hijaz and was appointed amir of Mecca.

Of Husayn's four sons, Abdullah was the most astute and politically ambitious. Born in Mecca in 1880, Abdullah received his education, which included military training, in Constantinople and in the Hijaz. Between 1912 and 1914 he was deputy for Mecca in the Ottoman Parliament, where he promoted his father's interests with acumen and enthusiasm. It was during this period that he developed his interest in Arab nationalism and began to link his father's desire for autonomy in the Hijaz to the broader and more radical ideas for Arab emancipation from Ottoman rule. In 1914 he returned to Mecca by way of Cairo, where he met Lord Kitchener, the British high commissioner, to explore the possibility of support in the event of an uprising against the Ottomans. Soon after his return home Abdullah became his father's foreign minister, political adviser, and one of the commanders of the Arab Revolt.

Abdullah was the thinker, planner, schemer, and driving force behind the Arab Revolt, though his younger brother Faisal assumed

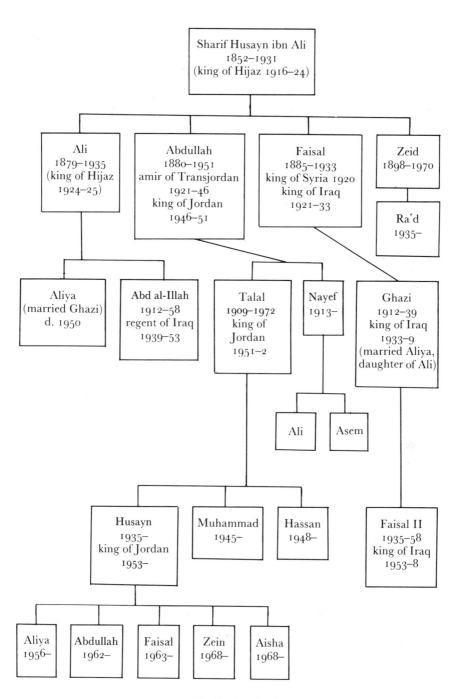

FIG. 1   The Hashemite dynasty

active control of the revolt as commander of the Arab army while the overall leadership was nominally in the hands of their old father. As Faisal himself confided to T. E. Lawrence, his liaison officer and most renowned chronicler of the 'revolt in the desert', the idea of an Arab uprising against the Turks was first conceived by Abdullah. It was only gradually and under constant prodding from Abdullah that the conservative sharif of Mecca raised his sights from the idea of home rule for his corner of Arabia inside the Ottoman Empire to complete independence for all its Arab provinces from Yemen to Syria. Husayn became a separatist only after he had tried and failed to attain his limited political objectives within the framework of the Ottoman Empire, whilst Abdullah became convinced of the necessity to break up the Ottoman Empire at the beginning of 1914. A further difference of an ideological character separated father from son: Husayn's idea of nationalism was based on the conservative concept of tribal and family unity, whereas Abdullah's was based on the theory of Arab preeminence among Muslims. Moreover, to have any chance of success in mounting an open rebellion against the mighty Ottoman Empire, the indigent rulers of the Hijaz province had to have the backing of another Great Power, and that Power could only be the British Empire, which had its own designs on Arabia. The guardian of the Holy Places of Mecca could not easily bring himself to embrace a Christian Power in his struggle against fellow Muslims. Divided counsel within his own family circle did nothing to ease his predicament. Faisal emphasized the risks and pleaded for caution; Abdullah wanted to play for high stakes and urged him to raise the standard of the Arab Revolt. Husayn warily plotted a middle course with the deviousness characteristic of oriental diplomacy: he made secret overtures to the British at the same time as he was seeking a compromise solution with the Turks.

The approach of war made the British much more receptive to Hashemite overtures, and to Abdullah fell the task of weaving the threads of this unholy alliance against the Sublime Porte. At the first meeting between Abdullah and Kitchener, the possibility of co-operation was raised but no commitment was made by either side. At a subsequent meeting with Ronald Storrs, the oriental secretary of the British Residency in Cairo, Abdullah was more forward: he asked whether Great Britain would present the sharif with a dozen, or even a half-dozen machine guns. When asked what could possibly be their purpose, he replied that they would be for defence against attack by the Turks. Storrs made it clear that Great Britain could not entertain the idea of supplying arms to be used against Turkey but he left the door wide open for further explorations.

Between July 1915 and March 1916 a number of letters were

exchanged between the sharif of Mecca and the British high commissioner in Cairo which came to be known as the McMahon–Husayn correspondence. In his first note the sharif, speaking in the name of 'the Arab nation', demanded British recognition of Arab independence in the entire Arabian peninsula and the area covered by present day Syria, Lebanon, Jordan, Israel, and the northern provinces of Iraq. To this absurdly inflated territorial claim was added a request for a British approval of a proclamation of an Arab caliphate of Islam. The note exhibited the vaulting ambition nursed by Abdullah, who remained the moving spirit and the 'power behind the throne' on the Sharifian side. After a year of desultory negotiation, Sir Henry McMahon conveyed the British government's agreement to recognize Arab independence over an area more limited than that to which Husayn had originally staked a claim, and the sharif undertook to join the Allies by mounting a rebellion against the Ottomans. The correspondence, conducted in Arabic, was shrouded in ambiguity, vagueness, and deliberate obscurity. It reveals a continuous thread of evasive pledges by Britain and compromises by the sharif, who appears to have been moved by dynastic interests and the wish to extend the power of his family rather than by the cherished dream of the Arabs for independence. His dream was to found an independent Hashemite empire, uniting the whole of the Arab Middle East, on the ruins of the Ottoman Empire. The British, who had their own interests to consider, failed to spell out the difference between his ambition and their commitments. Oriental diplomacy is not usually precise unless compelled to be so, and the methods by which the negotiations were conducted in 1915–16 left a great deal to be desired in this respect. In particular, the correspondence was imprecise as to whether the territory which became Palestine was, or was not included in the area within which Britain was prepared to recognize Arab independence. Conflicting interpretations over this issue were to plague Anglo-Arab relations after the war.[1]

As its origins make all too clear, the Arab Revolt which broke out in June 1916 and is remembered to this day as the Golden Age of Arab nationalism was in essence an Anglo-Hashemite plot. Britain financed the revolt as well as supplying arms, provisions, direct artillery support, and experts in desert warfare, among whom was the legendary and controversial T. E. Lawrence, popularly known as 'Lawrence of Arabia'. The Hashemites promised much more than they were able to deliver and their grandiose plans collapsed in shambles. A disappointingly small number of Syrian and Iraqi nationalists flocked to the Sharifian banner, while in Arabia itself a large number of Arab officers

[1] Elie Kedourie, *In the Anglo-Arab Labyrinth: The McMahon–Husayn Correspondence and Its Interpretations 1914–1939* (Cambridge University Press, 1976).

remained loyal to the sultan. The first phase of the revolt was confined to the Hijaz where Mecca, Taif, and Jedda fell in rapid succession to the rebel forces consisting of Hijazi bedouins commanded by the sharif's four sons, Ali, Abdullah, Faisal, and Zeid. Three of these units laid the siege on Medina and were tied down there until the end of the war. Only Faisal's unit was freed to assist the British offensive in Palestine and Syria and was allowed to enter Damascus first and hoist the Arab flag.

The military value of the Arab Revolt is a matter of some dispute. Lawrence, who did more than any other man to glorify the revolt and advertise its military successes, was rather disparaging about the role played by Abdullah. The picture which emerges from his account is that of a light-hearted and pleasure-seeking prince who wanted the rewards of victory but possessed none of the qualities necessary for successful leadership in war. 'The Arabs thought Abdullah a far-seeing statesman and an astute politician', wrote Lawrence. 'Astute he certainly was, but not greatly enough to convince us always of his sincerity. His ambition was patent. Rumour made him the brain of his father and of the Arab Revolt, but he seemed too easy for that. His object was, of course, the winning of Arab independence and the building up of Arab nations, but he meant to keep the direction of the new states in the family. So he watched us, and played through us to the British gallery.' He might be of some value, thought Lawrence, in the peace that would come after success, but during the physical struggle, 'when singleness of eye and magnetism, devotion and self-sacrifice were needed, Abdullah would be a tool too complex for a simple purpose, though he could not be ignored even now'.[2]

The post-war settlement

Indeed, Abdullah could not be ignored. He and the other princes who headed the revolt became the leading spokesmen for the Arab national cause at the peace conferences which ended the First World War and in the settlement following the dismemberment of the Ottoman Empire. For their contribution to the Allied war effort against the Turks, Britain had promised, or half-promised, to support Arab independence. But the territorial limits governing this promise were left so ineptly and obscurely defined in the McMahon–Husayn correspondence that a long and bitter wrangle was bound to ensue between the two sides, especially over the disposition of Palestine. Another major uncertainty surrounded the regime and institutions to be installed in the Arab areas which were indisputably marked for independence. Should this

[2] T. E. Lawrence, *Seven Pillars of Wisdom* (London: Jonathan Cape, 1935), 67 f.

independence take the form of a united kingdom, a federation, or an alliance between independent states? Was Britain committed only to recognizing Arab independence or also to Hashemite rule over these areas? One searches in vain for answers or even clues to these questions in the McMahon–Husayn correspondence. Husayn himself regarded Arab unity as synonymous with his own kingship and as an empty phrase unless so regarded. Arab unity meant little to him except as a means to personal aggrandizement. He aspired to head a united Arab kingdom consisting of the Arabian peninsula, Greater Syria, and Iraq, with his sons acting as viceroys. Such was the impatience of the Sharifians that within four months of the outbreak of the revolt, the grand sharif, at the instigation of his enterprising second son, was proclaimed king of the Arab nation. At first the British refused to recognize him, and when they eventually did so in January 1917, they recognized him only as king of the Hijaz.

The task of fashioning a new political order in the Middle East following the collapse of the Ottoman Empire was further complicated by other commitments undertaken by the British government after the initiation of its clandestine exchanges with the sharif of Mecca. Under the terms of the Sykes–Picot agreement of May 1916, the whole Fertile Crescent, comprising modern Iraq, Syria, Lebanon, Jordan, and Palestine, was divided into British and French spheres of influence. Each sphere was in turn divided into two zones, one to be placed under direct British or French rule and the other turned over to semi-independent Arab states or confederation of states. France and Britain were to supply advisers and enjoy economic privileges in the Arab states which would emerge within their respective spheres. The third and most famous promise made by the British government, in the Balfour Declaration of November 1917, was to support the establishment in Palestine of a national home for the Jewish people.

The peace conference found the Arabs free from Turkish control but ensnared in a more complex diplomatic web spun by rivalries of the Great Powers and the baffling array of pledges they made in their eagerness to inherit the Ottoman Empire. Faisal, who had formed a temporary administration in Syria, attended the Paris peace conference as the envoy of the king of the Hijaz. By temperament inclined to moderation and compromise, Faisal was enjoined by his authoritarian and crotchety old father to insist on nothing less than complete independence. Faisal possessed more than a touch of the romantic aura, gentle melancholy, physical grace, and perfect manners which many upper-class Englishmen found irresistibly attractive. But he was out of his depth in the world of Great Power diplomacy, and he left the conference empty-handed to face a rapidly deteriorating situation in Syria. Faisal tried to pursue a middle-of-the-road policy regarding the French, the troubles in Iraq, and the Palestinian Arabs' complaints against the Jews. But the clash with the French was made inevitable by the inflexibility of his Syrian nationalist supporters and by their insistence on a completely independent kingdom of Greater Syria, embracing Transjordan and Lebanon. A fervently nationalistic Syrian Congress meeting in Damascus in March 1920 offered Faisal the kingdom of Syria, which he hesitantly accepted, thereby embarrassing the British and antagonizing the French, who refused to recognize him. Brushing aside these Arab nationalist claims, the Supreme Council of the Peace Conference proceeded to San Remo to place Iraq, Transjordan, and Palestine under the mandatory authority of Britain, and Lebanon and Syria under the mandatory authority of France. In July 1920 came the final blow when French forces marched on Damascus, banished Faisal, and took over the government of the country. Thus was created the modern state of Syria, with a republican regime, under French protection, and on the ruins of the dream of a united Arab kingdom led by the Hashemites.

Many significant trends in Middle East politics have their origins in the events which unravelled in Damascus between 1918 and 1920, culminating in the fall of Faisal. The abiding mistrust of the French towards British intentions and policies in this part of the world goes back to these early post-war years. So does the grudge nursed by Syrian nationalists against the Western Powers for broken promises and cynical disregard for Arab rights. The Hashemites for their part constantly harked back to their short-lived kingdom in Damascus and based on it their various plans for Greater Syria. Finally, the fact that the Hashemites allied themselves with Britain in order to further their dynastic ambitions accounts for the estrangement and mutual suspicion between themselves and the more radical forces of Arab nationalism.

The foundation of the amirate of Transjordan

The eclipse of Faisal in Damascus gave Abdullah the opportunity to stage a comeback on the Arab stage after he had been soundly beaten on the battlefield by the Wahabi forces of Ibn Saud, denied admission to the peace conference by the Allies, and experienced growing difficulties with his father which led to his resignation as foreign minister. When the Syrian Congress elected Faisal to the throne of Syria in March 1920, a group of Arab leaders had nominated Abdullah to the throne of Iraq. But he received no encouragement from the British to seek that particular throne. Casting about for a principality to make his own, Abdullah turned his attention to the mountainous country lying east of the Jordan which nominally formed part of the British mandate but in practice had been left to its own devices and degenerated into a centre of brigandage and lawlessness. No troops had been left to administer this barren territory and only a handful of British political advisers (including Capt. Alec Seath Kirkbride), and there was no intention at that stage of forming it into an independent Arab state.

It was to this territory that Abdullah set off from Medina, with his father's blessing, at the head of a small band of retainers and tribesmen. On arrival in Maan in November 1920 he proclaimed his intention to march on Damascus, drive out the French aggressors, and restore King Faisal to his rightful throne. From Maan Abdullah moved northwards to Kerak where Capt. Alec Kirkbride, having received no instructions on how to deal with this unlikely contingency, decided to welcome the prince in the name of the National Government of Moab. This curious encounter between the Hashemite prince and the polite young Englishman marked the beginning of a warm personal friendship and a close political association severed only by the former's death thirty years later. Finally, in March 1921, Abdullah arrived in Amman and set up his headquarters, still with the declared intention of raising a larger force to mount an invasion of Syria from the south.

Abdullah's arrival in Transjordan threw into disarray a conference held in Cairo by Winston Churchill, the colonial secretary, to discuss Middle East affairs. Churchill had already promised the throne of Iraq to Faisal as a consolation prize for the loss of Syria. This offer was part of the 'Sharifian policy' favoured by Churchill, a policy of forming a number of small states in Arabia and the Fertile Crescent, all headed by members of the sharif's family and of course under British influence and guidance. This policy was threatened by Abdullah's bold march into Transjordan, and his well-advertised plan of reinstating Faisal in Damascus as a prelude to asserting his own claim to the Iraqi throne. Although such a move would have been doomed to failure from the start, it could embroil the British in difficulties with their suspicious French allies—and besides, Transjordan was needed by them as a link between Palestine and Iraq. The initial impulse of the eminent Arabists assembled in Cairo was to eject the upstart out of Eastern Palestine, by force if necessary, and administer the area directly. But on further reflection it was decided to accept the *fait accompli* and let Abdullah stay in Transjordan as the representative of the British government, on condition that he renounced his claim to Iraq in favour of his brother Faisal, undertook to prevent any hostile acts against the French in Syria, and recognized the British mandate over Transjordan as part of the Palestine mandate. Sir Herbert Samuel, the high commissioner for

Palestine, doubted Abdullah's ability to check anti-French and anti-Zionist activities in the area, but Churchill stressed the importance of securing the goodwill of the king of Hijaz and his sons, while Lawrence claimed that Abdullah was better qualified for the task than the other candidates by reason of his position, lineage, and very considerable power, for better or for worse, over the tribesmen. Lawrence was convinced that anti-Zionist sentiment would wane, and that Transjordan could be turned into a safety valve by appointing a ruler on whom Britain could bring pressure to bear to check anti-Zionist agitation. The ideal, said Lawrence, would be 'a person who was not too powerful, and who was not an inhabitant of Transjordan, but who relied on His Majesty's Government for the retention of his office'.[3] In other words, the British were looking for a stooge.

At a hastily arranged meeting in Jerusalem, Churchill himself, with the eager assistance and encouragement of Lawrence, offered Abdullah the amirate of Transjordan, comprising the territory between the River Jordan and the Arab Desert to the east, on condition that he renounce his avowed intention of conquering Syria and accept the validity of the British mandate. Abdullah, relieved to be quit of a military adventure with an extremely doubtful outcome, accepted the offer with alacrity and probably congratulated himself on his good fortune. In return for Abdullah's undertaking to forswear and prevent any belligerent acts against the French in Syria, Churchill promised to try to persuade the French to restore Arab government there, this time with Abdullah at its head. Abdullah's suggestion that he should be made king of Palestine as well as Transjordan was declined by Churchill on the grounds that it conflicted with British commitment to a Jewish national home. So Abdullah had to settle for a temporary arrangement, lasting six months, within the framework of the Palestine mandate and under the supervision of the high commissioner who would appoint a British adviser in Amman to help the amir to set up the administration. During this period, the amir was to receive from the British government a monthly subsidy of £5,000 to enable him to recruit a local force for the preservation of order in Transjordan. Thus, by the stroke of a pen on a Sunday afternoon, as Churchill was later to boast, he had created the amirate of Transjordan.

In April 1921 the first government was formed in Transjordan. The initial six months were full of problems as Abdullah, who was extravagant and absurdly generous towards his friends, squandered his allowances and indulged in an orgy of maladministration, while the country was swarming with Syrians bent on taking up arms against the

[3] Walid Kazziha, 'The Political Evolution of Transjordan', *Middle Eastern Studies* 15/2 (1979), 239–58.

French. Nevertheless, towards the end of the year, the temporary arrangement was given permanence when the British government formally recognized 'the existence of an independent constitutional government under the rule of His Excellency the Amir Abdullah Ibn Husayn', subject to the establishment of a constitutional regime and the conclusion of an agreement that would enable Britain to fulfil her international obligations in respect of this territory. This was the first step in a new trend which crept into Britain's policy, that of separating Transjordan from Palestine. The second step was taken in 1922 when Britain, in the face of strong Zionist opposition, obtained the necessary approval from the League of Nations for excluding the territory of Transjordan from the provisions of the Palestine mandate relating to the Jewish national home. In May 1923, the British government granted Transjordan its independence with Abdullah as ruler, and with St John Philby ('Philby of Arabia') as chief representative to administer a £150,000 grant-in-aid. It was largely Abdullah's own failure to fulfil the condition of constitutional government which prolonged the dependent status of Transjordan for another five years, until the conclusion of the 1928 agreement.

Another reason for the delay is to be found in the progressive deterioration in the relations between the British and Abdullah's illustrious father. At the Cairo conference some of the post-war problems in the Middle East were settled to the satisfaction of at least some of the parties concerned: Churchill got his 'economy with honour', Faisal got the throne of Iraq, and Abdullah got the amirate of Transjordan. In the summer following the conference, Colonel Lawrence was sent to Jedda to tie up some loose ends, only to discover that the grand sharif had become the greatest obstacle to the consolidation of Britain's Sharifian policy. Lawrence offered a formal treaty of alliance securing the Kingdom of the Hijaz against aggression, and indefinite continuation of the handsome subsidy paid annually to Husayn since 1917. But the obstinate old man, embittered by what he regarded as British bad faith and betrayal, refused to sign the treaty and angrily rejected the conditions that he should recognize the mandate systems and condone the Balfour Declaration. The consequent removal of British protection and the British subsidy left the king of the Hijaz exposed to the tender mercies of his great rival, Sultan Abdul-Aziz Ibn Saud of the Nejd. Only British diplomatic pressure and the payment of a subsidy to Ibn Saud had kept the rivalry between the two Arabian rulers dormant during the First World War—a rivalry accentuated by the support given to Husayn by the Foreign Office through the Arab Bureau while the India Office favoured Ibn Saud. After the war an inevitable trial of strength developed between the king who assumed that his sponsorship of the Arab Revolt entitled him to political authority over his neighbours and the chieftain whose determination revived the Wahabi movement and endowed it with a cutting military edge. The first serious clash occurred in May 1919 on the eastern border of the Hijaz when Ibn Saud's forces almost totally obliterated a Hashemite army of 5,000 men commanded by Abdullah. So complete was their victory that only Britain's intervention prevented the Wahabi forces from marching on Mecca. The decisive battle broke out in 1924. Ibn Saud conquered the whole of the Hijaz, forced Husayn into abdication and exile, and inflicted on him the crowning humiliation of assuming the administration of the Holy Places in Mecca and Medina, the two most sacred sites of Islam. Thus ended ingloriously the dream of a mighty Hashemite empire, and by a cruel historic irony it was in its own ancestral home that the Hashemite dynasty sustained its most monumental and shattering defeat.

Husayn's eclipse gave a dramatic illustration not only of his own folly and the price of obstinacy but also of the immense power wielded by Britain in shaping the fortunes of the Arab nations and their rulers. The political shape of the region did not evolve naturally, following its own internal laws, but was largely the product of British design tailored to fit Britain's own imperial needs. It was not the Syrians who expelled Faisal nor was it the Iraqis who raised him to the throne in their own countries. Abdullah could not gain power in Transjordan without Britain's approval, and had he tried to do so in defiance of Britain he would not have survived for very long. It was not the Hijazis who invited Ibn Saud but the arms supplied to him by Britain that enabled him to conquer their country. And just as the withdrawal of British support paved the way to the decline of the Hashemite kingdom in the Hijaz, so it was British protection, and only British protection, which could preserve the Hashemite amirate in Transjordan.

Ibn Saud was not content with his victory over Husayn. Driven by political ambition to expand his own realm and by the religious zeal of the Wahabi reform movement, he turned northwards with the intent of completing the destruction of the effete house of Hashem. Abdullah's incorporation of the provinces of Maan and Akaba, which formerly belonged to the kingdom of the Hijaz, into the amirate of Transjordan exacerbated the poor relations between the two rival dynasties. In 1924 Wahabi forces crossed the border into Transjordan, and had it not been for the RAF squadron from Jerusalem and the detachment of British armoured cars which furiously mowed down the column of camelry, Abdullah undoubtedly would have met the same sticky end which had befallen his father. Ibn Saud did not abandon his designs on

Transjordan, and the conflict continued to smoulder with occasional forays across the border and tribal clashes. The 1928 treaty, which recognized Transjordan's independence but left finance and foreign affairs under British control, was signed at the time when Wahabi raids were increasing. It was just as well for Abdullah that the British also undertook to defend the borders of the amirate because this time the Wahabis, fired by the fervour to sweep away all corruption and restore the pristine and puritanical brand of Islam, advanced upon Amman itself. Abdullah was quite firm in his friendship to Britain but none too firm in his hold over the amirate which faced an imminent threat of dismemberment by the fanatical Wahabi hordes. Once again it was only the swift and violent intervention of the RAF, this time assisted by the British-created Arab Legion, which repelled the invasion and kept the amir on his throne in Amman.

The principality which Abdullah had peacefully carved out for himself and from which he was in danger of being violently ejected was a political anomaly and a geographical nonsense. It had no obvious *raison d'être* and was indeed of such little political significance that the European Powers, in their generally acquisitive wartime diplomacy, tended to overlook it as an unimportant corner of Syria. The status of this vacant lot, as we have seen, remained indistinct until Abdullah's unexpected arrival on the scene. Transjordan was then created by the famous stroke of Churchill's pen, in mitigation of the sense of guilt felt towards the sharif, and in the hope of securing a modicum of stability and order east of the Jordan river at the lowest possible cost to the British exchequer.

The borders of the new principality did not correspond to any particular historic, cultural, or geographical unit. Bounded by the valley of the Yarmuk on the north, by the Arabian Desert on the east, by the River Jordan, the Dead Sea, and Wadi Araba on the west, it had no outlet to the sea until Abdullah, with British encouragement, grabbed Maan and Akaba from the expiring kingdom of the Hijaz. Effectively, Transjordan was a strip of cultivable land 270 kilometres long with a width tapering from 80 kilometres in the north to nothing in the south, and flanked by a great deal of desert; with a population of 350,000, one railway line and hardly any roads, no resources whatsoever, and no revenue except for a modest British subsidy. The capital and largest town of this backward and primitive kingdom was Amman—a drab and dusty place which could not even boast a glorious past. It was perhaps not altogether inappropriate that this one-horse town should serve as the capital of what was essentially a provincial backwater. And it was in a modest palace on the eastern hill overlooking Amman that Amir Abdullah settled down, 'loyally and comfortably', as Churchill had hoped, with two official wives and a charming black concubine.

Abdullah's ambition and the Greater Syria scheme

But Transjordan was a very insubstantial principality for so ambitious a prince. The contrast between the barren and insignificant patch of territory assigned to him to administer on behalf of the British mandatory and Abdullah's own heart's desire could hardly have been greater. He saw himself as the moving spirit behind the Arab Revolt. Proud of his race and descent, he was moved by an unshakeable faith that the true destiny of the Arabs lay in unity under Hashemite rule. Of Husayn's four sons, Abdullah was the brightest and most resourceful, and certainly the most ambitious; his family nickname was 'Ajlan'— the hurried one. From his father he inherited the belief in Arab greatness, the yearning to revive the glory of its past, and the vision of a mighty Hashemite empire and caliphate, but he did not inherit either the sanctimonious self-righteousness or the quixotic obstinacy which had brought his father's kingdom crashing down in flames. By all accounts, Abdullah, very far from being sanctimonious, was in fact the most irrepressibly individualistic, colourfully entertaining, resilient, and unpredictable member of the Hashemite clan. Kirkbride once described him as a 'king with a twinkle in his eye'. He loved pomp and ceremony but had a large store of good anecdotes and was also capable of laughing at himself. He was fond of poetry, horses, arcane customs, and desert lore. Yet, for all his love of tradition, there was an impish streak in Abdullah's character, and he took great delight in acting boldly, flamboyantly, and unconventionally.

Most upper-class Englishmen who came in contact with the Hashemites preferred Faisal to Abdullah, and there were not many Arabists who were not upper-class. 'More intelligent and more forceful than Faisal, he lacked Faisal's charm and, in consequence, lacked Faisal's ability to inspire trust and affection. Short of stature, and without Faisal's grace of body or grace of manner, he was not, like Faisal, a picturesque figure. He was never able to project his personality beyond the circle of his immediate advisers and so failed to command the support and loyalty commanded by those who deserved them less.'[4]

Among Arab politicians Abdullah was never a popular or trusted figure. In his own way he was an ardent Arab nationalist, but the

[4] John Marlowe, *The Seat of Pilate: An Account of the Palestine Mandate* (London, The Cresset Press, 1959), 5. For an extremely vivid and perceptive portrait, see James Morris, *The Hashemite Kings* (London: Faber and Faber, 1959).

authoritarianism which marked his approach to the affairs of state and the confidence he exuded of being marked out by destiny to lead the Arab world to independence did not endear him to other Arabs, especially when they happened to be fellow kings and rulers in their own right.

Given his pride in his heritage, the faith that he himself was destined to play a commanding role, his penchant for playing for high stakes, and the vaulting ambition he had nursed since his youth, it was inevitable that Abdullah would regard Transjordan as only the beginning, not the end, of his political career. The amirate was too small to contain his constantly bubbling ambition: the ambition to avenge the humiliation of his family, to hold sway over a kingdom worthy of his noble ancestry. He was, in the words of one of his contemporaries, 'a falcon trapped in a canary's cage, longing to break out, to realize his dreams and passions of being a great Arab leader; but there he was, pinned up in the cage of Transjordan by the British'.[5]

The direction in which Abdullah's ambition was channelled was Greater Syria—Syria in its historical or 'natural' dimensions. He could not forget that it was his family who sponsored the Arab Revolt, and that his brother Faisal was placed on the throne of Syria which purported to include Palestine, Transjordan, and Lebanon. The revolt was staged, as Abdullah recorded in his memoirs, with the object of establishing a unified Arab state, but after the war the Arab flags were hauled down in Damascus and Syria was trodden under foot: it was dismembered and divided into four parts.[6] Abdullah aspired, therefore, to realize the vision of Greater Syria with its capital in Damascus, the hereditary seat of the Umayyad caliphate, and with himself as king and overlord. He consistently maintained that Transjordan was only the southern part of Syria, and that his presence there was just a prelude to the attainment of complete Arab liberation in the pursuit of which his family had sacrificed the Hijaz. The motto he adopted was: 'All Syria to come under the leadership of a scion of the House of Hashem; Transjordan was the first step'. From his arrival in Transjordan until his assassination thirty years later, Abdullah nurtured this vision of a far-flung and powerful Arab kingdom united under his crown. The cherished notion of a great Arab empire which eluded the father would thus be realized by the son. Abdullah deliberately eschewed precision in defining the territorial limits of Greater Syria. Rather than commit himself to definite borders, he preferred to leave himself the greatest possible degree of tactical

[5] Larry Collins and Dominique Lapierre, *O Jerusalem* (New York: Pocket Books, 1972), 87.

[6] King Abdullah of Transjordan, *Memoirs*, ed. Philip R. Graves (London: Jonathan Cape, 1950), 247 f.

flexibility so as to be able to adjust his vision to changing circumstances and to take advantage of opportunities as and when they presented themselves. The obstacles standing in the way of realizing this vision were indeed formidable, but Abdullah was never a man to construe difficulty as impossibility. While holding before his eyes this lofty long-term ideal, he kept his feet firmly on the ground and pursued practical policies with limited objectives. Nor was he under any compulsion to try to accomplish his design in a great hurry. Despite his nickname, he was not in a hurry but, on the contrary, conscious of the importance of patience and self-discipline in carrying through his self-appointed mission to ultimate or even partial success.

In the early years of Abdullah's rule, frustrated Syrian nationalists and enemies of the French mandate descended on Amman in droves. Some of them found their way into Abdullah's embryonic administration while others, the more militant ones, were bent on pursuing their struggle against the French and even mounted some raids across the border. With Faisal keeping a low profile in Baghdad, and Husayn fighting a rearguard battle in his remote corner of Arabia, Abdullah emerged as a leading champion of Arab unity and Amman became a focal point for Arab nationalist politics. But the initial euphoria evaporated rapidly, and with the passage of time the gulf between his idea of Arab unity, based on Islam, autocracy, and the preservation of the old social order, and the younger nationalists' conception of unity as a means of attaining liberation from foreign rule and freedom and social reform at home, grew wider and resulted in mutual disenchantment. Abdullah's tendency to assume that what was good for the Hashemites was good for the Arabs did not gain him many friends, either at home or abroad. He himself began to focus more narrowly on his dynastic and personal interests at the expense of the broader political ideals. After the loss of the Hijaz to Ibn Saud and the expansion of his domain down to the Gulf of Aqaba, Abdullah settled down patiently to await opportunities for promoting his Greater Syria scheme. The scheme was modified following the death in 1933 of his brother Faisal. From now on he was to toy with various ideas for merging Iraq with Greater Syria, possibly in a Federation of the Fertile Crescent of which he, as the oldest member of the Hashemite family and the only surviving leader of the Arab Revolt, would be the natural ruler.

Abdullah worked industriously, if rather fitfully, to propagate the idea of Greater Syria, always harking back to Faisal's lost kingdom which should revert to himself just as Faisal's lineal heirs succeeded to the throne of Iraq. He cultivated assiduously a following in Syria itself and succeeded in enlisting the support of some of the conservative elements there: the Ulema (religious divines), the small landlords, and the tribal shaikhs scattered around the country. A not insignificant number of Syrians retained their monarchist sentiment and after Faisal's death in 1933 pinned their hopes on his aspiring older brother. But as long as the French remained in Syria and Lebanon, Abdullah's hopes had little chance of success, for the French regarded the Greater Syria movement as the unwary stalking horse, and Abdullah as the direct instrument of sinister British plots to undermine their own position in the area. In actual fact the British had never encouraged Abdullah to pursue his claims to Greater Syria; after the departure of the French, when Abdullah's expansionist plans were directed perforce against his Arab neighbours, they actively tried to discourage him.

Caught up in Great Power rivalries and in the cut and thrust of inter-Arab politics, the Greater Syria scheme ran for decades as a leitmotiv in the affairs of the Middle East, provoking suspicion, antagonism, and outright hostility towards Abdullah. The attack on his scheme in the Arab world came from every direction. The Lebanese emphatically refused to become absorbed in a unitary Muslim state. The republicans in Syria, who had struggled for so long to achieve independence from the Ottomans and the French, were not about to surrender their hard-won gains by subordinating their country to Hashemite rule. They also felt that if there was to be a Greater Syria they were better equipped to lead it than the ruler from the Hijaz, and that its core and political centre of gravity should be Syria itself rather than backward and feudal Transjordan. The Hashemites of Iraq and the nationalist politicians around them thought that their country was the natural leader of the Arab world; they devised their own plans for a federation under their leadership and gave Abdullah little support. The Saudis opposed any plan which might strengthen the Hashemites and were determined not to let Abdullah extend his power outside Transjordan lest he be tempted to reconquer the Hijaz. The Egyptians added their opposition to the concept of a Greater Syria seeing the Hashemite bloc as their principal rival for hegemony in the Arab world.

By posing as the champion of Arab unity, Abdullah thus ended up by antagonizing most Arab nationalists both inside and outside the boundaries of Greater Syria. The nationalists came to see Abdullah as the lackey and tool of British imperialism in the Middle East; they perceived his expansionist leanings as a threat to the independence of the other Arab states in the region; and they were critical of his accommodating attitude towards Zionism and the Jews in Palestine.

It was a measure of Abdullah's commitment and tenacity of purpose that he never abandoned his Greater Syria ambition even in the face of such formidable opposition. Because he knew where he was heading and had never made light of the difficulty of getting there, the obstacles and problems he encountered along the road could not easily deflect him. If he could not get to his ultimate destination today or tomorrow, that was no reason to give up the journey: conditions might change for the better and obstacles could be overcome through patience and perseverance.

Moreover, for Abdullah, Greater Syria was not an all-or-nothing proposition, nor was there only one path leading to its realization. If the whole of Syria in its historic dimensions could not be brought under Hashemite rule any extension of his domain would be welcome, in itself and as a further step in the right direction. Partial success might bring complete success; the road to Damascus might go through Baghdad or Jerusalem.

Without abandoning his larger goal, though he had so little to show for his initial efforts, Abdullah gradually began to change tack and to turn his thoughts and energy to Palestine. Palestine was only one of the four parts into which 'natural' Syria had been divided, and a small part at that. But for Abdullah it had importance out of all proportion to its small size. To want to rule over Palestine was not for him a vacuous ambition, nor was it an accident that at the very first meeting with Churchill he asked to be entrusted with its administration. Transjordan and Palestine were bound together by a complex network of political ties, trade relations, and routes of communication stretching back to the very distant past. The essential unity of the area lying on both sides of the Jordan, recognized by the League of Nations, was severed only by an arbitrary British decision which was opposed unsuccessfully by both Jewish and Arab inhabitants of the area. True, Abdullah had formally recognized the British mandate over Palestine and the Balfour Declaration—something his father had resisted to the bitter end—but he felt that he had no real choice in the matter. And there were compelling economic reasons for preserving the links between the two banks of the Jordan: Transjordan needed the capital, the markets, the trained manpower, and an outlet to the Mediterranean Sea which only Palestine could provide.

To Abdullah's way of thinking, gaining control over Palestine thus represented both an important end in itself and a possible means to a still larger long-term objective. The British attitude, here as always, was an important factor in Abdullah's calculations. He believed that the British would not look with the same disfavour on his plans for Palestine as they had always displayed towards his Greater Syria plan. The other two factors which had to be taken into consideration were the Palestine Arabs and the Jews. Accordingly, Abdullah's policy for furthering his design on Palestine can be seen as operating in three distinct but overlapping circles: in his relations with the British, in his relations with the Palestine Arabs, and in his relations with the Jews. In all three circles he used the same method—personal diplomacy.

Abdullah and the British

The circumstances surrounding Transjordan's birth go a long way towards explaining the character and evolution, the political system and the foreign policy of what turned out to be the only lasting progeny of the Anglo-Hashemite conspiracy. More than any other modern Arab state, Transjordan was the product of British imperial interests, of British will, and of British design. While the degree of independence afforded them by the colonial power and the struggle to expand it was a burning issue for all the Arab states, there can be no doubt that, in the case of Transjordan, the independence enjoyed was the most limited and the influence and control reserved by Britain for herself the most extensive. That control was no less effective for being indirect. Though the formative years and subsequent evolution of Transjordan were largely determined by the British, the hand of the British mandate was light and unobtrusive; unlike Palestine, the country was not over-weighed with British officials. A British Resident, supported by seven or eight officials, with a few technicians, sufficed to keep the country's administration under firm though indirect control.

In internal affairs of state the local ruler was granted considerable powers—powers which his upbringing and family traditions made him exercise in a thoroughly autocratic manner—but he was effectively placed under the superintendence and control of the British Resident in Amman and the high commissioner for Palestine. The paraphernalia of constitutional government were built to serve outward appearances rather than to limit the local ruler's autocracy *vis-à-vis* his own people. A dual pattern thus evolved, in the best tradition of British colonial government, whereby the local ruler enjoyed virtually absolute power at home in return for accepting his subordinate place in the hierarchy established by Whitehall. Viewed from Whitehall, this particular local ruler was not much more than a cog in the machinery of the mandate, notwithstanding all the appearances to the contrary.

Moreover, until the 1950s, the rulers of Transjordan, unlike most other Arab rulers, did not openly challenge or struggle to free themselves from this foreign domination; they accepted British control in principle and only strove to widen their own independence by persuasion and peaceful means. The amir of Transjordan set the model of Anglo-Arab cooperation. He was Britain's most loyal and devoted friend in the entire Arab world.

Abdullah's loyalty to Britain was free, however, of any illusions about Britain's motives or any romantic notions of Anglo-Arab partnership. Rather, it rested on a very sound appreciation of the needs of his dynasty, of his country, and of the Arab world at large. Abdullah perceived more clearly than Britain's strident critics that in her relations with the Arab world, Britain was motivated not by altruism but by her own interests. Unlike the critics, he also believed that Arab objectives could best be advanced through close co-operation with Britain and he acutely felt that opposition to Britain would be at best futile and possibly disastrous to the Arab national movement. Britain, he wished his fellow Arabs to realize, 'does not bestow her confidence on people who are untrustworthy or lacking in courage and resource. She does not believe in sentiment, but in realism and determination. Therefore be strong, loyal and alert and Britain will be with you and put her trust in you.'[7]

Abdullah certainly tried to practise what he preached, and once the amirate of Transjordan was established he bent all his efforts to win British backing for turning it into a larger and stronger Arab kingdom. While demonstrating loyalty to Britain and seeking to exact the maximum reward for his loyalty, he was not above resorting to intrigue, manipulation, and covert activities. Abdullah never really liked the British, but since the British had the last word he was careful not to challenge or antagonize them. He was well aware of the preference displayed by British officials towards his brother Faisal and felt that he himself had been misjudged, but he never allowed his disappointment and frustrations to sour his relations with the British. A sober realization of the limits of what the Arabs, himself included, could do for themselves, enhanced the value he attached to Britain's friendship. While pitching his demands very high he would settle for very little and would do so without bitterness, acrimony, or sulking in his tent. Abdullah's acceptance of the same British terms on Palestine which his father had so furiously rejected is an example of his general readiness to let Britain have the last word. No doubt the lessons he learnt from his father's mistakes helped him to manage relations with Britain altogether more smoothly and more successfully.

Although he did not speak English, Abdullah kept the conduct of relations with Britain in his own hands to the greatest possible extent and he imposed his distinctive personal stamp on every aspect of that relationship. Co-operation between the two countries was greatly facilitated by the warm friendship which linked the amir to Alec Kirkbride, the British Resident in Amman. It was largely due to Kirkbride's perfect command of Arabic, natural sympathy for the

[7] King Abdullah of Transjordan, *Memoirs*, 241 f.

Arabs, unrivalled knowledge of Transjordan, and accomplished diplomatic skills that British advice came to be seen in Amman as more of a support and less of a burden. Abdullah not only liked and admired Kirkbride but also knew him well—well enough to sense how the Englishman really felt about the official messages and advice he conveyed from the Foreign Office in London. Kirkbride had an equally penetrating insight, based on long experience, into the way Abdullah's mind worked, and without forgetting where his primary loyalty lay he presented Abdullah's case to London much more persuasively than Abdullah himself could ever hope to.

One of the factors which directly contributed to Abdullah's strength and durability as a ruler was his recognition of Transjordan's dependence on Britain and of the consequent inequality which pervaded the alliance between the two countries. He realized that Transjordan could not survive unless Britain supported her politically, assisted her financially, and underwrote her security. Despite this dependence, British officials treated Abdullah with unfailing courtesy and respect and outwardly upheld the myth of Transjordan's sovereign independence. But Abdullah was too shrewd to have any illusions. Making a virtue out of necessity, he accepted British advice and guidance with good grace and British subsidies with gratitude.

The British also built for Abdullah the ultimate prop of his regime—the Arab Legion. Established in 1921 by Col. F. G. Peake, the Arab Legion continued to be financed by Britain and led by British officers until 1956. Originally a small police force to defend the frontiers and protect the villages, it acquired, under the command of General John Glubb—Glubb Pasha—the organization and character of a regular army. It was widely considered to be the best trained, best equipped, most disciplined, and most effective fighting force among all the Arab countries. It served both as a praetorian guard to protect the Hashemite regime in Transjordan and as a dependable and powerful instrument in support of Abdullah's foreign policy.

Abdullah and the Palestinians

The interdependence of Transjordan and Palestine and the permeability of the border between them made it impossible for Abdullah to dissociate himself from the affairs of Palestine even if he had been inclined to do so. In fact, all his personal instincts and inclinations impelled him to concern himself very actively with the affairs of Palestine and to struggle ceaselessly to enlist the support of prominent Palestinians for his cause. Abdullah tacitly endorsed his father's claim that Palestine was included in the area over which Britain promised to support Arab independence; unlike his father he was not willing to pursue this claim to the point of an open rift with Britain. The pledge he secured from Britain in the summer of 1922 to exclude Transjordan from the orbit of Jewish settlement and from the undertaking to support a Jewish national home was seen by Abdullah as no more than an interim safeguard against Zionist encroachment. He made no effort to conceal his aspiration to incorporate Palestine in his own kingdom, possibly as a first step towards the realization of Greater Syria.

Abdullah's practice of employing Palestinians in high positions in his own government not only provided him with badly needed administrative and technical expertise but also enhanced his claim to be a legitimate spokesman of the Palestinian people. The administration of the amirate in the 1920s and 1930s included a large number of Palestinians at all levels, some of them veterans of Faisal's short-lived regime in Damascus. A significant proportion of Transjordan's leading statesmen were of Palestinian extraction, notably Ibrahim Hashim from Nablus, Samir al-Rifai from Safad, and Tawfiq Abul Huda from Acre. All three reached the post of prime minister and helped to steer the country to independence and through the stormy seas of the 1948 war and post-war era. All three gave Abdullah loyalty as well as service and they did not see themselves, nor were they perceived by others, as anything but true Transjordanians.

In addition, Abdullah had a substantial following among the Palestine Arabs, especially the Nashashibis, who urged unification with Transjordan and were willing to accept Abdullah as king of Palestine under British auspices. Pitted against the Nashashibis and against Abdullah was another powerful Palestinian family, the Husaynis, headed by Hajj Amin al-Husayni, the mufti of Jerusalem and president of the Supreme Muslim Council. The mufti represented the radical nationalist trend in Palestinian politics which, although socially conservative, was pan-Arab, pan-Islamic, committed above all else to the independence of Palestine, and rejecting any compromise on this score with the British authorities or the Zionist movement. The mufti himself, like the amir of Transjordan, was also an empire-builder, casting himself in the role of an Arab liberator who would banish the British from Palestine and use it as the base of a great pan-Arab and pan-Islamic empire. But there the similarity ended. Given the deep difference between their respective political outlooks and the absolute irreconcilability of their goals, not to mention the deadly personal antagonism between Abdullah and Hajj Amin, a head-on collision was inevitable. It was out of this deep-seated and many-sided conflict, which dominated Palestinian politics between 1917 and 1948, that the all-out struggle for power in Palestine was ultimately to develop.

2

THE HASHEMITE–ZIONIST CONNECTION

Early encounters

Of all the political friendships cultivated by Abdullah, the most controversial, the least well understood by fellow Arabs, and most damaging to his reputation was his friendship with the Zionists. No other aspect of his policy provoked such intense suspicion, stirred such strong passions, or brought him so much opprobrium. Abdullah's motives for seeking such an understanding were indeed complex but they can be reduced to two basic and seemingly inconsistent factors: his fear of Zionism and his perception of the opportunity it offered him to realize his own goals in Palestine. Much of the misunderstanding surrounding this aspect of Abdullah's policy stems from the failure to grasp this contradiction.

In an attempt to defend his grandfather against the charges so frequently levelled against him by his Arab critics, King Husayn, the present ruler of Jordan, has argued that in Abdullah's considered opinion 'the Zionist thrust and avalanche could have been blunted but not entirely thwarted. Morality and power-politics do not always match. The tragic undoing and dismantling of the Palestinian people, to which their leadership unwittingly contributed, was that they adamantly refused to understand or accept this unpleasant but elementary fact of life.' His grandfather, says Husayn, 'had perceived the Zionist iceberg and its dimensions, while others had seen only its tip. . . . His tactics and strategy were therefore attuned to circumventing and minimizing the possible consequences of a head-on collision. Others saw only the tip, and their responses were over-confidence, inflexibility, and outright complacency.'[1]

Although King Husayn is hardly a disinterested party in this great debate, one must recognize in all fairness the logic of his arguments in defence of his grandfather and in condemnation of the Palestinian leaders. It is perfectly true that Abdullah had a much more realistic and practical appreciation of the strength of the forces behind the Zionist

---

[1] King Abdullah of Jordan, *My Memoirs Completed: 'Al Takmilah'* (London: Longman, 1978), pp. xiv, xvi.

movement than most, if not all, of his Palestinian opponents. Whereas the latter indulged in facile optimism and hopes of an easy victory until overtaken by the disaster of 1948, he never underestimated the power, skill, and commitment which activated Jewish nationalism in Palestine. It is also true that because he realized that Zionism cannot be destroyed or ignored, and that the Arabs must one day compromise with it, Abdullah was regarded as a quisling by many Arabs less clear-eyed than he.

But all this is only one side of the coin. The other side of the coin, conveniently overlooked by King Husayn, is that his grandfather's policy towards the Zionists was also governed by an expectation of gains—gains which, at least in part, could only be realized at the expense of the Palestinian Arabs. For Abdullah was shrewd enough to recognize at an early stage in the game that the force of Zionism, if rightly channelled, could turn out to be not a barrier but a help in fulfilling his ambition of a greater Transjordan. Jewish enmity could only weaken his chances of being accepted by the world as the ruler of Palestine. On the other hand Jewish acquiescence, especially if it could be purchased at the price of autonomy under his rule, might pave the way to a greater Transjordan, incorporating part, or possibly all, of the Holy Land.

For the moderation he displayed towards the Jewish community in Palestine, Abdullah received praise from some quarters and was branded as a traitor in others. Both missed a crucial point because they failed to place the motives for his attitude in their proper historical context. They forgot that Abdullah received his political education at the centre of the Ottoman Empire before the Young Turks introduced new and alien concepts into its structure:

The empire was dynastic, Muslim, and supranational, with ethno-religious millets occupying their place in the appointed order of things. Although political power was firmly in Muslim hands, the millets—Armenians, Greek Orthodox, Jews—preserved their identity and their autonomy in matters of personal status and communal government. Their specific worth for the empire rested on their age old preoccupation with trade, finance, crafts, and the professions. It seems that Abdullah never ceased to regard the Jewish community of Palestine as some sort of modern millet, just as he saw Arab nationalism as a modern development of Islamic civilization and, mutatis mutandis, himself as successor to the Ottoman sultan, particularly after the death of his father Husayn (1931) and his elder brother Ali (1935) had made him head of his house. In this light the Jews of Palestine were potentially of immense value for their connections, their drive and their talents, and their reputed wealth, and Abdullah believed it was worthwhile to try and conciliate them with a generous 'autonomy'—provided, of course, they accepted their fundamental subjugation to an Arab–Muslim superstate with Abdullah as its benevolent sovereign.[2]

In his personal dealings with the Zionists, Abdullah was not hampered by any racist prejudice: hatred of the Jews did not burn in his heart and he stood above the fanatic anti-Jewish prejudices common among some members of his race. His unbiased and pragmatic attitude towards the Jews, while not unique and having several parallels, especially among conservative Arab leaders of which the present King Husayn is only one, did stand in marked contrast to the anti-Semitism of Ibn Saud, which verged on the pathological. Respect for the Jews, the People of the Book, was in fact for the Hashemites a family tradition, consistent with the teachings of the Koran. Abdullah's father refused to condone the Balfour Declaration not out of blind anti-Zionism but because it safeguarded only the civil and religious rights of the Arabs, disregarding what he perceived as their inalienable political and economic rights in Palestine. He was not opposed, indeed he was agreeable, to let the Jews live in peace beside Muslims in the Holy Land on the clear understanding that all the legitimate rights of the latter would be respected.

Faisal was the first Hashemite to discuss with a Zionist leader the possibility of co-operation between the Arab and Jewish national movements. In June 1918, as the military commander of the Arab Revolt, he received a visit from Dr Chaim Weizmann, the moderate Zionist leader, and their negotiations on this and subsequent occasions crystallized into the famous agreement signed by both parties on 3 January 1919. What is surprising is not that Faisal proved unable to ratify the agreement but that the talks ever got as far as they did. Although the Weizmann–Faisal agreement had no practical results, this episode in Hashemite–Zionist relations illuminates important trends in the thinking, expectations, and strategies of the two sides. Both sides based their strategy on an alliance with Britain, and it was the British who arranged the first meeting in the hope of allaying Sharifian fears of Zionism and of confirming them as the leaders of the Arab world. But while Weizmann sought agreement with the Sharifians at least partly so as to please the British, Faisal was interested in agreement chiefly as a means of furthering the Arab struggle for independence. Weizmann did not have any distinctive Arab policy of his own, having staked everything on the alliance with Britain. His policy was to a large extent only diplomacy, based on a very inadequate grasp of the political reality in Palestine and the desire to bypass local

<hr>

[2] Uriel Dann, *Studies in the History of Transjordan, 1920–1949: The Making of a State* (Boulder: Westview Press, 1984), 11.

opposition to Zionism through agreement with non-Palestinian Arab leaders. Hence his sympathy for the concept of pan-Arab nationalism based on the rejection of a distinct Palestinian national entity—a concept implicit in the Anglo-Sharifian alliance. Hence the inflated hopes he pinned on cordial relations with the Amir Faisal, whom he described as the greatest of the Arabs and a lifelong friend. Instead of grappling with realities, Weizmann devoted his consummate diplomatic skills to eliciting festive declarations from an accidental sympathizer on the unwarranted assumption that his attitude would have permanent influence on Arab behaviour towards Zionism. Faisal was similarly moved by exaggerated expectations of Jewish financial support (Weizmann mentioned the staggering figure of £40 million) and of political support in Europe and the United States for Syrian autonomy under the Sharifians. Whether or not he had the authority to sign an agreement affecting the Palestine Arabs, Faisal went back on it once his own hopes for Arab independence were dashed, following a shift in Britain's position from promoting Sharifian–Zionist co-operation to reaching a settlement with France. Let down by Britain and threatened by France, Faisal could not afford to go against the powerful nationalist tide running through Syria and Palestine. He was forced to declare that no separation of Palestine from Syria was acceptable, and that Zionist aspirations for a state clashed with Arab ideas.[3]

The Weizmann–Faisal intermezzo also highlighted the intrinsic difficulty in formulating precise and binding agreements when the Arab world-view was so different, a difficulty which was to bedevil Zionist diplomacy. Weizmann himself eloquently described this difficulty although he would have denied that it applied to his negotiations with Faisal.

The Arab is a very subtle debater and controversialist—much more so than the average educated European—and until one has acquired the technique one is at a great disadvantage. In particular, the Arab has an immense talent for expressing views diametrically opposed to yours with such exquisite and roundabout politeness that you believe him to be in complete agreement with you, and ready to join hands with you at once. Conversations and negotiations with Arabs are not unlike chasing a mirage in the desert: full of promise and good to look at, but likely to lead you to death by thirst.[4]

Amir Abdullah was thus not the first member of his family to discuss with a Jewish leader ways of bringing about reconciliation between their respective national movements. Soon after being made amir of Transjordan, Abdullah began his efforts to come to terms with the

[3] Simha Flapan, *Zionism and the Palestinians* (London: Croom Helm, 1979), 37–52, 124 f.
[4] Chaim Weizmann, *Trial and Error* (London: Hamish Hamilton, 1949), 271.

aspirations of the Jewish people, and he was to maintain intermittent contact with Jewish leaders over the next three decades. The opening move in his Jewish policy was an offer made to Dr Weizmann in London in 1922 to support Zionist demands and implement the Balfour Declaration if the Zionists, for their part, would accept him as amir of Palestine and use their influence with the British government to procure this appointment for him.

The basic solution to the problem, which he advanced at different times and in ever-changing forms, was a 'Semitic kingdom' embracing both Palestine and Transjordan, in which Arabs and Jews could live as of right and as equals and, needless to say, with himself as their hereditary monarch. Another small detail in this scheme which is worth noting is that Jews living abroad were not to have an automatic right to come to Palestine, and immigration controls of some sort would have to be imposed to ensure Arab preponderance and keep the Jews to a minority status in this 'Semitic kingdom'.

There was never any chance of Abdullah's offer of autonomy within a larger kingdom ruled by himself being acceptable to the official leadership of the Yishuv, the Jewish community in Palestine. The official leaders of the Zionist movement stood for nothng less than an independent Jewish state, and the offer of a limited autonomy under Arab rule fell far short of their expectations and was indeed incompatible with the basic aim of their movement. In the Hashemites they found a foreign Arab dynasty which could be used to bypass the opposition of the local inhabitants and to consolidate their toehold in Palestine. Confident in their ability to attain full independence and statehood by their own exertions, they were reluctant to place themselves under the benevolent umbrella held up by the Hashemites. They wanted good relations with Abdullah, but they had no wish to be his subjects. They saw self-reliance as the only path to genuine independence and felt that riding to power on Abdullah's esteemed coat-tails would incur unacceptable obligations. If this was the view of the Labour Zionists who dominated the political institutions of the Yishuv, further to the right were Zeev Jabotinsky's Revisionist Zionists who not only spurned any idea of subservience to an Arab ruler but were never reconciled to the partition of mandatory Palestine and continued to include the East Bank of the Jordan in their ambitious blueprint for a Jewish state.

Both Revisionist and Labour Zionists refused to come to terms with the exclusion of Transjordan from the Palestine mandate and both were intent on reversing the verdict of the 1922 White Paper, whether by political, military, or economic means. The Revisionists thought in terms of military conquest whereas the practical Zionists thought in terms of a more subtle and gradual process. It was Weizmann's belief and hope that 'the road along which we shall cross over to Transjordan will not be paved by soldiers but by Jewish labour and the Jewish plough'.[5] Ben-Gurion defined his movement's ultimate goal as the independence of the Jewish people in Palestine, on both sides of the Jordan, not as a minority but as a community of several millions. He was strongly attached to the empty spaces east of the Jordan and maintained that the opinion held by some Zionists that Transjordan was not Palestine rested upon ignorance of the history and geography of the country. The eastern border in Ben-Gurion's map of what he ambiguously termed the 'Jewish commonwealth' was not the Jordan River, but the Syrian desert, at the furthest edge of Transjordan.[6]

With hindsight, the aspirations of the Hashemite amir on the one hand and of the leaders of mainstream Zionism on the other appear so divergent that it is tempting to conclude that any attempt to reach agreement on his terms was doomed to failure from the start. But it should be recalled that in those early days when the future of Palestine was anything but certain, both sides were flexible, both had room for manœuvre, both were interested in finding a basis for mutual co-operation, and each side could reasonably hope that its vision would eventually prevail.

Moreover, conflicting aims in the long run did not preclude practical co-operation in the short run. Weizmann and his colleagues always stressed that the Jewish revival in Palestine, far from being prejudicial to the Arabs, would be directed at promoting their material welfare and progress. Transjordan was in dire need of foreign capital and skills and through *rapprochement* with the Jews Abdullah hoped to obtain them. A number of Jewish businessmen and entrepreneurs approached Abdullah in the early years with projects that promised to contribute to the development of his amirate and, directly or indirectly, to his personal riches. On the steamer which took him to England in 1922 he met Moshe Novomeysky, a Jewish mining engineer from Siberia who wanted to set up a chemical plant on the Dead Sea, and reviewed with him the prospects of Palestinian–Transjordanian co-operation and the mutual advantage the two countries could expect to draw from the proposed chemical industry;[7] in 1929 Novomeysky's Palestine Potash Company obtained the concession to exploit the enormous chemical resources of the Dead Sea. Similarly, in 1927 Pinhas Rutenberg,

[5] Meyer Weisgal, ed., *Chaim Weizmann: Statesman, Scientist, Builder of the Jewish Commonwealth* (New York: Dial Press, 1944), 57.

[6] Teveth, *Ben Gurion and the Palestine Arabs*, 35.

[7] M. A. Novomeysky, *Given to Salt: The Struggle for the Dead Sea Concession* (London: Max Parrish, 1958), 28 f.

another engineer from Russia, was granted the concession to set up a hydroelectric power plant in Naharayim, at the confluence of the Yarmuk and Jordan rivers. Public opinion in Transjordan was very much against it on the grounds that it would precipitate mass Jewish immigration to Transjordan,[8] but the agreement was signed because it was to the material advantage of the amir.

Col. Frederick Kisch, the chairman of the Palestine Zionist Executive, records in his diary interesting details of an official visit he paid to Amman in 1924. After an elaborate exchange of greetings and homilies about the historic bonds between the Semitic peoples, King Husayn of the Hijaz, who was staying with his son, told the delegation that he was ready to give land to the Jews free 'provided they entered through the door and did not make a breach in the walls'. Amir Abdullah, at a later meeting with the visiting delegation, said that in his previous conversations with Zionist leaders, including Dr Weizmann, he had declared his friendly attitude, but it looked as if the acts of the Zionists were not as good as their word. He feared that the Zionists had secret intentions. After being assured this was not the case, the amir, echoing his father's sentiments, declared that provided the rights of the Arabs were secure, they would welcome the presence of Jews not only in Palestine but in other Arab countries. He stressed the importance of hastening a solution of the difficulties lest the Arabs should lose patience. Kisch's suggestion of forming a joint committee of Jews and Arabs to discuss the Palestine question under the chairmanship of an Arab prince (meaning Abdullah) failed to elicit a positive response from the Hashemite court.[9]

Six years later, Abdullah issued an informal invitation to renew these conversations. Kisch was quite disposed to do so but felt constrained by the absence of a definite Arab policy on the part of the Jewish Agency. He did not mean in regard to matters of local relations between the Jews and the Arabs in Palestine, but in regard to the major issues that affected the neighbouring Arab states as well. A visit to Amman was duly arranged for February 1931 and Kisch once again went to pay his respects to the aged head of the Hashemite family, who had in the meantime lost his kingdom and was living in exile. Husayn recalled Kisch's earlier visit, declaring that what he had then said about kinship between Arabs and Jews had been spoken from the heart. He sent for Abdullah and told him that he should always respect that kinship and do his utmost towards establishing friendly relations between the two peoples. Afterwards, evidently under the impression of his father's

<hr>

[8] Sulayman Musa and Munib al-Madi, *The History of Jordan in the Twentieth Century* (Arab.) (Amman, 1959), 279.

[9] F. H. Kisch, *Palestine Diary* (London: Victor Gollancz, 1938), 96–107.

words, Abdullah relaxed his restraint and spoke freely about his past, about Arab aspirations, and about the Arab–Jewish problem in Palestine. Conflict between Arab and Jew would benefit neither, he said. He recognized and appreciated the Jewish connection with Palestine, which was even mentioned in the Koran, but a solution must be found which was not inconsistent with Arab aspirations for a united Arabia. His prime minister, Hassan Khaled Pasha, who participated in the talks, stated quite definitely that he saw no objection to Arabs and Jews from Palestine participating in the development of Transjordan.

As a consequence of Kisch's visit to Amman, a Jewish doctor was sent to treat a cataract in King Husayn's eye, and Amir Abdullah expressed his intention of bringing his son to see Dr Ticho in Jerusalem; undeterred by the efforts of the Arab Executive to spoil their relations, he sent Colonel Kisch a warm message of appreciation for his efforts in this regard.[10] Jewish medical attention to the Hashemite family was not the only outcome of Kisch's visit to Amman. It was at this meeting that Abdullah and his prime minister sowed the seeds which rapidly sprouted into a large-scale project of organized Jewish settlement in Transjordan to develop some of its uncultivated land. The idea itself was not entirely novel. As early as August 1926, Abdullah had made an impassioned plea for Jewish involvement in the development of Transjordan:

Palestine is one unit. The division between Palestine and Transjordan is artificial and wasteful. We, the Arabs and Jews, can come to terms and live in peace in the whole country, but you will have difficulty in reaching an understanding with the Palestine Arabs. You must make an alliance with us, the Arabs of Iraq, Transjordan and Arabia. We are poor and you are rich. Please come to Transjordan. I guarantee your safety. Together we will work for the benefit of the country.[11]

The statement is indicative both of Abdullah's tactics for circumventing the obstacles to co-operation posed by the Palestine Arabs and of his desire to harness Jewish capital, skill, and initiative for the development of his backward country. Jewish capabilities had been demonstrated in Palestine, giving Abdullah grounds for hope that Jewish capital and Jewish experts could do for the area east of the Jordan what they had done for the area to the west. Kisch was only too ready to oblige and asked one of his experts from the Jewish Agency to set up a Survey Office in Amman which would create a new and useful point of

---

[10] Kisch, *Palestine Diary*, 338, 387, 390.
[11] From the amir's statement on 18 August 1926 to Dr Saul Mizan, quoted in Aharon Cohen, *Israel and the Arab World* (Boston: Beacon Press, 1970), 28.

contact with Transjordan.[12] Kisch's efforts in Amman generated goodwill and led to the discussion of various joint projects for construction work, drainage, and electricity but yielded no significant political results.

When Chaim Arlozoroff replaced Colonel Kisch as the political secretary of the Jewish Agency Executive in August 1931, he embarked on a more purposeful policy designed to strengthen the moderate Arabs and weaken the extremists and to develop conditions for a Jewish state on both sides of the Jordan River. The shortage of land in western Palestine rekindled the Zionist interest in the sparsely populated spaces to the east, both as an outlet for Jewish settlement and as a refuge of last resort for Arabs displaced as a result of Jewish immigration to Palestine.

Arlozoroff was able to build on the work of his predecessor in developing and expanding the Jewish Agency's links with the amir of Transjordan. In March 1932, accompanied by Moshe Sharett, Arlozoroff went on an official visit to the amir's palace in Amman. As it was his first visit, Arlozoroff had no specific proposals to convey but simply set out to make personal contacts and gain first-hand impressions. His principal impression was that Abdullah seemed a stranger in his own country; that he could not forget the Hijaz and that his entourage was made up largely of Hijazis whom he knew and trusted. Arlozoroff also attributed Abdullah's caution in political matters to his shaky power-base and the need not to offend the susceptibilities of his subjects.[13]

Arlozoroff argued that the economic development of Transjordan could not proceed without a close link with Palestine and that the separation of the two territories was artificial. Transjordan needed access to the sea while trade and industry in Palestine needed a local market in order to grow, said Arlozoroff. Co-operation was bound to turn the two territories into one economic region. There were many instances of economic co-operation between countries leading in time to political unity. The Jews had made great strides in developing Palestine and were ready to act in neighbouring countries in need of capital, energy, and skilled manpower.

Abdullah replied that he himself was not afraid of the Jews and that his outlook was broader than that of the man in the street who viewed the Jews as he would a ghost. He, the amir, understood that the millions of Jews in the world could not give up their control of international finance and go to Palestine to starve. And since he knew that only a minority of the Jews would seek a place in Palestine, he was

[12] Kisch, *Palestine Diary*, 438.
[13] Chaim Arlozoroff, *Jerusalem Diary* (Heb.) (Tel Aviv: Mapai, 1949), 248–50.

not afraid of Jewish immigration. But whether or not the fear of Jews was justified, the fact was that this fear prevailed in Palestine and influenced public opinion in Transjordan as well. It created a political situation which had to be taken into account, and if the Jews wanted the kind of co-operation that Dr Arlozoroff referred to it was their duty to dispel the fears and to establish peaceful relations with the Arabs of Palestine.

During lunch the Jewish visitors tried to correct some of the popular misconceptions about the collective systems used in their agricultural settlements. The amir attacked these settlements for being breeding grounds of bolshevism and corruptors of morals. When the difference between political and economic communism was pointed out to him and his allegations of permissiveness and loose morals were rejected as being without substance, he persisted in arguing that economic equality and the collectivist way of life were contrary to the philosophy of Islam and to the traditions of the Arab inhabitants of the country. When invited to visit one of these settlements, the amir excused himself by saying that he could not ignore public opinion and what the press said. For the amir, Zionism's attraction clearly did not lie in its progressive social ideas.[14]

The saga of Ghaur al-Kibd

One of the strangest episodes in the history of Hashemite–Zionist relations followed from Amir Abdullah's offer to lease some of his own land in Ghaur al-Kibd, on the east of the Jordan, to Jewish entrepreneurs. The land, situated in the central Jordan valley between the Allenby Bridge and the town of Salt, was originally state property but was transferred to the amir's private domain in 1931. In the following year rumours reached Jerusalem that the amir was looking for capital to invest in the development of his land. Several unsuccessful attempts had been made to interest non-Jewish capitalists, and it was only after the amir had given up hope of finding any other source willing to undertake the work that rumours about his intentions began to reach Jewish circles.

Dr Arlozoroff was rather slow to react on account of the attendant political pitfalls, but two members of the Jewish Agency Executive, Emanuel Neumann and Herschel Farbstein, secretly went to see the amir to find out his real intentions. The amir told them that he would welcome Jewish economic initiative because it would help the country to develop. Jews and Arabs had much in common and should be friends, he said, and he felt that this project would promote the welfare

[14] Moshe Shertok, 'Visit to Amir Abdullah', 28 Mar. 1932, S25/6313, CZA.

of both. There was nothing startlingly new in these thoughts except for the fact that they were being uttered by the head of an Arab state.[15]

In January 1933 the secret negotiations culminated in the signature of an agreement between the amir and the Palestine Land Development Company granting the latter a 6-month option to lease 70,000 dunams—the equivalent of 7,000 hectares or 17,500 acres—against a payment of £P500. The lease, if made operative, was to run for a 33-year period and was renewable for two similar periods against the payment of an annual rent of £P2,000 plus 5 per cent of the profits made in the process of cultivation. The amir also undertook to procure the necessary authority for registering companies and for admitting any number of workers required by his tenant for the cultivation of the demised area.[16]

Despite the efforts of both sides to keep the deal secret, word got round and a storm of protest broke out in the Palestine press. The British authorities advised Abdullah that it was politically unwise to invite the Jews to settle and pressed him to renounce the agreement; they warned the Jews that Britain could not be responsible for the safety of potential settlers. Behind the official British position lurked an unspoken fear that the emergence of an Abdullah–Zionist axis would weaken their own hold over the two parties and over the Fertile Crescent as a whole. Particularly worrying was the prospect that the deal would provoke Ibn Saud to move his forces against Transjordan and in the process upset the British presence there.[17]

Under the combined pressure of the Arab nationalists in Palestine and the British authorities, Abdullah relented to the extent of telling the Arab press that he had never concluded a pact with the Jews. Behind the backs of the British authorities, however, he continued to renew the option and collect the payment for it. In 1935 he collected a lump sum of £P3,500 for a 4-year extension of the option, while his confidant, Muhammad al-Unsi, who conducted the negotiations on his behalf, received £P1,800 from the Jewish Agency for his trouble. The Jewish Agency seemed content to continue to pay for the option without ever exercising it. Clearly, it was not philanthropic instincts or any serious hope of eventual Jewish settlement in Transjordan that moved the Jewish Agency to keep up its payments to the amir, but the perceived need to secure the backing of an Arab ruler as a counterweight to Palestinian antagonism. What the settlement

[15] Emanuel Neumann, *In the Arena: An Autobiographical Memoir* (New York: Herzl Press, 1976), 121–30.

[16] Agreement Between Amir Abdullah and the Palestine Land Development Company, S25/3505, CZA.

[17] Kenneth W. Stein, *The Land Question in Palestine, 1917–1939* (Chapel Hill: North Carolina University Press, 1984), 192–9.

option did provide in this context was a thin veneer of legitimacy for what could otherwise be construed as the payment of a political subsidy.

In favouring the entry of Jews into Transjordan, Abdullah was expressing the wishes of many of his subjects, especially the land-owning shaikhs who were at least as eager as he was to lease their uncultivated land and much freer in giving vent to their anger with British interference. One of these shaikhs, Mithqal Pasha al-Faiz, head of the most important bedouin tribal confederation in Transjordan, the Beni Sakhr, went as far as establishing a new political party in May 1933. Named the Unity Party, it called for the removal of foreign officials from Transjordan and openly voiced its conviction that only Jewish settlement could save the country from the scourge of starvation which had afflicted it in recent years. Another influential supporter of joint economic enterprises with the Jews and the sale of land to them was Rufayfan Pasha al-Majali, head of the Majali tribe and leader of the ruling party in the Legislative Council. To counter the persistent efforts of the bedouin shaikhs to put their barren lands to some profitable use, the British authorities pressed for the enactment of a law restricting the sale or lease of land to foreigners. But the Permanent Mandates Commission of the League of Nations pointed out that the mandate could not prevent either the amir or the shaikhs from voluntarily permitting their land to be colonized, and the Transjordan Legislative Council rejected the draft law and affirmed its support for an 'open door' policy for the Jews. The British, however, won the last battle with the enactment of a Nationality Law, which prohibited the leasing of land to non-citizens, thereby closing to the Jews the gateway to the Arabian peninsula that the Transjordanian ruler and tribal chiefs were united in wishing to keep open.[18]

This setback did not end Abdullah's efforts at co-operation with the Zionists but marked the beginning of an intensified drive on his part to reach an understanding with them and to take a more active interest in the affairs of Palestine. If during the first decade of the amirate he had tended to keep himself aloof from developments there in order to consolidate his position at home, during the second decade he became increasingly preoccupied with the future of Palestine. It was in the early 1930s that he laid his claim to be first the religious leader and then the political spokesman of the Arabs of Palestine. With the Zionists he began to have more regular high-level contact, and the relationship became more political in nature after the move towards economic co-

[18] Benjamin Shwadran, *Jordan: A State of Tension* (New York: Council for Middle Eastern Affairs Press, 1959), 190–2; Y. Porath, *The Palestinian Arab National Movement, 1929–1939*, vol. ii, *From Riots to Rebellion* (London: Frank Cass, 1977), 71–3; Sasson, *On the Road to Peace*, 35–7.

operation had been blocked. Moreover, the conflict between Arabs and Jews provided Abdullah with a lever for extending his own influence in Palestine with a view to bringing the whole country under his crown. To the Jewish Agency he usually offered autonomy within a kingdom under his rule, asking them in return to pressure the British government to accept him as the ruler of Palestine and, secondly, to help him finance political activity designed to combat the Husaynis. The Jewish Agency was more responsive to the requests for financial help to combat common opponents than it was to pleas for diplomatic activity for a cause inconsistent with its own objectives.

In the spring of 1934, on the eve of a trip to London, Abdullah sent Muhammad al-Unsi, his trusted emissary, with a four-point proposal to the Jewish Agency: (*a*) Palestine and Transjordan would be united under the throne of Abdullah, (*b*) the Arabs would recognize the mandate, including its guarantee of Jewish rights, (*c*) each state would have its own Legislative Council and government but the two prime minsters would act under Abdullah's direction, and (*d*) an agreement would be reached between Jews and Arabs on Jewish immigration and land purchase which would be outside the jurisdiction of either Legislative Council. Al-Unsi conveyed Abdullah's proposal to Moshe Shertok (later Sharett), the head of the Political Department of the Jewish Agency, together with an invitation to talks in Amman. To lure the Jewish Agency, al-Unsi also intimated that Syria might join the united kingdom at a later stage, which would open up new vistas for Jewish enterprise. Two delegations of Palestinian Arabs, one representing the Husaynis and the other the Nashashibis, were also invited to discuss Abdullah's proposals. The Husaynis, although presented with a diluted version, nevertheless rejected the plan as incompatible with their basic demands for abrogation of the mandate and the Balfour Declaration and the granting of full independence to the Arab people. The Nashashibi leaders, on the other hand, pledged their loyalty to the amir, favoured the proposed union, and emphasized the urgent need for an agreement with the Jews. Abdullah's precise terms were not acceptable to the Jewish Agency, however, and this coming on top of the Husaynis' rejection sealed the fate of his plan.[19]

Abdullah had set a pretty substantial cat among the pigeons and in doing so he confirmed the worst suspicions of the Arab nationalists. For Hajj Amin, the union of Palestine with Transjordan under the Hashemite throne spelled death for his own political programme and for the most cherished national aspirations of his followers. He therefore mobilized all his forces in combating it and mounted a campaign of unrestrained personal invective against Abdullah, denouncing him as

[19] Porath, *The Palestinian Arab National Movement*, ii. 73 f.

'the Jews' friend' and his Nashashibi allies as traitors. As his conflict with Abdullah intensified over the Palestine question and the latter's moderation towards the Zionists, Hajj Amin, who had once served in Faisal's government in Damascus and enjoyed Husayn's patronage as mufti of Jerusalem, shifted his loyalty to Ibn Saud—the most deadly rival of the Hashemite dynasty. Abdullah maintained his moderate stand despite the deteriorating political and economic situation in Palestine, but the pressure of the Arab nationalists on the one hand and the British authorities on the other left him in a most uncomfortable position.

The Arab Revolt, 1936–1939

The influx of Jews from Hitler's Germany provoked deep anxieties and disturbances among the Palestine Arabs, and the ripples were felt in neighbouring states too. Abdullah, who was in close contact with the Arabs of Palestine and realized the genuineness and depth of their fears, repeatedly warned the British government of the disastrous consequences which would ensue unless it intervened to allay these fears with adequate safeguards. 'The Jews', he wrote in a letter to the high commissioner, 'have attempted and continue to attempt to go beyond the promises made in the Balfour Declaration and thereby have given rise in the minds of the Arabs to a fixed idea that a Jewish state is being created which is masquerading under the name of the National Home. The implications of this are causing fears to spread to the Arab countries outside of Palestine.' Arab fears, he continued, were accentuated by the failure of the Jews to give the slightest indication of their intention to integrate with the original Arab inhabitants of the country and if unrestricted immigration were allowed to continue, 'it will lead to evil and terrible results in the near future'.[20]

   Abdullah's forebodings came true in 1936 when the Arab Higher Committee declared a general strike with the aim of halting Jewish immigration, banning the sale of land to the Jews, and establishing an independent national government. The strike was accompanied by violent attacks on Jews and the spread of political disturbances which threatened to engulf the surrounding Arab states. The British authorities, who had persistently disregarded Abdullah's earlier warnings, now asked him to use his good offices to end the strike and prepare for the arrival of a commission of inquiry. Abdullah exerted himself to defuse the crisis by restraining his population; by influencing the rebels to appear before the commission; and by trying to persuade the Arab kings to adopt a united front, writing to them that the Arab–Jewish

---

[20] Abdullah, *My Memoirs Completed*, 80–3.

conflict would only find its satisfactory resolution in the holding of talks and not in the crossing of swords.

All Abdullah's lines of activity were equally in accordance with an independent appeal made to him by the Jewish Agency to use his influence to end the strike. This does not mean that Abdullah was acting on behalf of the Jewish Agency. After all, the invitation to act as mediator came from the British high commissioner, and Abdullah agreed to undertake the task in the express hope that the British government would intercede with France for the unification of Syria with Transjordan or, as an alternative, agree to the unification of Palestine with Transjordan. But the specific proposals made by Abdullah for ending the strike and the arguments he advanced in support of his proposals suggest at the very least that he seriously considered the advice that he and al-Unsi were receiving in letters from Sharett. Renewal of the strike in July forced Abdullah to adopt a tough public stand against permitting the influx of Jewish immigrants to continue. Privately al-Unsi suggested the stoppage of immigration for a limited period or its diversion to Transjordan on condition that Palestine would be merged with Transjordan. Although the Jewish Agency did not reply to this suggestion, Abdullah kept up his efforts to steer it towards a solution along these lines.[21]

Parallel efforts were made to find a satisfactory compromise through a series of talks between prominent figures from the two opposing camps. Musa al-Alami, a man of wide influence in the Arab community, participated in the talks with the amir's knowledge and approval. Pinhas Rutenberg, managing director of the Palestine Electric Corporation, headed the group and kept Dr Weizmann, whose moderate outlook he shared, informed about the course of the conversations. Rutenberg's view, summarized in a memorandum to the Jewish Agency, was that the aim of any serious attempt to find a way out of the Arab–Jewish imbroglio should not be a temporary agreement with Arab leaders in Palestine but a permanent settlement with the Arab world. Transjordan and Palestine, in his view, had to be considered as a single unit, and the government of Transjordan must be a party to any agreement between the two communities. But the detailed political arrangements he proposed involved a measure of Jewish independence that his Arab interlocutors could only regard as being at the expense of their own national aspirations and these talks, like so many others, foundered on this rock.[22]

It was the 'slow road' leading through Palestine's Arab neighbours

[21] Correspondence and reports, especially Shertok to Abdullah, 30 Apr. 1936, and Abdullah to Shertok, 6 May 1936, S25/3243, CZA.

[22] Ben-Gurion, *My Talks with Arab Leaders*, 70–84.

that Dr Weizmann recommended as the best way to get real results. Contacts with politicians in the neighbouring countries were seen as a way both of neutralizing their opposition and using their good offices to influence the Palestine Arabs. Amman was the main stop along this 'slow road', and the 'political subsidy' given by the Jews to Abdullah provided a basis for even closer political co-operation. But it was not just the Jews who sought co-operation with Abdullah; the British authorities also feared that the Transjordanian tribes might be drawn into western Palestine by the unrest. Abdullah therefore received special payments from both sources during the early months of the general strike, earmarked for 'the pacification of spirits', and the results were considered fairly satisfactory.[23]

Yet Abdullah's political value to the Zionists remained limited because he did not come out squarely on their side but continued to steer a cautious course between the contestants. Considerable skill was necessary to preserve his credibility simultaneously as a loyal ally of Britain, a sincere friend of the Jews and an Arab patriot defending the rights of his Palestinian brothers. In letters and meetings with Palestinian leaders, including Hajj Amin al-Husayni, he proposed ways of ending the strike without loss of face and offered his services as a mediator between them and the British. To the Jews he urged acceptance of a temporary halt to immigration to enable the Palestinian leaders to call off the strike and quell the violence, and here too he offered his services as a mediator. Abdullah coupled his short-term remedy of a voluntary suspension of immigration with a long-term solution based on the reunification of Transjordan with western Palestine. The Jews, however, categorically rejected the former and side-stepped the latter.[24]

---

[23] Neil Caplan, *Futile Diplomacy*, ii. *Arab–Zionist Negotiations and the End of the Mandate* (London: Frank Cass, 1986), 40 f.
[24] Ibid.

3

A JUDGEMENT OF SOLOMON

The Peel Commission

The British government's belated response to the outbreak of the Arab Revolt in Palestine consisted of appointing a Royal Commission, with Earl Peel as chairman, to investigate the problem. Announced in May 1936, the commission was appointed in August to ascertain the underlying causes of the disturbances which had broken out in the middle of April. It was also asked to inquire more widely into the implementation of the mandate, British obligations towards Arabs and Jews, the existence of grievances, and to 'make recommendations for the removal and the prevention of their recurrence'.

The first to give evidence to the Peel Commission after its arrival in Palestine were the British officials who told their sorry tale of trying to run an administration in the face of the conflicting pressures of 400,000 Jews and nearly one million Arabs and the thorny question of land sales and immigration that had provoked the general strike. The overall effect of this testimony was summed up by one percipient Jewish observer who compared the mandate to a minor English public school: 'There was the headmaster, the high commissioner, trying to be firm and impartial: but the assistant masters favoured the sporting stupid boarders (Arabs) against the clever swot dayboys (Jews) who had the deplorable habit of writing home to their parents on the slightest provocation to complain about the quality of the teaching, the food and so on.'[1]

As the members of the commission listened patiently to the rival claims of Jewish and Arab spokesmen, the idea of a territorial division of Palestine began to take root in their minds. Reginald Coupland, Beit Professor of Colonial History at Oxford and the commission's most cerebral member, was particularly persuasive in pushing the partition idea. 'Jewish nationalism is as intense and as self-centred as Arab nationalism', he and his colleagues were to conclude. 'Both are growing forces and the gulf between them is widening.'[2] Rumours about the possible partition of Palestine constituted the backdrop to Arab and

---

[1] Ian Black, 'A Judgement of Solomon That Could Not Save Palestine', *Guardian* 7 July 1987.
[2] Ibid.

Zionist diplomatic manœuvres during the commission's protracted deliberations.

Initial reactions inside the Jewish Agency were rather mixed. Weizmann, Ben-Gurion, and Sharett were generally in favour of partition. They were attracted to it as a way of securing independent control over Jewish immigration and settlement and they perceived it as an opportunity to realize the 2,000-year-old dream of a Jewish state—the ultimate if undeclared aim of the movement they headed. Chaim Weizmann was the most straightforward supporter of partition precisely because it involved a Jewish state. 'The Jews would be fools not to accept it,' he said, 'even if it were the size of a table-cloth.' Weizmann's natural optimism was not dimmed by the small area that was eventually allocated to the Jewish state. It was the beginning of a new chapter in Jewish history, he wrote. 'The Kingdom of David was smaller; under Solomon it became an Empire. Who knows? *C'est le premier pas qui compte!*'[3] The same logic prompted Ben-Gurion's conversion to the idea. A Jewish state in part of Palestine was preferable to no state at all, and it was only the beginnintg not the end.[4] Moshe Sharett was also prepared to settle for a Jewish state in part of Palestine, but he thought it would be a tactical mistake for the Zionist movement to declare its readiness too early in the game.[5]

Convinced that nothing less than the fate of the Zionist movement was hanging in the balance, Weizmann, Ben-Gurion, and Sharett spared no effort to create a favourable climate of opinion by the evidence they gave before the commission, by informal contact with its members, and by assiduous lobbying of British officials and members of Parliament. Consequently, these Zionist leaders played a greater role in crystallizing the Peel Report and its ultimate failure than they themselves were ever prepared to admit. The selection of partition in preference to establishing a legislative council with parity or cantonization; the borders of the projected states; the idea of a population exchange between them; and the choice of Abdullah rather than the mufti to head the Arab state were all influenced, if only marginally, by Zionist diplomacy.

The idea of Abdullah heading Arab Palestine was not part of the commission's original intentions, nor was it favoured by any influential British officials. Government circles in Jerusalem always saw Abdullah as more of a burden than an asset and none saw him as a decisive factor in the Palestine problem. For Foreign Office officials intent on solving

---

[3] Quoted in N. A. Rose, *The Gentile Zionists: A Study in Anglo-Zionist Diplomacy, 1929–1939* (London: Frank Cass, 1973), 128, 138.

[4] Ben-Gurion, *Letters to Paula*, 153–7.

[5] Moshe Sharett, *Political Diary*, vol. ii. 1937 (Heb.) (Tel Aviv: Am Oved, 1971), 178, 216, 235.

the problem in a way which would placate the Arabs, Abdullah was an embarrassing ally since any preference shown to him was bound to arouse Saudi resentment. In the Colonial Office, too, the wisdom of elevating Abdullah was questioned, on account of his unpopularity among the Palestinians and the Arab world generally. Members of the commission, however, were favourably impressed with Abdullah in the course of an unpublicized meeting during their visit and they began to pin their hopes for a solution on him and on the Nashashibi National Defence Party. The British officials would clearly have preferred the mufti, but his defiant rejection of partition as a solution worked in favour of Abdullah and in favour of merging the Arab state with Transjordan. Moreover, though Abdullah took the precaution of reserving his position on the subject of partition, it was generally assumed that he would go along with it provided the Arab part of Palestine was incorporated in Transjordan.

In March 1937 word got out that the commission was giving serious thought to the idea of partitioning Palestine between the Jews and the amir of Transjordan. For some Zionist leaders this was welcome news, though they did not dare say so publicly; for most Palestinian leaders it was anathema. For them a possible take-over of parts of Palestine by Abdullah was almost as objectionable as the Jews being given a state of their own on Arab soil. Thus, on hearing that the mufti was so hostile to the idea that he might make a deal with the Jews, the Turkish consul in Jerusalem offered to serve as a go-between.[6]

The Jews too were anxious to explore any possibility of an accord with the Arabs. Sharett wrote to Weizmann in April of his idea to offer the Arabs peace negotiations as the only way of escaping Solomon's judgement. Even if nothing was to come from such a meeting, Sharett felt that it would be interesting to learn something at first hand about the Arab frame of mind and he considered it 'important to go on record that at this eleventh hour before the cutting of the baby we have again offered peace'. But Sharett's suggestion of a common Jewish–Arab front against partition met with a firm rebuff. Awni Abd al-Hadi, the leader of the pan-Arab Istiqlal (Independence) Party, told Sharett: 'We will fight. We will struggle against the partition of the country and against Jewish immigration. There is no compromise.'[7]

Since there appeared to be no possibility of fruitful contact with the Palestinian Arabs, Sharett and his colleagues intensified their contacts with non-Palestinian Arabs and above all with Abdullah. The coronation festivities for King George VI brought to London many Arab dignitaries, including Abdullah, and it was there that Pinhas Rutenberg, with the knowledge and encouragement of Ben-Gurion,

---

[6] Caplan, *Futile Diplomacy*, ii. 63.   [7] Ibid.; Black, op. cit., n. 1 above.

approached the royal party with an offer of Jewish financial assistance in return for permission to settle Jews in Transjordan. The specific plan that Rutenberg had in mind was to create a development company with a capital of £P2 million and to pay the amir a substantial sum in return for which he would allocate one million dunams in Transjordan for Jewish settlers.

Ben-Gurion was interested both in gaining access for Jewish settlement in Transjordan and in eliciting Abdullah's views on the subject of partition. Accordingly, at Ben-Gurion's request, Dov Hoz and David Hacohen of the Jewish Agency made contact with Rutenberg in London and arranged to meet Abdullah. Ben-Gurion wanted a number of points to be stressed at the talks: Abdullah's dependence on Britain made his independence fictitious; Transjordan's economy and population were stagnating; Jewish capital for the settlement of Palestinian Arabs would give a boost to Transjordan and liberate it from financial dependence; a Jewish state would co-operate economically and militarily with Abdullah against Ibn Saud and his allies.

A preliminary meeting between the Jewish Agency representatives and Samir al-Rifai, chief secretary of Transjordan's delegation to London, took place on 14 May 1937. Rifai asked whether the Jews would accept a Palestine solution based on reunification with Transjordan under the amir. Rather than give an answer, Hoz asked another question: how would Transjordan react if Britain were to decree the creation of a Jewish state in Western Palestine? Rifai gave a blunt answer: such a state, however small, would be a danger to Transjordan and there would be no alternative to launching armed gangs from across the Jordan to fight it.

The next day Hoz and Hacohen met Abdullah himself and outlined a possible deal, along the lines suggested by Rutenberg, involving the settlement of Jews in certain parts of Transjordan in exchange for Jewish financial and diplomatic assistance. Abdullah was evasive, and all the efforts to draw him into a bilateral agreement that would stand whatever the commission concluded were to no avail. He insisted on awaiting Britain's decision before taking the next step.[8]

Rutenberg persisted in his own struggle to finalize his own business with Abdullah. Accompanied by his Sephardi aide, Elie Eliachar, who served as a translator, and three prominent British–Jewish business associates, he went to see the amir but the latter claimed that

[8] David Ben-Gurion, *Memoirs*, vol. iii, *1936* (Heb.) (Tel Aviv: Am Oved, 1973), 91, 238–40, 257, 280, 283; *Memoirs*, vol. iv, *1937* (Heb.) (Tel Aviv: Am Oved, 1974), 129–33, 174 f. 177–8, 192, 201–2; Caplan, *Futile Diplomacy*, ii. 65–7; Isaiah Friedman, 'The Palestine Partition Plan of the Royal Commission, 1937, and the British–Zionist–Arab Triangle' (Heb.), in *Studies in Partition Plans, 1937–1947* (Sde Boker: Ben-Gurion Institute, 1984), 9–20.

he could not conclude their tentative agreement owing to British objections.[9]

An interesting side light was thrown on this meeting by Blanche Dugdale, the niece of Arthur Balfour of the Balfour Declaration and confidante of Chaim Weizmann, and one of the most fervent and assiduous of the gentile Zionists. On May 20 'Baffy' recorded in her diary:

Dined with Peter Rutenberg in Whitehall Court. He told me about his negotiations with Abdullah for land. Also how Abdullah was paid to keep Transjordan quiet last year—but double-crossed by sending an anti-Zionist Memo to the Royal Commission. So when he asked Peter for £2,000 more before Coronation, he only got £1,000 and was told he must mend his ways before he got the rest. He excused himself, and promised. Then a Jewish jeweller in Jerusalem showed Peter a golden dagger ordered by Abdullah as a present to King George (with Peter's money!) and told Peter how the inscription was first to have been 'From the Emir of Transjordan', but later had it changed to 'the Ruler of the Transjordan lands'. Clearly the Royal Commission had consulted *him* about Partition! . . .[10]

In a post-mortem on the whole affair Sharett pointed out that both Ben-Gurion and Rutenberg had assumed that Abdullah could deliver the goods and that he would defy the British on the question of Jewish settlement in Transjordan. In Sharett's opinion both assumptions were totally erroneous, and had he known that Ben-Gurion pinned such hopes on a meeting with Abdullah in London he would have warned him so as to prevent disappointment. Sharett also suggested that Hacohen and Hoz could not possibly establish with Abdullah in one meeting the kind of frank relations that he himself had reached after a dozen meetings in the course of which the amir had poured out his heart about his weakness, his complete dependence on the British, his inability to take a stand until they informed him of their wishes, and on the thorn in his flesh, meaning Hajj Amin al-Husayni, which only the Jews could remove. Rutenberg's faith in the possibility of getting concrete results in direct negotiations with Abdullah without going to his British masters first, warned Sharett, carried the risk of losing a great deal of money and involving them in a political tangle.

Equally unflattering was Sharett's opinion of Abdullah's supporters among the Palestinian Arabs, the Nashashibis. He regarded the National Defence Party led by Ragheb al-Nashashibi as an unreliable partner in a political struggle because it was unstable, lacking in resolve, and prone to trim its sails to the prevailing winds of popular

[9] Elie Eliachar, 'An Attempt at Settlement in Transjordan', *New Outlook* 18/5 (1975), 71–5.

[10] Blanche Dugdale, *Baffy: The Diaries of Blanche Dugdale, 1936–1947*, ed. N. A. Rose (London: Vallentine, Mitchell, 1973), 42.

opinion. Veering from support for the principle of partition to strong denunciation of the plan showed just how unreliable and cowardly the Nashashibis could be. According to Sharett's theory it was right for the Zionists to support a political grouping possessing courage but lacking money or political backing. On the other hand, money would be to no avail where courage was lacking. Abdullah, for all his faults, lacked neither courage nor determination. His problem was that he could not confront his opponents, especially the mufti and Ibn Saud, secure in the knowledge that Britain stood behind him, which made it risky for the Zionists to stake everything on co-operation with him.[11]

The Peel Commission did not issue its final report until July 1937. Its major finding was that the mandate was unworkable, since the aspirations of the Jews and the Arabs were mutually contradictory. Partition was the only method it could see for dealing with the roots of the problem, and in recommending it to the British government, the commission marked a turning point in the tangled history of efforts at peacemaking between Jews and Arabs. Though the commission's proposals were not acted upon, the principle of partition guided all subsequent exercises in peacemaking right down to the UN partition resolution of November 1947. The Peel Commission envisaged a very small Jewish state—some 5,000 square kilometres—comprising the Galilee, the Jezreel Valley, and the coastal plain from Acre to Tel Aviv. All the rest of Palestine, bar an enclave from Jerusalem to Jaffa under a permanent British mandate, was included in the Arab state (see Map 2). The commission recommended an exchange of population between the two states, to avoid endless strife, and also a system of financial support for the Arab state from the Jewish state and the British government. It was also suggested that the Arab state be merged with Transjordan to form a United Arab Kingdom under Amir Abdullah.

Not unnaturally, Abdullah was overjoyed at the Peel Commission's offer of 80 per cent of Palestine, including the whole of the West Bank, the Negev, Jaffa, and old Jerusalem, as well as a £2 million annual subsidy from the Jewish state and a £10 million grant from Britain, although he took care not to appear too enthusiastic in his acceptance of the plan. Partition and annexation of the lion's share of Palestine represented a recurrent theme in his well-publicized ambition over the previous fifteen years and was the specific objective for which he had lobbied during the commission's investigations.

Privately, many leading Zionists welcomed the commission's recommendations but the official Zionist attitude was reserved. With only around 15 per cent of the country under offer it was an agonizing

[11] Sharett, *Political Diary*, ii. 150–1, 387 f.

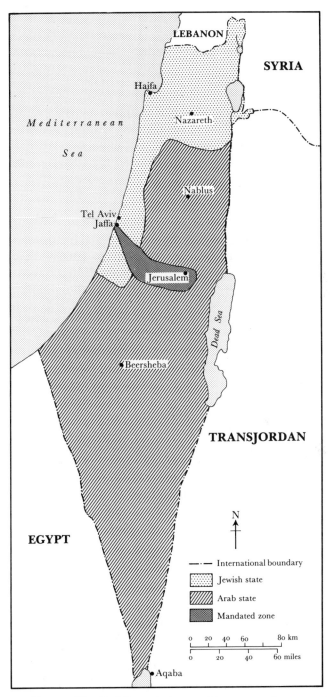

MAP 2   The Peel Commission partition proposal, 1937

decision to make; the Twentieth Zionist Congress, which met in Zurich in August, rejected the partition scheme as unacceptable but authorized further negotiations with the British government.

The real problem with the Zionist leadership's attitude to partition, both before and after the publication of the Peel report, lay in the realm of tactics. Convinced that open endorsement by the Jewish Agency would be the kiss of death for partition, Ben-Gurion looked for a group of Englishmen who might carry this particular banner. At the same time, he presented the Zionist movement as the wronged party whose reluctant acquiescence could only be purchased by substantial improvement on the Peel plan. This double game of private acceptance and public criticism of partition was as confusing as it was self-defeating. Had the Zionist movement accepted the proposal spontaneously and without delay, and had it mobilized its support behind a clear-cut, straightforward policy in favour of partition, it is quite conceivable that it might have been implemented. In the event, the pro-Zionist groups in Parliament accepted at face value the pleas for full implementation of the mandate, sharply attacked the government for betraying their protegés and in the process helped to wreck the Peel plan and to provide the government with an easy avenue of retreat from a path on which it was very reluctant to embark anyway.

By inadvertently obstructing parliamentary ratification, and hence government action on the Peel plan, Ben-Gurion's tactics also provided a breathing space during which the full weight of Arab opposition could make itself felt. The Arab Higher Committee, caught between its suspicion of Abdullah's expansionist designs on the one hand and of the Zionist aspiration to use the proffered base as a point of departure for transforming the whole of Palestine into a Jewish state on the other, rejected the Peel plan with vehemence. It also launched the second and unexpectedly effective phase of the Arab Revolt, which cast further doubts on the practicality of achieving partition by force and accelerated Britain's retreat from her traditional pro-Zionist policy.

In retrospect, the period from 1936 to 1938 can be seen as one of exemplary opportunity and unmitigated failure for the Zionist movement. The next world war and the holocaust of European Jews were just two years away. The contrast between the great hopes which attended the birth of the partition idea and the signal incapacity to carry it to fruition was very striking and weighed on the conscience of at least some Zionist leaders. Nahum Goldmann observed that 'if there had been a tragedy in the history of Zionism, it is the fact that largely through our fault, partition was not put into effect the first time it was proposed, in 1937 ... The Zionist movement's attitude towards partition was a major sin of our generation.'[12] Whether or not a sin, it was a major, costly, political failure. At the root of the failure lay lack of vision, self-defeating tactics, underestimation of the force behind Palestinian nationalism, and the unrealistically high hopes pinned on the alliance with the Hashemites.

Abdullah's twelve-point plan, the London conference and the 1939 White Paper

Once partition had been effectively removed from the political agenda by Zionist equivocations, uncompromising Palestinian nationalist opposition and mounting British doubts concerning its feasibility, Abdullah reverted to the opposite idea of a unitary solution for the Palestine problem. In May 1938, to everyone's surprise he sent the Woodhead Commission of Inquiry into the feasibility of partition a twelve-point proposal for the solution of the Palestine problem which was ingeniously framed to please the British, the Jews, and the Arabs without neglecting to further his own interests. Palestine and Transjordan were to constitute a United Arab Kingdom in which the Jews would enjoy self-government and representation in proportion to their numbers. In the designated Jewish districts, the Jews would be permitted a 'reasonable' level of immigration but they would have no right to buy land or settle immigrants outside those districts. The mandate would stay in force for ten years, though the British presence would be only in a 'supervisory capacity' and Britain's strategic interests would be safeguarded. After ten years the mandate would be terminated and a decision taken on the final form of this United Arab Kingdom.[13]

Once again Abdullah had put the cat among the pigeons. The Woodhead Commission declined to discuss his plan on the grounds that it fell outside its terms of reference, which were confined to implementing partition. Palestinian Arabs attacked him for failing to consult them and other Arabs before announcing his plan. The plan itself was variously criticized for not setting a clear limit to Jewish immigration, for entailing *de facto* partition, and for accepting the continuation of the mandate for another ten years before independence. The merger of Palestine and Transjordan, in the spirit of Abdullah's proposals, it was claimed, meant nothing less than capitulation to Zionist demands.

Abdullah hit back at his critics most forcefully. In a letter to the

---

[12] Nahum Goldmann, *The Autobiography of Nahum Goldmann: Sixty Years of Jewish Life* (New York: Holt, Rinehart and Winston, 1969), 179–81.

[13] Abdullah, *My Memoirs Completed*, 89 f.

president of the Young Muslim Men's Association in Cairo, he presented his own analysis of the Palestine problem and the case for union with Transjordan, which he claimed it was his religious and racial duty to promote in order to ward off the impending calamity. 'The pillars of Zionism are three', stated Abdullah, 'the Balfour Declaration, the European nations which have decided to expel the Jews from their territories and direct them to Palestine, and those partisans of the Arabs who will accept no solution but are content with weeping and wailing and calling for help from those who cannot aid them.' Palestine was thus in danger of being overrun by another people. The remedy for Palestine's malady lay in 'a speedy halting of the danger and in reducing the attack, then in considering how to put an end to it once and for all. Procrastination will mean the end of Palestine.'

At several points in this revealing letter, Abdullah returned to the charge that the Palestinians at the political helm were failing to prevent their compatriots from selling their land to the 'Jewish usurpers' and that 'the Arabs are as prodigal in selling their land as they are useless in wailing and weeping'. To the contention that by union with Transjordan the Palestinians would forfeit their rights, he gave very short shrift: 'The inhabitants of Palestine are 100,000 more than those of Transjordan and would ably take over the leadership of the administration of such a united state. There would be a parliament to represent the people and an army to defend them. Finances would be unified and the state would be well patrolled and its gates shut to prevent clandestine immigration.' The letter concluded with a dire warning that Palestine would become entirely Jewish in two years if the present state of affairs was allowed to continue.[14]

Faced with immovable Arab opposition to his twelve-point plan, Abdullah put out some tentative feelers to see if there was any chance of support from the Jewish side. One of his ministers contacted Chaim Kalvarisky, a prominent member of Kedmah Mizrahah, an unofficial association dedicated to the promotion of Jewish–Arab understanding, to suggest a meeting. Kalvarisky had been the Zionist Executive's liaison officer with the Arabs until his dismissal in 1928 and a prodigal dispenser of bribes and material rewards to an extensive network of informers and collaborators which he had built almost single-handedly. In and out of office, he was also the moving spirit behind numerous schemes for Jewish–Arab co-operation, some of which were eminently practical and successful, others tinged with astonishing political naïveté. One of his pet schemes called for the creation of a large Semitic federation in the Middle East consisting of independent states, including a unitary state of Palestine, which would not only permit

[14] Abdullah, *My Memoirs Completed*, 86–9.

unlimited Jewish immigration but even facilitate its extension to Transjordan.

After informing Sharett, Kalvarisky and Dr Jacob Thon, another prominent member of his association, met with the minister to learn details about the amir's plan for the unification of Palestine and Transjordan under his leadership, with provisions for limited Jewish immigration to those areas already settled by Jews. Kalvarisky put forward a counter-proposal: Palestine and Transjordan would have separate administrations but with a link to safeguard their common interests; Jewish immigration into Palestine would continue and would be governed by the absorptive capacity of the country. The minister agreed that the counter-proposal could serve as a basis for discussions and arranged for Kalvarisky and Thon to meet the amir himself. In the event, however, the amir merely confined himself to making reassuring generalizations about the avenues for Arab–Jewish peace that would be opened up.[15]

Kalvarisky continued to report to Sharett on the progress of his adventure with the amir. The amir's envoy, Mustafah Wahabi al-Tall, who was in contact with Kalvarisky and Thon, was sent to Egypt to mobilize support for the amir's merger plan. Because Kalvarisky hoped to steer the amir in the direction of his own pet plan for a Semitic federation embracing all the Arab states and Palestine and because he believed that by providing broader outlets for the amir's political ambitions he could deflect him from the idea that western Palestine must come under his rule, he attached great importance to al-Tall's mission to Egypt. He even went as far as to send him money and to promise him more, expecting the Jewish Agency to foot the bill. In the meantime, he carried on a lively correspondence with al-Tall on the subject of the plan: whether it should cover all of Palestine or the entire Semitic region. Kalvarisky showed Sharett a draft and a counter-draft, claiming that al-Tall had embraced the pan-Semitic doctrine enthusiastically; however, his report of al-Tall's belief that he, al-Tall, could guarantee full equality between Jews and Arabs in all the Semitic countries reminded Sharett of the joke about the chef in a restaurant who served minced meat made of equal parts of horse and chicken— one horse and one chicken.

The whole affair, in Sharett's view, had an air of unreality about it:

First of all, the amir is not a decisive factor in the situation. His wishes and activities would have only a slight weight in shaping events. His positive value lies only in his consent to a solution which will eventually be imposed by the British and in the fact that there is no anti-Jewish venom in his attitude. Our

---

[15] Moshe Sharett, *Political Diary*, vol. iii. 1938 (Heb.) Tel Aviv: Am Oved, 1972), 137 f.

direct links with the amir are decidedly sufficient to obtain from him, or through him, everything that can be obtained, when the time comes. One can forgive the amir his attempts to forge links with Jewish circles behind our backs in the vain hope that they might give him more than we. But it is difficult to understand Jews who know that they cannot bypass the [Jewish] Agency and yet believe that by cultivating an indirect link with the amir, they can discover new worlds.

To Kalvarisky, Sharett said bluntly that the Jewish Agency would have no truck with al-Tall's mission to Egypt. If he had gone there with the support of Kedmah Mizrahah, added Sharett, it was a mistake to be regretted. In any case, he and his colleagues on the executive would not give money to Kedmah Mizrahah to finance a dubious adventure of which they had been given no advance notice. Kalvarisky, who had evidently lost none of his zeal for using bribery to promote political aims, pleaded that the money be given, if not as a grant, then as a loan to Kedmah Mizrahah, whose members were falling behind in the payment of their subscriptions. Sharett replied that he was not in favour of the idea and that he would consult the Executive.[16]

The British government did not respond to Abdullah's twelve-point plan, but in November 1938 it issued a statement of policy on Palestine that rejected partition as impractical and invited representatives of the Jews, the Palestine Arabs, and neighbouring Arab States to a round-table conference in London to consider the future of Palestine. The possibility of incorporating any part of Palestine in Abdullah's king-dom thus fell by the wayside and there was a clear strengthening of the position of the mufti; the Arabs of Palestine acclaimed him as their sole representative and demanded that he be accepted as such by the other Arab statesmen. The British, in need of stability in the Middle East in order to concentrate on the challenge posed by Nazi Germany in Europe, hurriedly retreated from the three main prescriptions of the Peel Commission: partition, an independent Jewish state, and a direct role for Transjordan. Instead, they now offered to grant independence to a federal state after a transition period of five years, with restriction on Jewish immigration and on the sale of land to the Jews. The Jewish representatives were desperately opposed to the British plan and even considered walking out of the conference. The Arab statesmen and some of the mufti's own supporters urged him to accept it, underlining the magnitude of the British concessions, the value of having Britain on the side of the Palestinians in this struggle against the Jews, and the bright prospects it held out for further gains. But at this critical moment, when Arab leverage was at its peak, the leader of the Palestinian Arabs in effect rejected the British plan by insisting on a

[16] Sharett, *Political Diary*, iii. 219 f.

shorter transition period. A golden opportunity for creating an independent, unified Palestine was allowed to slip away. It was not the first blow inflicted by the mufti on the cause he was supposed to be serving nor was it to be the last, but it was probably the most devastating. Through the stubborn maximalism which had by now come to dominate his political outlook, he squandered the chance to have his own state, a chance that had emerged out of a unique set of historical circumstances. The London conference dispersed amid confusion and with an inaudible sigh of relief on the part of Abdullah and the Jewish representatives.

Disappointed with the failure of the Arab delegates to exercise a moderating influence on the mufti and his hard-line faction, the British government proceeded to issue, on 17 May, a White Paper on Palestine, based on the proposals which had just been spurned by both sides to the dispute. The White Paper represented the best deal that the Arabs could realistically hope for at that time and it conceded their most important demands: a unitary state which would be granted full independence after ten years, the prohibition of land sales to Jews in large areas of Palestine; and a drastic cut-back in immigration for five years, after which the Arabs would have exclusive control over the immigration policy and would thus be in a position to terminate Jewish immigration altogether. The 1939 White Paper also implied retreat from the mandate and the Balfour Declaration, and recognition instead of the Arab right to self-government in Palestine. Small wonder that the 17th of May went down as one of the blackest days in Jewish history and that the Yishuv prepared to fight the White Paper tooth and nail. Incredible as it may seem, the Arab Higher Committee headed by the mufti also came out against the White Paper, in a move which was as damaging to its own cause as it was consistent with the pattern of senseless rejectionism for which it was becoming notorious. Of all the Arab statesmen, many of whom conceded in private that the White Paper was the greatest victory in the struggle for Palestine scored by their side since the beginning of the mandate, Abdullah alone had the courage to welcome the White Paper publicly as a sound basis for co-operation between Britain and the Palestine Arabs.

Allies at war

The outbreak of the Second World War overshadowed the local problems of the Middle East and the conflict over Palestine remained largely dormant. The initial victories of Nazi Germany made a tremendous impression in the Arab east and tempted some Arab leaders, of whom the mufti was only the most notorious, to throw in their lot with what looked like a model for success worth emulating and a force capable of overrunning the mighty British Empire. However, most Arab governments waited to see which way the wind was blowing before declaring their loyalty to the Allies. Abdullah was the only Arab ruler who pledged his support for Britain at the beginning of the war and who remained unswervingly loyal even during its most difficult hours. In 1941 he sent his army to Iraq to suppress the rebellion of Rashid Ali al-Kilani, a nationalist leader with strong pro-Axis sympathies and a close associate of the mufti. This intervention won him the gratitude of the Iraqi branch of the Hashemite family and of the British authorities, but it also led to his being branded as a lackey of British imperialism by many Arab nationalists.

The war may have dimmed Abdullah's hope for Palestine and Greater Syria, but it did not extinguish it. Two factors in particular helped to keep these hopes flickering. First, the exile of the mufti from Palestine in 1938 and his prolonged stay in Germany as an ally of the Third Reich created a power vacuum in Arab Palestine which his great rival showed no reluctance in trying to fill. Second, Abdullah's firm stand on the side of the Allies ended his isolation in the Arab world and enabled him to play a dominant role in the discussions on Arab unity which took place in the later years of the war. Throughout the war Abdullah hardly missed an opportunity to press his own claims to Arab unity in the framework of a Greater Syria by addressing appeals to the political leaders of Syria, by issuing proclamations to the Syrian people, and by recruiting supporters in both Syria and Lebanon. Despite Abdullah's persistent lobbying, however, British support was never forthcoming, and the fact that he was not prepared to do anything to harm British interests as long as the mandate remained in force and the British remained in Palestine cast some doubt on the practical significance of his calls for a Greater Syria. It may well be that these calls were conceived by Abdullah, and were tolerated by the British, primarily as moves in the propaganda war against the Axis powers, to counter the appeal of the German promises which the mufti disseminated throughout the Muslim world from his headquarters in Berlin.

With the Zionists, Abdullah maintained close and friendly contact throughout the war, using Muhammad al-Unsi as the principal go-between. Several factors helped to strengthen these bonds of friendship, principal among which were common allies and common enemies. Both sides lent active support to Britain in the fight against Germany and consequently found themselves on the same side in the great divide created by the world war. For the Yishuv, co-operation with Britain was much more problematical than for Transjordan, on account of the British policy of restricting Jewish immigration to Palestine as laid down in the 1939 White Paper. A way out of this dilemma was found, however, and it was aptly summed up in David Ben-Gurion's slogan: 'We will fight with the British against Hitler as if there were no White Paper; we will fight the White Paper as if there were no war.' The best unifying factor, however, is a common enemy, and Abdullah and the Jews had in common not just one but two enemies: Hitler and the mufti. Hitler was the most diabolical foe ever to rise against the Jews in their long and tormented history. If his forces were to overrun the Middle East, it was not just political Zionism that stood to be crushed but the entire Jewish community in Palestine which faced extermination as total and as savage as that which had already claimed the lives of millions of Jews in central Europe. The threat of Hitler's forces overrunning Palestine reached its highest point between July and October 1942, when Rommel stood at al-Alamein on the border with Egypt. Desperate and pathetically inadequate defence plans were prepared by the Haganah, the military arm of the Yishuv, to meet this nightmarish possibility. Pro-Hashemite circles in Palestine realizing that they too would be doomed in the event of a German victory, began to seek a rapprochement with the Jews. Since Abdullah was also affected by the threat of a German invasion, albeit not to the same extent, he was told about some of these plans and tentative ideas of co-ordinated defence were also discussed. From his perspective, the inevitable consequence of a German victory would have been the handing over of Palestine to Hitler's ally—the mufti. The political leaders of the Yishuv, for their part, though divided on many questions unanimously preferred Abdullah to the mufti as their neighbour to the east. Zionist influence was therefore used to further Abdullah's cause in London, helping to transform a relationship of good neighbourliness into an incipient strategic alliance.

From time to time Abdullah sounded out the Jews about his plans for the future of Palestine. These plans were invariably linked to his long-term ambitions for Hashemite hegemony in the Middle East. An important meeting took place on 11 November 1942, when Moshe Sharett and Elias Sasson went to meet Abdullah and held a number of conversations with him on the subject of Greater Syria. He made it plain that he wished to rule over a united Syrian-Transjordanian state to which Lebanon and Palestine would be federated. He also offered secret negotiations and agreement on the question of Jewish immigration to Palestine in return for Jewish financial assistance and propaganda for his cause in Britain, America, and Syria.[17] Towards the end of the war Abdullah began to present variations on this federal theme. In January 1944 he proposed an administration in which Jews and

[17] Miriam Glickson to Moshe Shertok, 3 Mar. 1946, S25/10692, CZA.

Arabs would be represented in accordance with their numerical strength, and the inclusion of the whole of Palestine in a quadripartite federation with Transjordan, Syria, and Lebanon in which he would hold the position of king, president, or chairman.[18] Abdullah was very enthusiastic about this particular scheme, from which he expected numerous benefits for his backward country. To secure it he was ready to concede special rights to the Jews in Palestine and to the Christians in Lebanon.

The Jewish Agency, however, could not agree to a quadripartite federation any more than it could agree to any other variation on the federal theme. At the Extraordinary Zionist Conference held in May 1942 at the Biltmore Hotel in New York, a resolution was passed urging that Palestine be established as a Jewish commonwealth after the Second World War. This was the first time that the Zionist Organization officially came out in favour of a Jewish state in Palestine. This declared aim could be achieved in the context of partition but not in the context of a federation. Some Jews agreed to partition only because they regarded full sovereignty of the Jewish state as a measure of compensation for its limited territory. But if Palestine were to be part of an Arab federation, the Jews would always remain a small minority, even in the event of attaining majority status in Palestine. They were therefore reluctant to enter any political negotiations which did not concede at the outset the principle of an independent Jewish state. How to remain on good terms with Abdullah while rejecting his proposals for limited Jewish autonomy under his protection was a problem which the Jewish Agency was to encounter repeatedly after the end of the Second World War.

Post-war plans and strategies

For his wartime loyalty, Britain rewarded Abdullah by conferring formal independence on the erstwhile mandated territory of Transjordan in March 1946. The Agreement was replaced by a Treaty of Alliance, the Organic Law by a Constitution, the Legislative Council by a Parliament, and the Advisory Council by a Council of Ministers. Two months later, twenty-five years to the day since making his dramatic appearance in Amman, the amir was enthroned as king in oriental splendour and his amirate was officially renamed the Hashemite Kingdom of Jordan. But the change of titles did not betoken the acquisition of full-blown sovereignty and the 'independent' kingdom remained heavily dependent on British subsidies and British security assistance for its survival.

[18] Sasson, *On the Road to Peace*, 317 f.

In the foreign policy sphere, the most important sequel to the Treaty of 1946 was more active Jordanian interest in the affairs of Palestine and a renewed drive in the direction of Greater Syria. There is a view that holds that Abdullah began to press his claims to Palestine only in 1947, after the British had made it unmistakably clear to him that they would not support his Greater Syria scheme because it aroused widespread resistance in the Arab world and was incompatible with the pact of the Arab League, of which Transjordan was a founder member. Admittedly, the grant of independence could be interpreted as an attempt to cool Abdullah's zeal for Greater Syria while the possibility of British withdrawal made Palestine the more real and immediate question. But Abdullah had been alerted to this possibility during his meeting with Labour's foreign secretary, Ernest Bevin in London in February 1946, and from then on gaining control over Palestine assumed top priority in his political and diplomatic activity. Besides, Palestine and Greater Syria were not alternative or mutually exclusive goals, so that Abdullah did not have to abandon one in order to concentrate on the other. On the contrary, the two goals were closely linked in his long-term intentions and it was therefore only natural that he should pursue both goals simultaneously, merely changing his tactics and emphasis in response to changing circumstances.[19]

Abdullah's relations with the Zionists support the view that he started preparing for the coming crisis in Palestine well before 1947 and that he did so without irrevocably abandoning his wider ambition. Soon after the end of the Second World War he began to strive more purposefully towards an agreement with the Zionists on the future of Palestine. The constancy of his purpose was matched only by the fluidity of his ideas regarding the basis on which the agreement would rest. His preference was for incorporating the whole of Palestine in his kingdom with vaguely defined autonomy for the Jews, but he did not rule out the Zionist preference for partition and independence in one part of Palestine—provided, of course, that he would receive the other part. Yet another solution to spring out of his restless mind envisaged the simultaneous union of Transjordan with Iraq and the partition of Palestine which would be followed by annexing the Arab part to a United Hashemite Kingdom under Abdullah. Predictably, neither Iraqis nor Jews could be made to appreciate the virtues of this particular scheme or of their prospective partners within it. While a stream of new ideas continued to flow in private channels from the court of the recently elevated monarch, the Hashemite Kingdom of Jordan remained officially committed to seeing the region organized

---

[19] Joseph Nevo, *Abdullah and the Arabs of Palestine* (Heb.) (Tel Aviv: Shiloah Institute, 1975), 37 f.

along the lines of a quadripartite federation consisting of Syria, Lebanon, Jordan, and Palestine, with a measure of autonomy for the Jewish areas. Such a solution, as we have seen, was unacceptable to the Zionists even as a basis for opening formal negotiations. A much tougher kind of Zionism had been forged in the course of the Second World War, and the commitment to Jewish statehood became much deeper and more desperate in the shadow of the holocaust. The prospect of minority status under Arab rule was considered little better than a death sentence on the Jewish community in Palestine and on the survivors of the Nazi 'Final Solution'.

Although the rise of 'fighting Zionism' out of the ashes of the Second World War was scarcely conducive to political agreement between Abdullah and the Zionists, it must be remembered that in Abdullah's diplomacy personal relations counted above all else. At this level there were important changes which softened the impact of adverse circumstances. Until his death in 1946 Muhammad al-Unsi, who reached the position of minister of the interior and deputy prime minister, served as Abdullah's principal emissary in his contacts with the Jewish Agency. Al-Unsi was well known, and disliked, by many Arab politicians for his friendship with the Zionists and his close contacts with the Jewish Agency. He was certainly not a man to withstand a bribe, and his critics charge that he betrayed his country for financial rewards seems not to have been entirely without foundation.[20] Nor was it out of line with the practice of the Jewish Agency to pay Arabs for information and political services of various kinds. Al-Unsi supplied the Jewish Agency with valuable information about Jordanian, Palestinian, and inter-Arab affairs over a period of fifteen years but his motives were always suspect. He was not above deceiving either his master or his Jewish friends, and his reliability as a channel of communication between the two thus left something to be desired.

The man who maintained contact with al-Unsi on behalf of the Jewish Agency was Elias Sasson, who had been head of the Arab Section of its Political Department since 1937. Sasson was the most outstanding Arabist on the staff of the Jewish Agency and one of the leading architects of the Hashemite connection. Born in Damascus in 1902, he had grown up as an Arab among Arabs. As a young man he was an active member of the Arab National Club, which aspired to liberate the Arab world from Turkish rule. His public activities brought him to the attention of Faisal, who invited the 18-year-old nationalist and asked him to launch under his auspices and at his

---

[20] A report of 8 May 1938 by Mr Zagagi, head of the Finance Department of the Jewish Agency, shows that between April 1936 and April 1938 al-Unsi received nine payments totalling £P 800. File S25/3513, CZA.

expense, an Arab newspaper named *Al-Hayat* to spread the message of understanding and co-operation between Jews and Arabs in the Middle East. The paper enjoyed wide circulation for nine months but was closed down after the French entry into Damascus and the expulsion of Faisal. Following the collapse of the Syrian hopes for independence and the closure of the paper he edited, Sasson went to live in Palestine where he transferred his public activities from the Arab national movement to the Jewish national movement. In 1933 Moshe Sharett, then head of the Political Department of the Jewish Agency, recruited him into the Arab Section whose main function was to collect information and to cultivate friendly relations throughout the Arab world. During this stage of his career, which lasted until 1948, Sasson came into contact with hundreds of Palestinian, Transjordanian, Syrian, Lebanese, Iraqi, and Egyptian public figures, some of whom he had first become acquainted with as a student in Beirut or as a member of the Arab Club in Damascus. His natural empathy for Arabs, his fluency in Arabic, his broad understanding of the culture and mores of the Orient, and his remarkable grasp of the complexities of Arab politics enabled him to extend his circle of acquaintances and to carry out his task with great distinction. The difference in mentality and cultural gap that characteristically overshadow encounters between Israelis and Arabs was conspicuously absent in Sasson's case. Distinctive mental processes go with each particular language, and because Sasson was a native Arabic speaker the task of approaching Arabs, dealing with Arabs, and gaining their confidence came much more naturally to him than to any of his colleagues in the Jewish Agency. But Sasson was much more than what in today's language would be called a smooth operator. He represented a distinctive line of thought on Jewish–Arab relations. The crux of his strategy lay in setting goals that would be acceptable to Arabs as well as to his own side, and he also knew how to present the Jewish position to the Arabs in a way that was calculated to get them to concede Jewish rights in Palestine.

Muhammad al-Unsi was one of hundreds of Arab public figures with whom Sasson tried to keep in contact, but his closeness to Abdullah singled him out for specially attentive treatment. After al-Unsi's death, Sasson began to have frequent meetings with Abdullah himself. Despite the wide gap in status, the two men developed a warm personal friendship and a close political partnership which were to be of crucial importance in the coming years. As another formidable Jewish Arabist observed:

Until Sasson went into the talks with Abdullah, there was only stammering from our side. Sasson knew how to talk to Abdullah, and it was not just because he spoke Arabic. He had the sensitivities necessary for forging a true, sincere, and deep bond. He knew what had happened to the Hashemite family and understood its aspirations. He knew how to give and how to arouse sympathy. The way in which Sasson worked with Abdullah was diplomatic activity of the first order. It led to the fact that we did not have to fight the Arab Legion. He also planted in Abdullah's mind illusions which from our point of view were positive illusions. He was the architect and he was the builder.[21]

One of the first significant post-war meetings between Abdullah and Sasson took place in the king's summer palace in Shuneh, east of the Allenby Bridge, on 12 August 1946. An attempt by Britain to break the backbone of Jewish resistance in Palestine and an invitation to a round-table conference to discuss the Morrison–Grady plan for four self-governing cantons linked up in a federation constituted the backdrop to the meeting. Sasson had recently returned from a mission to Cairo where he had sought Egyptian assistance in breaking the deadlock between Jews and Arabs over Palestine. The senior government and palace officials he talked to realized that there was little chance that Britain would evacuate Egypt as long as the Palestine problem remained unresolved and a source of instability throughout the Middle East. They were therefore prepared to consider solutions based on partition, a binational state, or a federal state. But Sasson's greatest achievement in Cairo, and one which amounted to a major break-through for Zionist diplomacy as a whole, was to persuade Ismail Sidqi, the Egyptian prime minister, to agree to partition. Sidqi thought that it would be best if another Arab state supported Egypt in taking this stand and in resisting the demands of the Palestinian Arabs. Accordingly, Sasson went to Shuneh to secure Transjordanian backing for the Egyptian attempt to get the Arab League to adopt partition.[22]

During the meeting, which lasted an hour and a half, King Abdullah, at the request of his British allies, tried to influence the heads of the Jewish Agency to crack down on the dissident organizations respon-sible for the acts of terror and to agree to participate in the London talks unconditionally, notwithstanding their declared preference for a solution based on partition. Initially Abdullah suggested that the proposed federal plan would be better for the Jews than Peel's par-tition plan because, while not conceding a state, it opened the gates to immigration on a large scale. Later on, however, he declared himself to be a supporter of partition and the annexation of the Arab part to Transjordan. To Sasson's query whether he would continue to main-tain this position, Abdullah replied that it largely depended on their reaching an understanding between themselves. Asked to elaborate, he added in strict confidence that he aimed to enlarge Transjordan's

[21] Interview with Yehoshua Palmon.   [22] Sasson, *On the Road to Peace*, 364–6.

borders and to create one strong and unified Hashemite kingdom which would conclude alliances with Britain and Turkey and guard the British line of defence in the Middle East. Execution of the plan was to proceed in stages: (a) partition of Palestine and joining the Arab part to Transjordan; (b) the merger of Syria with Transjordan; (c) linking the enlarged Transjordan in a federation with Iraq; and (d) linking the Jewish part of Palestine in a federation or alliance with the Transjordanian–Iraqi federation.

Abdullah admitted that the British favoured postponement of all talks until after the Palestine problem was solved on the basis of their federal plan. The difference between him and the British, therefore, was one of sequence and not of principle. He saw partition and merger as the first stage, whereas they feared that it would arouse the hostility of the other Arab states and therefore preferred to start with a federal solution in Palestine.

The king also admitted that the Arabs of Palestine would not accept the federal plan, but nevertheless suggested that everything should be done to secure their agreement. Sasson's questioning of the Zionist interest in such an outcome brought forth a detailed and cogent royal reply:

First, so as not to close completely the gates of the Arab part and block the possibility of expansion. Second, so as not to assist with your own hands in the creation of an eighth Arab state, extremist and hostile, headed by your mortal enemies—the Husaynis. Third, it would be wiser for you Zionists to talk about the establishment of a Jewish state in two or three years when your numbers will be augmented by another hundred or two hundred thousand. Fourth, so as not to block the road to Transjordan's expansion and to the strengthening of the Hashemite family. Fifth, in order to ease things for Britain, improve relations with her and regain her sympathy for Zionism.

Still baffled by what he saw as contradictory arguments, Sasson wondered whether the king was for the federal plan or for partition. The explanation he elicited was that Abdullah was temporarily putting Britain's wishes before his own, but if the Jews believed they could get British, American, and UN support for partition he would back them. He was also confident that Iraq would back them even if it meant a rift in the Arab League. But he deemed the holding of secret tripartite consultations to be superfluous since he himself was authorized to speak on behalf of the Iraqis and in the event of the Zionists coming to an agreement with him, he would put them in touch with the head of the Transjordanian delegation in London.

Sasson wondered whether Abdullah had thought of ways of imposing the federal plan or the partition plan on the Palestine Arabs.

Abdullah replied that he had thought of little else in recent weeks and had actually worked out a plan of action which he was prepared to share with Sasson if the latter could visit him again in a week's time. Abdullah urged Sasson to bring back on his return the Jewish Agency's final answer to three questions: (*a*) which plan was acceptable to them? (*b*) were they willing to suppress all terrorist activity against the British and to try and mend their relations with them? and (*c*) were they prepared to back him 'sincerely and with all their might' in implementing his far-reaching plan? Abdullah also asked Sasson to bring him £P10,000 as a first payment. Asked why he needed the money just then and what was the total sum he needed from the Jewish Agency, Abdullah replied that over the next four or five months he needed £P25,000 to spend on the elections in Syria. His aim was to secure the election of a Parliament and the appointment of a government that would help him carry out the second stage of his plan, namely, the unification of Syria with Transjordan. This sum, claimed Abdullah, was small in relation to his needs, but the British had already promised him a sizeable sum for this purpose. Secondly, said Abdullah, over the next two or three months he would need £P10,000–15,000 to create a new agency representing the Palestinian Arabs, to supplant the Arab Higher Committee and implement the recommendations of the London conference. He had already talked to the candidates and had them approved by the British. When Sasson pretended that the sums envisaged by Abdullah, almost £P40,000, were rather large and he could not guarantee them, Abdullah said: 'One who wants to get drunk should not count the glasses', meaning that he who wants a state has to make the necessary investments. In Abdullah's opinion it was the right time to act, both for himself and the Jewish Agency, and he launched on a long explanation of the economic opportunities that would become available to an enlarged Hashemite kingdom.

As Sasson was about to leave, Abdullah took him by the arm and said: 'I am sixty-six years old. My remaining years are numbered. You do not have any realist Arab leader like me in the entire Arab world. You have two alternative paths: to join with me and work together or to give me up.' If the Zionists chose the first path, he said they had to meet his requests unhesitatingly, unreservedly, and soon. If they chose the second path, God be with them, but they must stop talking about co-operation and common interests.[23]

Six months had elapsed since a senior Zionist figure had met with Abdullah, and a great deal had changed in the intervening period. Sasson's visit to the royal palace therefore took the form of a prelimi-

[23] Report by Sasson, 12 Aug. 1946, S25/9036, CZA. An edited version appears in Sasson, *On The Road to Peace*, 367–70.

nary reconnaisance mission to appraise the king's thinking and disposi-
tions and, in particular, to see if he would back an Egyptian agreement
to the partition of Palestine. The king treated his visitor to a characteristically rambling discourse, full of contradictions and incon-
sistencies. The only conclusion that could be drawn from the king's
meanderings was that he himself had a plan for a Hashemite federation
but his hands were tied by the British. The breakdown of relations
between the British government and the Jewish Agency presented him
with an opportunity to serve as a mediator, or at least a messenger,
between the estranged parties. But he himself was kept on a perpetually
tight leash by his British masters and he looked to the Zionist
movement for material and political support in furthering his
ambitious scheme. In return for such support all the king could offer
was a vague and ill-defined promise to support partition if the international community could be persuaded to move in that direction.

Getting authoritative answers to King Abdullah's proposals was not
at all an easy task because one group of Jewish leaders, including
Moshe Sharett, had been detained in prison by the British authorities
since the crackdown on 'Black Saturday' while another group, headed
by David Ben-Gurion, was in Paris. It was in Paris that the Executive of
the Jewish Agency met and categorically rejected the Morrison–Grady
Plan. A less publicized but highly significant decision was also reached
in Paris at the suggestion of Nahum Goldmann: to agree to consider the
establishment of a viable Jewish state on an adequate part of Palestine.
This meant the acceptance of the principle of partition and a retreat
from the Biltmore resolution to set up a Jewish state over the entire area
west of the Jordan River. Even Ben-Gurion, who was generally
considered a militant, developed a plan for the establishment of two
independent states, 'Judaea' and 'Abdallia'. The latter was to
incorporate the hilly area west of the Jordan containing half a million
Arabs and to compensate 'Judaea' with an uninhabited stretch of land
to the east of the river.[24]

Meanwhile the Jewish Agency officials in Jerusalem managed to get
messages to and from Sharett by making a daily delivery of fresh milk in
a container fitted with a false bottom.[25] It was through this primitive
mailbox that Sasson sought guidance from his leader. But the use of
codes to reduce the value of the intelligence to the British in the event of
detection did not make for trouble-free communication. Sharett detected in Abdullah's words some truth, some lies, and some illusions but
the guidelines he prepared for Sasson's next meeting dealt with his

---

[24] Shmuel Dothan, *The Struggle for Eretz Israel* (Heb.) (Tel Aviv: Ministry of Defence, 1981),
332 f.

[25] Interview with Zeev Sharef.

questions one by one. Firstly, the Zionist movement had made clear and public its plan to strive for an independent Jewish state over the whole of or as much of Palestine as possible. That was the goal of the struggle. But if there was the prospect of an agreed solution with some influential Arabs, the movement would be prepared to pay a price. Of the various compromise plans under discussion, the movement preferred partition to the British federal plan, and by partition it meant the annexation of the non-Jewish part of Palestine to Transjordan with some minor territorial adjustments in favour of the Jewish state. Secondly, if the British genuinely wanted to improve relations with the Jewish community, it was up to them to make the first gesture such as releasing the detainees in time for the forthcoming conference organized by Bevin in London. Thirdly, Sharett was all for backing Abdullah provided there was a mutual agreement which obliged Abdullah to back them as well. As for 'the sweets', wrote Sharett in an obvious reference to money, it was evident that Sasson could not go empty-handed. He assumed that Sasson was reporting simultaneously to Paris but for his part Sharett felt that since they were dealing with a crowned king, they must 'steal, rob, mortgage and do without' in order to obtain £P5,000.[26] Sharett was not one of those Zionist leaders who believed that the basic aims of the Zionist movement could be significantly furthered by the payment of money to Arab politicians who professed themselves to be friends, and his agreement on this occasion should be seen in the context of his movement's political weakness, international isolation, and growing rift with the British authorities.

Sasson, on the other hand, felt that £P5,000 was the minimal sum with which he could return to Abdullah without disappointing him and spoiling the favourable climate. He also thought that he should have the authority to promise another payment in the event of concrete support by Abdullah and his emissaries for partition. Sasson had come away from his last meeting with Abdullah with the impression that Abdullah was not only talking about his far-reaching plan but was preparing to act and making a strong bid to carry the British with him. Sasson perceived the advantage of Sharett's subtle opposition to the Morrison–Grady Plan over Ben-Gurion's categorical rejection which placed the onus for the deadlock on the Jewish Agency. What troubled Sasson was the danger that they would sing different tunes to Abdullah and Sidqi and if the two Arab leaders chose to inform the British about their talks with the Jews it would create an impression of Jewish duplicity. It was true that both Sidqi and Abdullah were inclined towards partition but for very different reasons. The former wanted to avoid inter-Arab disputes and to win over the Palestinians by offering

---

[26] Unsigned letter by Shertok, 13 Aug. 1945, S245/105, CZA.

them full independence whereas the latter wanted to extend his own rule over the Palestinians.[27]

Sharett, however, saw no cause for concern. First of all, he advised Sasson, they should state what they themselves required: a substantial part of Palestine and sovereignty over it. What happened to the rest would not be up to them but up to the Arabs to decide. From this point on Sharett suggested slight variations in presenting the Zionist case to suit the taste of each listener. Abdullah should be told that they hoped that the remaining part of Palestine would be joined to his kingdom because they knew they could rely on his true friendship and intended to pledge their support to him in the framework of an alliance. But it should also be made clear to Abdullah that with all their support for him the Jews could not guarantee the agreement of his Arab brothers, and here it was he who must carry the main burden. Sidqi, on the other hand, should be told that it would be up to the Palestinian inhabitants to decide on the future of their territory. The Jewish Agency's view was that it would be better to unify west with east; separately, each leg would stumble, whereas together they would be able to stand up. But if the Palestinians preferred separation that was their affair. Finally, while agreeing to a present of £P5,000 if Sasson considered it really necessary, Sharett advised him to make no promises on the pretext that his bosses were out of reach.[28]

On August 19, Sasson once again went to meet King Abdullah in Shuneh. He was stopped and searched by officials on the eastern side of the Allenby Bridge. They found on him a number of Arab newspapers and the sum of £P5,000. Under persistent questioning Sasson stated that he had an invitation to see a high-ranking personality but declined to reveal the purpose of the meeting. Two hours later he returned to Jerusalem and when he was searched for the second time by the same officers, they found on him only £P1,000. Asked what he had done with the rest of the money, Sasson answered that it was none of their business.[29]

The king was none too pleased when he saw that Sasson had only brought him £P5,000. To prove that the sum he had requested was trivial in relation to his needs, the king showed Sasson dozens of letters and papers from Syrian and Druze notables referring to serious plans and actual deeds. Some of them even spoke of armed rebellion. Seeing his visitor's incredulity, King Abdullah took from his safe letters from Hijazi tribal chiefs which went even further, referring to plans for reconquering the Hashemite dynasty's lost kingdom. All

[27] Unsigned letter by Sasson, 16 Aug. 1945, S245/105, CZA.
[28] Shertok to Sasson, 18 Aug. 1945, S245/105, CZA.
[29] Al-Wahda, front-page article, 20 Aug. 1946.

the letters bore recent dates and dealt with two subjects: money and arms.

Sasson then told the king of the unfortunate incident on the Allenby Bridge and broached the question of employing a go-between. Agreeing that it was in neither side's interest to have frequent visits from the director of the Arab Section of the Jewish Agency's Political Department, the king returned £P1,000, and asked Sasson to give it to one of his emissaries who was staying in Jerusalem to hold talks and collect signatures for the 'partition and merger' plan. This man, whom he recommended to Sasson as thoroughly reliable, would serve as the go-between.

Sasson asked whether the British and the Iraqis knew of Abdullah's plans and approved of them. The British, replied Abdullah, claimed that nothing concrete could be done for the time being; they held that the ground had first to be prepared but when the time came they would support him fully and generously. As for the Iraqis, only a small number of people, family relatives and loyalists, knew about these matters, and they supported him unreservedly. All the money he had spent to gain support in northern Syria came from that source. Upon completing his explanation, Abdullah once again pressed for more money.

Acting on Sharett's instructions, Sasson raised the question of border modifications under Abdullah's 'partition and merger' plan, but was rebuffed with the observation that agreement in principle must precede the discussion of details. If border modification were to depend on him alone, Abdullah promised to be flexible. Besides, it was undesirable to raise the question when Ibn Saud was claiming Akaba and Maan. Sasson's insistence provoked a stern admonition: 'Don't be egotistical. Don't demand just what is good for you. Look at matters within the framework of the entire Arab Orient and its complications and not just within the framework of Palestine.' At this point Sasson offered a compromise, which the king accepted: to leave the detailed discussions of borders to their respective delegates to the London conference should the latter go in the direction of 'partition and merger'.

Abdullah explained that the Arab League's decision to insist on implementation of the 1939 White Paper was taken under pressure from the mufti and his men. The latter also demanded the boycotting of the London talks unless the mufti was invited but the Arab foreign ministers resolved to go without him. Speaking of the mufti, Abdullah observed that there was only one solution—to remove him from the scene. When Sasson recoiled, Abdullah added that he was ready to take it upon himself to arrange it. 'This man', he added, 'is the greatest obstacle to settling matters in Palestine, Transjordan, and Syria, he is hostile to you and to me, and he must be removed from the scene at any price and quickly.' The significance of this suggestion was not lost on the Jewish representative, but the only response it evoked was a troubled silence.

Abdullah had one final piece of advice for his Jewish friends: to resist every plan except 'partition and merger' which they should do everything in their power to attain. By doing so, he explained, they would jointly pave the way for the possibility that Britain would impose the federal solution on them and on the Palestine Arabs. This, he said, would represent a net gain. Admittedly, it would not give the Jews full satisfaction, but it could deal once and for all with the opposition of the Palestine Arabs to any solution which did not satisfy their demands. In the meantime, the immigration of 100,000 Jews would be made possible and they would be drawn closer to the Arab world.[30] Thus, with typically devious tactics, Abdullah proposed that they proceed by a partition route towards a federal destination, thereby throwing dust into their opponents' eyes along the road.

The two meetings in Shuneh were useful in identifying at least some common ground between Abdullah and the Zionists and in providing a basis for future co-operation between them. Using the newly designated go-between, Abdullah informed Sasson that he had given the head of the Transjordanian delegation to the London talks two instructions: to support partition and to make contact with a member of the Jewish delegation. Sasson appreciated Abdullah's gesture and later followed it up personally during his stay in London. Sasson also began to press for active Jewish support for Abdullah's planned take-over in Syria. His colleague, Ezra Danin, volunteered to meet Abdullah to examine the plan and supervise its execution. If it succeded, Sasson pointed out, the new reality would have to be taken into account by the London conference. If it failed, their loss would be purely financial.[31] Sharett was in favour of committing £P10,000 to the 'northern plan' though he was unclear as to Danin's precise role and the kind of control he would have over expenditure.[32] But before any move could be made to change the regime in the north, a very unwelcome change occurred in the south: Ismail Sidqi fell from power. His resignation nullified the Zionist break-through in Egypt and rendered all his promises to support partition worthless. Abdullah was now the sole Arab leader ready to work for a compromise solution with the Zionists.

This was the dominant assumption underlying a comprehensive

[30] Report by Sasson, 19 Aug. 1946, S25/9036, CZA. An edited version appears in Sasson, *On the Road to Peace*, 370–2.

[31] Sasson to Shertok, 11 Sept. 1946, S245/105, CZA.

[32] Shertok to Sasson, 12 Sept. 1946, S245/105, CZA.

plan of action which Sasson submitted to the leaders of the Jewish Agency in November 1946 with the aim of preparing the ground for the establishment of a Jewish state. In general, he argued for a more interventionist policy in Palestine and the Arab countries in order to foster trends conducive to this objective rather than letting events take their own course as they had been doing. Specifically, he argued that serious consideration be given to Abdullah's plan for engineering a pro-Hashemite government in Damascus, in order to annex Syria and parts of Lebanon and Palestine to a large kingdom which would change the balance of power in the Arab world. From the Jewish point of view, argued Sasson, such a plan would have distinct advantages. In its first stage, it would bring down the anti-Zionist nationalist regime in Syria. Similarly, it would divide the Palestine Arabs and thereby weaken the influence of the Husaynis and the general opposition to the Zionist enterprise. Second, in its subsequent stages, the plan would greatly assist any Jewish–Anglo-American move which would have as its end the creation of a Jewish state in part of Palestine. Third, if fully accomplished, the plan would tilt the balance in the Arab camp against countries such as Saudi Arabia and Egypt which took the lead in opposing Zionism. Fourth, the enlarged Arab kingdom would divide and possibly wreck the Arab League and expose the artificial base on which it was built. To the question whether it was desirable to have as a neighbour such a large Arab state, Sasson had a ready answer. It was desirable because it would prevent the emergence of a new Arab state headed by the mufti. It would assist the establishment of a Christian state in part of Lebanon. It would serve Britain's interests because Britain's loyal ally, Abdullah, would head it. And if alongside it a Jewish and a small Lebanese state did emerge, there would be a good chance that these three new states—the Christian, the Jewish, and Abdullah's—would conclude an alliance with Britain. In short, it would settle once and for all the problems of the region.[33] Sasson was unable to elicit any positive support for the proposed plan of action from his political superiors, but his memorandum is none the less significant as an example of the Hashemite orientation which was increasingly to colour the political outlook of the Jewish Agency and of which he himself was one of the most persuasive advocates.

Retreat from the mandate

The chances of mediation between Jews and Arabs, limited enough at the outset, faded away altogether during the second stage of the conference which opened in London in January 1947. The Jewish

---

[33] Sasson, *On the Road to Peace*, 378–82.

Agency would consider no solution other than partition; the mufti-led Arab Higher Committee would settle for nothing less than immediate independence in the whole of Palestine. No amount of British pleading or British pressure could bridge the gap between the two sides. Bevin's last proposal went a very long way in meeting the needs of the Palestine Arabs but it was nevertheless rejected, as in 1939, because it fell short of satisfying the maximalist demands of their leadership. The Arab states feebly endorsed the hard line laid down by the Arab Higher Committee. Even Abdullah was forced to declare his opposition to partition, if only to scotch rumours that his army was poised to occupy parts of Palestine and Syria and rebut the charge of sabotaging Arab unity in defence of Palestine. On February 18 a very bitter and disillusioned Bevin announced Britain's decision to refer the Palestine problem to the United Nations. Thus, without any serious preparation, a political hot potato was about to be dumped into the lap of the infant world organization.

To Britain's friends in the Middle East, news of her decision to wash her hands of the mandate was no less disturbing for having been expected. Abdullah made it known that he preferred Britain to solve the Palestine problem without the help of the UN. He declared that should the British evacuate any part of Palestine, his forces would immediately occupy it to save it from the danger of alienation. Reluctant as he was to see the British depart, he regarded their decision as irreversible and began to behave accordingly. A secret session of the Arab League opened in Cairo on 17 March 1947 to consider this unwelcome turn of events. In the course of its deliberations a consensus began to emerge in favour of implementing the secret decisions of the Bludan meeting of the previous June to furnish money, arms, and volunteers for Palestine so as to save it from a Zionist takeover and to apply economic sanctions against Britain and the United States. Transjordan's prime minister stated that his country reserved its freedom of action in connection with the Bludan decisions because his country was the second target of Zionism after Palestine. He asked the council to note that Transjordan, not being a member of the UN, must retain the right to fight independently for Palestine. On the last day he reiterated the Hashemite government's decision to reserve its freedom of action in Palestine in order to ensure that the Arab character of the country was preserved. To all those present in Cairo it was clear that the Transjordanian delegate's references to the UN and to Transjordan's duties only served to mask his master's determination to keep a free hand for military intervention in Palestine in pursuit of his plans for territorial expansion.

The heated dispute on the subject of Greater Syria, the other major bone of contention in Cairo, was soon transferred to the public arena. Abdullah appealed to the Syrian people over the heads of their leaders. The latter retorted that they would accept no Greater Syria unless it was republican and its capital was Damascus, adding that if Abdullah persisted in his attempts to subvert the existing regime in Syria, they would act to remove him from power and take over his country. In May, with elections impending in both Syria and Lebanon, a 300-page White Book was published in Amman, supporting Hashemite claims with documents that went back to the First World War and a Preamble which emphasized the compatibility of the Greater Syria plan with the Covenant of the Arab League.[34] The White Paper was an unco-ordinated collection of documents of no particular importance but it was prepared with the full knowledge and approval of the king and fairly represented his views. After the first outburst of irritation from Syria, Lebanon, and Saudi Arabia, it proved something of a damp squib. The British were mildly annoyed with Abdullah for injecting this additional irritant into Middle East politics and were moved to restate their complete neutrality on the question of Greater Syria.

Before the Greater Syria question was reopened in London, the Hashemite dynasty raised the level of its diplomatic representation in the British capital. Prince Abdul Majid Haidar was appointed as Transjordan's minister in London, while Prince Zeid was sent as the Iraqi minister. The former was Abdullah's cousin, the latter his brother. These appointments were not accidental: they reflected the determination to be on guard for the coming battle over Palestine and Greater Syria and to steer developments in a way which would enhance the Hashemite dynasty's influence in the Arab world. A much more significant move, undertaken with the same intention, was the conclu-sion, in April, of a Treaty of Brotherhood and Alliance between Transjordan and Iraq. The allies under this treaty committed them-selves to military co-operation against 'aggressors'—a term which could apply to other Arabs as much as it did to the Zionists. Syria on the one hand, and Saudi Arabia and Egypt who were lined up against the Hashemites on the other, were apt to view the treaty in this light. They also suspected Abdullah of wanting to make a deal with the Zionist 'aggressors'. One of the rumours circulating in Cairo was that Abdul-lah agreed to support a Jewish state in Palestine if the Jews would support the Greater Syria idea. This was denied by Fawzi el-Mulki, Transjordan's minister in Cairo. All Abdullah was prepared to sup-port, he assured the British ambassador there, was special arrange-ments and guarantees for communal life for the Jews in an integral

---

[34] Jordan, Ministry of Foreign Affairs, *The Jordan White Book on Greater Syria* (Arab.) (Amman, 1947).

Arab state. This was something quite different, he said, and anyhow there was no question of a bargain.[35]

As their rivalry with the Arab states escalated, the Hashemites turned their attention to Turkey as a potential ally. Abdullah went there on an official visit in January 1947, probably to win support for his Greater Syria idea. During his visit a treaty of friendship and amity was concluded between his kingdom and the Republic of Turkey. By means of these alliances it was hoped to strengthen the Hashemite bloc against the rival Egyptian–Saudi bloc which wielded greater influence within the Arab League. The support usually extended to the Arab Higher Committee by his rivals was a particular source of aggravation to Abdullah. He was most annoyed, for example, by the failure of the Arab League to dissociate itself from the Arab Higher Committee's refusal to co-operate with the UN fact-finding mission to Palestine. In a fit of exasperation, he told Christopher Pirie-Gordon (of the British Legation in Amman) that he had only joined the League as a personal favour to Sir Alec Kirkbride and now found himself committed to a series of ridiculous decisions by a lot of irresponsible politicians. But his assertion that now that both Transjordan and Iraq had treaties with Turkey it would be far simpler for them to leave the League and form a Hashemite–Turkish bloc was more indicative of a transitory state of mind than of the probability of adopting this course of action.[36]

Upon closer examination, the superficially plausible interpretation which holds that from the end of the Second World War until 1947 Greater Syria was Abdullah's top priority and that in 1947 he abandoned this broader ambition in order to secure part of Palestine for his kingdom thus becomes less and less tenable. The close interconnection between the two aims, both in Abdullah's policies and in his opponents' perception of those policies, renders artificial any attempt to separate them chronologically. What the survey of the period from 1945 to 1947 does reveal is a quickening of the pace and the start of a more frenetic drive by Abdullah to realize his territorial ambitions. In this connection, the impending British withdrawal from Palestine represented both a threat and an opportunity for Abdullah. It represented a threat in as much as he was accustomed to depend on Britain to hold the ring within which he could manœuvre in relative safety. Once Britain's firm hand was removed, Palestine was liable to be engulfed by chaos without any certainty as to who would come out on top. On the other hand, the very same fluidity which was bound to follow Britain's departure carried the prospect for enlarging his kingdom. It was the British, after all, who confined Abdullah to the east of

[35] Sir Ronald Campbell (Cairo) to FO, 19 May 1947, FO 371/61493, PRO.
[36] C. H. Pirie-Gordon to FO, 19 June 1947, FO 371/61493, PRO.

the River Jordan as part of the political order they sought to maintain in the Middle East. It was they who kept the falcon pinned up in a canary's cage. Now the transfer of responsibility for deciding Palestine's fate from the mighty British Empire to the toothless UN offered him the chance that had been denied him for a quarter of a century—the chance to break out of the cage, to carve out a kingdom to the measure of his territorial, political, and material ambition, and to assert his mastery over the Arab world. London's decision to surrender the mandate over Palestine to the UN also marked a turning point in Abdullah's relations with the British, with the Arab world, with the Palestinians, and above all, with the Zionists.

4

TWO KINDS OF PARTITION

UNSCOP's inquiry and partition plan

The transfer of responsibility for dealing with the Palestine problem from Britain to the United Nations compelled King Abdullah to reconsider his own position and the various alternatives available to him. A concrete policy objective emerged out of this process: the acquisition of the Arab part of Palestine and its merger with Transjordan. Abdullah's personal diplomacy in all the overlapping circles in which he operated was henceforth governed by this definite short-term objective. In the first place he had to co-ordinate his moves with Britain—Transjordan's protector and the principal imperialist power in the Middle East. Such co-ordination was all the more necessary since Transjordan was not a member of the United Nations whereas Britain was one of the permanent members of its Security Council. Secondly, he had to conceal his real intentions from the other members of the Arab League and from the Palestinian Arabs over whom he hoped to extend his rule, and this meant pursuing a pan-Arab declaratory strategy which was at total variance with his operational strategy. Thirdly, since acquisition of the Arab part of Palestine implied a partition of the country, he had to strive for an understanding with the Jews, who had their own territorial claims, behind the backs of his fellow Arabs.

Arab resistance to partition did not stem solely from their objection to the establishment of a Jewish state in part of Palestine but also from their disagreement on what should be done with the Arab part. Transjordan wanted to bring it under its own rule. Iraq supported this plan in the hope of merging with the enlarged kingdom of Transjordan and thereby gaining access to the Mediterranean. Syria and Lebanon opposed the enlargement of Transjordan for fear that it might jeopardize their independence and lead to the realization of the Greater Syria plan. Saudi Arabia was opposed to any change in the status quo which would extend the borders and strengthen the Hashemites of Transjordan and Iraq, lest they be tempted to try to reconquer their ancestral land in the Hijaz. The Arab Higher Committee was opposed to any partition plan so as to rule out altogether the possibility of merging the Arab part of Palestine with any of the neighbouring states. It took the view that the Arabs of Palestine had as much of a right to sovereignty as the Arabs of Transjordan, Iraq, Syria, or Lebanon, and that they had not struggled for thirty years against Zionism and the mandate in order to end up as the subjects of this or that Arab ruler but in order to become independent like the Arabs of the neighbouring countries. As for Egypt, it was opposed to partition so as to preserve as far as possible unity and solidarity within the Arab world.[1]

Interwoven with these endemic interstate rivalries there were others of a more personal and dynastic nature. The Jewish Agency was drawn into this complex web of rivalries and emnities that made up Arab politics in curious and often unexpected ways. King Abdullah was the foremost example of an Arab ruler who sought Jewish support to further his dynastic ambitions at the expense of Arab opponents. But he was not the only one. In the summer of 1947, for example, Sharif Fawaz al-Sharaf initiated a series of conversations with Elias Sasson at which he advanced some rather audacious and startling proposals.

Sharif Fawaz was a member of the Hashemite family, distantly related to King Abdullah and to Abd al-Illah, the regent of Iraq. Through his wife's family, Sharif Fawaz was also related to Amir Talal, the heir to the Transjordanian throne.

The sharif's proposals were as follows: Abd al-Illah, not as an Iraqi but as an individual and a member of the Hashemite dynasty and he, Fawaz, nurtured a dream of returning to the Hijaz, expelling Ibn Saud, and restoring the Arab kingdom to the Hashemites. In order to realize these dreams, which they considered as feasible from a military point of view, Abd al-Illah and his close associates (i.e. Fawaz) were prepared to consider receiving help from the Jewish Agency in return for recognition of its aspirations. The help sought involved both money and the use of the Zionist connections in the United States to influence the authorities and public opinion there. Fawaz thought that American support for Ibn Saud was based on the assumption that only he could preserve the peace necessary for the conduct of good business in the Arabian peninsula, but that it was possible to persuade the American public that the Hashemite dynasty would be no less effective in this respect. In exchange for such help, said the sharif, they would be prepared to recognize the establishment of a Jewish state in part of Palestine.

In all the talks Sasson stressed that the Jewish Agency had neither the means nor the will to get involved in plots against Ibn Saud. On the other hand it might be prepared to extend some practical assistance to the Hashemites of Iraq to help them carry out plans of their own

[1] Sasson, *On the Road to Peace*, 390.

without inquiring into the details and it would also be prepared to organize propaganda on behalf of the Hashemites in the United States.

To move the talks on to more practical lines, Sasson prepared a draft agreement. It was suggested that Fawaz would take this draft to Abd al-Illah and if the latter found it acceptable in principle, a meeting would be arranged between him and David Ben-Gurion in Europe to settle the detailed provisions and sign the agreement. After this draft was handed over to Fawaz, he requested another meeting in order to submit a counter-proposal.

A close reading of the two texts reveals a number of important differences. Fawaz's draft was much more cautious and reserved. Whereas Sasson envisaged that America and Britain should be let into the secret as soon as possible, Fawaz preferred that they should not be informed until after the necessary climate of opinion had been prepared in the Arab world. His draft also required formal recognition of the Hashemite dynasty and action by the Jewish Agency to bring about the merger of the Arab part of Palestine with Transjordan, whereas Sasson's draft spoke only of general willingness to recognize the Arab world's decision concerning the future of the Arab part of Palestine.

Sharif Fawaz set off for Iraq in early July, bearing both the original draft agreement and his own counter-proposal. He promised to speak to Abd al-Illah and return two or three weeks later with the regent's approval of one of them, or a new proposal, or a cancellation of the entire plan.

It was never made clear in the first place to what extent Fawaz had been authorized to speak in the name of the regent, and whether, indeed, he had spoken to him before approaching the Jewish Agency officials. But from the series of conversations they had with him, the latter formed the impression that he was not a simple adventurer and certainly not a liar. The Jewish Agency's archives do not reveal the sequel to this encounter, if any. But this intriguing episode at least gave a foretaste of the criss-crossing personal, dynastic, and interstate rivalries that were about to condition Arab handling of the Palestine problem in the UN context.[2]

These conflicting interests came to the surface during the visit of the United Nations Special Committee on Palestine (UNSCOP) to the Middle East in July 1947. The Arab Higher Committee insisted on boycotting UNSCOP on the grounds that the case of the Palestine Arabs was clear and should not be subject to a new investigation; that the UN had no jurisdiction in the matter; and that the end of the British mandate could be followed by nothing except the granting of full independence to Palestine. King Abdullah made an unsuccessful

[2] Yaacov Shimoni, 'Talk with the Sharif Fawaz al Sharaf', 16 July 1947, S25/3909, CZA.

attempt to persuade the Arab Higher Committee to call off the boycott, arguing that the Arabs should give evidence to UNSCOP and present their case before it. The representatives of the Arab states, at their meeting with the committee in Lebanon, were constrained to broadly reaffirm the rigid policy of the Arab Higher Committee, to reject partition, and even to threaten the use of force to prevent the establishment of a Jewish state in any part of Palestine. Arab diplomacy, with its tendency to adopt inflexible postures, created a very poor impression on members of the committee who had come with an open mind. It certainly eased the task of the Jewish Agency in presenting its case, in projecting an appearance of flexibility and moderation, and in gently nudging the committee in the direction of a solution based on partition, which its leaders strongly supported in the depth of their hearts.

Transjordan alone among the Arab states adopted a co-operative attitude and displayed some flexibility without breaking too blatantly the discipline of the Arab League. Having declined to send a representative to the collective appearances before the committee in Lebanon on the thin pretext that Transjordan was not a member of the UN, Abdullah invited its members to meet him in his capital. To cover himself against the charge of breaking rank, he stated in the invitation that 'Transjordan will take, as it always has, the same stand taken by the other Arab countries on the Palestine problem.'

The chairman of UNSCOP and some of its members and staff proceeded from Lebanon to Amman where they were received by King Abdullah. 'They found the King to be a small, poised, handsome man who spoke only Arabic in a most musical cadence, and who smiled frequently as he spoke.' Abdullah parried all questions relating to the type of solution he envisaged, saying that there were many such solutions, but what was necessary first of all, was to adopt one solution and enforce it firmly and unhesitatingly. 'Whatever the solution,' he said, 'the incontestable rights of the Arabs must be protected. It will be difficult for Arabs to accept a Jewish State even in part of Palestine.' Would partition lead to trouble in the Middle East, he was asked. He smiled. 'The Middle East already has much trouble', he countered. 'If the Jews were treated justly in all countries, there would be no Jewish and therefore no Palestine problem.'[3]

Transjordan's prime minister read a statement in English explaining his country's stand on Palestine—one which indeed paralleled that of the other Arab states. In an off-the-record conversation, however, Samir al-Rifai told the committee members that the Jews should be permitted to remain a minority with equal rights to those of the Arabs.

[3] Jorge Garcia-Granados, *The Birth of Israel: The Drama as I Saw It* (New York: A. Knopf, 1948), 208 f.

No more Jews should be permitted to enter Palestine, but those already there should be granted citizenship in the Arab state. When told that Arab representatives had implied in Beirut that if the United Nations decided on the establishment of a Jewish state they would consider it a state established by force and resist it by force, the prime minister seemed downcast and said: 'That is a very serious statement to make, for it clearly means declaring war on the United Nations if the Arab representatives really meant what they said. I should say that Transjordan would not take such an extreme attitude.' And on that important note the discussions ended.[4]

Abdullah's puzzling behaviour—first pressing for Arab co-operation with UNSCOP, then declining to participate in the discussions held in Beirut and finally meeting with it unilaterally and privately in Amman—gave rise to speculations that he had his own solution to propose which was not in accord with the Arab stand. In his public utterances, therefore, the king adopted a more uncompromising tone. He denied the very existence of the Faisal–Weizmann agreement which in 1919 promised 'the most cordial goodwill and understanding' between the future Arab and Jewish states in Palestine. He also denied having made unflattering remarks about the mufti, and sent the latter a collection of newly issued stamps depicting the deliverance of Palestine. But the secret sessions of UNSCOP in Amman, at which the relations between Abdullah and the mufti and the possibility of joining the Arab parts of Palestine to Transjordan were allegedly discussed, created persistent suspicions in pan-Arab circles, and there was even talk of asking the Political Committee of the Arab League to look into the matter.

These suspicions were not entirely without justification. Immediately after the UNSCOP visit to Amman, Abdullah sent a message to Bevin to say that although for reasons which were both tactical and political the Transjordanian government in its official evidence before UNSCOP had felt obliged to dismiss partition as a possible solution to the Palestine problem, he wished it to be known that these were not the real views either of his government or of himself. His real view was that partition was the only solution, and he hoped that every effort would be made to ensure that it was adopted. In the event of a partition scheme being finally promulgated, the question was bound to arise as to whether the new state should be independent or attached to Transjordan. Abdullah therefore wanted Bevin to know that in the latter event he would be perfectly willing to give his full co-operation and to take over all the Arab areas of Palestine, or as much of them as were offered to him, and to stand up to any abuse and criticism to which

[4] Ibid. 210.

this action might expose him from the other Arab states. Anticipating reproach from Britain for not having stated this opinion plainly to the committee, he explained that as Transjordan was the one Arab state which stood to gain substantially from partition, it was impossible that she should also be the only state publicly to advocate this course contrary to the official views of the whole Arab world. The king was under the impression that the Jewish state was unlikely to comprise more than the strip of coast between Haifa and Tel Aviv and seemed disappointed when told that the Jews were demanding the Peel Commission boundaries and the Negev in addition. In spite of this the king still maintained that he would be willing to take over whatever was left.

The prime minister confirmed to Pirie-Gordon that he was in agreement with the king on this subject, and that while he did not know what military implications might be involved in a proposal to hand Transjordan the Arab areas of Palestine when considerable opposition might be expected from the supporters of the Husayni party, he assumed that this difficulty would somehow be overcome at the time. He pointed out further that in his statement to the committee he had deliberately made his rejection of partition as a solution more a matter of administrative than of political difficulty.[5]

The Jewish Agency was less indulgent with regard to Abdullah's equivocal performance during UNSCOP's visit to Amman. Reports of the private conversations, including Abdullah's failure to come out for partition and Rifai's denial that the Jews had any right to self-determination, reached the Agency, and Ezra Danin was dispatched to see the king. The king received him cordially and stressed at the beginning of the conversation that the agreement between them was valid and firm and that he was doing everything for the common cause. He was even prepared to sign a written agreement. But his general view was that the Jews were too impatient and that they would gain much by waiting a year or two.

As for the anti-Zionist stand attributed to Abdullah in the press, he denied having sent a telegram to UNSCOP's chairman expressing support of the Arab League's position on the Palestine question. Secondly, he had not denied the existence of the Weizmann–Faisal accord, but simply explained that it was not binding because the conditions had not been fulfilled. Thirdly, he issued the stamps featuring defence of the Arab lands of Palestine in order to show that he was doing something whereas the other Arab kings were not doing anything. In proferring these explanations, Abdullah stressed that his position was exposed and that he was open to attack from Arab quarters.

[5] Pirie-Gordon to Bevin, 30 July 1947, FO 371/68176, PRO.

Nevertheless, continued Abdullah, he remained faithful to the common cause and wanted to pursue his activities in Syria. The British had not stood in his way, but he had the impression that they wanted to preserve the status quo. The unrest among the Druze and the Kurds he attributed to growing communist influence in Syria. If only his four brigades could be enabled to fight, the whole affair would be settled very quickly. Danin construed this as an indirect request for additional grants from the Jewish Agency.[6] He made no response to this allusion at the time but cabled Elias Sasson, who was active behind the scenes in Geneva, for his opinion.[7]

Sasson, who understood better than any of his colleagues the inter-Arab constraints that limited Abdullah's freedom of action or at least freedom of expression, was on this occasion totally unsympathetic. He argued that the appearance of Abdullah and his men before UNSCOP's delegates had been thoroughly unsatisfactory. They had talked about everything except the 'partition and merger' plan, and by failing to mention their willingness to annex the Arab part of Palestine they effectively let the plan be dropped, thereby damaging Transjordanian as well as Jewish interests. So incensed was Sasson with Abdullah's failure to act in accordance with their pre-arranged plan that he suggested that no further payment be made to him until he committed himself to a clear and specific agreement in writing.[8]

Sasson, who was expounding the virtues of partition to anyone in Geneva who would listen, found a very valuable ally in Omar Dajani, a Palestinian Arab who was politically close to Abdullah and served as his unofficial representative in UN circles. Dajani kept in close touch with Sasson throughout his stay in Geneva and engaged in numerous private conversations with UNSCOP members and staff to influence them in the direction of partition. From this informal and ill-defined co-operation, he then went on to become a paid collaborator of the Jewish Agency. Sasson reported to his colleagues in Jerusalem that Dajani had reinforced Zionist lobbying in Geneva, that he himself had obtained valuable information, and that he would be submitting proposals upon his return to Palestine. He asked them to treat Dajani with respect and trust and to take his proposals seriously.[9]

Once he was back in Palestine, Dajani promptly established contact with Yaacov Shimoni, Sasson's deputy in the Arab section of the Jewish Agency's Political Department. Born in Berlin in 1915, Shimoni was beginning to make his mark as a Middle East expert with exceptionally

---

[6] Ezra Danin's Talk with Abdullah, 21 Aug. 1947, S25/3960, CZA.

[7] Danin to Sasson, 22 Aug. 1947, S25/1961, CZA.

[8] Sasson to Danin, 23 Aug. 1947, S25/1961; Sasson to Zeev Sharef, 23 Aug. 1947, S25/6644, CZA.

[9] Sasson to Zeev Sharef, 23 Aug. 1947, S25/6644, CZA.

good knowledge of Palestinian Arab society and politics. In his report to Mrs Golda Meyerson (Meir), who was acting head of the Political Department in Sharett's absence, Shimoni described Dajani as 'our envoy to Geneva'. In a meeting which lasted three hours, Dajani gave Shimoni a full account of his discussions with UNSCOP members, of his successes in persuading them that partition offered the best possible solution, and of the favourable impression he had made on them. Although he was a faithful supporter of partition and the merger of the Arab part of Palestine with Transjordan, Dajani saw himself as a member of the group that had crystallized around Musa Alami. Alami did not support partition, but Dajani shared his hatred of the mufti and of the Arab Higher Committee and also felt that it would be easier to come to terms with him and his followers because they were more sensible and moderate than the mufti and his men. According to Dajani, Alami was determined to make the final break with the mufti and to organize his many followers in a new party. At this first meeting Dajani came across as boastful and prone to exaggerate his own achievements, but at the same time he impressed Shimoni as a sincere and competent individual, albeit a little audacious.

Dajani perceived his own role in the immediate future as covering three major areas. First of all, he wanted to visit King Abdullah and tell him that among the partition plans under consideration at the UN, not one involved annexing the Arab part of Palestine to Transjordan. Either Abdullah's evidence before UNSCOP was unclear or unsuccessful or it had been deliberately distorted. In any case, Dajani wanted to hear definitively whether Abdullah intended to act and whether there was any point in continuing the connection with him and working on his behalf. Should he find that there was no such hope, he was prepared to leave the king and to struggle for partition without him.

Dajani's second aim was to buy the weekly newspaper *Al Hadaf* and turn it into an effective mouthpiece for himself and his associates. He hoped that the Jewish Agency would supply the £P800 needed to buy the paper and thereafter contribute to the running costs. Another share of the running costs had already been promised to him by Musa Alami, even though their views about the solution to the Palestine problem were rather different.

Thirdly, Dajani wanted to go to New York to organize his followers and to strengthen Alami's group. Convinced that if the mufti and his men were to represent the Palestine cause before UNSCOP in New York all would be lost, he wanted to secure Alami's official nomination by the Arab states as their liaison officer with the UN.[10]

UNSCOP submitted its recommendations for solving the Palestine

[10] Shimoni to Meyerson, 27 Aug. 1947, S25/3300, CZA.

problem at the end of August in a majority report and a minority report. The majority report proposed the partition of Palestine into a Jewish state and an Arab state with an economic union between them and an international enclave around Jerusalem. The Jewish state under this scheme was much larger than that proposed by the Peel Commission, comprising the coastal plain, north-eastern Galilee, and most of the Negev. The minority report proposed a federal state in which the Jews would remain a permanent minority but with wide autonomy. The Jewish Agency gave the majority report a qualified welcome; the Arab League angrily rejected both. Azzam Pasha, the League's secretary-general, declared that any attempt to implement UNSCOP's recommendations would meet with total resistance on the part of the Arabs, and that if necessary they were prepared to fight.

In a last-minute attempt to find a peaceful solution, David Horowitz and Abba Eban, who had ably served as the Jewish Agency's liaison officers with UNSCOP, met Azzam Pasha in London through the good offices of the Jewish journalist Jon Kimche. To prove that they were serious, the Jewish spokesmen proposed a concrete plan for co-operation and compromise between Jews and Arabs in Palestine. Azzam's reply was courteous but firm: 'The Arab world is not in a compromising mood. The proposed plan may be logical, but the fate of nations is not decided by rational reasoning. Nations never give up. You will achieve nothing with talk of compromise and peace. You may perhaps achieve something by force of arms.' To the suggestion that it might be to the advantage of both sides to work out an agreement on the basis of the UN report, Azzam replied: 'Such an agreement is possible only on our terms. The Arab world considers you invaders, and is prepared to fight you. Conflicting interests of this kind between peoples cannot usually be settled except through war . . . You speak of the Middle East. For us there is no such concept; for us there is only the concept of the Arab world. Nationalism is the great force that moves us. We do not need economic development. For us there is only one test, the test of strength.'

Horowitz detected in Azzam's fanatical firmness a trace of the biological determinism of racist ideology and thought his nationalism verged on a fascist world view. Yet Azzam accurately reflected the hysteria and fanaticism prevalent in the Arab world at that time, a mood which he and his fellow politicians had helped to inflame for their own ends. Despite the cordial personal atmosphere in which the conversation was conducted, Horowitz sensed that it would be the last attempt to bridge the gap; the illusion that a solution might be achieved through peace and accord was finally shattered.[11]

[11] David Horowitz, *In the Service of an Emergent State* (Heb.) (Tel Aviv: Schocken, 1951), 256–8. See also Abba Eban, *An Autobiography* (London: Weidenfeld and Nicolson, 1977), 86 f.

The Political Committee of the Arab League met in Sofar, Lebanon, in mid-September to consider steps to be taken in the light of the UNSCOP Report. Transjordan was represented by its prime minister who claimed that his country was opposed to any form of partition. The meeting pledged its support for an independent Arab Palestine and its communiqué warned that any attempt to create a Jewish state would unavoidably lead to the outbreak of violence in the Middle East. In early October the Council of the Arab League convened in Aley, Lebanon, to consider preparations for military action in Palestine to prevent partition. It was resolved to implement the secret decisions of the Bludan meeting for the provision of money, arms, and volunteers to the Palestinian Arab community in the event of the solution adopted being in violation of Palestine's right to become an independent Arab state. But in view of Britain's imminent withdrawal and the existence of Jewish forces and terrorist organizations, the council also called on its members to alert their military forces along the borders with Palestine.[12]

Abdullah accepted the decisions calling for military, economic, and moral support for the Palestine Arabs, but he strenuously opposed the proposal of the Arab Higher Committee for the immediate formation of a Palestinian government headed by the mufti. A small delegation led by Azzam therefore went to Amman to try to get the king to withdraw his objection, but their efforts served only to make him reiterate his convictions that a Palestinian government would fail to obtain international recognition on the one hand, would spur the Zionists to form a government on the other, and would thus render permanent the fact of partition.

The decisions taken in Aley represented a fundamental change in the Arab League's policy towards Palestine. Since its inception in 1945 and more explicitly since the Bludan meeting of June 1946, the Arab League had supported the creation of an independent Palestinian Arab state. In keeping with this policy, it had submitted a comprehensive plan to the London conference in January 1947 for ending the mandate in stages and ultimately giving complete independence to a state in Palestine whose regime would ensure an absolute majority of Arab inhabitants. Once the announcement of Britain's resolve to withdraw from Palestine transformed the idea of an independent state from a theoretical notion into a practical possibility, the Arab states began to renege on their commitment. At Aley they took a decisive step, going beyond the pledge to support the Palestinian Arabs in their fight for independence and opening the

[12] Iraq, *Report of the Parliamentary Committee of Inquiry on the Palestine Problem* (Arab.) (Baghdad: The Government Press, 1949), 66.

door to direct intervention by the regular armies of the member states themselves.

It is for this reason that the mufti was so critical of the Aley conference in his book *Facts About the Palestine Question*. At first sight his critique is surprising because the Aley decisions and the invasion to which they led were undertaken ostensibly in support of the Palestinian claim for independence in the whole of Palestine. But on closer examination it becomes clear that the role assigned to the regular Arab armies in the struggle for Palestine did indeed hinder the ability of the Palestinians to shape their own destiny. At the Aley conference, claimed the mufti,

the British took steps to change the previously agreed Arab plan which determined that the Palestinians can be relied upon in the fight for Palestine and that the Arab states would supply them with arms and money and other forms of help but that the regular Arab armies would not enter Palestine. And I, when I noticed, at that time, the desire of some of the official Arab representatives to send their armies into Palestine and invade it in this way, was seized by great fear and even expressed the apprehension and suspicion that behind this desire lies a foreign intrigue and for this reason I opposed it very firmly. The majority of the Arab states did not express their agreement to the despatch of their forces into Palestine but persistent foreign pressure on some of the Arabs in responsible positions at that time was so great that it overwhelmed all resistance. Thus it came about that the Arab armies went into Palestine.[13]

One does not need to accept either Hajj Amin's account of the sinister part played by Britain in securing the Aley decisions or his implied claim that the Palestinians could have won the war against the Jews without the intervention of the Arab states in order to conclude that those decisions involved a major reversal of past positions and a disservice to the Palestinian cause.

To implement the decisions of the Aley conference, a military committee was set up under the chairmanship of an Iraqi general, Ismail Safwat. General Safwat, assistant chief of the Iraqi General Staff, had had no duties for two years, having lost the confidence of the army as a result of the disastrous Barzan campaign for which he was responsible. He was described by one British diplomat as 'typically an old fashioned Turkish officer, extremely brave and unutterably stupid'.[14] In the first report to the Council of the Arab League, he and his colleagues on the recently created Permanent Military Committee urged the recruitment and training of volunteers for Palestine, the

[13] Muhammad Amin al-Husayni, *Facts about the Palestine Question* (Arab.) (Cairo: Dar el-Kitab al Arabi, 1956), 22 f.

[14] Busk (Baghdad) to FO, 31 Dec. 1947, FO 371/68364, PRO.

supply of no less than 10,000 rifles to the Arabs of Palestine, the concentration of the bulk of the regular Arab armies on the border with Palestine, the use of aircraft to prevent supplies from reaching the Jews by sea, and the formation of a general Arab headquarters to which all these forces would be subordinated.[15]

From the very start, however, Transjordan's attitude was one of scepticism and extreme reluctance to co-operate on the basis of the joint plans for military intervention in Palestine. Transjordan had in fact no direct representative and was represented by the Iraqi member. This arrangement was designed to make it easier for Transjordan to repudiate any unpalatable decisions taken by the committee. Draft instructions prepared by Abdullah for the Iraqi member representing Transjordan consisted of a long list of questions about the commitment of the other members. The king's main objective was to bring home to the committee the enormous practical difficulties it faced. A secondary purpose was to relegate the mufti and the Arab Higher Committee to the background and to nip in the bud the formation of armed bands under their command. The king's idea was that the General Headquarters should be in Transjordan and under his command. He also showed interest in the provision of adequate funds to meet unforeseen military developments. Fundamentally, he realized how little the Arab states could do in the military field and how unlikely it was that anything concrete would emerge from the military committee's planning.[16]

Abdullah's partition plan and appeal to Bevin

It was to London that the king turned for reassurance and support in dealing with the grave problems that lay ahead. A background of apprehension mingled with ambition prompted him to address a series of messages and letters to Ernest Bevin. In his letter of August 30, he expressed the real anxiety he was feeling as to his future position in the event of a withdrawal of British forces from Palestine, together with his renewed interest in the matter of Greater Syria. He claimed that the Russian menace in the Middle East could only be met by the establishment of a Greater Syria, and that this was becoming a matter of urgency in view of the isolation of Transjordan which Britain's departure would entail. The king's allusions to the Russian menace were primarily intended to discredit the governments of Syria and Lebanon and thus to elicit British sympathy for his Greater Syria project. Since the letter would be interpreted as an invitation to His Majesty's government to co-operate with him in overthrowing the

---

[15] Iraq, *Report on the Palestine Problem*, 132 f.
[16] Kirkbride to Garran, 22 Oct. 1947, FO 371/61885, PRO.

Syrian Republic, it was inevitable that the reply would contain a reaffirmation of British neutrality and a reminder that Abdullah's public announcements in favour of Greater Syria were a cause of considerable embarrassment to His Majesty's government.[17]

Upon his return to Amman in early October after an absence of nearly four months, Sir Alec Kirkbride found the king in an acutely unsettled frame of mind. This condition was partly attributable to advancing years and partly to his diabetes, but mainly it stemmed from the fear that the basic policy that had governed his actions in the past might have been mistaken. Although he had never said so openly, Abdullah hoped that through a political and military alliance with Britain he would reach the dominant position in the Arab world for which his father had striven but failed to achieve. Now, Britain's withdrawal from India, her readiness to evacuate Egypt, and the probability that she might leave Palestine brought home to Abdullah the realization that his schemes were not only unlikely to reach fruition but that he could be left surrounded by hostile Arab neighbours with no British forces in the vicinity to protect him from aggression. His recent outburst of activity in connection with the Greater Syria scheme was probably motivated by the desire to achieve his objective before his position was irretrievably weakened by the withdrawal of British forces from Palestine.

On the subject of Palestine, Abdullah shared the general feeling of the people of Transjordan—a mixture of disbelief and anxiety lest Transjordan be isolated and possibly absorbed by a larger Arab state. His personal anxiety on the latter score was deeper because of the dynastic rivalries involved. Both he and his ministers appeared to take active intervention of the Arab states in Palestine in the event of fighting between Arabs and Jews to be a foregone conclusion. They realized that the Arabs of Palestine, without outside help, would be defeated by the more efficient and better organized Jews.

One thing was absolutely clear, according to Kirkbride:

If a Jewish state in Palestine is formed by the United Nations' Organization or forms itself, the authorities in Transjordan will make a determined bid to ensure that the remaining Arab areas become part of Transjordan. Such an outcome would be unwelcome to Syria and Saudi Arabia but it would not be contrary to British interests and geographically and economically Transjordan has the best claim to the residue of Palestine; in fact, after the formation of a Jewish state and British evacuation, Transjordan would find it difficult to continue to exist without the Arab parts of Palestine and the outlet to the sea which they afford.

[17] Abdullah to Bevin, 30 Aug. 1947, and Pirie-Gordon to Bevin, 10 Sept. 1947, FO 371/62226, PRO.

King Abdullah indicated more than once that he expected to be consulted under the terms of the Anglo-Transjordanian Treaty of Alliance before Britain took any decisive step regarding Palestine. The reorganization of the Arab Legion was a live issue which the possible evacuation of Palestine made all the more urgent. Kirkbride concluded his comprehensive report by pointing out that the king saw all his cherished schemes coming to nought and could obtain no word of comfort from his allies. It was not unnatural, therefore, that at times his anxiety and distress amounted to something approaching frenzy. Only the prospect of consultations could save him from becoming uncontrollable.[18]

London's response, following discussion in the Cabinet, contained no comfort or reassurance whatever for the troubled ruler of Transjordan. Kirkbride was instructed to tell him that while the government recognized their obligation to consult with him about their Palestine policy, they had made it quite clear to everyone concerned that they were in any case determined to give up the mandate and to withdraw from Palestine. They could only hope that the knowledge of the imminent British withdrawal would bring the two parties together and lead to an agreed settlement without bloodshed.

Aside from this bland message, Kirkbride was told, for his confidential information, that the policymakers in London were considerably preoccupied with the question of possible participation by the Arab Legion in Palestine after their withdrawal. Their tentative idea was that it would be necessary, on ceasing to be responsible for the administration of Palestine, to secure the withdrawal of all Arab Legion units from Palestine to Transjordan and to cease paying the expenses of these units. If at a later stage King Abdullah were to try to send units back to Palestine, they would probably have to withdraw those British officers who were seconded to the service of Transjordan and also have to reconsider the subsidy. It was felt that Abdullah should be warned in advance that this would be the British attitude, and Kirkbride was invited to telegraph his observations.[19]

Kirkbride's observations on the tentative ideas he received were sharply critical. Co-operation between Britain's forces and the Arab Legion, he pointed out, were of the closest and at one time appeared to be a model of what mutual defence arrangements between a small country and a great power should be. To take steps to cripple this tactical force because there was some prospect of its taking action in a matter in which the British government would no longer be directly concerned would be a poor advertisement of their policy. Likewise, he

---

18 Kirkbride to Bevin, 10 Oct. 1947, FO 371/62206, PRO.
19 FO to Amman, 26 Oct. 1947, FO 371/62226, PRO.

felt that Transjordan should not be penalized for being an ally of Great Britain if, as seemed likely, there was to be a general scramble for the Arab areas of Palestine following Britain's abandoning of the mandate and marching out.

The British approach to the Arab Legion depended to some extent on how the Transjordan authorities planned to use that force. As far as Kirkbride could judge, if Britain left a vacuum in Palestine Abdullah might act independently of the other Arab states to forestall the mufti. Kirkbride's own view, which he had been at pains to conceal from the king and al-Rifai, was that strategically and economically Transjordan had the best claim to inherit the residue of Palestine, and that occupation of the Arab areas by Transjordan would counteract the chances of armed conflict between a Jewish state and other Arab states—in particular Iraq, which he considered to be the most dangerous. He had already reported that Abdullah was prepared to acquiesce in the formation of a Jewish state provided Transjordan obtained the rest of Palestine, and he saw no signs of such an attitude on the part of other Arab leaders. A greater Transjordan would not be against Britain's interest, so even if they were not prepared to help he saw no reason why they should place obstacles in Transjordan's way. The alternative of a non-viable Palestine Arab state under the mufti was not attractive. The anti-Hashemite Arab states would no doubt blame the British for the outcome, but as they already blamed the British for almost everything the situation would not be abnormal.[20]

Abdullah's persistent epistolary and declamatory expression of his fears and hopes, and the sympathetic way in which it was viewed by the head of Britain's mission in Amman, eventually induced the Foreign Office to see what could be done to restore their ally to his normally more balanced outlook on international affairs. James Cable thought that the problem of Palestine, as it presented itself to King Abdullah, was simple enough: 'He knows that we are about to withdraw from that country and realizes that the establishment of a Jewish State in some portion of Palestine is probably inevitable. He is therefore naturally anxious to ensure that the remaining Arab areas of Palestine are united to Transjordan and looks to us, as his ally, to help him achieve this object.' Here, in view of Article 1 of the treaty of alliance, he was on strong ground and unlikely to be satisfied with a non-committal expression of British benevolence. In particular, Abdullah expected to be allowed the free use of the Arab Legion and to reach an agreement about the conditions of British withdrawal from Palestine which would enable him to occupy the Arab areas as quickly and as easily as possible.

[20] Kirkbride to FO, 29 Oct. 1947, FO 371/62226, PRO.

Cable agreed with Kirkbride that not only did their treaty of alliance make it extremely difficult for them to oppose this project of King Abdullah's, but that it would be against their own interests to attempt such opposition. The reasons he gave for the second and highly significant conclusion were that:

King Abdullah is the only Arab leader at present willing to acquiesce in partition which must now be regarded as inevitable. His acquiescence and his appropriation of Arab Palestine would undoubtedly be resented by Syria, the Lebanon and Saudi Arabia and might well cause some deterioration in our relations with those countries. On the other hand his action would command at least the tacit approval of Iraq. It would establish in a central and strategic position a state stronger than Transjordan as it now exists, but bound to us by ties not merely of friendship and obligation but also of dependence. The alternative, as Sir A. Kirkbride points out, would be a puny Arab Palestine dominated by the unreliable Mufti, incapable of maintaining its independence, and a sure source of unrest and even war.

Cable considered it unwise to express approval of Abdullah's ambitions at that stage because it was unlikely that he could keep such encouragement secret or even refrain from presuming too much thereon. Nevertheless he suggested that they should consider whether, assuming the UN agreed upon the principle of partition but not upon the method of its enforcement, they should not come to an understanding with the king along the lines outlined above. For the time being, a personal letter from Bevin, thought Cable, even if it contained nothing new, would reassure the king that his interests had not been forgotten by his allies.[21] No letter was sent, however, until a month later because it was felt that until some decision was reached on the future of the Arab Legion and its possible intervention in Palestine it would be unrealistic and almost disingenuous to write at all.[22]

Two conflicting strands may thus be seen as vying for mastery in Britain's foreign policy in the second half of 1947. The first strand involved a definite relinquishing of the League of Nations mandate over Palestine with all the constraints and restrictions it imposed on Britain and the possibility of maintaining British presence in the area under the terms of a less restrictive trusteeship arrangement to be conferred on Britain by the League's successor. With the increasing likelihood that the UN would opt for partition, however, the second strand of British policy, with which Kirkbride was most closely identified, began to move to the fore. This involved strengthening Abdullah internationally and regionally and encouraging him to impose his rule over as large an area of Palestine as he could seize.

---

[21] Minute by J. E. Cable, 4 Nov. 1947, FO 371/62226, PRO.
[22] Minute by B. A. B. Burrows, 13 Nov. 1947, FO 371/62226, PRO.

Diplomatic and military preparations

Britain's opposition to the Greater Syria project and her ambivalence on the question of Arab Palestine, the growing likelihood that the UN General Assembly would adopt UNSCOP's partition plan, the Arab League preparations to fight partition and its support for forming a Palestinian government headed by the mufti—all underlined for Abdullah the importance of co-ordinating his entry into Palestine with the Jewish Agency. Regular contact with the official representatives of the Jewish Agency had fostered a measure of understanding and confidence that the contents of their conversations would not be disclosed to third parties and this greatly facilitated the task of co-ordination. In recent talks Abdullah's objective had been to persuade the Jewish representatives to agree to, or at least tacitly endorse, his plans for enlarging his kingdom at the expense of the mufti. As with other Arab leaders, a wide gap separated the views about the Jews that Abdullah sometimes voiced in public from his private expressions of friendship, admiration for their achievements, and concern for their welfare. Unlike the great majority of other Arab leaders, however, he did not underrate the diplomatic and military capability of the opponent and he openly expressed his doubts about the outcome of an appeal to arms. Moreover, the most immediate danger facing Abdullah was that the mufti, with the help of Syria and Lebanon, would pre-empt him in capturing some of the strategic positions in Palestine, leaving Transjordan surrounded by enemies on all sides. A related danger was that the Arab Legion would be whittled down in the course of fighting in Palestine, and the capacity of the Hashemite dynasty to protect its position in Transjordan and to assert itself abroad would seriously diminish in the process. A prior understanding with the Jews that he and they would divide Palestine between them was one method open to Abdullah for keeping both dangers at bay. Such an understanding could assure him of obtaining the Arab part of Palestine while sparing his army. Since Abdullah was in a position to offer a promise of non-aggression against the Jewish state as the incentive for Jewish complicity in his plans for the conquest of Arab Palestine, the elements of a deal were already in existence. With characteristic pragmatism, Abdullah went about exploring the possibility of striking a bargain with the Zionists to divide Palestine between them.

The Zionist leaders had their own reasons for seeking an understanding with their Hashemite neighbour. While international pressures were now working in their favour, the local balance of forces placed them at a grave disadvantage. They were aware that ever since the formation of the Arab League in 1945, Britain had been building up the military power of the Arab states and took into account the possibility that this power might one day be used to destroy the Jewish national home and thereby rid Britain once and for all of the troublesome legacy of the Balfour Declaration. The decisions of the Arab League's conference at Bludan in June 1946 seemed to confirm these suspicions. As chairman of the Jewish Agency, David Ben-Gurion repeatedly alerted his colleagues to the growing danger of an armed attack by the neighbouring Arab states and to the need to prepare for that eventuality by all the means at their disposal.

After assuming formal responsibility for defence matters, Ben-Gurion requested a proposal for reorganizing the Haganah to make it able to withstand an assault by the regular Arab armies. The proposal he received, towards the end of May 1947, assumed that the Arab States could mount an invasion of Palestine with a combined force of 50,000 ground troops and considerable air support. The Arab Legion was identified as the best of the Arab armies on account of its modern equipment and partially British command, and hence also as posing the greatest danger to the Yishuv.[23]

In the orders he handed to the Haganah's high command on 18 June 1947, Ben-Gurion stated that the only answer to an armed attack by the Arab states would be Jewish military force, and that unless the Haganah was equipped and adapted for this role it would not fulfil its basic purpose and the Zionist enterprise would be exposed to destruction. Hostile acts by the Arab armies would be much more serious than terrorist action by local gangs and must be taken seriously. 'In Egypt, Iraq, Lebanon, and Transjordan there are over 120,000 military personnel of various kinds . . . The most advanced army . . . is the army of Transjordan . . . This army has modern equipment and its training is of a superior quality.' Preparing the Haganah to stand on this critical front and to defend successfully not only settlements but, when the time comes, also the country and their national future there, concluded Ben-Gurion, was the burning task of that era.[24]

On 7 November 1947 the High Command of the Haganah ordered a thorough reorganization of all its forces on a country-wide basis. The first paragraph of the order noted that the previous structure had been conceived in 1945 primarily in response to the danger of attack from the Arabs of Palestine; the growing danger of attack by the armies of the neighbouring Arab states necessitated a different structure and a different deployment of forces. The changes now elaborated marked the transition of the Haganah from a militia army

---

[23] Memorandum by Yohanan Ratner and Zeev Sheffer, 27 May 1947, Ben-Gurion's file on Security Affairs for 1947, Archive of the History of the Haganah.

[24] David Ben-Gurion, *When Israel Fought in Battle* (Heb.) (Tel Aviv: Am Oved, 1975), 14 f.

with territorial commands to a regular army organized on a nation-wide basis.[25]

All these developments clearly demonstrate that in the course of 1947, the political and military leadership of the Yishuv came to expect a full-scale military confrontation to take place following Britain's departure from Palestine, a confrontation in which they would have to face not only the Palestinian Arabs but the combined forces of the regular Arab armies. The Zionist leaders were united in seeing Transjordan's army as the most serious threat to their security. It was not its size but its quality and its strategic location in the heartland of Palestine that made that army such a serious threat. Given their estimate of the probability of invasion and of the relative strength of the Arab armies, it is not surprising that they should have sought an understanding with the master of the Arab Legion, even if it carried a political price.

In addition to the military considerations for wanting to neutralize the Arab Legion in the forthcoming confrontation, the Zionist leaders had weighty political reasons for looking to Amman. The problem about an independent Palestinian state alongside the Jewish state as envisaged by UNSCOP was that the Palestinian state would inevitably be headed by the mufti and fellow members of the Arab Higher Committee whose profound hostility to Zionism and the Jews ruled out any chances of a compromise. Abdullah was the only realistic political alternative to the mufti and the ground was gradually laid for another high-level meeting with him.

Both sides were anxious to restore the good relations and trust temporarily shaken by Abdullah's meeting with UNSCOP. In early September Abdullah informed Sasson that he was ready to sign an agreement on the partition of Palestine involving the establishment of a Jewish state and annexation of the rest of Transjordan. Sasson was in Paris at the time and suggested that Ezra Danin be sent to start negotiations with Abdullah and to find out whether Britain stood behind him. If it turned out that Britain knew and approved of the plan, Danin was to promise Abdullah that the Jewish Agency would give him its fullest support in his fight against Arab opponents plotting to get Transjordan expelled from the Arab League.

Sasson also urged that Omar Dajani be given the necessary funds to buy an Arabic-language newspaper to popularize the idea of partition along the lines recommended by UNSCOP. It was important, thought Sasson, that the paper be published quickly, even if it lasted only two or three months and even if the cost was high, so that it could be quoted during the forthcoming session of the UN General Assembly. The

[25] File 73/100, Archive of the History of the Haganah.

money for the paper could come out of their budget for expenses in connection with the UN.[26] But before this suggestion could be implemented, Sharett ordered his subordinates to send Dajani to join him in New York.[27]

In New York Dajani started talks with American officials, with the knowledge of the British, to secure American diplomatic recognition of Transjordan, and he cabled King Abdullah to ask for diplomatic credentials. Although Dajani appeared in the United States as Transjordan's representative, his expenses were borne by the Jewish Agency and he was in close touch with the Agency's officials. Intelligence reached Sharett from a Syrian source in New York that participation of the Arab Legion in the Arab League's military plans for Palestine was considered vital and that Iraq was pressing Abdullah to take part in the invasion of Palestine and to undertake to evacuate the country after the establishment of an Arab state. Sharett therefore wanted Danin to meet Abdullah immediately and tell him that they were aware of his endeavours to gain American recognition and were anxious to support him. At the same time Danin was to warn Abdullah against any action which would destroy his chances of getting support and compel them to use all their influence against him.[28]

Both the promise and the warning were promptly conveyed in writing. Abdullah sent back a message to say that he had not yielded to the pressure exerted on him during the Arab League meeting in Amman, and that all press reports on military plans and pan-Arab agreement were a bluff since no agreement had been reached between himself and the others or between the others themselves. Other sources independently confirmed that the pan-Arab front remained divided and that no military preparations had been agreed upon. These sources also indicated that the mufti's position was weak and that the main motive for his activation of disturbances on the 1936 pattern was his fear of Abdullah. It was therefore deemed necessary to alert Abdullah to the need to give a lead to his supporters in Palestine and start preparing actively for the occupation of the Arab centres of population. The planned meeting with Abdullah would provide an opportunity to apprise him of the situation in Palestine, although its main purpose would be to prepare a written agreement.[29]Another minor purpose which the meeting was designed to serve was to inform the king of Dajani's success in negotiating American recognition of Transjordan and of the help he had received from Jewish quarters in furthering the

[26] Zvi Maimon to Yaacov Shimoni and Reuven Zaslani, 14 Sept. 1947, S25/9013, CZA.
[27] Shertok to Meyerson, 9 Sept. 1947, and Meyerson to Shertok, 18 Sept. 1947, S25/1696, CZA.
[28] Shertok to Meyerson, 14 Oct. 1947, S25/1698, CZA.
[29] Shimoni to Shertok, 18 and 20 Oct. 1947, S25/1698, CZA.

king's cause in the United States. Dajani was most anxious to be appointed minister in Washington and he evidently counted on his Jewish friends to press his claims for obtaining the necessary credentials and fend off the rival claims of Prime Minister Samir al-Rifai who was also a possible candidate for the post.[30]

As they were planning and preparing for the meeting with Abdullah, the Jewish Agency's Arabists received a most interesting report about the thinking of the top men in Amman, based on off-the-record talks which two British correspondents had there with Sir Alec Kirkbride, Glubb Pasha, and Samir al-Rifai.

Kirkbride told the correspondents that Abdullah was showing signs of old age but that his mind was still as alert as ever. He was a reasonable man which meant that he took British advice, though there were occasions when Kirkbride had to argue with him. Abdullah was clearly keen to rule Nablus and Hebron—in fact, his ambitions were boundless— though Kirkbride was careful to mention that this solution had not been discussed officially. He did however say that in his own view it was the logical solution. At the Arab League meeting in Amman, Kirkbride reported, Abdullah had told Azzam and company very bluntly that the Arabs could not fight the whole world and that they were neither equipped nor organized to fight the Jews. 'They are all watching each other like cats and dogs,' said Kirkbride, 'fearful lest one should beat the other to it.'

Glubb Pasha also thought a move by Abdullah was 'the obvious thing', but said it was a matter of timing and that Abdullah might move too quickly. He discounted any large-scale move by Arab armies as did Kirkbride, and thought that the Arabs, after working themselves up, would eventually send money, arms, and volunteers to Palestine, as they had done on previous occasions. But whereas Kirkbride did not rule out Abdullah making a move which would be timed to prevent chaos and minimize strife in Palestine, Glubb thought the situation might have to be allowed to simmer for a while, until Jew and Arab were worn out, whereupon British intervention via Abdullah would be welcomed. 'By that time the Jews might be reasonable and give up Jaffa and the Negev. Western Galilee could go to Lebanon and Syria.' From these conversations the correspondents surmised that Abdullah was toying with the idea of annexing Arab Palestine and that his chief British adviser favoured such a move.

Samir al-Rifai, the 47-year-old prime minister of Transjordan, informed the British correspondents that the Arab League was determined to oppose the establishment of a Jewish state in Palestine by all means in its power as it would be a potential threat to the rest of

[30] Ruffer to Sasson, 27 Oct. 1947, S25/1698, CZA.

the Arab states as well as to the Palestinian Arabs. He would not like to
have a Jewish state on his eastern border.

The Jews are a people to be feared . . . look what they have done in only 27
years. They began with an insignificant community of 60,000 in 1920 and now
are 700,000 in Palestine, and have mobilized their money and influence to
obtain a state from the UNO. Give them another 25 years and they will be all
over the Middle East, in our country and Syria and the Lebanon, in Iraq and
Egypt. There are 150,000 of them in Iraq and they hold the commerce of the
country in their hands. It is the same in Egypt . . . They are responsible for
starting the two world wars we have known in our generation . . . yes, I have
read and studied, and I know they were behind Hitler at the beginning of his
movement.

After this remarkable statement, the prime minister said that if the UN
voted for partition, the Arab states might nevertheless take action in
Palestine, perhaps not officially. 'We all believe in the Greater Syria
scheme,' he added, 'and eventually Arab Palestine, Syria and
Transjordan will become one country, they must.'

From these three off-the-record talks, the writer of the report
deduced that the Transjordanians had the annexation of Arab
Palestine quite definitely in mind. Their strategy seemed to be to pull
the Legion out of Palestine, allow troubles to develop, then step in to
save the Arabs and thus have a strong claim to remain in Arab
Palestine, including Jaffa and the Negev. Abdullah himself was probably thinking of moving in smartly the moment the British withdrew
because he was afraid the Syrians might beat him to it.[31]

King Abdullah and Golda Meir: the first meeting

The long-awaited meeting with the ruler of Transjordan was eventually arranged for November 17 and Golda Meir (at this time still Golda
Meyerson) was chosen to represent the Jewish side at this historic
meeting.

Golda Meir went to see King Abdullah in her capacity as acting head
of the Political Department of the Jewish Agency. She was standing in
for Moshe Sharett, who was conducting the diplomatic struggle for
partition at the UN's temporary headquarters in Lake Success. She
was accompanied by two of the Jewish Agency's Arab experts, Elias
Sasson and Ezra Danin. On the way Danin, who had met with
Abdullah on several previous occasions, briefed her on the king's
general concept of the role of the Jews: he believed that Providence had
scattered the Jews throughout the Western world in order that they

[31] Off-the-record Talks in Transjordan of Two British Correspondents, 27 Oct. 1947, S25/
9038, CZA.

might absorb European culture and bring it back to the Middle East with them, thus contributing to its renaissance. Danin also warned her that while the king was certainly sincere in his expressions of friendship, these would not necessarily be binding on him.[32]

The meeting with Abdullah took place in Naharayim, at the house of Avraham Rutenberg, who had succeeded his father as the director of the Palestine Electric Corporation. The manager of the station, Avraham Daskal, who was also a liaison officer for the intelligence services of the Haganah, had made the elaborate arrangements for this clandestine meeting in close co-operation with his friend Muhammad Zubeiti who served as the king's private secretary and confidante. Sasson and Danin acted as interpreters since Mrs Meir spoke no Arabic.

Whereas Mrs Meir was visiting Naharayim for the first time, King Abdullah was a regular visitor there, ever since he had presided at the opening ceremony of the station in 1932. Relations of good neighbourliness had developed quickly between the amir and the first managing director of the Palestine Electric Corporation, Pinhas Rutenberg, and when Rutenberg died in 1942, his son, Avraham, kept up the friendly relations with the amir. Abdullah was particularly fond of Avraham Daskal, calling him 'Abu Yussuf' ever since hearing that, with two daughters, he was hoping for a son whom he would name Joseph. Twice a year, Daskal and Rutenberg and their wives were officially invited to dinner at the palace in nearby Shuneh. Daskal could also visit Abdullah informally whenever he chose to, and his wife, Hannah, became friendly with the ladies of the palace. On appropriate occasions, such as the birth of Abdullah's grandson Husayn ibn Talal, attractive presents were given to Abdullah and other members of his family. He himself fully reciprocated this generosity, on one occasion presenting Daskal with a gold watch inscribed with his name: 'Abdullah ibn Husayn'. The Jewish friends gladly rendered any help they could to the friendly amir, such as fitting the palace with electricity and a water-pump and supplying electricity to the house of Abdullah's beautiful and devoted black concubine. From time to time Abdullah used to accept invitations to go and stay in Rutenberg's elegant white house in Naharayim. He, his personal physician, and Muhammad Zubeiti were usually given the second floor; the rest of the royal party were accommodated in a sumptuous tent. The animated conversations continued well into the night. The Daskals remember Abdullah as a lively conversationalist with a good sense of humour and still cherish the memories of a sincere and genuine friendship with him.[33]

It was Daskal and Zubeiti who arranged for Mrs Meir to meet their

[32] Golda Meir, *My Life* (London: Weidenfeld and Nicolson, 1975), 175.
[33] Interview with Avraham and Hannah Daskal.

royal friend. Zubeiti had a plot of land and a house near Shuneh, a   t
was there that he arranged lunch for Daskal, King Abdullah, an
retinue. After lunch, following a pre-arranged plan, Daskal invite
king to go back with him for the customary midday siesta. Golda
and her companions were already waiting in Daskal's home and i
there that Abdullah met her for the first time.[34]

As they were sipping the ceremonial cups of coffee at the beginni
the meeting, the king was unable to conceal his astonishment th
woman should have been selected to head such an important poli
mission. He was told that Mrs Meir held the second highest position in
Jewish diplomacy and that it was precisely because of the importance
attached by the Jewish authorities to the meeting that she was sent in
person. Recovering his poise, the king said that he appreciated the fact
that Mr Sharett's successor had come to talk to him, and in an obvious
attempt to put the interview on a friendly footing he invited Mrs Meir
to pay an official visit some day to his palace in Amman.

In the course of the ensuing conversation Abdullah invited his
visitors to join him in thinking aloud: they had discussed partition in
the past and he was interested to know what their current thinking was.
But first he reported on recent developments in Arab affairs. Azzam
had come to visit him and he was the best of the bunch, intelligent and
of good character. Ibn Saud, President Quwatli of Syria, and King
Farouk had all ganged up against Abdullah but he had held out and
consequently everybody realized that he was powerful and that his
army was a force of some value.

The Arab League's Council had visited him in Amman and dined at
his table. He explained to them that he wanted peace, not war. He
spoke without fear and said what was in his heart. They took the view
that Palestine must take precedence over all other problems. Abdullah
agreed but stressed that it did not mean that he was retreating from his
Greater Syria plan. He was preparing a speech to make plain his hope
for an eastern union which would include Greater Syria.

Turning directly to the Jewish envoys, Abdullah continued his
monologue:

Over the past thirty years you have grown and strengthened yourselves and
your achievements are many. It is impossible to ignore you, and it is a duty to
compromise with you. Between the Arabs and you there is no quarrel. The
quarrel is between the Arabs and the British who brought you here; and
between you and the British who have not kept their promises to you. Now, I
am convinced that the British are leaving, and we will be left face to face. Any
clash between us will be to our own disadvantage. In the past we talked about

---

[34] Interview with Avraham and Hannah Daskal.

partition. I agree to partition that will not shame me before the Arab world when I come out to defend it. My wish is to take this opportunity to suggest to you the idea, for future thought, of an independent Hebrew Republic in part of Palestine within a Transjordan state that would include both banks of the Jordan, with me at its head, and in which the economy, the army and the legislature will be joint.

Noticing the unease evoked by this suggestion, Abdullah stressed that the Hebrew Republic would not be dominated by Transjordan but would simply be part of the Transjordanian monarchy. He did not press for an answer but simply explained that in the event of such a republic being formed, his kingdom could be expanded to embrace Greater Syria and even Saudi Arabia.

Mrs Meir drew attention to the fact that the Palestine question was under consideration at the UN and that her side was hoping for a resolution that would establish two states, one Jewish and one Arab, and that they wished to speak to the king only about an agreement based on such a resolution. Abdullah said he understood and that it would be desirable to meet again immediately after the UN pronounced its decision in order to discuss how they might co-operate in the light of that decision. At this point Abdullah asked how the Jews would regard an attempt by him to capture the Arab part of Palestine? Mrs Meir replied that they would view such an attempt in a favourable light, especially if he did not interfere with the establishment of their state and avoided a clash between his forces and theirs and, secondly, if he could declare that his sole purpose was to maintain law and order until the UN could establish a government in that area. Now it was the king's turn to be startled and he answered sharply: 'But I want this area for myself, in order to annex it to my kingdom and do not want to create a new Arab state which would upset my plans and enable the Arabs to ride on me. I want to ride, not to be ridden!' He also brushed aside a suggestion that he might secure his objective by means of a referendum in which his influence would be decisive.

He then raised the question of implementing the UN decisions, given that the British were leaving and the Jews were demanding an international force. Would such action not look like a violation of UN decisions? Mrs Meir explained that it was not they who had demanded Britain's departure but that Britain herself had announced her refusal to help with the implementation. It was this announcement that had forced the Jews to demand an international force. They had nothing against Britain, she confided, and had the latter shown goodwill and undertaken to carry out the decisions of the UN faithfully and sincerely, there would have been no objection from the Jewish side. As it was, they did fear deliberate interference by the British. Abdullah then asked whether he could convey this to the British and whether he could have it in writing in order to convince them. The Jewish envoys did not give a direct answer to this suggestion for fear of giving rise to additional complications, but they did make it clear that they were not disregarding Britain's interests. Abdullah preferred that the proposed solution be implemented by Britain, but if there was the slightest suspicion that she would not carry out the task willingly and faithfully he thought it would be better if she left the implementation entirely to the international force.

Abdullah expressed the wish that the international force supervise the Syrian and Lebanese borders with Palestine but not the Jewish–Arab border within Palestine. He would agree that Transjordan's border with Palestine be subject to international supervision though he saw no need for it. In any case, there was no need for a large international force; it should be only a symbolic one. Syria and Lebanon, he was confident, would not dare attack such a force. As for the Jewish–Arab border in Palestine, he was prepared to take the matter into his own hands and to ensure that no clashes took place between Jews and Arabs. Should the mufti attack the Jews, his advice to them was to reciprocate with devastating blows. It would be best, mused Abdullah, if the mufti were to disappear from the face of the earth . . .

The conversation turned to the preparations undertaken by the Arab world for intervention in Palestine. Abdullah claimed that he had notified the Arab states, including Iraq, that he would not permit their armies to pass through Transjordan. He had also given notice that he would not co-operate with any plan unless the arms, ammunition, vehicles, and workshops were concentrated in Transjordan under his command and for the express purpose of preserving order and reaching an understanding with the Jews. The situation and circumstances, he added, did not warrant war, but rather compromise.

As for the mufti, Abdullah said, he had demanded his removal to a distant place and the suppression of his activities. Were the mufti to be in Transjordan, he would certainly be able to take care of him! The Jewish representatives presented information regarding an alleged plot by the mufti to provoke a clash between the Arab Legion and the Haganah by dressing up some of his men in the uniform of the Arab Legion. Abdullah promised to give the necessary orders to his army and remarked that such an incident was beyond the realm of possibility and that they should put it out of their minds.

The Jewish representatives also drew attention to the fact that many of the mufti's political opponents among the Arabs of Palestine wanted to be organized by Abdullah and to appear with him in the public arena as his followers and supporters of his views but they had been waiting in vain for an invitation from him. Abdullah knew this to be the case and had even received some letters from these opponents of the mufti. If he hesitated to invite them it was only out of fear that they might not stand up to the test and for this reason he preferred that they come without an invitation. He graciously permitted Sasson and Danin to direct these Arabs to him in droves.

When the Jewish representatives sounded out the king about the British attitude to his various plans and especially his plan regarding Palestine, all he could say was that the British had not demanded anything of him and that the situation was unclear. No talks had taken place on this subject and he had some difficulty in accounting for Britain's silence.

Ezra Danin, who wrote the report on the meeting for the Jewish Agency, noted that in contrast to previous meetings Abdullah looked confident and resolute and seemed to have the situation under control. He was equally dismissive of the talk of armed invasion by Arab states and of the mufti's intrigues. Asked if he would be prepared to sign a written agreement in the event of a common denominator being identified in political, economic, and defence matters he replied affirmatively and asked them to produce a draft. In bringing the meeting to an end he reiterated that concrete discussions could only take place after the UN had made its decision and that they must meet again as soon as the decision was known.[35]

Sasson cabled a summary of the talk with Abdullah to Sharett in New York. Because this is the only other contemporary first-hand account we have, it is worth quoting extensively. He reported that Abdullah

will not allow his forces to collide with us nor co-operate with other forces against us. Belittled military power [of] Arab states. Believed would not dare break into Palestine. In case he will decide [to] invade Palestine will concentrate [on] Arab areas with a view to prevent bloodshed, keep law and order, forestall Mufti. Prepared [to] co-operate with us [in] this matter. Stated British did not suggest him any scheme, neither anti-Jewish [nor] pro-Arab, only repeatedly emphasising earnestness [of their] decision [on] evacuation. Abdullah advise we press UN for small international force of few thousand to concentrate [on] Syrian Lebanon frontiers only. Believe position Mufti weakened. Not to be expected head of Arab provisional government with support [of] Arab world. Abdullah ready [to] sign written agreement with us provided we agree [to] assist attach Arab part to Transjordan. Replied we prepared [to] give every assistance within frame [of] UN Charter. Agreed

---

[35] The foregoing account of the meeting is based exclusively on, and follows very closely, the report of Ezra Danin, 'Talk with Abdullah, 17 Nov. 1947', S25/4004, CZA.

meet after 25th of this month after UN decision . . . In conclusion Abdullah asked us [to] raise considerably our financial aid.[36]

Sasson's cable corresponds accurately in all essentials to the more detailed account of his colleague Danin. Between them the two reports prove beyond a shadow of doubt that a firm deal was concluded between the king and Mrs Meir on the division of Palestine between them and that the king was even willing to commit himself in writing.

Abdullah had once told Kirkbride that he had frequently obtained unexpected advantages by being willing to talk to anybody who was concerned with a problem and of being as charming as possible in the process. His charm did not fail him with Mrs Meir and helped to create a friendly atmosphere at the meeting. Kirkbride thought it a mistake, however, for the Israelis to be represented by a woman since Abdullah was very old-fashioned in his outlook, did not feel that women were the equals of men, and disapproved of their playing a political role. Moreover, the lady in question had little prior experience in dealing with Arabs and certainly none in negotiating with an Arab potentate. Royal dignity would have undoubtedly been better served if the other side had been represented by a man, especially by someone like Sharett who spoke the language and was familiar with the mental process of the Arabs.[37] Nevertheless, the meeting was as satisfactory as could be expected and both sides had reason to be pleased with the result. That result amounted to much more than an exercise in thinking aloud; it laid down guidelines for action by both sides upon termination of the mandate. Abdullah secured Jewish agreement for annexing to Transjordan that part of Palestine to be allotted to the Arabs by the UN. Mrs Meir, inexperienced though she was, had returned home with what amounted to a non-aggression pact with one of the leading Arab states. The ruler of that state and the master of the Arab Legion had promised that he would never attack the Jews or join with other Arabs in frustrating the establishment of a Jewish state. What is more, he was prepared to consider a formal pact embodying the terms of collaboration between Transjordan and the Jewish Agency. True, not everything said by Abdullah in the course of their cordial interview was music to Mrs Meir's ears: his remark about a partition which would not shame him in the Arab world implied that he expected a substantial, if unspecified portion of Palestine; his suggestion of a Hebrew Republic linked to the Hashemite monarchy of Transjordan implied that he was not resigned to the emergence of a sovereign Jewish state. These points

---

[36] Sasson to Shertok, 20 Nov. 1947, S25/1699, CZA.

[37] Sir Alec Kirkbride, *From the Wings: Amman Memoirs 1947–1951* (London: Frank Cass, 1976), 4 f.

were a source of constant uncertainty and worry to the leaders of the Jewish Agency in the coming months.

On November 29, only twelve days after the friendly meeting in the white house by the bridge over the River Jordan, the UN General Assembly convened in New York to pronounce its verdict on the future of Palestine. By a vote of 33 against 13 with 10 abstentions, the assembly adopted the partition plan recommended in UNSCOP's Majority Report. The passage of the resolution was accompanied by behind-the-scenes campaigns of unprecedented intensity and impropriety. The Arab states were helped by the oil companies in their campaign against partition. The Jewish lobby in the United States, with so much at stake, mobilized all its resources in the fight for partition and the tactics it used, involving threats, ultimatums, and bribes to Latin American delegates, were as effective as they were unsubtle.

The UN partition resolution laid down a timetable for the termination of the British mandate and for the establishment of a Jewish state and an Arab state linked by economic union, and an international regime for Jerusalem. Exceptionally long, tortuous, and winding borders separated the Jewish state from the Arab one, with vulnerable crossing points to link its isolated areas in the eastern Galilee, the coastal plain, and the Negev. Incorporation of the Negev in the Jewish state was one of the principal features of the UN plan. The borders of these two oddly shaped states, resembling two fighting serpents, were a strategic nightmare (see Map 3).

No less anomalous and scarcely more viable was the demographic structure of the proposed Jewish state. According to the plan of the majority of the Special Committee, the distribution of the settled population in the proposed Jewish and Arab states and in the city of Jerusalem would be approximately as shown in the following table.

1947 United Nations Partition Proposal: Settled Population and Proposed Demographic Structure

Area	Jews	Arab and other	Total
Jewish state	498,000	407,000	905,000
Arab state	10,000	725,000	735,000
City of Jerusalem	100,000	105,000	205,000

The unsettled population consisted of bedouins who lived for the most part in the arid Negev. According to an official British estimate, 22,000 bedouins were normally resident in the areas allocated to the Arab state under the plan proposed by the majority, while the balance of 105,000 resided in the proposed Jewish state. If these figures are taken into account, then the proposed Jewish state would have had a total population of 1,008,800, consisting of 509,780 Arabs and 499,020 Jews.

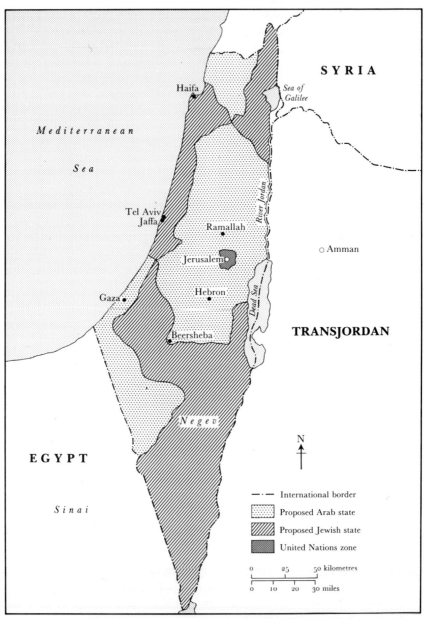

MAP 3   The United Nations partition plan, 1947

In other words, from the very beginning, the proposed Jewish state would have had an Arab majority.[38]

Yet the UN vote on November 29 was greeted by Jews everywhere with jubilation and rejoicing. While falling short of the full-blown Zionist aspiration for a state comprising the whole of Palestine and Jerusalem, it provided an invaluable charter of international legitimacy for the creation of an independent Jewish state. The UN decision alone could not guarantee the Jewish people a state of their own, but it represented a tremendous gain of international recognition and increasing momentum in its struggle for statehood.

Nevertheless, the Irgun, which had been founded in 1937 by the Revisionist Zionists, did not join in the general celebrations. It bitterly opposed the partition plan for carving up the homeland and warned that partition would lead to war. A day after the UN vote, Menachem Begin asserted the credo of the underground fighters: 'The partition of the Homeland is illegal. It will never be recognised . . . It will not bind the Jewish people. Jerusalem was and for ever will be our capital. Eretz Israel will be restored to the people of Israel. All of it. And for ever.'[39]

The UN partition resolution was roundly and bitterly denounced by Arabs everywhere. Even before the opening of the regular session of the General Assembly, the Arab League charged UNSCOP with a pro-Zionist bias and served notice that the General Assembly's approval of either the majority or the minority scheme would precipitate an Arab–Jewish war, and probably a world war. The Arab Higher Committee labelled the two plans 'absurd, impracticable and unjust'. The United Nations was warned that 'not a single Jew would be allowed to migrate to Palestine . . . the Arabs will fight to the last man to defend their country, to defend its integrity and to preserve it as an Arab country'.[40]

The passage of the partition resolution in the General Assembly was accompanied by renewed threats from the Arab League to resist its implementation by force. 'The partition line shall be nothing but a line of fire and blood', was Azzam Pasha's ominous warning.

When news of the UN resolution reached Palestine, the various Arab factions closed ranks in face of the new threat and proclaimed a three-day strike in protest, beginning on December 1. The Palestine Arabs were now determined to abort the partition scheme by demonstrating that a Jewish state would not be tolerated and could not be viable. Unlike the Jews, the Palestine Arabs 'made no serious efforts to plan ahead and work for the day when they might have to fight to save their homeland'. They did little 'to rebuild their forces, train their men in

---

[38] Khalidi, *From Haven to Conquest*, 677.
[39] Menachem Begin, *The Revolt*, rev. ed. (New York: Dell, 1977), 433.
[40] J. C. Hurewitz, *The Struggle for Palestine* (New York: Schocken Books, 1976), 299.

modern warfare, acquire sufficient modern arms, and seek more able military and political leadership. Thus, they were extremely ill-prepared militarily and politically when the struggle for Palestine reached its climax.'[41] Despite all these failures, for which they were soon to pay such a heavy price, the Palestine Arabs were convinced that they had justice and morality on their side in their fight against partition. Their case against the UN plan was eloquently summed up by the eminent Palestinian historian, Walid Khalidi:

The name of the plan was the old one of partition. But whereas in 1937 partition had been recommended by the royal commission of an imperial power it was now the ostensibly disinterested verdict of an impartial international body. This endowed the concept with the attributes of objectivity and even-handedness—in short, of a compromise solution. But a compromise by definition is an arrangement acceptable, however grudgingly, to the protagonists. The 'partition' of Palestine proposed by UNSCOP was no such thing. It was Zionist in inspiration, Zionist in principle, Zionist in substance, and Zionist in most details. The very idea of partition was abhorrent to the Arabs of Palestine and it was against it that they had fought their bitter, desperate and costly fight in the years 1937–39. Also, 'compromise' implies mutual concession. What were the Zionists conceding? You can only really concede what you possess. What possessions in Palestine were the Zionists conceding? None at all. Again, a compromise implies that you concede what in the last estimate is expendable in order to preserve the substance of your position. We all know what the 'concessions' demanded of the Arabs were in the UNSCOP plan, and what the residual Arab state in the country was to be after the concessions were made. Concessions of such a kind and scale are demonstrably alien to the very idea of compromise. It is surely utterly alien to this idea that one party should so revolutionise its position *vis-à-vis* the other, and at the latter's expense, that the relative positions between the two would be actually reversed. It surely goes against the grain of human nature to expect the party that would suffer this reversal to enter into the transaction just because some third party, itself affiliated to the potential aggrandiser, chose to befog the issue by calling this transaction a 'compromise'. One might say all this is very well except that it ignores the power factor. True enough, but if we are talking about power, then we should say so and not pretend that we are talking about compromise—except that UNSCOP and subsequently the UN General Assembly did talk about this process of dictation and blackmail as though it were indeed a genuine compromise transaction.[42]

The partition plan also marked the parting of the ways between the Palestinian Arabs and King Abdullah. During the General Assembly's deliberations Abdullah began to send troops into Palestine to demonstrate that the Arab Legion was the only force capable of

[41] Fred J. Khouri, *The Arab–Israeli Dilemma*, 2nd ed. (New York: Syracuse University Press, 1976), 40.

[42] Khalidi, *From Haven to Conquest*, pp. lxix f.

protecting the Palestine Arabs against the Jews. He also proposed to the Arab Higher Committee that in the event of a British withdrawal from Palestine, the Arab Legion, with its weapons and equipment, should undertake to look after the Arabs of Palestine and bring them under its control.[43]

On November 29, Ismail Raghib Khalidi, the youngest brother of Hussein Fakhri Khalidi, the secretary of the Arab Higher Committee, visited Amman to convey to the Hashemite monarch the committee's negative reply to his offer of protection. While the two men were talking, news of the UN partition vote was announced on the radio. Abdullah turned to Khalidi and said: 'You have rejected my offer. You deserve what will happen to you now.'[44]

Thus, by the end of 1947, not one but two partition plans had come into existence: one was born in New York on November 29, bearing the public seal of approval of the international community and calling for the creation of two independent states to replace the British mandate in Palestine; the other, secretly conceived in Naharayim, the progeny of an unholy alliance between the Zionists and the Hashemites, envisaged the creation of only one state and the annexation of the rest of Palestine to Transjordan. The second plan preceded the first chronologically by twelve days but was predicated on it. The Jewish community in Palestine was the principal beneficiary under both plans. Britain felt no particular enthusiasm for either. The Arab Higher Committee and the majority of the Arab states were irreconcilably opposed to the former plan and suspiciously hostile to the latter. Under the UN plan there was some recognition of Palestinian national rights, however inadequate in the Arab eyes, and the mufti was the obvious candidate to head the new Arab state. King Abdullah did not stand to gain anything under this plan but was the principal Arab beneficiary under the alternative plan for dividing up Palestine with the Jews. Herein lies the crucial difference between the two kinds of partition that sprang to life towards the end of 1947 in the attempt to jockey for the succession of the departing British Empire.

[43] Nevo, *Abdullah and the Arabs of Palestine*, 50.
[44] Told by Ismail Raghib Khalidi to his son Rashid Khalidi in May 1968. Interview with Rashid Khalidi.

THE COLLUSION

Arab pressures and British prevarications

The United Nations' vote in favour of partition provided not just international legitimacy for creating Jewish and Arab states but, unintentionally, the signal for a savage war between the two communities in Palestine. Arab guerrilla operations against Jewish targets in Palestine started the day after the UN vote. Popular identification with the cause of the Palestine Arabs was spreading so far and wide that no government in any Arab country could take a stand which might be interpreted as betraying that cause without endangering its own survival. As popular pressure for intervention in Palestine was building up all around him, King Abdullah became increasingly worried about the prospect of carrying out successfully his own secret plan. The uncertainty surrounding Britain's intentions only added to his anxiety.

An official statement of the British government's future policy concerning Transjordan was therefore both timely and reassuring. It enabled Sir Alec Kirkbride to check the issue of a somewhat explosive set of instructions to Transjordan's delegate to the coming meeting of the Arab League in Cairo. Abdullah had announced his intention to instruct his representative to table Transjordan's claim to the Arab areas of Palestine after the Jewish state had been formed, that is to say, to accept the UN decision regarding the partition of Palestine and then to determine unilaterally the future of the Arab areas. Prime Minister Samir al-Rifai went to see Kirkbride in despair and said that, apart from the wisdom or otherwise of showing one's hand so openly, he did not feel capable of going counter to the rest of the Arab League in such fashion, although he fully agreed with the king's ultimate aims. Kirkbride, too, while sympathizing with Abdullah's anxieties about the future of Transjordan if the Arab areas of Palestine fell into hostile hands, felt that the proposed step would be premature and harmful. At this juncture the telegram from London arrived, Kirkbride went immediately to see the king, gave him the message, and impressed upon him the importance not only of avoiding commitments but also of concealing his own intentions for the time being.

The king was delighted at the prospect of guidance from London and decided to send Samir Pasha himself with strict instructions to be entirely non-committal regarding Transjordan's plans and to urge moderation on the other members.[1] To Abdullah, an Arab state ruled by the mufti meant economic strangulation for Transjordan and could lead to its annexation to Saudi Arabia, Syria, or Iraq. Accordingly, he directed al-Rifai to oppose the giving of a free hand to the mufti in military and political affairs; to consider primarily the interests of Transjordan when voting; and under no circumstances to agree to the passage of Arab military forces through Transjordan.

Iraq's prime minister, Salah Jabr, stopped in Amman on his way to Cairo. His purpose was to pressure the king to allow the entry of an Iraqi detachment to Transjordan despite the latter's earlier protest to the regent of Iraq about the attempt to force the issue.[2] The king remained adamant: he could not permit a single Iraqi soldier to enter his country. Thus even though the regent was his nephew, Abdullah maintained a measure of reserve when it came to the question of Arab intervention in Palestine.

The Cairo meeting of the Arab League during the second week in December projected an outward appearance of strength and solidarity. It also reached important decisions but because of the conflicts of interest at play, these remained for the most part at the level of rhetoric and general principles. The basic resolution of the conference was to prevent the creation of a Jewish state and conserve Palestine as a united independent state. No general commitment to this course of action, however, still less willingness to make the necessary sacrifices, were revealed in the preceding deliberations. Most fundamental was the division about the military strategy to be adopted in fighting the Jews. The secretary-general of the Arab League and Egypt's prime minster, Mahmud Nuqrashi, were against the use of regular armies, preferring guerrilla warfare conducted by the Palestinian Arabs to wear down the Jews psychologically and economically in a long war of attrition. They still had some hope of a diplomatic solution that did not involve the setting up of a sovereign Jewish state and they were wary of making commitments of a military nature that might be regretted later.

Hajj Amin al-Husayni also wanted his own irregular forces to wage guerrilla war and resisted the idea of direct intervention by regular armies but for somewhat different reasons. What he feared most was a deal between King Abdullah and the Jews that would allow the former to occupy the Arab part of Palestine as defined by the United Nations plan. To keep the Transjordanians out, the mufti thought it necessary for his forces to crush the Jews before the departure of the British from

[1] Kirkbride to B. A. B. Burrows, 8 Dec. 1947, FO 371/62226, PRO.
[2] Kirkbride to FO, 29 Nov. 1947, FO 371/61580, PRO.

Palestine. But even if there was no deal, the mufti could not look with favour upon the intervention of the Arab Legion or any other Arab army for that matter. His aim was to set up a new Arab state over the whole of Palestine and he feared, not without reason, that if Arab armies marched into Palestine the country would be parcelled out between them.

It was exactly the same logic that lay behind the Iraqi and Transjordanian claims that the principal responsibility must be assigned to the regular Arab armies. The League Council took positive decisions to supply money, arms, and volunteers to the headquarters of Arab resistance that was being set up in Damascus under the command of Gen. Ismail Safwat. Despite some ambiguity about the details, and the virtually unanimous consensus not to allow Hajj Amin to direct policy, these decisions fitted into the context of an uprising under Palestinian leadership rather than of intervention by one or more of the Arab states. As for the future status of Palestine, the League Council chose to defer its decision until it had been finally freed from the Zionist threat.[3]

As is almost inevitable with international conferences, private conversations between the distinguished participants were much more intriguing than the Council's proceedings. Of the former we have more than an inkling, thanks to the voluminous reports compiled by Brig. I. N. Clayton, of the British Middle East Office, and Britain's unofficial ambassador to the Arab League. Clayton's experience of Arab affairs was considerable, going back to the heady days of T. E. Lawrence, but he tended to view the Middle East from a muscular perspective of British imperial interests and deeply engrained anti-Zionist convictions.

When they first met in Cairo, Samir al-Rifai told Clayton that the present situation was largely due to Arab intransigence in the past since they had refused outright measure after measure which might have enabled them to improve their position. Transjordan's opinion was that nothing could be achieved by guerrilla bands except chaos which might degenerate into internecine warfare. His view and that of the king was that some form of military action by regular troops would be required not necessarily for an attack upon the Jewish area but to maintain order in the Arab area and to resist any Jewish counter-attack which might take place as a result of regrettable attacks on Jewish settlements. He foresaw that other states would try and force the Transjordanian troops into taking offensive action and this he was determined to resist. What he envisaged was that as British troops

<hr />

[3] Iraq, *Report on the Palestine Problem*, 67; Barry Rubin, *The Arab States and the Palestine Conflict* (New York: Syracuse University Press, 1981), 178–84.

withdrew from the Arab area, the Transjordanians would move in to take their place and maintain as far as possible internal security.[4]

At a second meeting, on December 11, al-Rifai unexpectedly proposed to Clayton a detailed plan for joint action for which he invoked the authority of his sovereign. By way of introduction he observed that Transjordan's king and government were the only factors on which the British could really rely in the Arab world and he suggested that a long-term policy should be worked out to their common advantage. The plan he outlined was that as British troops marched out of Palestine, the Arab Legion would march in. This action would place the Arab Legion along the northern and southern frontier between the Jewish and Arab areas. He had no intention of permitting Iraqi forces to pass through Transjordan; these would consequently have to go to the Syrian or Lebanese frontiers. This deployment would place Transjordan's forces in virtual control of most of Palestine. They would not proclaim any formal annexation but would set up a military administration in the occupied territories.

From behind this frontier screen, irregular forces would exploit the disturbances which were bound to break out in the Jewish areas, but al-Rifai did not contemplate the incursion of regular troops into that area. After a period of one or two years they would attempt negotiations with the Jews, offering them the utmost autonomy in their own affairs and representation proportional to their size in a unified Judaeo-Transjordanian state in which questions of foreign policy and defence would be handled by the central government.

If such manœuvres were successful, he foresaw that the enlarged Transjordanian state, with the support of the Jewish economy, would become the most influential state in the Middle East and, by reason of its friendship with Great Britain, the outcome would also be to London's advantage.

Would the Jews accept his plan, having rejected similar offers in the past? Samir Pasha thought the extremist Jews in control would probably not do so, but sufficient elements within the Yishuv might well be glad to after a year of chaos. He brushed aside the suggestion that his plan might involve him in trouble with other Arab states though he said, of course, no whisper of it must reach them. To minimize bloodshed and destruction, could not the Arabs confine themselves to the Arab area and wait on events? To this Samir Pasha replied that he would have been satisfied with purely economic pressure to contain Jewish ambition had it been possible to trust the fixity of purpose of the Arab population. As it was, Transjordan could not stand back from the general Arab movement against the Jews. The

---

[4] Clayton to FO, 11 Dec. 1947, FO 371/62226, PRO.

movement was spontaneous now, even if catalysed by years of extravagant talk; no government could stand against it without being overthrown, and the king's position and even possibly his life as well as that
of his ministers might well be in danger if he tried.

Clayton's assessment, which he did not express in front of its author,
was that the whole plan was wildly optimistic from the Arab point of
view though if it led to talks of any sort with the Jews it would be a gain.
But in such talks any bargain struck was likely to be much more
favourable to the Jews than the prime minister of Transjordan was
willing to concede. In the short run the plan seemed unlikely to ease the
situation very much.[5]

Was Samir Pasha faithfully representing his monarch's thinking or
was he acting independently? Kirkbride pointed out that the monarch
had never given him reason to suppose that he contemplated the
execution of a plan such as that outlined by Samir to Clayton in Cairo.
His idea seemed to be to acquiesce in a Jewish state in order to secure
the remainder of Palestine. Samir, he added, was inclined to become
wilder in his views and statements when away from royal control.[6]

A change of prime minister had been pending for some time, but
Abdullah did not force the issue until after the Cairo meeting so as not
to enable Samir Pasha to pose as the hero who had been compelled to
resign by the king's unpatriotic policy of accommodation with the Jews.
There was also the problem of finding a successor who would ruthlessly
impose the king's kind of partition without trimming his sails to the
winds of popular opinion. Tawfiq Abul Huda fitted the bill, and when
al-Rifai resigned the choice fell on him to form a new government.
Another consideration in favour of Abul Huda was that he enjoyed the
confidence of the British. Not that al-Rifai had not been friendly and co-
operative, but Kirkbride had always found Tawfiq more discreet and
stable than Samir.[7]

Though Tawfiq himself was a Palestinian by origin he was
untouched by Palestinian national aspirations and could therefore be
instrumental in promoting the kind of solution to the Palestinian
problem favoured by the head of the British diplomatic mission in
Amman. For a number of years Sir Alec, who was well informed about

[5] Clayton to FO, 12 Dec. 1947, FO 371/62226, PRO. On 24 Feb. 1948 the Iraqi newspaper *Al
Yaqtha* published what it claimed was a 'most secret' report from Clayton about his conversation
with Rifai suggesting that Transjordan planned to implement partition as resolved by the United
Nations. Rifai allegedly assured Clayton that the Arab Legion would not attack any Jewish
settlements except for 'make believe' attacks that would be staged to remove any Arab suspicions.
Robert John and Sami Hadawi, *The Palestine Diary*, 2 vols. (Beirut: The Palestine Research Center,
1970), ii. 295 f. Reports of this kind fuelled Arab suspicions of a secret understanding between
Britain and Abdullah and between Abdullah and the Jews.
[6] Kirkbride to FO, 19 Dec. 1947, FO 371/62226, PRO.
[7] Kirkbride to FO, 25 Dec. 1947, FO 371/62226, PRO.

Arab opinion in Palestine, particularly in Galilee where he had served as district commissioner, had been pressing the view that if the Arabs were given a lead in favour of accepting inclusion in Transjordan, a large part of them could readily be persuaded to accept this. In Galilee the mufti was not at all popular, while Jerusalem, the stronghold of his family, was in any case excluded from the Arab zone. Kirkbride was therefore confident that with a strong British lead, a majority of the Palestine Arabs would opt for inclusion in Transjordan.[8] He was no less confident that the annexation of the Arab part of Palestine to Transjordan represented the best possible means to preserve British interests in the region and to prevent the spread of Soviet influence. This view, however, was strongly disputed by Brigadier Clayton, Sir Ronald Campbell, and other British officials, who argued that Egypt was the mainstay of British power in the Middle East and that Britain's influence with the Arab League would be undermined if she backed too blatantly the unpopular Hashemite ruler.

Kirkbride had his own contacts on the Jewish side and he used them to engage in some discreet lobbying on behalf of his candidate. On December 19 he asked his friend of long standing, Avraham Rutenberg, the director of the Palestine Electric Corporation in Naharayim, for his estimate of the Jewish Agency's reaction to Abdullah's plans and was told that the Jews preferred Abdullah as a future neighbour to any other Arab ruler. In that case, suggested Kirkbride, the Agency might influence the United Nations to give Abdullah control over the Arab part of Palestine. Rutenberg conveyed this suggestion to Ben-Gurion but the latter declined to commit himself without further assurances about the intentions of their prospective neighbour.[9]

Towards the end of 1947 Kirkbride stepped up the pressure for some form of British endorsement of Abdullah's plan for the partition of Palestine. The Transjordanian authorities, he argued, realized the delicacy of the British position regarding the occupation by Transjordan of the whole or part of the Arab areas of Palestine and they would not expect the British government to go to the point of encouraging them to take action on those lines. A hint that such a solution would not be unacceptable to them would be as far as they could be expected to go in that connection. What was more important was that no steps should be taken to reduce the efficacy of the means at the disposal of the Transjordanian government to control the Arab areas it occupied.[10]

Persistent pressure from Amman forced the officials at the Foreign

---

[8] Note for the secretary of state for the colonies, 30 Jan. 1947, box 60, file 5, Creech Jones Papers.

[9] Yoav Gelber, 'The Negotiations Between the Jewish Agency and Transjordan, 1946–1948', *Studies in Zionism* 6/1 (1985), 53–83.

[10] Kirkbride to FO, 5 Jan. 1948, FO 371/68367, PRO.

Office to assess the options open to Britain in connection with the surrender of the mandate and to choose that which would cause least harm to her position in the Middle East. Harold Beeley, Bevin's principal adviser on Middle East Affairs, was entrusted with this intellectually challenging task and, as one would expect from this highly intelligent former history don, the analysis he produced was both systematic and penetrating. Beeley's starting point was that the Arabs of Palestine would seek to prevent the implementation of the General Assembly's decision and that they would be assisted in some way by the governments of the Arab states. Broadly speaking there were three possible forms which such resistance might take: (*a*) the Arab states, or some of them, might send their regular forces into Palestine; (*b*) King Abdullah might on his own initiative send the Arab Legion into Palestine; (*c*) the Palestine Arabs, with or without the approval of the Arab League, might form a provisional government, refuse to co-operate with the UN Commission, and conduct guerrilla warfare against the Jews. Britain's interests in the Middle East generally worked against preventing the Arabs from trying to obtain a settlement more favourable to themselves than that proposed by the United Nations. It was to be feared, however, that open intervention by the Arab states collectively, or by Transjordan alone if her forces did not respect the UN frontier, would be more likely to place the British in an embarrassing position than action by the Palestinian Arabs themselves without the open backing of the states. This consideration suggested that the third method would be the most satisfactory from the British point of view. On the other hand, concluded Beeley, if King Abdullah were able to annex a large part of Palestine, to overcome the Arab opposition in Palestine, and to avoid a clash with any of the neighbouring Arab states, this solution would offer the advantage that the rights enjoyed by Britain under the treaty of 1946 would automatically extend to King Abdullah's newly acquired territories.[11]

To find out the probable attitude of the Arab states to an invasion of Palestine by the forces of King Abdullah, Beeley requested assessments from all British posts in the Middle East. The replies were summarized in another interesting and comprehensive survey. The Iraqi government wished Transjordan's forces to occupy the whole of Palestine including the Jewish areas. The Syrian government would 'intensely dislike' the occupation of any part of Palestine by a purely Transjordanian force, even if it was under the command of the Arab League. These sentiments were responsible for the Syrian government's support to the irregular forces which were being formed by

[11] H. Beeley, 'Possible Forms of Arab Resistance to the Decision of the United Nations', 22 Dec. 1947, FO 371/68864, PRO.

Fawzi al-Qawukji on their territory and which could provide an alternative to King Abdullah's troops as the nucleus for Arab resistance in Palestine. The Lebanese prime minister thought that if King Abdullah was considering occupying only the Arab areas, he might well end up losing Transjordan itself. Neither the population of Transjordan nor the Arab League would, in his opinion, stand for such a policy. If, on the other hand, the king could occupy the whole of Palestine, the prime minister and the other Arabs could only applaud him. Sir Ronald Campbell thought that as the Arabs would in any case control the areas allotted to them by the United Nations, Egypt would regard the occupation of those areas by King Abdullah as no more than an attempt to further Hashemite aggrandizement. On the other hand, a total occupation of Palestine by Transjordanian forces would be applauded as a quick solution. Ibn Saud would regard as 'treacherous and unjustifiable' any attempt by King Abdullah to seize any part of Palestine except under the authority of the Arab League. Finally, there was a report from Jerusalem indicating that the mufti's party would not quarrel with King Abdullah if his occupation covered the whole country and did not stop short at the frontier drawn up by the United Nations.

The general conclusion which emerged from this country-by-country survey was that King Abdullah could count on a large measure of support in the Arab world if his action involved defiance of the UN and invasion of the territory assigned by them to the Jewish state. But if he confined himself to occupying what the Arabs had already been given, his actions would be interpreted as personal aggrandizement and would isolate him from his neighbours and from Arab opinion generally.[12]

This remarkable consensus of opinion completely overlooked the very pertinent possibility that by defying the UN partition resolution, the Arabs might end up with a smaller, not a larger, portion of Palestine than that allotted to them under the terms of that resolution. It did not occur to the Arabs, or to the British officials who reported their probable attitude, that a less favourable form of partition than that offered by the UN might result from an appeal to arms. The implicit assumption was that the Arab part was secure and the only question was whether the Jewish part could be occupied in addition. But an attack on the Jewish part could place the Arab part in jeopardy if the Jews mounted a successful counter-attack. There was certainly no reason to assume that the Jews would go out of their way to afford the Arabs the luxury of a war of limited liability.

Rumours reached London that King Abdullah himself might want

[12] Minute by H. Beeley, 6 Jan. 1948, FO 371/68864, PRO.

to go beyond the limited objective he had confided to Kirkbride. Omar Dajani, the king's personal envoy, informed a British official that Abdullah was prepared to accept half of Palestine from the Jews with the intention of securing it all in something like a federal state as soon as a suitable opportunity presented itself. This was apparently a reference to the suggestion of a Hebrew Republic which Abdullah had made at his meeting with Golda Meir but had not pursued when he met with resistance. Dajani could have known about that meeting either directly from Abdullah or from Israeli representatives with whom he was in close contact in New York. In any case, went on Dajani, if Abdullah had the backing of the Arab states he 'would be willing to march his troops into the whole of Palestine, and "contain" the Jews in the coastal strip without further fighting, until the Jews were willing to come to terms'. According to Dajani, Abdullah would be willing to risk his forces on three conditions: (*a*) that he were given a public welcome as a liberator of Palestine; (*b*) that the British guarantee help for him in the Security Council even to the extent of using the veto, and (*c*) that other Arab states support him. Britain's reply was that the primary necessity was to maintain Arab unity and that no guarantees could be given regarding the Security Council because much would depend on the circumstances under which the case arose.

Dajani went on to say that Abdullah believed that the Jews must have their territory even in a unified Palestine and that it might be necessary to permit some further immigration but he would have nothing to do with the mufti's sovereignty in all or part of Palestine, whether that sovereignty was open or camouflaged. Abdullah wanted a revision of the Anglo-Transjordanian treaty because it would not be possible for him to be recognized as the liberator of Palestine so long as he was seen by the Arab public as subservient to Britain. He would not mind if there was a secret agreement guaranteeing Britain all she required in Transjordan as long as there was an overt revision of the treaty which would put him on a par with the other Arab states.[13]

Since Britain hoped to see Abdullah succeed to the Arab part of Palestine, there was considerable force in Dajani's last argument. In the Foreign Office it was readily conceded that a revised Anglo-Transjordanian treaty, on the lines of the new Anglo-Iraqi treaty, would help to boost Abdullah's position in Palestine.[14] After all, Bevin's grand design in the aftermath of the UN partition vote called for a system of defensive alliances to be concluded individually with

---

[13] Memorandum from TRL (Mr Little of the Arab News Agency), 7 Jan. 1948, FO 371/68864, PRO.

[14] Minute by M. Walker, 15 Jan. 1948, FO 371/68864, PRO.

each of the important Arab states. Under the new treaties, Egypt, Iraq, and Transjordan would be recognized as entirely independent and sovereign nations. Britain's avoidance of a pro-Zionist line at the United Nations was expected to make the Arab states turn to Britain for leadership. And the new alliances were expected to make Palestine expendable.[15] The Jews had always laughed at him, Bevin told his advisers, when he had told them that they might clear out of Palestine, and had maintained that the British never could do so since Palestine was strategically essential to them.[16] Bevin clearly intended to have the last laugh by first withdrawing from Palestine and then preserving Britain's strategic interests there through the extension of Abdullah's kingdom to include parts of the country.

In this new context, 'Mr Bevin's little king', as some of the Foreign Office officials called Abdullah, assumed the kind of importance in Britain's imperial plans that had always been denied him in the past. On 10 January 1948, the long-awaited message from Bevin was conveyed to Abdullah by the British ministers in Amman. Bevin's message covered three preliminary points at some length. First, he stated Britain's determination to remain in the Middle East and to strengthen her relations with the Arab states. Secondly, he suggested that Abdullah need not feel isolated following Britain's withdrawal from Palestine since some units would be stationed in Transjordan and Britain would seek to conclude defensive arrangements with all the Arab states. Thirdly, he assured Abdullah that Britain would continue to assist with the equipment and organization of the Arab Legion. On the subject of Palestine the text of Bevin's message was as follows:

We realise also that Your Majesty's objective in regard to Palestine is to assist in the establishment there, at the earliest possible moment, of a stable and democratic settlement, which would enable the people of Palestine to live in good relations with their neighbours, with the United Kingdom and with other peace loving countries. This entirely accords with our own hopes for the future of Palestine, but we feel sure that Your Majesty will not have underestimated the difficulties of the task or the risks which would ensue if Transjordan were to take steps which isolated her from other Arab states or which caused the Security Council to consider action against her. Greatly as His Majesty's Government in the United Kingdom sympathise with Your Majesty's desire to contribute to a speedy and peaceful settlement in Palestine, they might be in a position of considerable difficulty if either of these risks materialized.[17]

[15] Wm. Roger Louis, *The British Empire in the Middle East, 1945–1951: Arab Nationalism, The United States, and Postwar Imperialism* (Oxford: Clarendon Press, 1984), 106, 200.

[16] Egypt and Sudan, 10 Jan. 1948, FO 371/69192, PRO.

[17] FO to Amman, 11 Jan. 1948, FO 371/62226, PRO.

Every word in this message was carefully weighed and the consequent ambiguity was artfully contrived. The makers of British foreign
policy realized, as they informed Kirkbride, that what Abdullah really
wanted to know was whether they thought he should intervene in
Palestine contrary to the decisions of the Arab League and whether
they would protect him at the United Nations by using the veto if the
matter came before the Security Council. 'We do not feel that we can
give him any encouragement to act alone and the rather vague
generalizations at the end of the message are, I am afraid, the best we
can do.'

The Foreign Office's three hopes were: (*a*) to see the trouble in
Palestine localized and over as soon as possible; (*b*) that no situation
would arise that might call for Security Council action (where it was
unlikely that Britain would use her veto to protect an Arab aggressor),
and (*c*) 'that King Abdullah will take no action that might isolate him
from the other Arab states and thus give rise to the accusation that we
are using him to engineer our re-entry into Palestine and to the
possibility that he might unite the rest of the Arab world against him'.

So far as the makers of British foreign policy could see at the time, the
first and second requirements could be satisfied if King Abdullah
occupied certain Arab areas of Palestine and refrained from sending the
Arab Legion into the areas allotted to the Jewish state. This could not
however satisfy the third requirement, and they were unable to think of
any course of action which would satisfy all three requirements.[18]

Kirkbride delivered the message verbally on January 17 and, in view
of the king's habit of twisting verbal communications to suit himself,
also left an unsigned copy of the English text. Abdullah was pleased by
the verbal message and concentrated on the fact that he had not been
forbidden to move into the Arab areas of Palestine but the next day,
after he had gone through the text with a translation, he was depressed
and told the prime minister that the message was too non-committal, as
indeed it was. Kirkbride pointed out to Abul Huda that in view of the
king's notorious inability to keep a secret, he could not expect the
message to be anything else.[19]

Abul Huda and Bevin: the collusion

Britain was now skating on very thin ice. Fearing Abdullah's notorious
indiscretion and anxious to avoid the appearance of collusion in the
very partition scheme it had refused to support at the United Nations or
to help impose, the British government shrouded the degree to which

---

[18] FO to Amman, 10 Jan. 1948, FO 371/62226, PRO.
[19] Kirkbride to FO, 20 Jan. 1948, FO 371/68817, PRO.

its interests now marched with Abdullah's.[20] Neither Abdullah's interests nor its own would be served if he took action that was so blatantly contrary to the wishes of the other Arab states that they banded against him. This could have dangerous consequences for Abdullah's position and since he would be represented as Britain's tool, Britain would get a large share of the disapproval of the other Arab states.[21] One way out of the dilemma was to maintain the official posture of opposition to partition while secretly encouraging Abdullah to implement it. This kind of duplicity was not entirely alien to the spirit of British diplomacy but there was always the risk of exposure.

In the interests of secrecy, even some of the British officials most directly concerned were kept in the dark about the collusion with Abdullah. Sir Alan Cunningham, the British high commissioner for Palestine, had been given to understand that Kirkbride was instructed to warn Abdullah off on the grounds that any incursion by him into Palestine would embroil the British with the other Arab states. Cunningham was therefore surprised to discover that the Foreign Office now saw some advantage in intervention by Abdullah. Not surprisingly, Cunningham thought it most important that he be informed of his government's real intentions.[22]

The intentions of the British and Transjordanian governments emerged most clearly in the course of the visit of Tawfiq Abul Huda to London at the end of January. Tawfiq Pasha was invited ostensibly to renegotiate some of the technical clauses of the 1946 Anglo-Transjordanian treaty, but the real aim was to discuss the situation in Palestine. Before his arrival he requested that he personally should not be accommodated at the Hyde Park Hotel which he found too quiet, and his request was complied with. He was accompanied on this trip by Fawzi el-Mulki (the foreign minister), Glubb Pasha, and Christopher Pirie-Gordon, first secretary at the British Legation in Amman. Kirkbride thought it would be unwise to absent himself from the country at a time when the prime minister and the officer commanding the Arab Legion were also away. Someone had to stay in Amman to keep the king from ill-considered action, and Kirkbride thought he could do it more easily and with less friction than anyone else. He did however hope that it would be possible for the prime minister to have an interview with Bevin as both the prime minister and Abdullah attached great importance to personal contact.[23]

[20] Mary Christina Wilson, 'King Abdullah of Jordan: A Political Biography', D.Phil thesis (Oxford, 1984), 322.

[21] FO to Amman, 15 Jan. 1948, FO 371/68817, PRO.

[22] High commissioner for Palestine to secretary of state, 27 Jan. 1948, box iii, file 1, Cunningham Papers.

[23] Kirkbride to FO, 15 and 19 Jan. 1948, FO 371/68817, PRO.

When the treaty revisions were accomplished, Tawfiq Pasha himself asked Pirie-Gordon privately to request a further meeting with Bevin to explain to him his views on the situation in Palestine. As he spoke no English, Tawfiq Pasha wanted Glubb to be present as interpreter but did not wish his own foreign minister to know about the meeting. In making this curious request, Tawfiq Pasha explained that he wished to put to the secretary of state views on possible developments in Palestine which might not be altogether acceptable to Fawzi Pasha, who represented the younger and more nationalist current of opinion in their country, and he also naturally did not wish the foreign minister to know that the subject of Palestine had been discussed in his absence. Tawfiq Pasha said that he quite understood that any action Transjordan might take in Palestine was a matter of some delicacy for the British in view of their special relationship, and that while he considered it was only fair that Mr Bevin should be informed of his own views and intentions, he did not for his part expect Mr Bevin to give him any definite answer or comment unless he wished to do so. Pirie-Gordon strongly suspected that the request was made in response to direct orders from the king, contemplating some course of action in which an eventual understanding with the Jews was envisaged. Abdullah was believed always to have had such a policy at the back of his mind, and the previous prime minister, Samir al-Rifai, had also told Pirie-Gordon on several occasions in private that such a rapprochement with the Jews in the interests of Transjordan was the king's ultimate aim. The fact that it was so necessary to exclude the foreign minister from all knowledge of the meeting suggested that Tawfiq Pasha's proposals might be no less heretical than his predecessor's.[24]

Bevin was briefed with remarkable thoroughness for the conversation with the visiting prime minister. In view of the need for secrecy, the high stakes involved, and the fear of leaving traces of the collusion, Bevin's officials were determined to leave nothing to chance. In an early brief it was pointed out to Bevin that his recent personal message to Abdullah, which alluded to the risks of intervention in Palestine, had left the king in a dilemma. If he wished to annex territory forming part of Palestine, he had two courses of action open to him: (*a*) to occupy the areas which had been awarded to the Arabs by the United Nations; (*b*) to disregard the frontier drawn by the United Nations and to occupy, if not the whole country, at least those areas that were predominantly Arab in population. If he were to adopt plan (*a*), he would in effect be helping the United Nations to implement their plan, against which the whole Arab world had protested. If, on the other hand, he were to adopt plan (*b*), he would run the same risk of sanctions against him as any

[24] Minute by C. Pirie-Gordon, 28 Jan. 1948, FO 371/68366, PRO.

other Arab government which intervened openly in defiance of the United Nations.

Highly revealing of the emergent consensus within the Foreign Office was the passage which stated that 'it would perhaps be possible for King Abdullah to avoid both dangers, if he agreed to the participation of the Arab Legion in the Arab resistance in Palestine, on the understanding that it would not itself transgress the frontiers drawn by the United Nations, but would collaborate with the other Arab forces operating in the Jewish areas'.

Since it was impossible to suggest this course of action to the Transjordanian government, it was recommended that Bevin should speak on the lines of his personal message to Abdullah, emphasizing the embarrassment which would be caused to the British if their ally, Transjordan, was to fall foul of the United Nations or to become isolated from the other Arab states, with all of which Britain desired to have close and friendly relations.[25]

The secret meeting was arranged for 11.30 a.m. on Saturday 7 February. Not being in the same hotel as the rest of the Transjordanian delegation helped the prime minister to escape detection. No doubt this was a more important reason for his reluctance to be accommodated in the Hyde Park Hotel than the hotel's allegedly excessive quietness. On the Friday, Bevin was given a detailed brief by Michael Wright:

It seems likely that the Prime Minister may wish to put forward the idea of an action by Transjordan in Palestine which would lead to eventual agreement with the Jews. This might take the form of occupation by the Arab Legion after May 15th of some or all of the areas allotted to the Arabs by the United Nations, but without the occupation of any of the areas allotted to the Jews. Then after a suitable lapse of time, King Abdullah would come to a *de facto* agreement with the Jews that they would not encroach on each other's territory in return perhaps for a share of Jewish customs revenue.

Action along these lines, stated the brief, would not upset the United Nations, but unless handled very carefully indeed, would create very serious trouble with the other Arab states and thus possibly endanger King Abdullah's position. It was considered essential, therefore, that Bevin should take the opportunity to give a confidential warning that if Transjordan became involved in hostilities against the Jewish state or acted blatantly contrary to the United Nations, Britain would come under strong pressure to suspend her subsidy and to consider the position of the British officers seconded to the Arab Legion.[26]

Bevin received Abul Huda and Glubb on February 7 in his splendid

[25] Palestine, 23 Jan. 1948, FO 371/68818, PRO.
[26] Michael Wright, 'Brief for Conversation with Transjordan Prime Minister on Palestine', 6 Feb. 1948, FO 371/68367, PRO.

room in the Foreign Office where many borders had been drawn and redrawn in the imperial past with little or no reference to the wishes of the local inhabitants. On this occasion, with the future of Palestine under consideration, it was the prime minister of a neighbouring country who would be discussing likely developments following the termination of the British mandate. Glubb, who translated the statement of the prime minister sentence by sentence, later disclosed the content of this highly confidential interview in his book, *A Soldier with the Arabs*. Until recently this was the only first-hand account of the collusion and it has been quoted and misquoted by all historians of the period.

According to Glubb's account, Tawfiq Pasha began by observing that while the Jews had prepared a government, a police force, and an army to assume power upon termination of the mandate, the Palestinian Arabs had made no preparations to govern themselves, nor did they have the means of creating an army. If the situation was left as it was, Tawfiq Pasha forecast that one of two things would happen. One possibility was that the Jews would ignore the UN partition plan and seize the whole of Palestine up to the River Jordan. The other possibility was that the mufti would return and try to make himself ruler of Arab Palestine. Neither of these alternatives would suit either Transjordan or Britain, said Tawfiq Pasha, emphasizing that the mufti, who had spent the war with Hitler in Berlin, was the irreconcilable enemy of both countries.

During recent weeks, King Abdullah and his government had received, and were continuing to receive, many petitions from Palestine Arab notables begging for the protection of the Arab Legion after the withdrawal of the British forces. The Transjordanian government accordingly proposed to send the Arab Legion across the Jordan when the mandate ended and to occupy that part of Palestine awarded to the Arabs which was contiguous with the frontier of Transjordan. When Glubb finished translating thus far, Bevin interrupted by saying: 'It seems the obvious thing to do.' Glubb reminded Tawfiq Pasha, speaking in Arabic, that the Arab Legion could not occupy the Gaza area or Upper Galilee, which had also been allotted to the Arabs. Tawfiq Pasha made the appropriate qualification and Glubb translated it into English. 'It seems the obvious thing to do,' repeated Bevin, 'but do not go and invade the areas allotted to the Jews.' 'We would not have the forces to do so, even if we so desired,' replied the prime minister. To conclude the interview he pointed out that the treaty between their two countries called on the contracting parties to consult one another whenever a critical situation threatened to arise, and it was this provision that had prompted his call. Bevin thanked

Tawfiq Pasha for his frank exposition of the position of Transjordan and expressed his agreement with the plans put forward. The two visitors rose, shook hands cordially, and took their leave.[27]

It is interesting to compare Glubb's account with the official British record of the meeting which was released thirty years later. The latter was drafted by Bernard Burrows and sent by Bevin to Kirkbride with copies to the king and the Cabinet. It shows that Glubb was mistaken in suggesting that the meeting took place in the spring of 1948 but generally accurate on the content of the conversation. Being more detailed, it also helps to supplement and amplify Glubb's account on three points in particular.

First, Abul Huda conceded that the Arab Legion would have to leave Palestine before May 15 as part of the evacuation of the British forces but claimed that after that date, when the Legion would be controlled solely by Transjordan and would not be in any way under British command, it would be to the public benefit if it returned to the Arab areas of Palestine to maintain law and order.

A second point made by Abul Huda was that the presence of the Arab Legion in Palestine would not prevent the execution of any UN decision which might ultimately be taken, but would enable such a decision to be more easily enforced. If, as he hoped, some solution was ultimately adopted involving modification of the partition plan in favour of the Arabs, the Arab Legion would be able to help enforce such a solution. On the other hand, if the United Nations tried to enforce its original partition resolution, the presence of the Arab Legion would limit the ensuing chaos and not increase it. Abul Huda thought that it was possible that the Jews had opened their mouths too wide and that the United Nations would come to a similar conclusion, but even if this were so, the Arab Legion could not wait for the prior permission of the United Nations to enter the Arab areas of Palestine.

Thirdly, what Glubb represents as an explicit warning appears in the official record as a question: 'I asked his Excellency whether, when he spoke of the Arab Legion entering Palestine, he referred to the Arab areas as laid down in the United Nations' decision or whether he thought it would also enter the Jewish areas. Tawfiq Pasha replied that the Arab Legion would not enter Jewish areas unless the Jews invaded Arab areas. He saw that the entry of the Arab Legion into Jewish areas would create such strenuous United Nations opposition as to cause great difficulty for Transjordan.'

When Glubb's account is taken in conjunction with the briefs prepared for Bevin, it appears highly probable that the latter in fact used the opportunity to warn Abul Huda against attempting to seize

[27] Sir John Bagot Glubb, *A Soldier with the Arabs* (London: Hodder and Stoughton, 1957), 63–6.

any of the Jewish areas. On the other hand Abul Huda's acceptance of the United Nations partition lines was probably not as final and categorical as Glubb makes it out to be. Like his sovereign, Abul Huda, as the official record shows, hoped that the Jews would end up with less territory than they were due to receive under the UN plan. Even better than his sovereign, Abul Huda realized that an informal and non-committal understanding with Britain was the most that could be expected. When Bevin said he would study the statement made to him, Abul Huda repeated that he did not want a reply. If as a result of further study the British wanted to pursue the discussion he would be glad to do so, but otherwise he would not expect them to refer to the matter again.[28]

Abul Huda was reassured by Bevin's response to his presentation of the secret Transjordanian plan of action. He returned home with a definite sense that his mission had been accomplished. Bevin, too, had every reason to be pleased with the way the meeting went. Before the meeting he had been advised by Kirkbride that the Transjordanians were honest in their plan to restrict their occupation in Palestine to the Arab zone and to avoid a clash between the Arab Legion and the Jewish forces. Now he had that intention confirmed by the Transjordan prime minister himself.[29]

Bevin's meeting with Abul Huda was a major turning-point in Britain's policy towards the Middle East. Up to this point Britain had declined to enforce the UN partition plan but had failed to develop a clear strategy for defending her position in the area following the end of the mandate. There was a pro-Hashemite school which advocated an enlarged Transjordan as the principal bulwark of British power and influence in the Middle East. But there was also opposition to this line of argument inside the Foreign Office, on the grounds that siding with Abdullah against the rest of the Arab countries could lead to the destruction of the Arab League.[30] Abul Huda helped to persuade Bevin that the Transjordanians could be relied upon to act discreetly and moderately and that the proposed course of action would be to Britain's advantage. The keystone of British policy swung into place. From this

[28] Bevin to Kirkbride, 9 Feb. 1948, FO 371/68836, PRO.

[29] Kirkbride, *From the Wings*, 12. Haza al-Majali, a future Jordanian premier, defends Abdullah against the Arab charge that he acted on the basis of the UN partition plan. Majali maintains that Abdullah's support for the plan was simply tactical. According to Majali, Abul Huda's commitment to stay within the territories allotted to the Arabs in the partition plan was undertaken without Abdullah's knowledge or consent and the latter found out about it only on 16 May 1948. Haza al-Majali, *My Memoirs* (Arab.) (Beirut: Dar al Ilm lil-Malayin, 1960), 64. Majali's explanation is totally unconvincing and inconsistent with all the evidence that is now available about the Bevin–Huda meeting.

[30] Bevin to high commissioner for Palestine, 13 Nov. 1947, box ii, file 3, Cunningham Papers; minute by H. Beeley, 22 Dec. 1947, FO 371/68864, PRO.

point on Britain worked in close co-operation with Abdullah to secure the expansion of his kingdom over most of Arab Palestine.

In effect, Britain now became a party to an attempt to frustrate the UN partition plan and divide up Palestine instead between Abdullah and the Jews. This was the solution urged by the Jews on Abdullah and the basis of his agreement with Golda Meir at Naharayim. It was not the first time that Britain had heard about Abdullah's contacts with the Jewish Agency, but it was the first time that the Transjordanian government had asked for British advice on this matter.[31] Significantly, the only word of warning appended by Bevin to his acceptance of the Transjordanian plan was to refrain from invading the areas allotted to the Jews. Thus Bevin, who is portrayed by Zionist historians as irreconcilably opposed to the establishment of a Jewish state, appears, by February 1948, to be resigned to the inevitable emergence of a Jewish state but intent on frustrating the emergence of a Palestinian Arab state. It is hardly an exaggeration to say that he colluded directly with the Transjordanians and indirectly with the Jews to abort the birth of a Palestinian Arab state.

Immediately after his meeting with Abul Huda, Bevin spoke to his officials about ways of limiting the damage to Britain's relations with the rest of the Arab world which would be caused by the entry of Transjordan's forces into the Arab areas of Palestine. In particular, he wondered whether anything could be done to promote better relations between Saudi Arabia and Transjordan. Apart from this, he also directed that an urgent investigation be made into the possibility of general economic development in Transjordan, mentioning specifically the port of Aqaba. Whereas Bevin thought in terms of economic palliatives to counteract political tensions, his officials thought in traditional geopolitical terms of ways of countering the effects of the withdrawal from Palestine on the position of the British Empire in the Middle East.

'It is tempting to think', wrote Bernard Burrows, head of the Eastern Department

that Transjordan might transgress the boundaries of the United Nations Jewish State to the extent of establishing a corridor across the Southern Negeb joining the existing Transjordan territory to the Mediterranean at Gaza. This would have immense strategic advantages for us, both in cutting the Jewish state, and therefore Communist influence, off from the Red Sea and by extending up to the Mediterranean the area in which our military and political influence is predominant and by providing a means of sending necessary military equipment etc. into Transjordan other than by the circuitous route

---

[31] Ilan Pappé, 'British Foreign Policy Towards the Middle East 1948–1951: Britain and the Arab–Israeli Conflict', D.Phil thesis (Oxford, 1984), 22–3.

through Aqaba. It would of course be infinitely more difficult to obtain Jewish agreement for a move of this kind than for the occupation of United Nations Arab areas by the Arab Legion, which the Jews would probably welcome.

Burrows found it difficult to see how Ibn Saud could be compensated for the prospective extension of Abdullah's territory in Palestine: 'In the last resort, it might perhaps not be too far fetched to consider some kind of Saudi–Transjordanian condominium over a corridor leading from Aqaba to Gaza.'[32]

If with Saudi Arabia the problem was one of reconciling her to a move by Transjordan into Palestine, with Iraq Britain faced the opposite problem of curbing excessive zeal. Muzahem Pachachi, the Iraqi minister for foreign affairs, suggested to the British ambassador, Sir Henry Mack, that Transjordanian forces, supported by those of Iraq, should enter Palestine forthwith and establish themselves not only in Arab Palestine but in those parts of Palestine assigned to the Jewish state, since otherwise the situation would deteriorate and the whole Middle East would become involved in conflict. The Americans and the Zionists, claimed Pachachi, would acquiesce in a *fait accompli*, and as a result the peace of the Middle East would be served and the position of Britain's friend, King Abdullah, would be strengthened.[33] The Foreign Office attitude to this proposal was reserved because it was felt that action by Iraqi forces in conjunction with the Arab Legion would do nothing to remove Ibn Saud's hostility to Abdullah and might actually make him more alarmed. It was also thought that the Iraqi forces would find it more difficult than the Arab Legion to remain in the Arab areas of Palestine as defined by the United Nations; there would be more likelihood of their going beyond these boundaries and attacking the Jewish state. The British posts in Jedda, Damascus, and Beirut confirmed that the proposed action would increase local suspicions of King Abdullah and have unfortunate repercussions for Britain's own relations with the Arab states. Sir Alec Kirkbride expressed the hope that Tawfiq Abul Huda, when he visited Baghdad, would be able to correct Pachachi's ideas as to what action would be possible in Palestine.[34]

Uneasy allies

Britain's endorsement of Abdullah's limited plan did nothing to allay Jewish anxieties. At their meeting in November 1947, King Abdullah and Golda Meir had agreed to meet again after the United Nations vote

[32] Minute by R. A. B. Burrows, 9 Feb. 1948, FO 371/68368, PRO.
[33] Mack to FO, 2 Mar. 1948, FO 371/68368, PRO.
[34] Incursions into Palestine, 12 Mar. 1948, FO 371/68369, PRO.

on partition, but owing to the disorders overtaking Palestine the follow-up meeting did not take place. For a number of weeks the Jewish Agency was able to maintain contact with the king through his emissaries, but with the gradual slide to chaos in the early months of 1948 this contact became more tenuous and intermittent. The most important of the king's emissaries during this period was his personal physician, Dr Shawkat Aziz as-Sati. Unlike some of the king's other aides, who had a personal axe to grind, Dr Sati enjoyed Abdullah's absolute confidence and was entrusted by him to carry out the most sensitive of missions. It was Dr Sati who was usually sent to Jerusalem to convey the king's letters or verbal messages to Elias Sasson and Yaacov Shimoni. They for their part knew that 'the doctor' would not try to inject his personal views and preferences in the process of liaising between the two sides and that any money they handed to him would be faithfully delivered to the right destination.

To the Jewish officials it was rather disappointing that the king kept his relations with them on a strictly private and personal basis and that he did not see fit to involve his government in the talks or even to inform his ministers. Since the government was kept in the dark, there was always the danger that the prime minister and the king would pull in different directions. The king intimated that he could not rely on his ministers and that was why he used secret emissaries like Dr Sati. The Jewish officials could hardly insist that Abdullah involve his ministers but the fact that he did not was a constant source of concern for them.

Another factor which complicated the secret relationship was Jewish uncertainty about the extent of British knowledge and British support for the king's plan. Abdullah had hinted on a number of occasions that he preferred to reveal as little as possible about the nature of his relationship with the Jewish Agency to the British. The Jews had no direct link with the British government, and even if they had been told that Britain supported the division of Palestine between themselves and Transjordan they would not have believed it. Such was their mistrust of the abdicating mandatory power. So no tripartite collusion was possible and the triangle had only two arms, one linking Abdullah to Britain and the other to the Jewish Agency.

The Jewish Agency pressed Abdullah for a precise and written agreement. Its officials were very anxious to obtain a commitment in writing, a secret but written agreement, specifying the respective undertakings of the two sides. Abdullah, however, refused to be nailed down. He wanted the agreement to remain vague. It suited his temperament and it suited his political culture. The British had once tried to obtain his father's signature to a text but the Hashemites did not like precise or written agreements. Arab gentlemen keep such matters vague. Abdullah once sent a message to say that if there is trust, written commitments are unnecessary and if there is no trust, even written commitments would be of no avail.[35]

Yet, Yaacov Shimoni, who is in a very good position to judge, emphatically maintains that despite Abdullah's evasions, the understanding with him was

entirely clear in its general spirit. We would agree to the conquest of the Arab part of Palestine by Abdullah. We would not stand in his way. We would not help him, would not seize it and hand it over to him. He would have to take it by his own means and strategems but we would not disturb him. He, for his part, would not prevent us from establishing the state of Israel, from dividing the country, taking our share and establishing a state in it. Now his vagueness, his ambiguity, consisted of declining to write anything, to draft anything which would bind him. To this he did not agree. But to the end, until the last minute, and if I am not mistaken even during his last talk with Golda [Meir] in May 1948, he always said again and again: 'perhaps you would settle for less than complete independence and statehood, after all; under my sovereignty or within a common framework with me you would receive full autonomy or a Jewish canton, not a totally separate one but under the roof of the Hashemite crown'. This he did try to raise every now and again and, of course, always met with a blank wall. We told him we were talking about complete, full and total independence and are not prepared to discuss anything else. And to this he seemed resigned but without ever saying: 'OK, an independent state.' He did not say that, he did not commit himself, he was not precise. But such was the spirit of the agreement and it was totally unambiguous.

Incidentally, the agreement included a provision that if Abdullah succeeded in capturing Syria, and realized his dream of Greater Syria—something we did not think he had the power to do—we would not disturb him. We did not believe either in the strength of his faction in Syria. But the agreement included a provision that if he does accomplish it, we would not stand in his way. But regarding the Arab part of Palestine, we did think it was serious and that he had every chance of taking it, all the more so since the Arabs of Palestine, with their official leadership, did not want to establish a state at all. That meant that we were not interfering with anybody. It was they who refused. Had they accepted a state, we might not have entered into the conspiracy. I do not know. But the fact was that they refused, so there was a complete power vacuum here and we agreed that he will go in and take the Arab part, provided he consented to the establishment of our state and to a joint declaration that there will be peaceful relations between us and him after the dust settles. That was the spirit of the agreement. A text did not exist.[36]

When the rumours began to spread that the Transjordanian government had decided to join the other Arab states in an invasion of Palestine designed to seize the whole country, Golda Meir sent a

---

[35] Interview with Yaacov Shimoni.   [36] Ibid.

message to Abdullah asking whether his original promise to her still held. By her own account, the reply from Amman was prompt and positive. King Abdullah was astonished and hurt by her question. He asked her to remember three things: that he was a bedouin and therefore a man of honour; that he was a king and therefore doubly an honourable man; and finally, that he would never break a promise made to a woman. So there could not possibly be any justification for her concern.[37]

This triple reassurance, bedouin–royal–chivalrous, was not enough to calm Golda Meir's intensely suspicious mind, and her fears of betrayal fed on her ignorance of the intricacies of inter-Arab politics. Her doubts concerning Abdullah's reliability as a partner, though not her ignorance of the regional context in which he had to manœuvre, were shared by the man who led the struggle for a Jewish state, David Ben-Gurion. Ben-Gurion had at his disposal an effective intelligence-gathering service, fed by the Arab section of the Political Department and an additional network of secret agents and informers employed by the Haganah. The efficiency and secrecy with which this information was distributed to the leaders concerned and the central co-ordination of moves based on this information were no less outstanding. Ben-Gurion kept in close touch with both Moshe Sharett, who was leading the diplomatic campaign for independence in New York, and Golda Meir, who was acting head of the Political Department in Sharett's absence. Ben-Gurion encouraged both Sharett and Mrs Meir to cultivate the link with Transjordan while he himself remained sceptical about the viability of this link. A pessimist by nature, Ben-Gurion not only prepared for the worst but also expected the worst to happen. He was totally unshakeable in his belief that the Arab League would launch an all-out invasion of Palestine and was ever alert to the possibility that despite all Abdullah's private protestations of friendship he would ultimately throw in his lot with the rest of the Arab states.

Ben-Gurion was not terribly interested in the question of whether or not Abdullah genuinely wanted to live with the Jews in everlasting peace. He was much more concerned with the security problem, and his immediate purpose was to try and neutralize the Arab Legion. His entire strategy was governed by the twin imperatives of establishing a Jewish state and then defending it against what he saw as an inevitable Arab military onslaught aimed at destroying it at birth. The United Nations resolution of November 1947 had provided a charter of legitimacy for the establishment of a Jewish state but it did not afford this state any protection against attack by her neighbours. Ben-Gurion repeatedly warned his colleagues that the impending military

[37] Meir, *My Life*, 176.

confrontation would be not against gangs on the pattern of the 1936–9 Arab Revolt but against the regular armies of the Arab states. A well-trained and well-equipped regular army would therefore be needed to repel the attack. At that time the Jewish community in Palestine was weak in military terms, compared to the combined forces of the other side. Everything had to be tried, therefore, to reduce the strength of the opposing camp, and one way of achieving that was by splitting it. Ben-Gurion knew that the Arab Legion was the best and most dangerous of the regular armies surrounding Palestine, and that was why he was so keenly interested in breaking this link in the hostile chain. He also knew that King Abdullah was undecided on whether to join hands with the other Arab rulers, and therefore fully supported the efforts to persuade him not to go to war.[38]

On 9 December 1947, Ben-Gurion cabled Sharett that the situation was becoming grave, that the mufti held complete sway over all the Palestine Arabs, and that opposition to the Husaynis was practically non-existent. The king was also completely isolated, and could not be relied upon.[39] But the following day, Dr Sati came to meet Elias Sasson and Yaacov Shimoni with a reassuring report from the Hashemite monarch. The king, said Sati, was ready for a further meeting and was waiting for a visit. He had sent a cable to the mufti urging restraint and had also contacted Azzam Pasha and demanded that he issue an order to stop the disturbances in Palestine. To the Military Committee set up by the Arab League, Transjordan declined to appoint a representative because representation would have implied recognition of the League's authority to deploy Transjordan's forces. And Abdullah was not worried that Transjordan's absence would be exploited to intrigue against her.[40] Ben-Gurion's next report to Sharett was decidedly more optimistic: 'The king persists in his rebellion—he is helping neither the mufti nor the League; whether he will stand firm to the end is not clear to me, but there is a chance.'[41]

A week later, Dr Sati paid another visit to Sasson and Shimoni. The king was in an elated mood and had asked him to tell them that the League was not a League and its decisions were worthless. There were many details about the League's recent meeting in Cairo but Ben-Gurion wondered whether 'the doctor' heard them from the king, or from Samir Rifai or Fawzi el-Mulki or, as a local rumour had it, from Sasson himself. For the third time the king refused the request of Salah Jabr and Nuri Said to allow Iraqi forces passage through Transjordan,

---

[38] Interview with Gideon Rafael.

[39] Ben-Gurion to Shertok, 9 Dec. 1947, in ISA and CZA, *Political and Diplomatic Documents, December 1947–May 1948* (Jerusalem, 1979) 42 f. (Henceforth *Documents*.)

[40] Shimoni to Meyerson, 10 Dec. 1947, in *Documents*, 44–6.

[41] Ben-Gurion to Shertok, 14 Dec. 1947, in *Documents*, 59–61.

to station themselves on the border with Palestine. In response to a previous letter by Sasson about the Arab Legion, the king suggested that the Jewish press should loudly demand the transfer of the Legion to the Arab part of Palestine. Sasson now advised that the king should tell the British that the Syrians were buying arms and that this was directed against him, Britain's ally. The doctor promised to relay this advice. At this point Sasson made the boldest suggestion for a co-ordinated strategy: the Jews would deliver a fresh blow, this would supply an excuse for intervention by Abdullah, the king would come to the aid of the Arab part and then the Jews would help him with money.[42]

The outbreak of clashes between bedouins and Jews around Gaza alerted Ben-Gurion to the danger that the whole Negev could slip out of Israel's grasp. To reassert Israeli influence there, he appointed a special committee which included Ezra Danin. Elias Sasson was asked to appeal to King Abdullah to use his influence with the population of Gaza and with the bedouin tribal chiefs, who were considered his supporters, in order to quell the disorders. There was also a plan to organize a 'peace gang' under one chief, with moral backing from Abdullah and financial backing from the Negev committee, to beat up and banish the troublemakers. Danin was promised a budget of £P50,000 from which he thought a handsome portion could be diverted in Abdullah's direction.[43] Sasson expertly observed that if £P10,000–15,000 could be set aside for Abdullah, it would then become possible to ask him to take some concrete steps to calm down the Negev.[44]

A vitally important meeting was held under Ben-Gurion's chairmanship during the first and second days of January, 1948. The chiefs of staff of the Haganah and the Jewish Agency's Arabists were invited to participate in a comprehensive review of the situation. Many of the questions which were to dominate Israeli strategic thinking in the years to come were brought up in the discussion. Prominent among them were the questions of passive versus active defence, the role of settlements in the Yishuv's defence plans, the pros and cons of self-restraint as opposed to a policy of deliberate escalation of the conflict, and the perennial question of how and on what scale to retaliate against Arab

---

[42] Ben-Gurion's diary, 22 Dec. 1947, Ben-Gurion Archive, Sde Boker. See also David Ben-Gurion, *War Diary: The War of Independence, 1948–1949* (Heb.) 3 vols., Gershon Rivlin and Elhanan Orren, eds. (Tel Aviv: Ministry of Defence, 1982). These three volumes reproduce Ben-Gurion's diary from December 1947 to July 1949 with helpful introductions and annotations. Since the present book was already in progress when these volumes appeared, I have continued to give the dates of entries in the original diary rather than the page references in the published edition.

[43] Danin to Sasson, 23 Dec. 1947, S25/3569, CZA.

[44] Sasson to Danin, 29 Dec. 1947, S25/3569, CZA.

provocations. The confrontation between the political logic of the situation and the military logic of action ran like a central thread throughout the high-level debate.

Sasson advocated a selective but hard-hitting policy of military reprisals against the followers of the mufti because he did not believe that the opposition would stir itself into action against the Husaynis. If the volunteers being trained in the neighbouring countries heard about the devastating strength of the Haganah, argued Sasson, they would hesitate to come to Palestine and the mufti's stirring appeals to the Arab masses would fall on less receptive ears. Sasson also favoured hitting the Arab economy and communications in order to undermine the morale of the population and its capacity for waging war. But at the same time Sasson emphasized that Arab resistance could not be overcome by force alone, for it was not simply a matter of the indigenous Palestinian population but of the entire Arab world. Sasson appreciated the need for a strong army and for delivering crushing blows to Israel's enemies as the only effective means of deterrence. But he also insisted on the need to combine the use of force with political flexibility—indeed, to subordinate all military and tactical considerations to a clearly articulated political programme of action. 'We must not place our trust in force alone', he warned his colleagues. 'We have to find a way to an understanding with the Arabs.'

On the subject of Abdullah, which featured prominently in the discussions, Sasson had received some disturbing news suggesting that the king might have decided to join the Arab coalition and calling for a reversal of previous assumptions. One critical question was who would pay for the Arab Legion after the withdrawal of Britain from Palestine. Britain maintained the Legion at an annual cost of £2.5 million to herself. Transjordan's entire budget was £0.75 million per annum. There was now the possibility that Abdullah would lend the Legion to the Arab League, just as he had lent it to the British, and the League had already allocated £6.0 million for the struggle in Palestine. There were also rumours that the Legion would try to capture the whole of Palestine without entering the populated areas, to force the Jews to negotiate on the League's terms: autonomy for the Jewish community under a single regime for the whole country. These rumours reminded Sasson of Abdullah's words at the meeting in Naharayim about a partition which would not disgrace him in the Arab world and his suggestion of a small republic. They proved that this idea was not born recently but had always been there at the back of the king's mind.

Ezra Danin, who was charged with monitoring all the information and contacts with the Palestine Arabs, disputed Sasson's analysis and proposals. In his judgement, the arms purchases and military preparations by the opposition betokened not mere posturing but a serious intent to prevent a take-over by the mufti. The reinforcement expected to reach Palestine from outside was of no military value and its members would probably weaken the local inhabitants by making excessive demands on them. Internal squabbles would weaken the ability of the Palestinians to wage war against the Jews. Danin also opposed attacking Arab vehicles in areas where the inhabitants had not taken offensive action. His programme was to localize the trouble, reach agreement with as many villages as possible to prevent incidents, conserve Jewish force and resources, and aim to reach May 15 with as few casualties as possible. In other words, Danin's advice was to contain rather than purposefully escalate the developing military conflict.[45]

Ben-Gurion valued Danin as a good expert on the local Arab scene but he tended to side with Sasson. To help weld the opposition into a cohesive and organized force against the mufti, as Danin suggested, carried the risk that this force would one day rise up against its creator. Moreover, Danin's programme, pushed to its logical conclusion, was likely to lead to partition between the Jewish and Palestinian communities, whereas Ben-Gurion saw the Arab part as the prize with which to tempt Abdullah to break ranks with the Arab League. These considerations as well as considerations of timing influenced Ben-Gurion to seize the initiative and embark on a policy of 'aggressive defence' accompanied by economic subversion and psychological warfare. The escalation of violence would give Abdullah the pretext for intervention. The latest news made Ben-Gurion wonder whether Abdullah's previous pro-Jewish orientation or his new pan-Arab orientation would prevail in the end. So he adopted whole-heartedly the first part of Sasson's programme, neglecting the other half which called for political flexibility.

When Sasson looked back at the period which preceded the War of Independence from his vantage point as the Israeli minister in Turkey in 1951, one difference stood out as more fundamental and more durable than any of the others. During the period from November 1947 to May 1948, Sasson himself had argued more than once in discussions with Ben-Gurion that in their struggle against the Arab world they could win everything except formal, contractual peace agreements. The prime minister, on the other hand, was of the opinion that if they could defeat their enemies on the battlefield, they would be able to dictate the terms of peace in Damascus. This belief was no doubt coloured by his knowledge of European history where most wars not

[45] Ben-Gurion's diary, 1 and 2 Jan. 1948.

only started with a formal declaration of war but ended with the victors dictating the terms of surrender to the vanquished. Sasson, from his knowledge of the different political culture of the Middle East and Arab mentality, concluded that the European precedents were not valid points of reference for Zionist policy. In his view, even if they succeeded in conquering Damascus, they would not swiftly attain peace with the Arabs. The reason, according to Sasson, was that the Arab nation usually attaches such great importance to its prestige that even vital interests may take second place.[46] Ben-Gurion, nurtured in the European tradition of power politics and accustomed to placing the national interest above all other considerations, found this difficult to understand. His blind spot on the role of honour and prestige in Arab politics was a serious handicap for him in the struggle to promote Zionist interests.

Moshe Sharett suffered from no such handicap but the calls of international diplomacy diverted his attention from the local scene. When he returned home from New York in early January Danin immediately briefed him about a British plan attributed to Brigadier Clayton to substitute Arab League for British financing of the Arab Legion and to dispatch the Legion to impose cantonization on the Jews in the spirit of the Morrison–Grady Plan. Such a plan, explained Danin, would clear Britain of the direct responsibility for foiling the UN partition plan. The proposed Jewish counter-move was to tell Abdullah that such a deal would jeopardize his own immediate and long-term plans. Confrontation with the Jews would weaken him and force him to give up his Greater Syria scheme. There was every chance that after his rivals in the League made him dependent, they would stir up a military rebellion against him or cancel their grant and leave him in the lurch. But if he rejected this plan, the Jews would help him find a loan for his army for one year, and once he had captured the Arab part of Palestine they would reaffirm and continue their co-operation in the future. In addition, they would endeavour to enlist the support of America and possibly of Russia as well for his cause. From every point of view, co-operation with the Jews could be worth his while whereas co-operation with the League would be a disaster.

Sharett thought that if Abdullah looked like gaining control over the Arab part of Palestine either directly or through a stooge who would facilitate its annexation to Transjordan, they would be justified in making serious efforts to help him financially. Sharett's great worry was that the king was not to be trusted. That was why they had to take great care and remain vigilant. If they could be certain that there was a

---

[46] Sasson to Sharett, 29 Apr. 1951, 2401/12, ISA.

good chance that he would keep his promises—seizure and pacification of the Arab part and support for the establishment of the Jewish state— Sharett believed they could win the support of the Russians and the Americans for him. The Russians would be told that since he had been abandoned by Britain and no longer served Britain's interests and since they professed an interest in the establishment of a Jewish state, they should actively support Abdullah, or at least not oppose him. The Americans were definitely interested in the establishment of the Jewish state and if they could be convinced that the king would help to counter the prevalent extremism and stop the bloodshed, they would support him. As far as material assistance was concerned, Sharett doubted whether they would be able to lend Abdullah some of their own money to maintain the Legion during the period of transition. Nevertheless, he wanted Abdullah to be told that he did not visit him 'for fear of the evil eye which would harm him and malign him in his difficult present situation', and that the Jews were going to borrow money for themselves and that from whatever they obtain they would set aside a portion for him and his army.[47]

The task of composing the message to King Abdullah fell to Elias Sasson and he discharged it with the aureate but cunning and opaque style which flowed so naturally from the political culture of the Middle East. The letter mildly reprimanded Abdullah for not doing anything to put an end to the bloody riots in Palestine. It reminded him of his previous agreement concerning a peaceful solution to the problem of Palestine. It explained at great length and in lurid detail the intrigues of the Arab politicians to push him into the boiling cauldron in the cynical expectation that Transjordanians and Jews would exhaust one another in fighting and thereby rid the Arab League of both at little cost to itself. It insinuated that influential Syrian and Saudi politicians were behind the mufti's plot to establish a Palestinian Arab state which would frustrate by violence and terror any attempt to attach the Arab part to Transjordan. And it proclaimed the determination of the Jews to establish their own state and defend their independence with all their might. After the threats and the warnings, Sasson dangled the carrot in front of Abdullah's nose. 'My big brother' he said, meaning Sharett, has recently visited the country and among the questions discussed with him were:

(a) Our mutual agreement and its swift implementation.
(b) The strengthening of your international position and its prospects.
(c) The granting to you of an international credit and the ways to obtain it.
(d) Improving the relations between yourselves and the Americans and Russia and how to achieve it.

[47] Danin to Sasson, 4 Jan. 1948, in *Documents*, 126–8.

(e) Your intervention in the Arab part of Palestine and its capture, without
     protest from the Security Council.

In conclusion, the letter observed that all these matters were of great
importance and called for urgent talks between the Jews and Abdullah,
either directly or through an emissary.[48]

One go-between came from Amman, probably before the letter
reached its destination: Omar Dajani. He informed Sasson that Abdullah was under strong pressure from British and Arab statesmen to
occupy the whole of Palestine and award the Jews autonomy in the Tel
Aviv–Atlit area, a small enclave along the coast, and that he had been
promised several million pounds by Arab politicians for this purpose.
Abdullah had told Dajani about his promises to the Jews and said that
he was willing to keep them on condition that they get him American
and international support and agree to minor border adjustments to
enable him to show that he had achieved something for the Arabs, and
had asked Dajani to return immediately to the United States to work
for him in concert with the Jewish representatives there. He had even
promised Dajani written authorization to appear officially on his behalf
and on behalf of his government.[49]

Dajani, codenamed 'the orphan', may or may not have been an
orphan in the literal sense, but he certainly had two exacting employers
to please. This did not make him a double agent in the conventional
sense of the term since each employer knew and approved of his
association with the other. It did however complicate the problem of his
remuneration. Abdullah valued Dajani for his resourcefulness and
vigour and for the skilful manner in which he promoted his cause in
America. But with the meagre resources at his disposal, Abdullah
could not afford to keep Dajani in the style to which he was accustomed.
It suited him, therefore, to have Dajani on the Jewish Agency's payroll
even though such an arrangement was bound to cast some doubt about
his primary focus of loyalty. The irregularity of this arrangement in
terms of conventional diplomatic practice and protocol does not appear
to have caused Abdullah any loss of sleep. For the Jewish Agency it was
a major coup to secure the services of an agent with such excellent
Transjordanian, Arab, and international contacts. To them he was
useful not just for the light he shed on the darker corners of inter-Arab
diplomacy but also for his skill and ingenuity as a political operator.
The Jewish delegation at Lake Success was particularly anxious to
secure his services during the Security Council deliberations and 'the
orphan' was not a man to undersell himself. He was paid $2,000 plus

[48] E. Sasson to King Abdullah (Amman), 11 Jan. 1948, in *Documents*, 143–7.
[49] Sasson to Shertok, 13 Jan. 1948, in *Documents*, 156 f.

$300 travel expenses and $500 London expenses. And he was promised a monthly salary of $2,000 for his stay in New York in the coming year.[50]

In contrast to Dr Sati, who owed his undivided allegiance to Abdullah, Dajani had to please two masters and therefore had a personal stake in fostering better relations between them. On January 19, he returned from a second visit to Abdullah and reported to Sasson that the king complained that he had been misunderstood and wrongly accused of supporting the Arab League. His intention remained firm not to allow the Legion to attack Jews and not to intervene at all before the departure of the British. The king and his prime minister had told Dajani that they expected Britain to disclose her real attitude during the London talks to amend the 1946 treaty. The king's emissaries to London would take the line that he would accept partition, but a partition that would enable him to appear as an Arab nationalist and that would involve frontier changes. The king also promised to oppose with all his force the establishment of an Arab government or administration headed by the Husaynis.

Abdullah wanted an international loan to raise a militia in 'his part of Palestine', and had been told that the Jews would support it. He had also been promised that the Jews would help him get a loan to develop his whole country, and that rather than pay a subsidy to the Arab state envisaged in the partition plan they would assist him themselves with the money of the Jewish state. The king, reported Dajani, now wanted Jewish help to achieve these objectives. Sasson advised Ben-Gurion that Abdullah was sincere and that the promises should be kept.[51] The irony involved in the offer of Jewish finance for an Arab invasion of Palestine appears to have escaped Ben-Gurion's notice.

Sasson seized the opportunity to send a message to Amman to urge prompt Transjordanian intervention in Palestine to calm the mufti-instigated agitation. If this could not be done directly, he advised intervention by appropriate guidance to the king's supporters and followers there. Sasson also claimed that the Transjordanians ruled the Hebron area and that the recent clashes between Arabs and Jews in Hebron would not have occurred had preventive action been taken.[52]

A week later, 'the good doctor' resumed his shuttle between Amman and Jerusalem with a specific reply to Sasson's complaint. The king had invited the Hebron notables for talks and was also sending emissaries to the bedouins of the Negev. He asked the Jews to exercise

---

[50] Ruffer (Gideon Rafael) to Sasson, 19 Jan. 1948; Ruffer to Sasson, 25 Jan. 1948; Sasson to Ruffer, 29 Jan. 1948, S25/17001, CZA.

[51] Ben-Gurion's diary, 19 Jan. 1948; Sasson to Shertok, 19 Jan. 1948, in *Documents*, 186.

[52] Letter in Arabic, probably from Sasson to Abdullah, 19 Jan. 1948, S25/9038, CZA.

self-restraint. He himself was unable to intervene before renegotiating
the treaty with Britain and before learning Britain's real intentions
concerning Palestine. He asked Sharett to press for an international
force and the early arrival of the United Nations Commission in order
to frustrate the mufti's schemes and deter the Arab states. He also
asked Sharett to look into the question of an international loan for
Transjordan. In addition, he suggested a Jewish protest at the United
Nations regarding Syrian and Iraqi volunteers passing through
Transjordan on the way to Palestine without his consent; this, he said,
was a Syrian intrigue designed to bring him into conflict with the
United Nations. For his part, Abdullah intended to invite Fawzi al-
Qawukji, who commanded the volunteers from Syria, to win him over
and persuade him to direct his activities primarily against the Husayni
gangs. Abdullah expressed the hope that Sharett and Golda Meir, who
had joined Omar Dajani in New York, would assist him and treat him
as his loyal representative. Finally, Abdullah reiterated his request to
the Jewish leaders to trust him fully, to raise their financial support,
and to consider the possibility of border modifications.[53]

Since Abdullah's suggestion of frontier revision in his favour met
with stubborn opposition from the Jews, Dajani advanced the idea that
the international zone of Jerusalem should be occupied by the Jews and
the Arabs. The Jewish domain would be limited to the residential
quarters they already occupied; the remainder of the city and all the
countryside included in the international enclave would be added to
the Arab state. This would increase both the area and population of the
Arab state and establish Abdullah as the faithful saviour of Palestine.
Dajani was told that there was no point in propagating this idea
because it would turn the whole Christian world against Abdullah and
only add strength to his enemies. He was also told to stick to the terms
of reference which had been agreed in Jerusalem and Amman before his
departure for America. He was to negotiate with the State Department
for recognition of Transjordan; was to endeavour to raise an international loan for Transjordan; and was to serve as Transjordan's
unofficial representative at the United Nations with the aim of securing
his country's admission to that organization.[54]

Upsetting the United Nations scheme for international Jerusalem by
dividing the city with the Jews would have been a very poor recommendation for Transjordan's membership. Abdullah was unlikely
therefore to contemplate such a scheme at that particular time despite
the unquestionable attraction of becoming the protector of the Holy

[53] Sasson to Myerson, 27 Jan. 1948, S25/9138, CZA.
[54] Unsigned report 'From the Orphan After his Return from London, Palestine and
Transjordan', 18 Feb. 1948, S25/3569, CZA.

Places. The British had also cautioned him that he could not count on their diplomatic support if he incurred the wrath of the Security Council by taking unilateral action. Having worked so hard to get British acquiescence in his limited plan of intervention in Palestine, Abdullah was not about to forfeit it by going beyond the limits set by Bevin at his private meeting with Abul Huda in early February. On the other hand Abdullah could not openly declare that his policy was to occupy only the Arab part because then he would be denounced in nationalist Arab circles for accepting partition. To forestall such accusations, the king and his prime minister played a complicated double-game. They told the Arabs that they were going to try to occupy the whole of Palestine, fully aware that with the means at their disposal they would be unable to achieve more than the occupation of the Arab areas.[55]

A most authoritative account of Abdullah's military plans was given by Glubb Pasha on January 30 to Major-Gen. C. D. Packard, the director of Military Intelligence at the War Office. Since Glubb had arrived in London as a member of the high-level delegation from Amman, this conversation was 'off the record' and in this respect quite typical of the back-stairs methods by which Glubb continued to serve the British government. Glubb made it clear that there was no intention to move before May 15. He was also at pains to stress that King Abdullah would not march over the Jewish frontier. According to Glubb, the main objectives of the invading force would be Beersheba, Hebron, Ramallah, Nablus, and Jenin, with forward elements in Tulkarem and the area just south of Lydda. He thought it unlikely that the king would make any attempt on Gaza, which was also allocated to the Arab state, because he had no wish to come into conflict with the Jews. 'Jerusalem would of course be inviolate.'[56]

The change that had taken place in the British position on Palestine following Glubb and Abul Huda's visit to London was not detected by the Jewish side. Reliable information about Britain was in very short supply to the otherwise well-informed intelligence service of the Yishuv. Reuven Shiloah (Zaslani) persistently misunderstood and misrepresented British intentions to the Jewish policymakers during this period. The root of the problem was that he based his estimates on rumours regarding the British administration in Palestine and had no access to the highest levels in London where policy was determined. The result was a great deal of unjustified suspicion of the British role in the interim period from November 1947 to May 1948—suspicions

---

[55] Kirkbride to FO, 14 Feb. 1948, FO 371/68367, PRO.
[56] Maj.-Gen. C. D. Packard, War Office, to W. G. Hayter, FO, 5 Mar. 1948, FO 371/68369, PRO.

which led to underestimating the possibility of moving forward with Abdullah with tacit British agreement.[57]

In early February, Shiloah went to London to find out whether there was, as he suspected, a British plot against the Yishuv. Failing to catch the slightest whiff of the real plot that had just been hatched by Bevin and Abul Huda, Shiloah initially reported that the British were plotting to eliminate both the mufti and Abdullah from the Palestine settlement and to base it on Musa Alami and the Arab League. On the Jews the British were said to be preparing to impose ultimately a version of the Morrison–Grady plan.[58] On his return Shiloah asserted categorically that 'The Abdullah solution has, in the meantime, been set aside. Although there was strong pressure from the Army on the Cabinet to carry it out, Clayton was among its strongest opponents, stressing that the new policy of Britain must be built on Syria . . . Clayton's new plan is to rely on Syria, Iraq and Saudi Arabia and that leaves no room for Abdullah.'[59] It is difficult to conceive of a more erroneous or a more misleading estimate of British intentions, yet this was the basis on which Zionist policy was to proceed in the coming months.

Neutralizing the Arab Liberation Army

The presence of irregular Arab forces in Palestine before the termination of the mandate was as unwelcome to the Transjordanian government as it was to the British. But it proved impossible for Transjordan, already suspected by the other Arab states of having ulterior motives, to persist in its original policy of denying volunteers from Syria passage across its territory. Although in theory the irregular Arab forces were directed by a committee of the Arab League in which all the member states participated, in practice the control was in the hands of the Syrian government, and the Transjordanian authorities had no say in the matter.

The Arab Liberation Army was raised and financed by the Arab League in pursuit of its policy of preventing the establishment of a Jewish state without the official intervention of the regular Arab armies. It was commanded by the Syrian adventurer Fawzi al-Qawukji. Qawukji had had a chequered career in the course of which he had served in the Ottoman army, with the French against Faisal's short-lived kingdom in Damascus, as a military adviser to Ibn-Saud, and as a regular officer in the Iraqi army. During the Arab rebellion in Palestine in 1936–9, Qawukji had acquired a reputation as a successful

---

[57] Gelber, 'The Negotiations Between the Jewish Agency and Transjordan'.
[58] Zaslani to Shertok, 15 Feb. 1948, in *Documents*, 349 f.
[59] Report by Zaslani, 7 Mar. 1948, in *Documents*, 430–2.

guerrilla leader, but he owed this reputation more to his skill in manipulating the Arab press than in planning military operations. After being ignominiously banished from Palestine by the British he went to Iraq where he played a minor role in staging Rashid Ali al-Kilani's abortive pro-Axis rebellion. Having suffered a face wound when his car was machine-gunned from a British aircraft, which was for some reason taken as a mark of heroism rather than of incompetence or bad luck, he sat out the rest of the war in Germany and emerged from obscurity only in 1948 with his appointment to command the Arab Liberation Army. The Arab politicians who appointed Qawukji valued him more as a known enemy of and therefore potential counter-weight to the mufti than as the most promising military leader available to lead the fight against the Jews.

The first companies of the Arab Liberation Army, recruited and trained in Syria, reached Palestine via Transjordan in January 1948. Meeting no challenge from the British forces who were still responsible for law and order in Palestine, they established themselves in the Nablus–Jenin–Tulkarem triangle. Other companies followed at intervals, swelling its ranks from 2–3,000 in January to 4–5,000 in March and 6–8,000 in April. In mid-February, without proper preparations but with a great deal of theatrical fanfare, Qawukji ordered his forces to attack Kibbutz Tirat Zvi in the Jordan Valley. Instead of the victory intended to impress the Palestinian Arab population, Qawukji's 1st Yarmuk Battalion retreated in disarray, leaving behind 60 dead and a large part of its equipment.

Qawukji himself did not reach Palestine until early March, travelling by way of Amman. Earlier, when he had been stopped at the Syrian–Transjordanian border in January, he had declined the offer to go and see King Abdullah for fear that both of them would be suspected of plotting against the Arab League or against President Shukri al-Quwatli of Syria, but now, with Quwatli's subsequent turn against the mufti, his inhibitions about a meeting with Abdullah were reduced. In his political orientation Qawukji had always been anti-Husayni. He now apparently believed that Palestine should be joined to Transjordan and that the Jews should be forced to accept an autonomous but clearly subordinate position within this large Arab kingdom. Convinced that the mufti's lieutenants cared only about themselves and were taking the Arabs of Palestine along a road to disaster, he was ill-disposed from the start to any co-operation with them.

So by the time Qawukji was received by King Abdullah on March 5, there were three main Arab forces jockeying for position in Palestine. They were the mufti's paramilitary force, the Arab Liberation Army, and the seven infantry companies of the Arab Legion stationed in

Palestine to protect British military installations. Politically, these three separate forces were at loggerheads and if at any time two of the forces were to combine, the third would be of little value. Qawukji was invited to Amman to preclude the possibility of a clash between the Arab Legion and the Arab Liberation Army and to ensure that the mufti's force remained isolated.

Qawukji's anti-Husayni tendencies provided a basis for a dialogue not only with King Abdullah but also with the Jews. After the Arab Liberation Army had failed to capture Tirat Zvi, the Palestinian Arabs switched their tactics to cutting off Jewish lines of communication. In this they were much more successful and by the end of March they had ambushed a number of convoys and looked on the verge of winning the war for the roads. These military setbacks revived and reinforced Jewish doubts about Abdullah's reliability. 'Have you despaired of your king?' Ben-Gurion asked Sasson, half sarcastically, half accusingly. 'No,' replied Sasson, 'but the King is impotent.'[60]

On March 13 Sasson and Haim Berman, a colleague in the Political Department of the Jewish Agency, submitted the outlines of a new policy towards the Arab states. They noted that the Yishuv's political isolation was complete, that all contacts with the Arab states had been severed, and there was little chance of resuming them in their part of the world. Their proposal was to set up offices in France, Turkey, and India and seek direct links with the official representatives of the Arab states in these countries. Sasson and Berman also attached a plan to guide all future talks, a plan which involved an abrupt reversal of the Jewish Agency's previous political strategy. This plan envisaged the establishment of two republican–democratic states in Palestine, one Jewish and one Arab, in accordance with the UN partition resolution and its borders. The provisions for economic, political, and military cooperation between the two states went much further than those laid down in the United Nations scheme.[61]

As Yaacov Shimoni aptly observed in his written comments, 'The whole plan reeks of a change of our Arab political orientation, of despair of Abdullah.' Shimoni questioned the view that Abdullah had given up his special position and joined their enemies. If there was a rapprochement between Abdullah and the Arab League, Qawukji and the Syrians, it was possible, argued Shimoni, that it was the others who moved closer to Abdullah. 'If the contact between us and Meir [Abdullah was sometimes referred to by Jewish officials as 'Meir', an anagram of his title, emir] has been severed, the fault lies with us (and

---

[60] Ben-Gurion's diary, 8 Mar. 1948.

[61] E. Sasson and H. Berman, 'Outlines of a Policy Towards the Arab States', 13 Mar. 1948, in *Documents*, 456–8.

my hope is that we shall still be able to make amends, so that it will not become an unforgivable, historic guilt).' He saw the renewal of the contact with Abdullah, the development of the incipient contact with Qawukji's camp, and the potential link with the principal Arab representatives in America as much more realistic and promising than fresh diplomatic efforts in remote capitals.[62]

Sasson offered to go to Europe in person to renew the Jewish Agency's diplomatic links with various Arab quarters. On March 12 this proposal was considered at a meeting of the Political Department and no objections were raised. Golda Meir, however, wanted to know whether the proposed departure of Elias Sasson and Ezra Danin implied that all the work they had invested in Abdullah was being written off as a failure. Danin denied that there was any implication of this sort and Zeev Sharef insisted that 'no theory can justify the cancellation of the link with Meir. Everything must be done in order to preserve it'. Accordingly, Golda Meir vetoed the suggestion that Yehoshua Palmon should accompany Sasson on his trip abroad; in the event of their being able to renew the contact with 'Meir', she concluded, he would be needed at home.[63]

In the meantime, Palmon's linguistic and diplomatic talents were needed for the task of initiating a dialogue with Qawukji. Palmon was one of the Haganah's ablest intelligence officers; he had spent the Second World War as a secret agent in Syria and was later to become Ben-Gurion's adviser on Arab affairs. From following closely factional Arab politics, Palmon was aware of the bitter grudge which Qawukji bore the mufti. Back in 1947 Palmon had found wartime German documents bearing on this feud and he had put them in Qawukji's direction. These documents confirmed Qawukji's suspicion that it was the mufti who had instigated his arrest and incarceration by the German authorities. Qawukji expressed a desire to meet Palmon but on being appointed to command the Arab Liberation Army he dropped the idea. From the officers who arrived in Palestine before their chief, however, Palmon learnt that he was not hell-bent on fighting the Jews. He realized that such a war would be neither short nor easy and he was said to be open to suggestions for averting it.[64]

Palmon informed Ben-Gurion that a meeting with Qawukji could be arranged and that he wanted to try and persuade him to keep out of the fight between the Haganah and the mufti's followers. Ben-Gurion readily approved the idea provided no promises were made to limit

---

[62] Ibid. 458 f.

[63] Minutes of the Meeting of the Political Department of the Jewish Agency in Tel Aviv, 15 Mar. 1948, S25/426, CZA.

[64] Unsigned report, 16 Mar. 1948, S25/3569, CZA.

their own freedom of action to retaliate against any armed gangs.[65] Palmon went to see Qawukji at the latter's headquarters in the village of Nur Shams on April 1. After a great deal of beating about the bush, Palmon got down to the real business of the meeting, which was to turn inter-Arab rivalries to his side's advantage. A solution could have been found to the problems of Palestine, he said, had it not been for the mufti. Qawukji launched into a diatribe against the mufti's wicked ambitions, violent methods, and selfish lieutenants. When Palmon mentioned Abd al-Qadir al-Husayni, the mufti's cousin who commanded the Husayni forces in the Jerusalem area, and Hassan Salameh, who had his headquarters in Ramleh, Qawukji interjected that they could not count on any help from him and, indeed, he hoped the Jews would teach them a good lesson. Palmon then suggested that the Jews and the Arab Liberation Army should refrain from attacking each other and plan instead to negotiate following the departure of the British. Qawukji agreed but explained frankly that he would have to score one military victory against the Jews in order to shake his reputation clean of the mud of Tirat Zvi. Palmon would not promise to hand him a victory on a silver plate. If we are attacked, he said, we will have to fight back. Nevertheless, he went away with a clear impression that Qawukji would remain neutral in the event of a Jewish attack on the mufti's forces in Palestine.[66]

The promised attack took place on April 4 against Kibbutz Mishmar-Haemek, on the Jenin–Haifa road, under Qawukji's personal direction. It did little to rebuild his reputation, however, as despite the heavy odds in their favour his forces suffered another humiliating defeat. The flamboyant Qawukji proved himself little short of a menace to his own side.

The tide was now beginning to turn in favour of the Jews. Their military weakness in March had adverse repercussions on their international standing. The United States withdrew its support for partition and proposed instead a UN trusteeship which was vehemently rejected by the Jewish Agency because it involved a delay in the creation of a Jewish state. An advance party of the United Nations Palestine Commission was sent to the country but the British authorities and the Arabs refused to co-operate with it. The Jewish leaders realized that only military success would reverse the tide in their favour and that Jerusalem would be of overriding importance in the on-going struggle. On April 1, Operation Nachshon was launched to open the road to Jerusalem. First, Hassan Salameh's headquarters in Ramleh was

---

[65] Ben-Gurion's diary, 31 Mar. 1948.

[66] Interview with Yehoshua Palmon. See also Dan Kurzman, *Genesis 1948: The First Arab–Israeli War* (London: Valentine, Mitchell, 1972), 67–9; Collins and Lapierre, *O Jerusalem*, 269 f.

blown up. Although an Arab Liberation Army contingent with heavy guns was present in the neighbourhood it did not go to the rescue. Qawukji kept his word to Palmon. Next was the battle for the Kastel in which Abd al-Qadir al-Husayni was killed. Shortly before, Abd al-Qadir telephoned Qawukji to ask for an urgent supply of arms and ammunition to beat off the Jewish offensive. Thanks to the Arab League Qawukji had large stocks of war material, but according to the Haganah listening post that monitored the call, he replied that he had none. This conversation showed once more that the earnestness of his promise to Palmon was matched only by his disloyalty to his Palestinian comrades-in-arms. Abd al-Qadir was by far the ablest and most charismatic of the mufti's military commanders and his death led to the collapse of the Husayni forces in Palestine.

Encouraged by the success of Operation Nachshon, the Haganah pressed on with the highly ambitious 'Plan D'. Its aim was to secure all the areas allocated to the Jewish state under the UN partition resolution, as well as Jewish settlements outside these areas and corridors leading to them, so as to provide a solid and continuous territorial basis for Jewish sovereignty. The novelty and audacity of the plan lay in the orders to capture Arab villages and cities, something the Haganah had never attempted before.

Once the tide had turned in their favour, the Jews no longer felt constrained to remain within the narrow and awkward boundaries laid down for them by the UN cartographers—after all, the Arab Higher Committee had rejected the 1947 partition resolution lock, stock, and barrel, and they were thus hardly in a position to complain if the Jews chose to disregard selected boundary provisions. The only practical constraint on Jewish expansion stemmed from their understanding with Abdullah to let him take the Arab part as defined by that resolution. Once Abdullah was thought to be wavering in his commitment to the agreement, they too began to consider themselves free of the reciprocal obligation to him. Yaacov Shimoni was undoubtedly right in holding that it was they themselves who were responsible for the loosening of the contact with Abdullah, but Shimoni's capacity for self-criticism was not generally shared. The men at the top mostly believed that it was Abdullah who was backsliding, and their suspicions of him were only reinforced by his repeated attempts to reopen the questions of borders and autonomy. Though they had not given up hope that Abdullah would stand by his original promise, they were assailed by mounting doubts about his reliability and fears of betrayal. The pact between the Zionist movement and the ruler of Transjordan, though just a few months old, was showing signs of breaking up under the combined strain of external pressures and mutual suspicion.

6

THE TORTUOUS ROAD TO WAR

Britain, Abdullah, and the Jews

As the British mandate was approaching its unhappy end, the Jewish community in Palestine remained greatly troubled by the thought that the British were not really resigned to partition and were plotting to prevent the establishment of an independent Jewish state. There was widespread fear that the British were not going to carry out a complete withdrawal or, alternatively, that they would leave but seek re-entry in the wake of an Arab victory which would reduce the Jews to begging for British protection. In Jewish political circles it was seriously believed that Britain was conspiring with the Arab rulers, and particularly with the ruler of Transjordan, to invade Palestine and impose a settlement along the lines of the Morrison–Grady plan, giving the Jews an autonomous area along the coast, the rest of the country to the Arabs, and bases with secure lines of communication to the British Empire. Ben-Gurion in particular was convinced that Britain's cynical ploy was to permit the neighbouring Arab countries surreptitiously to send armed forces into Palestine in sufficient quantity to destroy the Jewish community and capture the country after the termination of the mandate.[1]

These suspicions of sinister British imperial machinations are faithfully reproduced by Zionist historians. Some had explicitly charged that during the twilight of British rule in Palestine, the objective which dominated British policy (perhaps more accurately, the objective of those whom the Cabinet entrusted with the execution of its policy—the Foreign Office, the chiefs of staff, and the Palestine administration) was to see the Jewish national home physically destroyed.'These men were determined' alleges Jon Kimche, 'if the British had to leave Palestine, to put no obstacles in the way of the Arabs driving the Jews into the sea.'[2]

But Zionist historiography seriously misrepresents the reasons and motives behind the surrender of the British mandate. Far from wanting

[1] Ben-Gurion's diary, 11 Mar. 1948; high commissioner for Palestine to secretary of state, 11 Mar. 1948, box iii, file 2, Cunningham Papers.
[2] Jon Kimche, *Seven Fallen Pillars* (London: Secker and Warburg, 1950), 199.

to cling at any cost to their position as the ruler of Palestine, the makers of British foreign policy longed to get out and give up the thankless task of trying to reconcile Jews and Arabs. There is very little evidence in the official British archives to support the Machiavellian view of British policy during the final phase of the mandate. Most of the evidence points in the opposite direction. It supports the view that 'the long history of rebellion and terrorism had exhausted the patience and disillusioned the British ministers to such a point that their one desire was to divest themselves of all future responsibility for what might happen in that troublesome country'.[3]

To be sure, there were many officials in the Foreign Office who did not welcome the retreat from Empire and hoped for a much weaker and smaller Jewish state than that laid down by the United Nations, just as there were many anti-Jewish officials in the Palestine administration who implemented policy on an everyday basis in a manner calculated to hurt the Jewish community. But the basic thrust of British official policy was not to prevent by force the establishment of a Jewish state. On 23 March 1948, the Cabinet decided to accelerate the pace of withdrawal from Palestine and do nothing to oppose either an attempt by the Jews to set up a Jewish state before May 15 or by the armed forces of Transjordan to enter Palestine before that date.[4]

Bevin and his colleagues had to see the Palestine problem in a wider context than the Jews. They had to consider the need for peace in the Middle East, the need to keep an eye on Russia, the need to keep the friendship of the Arabs and not to alienate the Muslims in the British Empire. They also wanted to involve the United States in sharing responsibility for a Palestinian settlement that would safeguard Western interests. Arthur Creech Jones, the colonial secretary who played a major role in the surrender of the Palestine mandate, rebuts the charge that Bevin's policy was inspired by anti-Semitic prejudice; although he was angered by the Jews, he never allowed personal feelings to dominate his judgement. He refused to forget the wider implications of any Palestine settlement, as he thought Truman did. Equally emphatic was Creech Jones's rejection of the charges made by Labour Party critics, such as Harold Laski, that the British government deliberately tried to create confusion and let things go in the months before withdrawal.[5]

---

[3] Kirkbride, *From the Wings*, 26.

[4] Cabinet 24 (48), minute 6, 22 Mar. 1948; and secretary of state to high commissioner for Palestine, 24 Mar. 1948, box iii, file 2, Cunningham Papers.

[5] Elizabeth Monroe's interview with Arthur Creech Jones, 29 Oct. 1958, Papers of Elizabeth Monroe. See also id., 'Mr Bevin's "Arab Policy"', St Antony's Papers, no. 2, *Middle Eastern Affairs*, ed. Albert Hourani (London: Chatto and Windus, 1961), 39; id., *Britain's Moment in the Middle East, 1914-1971* (London: Chatto and Windus, 1981), 161–70; Avi Shlaim, Peter Jones, and

The fiercest critic of Bevin's Palestine policy to emerge from within the ranks of the Labour Party was Richard Crossman. Where others blamed the Attlee government for abdicating its responsibility and failing to carry out an orderly transfer of power, Crossman attributed to Bevin personally a vindictive and purposeful policy designed to cut the Jewish state down to size:

> Once it had been decided . . . to end the mandate, Bevin's aim, apparently, was to ensure that Abdullah's Arab Legion should overrun most of Palestine, leaving a rump Jewish State, so weak that it would have to throw itself on the mercy of the British Government. This aim was so shameful that it was never revealed to the Cabinet and so could not be expressed in clear directives to the men on the spot. Hence the dreadful impression of weakness and indecision, combined with malignant anti-Jewish prejudice which characterized British policy throughout.[6]

Crossman's conspiracy theory was grist to the mill of all those who sought to portray Bevin as a prejudiced, callous, and brutal enemy of the Jewish state, but the factual evidence on which it was constructed is exceedingly flimsy. It is true that Bevin gave the green light to Abdullah's Arab Legion to enter Palestine. But, as we have seen, the initiative came from the Transjordanian side, and Bevin gave his consent only on condition that the Legion stopped at the border of the Jewish state. What this stand clearly implied was that far from being driven by blind anti-Semitic prejudice to unleash the Arab Legion against the Jews, as Zionist historiography frequently charges, Bevin had in fact pragmatically resigned himself to the emergence of a Jewish state and was urging moderation on the potential Arab attackers of this state. Attlee's approach to the Jewish–Arab conflict was strongly influenced by the analogy of India. He thought that there might be a bit of fighting in Palestine, but that both sides would be better off in the end. He only envisaged clashes of the kind between Hindus and Muslims that had accompanied his government's grant of independence to the Indian subcontinent in 1947.[7]

By April 1948 the British saw that the indigenous Palestinian society was rapidly disintegrating and that it was in no position to form a government. This only strengthened them in their view that the best

---

Keith Sainsbury, *British Foreign Secretaries since 1945* (Newton Abbot: David and Charles, 1977), ch. 2; Alan Bullock, *Ernest Bevin: Foreign Secretary, 1945–1951* (London: Heinemann, 1983); Kenneth O. Morgan, *Labour in Power, 1945–1951* (Oxford: Clarendon Press, 1984), 208–18; Ritchie Ovendale, *The English-Speaking Alliance: Britain, the United States, the Dominions and the Cold War, 1945–1951* (London: Allen and Unwin, 1985), chs. 4 and 5; Wm. Roger Louis, 'British Imperialism and the End of the Palestine Mandate', in Wm. Roger Louis and Robert W. Stookey, eds., *The End of the Palestine Mandate* (London: I. B. Tauris, 1986), 1–31.

[6] Crossman in *New Statesman* 23 July 1960.
[7] Elizabeth Monroe's interview with Frances Williams, October 1959, Monroe Papers.

solution would be for Transjordan to take over the Arab part. At that stage they still had some hope that Abdullah would simply 'inherit' the Arab part without any large-scale hostilities and bloodshed. A smooth partition of the country between Abdullah and the Jews was, from a British point of view, a highly desirable outcome. Creech Jones was one of the principal advocates of a Transjordanian–Jewish understanding. But he was not the only one. It was the general policy of the Labour ministers to encourage Abdullah to reach an understanding with the Jews for partitioning Palestine peacefully between them.

The British also tried to use what little influence they had with the Jewish side in order to foster such an understanding. Col. Oskar Norman, the intelligence chief of the Palestine administration and one of the few British officers who remained sympathetic to the Jewish side, told Vivian (Chaim) Herzog, the head of the Jewish Agency's Security Department and a future president of the state of Israel, that he could see no way out of a war unless the Jews were sensible enough to get together and come to some agreement with Abdullah. Herzog interjected that in other words they would have to come to an agreement with the Foreign Office. Colonal Norman nevertheless thought that they were not being wise in failing to do their best with Abdullah, especially at a time when he was out of favour with the Arab League, whose member states were extremely jealous of him.[8]

On the same day Elias Sasson wrote to Dr Sati to say that he had been waiting for eight weeks for a visit or a message from him and that the silence from Transjordan was all the more puzzling in view of the gravity of recent developments. Sasson wanted to know why the Transjordanians opened their gates to permit guests to enter Palestine in contravention of their promise to the Jews. He had also heard that Transjordan had entered into agreements with its neighbours which contradicted the agreement with the Jews and he wanted to know whether this was indeed the case. With a hint that the Jews still intended to carry out their part of the agreement, Sasson called for an urgent meeting to exchange views on the deteriorating situation.[9] At a meeting of the Arab Section of the Political Department held three days later, Sasson reported that contact with Abdullah was virtually non-existent. Sasson was in favour of efforts to continue the dialogue with Abdullah but without expecting too much to come out of it. Abdullah, he explained, had only influence, not the authority to decide. In defiance ·of the Arab League, he had signed a new treaty with the

---

[8] Vivian Herzog, 'Notes of a Conversation with Colonel Norman', 5 Apr. 1948, S25/5634, CZA.

[9] Unsigned letter in Arabic which does not name the addressee, but most probably Sasson to Dr Sati, 5 Apr. 1948, S25/9038, CZA.

British. After May 15, the British would hide behind him and his influence would consequently grow. A document from American intelligence indicated that the agreement between the Jews and King Abdullah was a wise move, spoilt only by the publicity given to it.[10]

Publicity of a totally different order was given to the atrocity of Deir Yassin committed by Jewish dissidents while Operation Nachshon was in full swing. Deir Yassin was a small Arab village lying along the western approach to Jerusalem. It had concluded a non-aggression pact with the Haganah and scrupulously observed it. But on April 9, a contingent of Irgun and Stern Gang fighters, without the agreement of the Haganah, fell upon the village with the purported intention of forcing its inhabitants to flee. When the inhabitants offered resistance, the attackers opened fire indiscriminately and savagely massacred some 245 men, women, and children. Some of the villagers were driven in a lorry through the streets of Jerusalem in a 'victory parade' before they were taken back to the village and shot against the wall. News of the massacre spread like a whirlwind through the land, striking terror into Arab hearts. More than any other single event, it was responsible for breaking the spirit of the civilian population and setting in motion the mass exodus of Arabs from Palestine.

The spokesmen of the Jewish Agency and the Haganah immediately repudiated responsibility for the massacre. With the approval, and possibly on the initiative, of Ben-Gurion, the Jewish Agency also sent a telegram in Arabic to King Abdullah disclaiming responsibility and denouncing the Irgun for having committed this 'brutal and barbaric deed'. The message ended with an appeal to all concerned to ensure that the Palestine dispute is conducted in accordance with the laws of war of civilized nations, if it could not be averted and stopped altogether.[11] No such message was addressed to the other Arab leaders. Ben-Gurion's biographer gives three reasons for this unusual step. First and foremost, there was the secret understanding with Abdullah. Ben-Gurion feared that the Deir Yassin atrocity would inflame Arab fear and hatred of the Jews and intensify the pressure on Abdullah to throw the Arab Legion into the battle. A second reason was Ben-Gurion's fear that the Deir Yassin incident would plunge the Arab and Jewish communities in Palestine into total war with mass extermination and uncontrollable bloodshed. The third reason was connected with the diplomatic campaign at the United Nations. The flight of the Palestinian Arabs served the military needs of the Yishuv but endangered its international position. A major contention of official Zionist propaganda was that peaceful relations between Arabs and

---

[10] Minutes of the Meeting of the Arab Section, 8 Apr. 1948, S25/5634, CZA.
[11] The Jewish Agency to King Abdullah (Amman), 12 Apr. 1948, in *Documents*, 625.

Jews were possible, and Ben-Gurion himself repeatedly declared a Jewish–Arab alliance to be one of the three main objectives of his policy. Any sign of deterioration, any incident liable to plunge Palestine into a bloodbath, naturally encouraged the opponents of partition. Ben-Gurion therefore did all he could to prevent his thesis about Jewish–Arab peace from collapsing in front of the eyes of world public opinion.[12] Deep in his heart, he rejoiced at the flight of the Arabs from the areas allotted to the Jewish state. His calls on them to stay and promises of a just and humane treatment resulted from tactical considerations not from his fundamental position. When the Arabs began to run away from Haifa *en masse*, Ben-Gurion stressed that 'it is not our function to see to the return of the Arabs'. And in a crucial political–military meeting he ordered 'the destruction of the Arab islands between the Jewish settlements'.[13]

The head of the Royal Diwan acknowledged receipt of the message and remarked that the Jewish Agency could not divest itself of responsibility for anything that happened in Palestine.[14] This non-committal message did not convey the full extent of Abdullah's outrage at the massacre of Deir Yassin. He wrote a letter to Kirkbride asking him to secure British assent to the posting of detachments of the Arab Legion in Palestine to defend Arab villages from Jewish aggression. When Kirkbride saw Abdullah the next day, he advised him against any message to the British government as it would be impossible for them to permit the regular army of an Arab state to function independently in Palestine before the end of the mandate. He also pointed out that there were so many Arab villages liable to attack that the whole of the Arab Legion could not provide them with separate guards. After some further discussion they agreed that Glubb should explore with the officer commanding the British forces in Palestine the possibility of using the Arab Legion units under his command to improve security in the Arab areas. This formula satisfied the king even though it was unlikely to have any practical effect.[15] One official in London remarked that Abdullah would be well advised to leave the strategy to his army commanders and concentrate on the propaganda side at which he was much more competent.[16]

[12] Bar-Zohar, *Ben-Gurion*, ii. 701 f.

[13] Ibid. 702 f.

[14] Head of the Royal Diwan to Jewish Agency, 12 Apr. 1948, S25/5634, CZA. Abdullah told *Al-Ahram* on 17 Apr. 1948 that he interpreted Deir Yassin as tantamount to a declaration of war on Transjordan and the Arab states, that he did not recognize the existence of a Jewish state, and that he gave no weight to the telegram he received from the Jewish Agency. Mohammad Ibrahim Faddah, *The Middle East in Transition: A Study of Jordan's Foreign Policy* (London: Asia Publishing House, 1974), 23.

[15] Kirkbride to Burrows, 15 Apr. 1948, FO 371/68852, PRO.

[16] Minute by M. T. Walker, 23 Apr. 1948, FO 371/68852, PRO.

Abdullah's offer, Azzam's acceptance, and Ben-Gurion's suspicions

The general collapse of Arab morale in Palestine and the military defeat of Qawukji's forces at Mishmar Haemek and of the Husayni forces in the Jerusalem area forced the Arab League to recognize that the volunteers on their own, even if reinforced in numbers and equipment, could not stand up to the Jewish forces and that regular armies might have to be used to check the Jewish military offensive. King Abdullah was quick to exploit this general Arab predicament and to volunteer the Arab Legion for the task of saving Palestine. Excessive Hashemite zeal to intervene in Palestine was liable to arouse the suspicion of the Arab states who were in no position to take part in the invasion. To forestall these suspicions, Abdullah made it clear that he himself was determined to go to the rescue when the British withdrew and that he would welcome the participation of the other Arab countries in this rescue operation provided they recognized that he was in overall charge and that anyone who wished to co-operate must go to Amman.

The deteriorating situation in Palestine and the declared intention of one of its members to act formed the backdrop to the Arab League's meeting in Cairo on April 10. According to a contemporary report, Syria and Lebanon presented a proposal for the formation of an all-Arab expeditionary force to capture Palestine after the end of the mandate. Fear that King Abdullah would follow up his unilateral action by an attempt to realize his Greater Syria plan was said to be the motive behind the Syrian–Lebanese proposal. But the Egyptians voiced strong opposition to the use of regular forces. An alternative proposal which originated with King Farouk asked the League to determine that the occupation would be temporary and that the Arabs of Palestine alone would have the right to choose the regime and government for their liberated country.[17] This formula proved readily acceptable to all the members because it entailed no commitment to send regular armies and at the same time provided some sort of safeguard against a unilateral annexation of Palestine by Abdullah. To everyone's relief, Abdullah, against whom this decision was primarily directed, sent a telegraphic message to the Political Committee in Cairo offering to undertake the rescue of Palestine.[18]

---

[17] *Akhbar al-Yawm* (Cairo), 10 Apr. 1948. The League's decision of April 12 stated that 'the entry of the Arab armies into Palestine should be seen as something temporary, without any intention of occupying or dividing it; after liberating Palestine, they will restore the country to its rightful owners to rule as they desire'. The Arabs of Palestine were extremely happy when they learnt of this decision. Aref el-Aref, *The Disaster* (Arab.), 6 vols. (Beirut and Sidon: al-Maktaba al-Asriya, 1956–1960), ii. 345.

[18] On the League's meeting, see also Jon and David Kimche, *Both Sides of the Hill* (London:

Azzam Pasha, the secretary-general of the League, wrote to Abdullah on April 15:

The Committee has decided, at its meeting today, to thank Your Majesty for your magnanimity and Arab zeal. It was also decided to delegate General Officer Commanding Ismail Safwat Pasha, to discuss with Your Majesty the necessary measures to be taken to liberate the besieged Arabs and to prevent more massacres taking place as happened at Deir Yassin village and other localities. The Committee are of the unanimous opinion that the presence in Palestine of the Arab Legion makes it possible for the Legion to accomplish this important task with the required haste. The Political Committee adjures Your Majesty to allow please the Transjordan Arab Legion to do this duty. I avail myself of the opportunity of presenting the Committee's thanks to Your Majesty for the well appreciated magnanimity and generous preparedness you have shown. May God watch you with his care and give you success.[19]

One has to strip away a substantial layer of rhetoric to get to the real reasons behind the League's surprising *volte face* in accepting Abdullah's offer. As Azzam himself confided privately, it had been evident for some time that Fawzi al-Qawukji was no good and that the Arab states were unable to supply sufficient resources to the partisans in Palestine to enable them to defeat the Jews. In the circumstances Azzam felt that there was no alternative to letting Transjordan do the job, on condition that Palestine as a whole remained an Arab state and that there was no acceptance by Transjordan of partition. In the discussion by the committee, the prime minister of Syria and Hajj Amin al-Husayni were opposed to acceptance of Abdullah's offer, but this opposition was overcome by the Egyptian prime minister who accused them of being prepared to sacrifice Palestine for their personal jealousies. Azzam's letter was so worded that it did not constitute unqualified approval of Transjordan's intentions. His idea was to try and use the Arab Legion under the control of the League. On the other hand, if the Legion did occupy parts of Palestine, it would no longer be possible, in view of the letter, to accuse Abdullah of having acted in defiance of the League.[20] Besides, once the Legion had occupied parts of Palestine, the League, as Abdullah surely realized, would have no way of dislodging it.

While the Political Committee continued its discussions in Cairo, a statement from the Royal Hashemite Diwan asserted Transjordan's special position regarding Palestine. It declared that the Hashemite kingdom and Palestine were a single entity, comprising a coast and a

Secker and Warburg, 1960), 107 f.; Joseph Nevo, 'Abdullah and the Arabs of Palestine', *Wiener Library Bulletin* 31/45–6 (1948), 51–62; Walid Khalidi, 'The Arab Perspective', in Louis and Stookey, *The End of the Palestine Mandate*, 128–30.

[19] Copy in FO 371/68852, PRO.
[20] Kirkbride to Bevin, 16, 17, and 19 Apr. 1948, FO 371/68852, PRO; high commissioner for Palestine to secretary of state, 20 Apr. 1948, box iii, file 3, Cunningham Papers.

hinterland. Transjordan, it went on to say, 'opposed vigorously partition and trusteeship in defence of its own interests and for the preservation of national existence'.[21]

The same independent attitude was displayed by the king himself at his meeting with General Safwat who came to Amman bearing Azzam Pasha's letter. After meeting Safwat for the first time, Abdullah remarked that he had imagined that his type had died with the Ottoman Empire. Now Safwat talked as though the Arab Legion were to be placed under his command, while King Abdullah made it clear that he expected the army of liberation to be placed under Transjordanian command. The king also made the point that the Arab Legion would not gain freedom of action in Palestine before May 15. Safwat asked if there would be any objection to a brigade of the Iraqi army being brought to Transjordan in readiness for operations after May 15. Abdullah replied that there would be no objection provided the brigade came under Transjordanian command.[22]

Abdullah made the same points in his reply to Azzam Pasha's letter. He also pointed out that the Arab Legion could not be dispersed in order to protect Arab villages as this action would leave the Arabs without a striking force to cope with the enemy offensive expected after May 15. Air support would also have to be provided by the members of the Arab League as the Arab Legion had no aircraft. Abdullah's final observation was that the Arab League had to share responsibility with Transjordan for action in Palestine and act jointly in dealing with any international reactions in the future.[23] Abdullah had obviously taken to heart British advice that he should keep in step with the other Arab states, and he was exploiting to the full the fact that he alone disposed of a force suitable for rapid and effective action in Palestine.

The fall of Tiberias, Haifa, and Jaffa into Jewish hands in the second half of April and the flight of their Arab inhabitants from these mixed towns led to a growing volume of pressure from both inside and outside Palestine for the immediate intervention of the Arab Legion to contain the Jews. The flood of refugees reaching Transjordan put a great strain on the neutrality of the Legion and pushed it towards greater participation in the military and political affairs of Palestine. Without waiting for the end of the mandate, units of the Legion began to move across the river Jordan. They actively participated in the attack on a Jewish suburb of Jerusalem; gave aid and protection to Arab bands operating in different parts of the country; and provided patrols to accompany

[21] Statement by the Royal Hashemite Diwan regarding the position in Palestine, 17 Apr. 1948, copy in FO 816/117, PRO.
[22] Kirkbride to Bevin, 17 Apr. 1948, FO 371/68852, PRO.
[23] Kirkbride to Bevin, 21 Apr. 1948, FO 371/68852, PRO.

Arab traffic along the roads between Jerusalem and Hebron, Ramallah, and Jericho. They also undertook guard duties in Arab villages in different parts of the country to release Arab irregulars for combat missions and to prevent counter-attacks by Jewish forces.

These activities were also of some political significance because they brought the commander and officers of the Legion into contact with Arab notables in Palestine and fostered a growing body of support for Abdullah as the only effective protector. Glubb Pasha himself went on a number of trips to persuade mayors and other influential public figures that their interests would be better served by co-operation with Abdullah than by co-operation with the mufti.[24] The activities of the Legion were accompanied by a propaganda campaign directed against the Jewish forces. These and Abdullah's frequent statements that he would send his army to protect the Arabs of Palestine all contributed to the Jewish perception that the Legion had abandoned its earlier neutrality.

Ben-Gurion was concerned about this trend and asked Sasson to brief him on April 20. Sasson told him that Abdullah's power was rising because everyone recognized that his force, the Legion, would have to be used. Britain wanted to secure her lines of communication between the Mediterranean, Transjordan, and Iraq. Legion units were accordingly stationed on the route passing through Gaza, Beersheba, Hebron, Jerusalem, and the Allenby Bridge. Britain herself would remain in Haifa, ensuring the route to Transjordan through Beisan and Naharayim with the help of the Legion, whose forces were being deployed along this route. The commander of the irregular bands in Haifa was a Transjordanian, and that was no accident. His predecessor, who had been killed, had also been a Transjordanian. Without the Legion Britain could not secure these routes and she could not use the Legion without the consent of the Arab League. The League, seeing how hard-pressed the Palestinian irregulars had become, realized that regular armies would be needed, above all the Legion. From the Arab press it emerged that the League had decided to use the regular armies of Lebanon, Syria, Iraq, and Transjordan, and possibly Egypt. Abdullah believed that all these armies would not last very long and only he would be able to take their place because only he had an army which was not needed at home. Sasson concluded his briefing with the recommendation that they initiate a clash with the Legion before May 15.[25]

The fact that a Jewish initiative to attack the Legion before the end of the mandate could even be contemplated reveals the speed with which

[24] Nevo, 'Abdullah and the Arabs of Palestine'.
[25] Ben-Gurion's diary, 20 Apr. 1948.

relations had deteriorated and Jewish assumptions had changed. Whereas previously it had been assumed that Abdullah would use his army to give effect to his secret agreement with the Jewish Agency, the new working assumption was that the agreement was dead and that Britain would direct the operations of the Legion to meet her needs and the wishes of the Arab League. Abdullah did not help matters by issuing a stream of public statements designed to establish his credentials as an Arab nationalist, and which for that very reason were seen by the Jews as incompatible with his earlier pledge. On April 21, Abdullah declared in a statement to the Arab News Agency that after the incidents of Deir Yassin, Haifa, and Tiberias he had given up hope for a peaceful solution to the Palestine problem. If invited to defend Palestine, he would accept. The Jews still had time to settle the dispute if they agreed to the constitution of Palestine as an Arab state with autonomy for the areas where the Jews formed a majority.[26]

The Arabists of the Jewish Agency took the statement to mean that Abdullah was intending to impose a solution and that he was thinking of a variation of the Morrison–Grady Plan, giving the Jews autonomy within his state. Even Yaacov Shimoni confessed that up to that point he had believed that Abdullah would capture the Arab part while avoiding a clash with them, and that after he had consolidated his position in the Arab part he would start negotiating with them. But now Shimoni was no longer certain: he conceded that Abdullah's thinking might have changed as a result of recent events.[27]

For military as well as political reasons, Ben-Gurion was reluctant to provoke a showdown with the strongest of the Arab regular armies, but he authorized Sasson to issue a warning to Abdullah. Following Abdullah's statement, Sasson sent a telegram in Arabic to the royal court to say that peace in Palestine and mutual understanding between Jews and Arabs could not be achieved by threats based on biased and misleading propaganda. Nor could it be achieved by one side dictating conditions to the other. Real understanding could only be achieved by direct and quiet negotiations guided by a sincere intention to guarantee the rights and independence of Arabs and Jews alike. Sasson believed that the Jews would welcome any step in that direction and volunteered his personal services for the task.[28]

The wording of this telegram was more abrupt than the earlier communication from the Jewish Agency to the king following the Deir Yassin massacre. The new message was a judicious mixture of menace

---

[26] In *Documents*, 667; high commissioner for Palestine to His Majesty's minister, Amman, 25 Apr. 1948, box iii, file 4, Cunningham Papers.

[27] Minutes of the meeting of the Arab section, 22 Apr. 1948, S25/9664, CZA.

[28] Sasson to head of the Royal Diwan, Amman, 22 Apr. 1948, in *Documents*, 667–77.

and readiness to negotiate. The following day Sasson received the following reply from the head of the Royal Diwan:

I found nothing in your telegram to warrant my bringing it to His Majesty's notice since His Majesty's statement was quite unambiguous. There can be no question of threat or intimidation after what happened in Deir Yassin, Tiberias, and Haifa. As to your personal services, they will be acceptable if you comply with what is stated in His Majesty's declaration, namely, that the sovereignty of the Arabs in their country may not be contested, and that the Jewish community will be granted citizenship, with the same rights and obligations as the Arabs, and with a decentralized administration in those areas where they form a majority.[29]

In confidence Abdullah told Kirkbride that in view of the publicity attending his exchanges with the Jewish Agency, the offer of an autonomous Jewish administration in an Arab state was as far as he could go. He did not expect the Jews to accept such terms but his purpose was to keep the door open for negotiations when both sides were in a more reasonable frame of mind.[30]

There was indeed no chance whatever of the Jews accepting such terms and their very mention put them in a more belligerent frame of mind. Even the diplomatic Sharett cabled his suggestion from New York that Abdullah be warned privately that if the Legion went into action, the Jews had the means to wipe out whole units and would use them.[31] It was precisely the possibility of an armed clash with the Legion which dominated Ben-Gurion's military calculations. Probably with a sigh of relief he recorded in his diary on April 24: 'At long last I received the news that the first cannons have arrived—there should be 31 with shells . . . This changes the situation once more in a radical fashion—we shall not stand defenceless against the tanks of the Legion and its cannons.'[32]

It was typical of the two leaders that while Ben-Gurion devoted his formidable organizational powers to arming the Haganah for the forthcoming battle, Abdullah concentrated on the propaganda war at which he was a past master. Immediately after the Transjordanian Parliament had ratified the decision to send the Legion into Palestine, Abdullah told a press conference that 'All our efforts to bring about a peaceful solution have failed. The only way left to us is war. To me has fallen the honour to save Palestine.'[33] This statement was a bitter blow to the Jewish officials. It was generally construed as a declaration of

[29] Head of the Royal Diwan to Sasson, 23 Apr. 1948, S25/5634, CZA.
[30] Kirkbride to Bevin, 24 Apr. 1948, FO 371/68852, PRO.
[31] Shertok to Zaslani, 25 Apr. 1948, in *Documents*, 674.
[32] Ben-Gurion's diary, 24 Apr. 1948.
[33] J. and D. Kimche, *Both Sides of the Hill*, 108.

war on the Jews. With its emphasis on the inevitability of war and on
Abdullah's self-appointed role as saviour, it shattered what was left of
the hopes that he and his Legion would stay neutral. To Ben-Gurion,
however, the news, though disappointing, came as no surprise. The
newspapers, he noted calmly in his diary, announced that Abdullah
had 'declared war' on the Zionists. Whether Abdullah declared or did
not declare, he wrote, made very little practical difference. 'It was
obvious all along that we should expect two things: aerial bombardment by the forces of Egypt, Iraq and others, and the attack of the Arab
Legion.'[34]

The Arab League's decision to fight separately

These were precisely the two things that the Arab chiefs of staff,
following the military logic of the situation, recommended to their
governments in the course of the Arab League discussions in Amman in
the last week of April. The Military Committee, after hearing a report
from General Safwat, concluded that in order to overcome the Jewish
forces, the invasion must be supported by no less than five fully
equipped divisions and six air force squadrons operating under a single
command. This conclusion was passed on to the Political Committee
which convened in Amman at the same time.[35] In addition to the voices
of the soldiers, the full weight of public opinion was brought to bear on
the Arab leaders to dispatch regular troops to Palestine immediately.

The leaders, however, were very apprehensive of embarking on a
campaign against forces of unknown strength. Kirkbride gave a
graphic description of their mood:

There is a general slump of Arab morale and an inclination to indulge in
recriminations instead of planning to deal with the situation. King Abdullah
having got what he has always demanded, freedom to act, is losing his nerve.
The Regent gave me the impression that his main objective was to calm public
opinion in Iraq rather than to save Arab Palestine. The Prime Minister of
Transjordan and his colleagues are counselling prudence and are resisting in
admirable manner the hysterical demands for armed intervention by which
they are inundated. I have added my own voice to theirs.[36]

No agreement was reached at the first meeting with King Abdullah
at which neither Egypt nor Syria was represented. The only practical
outcome was to send the Lebanese prime minister, Riad al-Sulh, to
Cairo with a letter from King Abdullah to Azzam Pasha saying that
Transjordan could not cope with the situation alone and before moving
must be assured of the full support of the Arab states in men, money,

---

[34] Ben-Gurion's diary, 27 Apr. 1948.   [35] Iraq, *Report on the Palestine Problem*, 131.
[36] Kirkbride to FO, 25 Apr. 1948, FO 371/68370, PRO.

and material.[37] Al-Sulh laboured indefatigably to dispel the mutual suspicions between the Hashemite bloc on the one hand and Egypt, Syria, and Saudi Arabia on the other and to try and work out, as far as possible, a unified Arab strategy. Though he himself had never been a great protagonist of Greater Syria, he was now ready to see King Abdullah annex the whole of Palestine. In a private interview he reminded Abdullah that the departure of King Faisal from Damascus in 1920 was largely due to Syrian conceit and intransigence and said that unless they were very careful another Arab defeat would be in the making this time. Abdullah replied that he had never worked for Greater Syria in his personal interest but was striving for the good of the Arabs as a whole. He went on to say that in any case the Palestine problem was now much more important and urgent than any other question.[38]

In Cairo, al-Sulh, with the help of the Iraqi regent, pressed for Egyptian participation in an invasion of Palestine and pleaded with King Farouk that Egypt could not continue to do less for Palestine than other Arab countries without losing prestige. However, he met with strong resistance from Egypt's prime minister, Mahmud Nuqrashi. The conservative Nuqrashi, nicknamed 'the timid sphinx' by Egyptians and 'Old Nokkers' by British officials, was opposed to such action generally and by Egypt in particular.

Although the Egyptian government reserved its position, at the last meeting of the Arab summit in Amman, on April 29, a decision was reached, in principle, in favour of intervention by the regular Arab armies. On the question of date there was a heated discussion because King Abdullah said he could not intervene before May 15 whereas the other leaders felt that waiting until then to move their troops would give the Jews a great tactical advantage. It was secretly decided that Syrian, Iraqi, and Lebanese troops, in the guise of volunteers, would start crossing into Palestine on May 8 under instructions to avoid all contact with British and Jewish forces before May 15. It was also agreed that British representations on the subject should continue to be met by promises to do nothing before the end of the mandate and that if the presence of the so-called volunteers in Palestine was discovered, the Arab governments should deny all knowledge. Kirkbride, who learnt about this ploy from a source he regarded as entirely reliable, did nothing actively to foil it.

The real argument was over the question of command. King Abdullah maintained that command should be in the Transjordanian hands

[37] Ibid.
[38] Kirkbride to FO, 24 Apr. 1948, FO 371/69403; Beirut to FO, 2 May 1948, FO 371/68371, PRO.

and with a headquarters in Amman. Azzam Pasha was in favour of continuing the current arrangements with a headquarters in Damascus under Ismail Safwat or another Iraqi general. The Iraqis wanted an Iraqi in overall command wherever the headquarters might be situated. Abul Huda said resolutely that Transjordan would not place the Arab Legion under the existing command at Damascus. To break the deadlock, it was agreed by those present that each state should retain its independent command and be allocated an operational zone in Palestine. The Arab League allocated £1,500,000 to finance the opening stages of the operation; the secretary-general was given control over these funds, and representatives of the General Staffs of the armies concerned were invited to Amman to work out the technical and logistical details.[39]

When the conference was over, Maj. Charles Coaker, one of the Legion's British officers, drove a high-ranking Iraqi from the royal palace back to the centre of Amman. 'How did the meeting go?' he politely asked his passenger. 'Splendid', was the reply. 'We all agreed to fight separately.'[40]

In contrast to her ill-tempered disagreements with the other members of the Arab League, Transjordan remained amenable to British advice and guidance. As the other Arab countries were getting more difficult to control, Britain moved closer behind Transjordan. The crisis underlined Transjordan's value as a strategic asset to the guardians of the British Empire. A private directive from the chiefs of staff for the British members of the Anglo-Transjordanian Joint Defence Board described Transjordan as being:

of considerable importance to British strategy in the Middle East for the following reasons:
(a) It lies astride one of the main lines of approach from the Caucasus and the Caspian to the Suez Canal and the Delta.
(b) It covers the direct route from the head of the Persian Gulf to Aqaba and thence to the Suez Canal and Delta.
(c) It flanks our possible defence position across Palestine.
(d) It is potentially an area in which forward air bases could be established.
(e) The Arab Legion is the only properly organized, trained and equipped force in the Middle East. It is much to the advantage of HMG to ensure that this force remains in a high state of efficiency since it would prove of considerable value in time of war.[41]

Rumours that the Arab Legion was poised for intervention in Palestine alarmed the American policymakers and caused serious

[39] Kirkbride to Bevin, 29 Apr. and 2 May 1948, FO 816/118, PRO.
[40] Collins and Lapierre, O Jerusalem, 354.
[41] Draft dated 19 Apr. 1948, FO 371/68821, PRO.

strains in Anglo-American relations. Bevin's failure to inform the Americans of his secret understanding with Abul Huda meant that the Americans were unaware of the real basis on which British policy was proceeding and in these circumstances a crisis of confidence was bound to occur sooner of later. Bevin informed Creech Jones, who was with the British delegation to the United Nations in New York and kept in close touch with the US delegation, that failing the imposition of a political settlement, 'King Abdullah would no doubt try to carry out the programme mentioned to me secretly by the Transjordan Prime Minister on 7th February, i.e., the occupation of the "Arab areas" of Palestine in order to maintain law and order. Even so he would have to steer a very careful course if he was to avoid either major hostilities with the Jews or a major quarrel with the Arab League.' Bevin specifically enjoined the colonial secretary not to discuss this eventuality with the Americans and to confine himself to saying that if fighting breaks out the best contribution any outside state can make will be to limit the conflict and prevent the entry of additional arms or reinforcements for either side.[42] Creech Jones sought authority to speak to the Americans about this eventuality.[43] But after further reflection Bevin concluded that it would be too risky to give them his plan or to discuss with them the measures to be taken if no truce or settlement were achieved.[44]

Secretary of State George Marshall reacted to reports that Abdullah was planning an invasion of Palestine and that the armed forces of the other Arab states might also cross the borders by instructing his ambassador, Lewis Douglas, to see Bevin and Attlee urgently and demand that they use all their influence to restrain Abdullah from engaging in such an adventure.[45] Douglas called on Attlee and Bevin in the House of Commons on April 28 and the first point he raised was the question of the threatened invasion of Palestine by Abdullah's troops. If that took place, said Douglas, it would be regarded by the Security Council as aggression. Bevin leapt to the defence of his 'little king'. What was Abdullah to do? First of all, he had never been admitted to the United Nations, so how did the charter apply to him? Secondly, were the Jews to be allowed to be the aggressors on his co-religionists and fellow Arabs in the state of Palestine while he had to stand idly by and do nothing? All the aggression came from the Jews, claimed Bevin, adding for good measure that it seemed to him that 'United States policy was to allow no Arab country to help their fellow Arabs

[42] Bevin to Creech Jones, 20 Apr. 1948, FO 371/68543, PRO.
[43] Creech Jones to Bevin, 20 Apr. 1948, FO 371/68544, PRO.
[44] Bevin to Creech Jones, 22 Apr. 1948, FO 371/68544, PRO.
[45] *Foreign Relations of the United States, 1948* (Washington, DC: Government Printing Office, 1976), v, 865, 876 f. (Henceforth *FRUS*.)

anywhere, but for the U.S. themselves to assist the Jews to crush the Arabs within Palestine and to allow the slaughter to go on, and then to ask the British Government to restrain Abdullah.'

Attlee followed up Bevin's attack on the Jews and the Americans with some vehemence. Was it aggression, asked Attlee, for Arabs to come into Palestine from their own countries and non-aggression for the Jews to come in by sea in their thousands? Douglas said that the Jews were coming in unarmed and were not fighting men, but Attlee pointed out that that was just Hitler's method. He put people in as tourists, but they were soon armed once they got in. Following Bevin's lead, Attlee urged strong American pressure on the Jews in order to bring about a cessation of the fighting in Palestine.

Douglas was assured that the British would use all their influence to prevent an invasion of Palestine by Transjordan or any other Arab country provided the Jews did not attack and refrained from disorder while discussion of a settlement was still proceeding at the United Nations. Further, if Arab–Jewish agreement was reached on a truce and the British were asked to play a part alongside others in enforcing it after May 15, they would consider doing so though no assurance of military participation could be given. They feared that they would be left to carry the whole weight again and this they could not and would not undertake to do.[46]

The British, however, rated very low the prospect of a truce acceptable to both sides given the manifest Jewish intention to go ahead steadily with a separate Jewish state by force of arms. Bevin assumed that the Jews would win the first battles in a war which he was anxious to contain and localize. The real bloodshed might not come for some time, he told Creech Jones, but he was certain that it would come and would create a very dangerous situation.[47]

Harold Beeley was not only convinced that the future of Palestine would be determined by fighting between Jews and Arabs but thought that this might result in a more stable settlement than could be achieved by any other means.[48] But he was troubled by the possibility that resounding Jewish victories might result in Arab appeals to Britain for assistance and wrote to the head of the Eastern Department:

You may think that I am plunging . . . into the realm of fantasy when I suggest that we ought to be considering the risk, which admittedly may be remote, that Jewish forces might in the course of the struggle succeed in invading Transjordan. After all, the Arab armies cannot be classed as formidable, the

[46] Roberts to Inverchapel, 30 Apr. 1948, FO 371/68649, PRO; CM (48) 8, 29 Apr. 1948, CAB 128/12; Bevin to Creech Jones, 29 Apr. 1948, box 60, file 2, Creech Jones Papers.
[47] Bevin to Creech Jones, 22 Apr. 1948, box 60, file 3, Creech Jones Papers.
[48] Beeley to Burrows, 'Personal and Confidential', 24 Apr. 1948, FO 371/68546, PRO.

Jews may be very well armed, it appears that the relative strength of the Irgun is increasing, and we know that the Irgun . . . claim that Transjordan as well as Palestine should be included in the Jewish State. I assume that, if matters came to this pass, H.M.G. would take action to preserve the integrity of Transjordan. If this were not done, our prestige in the Middle East would be irremediably destroyed.[49]

Jewish aggressiveness, coupled with the inability of the United Nations to curb it, exhausted Abdullah's patience. To an appeal by a Truce Commission for Palestine established by the Security Council on April 23 and consisting of the consul-generals of the United States, France, and Belgium, in Jerusalem, asking Abdullah to refrain from intervening in Palestine, he replied that if the commission could guarantee that there would be no aggression from the Jews, then there would be no aggression from the Arabs. 'It is known', he said, 'that the Arab Nation, including her member states of the United Nations Organization, have rejected partition as well as the establishment of a Jewish state which would compete with the Arabs for their sovereignty in their homeland. You should compel them to remove any aggression and abandon the idea of establishing a Jewish state thus making it possible to establish peace in the Holy Land.'[50] Once again Bevin rallied to protect his ally. He felt that it was unfair that Abdullah should be singled out for this admonition at a time when actual aggression was coming from the Jews. He made some scathing remarks about the totalitarian form of government which the Jews were preparing and insisted that the Americans must act resolutely to stop Jewish aggression if they wanted him to continue to do his best to keep the Arabs in check.[51]

Kirkbride, who was charged with the task of steadying the mercurial Hashemite ruler, was himself beginning to reveal signs of weariness. 'I am having a very trying time in keeping His Majesty from kicking the traces altogether', he complained. 'He spends his days, and some of his nights, in alternate moods of lucidity and something approaching complete nervous breakdown.' Kirkbride wished that Abdullah would stop making statements to the press but, like a psychiatrist explaining the behaviour of a difficult patient, he added that 'some outlet for his fury seems to be essential'.[52]

Abdullah gave vent to his fury by serving notice to Sir Alan Cunningham that he was proceeding immediately to Jerusalem at the

[49] Beeley to Burrows, 'Secret and Personal', 30 Apr. 1948, FO 371/68554, PRO.
[50] Text in Kirkbride to FO, 30 Apr. 1948, FO 371/68546, PRO.
[51] Minute by Burrows, 29 Apr. 1948, FO 371/68545; Bevin to Creech Jones, 30 Apr. 1948, and Bevin to Washington, 30 Apr. 1948, FO 371/68546, PRO.
[52] Kirkbride to Burrows, 29 Apr. 1948, FO 371/68372, PRO.

head of a force to protect the Holy Places. Kirkbride secured a cancellation of this part of the message and frightened King Abdullah in the process. He also took advantage of the incident to press the importance of securing a truce in Jerusalem. But the fact that the king seriously contemplated sending his original message was taken by Kirkbride as a symptom of his state of mind. Although the threat to march on Jerusalem had been withdrawn, Kirkbride was doubtful whether some such precipitate action could continue to be prevented in the face of continuing Jewish provocations.[53]

The reasons for Abdullah's restlessness were essentially political rather than psychological. Amman was a vortex of conflicting pressures from the Arab world, the Palestinians, the Zionists, the British, and now the Americans as well. Abdullah's hopes of a clean and peaceful division of Palestine with the Zionists had been dimmed, if not extinguished, by the rising tide of violence sweeping through the country. The success.of the Haganah's military offensive generated powerful pressures for intervention by the regular armies of the Arab states. Abdullah was now impaled on the horns of a dilemma which was at least in part of his own making. If he threw in his lot with the Arab world, he would forfeit any claim on Jewish goodwill and material support. If he tried to remain neutral, he would be denounced as a traitor to the Arab cause and could end up by losing not only Palestine but his throne. From the very beginning Abdullah's agreement with the Jews suffered from a built-in constraint: he could not divulge to his own ministers, let alone to other Arab politicians, the fact of its existence. Under these circumstances it was not always possible to prevent lower-level violations of the agreement.

The first open violation of the agreement occurred on the night between 28 and 29 April when the Arab Legion attacked Kibbutz Gesher which lay just north of the hydroelectric works in Naharayim and guarded an important point of entry into the country. It was the first major attack by the Legion across the border and as such was a violation of the promise that Abdullah had made to Golda Meir and Abul Huda had made to Bevin not to attack the area allotted by the United Nations to the Jews. Since it also proved to be the last attack, it may well have been, as a British officer of the Legion claimed afterwards, an unfortunate local misunderstanding. The immediate cause for the attack was the seizure by the settlers of Gesher of a nearby British police fortress. According to Abdullah al-Tall, an officer in the Legion who was to achieve both fame and notoriety, when the British officers evacuated this important fortress they invited Glubb Pasha to

[53] Kirkbride to high commissioner for Palestine, 4 May 1948, box iii, file 5, Cunningham Papers.

take it over but he declined the offer because he knew of the general plan which forbade the capture of any point situated according to the UN partition resolution within the Jewish state. In any case, once the Jewish settlers had occupied the fortress and turned down an ultimatum to hand over the fortress and their settlement, the Legion mounted a co-ordinated attack with infantry, artillery, and armour. The settlement would have fallen into the hands of the Legion but for Abdullah contacting his son Talal, who was on the scene, and telling him to order the battalion commander to halt the attack.[54]

Avraham Daskal, the manager of the hydroelectric works, throws an interesting sidelight on the circumstances that led to the royal order to call off the highly effective opening attack by his army across the Jordan. When the settlement was under fire, one of the settlers came swimming down the river to call for help. Daskal, whose telephone line no longer worked, drove to the nearest police station and called the palace. He was promised, by Muhammad Zubeiti, a cease-fire of one hour. This made it possible to evacuate the women and children and to rush in reinforcements. In Naharayim itself there was a quantity of arms, both legal arms given by the British and illegal arms made in Poland and hidden in caches, all of which were transferred to the settlement. In co-ordination with the Haganah commander, Daskal also opened the dams north of Gesher to flood the Jordan, thus making it impossible for tanks to cross over to the Jewish side.[55]

Daskal's success in arranging a cease-fire raised a flicker of hope in Ben-Gurion's heart that an official attack by the Legion might still be averted. The Haganah force sent to defend Gesher was authorized to blow up the bridge over the river near Naharayim. On hearing that such action would constitute a violation of the agreement with Transjordan, he gave an order not to destroy the bridge.[56] Though badly damaged, both the settlement at Gesher and the police fortress remained in Jewish hands and later played an important part in impeding the crossing of the Iraqi forces into Palestine.

A message from Glubb Pasha

Glubb Pasha was at least as anxious as King Abdullah to avoid a head-on collision between the Arab Legion and the Haganah—not out of love for the Jews but out of profound concern for the well-being of the Arab Legion. Having dedicated the best part of his professional career to building up the Legion, he was exceedingly reluctant to throw it into battle against heavy odds and run the risk of its destruction. As a wise

[54] Abdullah al-Tall, *The Palestine Tragedy* (Arab.) (Cairo: Dar al-Qalam, 1959), 22.
[55] Interview with Avraham Daskal.   [56] Ben-Gurion's diary, 30 Apr. 1948.

and prudent soldier, Glubb's first concern was to conserve his tiny force and not expose it to the threat of attrition at the hands of the Jewish forces who had already shown their mettle on the battlefield. Although King Abdullah was the titular head of the Arab Legion, effective control was in the hands of its British commander. Commanded, officered, and financed by the British, it was primarily an instrument of British policy rather than of Transjordanian or Arab policy. Both Glubb and Kirkbride treated Abdullah with the utmost deference but he knew and they knew that in the final analysis he could not use it in defiance of Britain's wishes. Glubb's aims, as his intervention in the Bevin–Huda meeting had suggested, were slightly more modest than those of King Abdullah. He wanted to use the Legion to gain control only over those Arab areas on the West Bank which were contiguous with Transjordan. He wanted to prevent the mufti and the Husaynis from gaining control over this area and this task was relatively easy because the British administration in Palestine could simply hand over this area to the Legion at the end of the mandate. The real problem lay in averting a clash with the Jews amidst the confusion and chaos that accompanied the termination of the mandate.

Glubb remained undisturbed by the setbacks of Qawukji and the death of Abd al-Qadir Husayni. Nor was he prepared to send reinforcements in response to the Palestinian pleas for help in Tiberias and Safed because these towns were included by the United Nations in the Jewish state. He was, however, disturbed by signs that the Jews were preparing to capture areas that had not been allocated to them and he was alarmed by the mounting Jewish offensive in Jerusalem which culminated in the capture of Katamon on April 30. An Arab quarter in southeast Jerusalem, Katamon was important to the control of the Jewish and Arab parts of the city alike. A danger that Glubb could not ignore was that the Haganah would not be content with securing the new Jerusalem but would make a bid to capture the Old City as well. He therefore resolved to establish direct contact with the Haganah to elicit what its real intentions were and to avert a major clash if at all possible.

Brig. Norman Lash, Glubb's second-in-command and trusted lieutenant, was asked to arrange the contact with the enemy. Lash summoned Col. Desmond Goldie, a senior British officer serving with the Arab Legion, to his headquarters in Mafraq and entrusted him with this unusual liaison mission. The gist of the verbal message that Goldie was to convey was an offer from Glubb to delay the forward move of the Arab Legion in order to give the Haganah time to establish control over the Jewish areas and then fight a kind of mock war if they had to.

Lash told Goldie to wear civilian clothes and go in his own car, a Ford V8, to meet the Haganah officers in Naharayim on May 2. The trip to Naharayim had all the ingredients of a cloak and dagger operation. When Goldie reached the Majami Bridge, the 4th Infantry Regiment commanded by Lt.-Col. Habis Majali was firing on the high ground by the river. Goldie got out to explain to Habis that he was on a liaison mission and to ask him to stop firing. To the Transjordanian officer, who was later to become a field-marshal, the whole affair looked rather odd; his suspicions were not laid to rest by Goldie's explanation that he was acting as a messenger for the pasha. On reaching the other side of the bridge Goldie was surrounded by a band of angry Arabs and the encounter could have cost him his life had he not been recognized by one of them and permitted to continue on his journey.

Given the importance of the mission and the dangers involved, it is strange that Glubb delegated to Lash the task of briefing Goldie rather than doing it personally. Goldie himself cannot explain this casual procedure; he can only guess that the motive was to protect Glubb in the event of things going wrong, to enable him to say that he had nothing to do with it. Regarding Glubb's motive for seeking contact with the Haganah in the first place, however, there is no uncertainty in Goldie's mind; 'Glubb's prime concern was to protect the Arab Legion. He did not want his little army to get a bloody nose.'[57]

Colonel Goldie had been seconded by the War Office to the Arab Legion in 1947 and he stayed with them until 1949 as the commander of the 1st Brigade. He was a professional soldier with limited knowledge of Middle East politics and no strong views on the Arab–Jewish dispute. He was the perfect complement to Glubb, who had very limited experience of actual soldiering or logistics but loved politics and was highly skilful at handling soldiers and politicians, as Goldie himself recalls:

There was a terrific pressure on the pasha to fight, but we wanted to hold back as far as possible. In the end we had to go in. The pasha did not want to go to war. For one thing, there was a shortage of ammunition. The ammunition came from Britain and was strictly rationed. The pasha applied for stocks but the British government delayed. For political reasons it was keeping a close rein on ammunition. It did not say you can have whatever you want. If we were to run out of ammunition, we would have had to withdraw anyway. So it made no sense to rush in in the first place.

Goldie was emphatic that his commanding officer did not hate the

[57] Interview with Col. Desmond Goldie, Wallingford, 15 Sept. 1985; Goldie to Glubb, 13 Jan. 1971 plus enclosures, private papers of Col. Goldie; James Lunt, *Glubb Pasha: A Biography* (London: Havrill Press, 1984), 136–7; letter from Maj.-Gen. James Lunt to the author, 3 Mar. 1985.

Jews: 'The pasha was a very worthy, a Christian man. He was carrying out his duty as a British servant. He did not hate the Jews but he did his best for the Arabs. He did not want them to get a bloody nose. Besides, he had to do what Kirkbride told him because Kirkbride was the chap who was getting the policy from the British government.'

Goldie himself had no illusions about the prospects of an Arab victory and, as a professional soldier, scrupulously carried out the orders of his superiors. 'I was completely neutral,' he explained, 'but I was posted to an Arab unit so I had to do my best for that unit. Had I been posted to a Jewish unit, I would have done my best for the Jewish unit. Politically I was neutral.'[58]

The meeting with the Jewish officers took place in Naharayim at the house of Avraham Daskal on May 2—two weeks before the end of the mandate. Goldie was accompanied by Maj. Charles Coaker, who was about to assume the command of the 1st Mechanized Regiment and be promoted to the rank of lieutenant-colonel. The General Staff of the Haganah was represented by Shlomo (Rabinovich) Shamir, who was about to assume the command of the 7th Brigade. Shamir had served as a major in the British army during the Second World War and was therefore familiar with the way of thinking of British officers. He was also considered by Ben-Gurion as one of the more politically reliable commanders of the Haganah who could be entrusted with sensitive missions. On this mission Shamir was accompanied by Nahum Spiegel, the operations officer of the Golani Brigade.

Colonel Goldie opened this extraordinary meeting by stressing that they were speaking in Glubb's name and that they were anxious to make arrangements for further meetings. He himself was worried that the Arabs would suspect him of meeting the Jews and kill him, so Major Coaker would come on his own in future because as a staff officer he was less well known to the Arabs serving in the Legion and therefore less likely to arouse suspicion. The pasha had suggested Kalia, near Jerusalem, on the northern shore of the Dead Sea as a meeting point; Shamir agreed but suggested they maintained contact through Daskal. Goldie then explained that their reason for initiating this contact was to avert a clash between their respective forces. Shamir responded by saying that provided the Legion did not fight them, did not cover offensive Arab operations, and did not go anywhere it should not be, he saw no reason for a clash.

Next, Goldie tried to elicit the Jewish intentions: did they plan to capture the whole country? The reply he received was deliberately non-committal: the borders of the Jewish state are a matter for the politicians to determine but if military needs so dictated, the Haganah

[58] Interview with Col. Goldie, Wallingford, 12 Nov. 1985.

was capable of capturing the whole country. The situation in Jerusalem was of particular concern to Goldie and he asked: how can a clash be averted there? To this Shamir replied that their position on Jerusalem was well known. If the Legion refrained from attacking the Jewish sector of Jerusalem, if the road to it remained open, and if the Jewish settlements around Jerusalem and the roads leading to them were not endangered he thought there would be no reason to clash.

In an apologetic tone Goldie explained that the British did not want to clash with the Jews but they could not afford to appear to be blocking and betraying the Arab cause; what should they do? Without saying so outright, Shamir implied that that was a British problem—his side had to look after its own security and clashes might prove inescapable under the circumstances. Turning to Coaker, Goldie said he thought they could somehow settle the matter. Coaker wanted to know whether the attack by the Jewish forces on Jaffa presaged a plan to expand over the whole of Palestine. No, said Shamir, Jaffa interfered with traffic between Tel Aviv and Jerusalem, and since the British officer commanding could not guarantee the road they had no choice but to do the job themselves. When Shamir asked whether the Legion planned to enter Palestine, Goldie replied that the pasha might know something but, as far as he knew, nothing had been decided.

The conversation then turned on the quality of the various fighting forces. The British officers looked down on the Arab fighters, with the exception of the bedouins; they conceded that the Jews had won the first round, and thought that Arab morale would collapse, but they did not anticipate the speed with which this would happen. Switching back from soldiers' talk to the real purpose of the meeting, Goldie reiterated that they wanted to avoid a clash. Shamir contented himself with the observation that the Legion was twenty-six years old and had acquired a reputation as an important force in the Middle East, and it would be a pity to damage that reputation by allowing it to be defeated. He also wondered how the attack on Gesher could be reconciled with the professed desire for peace. Goldie immediately launched into a long and complicated explanation designed to prove that it was all the responsibility of the Transjordanian battalion commander, who had been severely reprimanded by the pasha. The meeting lasted over an hour and remained friendly throughout. It ended cordially with an agreement that Coaker would go to Daskal on May 5 to get details of the next meeting.

Shamir went away with the impression that Glubb's secret emissaries wanted, first, to establish a regular channel of communication; second, to probe the Haganah's plans and likely response should the Legion defend the Arab area; and third, to come to an arrangement about Jerusalem, where the situation was giving them cause for worry.[59]

Shamir's own purpose in going to this meeting was essentially the same as that of his British counterparts: to gain a first-hand impression of what the Arab Legion planned to do after the withdrawal of the British from Palestine and, secondly, to establish a more or less regular channel of communication for future use. With the benefit of hindsight General Shamir gave a balanced account of the aim and nature of the meeting and of its significance for the relations between the Haganah and the Arab Legion:

Colonel Goldie represented for us a potential enemy. It was only natural that we would want to probe the intentions of the enemy. We also wanted to find out whether it would be possible to reach an understanding and accord at the military level, but I was not asked to convey any specific message to Abdullah or to Glubb Pasha. There was talk of a kind of mutual neutrality: if they did not attack us, we would not attack either. One should not exaggerate the importance of this meeting . . . Goldie had no mandate to put to us practical and specific suggestions, nor did we . . .

They were particularly interested in our intentions regarding Jerusalem. But even on this matter we did not speak in a concrete fashion. No borders or demarcation lines were mentioned. We asked them whether they intended to enter Jerusalem, and in general whether they would stay within a limited framework or go to war and then *à la guerre comme à la guerre*.

I got from them the impression that they had a very high regard for the Haganah. In general it can be said that in the War of Independence we had an inflated view of the Arab potential and they exaggerated our capability. The Haganah had no military intelligence worthy of the name. We did not know, for instance, how much ammunition the Legion had and how long it could go on fighting. We did not even know how many battalions the Legion had and we certainly did not know the precise number of cannons and armoured cars in its possession. The British officers for their part were very cautious and very respectful.

One of the main points was to establish a procedure for future contact. In the end I did not have a second meeting because the whole matter was transferred to a more senior level and gave birth to the meeting between Golda Meir and Abdullah. I myself was swept along by events and preparations for the invasion. I set up the 7th Brigade and met the Legion on the battlefield in Latrun where Goldie was the commander of the brigade that fought against us.

It should also be remembered that although the Legion was withdrawn east of the Jordan, there were in Palestine about twelve companies of the Transjordan Frontier Force which were not subordinate to the Legion but owed their loyalty directly to the king. The king had to demonstrate that he

[59] Report on a Meeting with Representatives of the Arab Legion, 3 May 1948, 130.11/2413/2, ISA.

was taking part in the fighting, and that is why he invaded and attacked at a number of points. Glubb, on the other hand, was very worried that his small force would be worn down by attrition, because after all the king depended on the legion as his main base of support.

If Abdullah had dared to come to a real agreement with the Haganah it could have been done, but it would have required a much more serious effort than the one made at that exploratory meeting between me and Colonel Goldie.[60]

Little wonder that 'the pasha', as his subordinates reverently called him, makes no mention whatever of this friendly little meeting in his admirably detailed and elegantly written memoirs. The title of these memoirs, *A Soldier with the Arabs*, neatly bypasses the hierarchical question of whether he served the Arabs or ruled over them. Arab nationalists like Abdullah al-Tall denounced him as the instrument of British imperial domination over Transjordan and suspected him of collusion with the Zionists to prevent the establishment of a Palestinian state, and the cloak and dagger meeting in Naharayim was incriminating on both counts. There was something bizarre about this meeting at which the army of a supposedly independent Arab state was represented by two British officers who spoke in the name of another British officer, and the lengths they went to in concealing all knowledge of their mission from their Transjordanian colleagues makes it tempting to conclude that the entire mission was designed to serve specifically British interests rather than Transjordanian ones. It is not that King Abdullah was opposed in principle to a dialogue with the Jews or that the purpose of the meeting—preventing war between the Legion and the Haganah—was unacceptable to him, but rather that in this instance his most senior military officer went behind his back in contacting 'the other side'. From the Jewish point of view the attempt to prevent a war would have been much more convincing had it been made in the name of Glubb and Abdullah jointly.

As it were, the Goldie–Shamir meeting was one of some value to the commanders of the Haganah because it showed that the British considered them a military force to be reckoned with and it gave them some indication of the Legion's operational plans. But it gave them no indication as to how, if at all, these British plans were related to King Abdullah's overall political orientation. Ben-Gurion accurately summarized Shamir's report on the meeting in his diary but gave not a hint of the conclusions he drew from it. It was Golda Meir who, a day before

[60] Interview with Maj.-Gen. Shlomo Shamir (Rabinovich), Tel Aviv, 3 Aug. 1986. I am grateful to my friend Col. Mordechai Bar-On for conducting this interview on my behalf. Shamir saw a draft of the present chapter and remarked that the treatment of the background and substance of his meeting with Col. Goldie is accurate.

the Goldie–Shamir meeting, expressed to Ben-Gurion her interest in going to see King Abdullah again. Ben-Gurion was obviously in two minds. 'I agree to the attempt,' he wrote, 'although I do not expect much, but it is worth trying to prevent awkward developments before or after May 15.'[61] The report on the Goldie–Shamir meeting probably heightened his interest in such an attempt.

Considerable importance was attached to this single meeting both in London and later in Washington. In the Foreign Office and in the State Department the meeting was thought to mark the beginning of military co-ordination at the operational level between Abdullah and the Jews. In fact, despite the elaborate arrangements made for future contact, no further meeting of this kind took place.[62]

Yet there was a growing number of signals that the British government was reconciled to the establishment of a Jewish state. On May 1, Arthur Creech Jones, the colonial secretary, went up to Moshe Sharett in the delegates' lounge at Lake Success and said he knew the Jews thought the British were full of sinister designs and were inciting the Arab states to swoop down on the Jews after the termination of the mandate. He wanted to assure Sharett that they had in mind nothing of the sort but, on the contrary, were exerting their influence in the Arab capitals to the utmost to prevent anything of that kind happening. Creech Jones claimed that he and his colleagues, including Bevin, were anxious to localize the trouble and prevent it spreading into a major conflagration and that is why they were anxious to keep the Arab states out of the fray. As for Abdullah, the colonial secretary was sure that notwithstanding his high-sounding statements he actually intended to get hold of the Arab part of Palestine, and it was no part of his design to attack the Jews. Sharett did not take all these assurances at face value, but the coincidence between what Goldie had told Shamir and what Creech Jones told him seemed to him significant.[63] Ben-Gurion, on the other hand, was not prepared to base his strategy on these vague British promises.

The sentiments conveyed by Goldie at the operational level and Creech Jones at the political level were widely shared within the Palestine administration. Gen. Gordon MacMillan, the officer commanding the British troops in Palestine, preferred a regular army to occupy the Arab areas during a truce in place of 'Qawukji's filthy rabble'. He also asked for secret meetings with the Haganah to discuss evacuation plans.[64] MacMillan referred to Abdullah as 'a sly old fox'

---

[61] Ben-Gurion's diary, 1 and 2 May, 1948.

[62] Michael J. Cohen, *Palestine and the Great Powers 1945–1948* (Princeton: Princeton University Press, 1983), 333.

[63] *Documents*, 712, 758 f.

[64] Herzog to Shertok, 4 May 1948, in *Documents*, 722.

who made warlike declarations on the one hand to frighten the Jews and on the other to satisfy the Arab world which was urging him to act. The general thought it not unlikely that Transjordanian troops would move into the Arab areas of Palestine with fanfare after the mandate ended but that Abdullah would be 'jolly careful' not to risk his army in battle with the Jews.[65]

MacMillan's head of intelligence, Colonel Norman, thoughtfully offered British assistance in arranging a meeting between the Jewish Agency and Abdullah on learning that physical difficulties stood in the way. Norman told Vivian Herzog that Abdullah was unhappy about the invasion because he stood to lose his position if his forces were defeated, and he was not overenthusiastic about the gamble. Herzog pointed out that the Jews would not bother him if he merely sat down in Nablus and kept quiet but they would have to resist any attempt to encroach on Jewish state territory. Norman replied that of course Abdullah would not dream of attacking Tel Aviv or Haifa, but he had to show something to satisfy public opinion in the Arab world.[66] The message Ben-Gurion received was that Abdullah wanted a meeting and he urged that arrangements be made quickly but that the meeting should not be made open and official as Elias Sasson was thought to have suggested.[67]

If Abdullah really wanted a meeting, there was no sign of it in his public utterances. On the contrary, he issued a direct appeal to the 'Jewish community in Palestine', repeating his offer of equal rights and autonomy in the predominantly Jewish areas and warning that they would only have themselves to blame if they rejected the offer.[68] Sasson responded by sending a long letter in Arabic to one of his many friends in Amman, a letter conveyed by a foreign correspondent, probably to Dr Sati. Sasson reprimanded his friend for making no effort to contact him and expressed bitterness at Abdullah's failure to reply to his two-week old request for an interview to renew the agreement between them. As for the threats and conditions issued by Abdullah, Sasson asserted that they were incompatible with the spirit of the agreement between them. No practical results would be yielded by public statements and proclamations, warned Sasson; on the contrary, they could only deepen the conflict. The Jews had not gone back on the promise they had made at Naharayim and were ready to meet again to renew the agreement and make the necessary arrangements for its implementation. But they

---

[65] Wasson to Marshall, 2 May 1948, the Rusk Papers, National Archives (NA), Washington, DC.

[66] Herzog to Meyerson, 7 May 1948, in *Documents*, 755–7.

[67] Ben-Gurion's diary, 7 May 1948.

[68] Text of Abdullah's statement to the Jewish community in Palestine, 6 May 1948, S25/9038, CZA.

were not ready to countenance any attempt to impose new conditions which contradicted the original agreement. They wanted to bring peace to their part of the world but not at the expense of their security or independence.

Sasson hinted that they had received offers from Abdullah's rivals to settle the dispute but had declined them so far on account of their promise to Abdullah and their common interests. From the king's statements Sasson inferred that Transjordan and Iraq planned to attack and he warned that any hostile act would bring calamity on both countries. The beginning of aggression, he observed, is always clear, but its end cannot be foreseen and a particularly fearsome punishment was reserved for Iraq should it take the initiative. Transjordan's attack and conquest of the Arab part, however, was acceptable to the Jews provided it was in line with their earlier agreement and did not include an attack on the other part. The letter concluded by saying that it was not too late to meet again and settle matters amicably and that it was up to Abdullah to choose between reconciliation, which they would welcome, or attack, which would bring forth a counter-attack.[69] In its tone this was the most incisive and trenchant letter ever addressed by Sasson to Abdullah before or after. In substance it was the usual mixture of threats and blandishments but with the emphasis very much on the former.

The truce neither side wanted

The spread of chaos and violence in Palestine and Britain's persistent refusal to effect an orderly transfer of authority to the United Nations Commission led to another major American diplomatic initiative less than two weeks before the end of the mandate. The British government seemed to be saying that until May 15 it was the only ruler of Palestine and would not share its authority with any partner, local or international, whereas after May 15 it would no longer exercise any responsibility nor did it care who succeeded it. As Sharett aptly observed, this attitude combined the slogans of two famous French kings, Louis XIV and Louis XV, for the former used to say *l'etat c'est moi* whereas the latter used to say *après moi le déluge.*[70]

If London's policy seemed to the outsider a combination of these two French mottoes, Washington's policy appeared to be a series of pendulum swings between a bureaucracy which did not want to fight the Arabs and the Democratic Party which did not want to fight the Jews. The latest swing by the anti-Zionist bureaucracy took the form

---

[69] Unsigned letter from Sasson, probably to Dr Sati, 7 May 1948, S25/9038, CZA.

[70] Moshe Sharett, *At the Gate of the Nations 1946–1949* (Heb.) (Tel Aviv: Am Oved, 1958), 156.

of an emergency proposal for an unconditional cease-fire and an extension of the mandate by ten days. Implicit in this proposal was a call to postpone the declaration of a Jewish state. Secretary of State Marshall even offered the president's private plane to fly to Palestine the representatives of the Jewish Agency, the Arab Higher Committee, the Arab states and the members of the Security Council's Truce Commission (United States, France, Belgium) to expedite the truce negotiations.

The leaders of the non-Hashemite Arab states gave serious consideration to this dramatic American proposal. Despite the agreement in principle they had reached in favour of official intervention in Palestine, they still preferred a solution which would make it unnecessary for them to be drawn into war. They wished to avoid an armed conflict so as to deny Abdullah the opportunity to pursue his expansionist aims. And they hoped that the American proposal would delay partition and render an invasion unnecessary. Azzam Pasha spoke to King Abdullah on May 4 from Damascus and said that in view of the deterioration of the situation in Palestine, the representatives of the Arab states at Damascus and the chairman of the Arab Higher Committee had decided to accept the proposal for a cease-fire over the whole of Palestine, a prolongation of the British mandate, and on-the-spot negotiations on the future of Palestine.[71] Abdullah did not believe that the representatives in Damascus genuinely intended to accept the American proposal for a cease-fire and viewed Azzam's message as nothing other than an attempt to force his hand. Abdullah's suspicion grew when, following their telephone conversation, Azzam went back to Amman in order to make a supreme effort to engage the Arab Legion. Both the king and his prime minister refused to be rushed into premature action.[72]

Worried by the timing and the substance of the American proposal, Abdullah asked the British what action he should take. The British themselves turned down the proposal to extend the mandate by ten days but they advised Abdullah not to stand out against the truce and not to use Transjordan's non-membership of the United Nations as a pretext for his refusal. Abdullah accordingly decided to do nothing to prevent the acceptance of the truce by the Arab League but to insist that the members of the League who were members of the United Nations take the decision.[73] Thus without incurring the responsibility for sabotaging the truce, Abdullah ensured that there would be no

[71] Kirkbride to Bevin, 5 May 1948, FO 816/119, PRO.

[72] Kirkbride to FO, 8 May 1948, box iii, file 5, Cunningham Papers.

[73] Bevin to Kirkbride, 11 May 1948, FO 816/119; Kirkbride to Bevin, 13 May 1948, FO 816/119, PRO.

unanimous acclaim by the Arab League for the American proposals. The Arab Higher Committee should have realized that the British were playing their Abdullah card and that by accepting an American-sponsored truce they themselves could beat both Abdullah and the British. But as usual Abdullah out-manœuvred his Husayni opponents.

The Jewish Agency formally rejected the American truce proposal and the reasons for that rejection emerged very clearly in the course of the lengthy meeting that Sharett had with General Marshall on May 8. Stressing that King Abdullah held the key to the problem of Palestine, Sharett related that Arthur Creech Jones had told him that Abdullah would enter the Arab portions of Palestine but there was no fear that his forces, with their British officers and subsidies, would seek to penetrate the Jewish areas. Sharett also read Marshall a telegram from Tel Aviv reporting that Glubb's assistant, Colonel Goldie, had made contact with the Haganah to co-ordinate their respective military plans in order to 'avoid clashes without appearing to betray the Arab cause'. Marshall and his State Department aides were left in no doubt that these two overtures caused an abrupt shift in the position of the Jewish Agency. Only a week previously, the Jewish Agency seemed seriously interested in a truce. 'Now, however, their attitude had shifted and they seemed confident, on the basis of recent military successes and the prospect of a "behind the barn" deal with Abdullah, that they could establish their sovereign state without any necessity for a truce with the Arabs of Palestine.'[74]

Marshall warned Sharett that the Jews were taking a grave risk in gambling on Abdullah and that they should not come running to America for help if the gamble did not come off. But Marshall's real mistrust and resentment was now reserved for the British for having double-crossed him. For Bevin had welcomed the American truce proposal although Creech Jones's assurances to Sharett made them superfluous. In view of these conflicting reports, Marshall demanded a prompt indication of Bevin's real policy. Bevin replied that he did not know exactly what the colonial secretary had said but that it had always been their hope that the Jews would act sensibly and keep to their own zones, that Jerusalem would be put under a truce, and that King Abdullah might use his forces temporarily to maintain order in the Arab areas. This would allow time to discuss the whole situation. But even if there was no truce, added Bevin significantly, the colonial secretary's proposal could still be adopted.[75] Marshall's anger was not

---

[74] Marshall to Bevin, 8 May 1948 and Memorandum of Conversation, 12 May 1948, in *FRUS 1948*, v. 940–5, 972–6. For Shertok's account of the meeting see *Documents*, 757–69.

[75] Bevin to Kirkbride, 11 May 1948, FO 816/119, PRO.

assuaged by this explanation. 'It was generally agreed', he said to President Truman, 'that the British had played a lamentable, if not altogether duplicitous role, in the Palestine situation.'[76]

No outsider, however, played a more lamentable or duplicitous role in the Palestine situation than President Truman himself. For while the State Department was making every effort to avert war in Palestine by means of a cease-fire and a temporary postponement of Jewish state-hood, the president informed Chaim Weizmann in the greatest secrecy that he would recognize a Jewish state if they went ahead and declared it. Truman kept the British and the State Department totally in the dark about this verbal message which he sent to the Zionist leader through a secret emissary.[77] For the Zionists the implications of this message were unmistakable: they could disregard the pressures from the State Department to negotiate and the accompanying threats of action by the United Nations in the knowledge that they had the president on their side. That is why the normally cautious Weizmann entreated his colleagues not to weaken and on no account to delay their proclamation of a Jewish state. That is why Sharett could afford to disregard the advice and warning of the American secretary of state. And that is one of the reasons for Ben-Gurion's insistence, as we shall see, on rejecting the American truce proposal and going ahead with a declaration of independence.

The principal uncertainty on the Zionist side concerned British policy, and on May 11 Dr Goldmann, the moderate American Zionist leader, arrived in London to find out. He went to see Hector McNeil, the minister of state at the Foreign Office with responsibility for Palestine. McNeil told Goldmann that he was convinced that Abdullah would not attack the Jews and, if he did, Britain would withdraw all her officers serving in the Arab Legion. McNeil thought that if Abdullah stopped at the border or returned to the border after some token forays, there would be a possibility of a truce between the Jews and Abdullah. The principal objective, said McNeil, was to work out an arrangement which would permit Britain to develop relations with both sides. Abdullah had completely eclipsed the mufti and the Arab Higher Committee, said Goldmann, and that was all to the good. But every-thing depended on where Abdullah stopped and that posed a delicate problem for the Jewish Agency: 'Relations had always been good with Abdullah, and he would make the best possible neighbour. If he stopped short at the frontier of the Jewish state the Jewish Agency would be glad to have him there. Any truce signed between Abdullah and the Jewish Agency would be far more valuable than one signed

[76] *FRUS 1948*, v. 974.
[77] Cohen, *Palestine and the Great Powers*, 376; Louis, *The British Empire in the Middle East*, 514 f.

between them and the AHC.' When asked why the Jews were being so intransigent regarding a truce, Goldmann, who was himself the most fervent advocate of that proposal and the postponement of statehood among the Zionist leadership, referred to some technical points. He made it clear, however, that since Abdullah was still the uncertain factor and at the same time the best Jewish hope on the Arab side, the technical objection of the Jews might alter with circumstances, especially if the truce was negotiated with Abdullah and not with the Arab Higher Committee.

The weak point in Goldmann's argument was that Abdullah was interested not in a truce but in a war which would provide him with the pretext for intervention and later legitimize his territorial expansion. Whereas Ben-Gurion and Sharett were perfectly logical in spurning the truce precisely because they wanted to come to an arrangement with Abdullah, Goldmann's support for both Abdullah and the truce represented an attempt to square the circle. In any case, Goldmann was convinced, on the basis of recent British behaviour and his conversation with McNeil, that a major change had taken place in the British position: not only did the British agree to a Jewish state but they showed themselves to be very friendly and did good work in curbing Arab militancy.[78]

Kirkbride gave the Transjordanian authorities and Azzam Pasha the latest draft of the truce proposal on May 10. After studying the text, Azzam seemed to incline in favour of acceptance. Abdullah and his prime minister claimed that they were anxious for a peaceful solution in Palestine, especially in view of the pressure being brought to bear on them by the other Arab states on the subject of the Arab Legion. But they emphasized the practical difficulties of giving effect to the obligations which the proposed truce would impose on the Arabs. Both wanted to retain freedom of action vis-à-vis the other Arab states by exploiting the fact that Transjordan was not a member of the United Nations.

Abul Huda said that if the Arab League refused the truce he did not want to be implicated inevitably in a war with the Jews and that if the Arab League accepted the truce, he did not wish the Arab Legion to be automatically debarred from being used for security purposes in the Arab areas of Palestine. The Transjordanian delegate to the meeting in Damascus was therefore going to insist that the formal decision of the League on this subject must be taken only by member-states who were also members of the United Nations.[79]

In urging the other Arab states to accept the truce the Foreign Office

[78] 2081 from London, 12 May 1948, in 867N.01/5-1248, box 6764, NA.
[79] Kirkbride to Bevin, 10 May 1948, FO 816/119, PRO.

took the line that it would be better for the Arab governments to stand fast against popular demand for intervention than to intervene unsuccessfully, for in the latter event they could not hope to weather popular rage at failure.[80] It was not only popular clamour for intervention, however, but the knowledge that Abdullah would intervene whatever happened that pushed the Arab governments, with Syria at their head, to the brink of war. From a military point of view, the Syrians had no illusions about their ability to handle the job alone. But from a political point of view they continued to see Abdullah as their principal enemy and were impelled to intervene, if only to prevent him from tipping the balance of power in the region against them. The anxiety bordering on hysteria that seized the Syrian leadership was evident in the report of Dr Muhsin Barazi, the foreign minister, to the American ambassador in Damascus:

Barazi said seemingly fantastic story, now widely believed here, that Abdullah had made a deal with the Jews 'not without foundation'. According story Haganah will counter-invade Syria after crushing Syrian Army then return quickly to Jewish Palestine as Abdullah rushes to rescue. Abdullah would receive plaudits of grateful Syrian population and crown of Greater Syria . . . Barazi added Syria would not tolerate Abdullah with his royal airs and black slaves . . . he added 'We must invade, otherwise the people will kill us.'[81]

Ibn Saud's fears of Greater Syria were also reawakened and he began to consider ways of thwarting Abdullah's expansionist designs. He knew that his army was incapable of effective field operations; tribal raiding designed to make Abdullah nervous about his rear was the most he could do. There were rumours that Saudi irregulars ostensibly bound for Palestine were really intended for attacking Amman. But Ibn Saud was sensitive to the charge of opening a second front for the Jews. He was therefore unlikely to go beyond a war of nerves against his old Hashemite enemy.[82]

Such were the fears of the Arab rulers when the Political Committee of the Arab League convened on May 11 in Damascus for a crucial session that lasted three days. In this atmosphere, no Arab politician dared speak out openly in favour of the American proposal for a truce for the whole of Palestine or for the subsequent British proposal for a truce covering Jerusalem. The burning question was Jerusalem, and the Arab politicians were torn between the fear of the Jews acquiring control over all the Holy City on the one hand and the realization of their own unpreparedness to meet the danger and the British insistence

[80] *FRUS 1948*, v. 985 n. 4.
[81] 266 from Damascus, 10 May 1948, 687N.01/5-1048, NA.
[82] His Majesty's ambassador, Jedah, to the high commissioner for Palestine, 26 Apr. 1948, box iii, file 4, Cunningham Papers.

that nothing must be done while the mandate still existed on the other.[83] At its meeting on May 12, the committee considered Bevin's note to some of the member governments on the conclusion of a truce for Jerusalem between the Jewish Agency and the Arab Higher Committee. 'After the Mufti's opinion had been heard, it became clear that the plan had not been officially presented yet to the Arab Higher Committee; consequently, the Political Committee decided to enable each country to reply to the memorandum as it saw fit—but stressed that the reply would be in the same spirit and that it was best to send this reply a short time before May 15, 1948.'[84] This decision deprived the committee—which had been appointed by the League itself to represent the Palestine Arabs—of the possibility of exercising any independent judgement on a matter that concerned them most directly by using the thin pretext that it had not been formally approached by Britain. Coming on top of Jewish evasion, this decision sealed the fate of the British proposal.

Thus before launching their proposal, the British thought that all the ingredients for a truce for Jerusalem between the Jews and the local Arabs were in existence. The claim by an Israeli historian that the British forces remained in Jerusalem until the end of the mandate with the express intention of preventing an early Jewish takeover and facilitating a takeover by Abdullah is unjustified.[85] It was the Jews who could not wait for the departure of the British, with whom relations had become thoroughly poisoned by this time. Another reason for their lack of interest in negotiations was that they were constantly advancing their line as Arab resistance in Jerusalem collapsed. A Jewish Agency representative was invited to a meeting with the British high commissioner in Jerusalem but the Agency did not send a representative, claiming that the journey was too dangerous because the British were not guarding the roads.[86]

The representative in question was Golda Meir, who at this very moment, as we shall see, was on her way to Amman to meet King Abdullah. Though the dangers of this journey were much greater, they did not deter her from going to Amman. So safety on the roads in Palestine could not have been a reason but merely an excuse for the failure to engage in high-level truce negotiations with the British authorities.

[83] Secretary of state to high commissioner for Palestine, 2 May 1948, box iii, file 5, Cunningham Papers.

[84] Iraq, *Report on the Palestine Problem*, 192.

[85] Yigal Elam, *Hagana: The Zionist Way to Power* (Heb.) (Tel Aviv: Zmora, Bitan, Modan, 1979), 294.

[86] Diary of Sir Henry Gurney, St Antony's College, Oxford, 4 and 5 May, 1948; interview with Gershon Avner.

With every further excuse the basic Jewish reluctance to negotiate became more obvious to the British officials in Jerusalem. Sir Henry Gurney, the chief secretary, recorded in his diary on May 10 that 'The Jews are still rankling at their not having been told of our meeting with the Arabs in Jericho. It has wounded their vanity, and has exposed them to the charge of refusing to agree to obviously reasonable terms for peace in Jerusalem. At this stage they do not really want a truce at all. They always in any case want something more than they have got.'[87]

The next day the Jews declined to go and see the high commissioner and sent a formal protest for not having been consulted before the Arab decision to cease fire was announced. 'As the Arab cease-fire was obtained only after seeing the Jews, who have been saying for months that they would stop shooting as soon as the Arabs did, this is a bit odd', remarked Gurney, 'But the Jews are evidently determined not to have any British-made agreement.'[88] The Jews got their way.

Gurney and his colleagues spent the afternoon playing tennis. They had in fact run out of work. The British mandate in Palestine had only four more days to go. Everything was beginning to have an 'end of term' air about it.[89]

[87] Sir Henry Gurney's diary, 10 May 1948.
[88] Ibid. 11 May 1948.
[89] Ibid. 10 and 11 May, 1948.

7

ON THE BRINK

Two invasion plans

After settling on evasive replies to the American and British truce proposals, and after elbowing aside the Palestinian Arabs from the struggle for Palestine, the Arab League politicians began to address in Damascus some of the military issues that, with only four days to go until the termination of the mandate, could no longer be evaded. These discussions revealed the incompetence and the folly of the Arab politicians and the fatal weakness of insisting on rights without regard to practicality. Glubb Pasha illustrates this weakness by quoting a despairing comment of King Abdullah after one of the meetings of the Arab League's Political Committee:

> If I were to drive into the desert and accost the first goatherd I saw and consult him whether to make war on my enemies or not, he would say to me, 'How many have you got and how many have they?' Yet here are these learned politicians, all of them with university degrees, and when I say to them, 'The Jews are too strong—it is a mistake to make war', they cannot understand the point. They make long speeches about rights.

King Abdullah's inability to see eye to eye with the Egyptians was attributed by Glubb not solely to a clash of interests but also to some organic difference in their mental make-up. For the king was 'a practical man, always ready to make a bargain or consider a compromise'. A Palestinian, on the other hand, had told Glubb, 'Better for us all to be exterminated than for us to agree to give a yard of our country'. This peculiarity was attributed to the mentality of the Levantine Arabs. Glubb conceded that there was something admirable in this resolution to demand that which was right, regardless of the cost; he merely observed that the effect on the fate of the Palestinian Arabs was utterly disastrous.[1]

King Abdullah was unquestionably more pragmatic than the other Arab politicians, and the differences in the outlook of their leaders undoubtedly imposed strains on the relations between the member states of the Arab League. This, however, should not be allowed to

[1] Sir John Bagot Glubb, *A Soldier with the Arabs* (London: Hodder and Stoughton, 1957), 152.

obscure the fact that the strains within the League, which were to have such disastrous consequences for the Arab cause, had their roots in a clash of interests and an abiding mistrust between the Hashemite and the anti-Hashemite blocs. Suspecting Abdullah of collusion with the Zionists, the anti-Hashemite states stepped up the pressure for invading Palestine, if only to curb Abdullah's territorial ambition and stall his bid for hegemony in the Arab world. Diplomatic, strategic, and military co-ordination became extremely difficult, if not impossible, to achieve under the circumstances.

A prime example was the question of a unified military command which the politicians were called upon to settle. Gen. Ismail Safwat had been the key figure in the Arab League's military planning and preparation for the conflict in Palestine since October 1947 and was therefore the obvious candidate for the post of supreme commander for all the regular and irregular forces involved in the invasion of Palestine. Though a former Iraqi chief of staff, he was politically acceptable to the anti-Hashemite governments on account of his personal integrity. It was this very integrity and the insistence on serving the Arab League rather than individual members that brought Safwat into conflict with King Abdullah. Under pressure from Abdullah and the Iraqi regent, the Political Committee was forced to replace Safwat with another Iraqi general, Nur al-Din Mahmud, who was weaker in character, less anti-British, and more amenable to the influence of Abdullah and Glubb. Since Abdullah demanded the position of supreme commander for himself, the committee designated Nur al-Din Mahmud as his deputy.[2] Within a matter of days, however, it became clear that the notion of a commander-in-chief and a unified command was nothing but a fiction since none of the countries bothered to consult or co-ordinate their activities. In his memoirs Abdullah delivered a crushing indictment of his Arab comrades in arms:

Unity of command existed in name only and the Commander in Chief was not permitted to inspect the forces which were supposed to be under him. The Arab troops entered Palestine and their lack of progress, their confusion and absence of preparation, were complete . . . If it were not necessary to keep certain things confidential out of brotherly feeling and hope for the future . . . I could mention what befell Palestine and its people at the hands of its leaders and those member states of the Arab League which put confidence in these leaders and supported them. History will record the consequence with pain and regret; the grandsons of these men will blush with shame at the deeds of their grandsires.[3]

---

[2] Iraq, *Report on the Palestine Problem*, 105; Taha al-Hashimi, *The Memoirs of Taha al-Hashimi, 1942–1955*, vol. ii. *Syria, Iraq, Palestine* (Arab.) (Beirut: Dar al-Talia, 1978), 219–22.
[3] Abdullah, *My Memoirs Completed*, 10 f.

Another vitally important task on the agenda of the politicians who assembled in Damascus, with or without their university degrees, was to put the finishing touches on the plan prepared by their military experts for the invasion of Palestine. Whether or not such a plan existed at all is a matter of some dispute. Syed Ali el-Edroos, a retired brigadier from the Pakistan Army and a historian of the Arab Legion, claims that

Prior to the invasion of Palestine no joint Arab plan for operations was drawn up. No preliminary planning or coordination in the field of a unified Arab strategy or concept of operations was either considered or approved by the Unified Military Command of the Arab League. Though preliminary political and military discussions had been held by Egypt and Syria under the auspices of the League, the strategy drawn up for the campaign was amateurish in the extreme. No proper and balanced military appreciation of the Israeli forces had been undertaken, with the result that operational plans were based more on sentiment and emotion than on a cool, balanced and professional assessment of the existing operational situation. It was only on May 13, 1948 that the Arab League Secretary General, Abdul Rahman Azzam Pasha, informed King Abdullah of the Unified Arab plan for the campaign. From the 'Joint Plans' which finally emerged it appears that the Arab concept of operations envisaged a many-fronted, multi-pronged advance from Lebanon, Syria, Transjordan and the Sinai directed at the destruction of the Haganah and the occupation of Palestine . . . As a result of the five-pronged, concentric thrusts, launched on a 180° arc extending from the Mediterranean port of Acre through Galilee, the highlands of Central Palestine to Gaza and Beersheba, it was hoped that the over-extended Zahal, in attempting to stem the Arab offensive across the entire length of the border, would be overwhelmed and annihilated, and Palestine occupied in its entirety . . .

The Israelis were later to claim knowledge of an Arab 'Master Plan', combining the strategy of all the Arab armies. No such plan existed, nor had any attempt been made to prepare one. As stated earlier, the so-called Arab strategic plan, drawn up by the Arab League, was amateurish and nonprofessional in the extreme. In professional military terms, there was, in fact, no plan at all.[4]

The amateurism in operational matters displayed by Arab politicians was fully matched by the political amateurism of the Arab military some of whom embodied the worst vices of both groups: the politicians' bombastic trumpeting of Arab rights without due regard for the balance of forces, and the officers' tendency to be diverted from their true task by political interests and political considerations. Safwat had at his disposal a handful of officers of different nationalities who turned his headquarters into a hive of conflicting interests and ambitions. 'A swarm of Syrian and Iraqi officers buzzed around the building seem-

[4] Brig. Syed Ali el-Edroos, *The Hashemite Arab Army, 1908-1979* (Amman: The Publishing Committee, 1980), 244 f.

ingly more familiar with the science of political intrigue than with that of warfare. The distribution of funds, of commands, of rank, of operational zones, of arms and materials, all were objects of bargaining as intensive as any displayed in the city's souks.'[5]

General Safwat himself was incapable of giving a lead in undertaking the intelligence gathering, logistical preparations, staff work, and operational planning that are essential to success in modern warfare. Boosting the morale of his troops with promises of a triumphant march on Tel Aviv was a poor substitute for actual preparations. Capt. Wasfi al-Tall, his operations officer, who later became prime minister of Jordan, warned that the promised march on Tel Aviv might turn into a rout because of the deplorable state of their forces. But Safwat angrily locked up the prescient report on the grounds that if some of the Arab governments read it, they would refuse to take the risk of sending their armies to Palestine.[6]

Despite Safwat's selective, ostrich-like behaviour, by the time the Political Committee arrived in Damascus there was in existence a detailed military plan, accompanied by maps, for the invasion of Palestine. Prepared by the clear-eyed and hard-headed Wasfi al-Tall, this plan reportedly called (see Map 4) for

a northern thrust by the Lebanese, Syrian and Liberation armies, spear-headed by an Iraqi armoured force to capture the port of Haifa, while a narrow southern thrust by the Egyptian army up to the coastal plain would seize Jaffa. Thus the new state would be deprived of the ports that Tall knew it would need to bring in men and arms after the British left. At the same time, the Arab Legion and the balance of the Iraqi Army would aim to cut the Jewish settlement in half by thrusting across the coastal plain from the Judaean hills to the sea north of Tel Aviv.

Eleven days was the estimated duration of the campaign. To carry it out Tall asked that virtually all of the Arab armies be placed under one supreme commander. In the opinion of informed observers, if those forces, prepared or not, could have been made available, Tall's plan would have had every chance of success—'It was the stuff of which Ben-Gurion's nightmares were made.'[7]

But the forces demanded by the young and very capable operations officer could not be made available and as a result Ben-Gurion's worst nightmare did not come true. The forces actually made available by the Arab states for the campaign in Palestine were well below the level demanded by the Military Committee. Immediately following his appointment as deputy to the supreme commander, General Mahmud was instructed by the Political Committee to prepare a plan for driving

---

[5] Collins and Lapierre, *O Jerusalem*, 159 f.   [6] Ibid.   [7] Ibid. 300 f.

PLAN IMPLEMENTATION

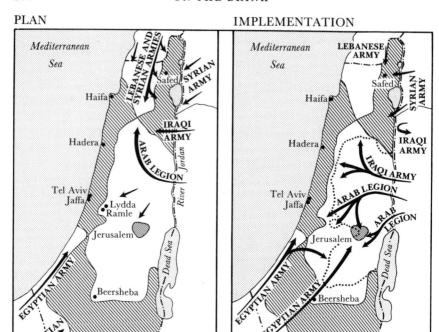

MAP 4   The 'Damascus plan' compared with the actual invasion

a wedge between the area around Tiberias and the coastal plain. Tall's ambitious plan was therefore hurriedly scaled down by Mahmud and the other Arab military chiefs.

The revised plan required the Syrian and Lebanese armies to move from north to south, through Safed to Nazareth; the Transjordanian and the Iraqi armies to move westward through Afuleh to Nazareth; and the Egyptian army to move towards Tel Aviv to pin down and destroy Jewish forces and thereby help the other armies to accomplish their particular missions.[8] As Salih al-Juburi, the Iraqi chief of staff, points out in his memoirs, the aim of this plan was to detach the north-eastern part from the Jewish state through simultaneous thrusts by four Arab armies. The specific objective was to cut off the lines of communication between Huleh, Tiberias, Beisan, and other Zionist settlements along the Jordan River from cities along the Mediterranean. This was to be achieved by proceeding step by step through Jenin, Afuleh, and Nazareth so as to surround the Zionist villages and settlements to the east. From these forward positions the Arab armies were intended to move, if conditions were favourable, to occupy Haifa and Tel Aviv.[9]

This revised plan was much more modest, at least in its initial aims, than is commonly believed or the slogan of 'throwing the Jews into the sea' would imply. But as the Israeli military historian Meir Pail has pointed out, it was precisely because the plan was so cautious and tailored to the ability of the regular Arab armies that it posed such a threat to the Jewish state. Firstly, the assignment of four or five regular Arab armies to the task of encirclement gave the plan a very realistic chance of success. Secondly, the loss of the lower Galilee and the valleys of Beisan and Jezreel could have dealt a body blow to the embryonic Jewish state and placed its survival in the balance even without attempting a pincer movement in the second stage, with one arm aiming at Haifa and the other at Tel Aviv.[10]

The danger to the Jewish state did not materialize however, because the Damascus plan was not put into operation in the way that the Arab chiefs of staff had originally recommended. General Mahmud changed the plan by moving the Syrian army from the north to the southern tip of Lake Tiberias, alongside the Iraqi army. This change was made at the request of the Transjordanian authorities. The Transjordanians insisted on the concentration of their forces in the Jerusalem area, Hebron and the Nablus–Jenin–Tulkarem Triangle, and despite all his efforts Mahmud was unable to persuade them to act in accordance with the original plan.[11]

General Juburi did not learn about the change until May 14. He was dismayed to discover that because of the Transjordanian refusal to co-operate, the Lebanese army would be left alone in the north and insufficient forces would be available to occupy the Beisan area which he considered to be of great importance. Unable to intervene directly with the Transjordanian HQ, Juburi informed the Iraqi regent and

[8] Iraq, *Report on the Palestine Problem*, 194.

[9] Salih Saib al-Juburi, *The Palestine Misfortune and its Political and Military Secrets* (Arab.) (Beirut: Dar al-Kutub, 1970), 168 f.

[10] Meir Pail, 'The Problem of Arab Sovereignty in Palestine, 1947–1949' (Heb.), *Zionism*, 3 (1973), 439–89.

[11] Iraq, *Report on the Palestine Problem*, 194–5; Hashimi, *Memoirs*, ii. 220–2.

Azzam Pasha of his concern and they agreed to urge King Abdullah to adhere to the original plan. The regent, Azzam Pasha, Juburi, and Mahmud went together to plead with King Abdullah, and he agreed to send one unit through the Allenby Bridge to Beisan and to move another unit from Jenin to Afuleh in accordance with the plan that had been agreed upon in Damascus. In their presence the king issued the necessary orders to the HQ of his army but those orders were not carried out, possibly because they were countermanded by the wily old man himself after his visitors had left the palace.[12]

By insisting on this last minute change King Abdullah wrecked the Damascus plan, with disastrous consequences for the invading armies. Abdullah had never asked for or wanted Egyptian or Syrian or Iraqi or Lebanese intervention. He probably estimated that even with Transjordan's co-operation the Arab forces would not be capable of reaching Haifa and Tel Aviv. What he told his partners in effect was that they could decide whatever they wanted but he in any case was going to give priority to his part of Palestine, and his part was the central area contiguous with his country, not the north or the south or the west.

Whereas the political objective implicit in the Arab League's plan was to prevent the partition of Palestine, Abdullah's objective was to effect the partition of Palestine by war and to bring the central part under his crown. By concentrating his own forces in the West Bank, Abdullah intended to eliminate once and for all any possibility of an independent Palestinian state and to present his partners with annexation as a *fait accompli*. It was only in the light of this political objective that the modifications demanded by Transjordan made any strategic sense. From the military point of view the Hashemite plan had every chance of success because it did not necessitate a full-scale war with the Jewish forces; it did not require the co-operation of the non-Hashemite states, and was not likely to encounter any serious resistance on the part of the Palestinian inhabitants of the West Bank.

Both the Damascus plan and the Hashemite plan were characterized by total disregard for the rights, interests, and even military potential of the Palestine Arabs. Neither plan assigned any significant role to the people who had started the war in December 1947 in order to 'wipe out in red what had been written in black'. In the coming offensive to save Palestine from the Jews, the Palestinians were not even requested to carry out guerrilla operations against the Jewish forces or to perform any combat-support missions. This exclusion reflected both the contempt felt by the Arab League's chiefs of staff for guerrilla warfare and, more significantly, the refusal of the politicians of the League to treat

[12] Juburi, *The Palestine Misfortune*, 169 f.

the Palestinian community as a political partner with a legitimate claim to a state of its own. The tacit assumption behind both the Damascus plan and the Hashemite plan was that Britain was leaving behind a power vacuum in Palestine; that the neighbouring Arab states would rush to fill this vacuum, and that the Palestinian community could be excluded from the eventual division of the territorial spoils. In short, both the Hashemites and the anti-Hashemites were preparing for a general land grab.

A more contentious issue was the role of the Arab Liberation Army in the planned Arab offensive. Fawzi al-Qawukji was playing a clever waiting game in order to be able to join the winning side. The Syrians were worried by rumours that Qawukji was moving closer to their Transjordanian rival. Abdullah, however, wanted to clear the field for his own regular troops and did not place much faith in the Arab Liberation Army, especially since the Syrian government was trying to gain control over some of its formations, so he demanded that it be disbanded. Two days before the invasion a compromise was reached to move it from the central zone to the Galilee, to operate in conjunction with the Syrian and Lebanese armies.[13]

The fundamental difference between the Damascus plan and the Hashemite plan lay in their responses to the challenge of the emergent Jewish state. The former envisaged crippling the Jewish state by the co-ordinated attack of four Arab armies on its northern part where much of the manpower, water, and agricultural resources were located. In the less definite second stage it was hoped to reach Haifa and deprive the Jewish state of its major seaport. The Hashemite plan, on the other hand, did not envisage an attack on Jewish territory and was not directed at preventing the establishment of a Jewish state. An armed confrontation with the Jewish state was precisely what Abdullah was anxious to avoid, hence his objection to the Damascus plan. The success of that plan spelled doom for his own. Were the Jewish state to disintegrate and the Syrian and Egyptian armies to emerge victorious, it would have been unlikely, to say the least, that the Arab League would have allowed Abdullah to take the West Bank. His plan assumed and even required a Jewish presence rather than a military victory by his Arab rivals.

It is tempting to conclude that only a tacit agreement with the Jews could account for the Hashemite invasion plan which proved so fatal to the strategy of the Arab League and to the hopes of an independent Palestinian Arab state. But such a conclusion is not wholly warranted

---

[13] For a partisan account of these political manœuvres see Fawzi al-Qawukji, 'Memoirs, 1948', pt. ii, *Journal of Palestine Studies* 2/1 (1972), 3–33. See also Ali Muhafaza, *Jordanian–British Relations, 1921–1951* (Arab.) (Beirut: Dar al-Nahar, 1973), 187 f.

by the facts. In essence, Abdullah's decision not to attack the Jewish state was not part of a bargain but a one-sided choice which flowed from a realistic appraisal of the balance of forces. No doubt the original agreement that the Jews would not stand in his way played a part here. Nevertheless, Abdullah did not subvert the Arab League's invasion plan in collusion with the Jews; he replaced it with a different plan tailored to serve his specific dynastic ambitions.

In the past the shrewd Hijazi chieftain had always believed that the Palestinian community was weak and divided and that he could therefore dominate it, but that the Jewish community was too united, strong, and advanced to be destroyed and should therefore be turned into an ally. But in the circumstances of May 1948, he did not need the permission of the Jews to move into Palestine and impose his rule over the Palestinians. He already had the Arab League's official sanction for intervention, however reluctant, and Britain's unofficial support, as well as considerable political backing on the West Bank. All he was waiting for was the official end of the mandate and the outbreak of hostilities that would justify the crossing of the Jordan and the annexation of central Palestine.

If Abdullah double-crossed his partners just as they were about to do battle with the Zionist enemy in Palestine, none of those partners appear in retrospect to have been a shining example of integrity or altruism. All betrayed by their actions the pan-Arab ideal they professed to be serving in their rhetoric. All displayed suspicion and anxiety lest their rivals should exploit the Palestinian Arab cause as a vehicle for promoting their separate regional ambitions. Indeed, it may be argued that the Arab League's decision to intervene was rooted not in a common interest to save Palestine for the Palestinians or to defeat Zionist ambitions but in inter-Arab fears and rivalries.

Under these circumstances military co-ordination and joint planning for the invasion of Palestine were bound to flounder, regardless of the level of professionalism of the officers concerned. Arab politicians, after all, had persistently disregarded the information and advice supplied by their military experts. As Wasfi al-Tall was to claim in a brutally honest post-mortem on the causes of the Arab military defeat in Palestine, the Arab politicians who took the decision to invade Palestine proceeded on the basis of hopelessly unrealistic assessments of their own strength and the strength of the enemy. Their estimate of the situation was influenced by the attitudes of the mob, by excessive emotionalism, by rumours and legends about the cowardice of the Jews and the heroism of the Arabs. So deficient was the estimate of the situation by those responsible, according to Tall, that it became a vehicle for self-deception rather than for combating the enemy.

Tall was contemptuously dismissive of the stories about betrayals and conspiracies that were later invented in order to explain the Arab military defeat in Palestine, on the grounds that the Arab military effort, without treason, conspiracies, and imperialist plots, was insufficient to attain victory or to prevent the disaster. It was futile, argued Tall, to seek foreign scapegoats for Arab shortcomings and misdeeds and he warned that the Arabs would bring upon themselves further disasters unless they stopped behaving like ostriches and started facing up honestly to their own weaknesses and drawing lessons from their past mistakes.[14]

It is because the Arab military effort in May 1948 was in itself inadequate and related to wider societal factors and temperamental peculiarities, and because suspicion and conflicts of interest among the Arabs themselves was so pervasive, that it would be misleading to single out Abdullah's deviousness and duplicity as the sole reason for the marked disarray in Arab League quarters on the eve of battle. Such a single-factor explanation may seem superficially plausible but it does not survive a more penetrating analysis of the kind offered by Wasfi al-Tall.

Golda Meir and Abdullah: the last meeting

The last ditch attempt to dissuade Abdullah from joining in the invasion of Palestine was made by Golda Meir while the Arab League was putting the final touches on the invasion plan in Damascus. Abdullah had already made his own last attempt to keep his country from becoming involved in the threatening conflict: through Muhammad Zubeiti, his trusted private secretary and confidant, he inquired whether the Jewish leaders would be prepared to cede to him some of the territory allotted to them by the United Nations so as to provide him with an argument to persuade the Arab world to settle for partition. The answer given to his emissary was that there could be no question of any territorial concessions and, moreover, acceptance of the United Nations borders was subject to the partition scheme being implemented peacefully. If the Arabs went to war, the Jews would no longer be bound by the UN borders and everyone would take whatever was in his power to take.

Nothing further was heard from the king after Zubeiti's return to Amman with this message. But with an Arab invasion looking ever more likely, Golda Meir pressed for another direct meeting with him before it was too late. A great deal hung in the balance: not only was the

---

[14] Asher Susser, *Between Jordan and Palestine: A Political Biography of Wasfi al-Tall* (Heb.) (Tel Aviv: Hakibbutz Hameuhad, 1983), 23–5.

Legion by far the best Arab army but, if by any remote chance it could be kept out of the conflict, the Iraqi army might not reach Palestine to participate in the attack. Ben-Gurion was of the opinion that there was nothing to be lost by trying and it was he who personally contacted Avraham Rutenberg to request an interview for Golda Meir with King Abdullah.

Rutenberg referred the request to Avraham Daskal, who immediately contacted his old friend Muhammad Zubeiti. Zubeiti thought a meeting was out of the question but after obtaining the king's agreement to see Rutenberg and Daskal, he drove them the 180 kilometres from Naharayim to his house near the royal palace in Amman. Abdullah came from the palace, where the Jewish visitors would have been recognized, to Zubeiti's house. Looking pale and sad, he complained that the Jewish Agency had waited so long before sending someone to see him and said he did not see how he could receive Mrs Meir after the Jewish atrocities in Deir Yassin and elsewhere. It took a great deal of persuasion to get him to relent, but eventually he did.

On hearing that Abdullah had agreed to see Mrs Meir, Ben-Gurion arranged for a plane to pick her up in Jerusalem, which was under siege, bring her to Tel Aviv for consultations, and then take her to Haifa whence she would proceed to Naharayim by car. In a cable Ben-Gurion informed her that she must get to the meeting urgently and that he himself preferred this arrangement to an official meeting. 'We brought Golda from Jerusalem', wrote Ben-Gurion in his diary, 'so she can travel to meet the friend. For the time being we have settled on two guidelines: (1) agreement based on the UN [resolution], (2) or mutual border rectification.' Elias Sasson was supposed to accompany Mrs Meir to the meeting with 'the friend' but for some reason failed to await her in Haifa and serve as interpreter at the meeting, and Danin went with her instead. Just before they set off on the long journey, he remarked that he thought nothing would come out of it and asked Mrs Meir why she was going, implying that the mission facing them could be dangerous as well as difficult. Her reply was that if there was the smallest chance of saving the life of one of their soldiers, she was determined to try. 'Are you afraid?' she asked. 'I have stared death in the face many times', replied Danin. 'I am not afraid. I have been summoned. It is my duty to go.'

They arrived at Daskal's house in Naharayim in the afternoon of May 10. There, to avoid arousing the suspicion of the numerous Legionnaires stationed along the road, Danin put on the traditional Arab headgear and Mrs Meir changed into the voluminous black robes worn by Arab women. Security precautions were particularly elaborate on this occasion because news of the meeting had leaked out and widespread rumours and speculations about it increased the risks of detection. Abdullah declined to come to Naharayim this time because it was too dangerous and because he could not afford to inflame any further Arab suspicions of his collusion with the Zionists. So Muhammad Zubeiti, who had run many dangerous errands for Abdullah in the past, arrived after dark to collect the visitors and drive them to his own house in Amman. Danin had been a close associate of Zubeiti over a period of several years when they had owned 'orchards in partnership on the border, selling the fruit in Palestine where prices were higher than those current in Transjordan or the neighbouring Arab countries, but despite this long association the tense silence of this particular journey to Amman was broken only on approaching one of the dozen or so Arab Legion checkpoints by Zubeiti shouting his name and being waved on.

Abdullah received the visitors cordially but he looked depressed, troubled, and nervous. Through Zubeiti he had already sent his offer: the country would remain undivided, with autonomy for the areas in which the Jews predominated. This arrangement would last one year and then the country would be joined with Transjordan. There would be one Parliament, in which the Jews would have 50 per cent of the seats, and a Cabinet in which they would also be represented. Abdullah opened the talk by asking whether they had received his offer. Mrs Meir replied affirmatively, adding that she had thought it necessary to come and meet him in person even though his offer was totally unacceptable. Abdullah talked about his desire for peace and avoiding the destruction of agriculture and industry. All along he had been for peace but now the only way to prevent war was to acept his offer. Why were the Jews in such a hurry to proclaim their state anyway?

Mrs Meir said she didn't think that a people who had waited two thousand years could be described as being in a hurry. She reminded Abdullah that they had made an agreement, and that the Jews counted on this agreement and on the long-standing friendship and mutual understanding with him. Having common enemies was one of the bases of that friendship. During the previous five months they had beaten those enemies: the power of the mufti in Palestine had declined markedly as a result of their military successes, while the foreign troops had been chased out of the country. As a result of their efforts, the road was now paved for Abdullah too as it had never been before.

Mrs Meir suggested that instead of Abdullah's new offer they should adhere to the original plan on which there was an agreement and an understanding between them. Abdullah did not deny that that was his wish, but things had happened in Palestine since, like the atrocity of

Deir Yassin. Before he had been alone, now he was one of five; he had no choice and he could not act differently.

Mrs Meir remarked that they knew he was one out of five but they always thought of him as someone who stood against the current. She also hinted that his difficulty was not only the other Arabs but the British who had already secured their position and stood to lose nothing even if he were to be defeated. Moreover, Jewish strength was not what it had been five months previously or even a month previously, and if there was war they would fight with all their strength. Abdullah accepted that they would have to repel an attack. Mrs Meir then stated that they were prepared to respect borders as long as there was peace. But in the event of war they would fight everywhere and with all their power. Again and again Abdullah repeated his warning, though not in a threatening manner. Throughout, the conversation remained friendly though he showed signs of strain and depression. He regretted the destruction and bloodshed, but he had no choice. He asked the Jews to think it over and if their reply was positive, it had to reach him before May 15. He would invite the Palestinian leaders who backed him and some of the moderate Arabs and would ask the Jews to send moderate representatives too and then the matter could be settled. Similarly, in the Cabinet there would be no extremist Arabs or Jew-haters but only moderate Arabs.

Mrs Meir reacted by saying that she did not want to delude Abdullah and therefore had to make it clear that his suggestion could not even serve as a basis for negotiations, not only would the responsible authorities not accept it but there would not be ten Jews who would lend their support to his autonomy plan. Her answer was immediate and categorical: it was out of the question. If Abdullah was going back on their agreement and if he wanted war, then they would meet after the war and after the Jewish state was established.

Abdullah said he had heard that Moshe Sharett was in France and wondered whether one of his men could meet Sharett there. Mrs Meir thought her colleague would stay in France only a short time and though he would no doubt be glad to meet, there could be no change in their position as she had stated it. On a slightly more hopeful note Abdullah proclaimed: 'We do not need America and Europe. We, the children of the Orient, must show this miracle to the world. Let us get around one table and secure the peace between us.'

Towards the end of the conversation, which lasted about an hour, the king turned to Danin and asked in a fatherly voice why he, who was also a native of the Orient, did not help him in this conversation. Danin, who up to this point had scrupulously kept to his role as interpreter, now mustered his courage and warned the king against making a fatal mistake. The king, said Danin, had no real friends in the Arab world. And he was relying on the armoured cars of the Legion just as the French had relied on the Maginot Line. The Jews could smash his armour. It would be a pity if Abdullah destroyed with his own hands what he had built with so much toil. It was not too late to change course. Abdullah replied: 'I am very sorry. It would be a shame to shed blood and cause destruction. Let us hope we shall meet and not break off the contact between us. If you see any need to come and see me after the battles start, do not hesitate to come. I shall always be glad to meet you.' 'But how will I be able to get to you?' asked Danin. 'Oh, I trust you to find a way', said Abdullah with a smile.

Before they parted, Danin warned the king to put an end to his practice of allowing his followers to kiss the hem of his garment and to take more precautions against the evil-doers who were plotting against his life. 'My good friend,' replied the astonished monarch to Danin, 'I shall not abandon the customs of my ancestors. I was born a bedouin, a free man, and I shall never become the prisoner of my own guards. Come what may, I shall not stop my subjects from showing their affection towards me.' Then he bid his visitors farewell and left.

Over dinner Zubeiti told Mrs Meir and Danin that he did not want this war and that the king did not want it either. To illustrate the depth of the king's feelings, Zubeiti said that if he had to choose between a room full of pearls and the duty to go to war or peace without the treasure, the king would have forgone the pearls and opted for peace. It was the British who were pushing him, said Zubeiti, and involving the Iraqis too, because the Iraqis had refused to sign a treaty and the British therefore wanted to send them to the front so that they would be beaten and brought to their knees. Even Abdullah's eldest son Talal, who was more radical than his father, was according to Zubeiti opposed to this war and regarded defeat as a foregone conclusion.

Zubeiti promised to continue his efforts to persuade Abdullah. But in Mrs Meir's judgement, Abdullah was so deeply involved that he was unable to retreat. In a previous conversation Abdullah had said that he had informed the Arabs that unless they put him in charge he would not touch the Palestine affair. Now he had apparently got what he wanted. Nevertheless, Mrs Meir had the feeling that he was afraid of his partners and possibly of the British as well. She thought he was well aware of his predicament in relation to the Arabs and Britain. She gained the distinct impression that he was not going forward with any great joy but because he was caught up in a web and did not know how to extricate himself.

It was nearly midnight when Mrs Meir and her escort set off on the long journey back to Naharayim. On the way they saw the Iraqi force with its field artillery and heavy equipment massing in Mafraq. The journey could have easily ended in disaster because the car driver lost his nerve and dropped his passengers a couple of miles short of their destination, leaving them to complete the trip on foot. But by around 3 o'clock in the morning they staggered into Daskal's house, and from there Mrs Meir proceeded directly to Tel Aviv to report the failure of her mission and the inevitability of invasion.[15]

A legacy of suspicion

Did the meeting between Mrs Meir and King Abdullah really end in failure? That is a question of paramount historical significance. The story of the meeting has spread far and wide and has come to be surrounded by numerous legends and misconceptions. Four decades after the event, the historian still faces a daunting task in trying to disentangle the core of hard evidence from the penumbra of tendentious interpretations and Oriental embellishments. On June 11 the palace issued an official denial that King Abdullah had met with Mrs Meir. But Kirkbride reported in response to a query from London that he had reason to believe that the lady in question did see the king on May 10 and that the proceedings consisted of both parties stating their case and agreeing to differ: 'The lady said that the Jews would accept nothing less than United Nations partition and the King said he could not go further than Jewish autonomy in an Arab state.'

To Kirkbride it seemed that the Jewish leaders had based all their plans on the assumption that Transjordan would not intervene in Palestine and since the Transjordanian army was the most effective opposition with which they had to contend, they were very cross about it. Among the Jews two different lines were taken on the subject. Haganah broadcasts said that the politicians were tricked by the king, who was the Jews' worst enemy. The politicians, on the other hand, were trying to make out that Abdullah would not be so bad if only he could be freed from British control.[16]

In Zionist historiography the meeting is usually presented as a valiant but utterly futile and unsuccessful attempt to avert the outbreak

---

[15] The foregoing account is based essentially on Golda Meir's verbal report to the 13-member Provisional State Council on 12 May 1948. ISA, *Provisional State Council: Protocols, 18 April–13 May 1948* (Heb.) (Jerusalem, 1978), 40–4. Additional information was drawn from Meir, *My Life*, 176–81; Zeev Sharef, *Three Days* (London: W. H. Allen, 1962), 72–8; Kirkbride, *From the Wings*, 21 f.; Ben-Gurion's diary, 8 May 1948; Ben-Gurion to Meir and Sasson, 8 May 1948, 2513/2, ISA; interview with Avraham Daskal; interview with Ezra Danin; record of conversation between Ezra Danin and Dr Joseph Johnson of the UN on 18 April 1962, Ezra Danin's private papers. I am grateful to Mr Danin for giving me a copy of this record, which throws some light on his relations with Muhammad Zubeiti and the meeting with Abdullah.

[16] Kirkbride to FO, 14 June 1948, FO 371/68821, PRO.

of war. Mrs Meir herself helped to propagate the view that King Abdullah broke his promise to her; that the meeting ended in total disagreement and that they parted as enemies. Quite a few Zionist leaders thought Abdullah could not be trusted, and his words to Mrs Meir were readily seized upon as evidence of treachery and betrayal on his part. In essence, the Zionist charge against Abdullah is that when the moment of truth arrived, he revoked his pledge not to attack the Jewish state and threw in his lot with the rest of the Arab world. This charge helped to sustain the legends that grew up around the 1948 war of a carefully orchestrated and monolithic all-Arab invasion plan directed at strangling the Jewish state at birth.

First- or second-hand Jewish accounts of the meeting, however, do not cast Abdullah quite so unambiguously in the role of villain and traitor reserved for him by subsequent Zionist writers. To begin with, Golda Meir's own account of her mission, given to her colleagues on the Provisional State Council shortly after her return from Amman, was nowhere as unsympathetic and unflattering about Abdullah's behaviour as the account she later wrote in her memoirs. In her first account she did not claim that the king had gone back on his promise not to attack the Jewish state. He even recognized that if the Jews were attacked they would have to repel the attackers. What he said to her was not that he no longer wished to abide by their earlier agreement but that changing circumstances made it impossible for him to carry it out to the letter. In particular, Arab pressure reduced his room for manœuvre and forced on him a change of tactics, but not the abandonment of his original scheme. Chaim Weizman said in a press conference in Paris that Mrs Meir had seen King Abdullah and received the impression that he was not anxious for war but was being subjected to foreign pressure.[17]

The most balanced and perceptive assessment of Abdullah's position was presented by Yaacov Shimoni at the meeting of the Arab Section of the Political Department of the Jewish Agency on May 13 in Jerusalem: 'His Majesty has not entirely betrayed the agreement, nor is he entirely loyal to it, but something in the middle. He will not remain faithful to the borders of 29 November, but nor would he try to conquer all our state.' An American journalist had told Shimoni that the Legion would stop at the border of the Jewish state. He was absolutely certain of this on the basis of talks with Abdullah and with Arab and British officers from the Legion. Shimoni's own view was that they had to stay with Abdullah to the end and that it was too late to change the policy and start cultivating new contacts at one minute to midnight.[18]

If at one end of the spectrum there is the Zionist contention that at

[17] FO to Amman, 14 June 1948, FO 371//68821, PRO.   [18] Documents, 789–91.

the second meeting with Mrs Meir, Abdullah reneged on the under-standing they had reached during their first meeting, at the other end of the spectrum there is the nationalist Arab contention that this meeting only served to confirm the long-standing collusion between the unpatriotic monarch and the Jewish Agency. Whereas the Zionists accused the king of turning his back on them in their hour of need and behaving like all the other Arab nationalists, the Arabs levelled at him the opposite charge of betraying the Arab cause for the sake of a cynical deal with the Zionist enemy. Thus Abdullah al-Tall, the self-appointed spokesman of Palestinian nationalism, claimed that King Abdullah had assured Mrs Meir that the Transjordanian and Iraqi armies would not cross the border laid down by the United Nations in its partition plan. According to al-Tall's far from reliable acount, one of Mrs Meir's conditions was that the king should declare peace with the Jews and refrain altogether from sending his army into Palestine. This condition was rejected because it would have manifestly contravened the unanimous decision of the Arab states to send their armies to rescue Palestine. However, alleges al-Tall, the king gave her a pledge that the Transjordanian and Iraqi armies would not go to war against the Jews but stop at the United Nations partition border. After some threats on the part of 'Golda' and warnings on the part of the king, concludes al-Tall, she bowed to the king's opinion and received a commitment from him that his armies would not attack.[19]

The one thing on which most commentators seem to agree is that sending a woman to meet an Arab king was a mistake. Abdullah himself was later to claim that if any one person was responsible for the war it was she. He even made jokes, according to Abdullah al-Tall, about the coarseness and arrogance of the Jewish woman.[20] Sir Alec Kirkbride, who thought it was a mistake for the Jews to be represented by a woman at the November 1947 meeting because of the king's old-fashioned views on the position of women, wrote off the May 1948 meeting as a completely futile exercise.[21] A number of Jewish officials also admitted with hindsight that it was an insult to send a woman to negotiate with an Arab king and that royal dignity would have been better served if someone like Moshe Sharett had undertaken the mission. Gideon Rafael regarded the mission itself as a necessary part of Ben-Gurion's strategy of deterrence, a strategy based on a correct analysis of the strength of the other side and of the role of the Legion as the crucial link in the hostile coalition facing Israel. Yet, it was a grave mistake in Rafael's view to entrust Mrs Meir with such a sensitive political mission. For all her courage and the risks she bravely took

---

[19] Tall, *The Tragedy of Palestine*, 67.   [20] Ibid.
[21] Kirkbride, *From the Wings*, 5, 21 f.

upon herself, it was absurd under the circumstances to send her to talk with Abdullah.[22]

Yehoshua Palmon, who had conveyed Mrs Meir and Danin from Haifa to Naharayim, also thought that the mission's primary purpose was to serve an ultimatum to Abdullah, to say to him 'If you join the invasion, we will take off the velvet gloves.' He was actually disappointed that there was no room for him to complete the journey to Amman because he liked cloak and dagger exploits and his success with Qawukji had whetted his appetite for more. But he was given to believe that Golda Meir was going not to negotiate with Abdullah but to warn him that the Jews would retaliate without inhibition or restraint if he lent a hand to the Arab attack on their state. That was the basic message, the rest was just window dressing. As a Muslim, argued Palmon, Abdullah could not accept Jewish sovereignty over an Arab land. He wanted to be the supreme ruler himself and used the Turkish concept of autonomy to induce the Jews to accept him in that position. From this perspective Abdullah was not opposed to the Jews building a national home for themselves in Palestine provided they recognized his claim to overlordship. In the past the Jews had refrained from telling Abdullah too bluntly that he was mistaken in his assumption because they wanted to strengthen him rather than the Husayni tendency of unrelenting opposition to the growth of a Jewish national home. But by May 1948, according to Palmon, the time had come to make it unmistakably clear that the Jews would settle for nothing less than full independence and formal sovereignty and Golda Meir was sent to disabuse him of any notion that he could impose his solution by resorting to force. Although ultimate control over the Legion was kept in Glubb's hands, Palmon considered that it did make sense to send an envoy to impress the nominal ruler with a show of Jewish strength and resolution.[23]

A clear distinction should be made between the point of a face-to-face meeting with Abdullah and the choice of a particular person to represent the Jewish side at such a meeting. While the exercise itself was not futile, the choice of Golda Meir to conduct it ranks as one of the worst blunders in the annals of Zionist diplomacy. The complex situation that had developed by the end of the mandate warranted not only resolution but political subtlety. Now whereas Mrs Meir possessed the former quality in abundance, she was totally lacking in the latter. Although she was apparently authorized to discuss mutual territorial modifications, she clung with the utmost tenacity at her meeting with Abdullah to the unnatural and arbitrary borders of the 1947 partition resolution. There was not the slightest hint of flexibility

[22] Interview with Gideon Rafael.   [23] Interview with Yehoshua Palmon.

about the posture she struck. Nor did she display any imagination or resourcefulness in devising ways of helping the king out of his predicament which would be to their mutual advantage. No Zionist could quarrel with her refusal to compromise the overriding Zionist aim of statehood for the sake of a dubious compromise with a solitary Arab ruler. But she was very prone to seeing everything in black and white and largely blind to the possibility of intermediate solutions and roundabout tactics. It should not have been beyond the realm of possibility to preserve the spirit of the November agreement by adopting new tactics—by staging mock battles, for example—to enable Abdullah to pose as a great Arab nationalist while at the same time averting a real military clash. But King Abdullah did not find in Mrs Meir a congenial partner, while she for her part judged him by the simplistic criterion of whether or not he was prepared to observe the earlier agreement between them to the letter.

Jewish military predispositions

After the hazardous journey back from Amman, Mrs Meir proceeded from Naharayim directly to the Mapai headquarters in Tel Aviv where a meeting of the party's central committee was in session. To Ben-Gurion who had been anxiously awaiting her return she scribbled a note: 'We met amicably. He is very worried and looks distraught. He did not deny that there had been talks and understanding between us about a desirable arrangement, namely, that he would take the Arab part, but now he is only one among five. This is the plan he proposed— a unitary state with autonomy for the Jewish parts, and after one year this would be one country under his rule.'

If Ben-Gurion had any shred of a hope left that Transjordan would stay out of the war, this note destroyed it finally and irrevocably. The conclusion he drew was instantaneous and unequivocal. He walked out of the meeting, rushed to the Haganah headquarters, summoned Israel Galili, the head of the National Command, and Yigael Yadin, the acting chief of staff, and demanded that they prepare all their units to advance, press on with the recapture of the road to Jerusalem and the Arab enclaves in Jewish areas, and prepare a plan to meet a general Arab invasion.

Yadin wanted to know whether they would still be bound by the partition borders if the Arabs launched a general invasion in disregard of these borders. Should they fight Abdullah if he crossed the borders of mandatory Palestine or only if he crossed the borders of the Jewish state? He also wanted to know with regard to Beersheba, which was included in the Arab state, whether they should try and capture it

immediately or not. Ben-Gurion's reply was evasive: only the Provisional State Council could decide. To Gen. David Shaltiel, the
Haganah commander in Jerusalem, wanting to mount an offensive at
the end of the mandate, Ben-Gurion replied that this too was a political
question. It was clear that they had to attack along the entire front on
zero day but Jerusalem was a special case; an attack there was liable to
antagonize the Christian world. In the evening, at another meeting to
discuss the anticipated invasion, Yadin once more raised the key
question: when and where should they meet Abdullah's forces—only
inside their own state, anywhere in Palestine, or perhaps in
Transjordan? Once again, however, Ben-Gurion declined to commit
himself to a particular line of policy in advance of the meeting of the
State Council.[24]

Ben-Gurion's belief in the inevitability of a full-scale invasion of
Palestine spearheaded by Transjordan seemed to be confirmed when
Arab Legion detachments opened an all out attack with armoured cars
and cannons on the Jewish settlement of Kfar Etzion on the morning of
May 12. Such a ferocious attack aimed at destroying a Jewish settlement could not indeed be reconciled either with Abdullah's earlier
protestations of friendship or Glubb's professed interest in avoiding
serious fighting. A number of factors, however, should be recalled to
help place the attack in its proper political context. First and foremost,
the Etzion bloc with its four Jewish settlements astride the Jerusalem–
Hebron road was in the middle of a purely Arab area and had been
assigned to the Arab state by the United Nations. Secondly, on orders
from above, the soldiers and settlers of Kfar Etzion had ambushed
passing vehicles and cut the road to stop the Arab Legion reinforcements from reaching Jerusalem during the Palmach offensive in
Katamon. Thirdly, despite their proximity to the Legion's supply line
from the Suez Canal zone to Amman, Glubb had no wish to tangle with
the Jewish forces in Kfar Etzion and had even called off an earlier
attack led by Abdullah al-Tall on May 4, ordering him to return to
base. Vowing to liquidate this troublesome Jewish enclave, Major Tall
secretly ordered a subordinate to provoke a clash with Kfar Etzion and
appeal to the commander of the Legion for help. On May 12 Tall
received the expected call from Glubb to rush reinforcements to the
unit which was falsely reported to have been trapped in a Jewish
ambush; he personally led the column which crushed the four Jewish
settlements, inflicted heavy casualties, and took 350 prisoners to
Amman.[25] For all these reasons it is misleading to regard the attack on

---

[24] Ben-Gurion's diary, 11 May 1948.
[25] Tall, *The Tragedy of Palestine*, 31–4; Pappé, 'British Foreign Policy Towards the Middle East',
37 f.

the Etzion bloc as part of a premeditated plan on the part of either the king or Glubb Pasha to engage the Jewish forces in battle before the expiry of the British mandate over Palestine.

News of the fall of the Etzion bloc reached Ben-Gurion in the middle of a crucial meeting of the State Council which was called upon to decide whether to accept the proposal for an armistice and postpone the declaration of independence or carry out the original plan of proclaiming the establishment of a Jewish state despite all the dangers, uncertainties, and international pressures. It was at this meeting that Golda Meir reported on her talk with King Abdullah and Moshe Sharett conveyed the warning he had received from General Marshall in Washington. Yadin and Galili presented a rather pessimistic appraisal of the military situation and warned that the chances of victory and defeat were equally balanced. Yadin's estimate that the Yishuv had only a 50–50 chance of survival was based on the assumption that the Yishuv would have to withstand an attack by all the Arab armies, including the Arab Legion. He totally discounted any possibility that the legion would stay out of the war. He did not even know, he was later to claim, that there were political contacts with Transjordan. The fact that Ben-Gurion did not tell him about these contacts was in Yadin's view conclusive proof that Ben-Gurion himself did not believe that there was any possibility of an understanding with Abdullah. Such an understanding would have had important operational implications and Ben-Gurion therefore would have been bound to inform Yadin. In actual fact they did not even discuss this possibility. According to Yadin, Ben-Gurion's estimate was that the clash with the Legion was inescapable.[26]

Ben-Gurion was absolutely convinced that they should proclaim independence without delay lest they miss a historic opportunity but he had the problem of convincing the waverers on the State Council. The real question, as he formulated it, was whether they had a realistic chance of resisting invasion and his assessment was that they had every prospect of success. The Etzion disaster did not shake Ben-Gurion's confidence. 'I expected such reverses', he said, 'and I fear we shall have even greater ordeals. The matter will be settled when we destroy the greater part of the Arab Legion. Then they will fall. Destruction of the enemy forces is always the determining factor in war, not the occupation of this or that point.' Ben-Gurion also argued that the attack on the Etzion bloc constituted an invasion and made the question of a truce largely academic.[27] When the vote was taken on whether to accept the truce, six voted against and four voted for. Sharett cast the deciding vote in favour of proclaiming the establishment of a Jewish state. It was

---

[26] Interview with Gen. Yigael Yadin.   [27] ISA, *Provisional State Council: Protocols.*

also decided, following Ben-Gurion's strongly expressed preference, not to indicate the borders of the new state in the declaration of independence so as to leave open the possibility of expansion beyond the United Nations borders. The name of the new state was to be Israel.

Once the historic decision had been made, attention shifted towards the operational problems of repulsing the anticipated Arab invasion. First there was a question of whether to attack the Arab Legion detachments on their way back from the Etzion bloc. The military experts were fairly evenly divided into those who favoured such an attack and those who thought it would be too risky. Ben-Gurion argued that it would be a fatal mistake to allow the Legion to leave the country or to roam freely inside it, especially as it could endanger the Jewish position in Jerusalem, and it was agreed to launch an attack from Jerusalem if adequate reinforcements could be mobilized.[28]

At four o'clock in the afternoon of May 14 Ben-Gurion read out the Declaration of Independence and proclaimed the establishment of the State of Israel. 'Its fate', he wrote laconically in his diary, 'is in the hands of the defence forces.' The fundamental differences between Ben-Gurion and the chiefs of the defence forces on the strategy to be adopted for dealing with the invasion persisted. Ben-Gurion pressed for an offensive strategy to capture various areas round the Tel Aviv–Jerusalem road in order to secure Israel's hold on Jerusalem. But he met with resistance from the General Staff on the grounds that they did not have sufficient strength to dislodge the Transjordanian forces and did not know the enemy's plans.[29] Whereas the General Staff saw the southern front as the critical one, Ben-Gurion was convinced that it was the Jerusalem front that might well determine the result of the entire campaign.

On Jerusalem there was certainly no understanding with Transjordan, nor had the subject been raised by Golda Meir at her first or second meeting with Abdullah. Under the UN plan Jerusalem was to be an international zone so there was no compelling reason to try and reach an understanding. Each side kept its thoughts and its hopes to itself. But with the collapse of the secret plan for a peaceful partition, the future of Jerusalem became a burning concern to both sides. Because he considered Jerusalem to be so vital to the Yishuv's prospects of surviving the Arab invasion, Ben-Gurion pressed for concentrating massive resources there, even at the cost of exposing the other fronts. A senior member of the General Staff calculated that a third of their forces were deployed in and around Jerusalem. Had there been an understanding with Transjordan they would not have done that; on the contrary, they would have sent more forces to the southern

[28] Ben-Gurion's diary, 13 May 1948. [29] Ben-Gurion's diary, 14 May 1948.

front. In fact, on May 15, they did the reverse, moving troops from the south for the battles in Latrun, to wrench control of the north-eastern approaches to Jerusalem from the Arab Legion.[30]

Britain and the Arab Legion

There had been many ups and downs in the relations between the Zionist movement and King Abdullah over the previous six months but by mid-May 1948 they had hit rock bottom. Among the reasons for this estrangement was the persistent Zionist distortion of Britain's intentions. The intelligence experts, working with very inadequate sources of information about policymaking in Whitehall, perpetuated the mistrust felt by the political echelon towards Britain. It was widely believed that there was a British plot against the Yishuv and that Abdullah was the tool of British imperialism and that even if he wanted to come to terms with them, the British would not let him. Ben-Gurion's great mistake, sustained by an obsessive hatred of Bevin, was in believing for so long that Britain was the main enemy. All the signals pointing to Britain's aceptance of a Jewish state, notably those conveyed by Creech Jones and Colonel Goldie, and, indeed, the desire that the Jews should co-ordinate their strategy with Abdullah, left Ben-Gurion unmoved. Glubb too was perceived as an implacable enemy and hence a willing accomplice in Bevin's machinations to frustrate the establishment of a Jewish state. All these fears, suspicions, and mis-perceptions not only poisoned Zionist–British relations but rendered difficult in the extreme the task of preserving the accord with King Abdullah.

The real indictment of British policy was that it refused to hand over authority in Palestine to the United Nations and to effect an orderly transfer of power. This, as Sir Alec Kirkbride was later to admit, was inexcusable.[31] The manner in which the withdrawal from Palestine took place was unprecedented in the history of the British Empire. But the contradictions in British policy and the doubts to which these contradictions gave rise in the minds of those most directly affected were better appreciated by British officials who served in the Middle East than by the politicians at home. A diary entry made by Sir Henry Gurney, the tough-minded chief secretary to the British administration in Palestine, was symptomatic of the frustration felt by British officials as the mandate was nearing its unhappy end:

In fact the last 30 years in this country have seen nothing but fluctuations of policy, hesitations, or no policy at all. When Monty asked me here last year

[30] Interview with Gen. Yoseph Avidar.
[31] Elizabeth Monroe interview with Kirkbride, Sept. 1959, Monroe Papers.

what was really wrong with Palestine, I said, 'Merely a lack of policy with which nobody agrees.' It is this continual surrender to pressure of one sort or another—American Jewry or Arab rebellion—that has made British policy in Palestine, with all its first-class administrative achievements, unintelligible and mistrusted by both sides.[32]

Sir Henry, who was once described by a member of UNSCOP as having 'a strong sense of superiority concealed under an icy courtesy', gave what was perhaps the supreme example of the breakdown of government in his diary entry for May 14:

The Police locked up the stores (worth over £1 million) and brought the keys to the UN, who refused to receive them. I had to point out that the UN would be responsible for the administration of Palestine in a few hours' time (in accordance with the November resolution) and that we should leave the keys on their doorstep whether they accepted them or not; which they did.[33]

Confusion was compounded in the last days of the mandate by the long-standing conflict between the Palestine administration and the British diplomatic mission in Amman. Until Transjordan received its independence Kirkbride had been subordinated to the Colonial Office in London and the high commissioner in Jerusalem, but the high commissioner continued to treat him as an underling even after his elevation to the rank of minister. Kirkbride did not give in: 'Both Cunningham and Gurney seemed to find it difficult to accept me as a genuine head of a diplomatic mission, and tended to give me instructions, which they had no right to do and which I had no intention of obeying unless I happened to agree with them.' Moreover, 'They were on the way out and did not care if the edifice of government was on the point of collapse, but I was to stay on and I was anxious to save something from the wreck.'[34]

The foreign secretary in London bore a large share of the blame for the elephantine clumsiness and for the sheer bloody-mindedness which characterized the British withdrawal from Palestine and which left such an unpleasant taste in the mouths of Arabs as well as Jews. Bevin was personally guilty of duplicity in pretending to favour the last minute American efforts to secure a truce while working for partition and the enlargement of Transjordan at the expense of the Palestinian Arabs. But there is precious little evidence in the official British documents of this period to support the Zionist charge that Britain deliberately engineered disorder and chaos in order to frustrate partition and permit the Arabs to crush the Jews upon withdrawal of the British forces. Arthur Creech Jones, who as colonial secretary had

---

[32] Sir Henry Gurney's diary, 25 Mar. 1948.   [33] Sir Henry Gurney's diary, 13 May 1948.
[34] Kirkbride, *From the Wings*, 11.

worked very closely with Ernest Bevin over Palestine, insisted most emphatically that 'we had absolutely no desire to create chaos in Palestine on our withdrawal in the hope that the Arabs would win the struggle. It is an evil suspicion on the part of those who have made it.'[35] Indeed, whatever the faults of the manner in which Britain surrendered the mandate, and they are many, the historian who examines the documentary record is bound to conclude that the theory of an officially instigated 'Operation Chaos' remains unproven.

Machiavellism in British policy there emphatically was, but Machiavellism of a different kind from that usually attributed to Britain by her critics. The real Machiavellism consisted of conspiring directly with Abdullah and indirectly with the Jews to abort the birth of a Palestinian Arab state. Although the Zionists habitually accused Britain of partisanship in favour of the Arabs, the Palestine Arabs firmly believed that Britain's sympathies lay with the Zionists and saw the creation of the State of Israel as the culmination of the process that had begun with the Balfour Declaration. Particularly sinister in the eyes of the Palestinians was the combination of the United Nations partition resolution of November 1947 and the British withdrawal six months later. As Walid Khalidi has argued: 'Since the UN had not provided for an international force to implement its resolution, the British decision to withdraw was an invitation to both sides to fight it out. Given the balance of power inside Palestine, which was crushingly in favour of the Zionists—a fact of which all parties were well aware— the British withdrawal was an open invitation for a Zionist military take-over of the country.' Moreover, British presence in the remaining six months of the Mandate 'acted virtually as a shield against external Arab help behind which the Zionist military forces could conduct their business'. Even the pattern of British withdrawal, argues Khalidi, increased the fragmentation of the Arab scene while it furthered the cumulative consolidation and extension of Jewish power.[36]

The real aim behind British policy, however, was the consolidation and extension of Abdullah's power. Ernest Bevin had never accepted the case for creating a separate Palestinian Arab state. Time and again he returned to the idea that if Palestine had to be partitioned, the Arab area should not be left to stand on its own but should be united with Transjordan.[37] British hostility to Hajj Amin al-Husayni and to the idea of an independent Palestinian state was a constant and important feature of British policy during the period 1947–9.

[35] Creech Jones to Elizabeth Monroe, 23 Oct. 1961, box 32, file 6, Creech Jones Papers.
[36] Khalidi, *From Haven to Conquest*, p. lxxvi.
[37] Sir Harold Beeley, 'Ernest Bevin and Palestine' (unpublished text of the George Antonius Lecture, St Antony's College, Oxford, 14 June 1983).

In official British circles, such a state was almost invariably referred to as a 'mufti state' and as such met with resistance and even revulsion. On the other hand, in those same circles, Abdullah, as we have seen, occupied a special position as 'Mr Bevin's little king'. With varying degrees of enthusiasm, the makers of British imperial policy concluded that the annexation of the Arab part of Palestine to Abdullah's kingdom was, from their point of view, the best available option for filling the power vacuum they were about to leave behind them. Their dilemma was that if this 'born land-grabber', as Sir John Troutbeck had called him, cast his beady eye on Jewish territory and used the Arab Legion to grab it, Britain herself would be held to acount at the United Nations. Conversely, if Abdullah stopped at the borders of the Jewish state, Britain's prestige and influence in the rest of the Arab world would suffer and she would be accused of selling out Palestine to the Jews.

Of the two scenarios the former was more worrying, especially in its implications for Anglo-American co-operation; hence the hope that Abdullah would not fall foul of the United Nations. To this end an understanding between Abdullah and the Jews was in fact highly desirable. On May 8, Kirkbride was guardedly optimistic that open warfare between the Arab Legion and the Jews could be avoided. For Bevin's top secret information he added that 'there have been recent Transjordan contacts with the Jewish Agency and Haganah which indicate that the Jews too do not wish to clash with the Arab Legion. The danger is that some unforeseen incident will at the crucial moment bring about a general battle which neither side wants.' Unless and until open warfare broke out, Kirkbride thought it would be a mistake to take any action to deprive the Arab Legion of its British officers. He suggested that combat officers must accompany their units into the Arab areas of Palestine. Only departure from the scheme put by Abul Huda to Bevin in London that there should be no aggression against the Jewish areas could justify, in Kirkbride's view, the withdrawal of British officers. Clearly, such a departure was considered improbable: 'In spite of statements made for publicity purposes, the intentions of both King and the Prime Minister remain basically as explained to you. It is not possible however in the present circumstances for them to indicate to the Arab world that they propose in effect to accept partition.'[38]

Bevin attached great importance to the recent contacts between the Transjordanian authorities and the Jews. He brought Kirkbride's report to the attention of the minister of defence on May 13, adding in confirmation that the Jewish Agency had informed Marshall that there

---

[38] Kirkbride to FO, 8 May 1948, FO 371/68852, PRO.

had been negotiations between the Arab Legion and the Haganah which had been conducted by a British officer of the Arab Legion. 'It is understood', continued Bevin, 'that the object of these top secret negotiations is to define the areas of Palestine to be occupied by the two forces.' In a highly revealing passage Bevin added: 'I am reluctant to do anything which might prejudice the success of these negotiations which appear to aim at avoiding actual hostilities between the Arabs and the Jews. Since their conduct, and no doubt also their implementation, seem to depend to a considerable extent on British officers serving with the Arab Legion, I feel we ought not to withdraw the latter prematurely.'[39]

For this reason Bevin agreed with Kirkbride that they should wait on events: 'In the event of hostilities breaking out between the Arab Legion and the Jewish State, as a result of a Transjordanian attack on the Jewish State within the frontiers laid down by the Assembly, we shall of course have to order all regular British officers to withdraw from and remain outside Palestine but if hostilities do not in fact occur, there seems actually to be advantage in leaving these officers in their present positions.' Bevin felt, however, that they should be able to act quickly in the event of hostilities. So while agreeing to let the British officers remain, he asked Kirkbride to make arrangements for such instructions to reach all officers concerned with the least possible delay, should it become necessary to issue them.[40]

Not only was Bevin resigned to the establishment of a Jewish state but, ironically, he did what he could to ensure that it would not be attacked by Transjordan. Far from plotting to unleash the Arab Legion against the Jewish state, Bevin took some pains to ensure that hostilities would not break out. Bevin's motives for deciding to keep the British officers at their posts and allowing them to accompany their units into the Arab parts of Palestine were in fact the exact reverse of the motives attributed to him by his Zionist and pro-Zionist opponents. It was not in order to lead the Transjordanian forces into battle that Bevin needed the British officers but in order to restrain them and, more particularly, in order to reach and enforce an accord with the Haganah. If there was no follow up to Colonel Goldie's approach to the Haganah, it was not due to lack of interest on the part of Bevin but to ineptitude or indifference on the part of the Haganah.

The Zionist charge that Bevin wanted a war and gave the Arabs encouragement and arms to attack Israel represents the exact opposite of the historical truth. The crisis in Palestine coincided with the start of the European Recovery Programme under the Marshall Plan, which

[39] Bevin to secretary of defence, 13 May 1948, FO 800/477, PRO.
[40] FO to Amman, 14 May 1948, FO 371/68852, PRO.

depended on a steady flow of oil from the Middle East to Europe. It also coincided with the Western confrontation with the Soviets in Berlin which threatened to turn the Cold War into a hot war. To encourage hostilities in the Middle East at such a critical juncture in East–West relations would have been sheer madness on Bevin's part.[41]

Glubb Pasha, out of a realistic appraisal of the balance of forces, was fully committed to the policy of restraint. He was in no mood to roll the dice and risk losing everything in a fight to the finish with the Haganah. The gradual slide to chaos underlined to him the importance of preserving his tiny force for subduing the Palestinians on the West Bank and as an adjunct in future negotiations with the other side. As the message he had sent with Goldie to the Haganah demonstrated, Glubb was anxious to avoid an appeal to arms. But Glubb had his own contacts on the other side and he used them to explore the possibility of negotiations. His contacts were Jewish businessmen connected with the Palestine Potash Company who were anxious to ensure that their works on the north end of the Dead Sea would not be wrecked by war. Although he had few illusions he was willing to clutch at any straw.[42]

On May 13, the day after the Arab Legion reduced the Etzion bloc to rubble, Glubb met Moshe Novomeysky, the director of the company, and offered a truce covering the works and nearby hotel and to guarantee their protection provided all the Haganah personnel were withdrawn and only sufficient guards retained to prevent pilfering. Novomeysky said he would welcome such an arrangement but he would have to obtain the assent of certain unspecified Jewish authorities. No reply came from Novomeysky but on May 21 the works were abandoned with some store houses in flames and some of the machinery damaged.[43] As Novomeysky had told Glubb, the men with the guns were now in control.

Even more revealing of Glubb's determination to avoid war was his refusal to make any serious preparations for the defence of Jerusalem. Appalled by the low level of military preparations on the Arab side regarding arms, ammunition, and training, Abdullah al-Tall contacted Glubb repeatedly and sought permission to leave at least one company of the Arab Legion in Jerusalem in order to hold strategically important bases, encourage and help the Palestinian irregulars, and deter the Jews from trying to break into the Arab quarters. Glubb resisted these

[41] Monroe, *Britain's Moment in the Middle East*, 159 f., 169 f.; Bullock, *Ernest Bevin*, 594; Avi Shlaim, *The United States and the Berlin Blockade 1948-1949: A Study in Crisis Decision-Making* (Berkeley: University of California Press, 1983), 198, 212–15; id., 'Britain, the Berlin Blockade and the Cold War', *International Affairs* 60/1 (1983-4), 1–14.

[42] Lunt, *Glubb Pasha*, 136.

[43] Kirkbride to Bevin, 14 May 1948, FO 800/488; Kirkbride to Burrows, 7 June 1948, FO 816/123, PRO.

requests, saying that His Majesty did not agree to leave any soldiers in
Jerusalem because the Arab League wanted to spare the city and had
excluded it from its plans for operations by the Arab armies. In reply
Tall suggested that they leave one company dressed like the Palestinian
irregulars so as to avoid detection by the British and the Americans.
But Glubb did not yield and on the evening of May 13 removed the last
soldier from Jerusalem, 'leaving the city at the mercy of the Zionist
gangs'.

The reason given by Glubb for withdrawing the army from Palestine
was that the British government had ordered the withdrawal before
May 15 in accordance with the promise of the high commissioner to the
Security Council. Tall recalls this fact as evidence for his claim that
'The Arab Legion was a British division stationed in the heart of the
Arab world.' The Arab Legion was withdrawn from Palestine or, more
precisely, from the important and sensitive parts of Palestine. Some
units remained in the parts allotted to the Arabs in the partition
resolution and this fact is adduced by Tall as further evidence of the
plot hatched by Britain to attach the Arab parts of Palestine to
Transjordan. Tall gives a detailed list of the location of all the units of
the Arab Legion on the evening of May 13. From this list it is evident
that Glubb did not leave any Arab Legion troops in Palestine, except in
those areas allotted to the Arabs by the United Nations.[44]

Glubb Pasha was really an imperial proconsul, for all his insistence
on having served not Britain but the Hashemite dynasty. This is not to
say that he was disloyal to King Abdullah, but his primary loyalty was
to Britain. Odd as it may seem, on most important political matters, the
Arab potentate and his British general held similar views and when
differences arose, they were rarely pressed to the point of an open rift.
Regarding Palestine, the two men were united by a common purpose,
by a common strategy, and by a secret agreement that bound both to
the British foreign secretary. With perfect sincerity Glubb could
therefore argue that by accepting the partition of Palestine and seeking
to avoid a bloody war, he was not furthering the interests of the British
Empire at the expense of Transjordan but acting in the best interest of
both countries.

On the brink

While sharing the general Arab feeling of moral outrage over Jewish
encroachment in Palestine, Glubb contrasted the realism of Abdullah
with the irresponsibility and incompetence of the other Arab leaders:

The Arabs had to a great extent been deluded by their own enthusiasm. Fond

[44] Tall, *The Tragedy of Palestine*, 35–9.

of studying and retailing in public the story of the Arab conquests thirteen centuries ago, they believed themselves to be a great military people, and regarded the Jews as a nation of shopkeepers . . . The Arab governments did immense harm to the cause of the Palestine Arabs, because they encouraged them to be defiant, and when it came to violence, they failed.

Only King Abdullah and Jordan were in a position to take a balanced view. They were near enough to know the extent and thoroughness of the Jewish preparations. They were in sufficiently close touch with the Arabs to know their inefficiency. One of the major causes of the Arab failure in 1948 was their unwillingness to face facts. Not only did they fail to study the potential military strengths of both sides, but they accused of treachery any man with the courage to speak the unpalatable truth. King Abdullah always possessed the moral courage to say what he thought. He deprecated the idea of fighting and was immediately covered with bitter reproaches, and charged with treachery in the most opprobious terms.[45]

Given his low opinion of the Arab politicians and of the combat ability of the other Arab armies, Glubb was troubled by the growing militancy exhibited by King Abdullah in his public statements. To a large extent this militancy was inspired by universal Arab clamour for immediate military action and by the appeals for help from the Palestinian Arabs. To cover up his own fears, Abdullah resorted to increasingly bellicose public statements—statements which were interpreted by the Jewish Agency as a declaration of war. But to some extent Abdullah was the victim of his own rhetoric. He came to see himself as the protector of the Palestine Arabs and was overcome by a sense of mission to uphold Arab honour by meeting the Zionist challenge head-on. If he were to evade the challenge, to disappoint the widespread hopes that had come to rest on him personally, he was sure to be denounced as a traitor and might end up by losing his throne. The risks of resorting to military action to defend Arab land and honour were great but the risks of inaction seemed scarcely less so.

Arab pressures on King Abdullah to fight the Jews were mounting at an alarming pace. The centre of gravity of Arab policy in Palestine had shifted decisively from the Palestine Arabs under the mufti of Jerusalem to the Arab states loosely gathered in the League under the leadership of an Egyptian secretary-general. On May 12, Abdullah's foreign minister returned from Cairo with a message from King Farouk promising Egyptian intervention in Palestine after the end of the mandate and offering to send Egyptian staff officers to Amman to co-ordinate a plan. This message temporarily dispelled Abdullah's caution and the politicians in Amman started wildly discussing plans for action after the end of the mandate.[46]

[45] Glubb, *A Soldier with the Arabs*, 78 f.
[46] Kirkbride to FO, 12 May 1948, FO 371/68372, PRO.

This message from Cairo amounted to a reversal of Egypt's and the Arab League's decision not to send regular armies into Palestine but confine themselves to concentrating troops on the border and extending help to the Arab Liberation Army and Palestinian guerrilla forces. King Farouk personally took this decision which upset the Arab League's strategic consensus and forced the other Arab states to follow suit by sending their regular armies into Palestine. The decision arose out of a growing realization that King Abdullah was determined to send his army into Palestine at the end of the mandate whether the Arab states agreed or resisted, and whether they participated in the invasion or remained on the sidelines. It was also clear to the Egyptian and the other Arab leaders that whatever the reason given for the entry of the Arab Legion into Palestine, the ultimate intention would be to obtain new territory for King Abdullah. Many suspected that Abdullah would not try to conquer the whole of Palestine by force of arms but would try to reach—and had perhaps already reached—an agreement with the Jews for sharing the spoils. Here lies one of the principal reasons for the reversal of Egypt's earlier stand and the decision taken against the advice of the military experts to send the Egyptian army into Palestine. An invasion by Abdullah and the partition of Palestine between him and the emergent Jewish state, regardless of whether accomplished peacefully or as a result of armed conflict, would have dealt a death blow to the vision of Arab unity, to Egypt's hegemonial aspirations, and to Egypt's prestige in the Islamic world. A desire to prevent a unilateral invasion and the conquest and annexation of Palestine was accordingly one of Egypt's primary war aims and a major factor in forcing her government to decide at the last minute on the dispatch of the Egyptian army to Palestine.[47]

Azzam Pasha had his own suspicions that the imminent redeployment of the Arab Legion in Palestine was intended to serve Abdullah's private interests rather than pan-Arab ones. On May 13, Azzam arrived in Amman to see if the Transjordanian authorities could be induced to play the part assigned to them by the Arab League planners. He informed the authorities that the Arab League had decided to fight and that the Egyptian army would invade Palestine. 'This announcement', Glubb was later to claim, 'destroyed King Abdullah's plan of an agreement with the Jewish state on the lines of the partition plan.'

In the course of discussions with Glubb Pasha it emerged that the secretary-general's concept of war was hopelessly naïve and impractical. Glubb could not be impressed by the fact that the Arab League had decided to fight without even asking how many men they had and how

[47] Yaacov Shimoni, 'The Arabs and the Approaching War with Israel, 1945–1948' (Heb.), *Hamizrah Hehadash* 47/3 (1962), 191–211.

many constituted the enemy. According to him the forces engaged by the Arab League comprised 10,000 soldiers from Egypt, 4,500 Arab Legion troops, and 3,000 each from Syria and Iraq, giving a total of 20,500. The enemy forces were estimated by Glubb at 60,000.[48]

Azzam surprised Glubb even more by offering him the post of commander-in-chief of all the Arab armies in Palestine. Both Glubb and Kirkbride were convinced that the offer was made in bad faith and that none of the other Arab governments would consent to place their troops under the command of a British officer, even if he was technically the servant of the Transjordanian government. They suspected that the hidden idea behind the offer was to prepare a scapegoat for future failures. A British commander-in-chief could be disregarded if the operations went well but would provide a ready-made scapegoat if the war ended in defeat. Anyway, Glubb politely declined the honour. The only positive result of Azzam's visit was the payment of a sum of £250,000 to the Transjordanian government out of an Arab League war chest of nearly £4 million. Azzam presented the payment as the first instalment of a larger sum of up to £3 million from the same source, but in the event he did not honour the promise to pay the balance. Having been rebuffed when he asked the Transjordanian prime minister for supplementary financial allocations to meet the cost of fighting a war, Glubb was obviously grateful for small mercies.[49]

Azzam's extraordinary conduct reflected the inability of the Arab League to choose between war and its sacrifices or peace and its compromises. The utterly irresponsible and unprofessional manner in which Azzam approached the conflict over Palestine emerged again during his meeting with Kirkbride. When they had met five days earlier his mood had been more subdued and he had said that it was necessary to do something to re-establish the prestige of the Arab world and to bring the Jews to a reasonable state of mind after which the negotiation of a settlement might be possible. He even hinted that a reduced Jewish state might be accepted if it took the form of an act of generosity on the part of the Arabs after they had re-established their position.[50] This was a remarkable change from the earlier objective of occupying the whole of Palestine and making it an independent Arab state.

Now, however, after much havering, Azzam stood up, struck a pose and said dramatically: 'It is my duty to announce to you the intention of the Arab armies to march into Palestine tomorrow at midnight.' Kirkbride retorted that the news did not surprise him. Azzam went on

---

[48] John Bagot Glubb, *The Changing Scenes of Life: An Autobiography* (London: Quartet Books, 1983), 142 f.

[49] Glubb, *A Soldier with the Arabs*, 82–5; Kirkbride, *From the Wings*, 22–4.

[50] Kirkbride to FO, 8 May 1948, FO 816/119, PRO.

to enumerate the strengths of the various Arab armies available for the invasion; when asked for the size of the Jewish forces, he waved his hands and said: 'It does not matter how many there are. We will sweep them into the sea.' On being told that when considering a military problem it was normal to take into account the courses open to the enemy as well as those open to oneself, Azzam became peevish and the meeting ended on a frosty note. To Kirkbride Azzam seemed to be suffering from acute anxiety, though in public, like other Arab politicians, he affected to be utterly confident about the outcome of the pending conflict.

To Kirkbride's dismay, Transjordanian politicians were also infected by the sudden surge of Arab war psychosis. He experienced a feeling of helpless horror in much the same way as a bystander watching an impending motor accident knows he can do nothing to prevent it.[51] King Abdullah was thrown off-balance by the cacophony of Arab voices clamouring for the liberation of Palestine. Even the sensible and level-headed prime minister, who rarely took a step unless it had the blessing of the British, appeared to throw all caution to the winds and to be resigned to letting events take their own course.

On May 15, the day after the mandate ended, Kirkbride reported to London that for no better reason than that which existed for the recent collapse of morale, the Arabs were now full of optimism and in no mood to listen to advice. 'A reverse in the operations now being undertaken by the regular Arab armies would doubtless dispel this feeling in a matter of hours and advantage should be taken of such an occasion to preach moderation. The present is not the moment.' In an informal talk with Abul Huda, Kirkbride warned him that if Transjordan went beyond the plan regarding the Arab areas of Palestine, His Majesty's government would have to reconsider their subsidy and the loan of British officers to the Arab Legion. Abul Huda gave him an opening by forecasting total Jewish defeat within a fortnight.

Abul Huda took the warning in good part and said that while he and the king adhered basically to their original intentions, it would be impossible for Transjordan to stop at the frontier of the Jewish state if the other Arab armies were sweeping all before them. In such an event (which Kirkbride interposed was unlikely) Abul Huda promied he would spare them the embarrassment by releasing the British officers concerned beforehand. If the subsidy was withheld, Transjordan would just have to beg for funds from the other Arab states.[52]

In his memoirs, Sir Alec Kirkbride, who had himself played a role alongside the legendary T. E. Lawrence in instigating the Arab Revolt

---

[51] Kirkbride, *From the Wings*, 23–5.
[52] Kirkbride to Bevin, 15 May 1948, FO 800/488, PRO.

against the Ottoman Empire and had recorded with considerable literary grace his early experiences in *A Crackle of Thorns*,[53] gives a colourful eye-witness account of the opening shot in the 1948 Arab–Israeli war:

At a few minutes before the hour of midnight on May 14–15th, 1948, King Abdullah and members of his personal staff stood at the eastern end of the Allenby Bridge across the river Jordan waiting for the mandate to expire officially. They need not have waited because the British personnel had already gone. At twelve o'clock precisely the King drew his revolver, fired a symbolical shot into the air and shouted the word, 'forward'. The long column of Jordanian troops which stretched down the road behind the bridge, already had the engines of their cars ticking over and, as they moved off at the word of command, the hum of their motors rose to a roar. They passed through Jericho and went up the ridgeway which had been prepared for them and, when daylight came, the first regiment was in position on the Ramallah ridge which was their objective in the Judean highlands. Other units moved up the Wadi Fara into the heart of the Samaria district.[54]

As the troops marched into Palestine, the politicians of the Arab League continued their backstage manœuvres, labyrinthine intrigues, and sordid attempts to stab each other in the back—all in the name of the highest pan-Arab ideals. Politics did not end when war started but was inextricably mixed with it from the moment the first shot was fired until the guns finally fell silent and beyond. On May 15 an event took place which presaged much of what was to follow and exposed the lengths to which Arab politicians were prepared to go in their attempts to outwit their partners. King Abdullah, whose own skills lay decidedly in the realm of politics rather than that of warfare, received a phone call from Damascus. The conversation which ensued is described by the king in his memoirs:

Damascus called Amman, saying that it was doing so because of certain thoughts which President al-Quwwalti (who at the time was being visited by Arab League Secretary General Azzam Pasha) wished to express. The message referred to the necessity of refraining from advancing into Palestine and of providing the Palestinians with all possible arms and funds, and promised that if the Arab uprising actually got under way and needed effective assistance such aid would then be given.

Because of Azzam Pasha's presence in Damascus I was not sure at the time whether this really had been suggested to Damascus by Egypt or whether it was due to some distrust of me which had arisen in their minds and aroused a desire to discover my true intentions. At any rate, it was a moment that touched my soul with apprehension and anxiety, for the Arab Legion was

[53] Alec Seath Kirkbride, *A Crackle of Thorns* (London: John Murray, 1956).
[54] Kirkbride, *From the Wings*, 28.

engaged in a violent struggle for Jerusalem and had advanced to the coastal plain in the vicinity of Bab al-Wad, Lydda, and al-Ramlah on one hand, and Tulkarm and al-Affulah on the other. My answer was a flat rejection of this strange proposal and I requested to speak to the Secretary General of the League himself, who protested that my suspicions were entirely unfounded. They naturally agreed with me immediately as to the necessity of persevering in our course, but added by way of excuse that the state of preparation did not permit assistance to other fronts.[55]

The die was cast. It was too late for second thoughts. Once the invasion had been set in motion, it could not be reversed by a mere telephone call from one Arab capital to another. If King Abdullah's relations with his fellow Arab leaders had sunk to one of their lowest points, his contact with the Jewish Agency had been severed altogether. At this critical juncture when Britain had finally relinquished the mandate over Palestine, the secret agreement which Abdullah had concluded with Ernest Bevin through the good offices of his Palestinian-born prime minister seemed at the point of being overwhelmed by the momentum of the invasion and by the popular Arab clamour for doing battle with the Zionists and liberating the whole of Palestine.

The Jews were in a similarly truculent and uncompromising mood; they had proclaimed their independent state and they were determined to fight for it, come what may. It was an ultimatum that Mrs Meir had gone to give King Abdullah, not sympathy or help in overcoming his inter-Arab problems. After Golda Meir's return from her mission, the Jewish Agency used its contacts in Washington to induce President Truman, who had already decided to recognize the Jewish state as soon as it was proclaimed, to warn Abdullah against invasion.[56]

The Hashemite–Zionist accord, which had been thirty years in the making, abruptly dissolved in bitter recriminations. Five Arab armies were on the move, dashing the hope of the peaceful partition of Palestine that lay at the heart of that accord. Popular sentiment throughout the Arab world proved more powerful than either the assurances conveyed to Mr Bevin or the royal promises that had earlier been expressed to Mrs Meir. As the soldiers took charge on both sides, the prospects for salvaging anything from the ruins of the Hashemite–Zionist accord looked at best uncertain.

[55] Abdullah, *My Memoirs Completed*, 20 f.

[56] Lowenthal to Clark, 11 May 1948, George Elsey's Notes of White House Meeting on 12 May 1948 and memorandum for the President, 14 May 1948, Clark M. Clifford Papers, Harry S. Truman Library, Independence, Missouri.

8

THE INVASION

Ben-Gurion's grand strategy

There have been countless studies of the military operations of the 1948 Arab–Israeli war but very few writers have studied seriously the politics of that war. One notable exception to the general tendency to dwell on the military course of events in 1948 while paying insufficient attention to the political objectives of the principal participants is a book written by a highly controversial Israeli expert on strategy, Dr Israel Ber.

Ber was born in Austria, studied literature and philosophy at the University of Vienna, fought with the international brigade during the civil war in Spain and joined the Haganah in 1940. With the outbreak of war in 1948, he became one of the principal aides to the head of the Operations Branch of the Israel Defence Forces (IDF), General Yadin. After the war, as a lieutenant-colonel, he was placed at the head of the planning and operations division of the IDF General Staff. But when thwarted in his ambition to become deputy chief of staff, he left the army and joined the left-wing party Mapam, which was pro-Soviet in those days. In 1953 Ber switched his political allegiance from Mapam to Mapai and began to extol the leadership of David Ben-Gurion of whom he had been highly critical in the past. With Ben-Gurion's support he became the semi-official historian of the IDF. He had a secretary and an office in the Ministry of Defence and a free access to the IDF archives. In the late 1950s he once again became critical of Ben-Gurion's leadership and particularly of his close alliance with the west. He began to meet with Soviet diplomats and to give them information about the situation in Israel as well as extracts from Ben-Gurion's diary to which he had access in connection with his historical work on the War of Independence. In 1961 Ber was arrested and sentenced to fifteen years' imprisonment for his contacts with the agents of a foreign power. It was in prison that Ber wrote his book *Israel's Security: Yesterday, Today, Tomorrow* and it was in prison that he died in 1966. 'My actions in the years 1957–1961', wrote Ber in the Preface, 'were guided by the conviction that if Israel's foreign and defence policy is not changed, another historic catastrophe would be inescapable.'[1] His chapter on the 1948 war is thus part of a more comprehensive, and polemical, critique of Ben-Gurion's foreign and defence policy. Ber's own controversial career certainly casts some doubt on the objectivity and intellectual integrity of his analysis. But the fact that he had a personal and an ideological axe to grind does not entirely invalidate his analysis. His book is biased and inaccurate but it contains many original ideas and penetrating insights.

Ber argues that the final balance-sheet of the Jewish side in the 1948 war was determined not by the military capability of the IDF but by the political objectives of the man who directed the Jewish forces—David Ben-Gurion. Ber dwells at great length on the contrast between Ben-Gurion's declared political objectives and his actual objectives as they emerge from his direction of the war effort. In his speeches Ben-Gurion consistently called for resistance to imperialism, peaceful accommodation between Israel and the Arabs, an orientation on the progressive and revolutionary forces in the Arab world, and neutrality on the international stage. But his actions and the ideas that determined the strategy of the war are said to have their roots in the policy of the Jewish Agency during the decade from 1936 to 1946: striving for an alliance with Britain, joining the Western camp and an orientation on Arab feudalism.

Ben-Gurion's Big Plan, as Ber calls it, was based on the assumption that the British Empire in the Middle East would survive and that if it could be demonstrated that Zionism could not be destroyed, the pragmatists in Whitehall would try to turn the existence of the Jewish state to their advantage. Israel's war leader was prepared to facilitate Britain's continuing rule over the Middle East but on his own terms, which included modification of the original partition plan and, above all, firm control over Jewish Jerusalem and the approaches to it. In exchange, Ben-Gurion was ready to reach an agreement with Britain's chief agent among the Arabs, King Abdullah, and give the latter part of the area allotted by the United Nations to the Arabs as his reward for the deal. From the outset, claims Ber, the Big Plan—reconciliation with Britain through an agreement with Abdullah—constituted Ben-Gurion's real objective rather than his pronouncements in favour of non-alignment, solidarity with the Arab revolution against imperialism, and peace in the Semitic region. Once the Jewish state was an accomplished fact and the conditions for realizing his Big Plan developed in the course of the first truce, Ben-Gurion adopted two different

[1] Israel Ber, *Israel's Security: Yesterday, Today, Tomorrow* (Heb.) (Tel Aviv: Amikam, 1966), 21.

lines of action: a limited strategy towards his rival–partner Abdullah, and a strategy of defeating the rest of the Arab countries, especially Egypt.

To Abdullah, Ber similarly attributes two different strategies: one towards his official Arab allies who were in fact his rivals and one towards the official opponent who gradually became an ally—Israel. Abdullah's principal objective in the context of the first strategy was to prevent the Egyptians and the Syrians from establishing a permanent presence in Palestine. To this end he changed the invasion plan worked out by the Arab League in Damascus, did his best to disrupt any attempt at a co-ordinated Arab war effort, and took steps to disband Qawukji's Arab Liberation Army. The evolution of Abdullah's strategy towards his allies–rivals was linked to the second strategy of trying to co-ordinate his plans with those of the Jewish leader.

Ber identifies four distinct phases in the relations between the two rulers. First there were the contacts in April and May 1948 that nearly led to a complete and prior understanding between the two sides. But the dialectics of the situation produced exactly the opposite result. The danger of an agreement between Tel Aviv and Amman, and of Hashemite expansion resulting from this agreement, pushed the reluctant Arab countries along the adventurous path of invasion. This created another paradoxical constellation: the Israeli and Transjordanian war leaders threw their forces into bloody battles for the sake of objectives that they could have attained, and indeed planned to attain, round the conference table. It was a phase of tension and mistrust between the two war leaders with each suspecting the other of an all-out strategy instead of a strategy of deliberate restraint. A new phase, the third, was opened with the renewal of hostilities after the first truce. During this phase both sides supplied convincing proof that these suspicions were unfounded and turned their mutual restraint increasingly into a complementary strategy. This situation lasted until the end of 1948.[2]

In short, Ber puts forward a double thesis: collusion between Abdullah and Ben-Gurion in a limited strategy for the eastern front of the Jewish state and, secondly, the presentation of this collusion as a form of partnership within a British imperial framework.

According to Ber, the principal actors in the drama of 1947–9, the Zionist labour leader and the bedouin sharif, grasped the crucial importance of the holy city of Jerusalem for their respective 'big plans'. On the one hand, no Jewish state would be viable, from either the geopolitical or the moral point of view, without Jerusalem as its capital. On the other hand, Abdullah was convinced that the prestige of being

[2] Ibid. 125–35.

the guardian of the Holy Places of Jerusalem was essential for realizing his Hashemite dreams. Consequently, from the very start the two parties had a supreme interest in common: opposition to the UN internationalization plan. Both were sufficiently shrewd to realize that total victory in the battle for Jerusalem could only bring in its wake a total political defeat. Ben-Gurion understood that forces in the Christian world would oppose Jewish sovereignty over the Holy Sepulchre, the Al-Aksa Mosque and the Dome of the Rock, just as Abdullah understood that he could neither destroy nor include in his kingdom the 100,000 Jews of Jerusalem.

The only alternative to the internationalization of Jerusalem to which both sides could agree was partition. In the context of partition the logical aim for the Jews was to secure the new city and a firm corridor linking it to the coastal plain, while the Transjordanian aim was to secure the Old City inside the walls and complete control over the routes leading to it: the Jericho road in the east, the Ramallah road in the north, the Bethlehem–Hebron road in the south. Had the early assumptions about a comprehensive settlement by peaceful means proved realistic, these aims could have been attained by negotiations. But since the course of events, according to Ber, imposed on Ben-Gurion and Abdullah an armed conflict against their will, the Jerusalem front became the touchstone of the limited and then complementary strategy of the two rivals.[3]

The part of Ber's thesis that can most swiftly be disposed of concerns the place of the British Empire in Ben-Gurion's putative Big Plan. Ber's repeated assertions that Ben-Gurion was willing to offer concessions and privileges to the British so that Israel might be fitted into the imperial order in the Middle East are no substitute for evidence. All the available evidence suggests that Ben-Gurion was not prepared to even consider the extension of the mandate by ten days, that he jealously guarded Israel's independence when it was finally achieved, and that he was to remain totally uncompromising on the subject of Israeli sovereignty. It is true that Ben-Gurion underestimated the speed with which British power was declining after the war, not least in the Middle East. It is also true that he was anxious to avoid an armed clash with British forces and was indeed to lay it down as one of the basic tenets of his security doctrine that Israel should only go to war against an Arab country when assured of the backing of a Great Power. Equally, Ben-Gurion had no ideological inhibitions about collaboration with 'imperialist' powers against 'progressive' Arab regimes, as the Suez affair was to demonstrate. But in 1948 Ben-Gurion was bent on consolidating Israel's independence, defending it against real and

[3] Ber, *Israel's Security*, 145 f.

imagined British machinations and preventing Britain's re-entry through the back door.

The part of Ber's thesis that deserves to be taken more seriously concerns the complex and paradoxical relationship—the adversary partnership—between Israel and Transjordan in 1948. Here again Ber spoils a good case by overstating it. He rightly emphasizes the limited nature of the strategy pursued by both Ben-Gurion and Abdullah after the first truce but he errs in attributing it to 'collusion' between them. There was no collusion between the socialist leader and the feudal warlord: the contact was severed in May and it was not renewed until four months later. Hence, the most that can be claimed is that during the latter part of this period there was a tacit understanding between the two rulers to avert a major collision between their armed forces. This tacit understanding was based on perceived interests that the two had in common and which neither shared with their Arab partners—opponents. And it was this perceived interdependence or overlap of interests that led each ruler independently to exercise a measure of self-restraint in relation to the other.

The distinction is not purely semantic. 'Collusion' presupposes a direct and explicit agreement and it carries the connotation of a shabby and secret deal. 'Tacit understanding', on the other hand, can issue from mutual mind-reading, leading to awareness that co-operation between adversaries can work to their mutual advantage but without any direct contact or explicitly formulated plan of action. The difference between the two is small but significant. For if there had been collusion between the Zionist leader and the Hashemite monarch, how is one to account for the fierce fighting that took place between their respective armies in the central front? Surely the whole point about collusion is that it enables politicians to avert a head-on clash and limit the bloodshed. A tacit understanding, by contrast, is much more vulnerable to miscalculation by the policymakers and confusion on the part of their subordinates.

Some of the aspects of the 1948 war, at any rate, can be understood in terms of plain military realities, without resorting to elaborate conspiracy theories. At various stages in the war there were military considerations rather than political ones that led the Israeli side to avoid a clash with the Arab Legion. But if Ben-Gurion's conduct of the war was dictated by an overall political conception, the men serving under him were not aware of it. Many of his senior military advisers were later to testify that he did not impose operational restrictions on them and some specifically rejected the charge of collusion with Transjordan.

Yigael Yadin, the chief of operations who dominated the General

Staff and was the prime minister's principal military adviser throughout the war, dismissed collusion as a myth:

Contrary to the view of many historians, I do not believe that there was an agreement or even an understanding between Ben-Gurion and Abdullah. He may have had wishful thoughts; Sasson may have planted hopes in his heart, but until 15 May 1948, he did not build on it and did not assume that an agreement with Abdullah would neutralize the Arab Legion. On the contrary, his estimate was that the clash with the Legion was inevitable. Even if Ben-Gurion had an understanding or hopes, they evaporated the moment Abdullah marched on Jerusalem. First there was the assault on Kfar Etzion, then the capture of positions in Latrun in order to dominate the road to Jerusalem and then there was the entry into Jerusalem. From these moves it was clear that Abdullah intended to capture Jerusalem.

If there had indeed been an agreement between Ben-Gurion and Abdullah, it was violated and it was Abdullah who violated it. That was the turning point in Abdullah's policy. He cancelled any agreement and any understanding. His armies entered the battle and the clash was unavoidable. The contact with Abdullah was severed and it was not renewed at any level until September.

After May 15, Ben-Gurion saw the Legion as the number one enemy. He strove towards a showdown with the Legion. For Ben-Gurion Jerusalem was the focal point of the entire War of Independence and he concentrated all the forces in order to gain the upper hand over the Legion in Jerusalem. I, for military reasons, saw Egypt as the number one enemy. But Ben-Gurion did not want to clash with Egypt. It was with difficulty that he was persuaded to divert forces to the southern front when the war broke out.[4]

Equally categorical in denying any collusion or preferential treatment of Transjordan was the commander of the northern front, Maj.-Gen. Moshe Carmel. According to General Carmel:

The link with Transjordan had no influence whatever on the military side of the War of Independence. The assumption was that we were facing all the Arab states and that Transjordan, like the others, was poised to invade. And, indeed, the Transjordanians were the first to invade. On Shlomo Shamir's meeting with Colonel Goldie I did not hear. I did not participate in the political moves nor was I alert to the political side. I knew that Golda had met Abdullah but that did not concern us. We were in charge of the military side.

Politically, Ben-Gurion had a tendency, a predilection, to reach an understanding with Abdullah, but when the invasion started and there was war, Ben-Gurion had no inhibitions about the actions of our forces against the Arabs, including Transjordan.

I say categorically that from the moment of the invasion to the end of the war I did not hear about any political constraints regarding Transjordan. Everything we were capable of doing we did, and all the authorizations we requested

---

[4] Interview with Gen. Yigael Yadin.

were granted. From the time I was appointed commander of the northern front in June and carried the responsibility for repelling the Arab invasion into Israel by the forces of Lebanon, Syria, Transjordan, and Iraq, I did not experience any political constraints in the way of military operations against the forces of Transjordan or the Iraqi forces that were stationed in Transjordan. All of us felt that *à la guerre comme à la guerre* and that we had to act against all the Arab forces that had invaded the country.[5]

But perhaps the best guide to Ben-Gurion's thinking is to be found in his own diary rather than in the retrospective interpretation offered by his generals. There are a number of different entries on the subject of war aims in the diary, reflecting changes in the military balance of forces as seen by the writer, but the first and most comprehensive statement appears on May 24—ten days after the declaration of independence. On that day, Ben-Gurion suggested to the General Staff that they prepare

an offensive directed at crushing Lebanon, Transjordan and Syria. We have to hold on in the Negev, and the plan for this week: the liberation of Jerusalem and the area around it. To this end we have to add forces, especially heavy arms, because it should be assumed that large reinforcements will be sent to Jerusalem. The battle for Jerusalem is the crucial one from a moral-political point of view and to some extent also from a military point of view . . . with the arrival of the cannons we should destroy Ramle and Lydda. We have to organize immediately the division . . . which would be directed against Jenin and towards the Jordan Valley.

Makleff should get reinforcements and his task—the capture of southern Lebanon—with the aid of aerial bombardment of Tyre, Sidon and Beirut. Beirut we should bomb from the sea too.

Yigal [Allon] should be charged with hitting Syria from the east and from the north. Our air force should bomb and destroy Amman.

The weak link in the Arab coalition is Lebanon. Muslim rule is artificial and easy to undermine. A Christian state should be established whose southern border should be the Litani. We shall sign a treaty with it. By breaking the power of the Legion and bombing Amman we shall also finish off Transjordan and then Syria will fall. If Egypt dares to fight—we shall bomb Port Said, Alexandria, and Cairo.[6]

A number of conclusions may be drawn from this early presentation by Ben-Gurion of his strategic objectives before the General Staff. First, he had a clear order of priorities: Jerusalem, Galilee, and the Negev. Second, he favoured an offensive rather than a defensive strategy and saw air power, and especially the bombardment of Arab capitals, as the key to destroying the enemy's will to fight. Third, his method for dealing with the hostile Arab coalition, and one which was to be a

---

[5] Interview with Gen. Moshe Carmel.   [6] Ben-Gurion's diary, 24 May 1948.

central tenet in Israel's security doctrine, was to pick off the Arabs one by one: to attack in one front at a time while holding on in the other fronts. Fourth and most important, it shows that Ben-Gurion did indeed regard the Arab Legion as the number one enemy and that he wanted to force a showdown with it in the belief that once the mighty Legion had been defeated all the other Arab armies would rapidly collapse.

It would appear, therefore, that Ben-Gurion did have an overall strategic plan for winning the war, but it was not the Big Plan attributed to him by Dr Ber. The most decisive proof that the Zionist leader did not aim at sustaining the British imperial order in the Middle East through a partnership with Abdullah is available in that very same diary from which Dr Ber thoughtfully copied extracts for his Soviet associates. The hope, however faint, of an understanding with Abdullah was there all along in Ben-Gurion's mind, but once the Legion invaded, there was no holding back, at least not initially. Later in the war, Ben-Gurion and Abdullah did appear to be pursuing a more limited strategy towards one another but the reasons behind these strategies are far too complex to be explained in terms of plots, collusions, and 'big plans'. The importance of Ber's book lies in the attempt to relate strategy to the political context in which it was formulated. One may, therefore, discount Ber's specific charges of collusion but follow his example in probing the political as well as the military considerations that shaped the strategy of the principal actors in the 1948 war.

The battle for Jerusalem, May 1948

Jerusalem was the principal battleground and the most coveted prize in the 1948 Arab–Israeli war. The Holy City was of profound spiritual and religious importance to Muslims, Jews, and Christians throughout the world. It was also the strategic key to the whole of Palestine, being perched on the mountain ridge at the junction of the main roads from Tel Aviv to Jericho and from Nablus to Hebron. The future of Jerusalem was therefore uppermost in the minds of both Ben-Gurion and Abdullah as their armies went into battle.

Under the United Nations partition plan, Jerusalem was to be an enclave under an international regime inside the Arab state, a separate body or *corpus separatum*. If the Jewish Agency or the Transjordanian government had objections to this plan, they failed to communicate them to the United Nations. Both behaved as if they accepted the plan to internationalize Jerusalem. In the unwritten agreement between the Jewish Agency and King Abdullah there were no provisions for

Jerusalem. The king undertook not to interfere with the establishment of a Jewish state within the partition borders while the Jews undertook not to interfere with his invasion into the Arab parts of Palestine. Jerusalem was not even mentioned in the talks because it was tacitly assumed that it would constitute a separate body under an international regime. The fighting broke out in Jerusalem precisely because it was not covered by any kind of agreement or understanding between the two sides. Everywhere else, as we shall see, the Arab Legion respected the partition borders and made no' attempt to seize Jewish territory.

Glubb's original plan for the deployment of his four regiments in Palestine did not cater for the occupation or even the defence of Jerusalem. As he later explained,

The Arab Legion had crossed the Jordan on May 15, with the approval of the British government, to help the Arabs defend the area of Judaea and Samaria allotted to them. We were strictly forbidden to enter Jerusalem, which had been declared by the United Nations to be an enclave or to enter any area allotted to the Jewish state in the partition plan. Our plans were therefore strictly in accordance with the orders of the United Nations and the approval of the British government.[7]

None of Glubb's own orders to his officers was more categoric than that which warned them against getting involved in fighting in Jerusalem. The wishes of the British government and resolutions of the United Nations were important considerations. The small size of his army in relation to the 260-kilometre front from Hebron to Nablus which he wanted to hold also made Glubb reluctant to assume any additional responsibilities. Moreover, his bedouin soldiers were not trained for town fighting; it was not their natural habitat. Fighting in Jerusalem's narrow lanes and cramped bazaars was likely to be very costly in casualties and Glubb did not want to see his life's work torn apart in streetfighting. Finally, even at this late hour, Glubb had lingering hopes of limiting hostilities to a semblance of war—a few skirmishes, a few token forays, and then allowing the dust to settle. For all these reasons he laid down a strict policy of non-involvement in Jerusalem, leaving the defence of the city to the various bands of Palestinian irregulars.

There was no parallel restraint on the Israeli side. The truce covering Jerusalem was broken immediately the mandate ended. Hardly had the British evacuated the town when a well-planned and vigorous Israeli offensive, Operation Pitchfork, was launched to seize all the Arab and mixed zones of the new city and form a solid Jewish area

---

[7] Glubb, *The Changing Scenes of Life*, 148.

going all way up to the Old City walls. Another objective of the operation was to capture the Arab quarter of Shaikh Jarrah and establish a secure link with the Jewish enclave containing the Hadassah Hospital and the Hebrew University on Mount Scopus.

The Jewish Quarter inside the Old City represented a particularly difficult problem for the Israeli command. It occupied an area of 450 by 325 metres and had a non-combatant population of 1,700 and a garrison force of 150 lightly armed men. Surrounded by 20,000 hostile Arabs, this small enclave was virtually indefensible. The Israelis had the option of taking the fighters out and leaving the Jewish Quarter under a Red Cross flag. But David Shaltiel, the commander of the Jerusalem front and a loyal supporter of Ben-Gurion, declined the offer of voluntary evacuation. Instead, he planned to hold on to the Jewish Quarter and use it as a springboard for capturing the entire Old City.[8]

The first task was to break through the massive sixteenth-century stone ramparts that enclosed the Old City and effect contact with the forces defending the Jewish Quarter. A first attempt was made on the night of May 16 to break into the Old City through the Jaffa Gate but the attack was repelled by the Arab defenders. A second attempt was made to break in at the same point the following night but this too failed. At the third attempt, on May 19, a Palmach unit succeeded in forcing its way through the Zion Gate and linking up with the Jewish Quarter. But instead of keeping up the offensive to complete the capture of the Old City, as Shaltiel expected, the Palmach handed over to another unit, which relapsed into a static defence of the Jewish Quarter. Such defence was doomed to failure from the start. Daily attempts were made to breach the massive city walls in order to reinforce the beleaguered garrison but on May 28 the Jewish Quarter finally and formally surrendered to the Arab Legion.

The Israeli attempt to capture the Old City triggered off a chain of events that ended up by overturning Glubb's careful policy of non-involvement. The king and his ministers were inundated with desperate appeals for help from the Arabs in the Old City. A National Committee had been elected and entrusted, belatedly, with organizing the defence of Jerusalem in face of the accelerating violence. Anwar Nuseiba, a prominent member of the committee recalled that 'A delegation was sent to see King Abdullah to tell him that we needed support and we badly needed arms. We were supposed to be the radicals—from Jerusalem, the seat of the mufti. Abdullah rebuked us for not having listened to his advice. Even then he was concerned to carry Palestinian opinion with him, and seek a solution through means

[8] David Shaltiel, *Jerusalem 1948* (Heb.) (Tel Aviv: Ministry of Defence, 1981), 173–5.

other than violence.'[9] Ahmad Hilmi, the leader of Arab Jerusalem, cabled the government in Amman: 'Unless you rescue us immediately, Jerusalem will fall finally into the hands of the Jews.'[10]

Glubb held out against the mounting pressure to commit his troops to the defence of the Old City for as long as he could. He suspected that the likelihood of an imminent fall into Jewish hands was exaggerated and he clung to the hope that the Consular Truce Commission would succeed in its efforts to arrange a cease-fire in Jerusalem.

King Abdullah, whose father was buried in the precincts of the Great Mosque, was torn between carrying out his duty as a Muslim and a Hashemite and going to the rescue on the one hand and displeasing his British allies on the other. As the calls for help from Jerusalem became more frantic, he decided to act. At half past eleven in the morning of May 17 Glubb received the following message: 'His Majesty the King orders an advance towards Jerusalem from the direction of Ramallah. He intends by this action to threaten the Jews, in order that they may accept a truce in Jerusalem.'

Half an hour later Glubb received another and longer telegram from the defence minister. It read as follows:

His Majesty the King is extremely anxious and indeed insists that a force from Ramallah with artillery be sent to attack the Jewish quarters of Jerusalem. The Jews are attacking the gates of the Old City in order to break into it. An attack on the Jews would ease the pressure on the Arabs and would incline the Jews to accept the truce for Jerusalem. The Belgian consul has been here and His Majesty has gathered from him that such action on our part might frighten the Jews and make them less obstinate. His Majesty is awaiting swift action. Report quickly that the operation has commenced.[11]

The king realized that he had embarked on an enterprise that could carry him beyond the original scheme for which he had secured Bevin's agreement. To limit the damage to his relations with Britian, he followed up his orders to Glubb with a letter of explanation to Kirkbride. Kirkbride proposed to tell him that any departure from the original scheme would necessitate a reconsideration of Britain's own position,[12] but by the time Kirkbride received instructions from London to warn Abdullah against a full-scale Arab Legion attack on Jerusalem, the die was cast.[13]

The king's unusually insistent orders to Glubb could not be lightly ignored. For 48 hours Glubb had been opposing both the king and the government for reasons that were partly political and partly military.

[9] Interview with Anwar Nuseiba.   [10] Majali, *My Memoirs*, 67.
[11] Glubb, *A Soldier With the Arabs*, 110.
[12] Kirkbride to FO, 17 May 1948, FO 371/68853 PRO.
[13] FO to Kirkbride, 19 May 1948, FO 371/68853, PRO.

Now the situation had become too critical to permit any further delay. On May 18 Glubb gave the orders to an infantry company of about 100 men stationed on the Mount of Olives to go into the Old City. The following day, to prevent the Old City being cut off, Glubb ordered a force of 300 men to break into Jerusalem from the north, clear Shaikh Jarrah, and establish contact with the Old City (see Map 5). There were also political reasons for Glubb's decision to intervene in Jerusalem, as Kirkbride noted in his report to London:

Glubb had the choice of turning outwards on an operation which might ultimately lead him into a Jewish area or inwards to relieve the Arab areas of Jerusalem. He chose the latter, I think wisely. To have saved the Holy Places of Jerusalem would give Transjordan great merit in the Arab world and the troops can be given the battle for which they are clamouring without the risk of being involved in what might be described as an act of aggression against the Jewish state.[14]

The Arab Legion's effective intervention to save the Old City raised Abdullah's prestige in the Arab world but it also exposed him to growing pressure to nullify the partition plan. At a meeting of Arab statesmen and military commanders at Deraa, in southern Syria, on May 19, it soon became clear to Abdullah that the real purpose of his allies was to involve the Arab Legion still further, and in particular to get it to move against the Jewish state. Lieut. Gen. Taha al-Hashimi, the head of the Arab League's Military Committee, touched off an explosion of royal wrath by insisting that the Arab armies should not be used for political purposes. The king retorted that after the deplorable shows put up by the Syrian and Lebanese forces they were in no position to criticize the Arab Legion, and that no one with any sense would propose attacking the Jewish state.[15]

President al-Quwatli of Syria demanded that they implement the Arab League plan for the Syrian army to move through Bennt Jbail in southern Lebanon towards Nazareth and from there to capture Afuleh in order to link up with the Iraqi army in Jenin and cut off the Jewish settlements in the Jordan Valley. Abdullah, however, was opposed to this plan and insisted that the Syrian army should move westward through Samakh towards Tiberias. This was the route that the Syrian army took, but after capturing Samakh it was stopped in Degania and in effect lost the battle for the Jordan Valley.[16] Of his nephew, Abd al-Illah, the regent of Iraq, Abdullah asked that the Iraqi forces be moved into Samaria in order to defend the new Hashemite conquests and relieve the Arab Legion for other missions in the Jerusalem area.

[14] Kirkbride to FO, 19 May 1948, FO 816/120, PRO.
[15] Kirkbride to FO, 22 May 1948, FO 371/68873, PRO; Hashimi, Memoirs, ii. 223 f.
[16] Tall, The Palestine Tragedy, 190 f.

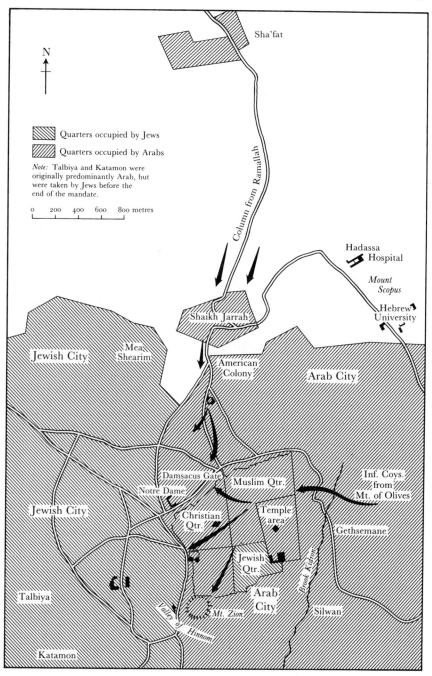

MAP 5 Entry of the Arab Legion into Jerusalem

The Jewish offensive in Jerusalem having been halted, the focal point of the battle moved to Latrun, a hill spur with fortifications that dominated the main route from Tel Aviv to Jerusalem. That road was the lifeline of Jerusalem's 100,000 Jews, and Latrun was its most vulnerable point. From this towering position the New City—Jewish Jerusalem—could be blockaded and its population starved into submission. Yet despite the immense strategic importance of Latrun, Qawukji's troops withdrew on May 15 without handing it over properly or even notifying the Arab Legion. Because of poor intelligence and the need to transfer forces to the Negev to deal with the invading Egyptian forces, the Israeli command made no attempt to move into the positions vacated by the Arab Liberation Army. Thus Latrun remained unmanned by either side for three days until Glubb ordered the 4th Regiment to occupy it; only with the arrival of the Iraqi troops to the Nablus–Jenin–Tulkarem triangle could the 4th Regiment be spared to assume this vital mission on the road to Jerusalem.

The deployment of the 4th Regiment in Latrun was typical of Glubb's entire strategy. Having only four infantry regiments at his disposal, no strategic reserves, and little prospect of recruiting and training additional reinforcements, he opted for a defensive deployment of his forces in key Arab areas. His objective was to gain control over the Arab areas of Palestine in order to prevent their capture by the Israelis and ultimately to annex them to Transjordan. This defensive strategy was contrary to the Arab League's wish to create a unitary Arab state over the whole of Palestine but it accorded with Britain's preferences and Abdullah's territorial ambitions. Latrun was well within the zone allotted to the Arabs so the Transjordanian occupation of it could be regarded as legitimate. Whereas a direct attack to conquer the New City of Jerusalem would have constituted a violation of the UN plan, blockading it from inside Arab territory did not. Glubb did not occupy Latrun in order to expand westward into Jewish territory although it was potentially a good springboard for attack. Had he wanted to break through the lines of the new state an even better route would have been from Kalkilya to Kfar Saba, 40 kilometres north of Latrun. But he made no attempt to expand. His order to the 4th Regiment was to do nothing to disturb the peace, but be prepared to repel an Israeli attack.[17]

The bloody battles fought in Latrun were not the result of offensive operations by the Legion but of Israeli attempts to capture it so as to break the stranglehold on Jerusalem. Ben-Gurion was determined to meet the challenge head-on because to his way of thinking the fate of Jerusalem and therefore the fate of the entire state hung in the balance.

---

[17] Mahmud al-Rusan, *Battles of Bab el-Wad* (Arab.) (n.p.: 1950), chs. 2 and 3.

Fearing that Jerusalem might fall or that the United Nations would impose a truce before the siege was broken, he pressed remorselessly for an immediate frontal attack on Latrun. Yadin wanted time to prepare his forces and presented an ingenious plan based on Liddell Hart's strategy of the indirect approach but he was overruled. Three frontal attacks were mounted on Latrun, all of which failed (see Map 6). Shlomo Shamir's hastily improvised 7th Brigade was badly mauled in the process. The Arab Legion beat off all the attacks, inflicted very heavy casualties on the attacking forces and retained control of the battlefield throughout. Shamir must have regretted that there was no follow up to his meeting with Colonel Goldie and that his own side did not take more seriously Glubb's offer to keep out of each other's way or fight only mock battles. But it was too late for second thoughts. Having failed to dislodge the Arab Legion from its heavily fortified position at Latrun he improvised an alternative route to Jerusalem—the so-called Burma Road which was completed just before the United Nations truce put an end to the first round of fighting.

Britain reins in the Arab Legion

The battle for Jerusalem threatened the United Nations internationalization plan to which Britain remained strongly committed. As the battle unfolded, the relations between London and Amman became seriously strained. London recognized that the Arab Legion could not stand idly by a few miles away while the Israeli truce-breakers tried to overrun the third most holy shrine of Islam. London could not, however, tolerate an attempt by the Legion to capture the whole city because such an action would have involved Britain herself in an open rift with the United Nations. Maj. Abdullah al-Tall sought the king's permission to mount a major counter-offensive designed to liberate the whole of Jerusalem but Glubb exerted countervailing pressure. Only one attempt was made, by the 3rd Regiment on May 24, to penetrate into the Jewish quarters in the north of the city. When this attempt was checked in the Monastery of Notre Dame, it was not repeated.

Because of the British subsidy, the loan of British officers, and the supply of war material, Britain was generally held to be responsible for the actions of the Arab Legion. The British government was therefore subjected to growing international pressure to bring to an end the fighting in Jerusalem. Particularly worrying was the American threat to lift the embargo on the supply of war materials to the Israelis unless the British cut off supplies to the Arab armies and joined in the United Nations efforts to impose a truce in Palestine. Since by now Britain was utterly dependent on American aid for her economic recovery and for

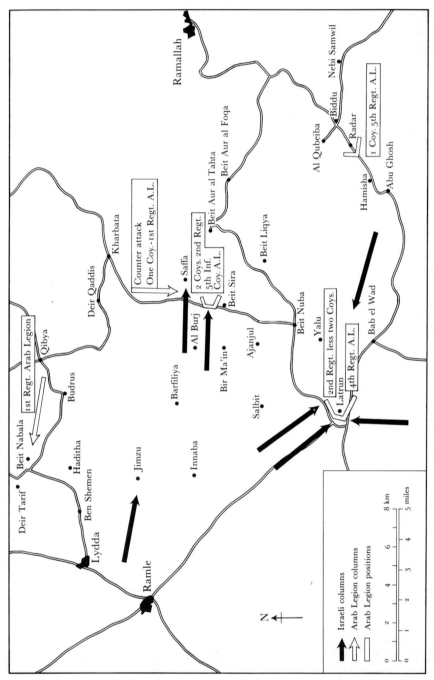

Ramallah

Nebi Samwil

Biddu

Al Qubeiba

Radar

1 Coy. 5th Regt. A.L.

Abu Ghosh

Hamisha

Beit Aur al Foqa

Beit Aur al Tahta

Counter attack
One Coy.–1st Regt. A.L.

Kharbata

Saffa

Beit Liqya

Al Burj

2 Coys. 2nd Regt.
5th Inf.
Coy. A.L.

Beit Sira

Deir Qaddis

Beit Nuba

Bir Ma'in

Yalu

2nd Regt. less two Coys.

Bab el Wad

Ajanjul

Barfiliya

Latrun

4th Regt. A.L.

1st Regt. Arab Legion

Qibya

Budrus

Salbit

Haditha

Innaba

Jimzu

Deir Tarif

Ben Shemen

Beit Nabala

Lydda

Ramle

N

Israeli columns

Arab Legion columns

Arab Legion positions

0   1   2   3   4   5   6   8 km

0   1   2   3   4   5 miles

Map 6   Abortive Israeli offensive against Latrun

securing Western Europe against Soviet domination, the British government could not afford to fall out with the Truman administration over Palestine.

Bevin, for whom the alliance with the United States took precedence over all other considerations, took immediate steps to persuade his opposite number that British policy in Palestine was in conformity with the decisions of the United Nations. In a top secret message to Marshall on May 24, Bevin revealed that the British officers on secondment to the Arab Legion had been instructed to withdraw to Transjordan if the Legion became involved in hostilities with the Jewish state as a result of an attack on that state within the frontiers recommended by the General Assembly. Bevin confirmed the information previously given by the Jewish Agency to Marshall that contact was being maintained between the Jews and the Arab Legion through the intermediary of a British officer. Without naming Colonel Goldie, Bevin made the point that the British had always favoured giving the Haganah and the Arab Legion responsibility for maintaining law and order in different areas. The Arab Legion, he emphasized, had not entered any part of the area recommended for the Jewish state by the Assembly. The Legion's attack on parts of Jerusalem was presented by Bevin as the direct consequence of the Jews' breaking the cease-fire. He was confident that the attack would not have taken place if the Jews had accepted a truce in Jerusalem. Bevin's latest information was that henceforth the Arab Legion would be mainly on the defensive in Jerusalem.[18]

At the same time Bevin took steps to ensure that the Arab Legion would indeed remain on the defensive and he began to exert the strongest possible pressure on the Arab leaders to accept the cease-fire resolution that Britain tabled before the Security Council. King Abdullah was reminded of the assurances he had sent with Abul Huda to enter only the Arab parts of Palestine and not to cause difficulties for Britain by getting involved in large-scale hostilities. Now that the stated objectives had been achieved and the Muslim Holy Places in Jerusalem had been protected, there was nothing to be lost by agreeing to a cease-fire. Refusal by King Abdullah would imply that he had other objectives in mind, in which case the British government would be forced to reconsider her entire position with regard to the Arab Legion.[19] Faced with this thinly veiled threat, Abdullah not only agreed but promised to do his best to get the other Arab leaders to accept the British-sponsored cease-fire.

When the Arab League's Political Committee met in Amman on May 25, there was strong resistance from the Egyptian and Syrian representatives to the cease-fire proposal. Acceptance of a cease-fire

[18] *FRUS 1948*, v. 1038 f.   [19] Bevin to Kirkbride, 24 May 1948, FO 800/488, PRO.

was thought to signify an admission of defeat for which the Arab public, fed with false accounts of Arab military successes, was totally unprepared. Only Abul Huda spoke in favour of the British proposal and threatened that the Arab Legion would not continue to carry the main burden if the fighting continued. In the end the committee rejected the Security Council's request that both sides should observe a cease-fire order but asked the council to make new proposals for a solution to the Palestine problem. For Transjordan to accept the cease-fire alone would have been too risky. Politically Abul Huda could not survive such an action, nor could the Hashemites in either Iraq or Transjordan.[20]

The Arab rejection, following an Israeli acceptance of the British proposal, placed Bevin in an awkward position. Pressure for withdrawing the British officers and subsidy was building up both at home and in the United States. As Bevin explained to the Cabinet, it had originally been assumed that no difficulty would arise if these officers accompanied the Legion into those parts of Palestine which were to remain in Arab hands under the partition plan, and it was thought that their presence would have a restraining effect on the Arab legionaries. A different situation had arisen now that the Legion had become engaged in military operations against the Jews, and it was necessary to make a further statement on British policy.[21]

To enable Bevin to make his speech, orders were given to the Transjordanian authorities to withdraw all the regular British officers from Palestine within 48 hours. This decision was supposed to indicate the lengths to which Britain would go to uphold United Nations resolutions. But once Bevin had made his speech, the British officers were allowed to recross the Jordan and join their units in Palestine. King Abdullah and his prime minister helpfully played the role assigned to them in this British charade and even promised that they would continue, as in the past, to get the other Arab states to follow Bevin's advice.[22]

Having had its first resolution turned down by the Arab League, Britain put before the Security Council another resolution which called for a cessation of all acts of armed force for a period of four weeks, with a ban on the introduction of fighting men and war material into Palestine. Indirectly this resolution carried the threat of sanctions against the Arab states. Like the withdrawal of the British officers, however, it was a hollow gesture designed to restore Britain's

[20] Kirkbride to FO, 25 and 26 May 1948, FO 816/121, PRO.

[21] CM 33(48)7, 27 May 1948, PRO.

[22] Bevin to Kirkbride, 27 May, Kirkbride to Bevin, 28 May 1948, FO 816/121, PRO; interview with Col. Desmond Goldie.

credibility in the eyes of the United Nations. The Cabinet noted that compliance with the embargo on the movement of war material might involve some breach of Britain's contracts for the supply of arms to the Arab state, but Bevin assured his colleagues that there was no intention of modifying Britain's long-term obligations under the treaty of alliance with Transjordan.[23] The Security Council adopted the British resolution on May 29 and the task of implementing it was entrusted to the United Nations mediator for Palestine, Count Folke Bernadotte.

The British had supported the appointment of Count Bernadotte as the mediator for Palestine. He was a member of the Swedish royal family, president of the Swedish Red Cross, and had saved thousands of Jews from extermination by negotiating with the Nazis during the Second World War. Another qualification, as far as Britain was concerned, was his privately held opinion that the United Nations partition resolution had been a mistake. The British considered it unrealistic, as they repeatedly told their Arab allies, to propose the abolition of the Jewish state in favour of a unitary Arab state over the whole of Palestine. But they did not consider it unrealistic to try and change the boundaries recommended by the General Assembly and they had reason to believe that Bernadotte would be amenable to their suggestions.

British thinking proceeded on the assumption that the Arab governments would in fact prefer not to set up a separate Arab state in Palestine but to appropriate the Arab areas to themselves. The British expected Transjordan to annex the central Arab area and hoped that Egypt and Transjordan would share the Negev between them, even if it meant that the western Galilee would have to be ceded to the Jewish state in compensation for the loss of the Negev. An arrangement along these lines, it was believed, would create a strong barrier against Jewish and communist expansion south and would provide Britain with an extended area of friendly Arab country in which she would have strategic facilities, whereas a separate Arab state in Palestine would be so small and weak that it might well succumb at some stage to Jewish pressure. Before putting these ideas to Bernadotte, Bevin wanted Kirkbride to have a frank discussion with Abdullah.[24]

A preliminary discussion with the prime minister revealed that the Egyptian government, probably at the insistence of the mufti, had recently put forward a suggestion that the Arabs set up and recognize a unitary state over the whole of Palestine. This suggestion was opposed by Transjordan and Iraq, and it was decided to maintain the original decision of the Arab League that whatever part of Palestine was

[23] CM 34(48)1, 31 May 1948, PRO.
[24] Bevin to Kirkbride, 27 May 1948, FO 816/121, PRO.

rescued should be placed under military rule until its inhabitants were in a position to choose their future status for themselves. Abul Huda felt that any other decision would have provoked a dispute between the Arab states while they were still in combat with the Jews. This dispute was bound to arise later, but he was confident that by then the inhabitants in the areas controlled by the Legion would be unanimous in asking for union with Transjordan. Steps to secure that were being taken. Abul Huda personally saw no objection to Egypt acquiring the Negev provided Transjordan acquired access to the sea in the Gaza area. But he urged Kirkbride not to suggest any other course of action to King Abdullah so as to avoid creating an open breach among the Arab states at a critical time.[25]

Count Bernadotte flew to the Middle East at the end of May and worked tirelessly to secure a cease-fire. King Abdullah informed him that his country would accept the cease-fire. The Political Committee of the Arab league reconvened in Amman to discuss the latest proposals. Egypt and Transjordan pressed for acceptance and were soon joined by Iraq. Syria, Lebanon, and Saudi Arabia were more difficult to convince because of their concern for local public opinion, but they finally voted for acceptance. After adopting this resolution, the Syrian, Lebanese, and Saudi Arabian delegates proposed an additional resolution stating that all Arab states rejected a Jewish state and that anybody entertaining contrary ideas was a traitor to the Arab cause. Tawfiq Abul Huda told the three delegates that this matter was entirely outside the scope of the meeting and that the proposed resolution was a direct attack on the Hashemites. He abruptly declared the meeting closed and walked out.[26]

An American official confirmed that there was a widespread desire in Amman to see an end to the war if an honourable way out could be found for Transjordan. King Abdullah told him that he did not hate the Jews, that he had never wished to make a war on them, that it had been forced on him by the Arab League and that he would be glad to see it come to an end. Sharif Husayn Nasser, Abdullah's son-in-law and chief of the royal court, told the American official that the king realized the strength of the Jews and did not wish to risk losing his army as this would undermine his strong position *vis-à-vis* the other Arab states. Sharif Nasser spoke almost pleadingly for a solution that would save the king's honour. Further talks with the prime minister, the foreign minister, Kirkbride, Glubb, and others in and out of the government revealed a consensus of opinion that the war had gone on long enough, that it could not possibly end in victory for the Arabs, and that time worked in favour of the Jews. Various persons pointed out that the

[25] Kirkbride to Bevin, 19 May 1948, FO 816/121, PRO.   [26] *FRUS 1948*, v. 1086.

Arab Legion had not yet attempted any large-scale operation against the Jews in Jewish territory. The operation in Jerusalem was relatively small and limited. Operations in Latrun had resulted in no gains by either side, although the Tel Aviv–Jerusalem road remained closed. British officers in the Arab Legion appeared to be proceeding very cautiously to avoid any major engagement with the Jews.[27]

The battle for the Triangle, June 1948

While British officers were holding back the Transjordanian forces in the Jerusalem front and British diplomats were pressing for an Arab acceptance of a cease-fire, a major battle was fought in Samaria between the Hashemite army of Iraq and the Israeli army. The battle was for control of the Triangle defined by the large Arab cities of Jenin in the north, Nablus in the east, and Tulkarem in the west. From this hilly area an attack launched in the direction of the Mediterranean could cut the state of Israel in two. To the Israeli military planners, this seemed to be the objective of the Iraqi expeditionary force which advanced along the Tulkarem–Natanya road to within only six miles of the Mediterranean coast.

To defend Israel's narrow waistline, the Israeli Command ordered its first large-scale offensive operation of the war. The plan called for a co-ordinated attack by the Golani and Carmeli brigades on the northern flank of the Iraqi army in Jenin and a diversionary attack to be mounted on Tulkarem from the south by the Alexandroni Brigade. Between June 1 and 3, Moshe Carmel, the commander of the northern front, staged an attack which led to the capture of Jenin, but the Alexandroni Brigade, commanded by Gen. Dan Even, unaccountably failed to mount the attack on Tulkarem. All the power of the Iraqi forces was then turned against the northern spearhead which suffered heavy casualties and was forced to withdraw from Jenin. The two-pronged Israeli strategy thus failed to make a dent in the Arab positions overlooking the coastal plain. A major opportunity to widen Israel's narrow waist was lost.

Israel Ber has suggested that the passivity of the Alexandroni Brigade during the battle for the Triangle may have been partly inspired by political considerations. He dismisses Dan Even's explanation that his brigade did not have sufficient fire power and ammunition to carry out its orders, and declines to comment on the extent to which Even's behaviour was determined by objective conditions, by military incompetence, or by political intention. The important point, according to Ber, is that, whether deliberately or inadvertently, Even's

---

[27] Ibid. 1105 f.

behaviour saved Ben-Gurion's Big Plan from a serious complication. Since Jenin could not be maintained as the only foothold in the Triangle, an initial penetration would have necessitated consolidation and expansion which would have eventually entailed a major engagement with the Iraqis and possibly the conquest of the whole of this purely Arab area. What began as a defensive step could thus have ended up by endangering Ben-Gurion's plan for partitioning Palestine with Abdullah and accommodation to the British imperial order in the area. Thus, whatever the reason for Dan Even's passivity in the first week of June, concludes Ber, it had far-reaching consequences.[28]

Moshe Carmel disputes Ber's claim that Israel's strategy in the battle for the Triangle was not pursued more vigorously because Ben-Gurion hoped for an accommodation with the Hashemites. It was not political reservations on the part of Ben-Gurion or the General Staff but objective military factors that determined the course and outcome of the battle, says Carmel:

It is obvious that if the attack on Jenin had succeeded, we would have stationed our forces in Jenin itself and on the hills east of Jenin. This would have changed our position in Judaea and Samaria; it would have secured the valley of Jezreel. But there were no political inhibitions here. The plan was that when we attacked Jenin, Dan Even was to attack in Tulkarem in order to cause a diversion and force the enemy to disperse his forces. We took Jenin and captured the police station and were then subjected to a serious counter-offensive mounted by the Iraqis. It became clear that the Alexandroni Brigade was doing nothing and all the Arab forces turned against us.

Ber's claim that there were political reasons for Dan Even's passivity is baseless. The reason was not political but the nature of the brigade and its order of priorities. Alexandroni was not an aggressive brigade; it was organized for defence and it could not muster enough forces for an operation in Tulkarem.

The best proof that no political constraints were imposed on us is that on the night of the Iraqi counter-offensive I contacted Yigael Yadin and reported that our position was precarious and that we had carried out a partial withdrawal. I said that if Alexandroni could attack Tulkarem in accordance with yesterday's plan, I was for holding on to the territories and continuing the operation, but if this could not be done, we would have no choice but to withdraw and establish ourselves in a line north of Jenin. Yigael said he would find out. Two hours later he called and said: 'I am sorry, an attack on Tulkarem is not possible, and if you have to retreat, then so be it.' There was no political element whatsoever in this decision. There was only one consideration: to fight the war and repel the attack.[29]

Political considerations of a different kind interfered in the Hashemite involvement in the battle for the Triangle. According to the

[28] Ber, *Israel's Security*, 170–2.   [29] Interview with Gen. Moshe Carmel.

Iraqi chief of staff, Salih Saib al-Juburi, it was the failure of the Arab Legion to carry out the mission assigned to it in the overall Arab invasion plan that exposed his own army to attacks from the Israelis and prevented it from achieving its aims. Although there was one headquarters for all the invading armies, headed by an Iraqi general, Nur al-Din Mahmud, it had no effective control over those armies, and the military operations did not follow the agreed plan. Only the Iraqi army, Juburi claims, obeyed the HQ; the Legion acted independently throughout, with terrible results for the general Arab war effort.[30]

On May 14, specific instructions were issued by the HQ to the Arab Legion to reinforce the small unit it had already sent to guard the Allenby Bridge and to send one infantry regiment to Nablus and one armoured regiment to Ramallah. The Legion did nothing on either count. This provided the opportunity for the Israelis to move against the Iraqi forces in this area and to send reinforcements to Gesher, along the Jordan, to help the local settlers repel the Iraqi offensive.

In view of the situation of the Iraqi and Syrian armies, on May 16 HQ asked the Legion to send a force to Jenin and from there proceed to attack Afuleh. The reply was that they would study the situation but no action was taken. So two days later General Mahmud went to Ramallah to see Glubb in a vain attempt to discover the reasons for the Arab Legion's inaction.

Juburi, Glubb, and senior Egyptian, Syrian, and Lebanese officers went to the palace in Amman on May 20 for a meeting with King Abdullah, Abd al-Illah, and Azzam Pasha. The king opened the meeting with a general survey and made some favourable remarks on Glubb's energetic contribution to their common objectives. Azzam added that everybody was grateful to Glubb for his loyal and distinguished service to the Arab cause over a long period of time. Behind this flattery, Juburi detected a desire to elicit a more co-operative attitude but he himself was convinced that Glubb was not the kind of man who would allow Arab flattery to deflect him from carrying out the orders of the British government. At the time Juburi had no knowledge of the secret meeting between Bevin, Glubb, and Abul Huda, but when he learnt about it after the war it confirmed his suspicions that Glubb's direction of the operations of the Arab Legion in 1948 conformed to a plan that had previously been settled in London.

At the meeting in the palace there was some discussion of the reasons that had compelled the Arab armies to depart from the invasion plan that had been agreed in the joint HQ. Glubb suggested that some units of the Iraqi army remain at the Majami Bridge to guard the frontier while other units be moved to occupy Nablus. Juburi resisted this

---

[30] Juburi, *The Palestine Misfortune*, 189 f.

suggestion on the grounds that it would split the Iraqi army into two parts operating in two widely separated areas. He wanted the Iraqi army to stay as one unit so that it could operate more effectively in an offensive capacity. The Egyptian representative, General Sabour, agreed with Juburi. To forestall an open rift between the military and to deprive Glubb of the excuse for acting independently, some of the politicians suggested that it be left to Glubb and Mahmud to work out jointly a new operational plan.

Just as the Iraqi army was preparing to launch another offensive in Gesher, it received the instruction from the joint HQ to move to Nablus. Consequently, it had to abandon Gesher and proceed to Nablus where it confronted the enemy single-handed in the battle for the Triangle.[31] As we have seen, the Iraqi army fought tenaciously in the Triangle, held the line against Israeli advances, and succeeded in forcing the Israelis to retreat from Jenin under heavy fire. Nevertheless, there is some strength in Juburi's argument that had the Arab Legion followed the instructions of the joint HQ and had it not exposed the southern flank of the Iraqi force to encirclement by the enemy, better results overall could have been secured for the Arab side. Juburi's analysis is particularly noteworthy for highlighting the discord and mistrust between the Iraqi and the Transjordanian commanders who, of all the Arab commanders, were supposed to be collaborating in the service of the Hashemite dynasty.

Whether the result of the lack of Transjordanian co-operation or the objective balance of forces, by the end of the first week in June a clear stalemate had developed on the central front and a similarly inconclusive situation prevailed on all the other fronts. Recognition by the opposing parties that from the military point of view they had reached a stalemate, at least temporarily, facilitated Count Bernadotte's task in arranging a truce. On June 7 he notified the parties that the truce would begin on June 11 and gave them two days to communicate their unconditional acceptance.

The Israelis were first to announce their acceptance, and this time the Arab League followed suit. To the Israelis the truce came, in Moshe Carmel's words, like dew from heaven. Though they had succeeded in halting the Arab invasion, their fighting forces were stretched to the limit and badly needed a respite to rest, to reorganize, to bring in arms from abroad, and to train 40,000 new recruits. Despite all their efforts, the main road to Jerusalem remained blocked. At Ben-Gurion's insistence, a further attempt was made to take Latrun on June 9 but the Israeli attack broke up in disarray just before the truce came into effect (see Map 7).

---

[31] Juburi, *The Palestine Misfortune*, 176–82.

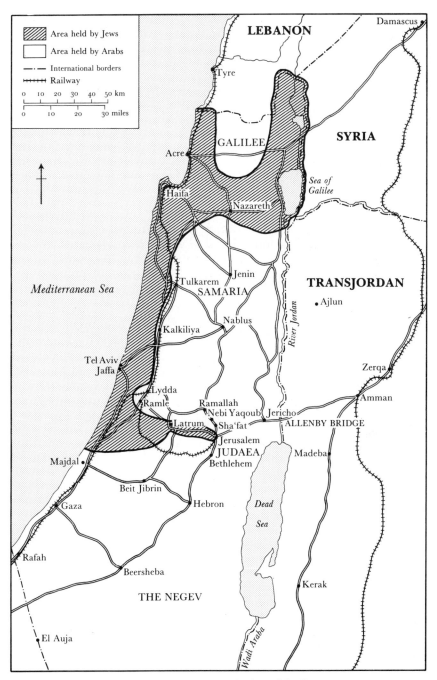

Area held by Jews

Area held by Arabs

International borders

Railway

| 0 | 10 | 20 | 30 | 40 | 50 km |

| 0 | 10 | 20 | 30 miles |

Damascus

LEBANON

Tyre

GALILEE

SYRIA

Acre

Sea of Galilee

Haifa

Nazareth

Mediterranean Sea

Jenin

TRANSJORDAN

Tulkarem

SAMARIA

Ajlun

Kalkiliya

Nablus

River Jordan

Tel Aviv

Jaffa

Zerqa

Lydda

Amman

Ramle

Ramallah

Nebi Yaqoub

Jericho

Latrum

Sha'fat

ALLENBY BRIDGE

Jerusalem

JUDAEA

Madeba

Majdal

Bethlehem

Beit Jibrin

Hebron

Dead Sea

Gaza

Rafah

Beersheba

Kerak

THE NEGEV

El Auja

Wadi 'Araba

MAP 7   Situation at the beginning of the first truce

Ben-Gurion himself had no faith in the United Nations' ability either to arrange or to enforce a truce and on June 11, as the soldiers were laying down their arms, he formulated his own strategy for continuing the fight. As he saw it there were three fronts:

The Jerusalem and central front (including the Triangle) where our task is to destroy the Legion and capture the Triangle; the southern front, including the Negev; and the Galilee front, including Haifa. In the Galilee, the principal enemy is Lebanon and Syria, and our target is to hit Beirut (Tyre and Sidon) and bring about a Christian uprising, and, on the other hand, Kuneitra and Damascus. In the south we would have to stand mainly against Egypt and her turn will come after we break the power of the Legion and take Lebanon out of the game.[32]

Clearly, Ben-Gurion expected only a temporary lull in the fighting and he continued to view the Arab Legion as the prime enemy.

In contrast to Ben-Gurion, Abdullah was immensely satisfied with the achievements of his army in the first round and determined to do what he could to prevent the outbreak of a second round. His own star was in the ascendant as a result of the Legion's intervention in Jerusalem and staunch resistance in Latrun. But his army needed a respite to replenish its dangerously depleted stocks of ammunition and to recruit and train new fighters to replace those who had died in battle. It also needed time in order to consolidate its position for an eventual takeover of the West Bank. International pressure provided Abdullah with an honourable way of bringing the fighting to an end. The continuation of hostilities could only wear out the small army which was also his principal defence against his Arab antagonists.

[32] Ben-Gurion's diary, 11 June 1948.

9

THE COUNTER-OFFENSIVE

Count Bernadotte's proposals for a settlement

Amman became increasingly a centre for Arab political and military decisions as a result of its successes in the first round of fighting. From the military point of view, however, the four weeks' truce was largely wasted by the Arab side. No serious preparations were made by any of the Arab countries to reorganize and re-equip their armies so that they would be better placed in the event of the war being resumed. When Glubb explained the precarious position to Abul Huda and asked him to sanction further enlistments in the Arab Legion, he was firmly told that there will be 'no more fighting and no more money for soldiers'.

King Abdullah went on a tour of Arab capitals to consolidate his leadership and to achieve greater unity on the fundamental questions of war and peace in Palestine. He made no secret of his view that the resumption of the war would be disastrous to the Arabs and the real purpose of his visit was to generate what goodwill he could for his plan to incorporate parts of Palestine in his kingdom. Knowing that Count Bernadotte was about to propose a territorial settlement that would be favourable to Transjordan, Abdullah visited King Farouk of Egypt and King Abdul Aziz Ibn Saud of Saudi Arabia in an effort to allay their anxieties. The visit was successful in creating the outward impression that the Arabs were united, particularly on the Palestine issue, but politically it achieved very little.[1]

Abdullah fared rather better in his search for international support for the enlargement of his kingdom. The Americans began to appreciate his pragmatism and to favour a settlement based on a *rapprochement* between Transjordan and Israel. The main lines of the new American thinking were to redraw the frontiers of Israel so as to make it more compact and homogeneous; the remainder of Palestine to go largely to Transjordan with appropriate transfer of populations; Jerusalem to remain an international entity with free access to the outside world; the boundaries of Israel and the enlarged Transjordan to be guaranteed mutually between themselves and the United Nations; and a customs union between the two countries to enhance their economic prosperity.

[1] Muhafaza, *Jordanian–British Relations*, 187–90.

In discussions between American and British officials, Abdullah was even described as the 'trump card' for persuading the Arab states to accept a Jewish state as a permanent feature of the Middle Eastern landscape.[2]

Count Bernadotte was strongly influenced by Anglo-American thinking on how to bring about a peaceful adjustment of the Palestine conflict. He also realized that the fate of any proposals he might make would depend to a large extent on the attitude of the Great Powers. The Palestine problem was complicated by the fact that there were so many countries and groups with different interests involved. The position of the Arabs was particularly confused and confusing. It was axiomatic that no solution of the Palestine problem could satisfy both Jews and Arabs, but no solution could satisfy all the Arabs either.

Bernadotte's knowledge of the Middle East was rather slight. His assistants told him that the Palestine Arabs had not developed any distinctively Palestinian nationalism; that the demand for a separate Arab state in Palestine was consequently weak; and that in the existing circumstances most of the Palestine Arabs would be quite content to be joined with Transjordan. King Abdullah, on the other hand, had more at stake in the Palestine conflict than any of the other interested parties: 'If he succeeds in incorporating the Arab parts of Palestine in his dominions, he will expand his country's economic resources and make himself more independent of his [British] protectors. That will also be the case if he brings about a political and economic agreement with the Jews.' Syria's attitude was thought to be determined by considerations of home policy and by her relations with Transjordan: 'The Syrian Government regards an Arab Palestine as a useful counterbalance to King Abdullah's empire. Abdullah has been dallying for years with a plan to unite Syria, Lebanon and his own country into Greater Syria, to be ruled from Amman. Abdullah's Arab Legion is consequently regarded in Damascus as a permanent threat.'

In formulating his suggestions for a settlement, Bernadotte tried to bear in mind the aspirations of the Jews, the political difficulties and differences of opinion of the Arab leaders, and the strategic interests of the Great Powers.[3] The deeper he delved, the more convinced he became that the United Nations resolution of 29 November 1947 did not constitute a sound basis for a settlement.

Bernadotte's suggestions for a settlement, issued on 27 June 1948, omitted all reference to the UN plan for an independent Arab state in part of Palestine. Instead, he proposed that the whole of Palestine as defined in the original mandate—that is, including Transjordan—

---

[2] *FRUS 1948*, v. 1133 f., 1205.
[3] Folke Bernadotte, *To Jerusalem* (London: Hodder and Stoughton, 1951), 113–15.

might form a union comprising two members, one Arab and one Jewish. The functions of the union would be to promote the common economic interests, operate the common services, and co-ordinate foreign policy and measures for common defence. Attached to the proposals there was an annex dealing with territorial matters in which Bernadotte suggested the inclusion of the whole or part of the Negev in the Arab territory and the inclusion of the whole or part of western Galilee in the Jewish territory. He further proposed that Jerusalem should be Arab, that Haifa be a free seaport, and Lydda a free airport.[4]

One of the surprising features of Bernadotte's plan was that he looked at Transjordan and Palestine as a single unit and proposed that this entire area be repartitioned on the principle that the Arab part of Palestine should be annexed to Transjordan. This proposal was reminiscent of what the Peel Commission had recommended in 1937, namely, that a Jewish state be established in the western part of Palestine and the rest attached to Transjordan. The difference between the Peel plan and the Bernadotte plan was that the former envisaged two sovereign states, while the latter included both states in a union with economic and political powers.

Bernadotte's suggestions were angrily rejected by both sides. In Israel he was generally regarded as a British stooge. On reading his suggestions Ben-Gurion remarked that the suspicion that the count was Bevin's agent was not entirely unjustified.[5] In Israeli eyes the suggestions represented complete capitulation to Anglo-Arab pressure, a disastrous blunder. One of the Hebrew papers called it an attempt 'to harness our defence and foreign policy to the chariot of Abdullah's master, Britain'. Bevin was said to be trying to squeeze Israel into boundaries 'the size of a coffin'.[6] In its official reply the Israeli government excoriated Bernadotte for ignoring the resolution of the General Assembly of 29 November 1947; it rejected any infringement of Israel's sovereignty; it stated that it would never acquiesce in the imposition of Arab domination over Jerusalem; and it advised him to reconsider his whole approach to the problem.[7]

The Arabs rejected the suggestions out of hand and condemned Bernadotte for denying them everything they sought while giving the Jews everything they were seeking. The Arab reply was accompanied by a counter-proposal which amounted to a repetition of the old Arab demand that Palestine should be constituted as a unitary state with protection for the Jewish minority. The Arabs objected to Bernadotte's

[4] Ibid. 126–31.
[5] Ben-Gurion's diary, 29 June 1948.
[6] Harry Levin, *Jerusalem Embattled* (London: Victor Gollancz, 1950), 257, 280.
[7] *Documents on the Foreign Policy of Israel*, vol. i. *14 May–30 September 1948*, ed. Yehoshua Freundlich (Jerusalem: Israel State Archives, 1981), 262–4. (Henceforth, *DFPI*.)

suggestions not only because they ratified the existence of an independent Jewish state but also because they would have increased the threat posed by King Abdullah. Jamil Mardam, the Syrian prime minister, declared that the proposed union was worse than partition since, if accepted, it would make Transjordan a Jewish colony and constitute an even greater menace to the Arab world.[8]

Great disappointment was felt in Amman that the other Arab capitals refused to accept Bernadotte's proposals even as a basis for negotiations. King Abdullah must have been surprised by the mediator's extraordinary partiality towards him. Not only was he to receive the areas of Palestine previously earmarked for the Arab state but the Negev and the whole of Jerusalem as well. Had Britain herself drafted the proposals they could have scarcely been more favourable. Britain, after all, accepted the internationalization of Jerusalem, whereas Bernadotte proposed to give it to Abdullah as his capital. Yet, since both Israel and the Arab League rejected the proposals, it would have been pointless for Abdullah to accept them. To avoid being denounced as a traitor to the Arab cause, he reluctantly toed the official Arab League line.

Bernadotte's first attempt at a political settlement of the Palestine problem was thus an unmitigated failure. It damaged his own prestige and left behind a legacy of suspicion and mistrust of the United Nations. Fawzi al-Qawukji, whose Arab Liberation Army controlled the western Galilee, was bound to resent the suggestion to turn it over to Israel just as much as the Egyptians were bound to resent the suggestion that the part of the Negev that they had captured should be given to Abdullah on a silver salver. There was a belief among the Arab states that Britain was manipulating international diplomacy for the benefit of Abdullah and a consequent fear that even if they were to step up their military involvement, they would be robbed of the fruits of their victory. Rather than try to preserve a united Arab front, each country therefore increasingly looked after its own interests.

In Israel, too, Bernadotte's failure undermined the authority of the United Nations and encouraged the tendency to act unilaterally. It was with great reluctance that Israel had accepted the 1947 provision for the internationalization of Jerusalem as part of the UN package that offered independent statehood. Now that the UN's own representative himself had violated that provision by offering to place Jerusalem, with its 100,000 Jewish inhabitants, under Arab rule, Israel no longer felt herself bound by it. Ben-Gurion had already concluded that the 1947 partition resolution was a dead letter since the UN had failed to enforce it. On June 24 he told the other twelve members of the State Council

[8] *FRUS 1948*, v. 1159.

that the problem of Jerusalem was no longer a political question but essentially one of military capability and that, like any area that was under the control of the IDF, it formed part of the state of Israel.[9] Bernadotte's proposal only reinforced Ben-Gurion in his view that Israel must capture the Old City, remove the danger of encirclement by the Arab Legion, and establish a wide and safe corridor to link Jerusalem to the rest of the state.

Having failed to promote a settlement of the Palestine problem, Bernadotte proposed an extension of the truce which was due to expire on July 9. Abdullah came under strong pressure from Britain to agree to the proposal. Glubb impressed upon the government that the Arab armies had lost the momentum and were running short of ammunition and equipment. Tawfiq Abul Huda was sent to the Arab League meeting in Cairo with clear instructions to work for the prolongation of the truce, but in Cairo he found himself in a minority of one. Nuqrashi Pasha, on whom Abul Huda had counted for support, made a speech in favour of renewing the fighting—a gesture designed to appease the belligerent Egyptian public. All the Arab military leaders pointed to the gravity of their supply position but the politicians voted unanimously not to renew the truce. To deal with the difficulty of resuming hostilities when their arsenals were depleted, the Arab politicians settled on a defensive strategy of holding on to existing positions.

Abdullah suspected that the Cairo decision was taken with the sinister intention of undermining his diplomatic strategy and embroiling his army in a potentially disastrous war with the Israelis. He therefore summoned Count Bernadotte to Amman to express his extreme uneasiness at the prospect of war breaking out afresh and to urge him to use the full power of the United Nations to bring about a reversal of the Arab League's warlike decision.[10] But the Egyptians pre-empted by attacking on July 8, thereby ending the truce and committing the Arab side irreversibly to a second round of fighting.

The ten days' fighting, 8–18 July 1948

The Arab leaders' decision to renew the war for political reasons but remain on the defensive for military reasons left the initiative in the hands of the enemy. Whereas the Arab leaders had frittered away the first truce in sterile political wrangles, the Israelis had used it to retrain and reorganize their forces and to bring in volunteers and large

[9] Ben-Gurion, *When Israel Fought in Battle*, 179–83.
[10] C. M. Pirie-Gordon to B. A. B. Burrows, 25 July 1948, FO 371/68822, PRO; Bernadotte, *To Jerusalem*, 163 f.; Aref, *The Disaster*, iii. 592.

quantities of modern weapons, including tanks and aircraft, mostly from the Soviet bloc, thus tipping the military balance decisively in their favour. They also had very detailed operational plans for the deployment of their newly, and illicitly, acquired military capability. In contrast to the divisions that existed between the political and the military echelons at the outbreak of the war, there was now a general consensus that Israel must open the second round with an offensive on the central front against the Arab Legion. Ben-Gurion summed up the agreed strategy at a meeting with the General Staff on June 18:

If the war is renewed, our task will be to stabilize as far as possible the two fronts in the north and in the south and to prepare a force and a plan for breaking the Legion and capturing Nablus. This calls for a unified command over the area of the entire Triangle (Jenin, Tulkarem, Latrun, etc.)—with its headquarters in Jerusalem. The war for Jerusalem and its environs—sentimental considerations apart—is the war for the country. If we win there, we will have won altogether.[11]

When hostilities were resumed, the IDF quickly seized the initiative on the central front with Operation Danny. In the first phase the objective was to eliminate the Lydda–Ramle wedge which threatened Tel Aviv as well as the road to Jerusalem; the second phase called for opening a wide corridor to Jerusalem by capturing Latrun, and Ramallah. All these places—Lydda, Ramle, Latrun, and Ramallah— had been assigned to the Arabs and fell within the perimeter held by the Arab Legion.

Glubb was faced with a difficult choice. If he spread his forces thinly across the entire front, Latrun, the real objective of the Israeli attack, might be overrun; if he concentrated his forces at Latrun, Lydda and Ramle would have to be sacrificed. Glubb had two battalions at Latrun and he came under pressure to send one of them to reinforce the garrisons in Lydda and Ramle, but he feared that it would be cut off and surrounded by the Israelis who would then move against the remaining battalion at Latrun. Latrun commanded not only the main road to Jerusalem but also the road leading to Ramallah. Consequently, if Latrun fell, the Israelis would march on Ramallah and from there overrun the Transjordanian forces north of Jerusalem and attack the Iraqi forces in the Triangle from the rear. Latrun was thus the key to the whole front and Glubb decided, with the agreement of the king and the prime minister, to sacrifice Lydda and Ramle in order to defend it.[12]

While Glubb prepared to meet the Israeli offensive, Abdullah made a last bid to restore the truce. He sent a telegram to the other Arab states saying that the Arab Legion was short of ammunition and that

---

[11] Ben-Gurion's diary, 18 June 1948.   [12] Glubb, *A Soldier with the Arabs*, 142 f., 157 f.

unless they undertook an immediate and victorious offensive, they would be defeated in a long defensive war. He went on to say that unless his government could be assured of such an offensive, they would with regret have to withdraw their troops from the fight. The Arab League was thrown into utter confusion and indignation. It was not understood how Abdullah could say this a few hours after the declaration that 'the cannon must now speak'. The lack of ammunition was therefore simply not believed, and Abdullah's intention to stop fighting was put down to treachery.[13]

When the Israeli forces, meeting with little resistance, captured Lydda and Ramle on July 12 and forced their inhabitants to flee across the Jordan, it was Glubb's turn to be accused of treachery by the Arabs. The fact that he had repeatedly warned both the king and the government that these towns could not possibly be held in the event of fighting being resumed, was considered in some quarters as evidence that the British commander had deliberately lost them on orders from London designed to ensure that Transjordan accepted a truce at all costs. Demonstrations against the Arab Legion took place in Nablus and Salt, and Glubb was summoned to attend an unpleasant interview with the king and Council of Ministers during which it was made clear to him that his stories of ammunition shortages were not believed. The king took the opportunity to tell him that if he did not want to serve the country loyally, there was no need for him to stay. To deflect public criticisms from themselves, some of the ministers put it about that Glubb and the British officers were purposely leading the Arab Legion to destruction to further Bevin's wicked intrigues.[14]

Following the fall of Lydda and Ramle, Glubb visited the Arab Legion positions in Palestine and reported to the government that if Israeli pressure were to continue, the position would become critical in a few days owing to exhaustion of supplies of artillery and mortar shells. He expressed the opinion that the Arab Legion should begin to fall back while it still had ammunition to extricate its units intact. The government, however, rejected this advice and ordered him to hold on at all costs. The prime minister and the foreign minister went to Kirkbride to plead for supplies. They pointed out that the Arab Legion had nowhere departed from the policy which the prime minister had described to Bevin and that its activities had been limited to the Arab areas of Palestine. They had no desire to continue the fight but could not act independently of the rest of the Arab League except to the extent of ordering the Arab Legion to stay on the defensive if more ammunition

[13] Kirkbride to FO, 8 July 1948, FO 800/477; Sir Ronald Campbell (Cairo) to FO, 16 July 1948, FO 371/68574, PRO.
[14] Pirie-Gordon to Burrows, 25 July 1948, FO 371/68822, PRO.

was forthcoming. They felt it inconceivable that Bevin should allow the Arab Legion to be destroyed and so endanger the existence of the Arab state most closely bound to Britain.[15]

Glubb approached the Iraqi chief of staff, Salih Saib al-Juburi, with a request for shells but was told that the Iraqi army, with its supplies cut off by Britain, had none to spare. Pointing out that to carry on fighting in these conditions was bound to end in disaster for their side, Glubb suggested that both of them should resign. Juburi, suspecting Glubb of playing a double game and of trying to involve him in it, replied that Glubb was free to resign as he was a foreigner but he himself had his national duty to perform. Military defeat, added Juburi, was likely to provoke political unrest and revolutions throughout the Arab world.

From the Iraqi regent, Juburi heard that Glubb had sent a report to Abdullah suggesting the withdrawal of the Arab Legion from Palestine and that the king's answer, written on the report, said: 'If you want to withdraw, I will go to lead the army. Thank you for your service until now.' Abd al-Illah also informed Juburi that there was a suggestion that Iraqi officers might be appointed to lead the Arab Legion instead of the British officers.[16]

King Abdullah took the initiative in arranging a further session of the Political Committee to reconsider the situation in Palestine and to discuss ways and means of making good the Legion's deficit. Azzam arrived in Amman on July 12, representing not only himself but the Egyptian government, full of suspicions as to what plots Abdullah might have been making with Bernadotte and determined to ensure that the good work done in Cairo was not reversed in a moment of panic. Jamil Mardam, the Syrian prime minister, and Riad al-Sulh, the Lebanese prime minister, duly joined the party the next day. Among the questions discussed at the meeting were Glubb's position and his suggestion for the withdrawal of the Arab Legion from Palestine. The possibility that Transjordan would back out of the war evoked anxiety on the part of all the other participants. General Juburi, who accompanied Abd al-Illah to the meeting, bitterly criticized Transjordan for abandoning Lydda and Ramle without considering the effect of this action on the other Arab armies. The meeting ended somewhat inconclusively. Syria and Egypt having made vague promises to provide the ammunition required by the Arab Legion, it was resolved to continue with the fighting, and the Committee dispersed pending receipt of some communication from the Security Council.[17]

[15] Kirkbride to FO, 12 July 1948, FO 800/477, PRO.
[16] Juburi, *The Palestine Misfortune*, 234 f.
[17] Ibid. 235–7; Pirie-Gordon to Burrows, 25 July 1948, FO 371/68822, PRO.

The Israeli army, having successfully carried out the first phase of Operation Danny, made a determined effort to outflank Latrun from the north and cut it off from Ramallah. To forestall the danger of encirclement, the Legion committed its only reserve regiment to Latrun and mounted there some of its fiercest counter-attacks of the entire war. Both sides fought bravely and tenaciously but in the end the Israeli offensive was repulsed.

The fighting in Latrun used up the dwindling supplies of ammunition at the Legion's disposal at an alarming rate and the Syrians and Egyptians failed to deliver the supplies they had promised. On July 17 Glubb estimated that he had sufficient artillery ammunition to hold the front until the evening of the following day. As he had written orders from the king in no circumstances to retreat, only a truce could save his forces from total isolation in the area of Bab el Wad.[18]

While maintaining the pressure in this area, the Israelis also made a last minute attempt to capture the Old City of Jerusalem. With the renewal of the fighting they took the Malha and Ein Kerem quarters and thus succeeded in widening the southern part of the corridor. On the eve of the second truce, they mounted a further attack with a view to capturing the Old City. The order of the GHQ of July 16 called for two simultaneous attacks, one on Shaikh Jarrah and the other to establish a bridgehead inside the Old City. Although the order stated that if only one operation was possible that evening, priority should be given to Shaikh Jarrah, the local commander, David Shaltiel, chose to mount the other attack, code-named Operation Kedem. It ended in total failure and the Old City remained in the hands of the Arab Legion during the second truce. Israel Ber has argued that Shaltiel deliberately staged the abortive operation in order to further Ben-Gurion's aim of reconciliation with Abdullah. But it appears much more likely that the mission was not accomplished because of failings in the manner in which it was planned, co-ordinated, and executed. In other words, it was not political intrigues or political constraints but the military incompetence of the local command that caused the failure of Operation Kedem. In his letter of July 23 accepting Shaltiel's resignation, Ben-Gurion specifically mentioned his disappointment at Shaltiel's failure to liberate the entire Old City and to capture Shaikh Jarrah.[19] To replace Shaltiel, Ben-Gurion appointed a much more aggressive commander with combat experience: a young major named Moshe Dayan who had won his spurs by leading the daring commando raid into Lydda and Ramle.

[18] Pirie-Gordon to Burrows, 25 July 1948, FO 371/68822, PRO.
[19] Ben-Gurion's diary, 16 and 17 July 1948; Shaltiel, *Jerusalem 1948*, 204–7; Ber, *Israel's Security*, 165–7.

On July 15 the Security Council passed a resolution calling for a cease-fire. In contrast to the first truce, this time the Security Council did not wait for the combatants' reply but took a strong line, threatening to resort to sanctions against any party that failed to issue a cease-fire order within three days. Moreover, no time limit was fixed for the duration of the truce: it was to continue until the mediator came up with proposals for a permanent settlement. The Arab League's Political Committee assembled in Aley, Lebanon, to consider the order. With the exception of the Arab Legion, all the Arab armies had lost ground during the previous ten days, and continuation of the fighting carried the risk of even greater disasters. Arab politicians were anxious to find an excuse to stop but needed some scapegoat on whom to lay the blame. By supporting the American call for sanctions and threatening the Arabs with serious political and military consequences if they defied the Security Council, Britain presented herself as a convenient scapegoat. Britain had reversed her policy, it was claimed, and joined the United States and the Jews in opposing the Arabs. The fact that the Syrians, Iraqis, and Egyptians had all suffered reverses was brushed aside. The extremists could not eradicate the impression that the Arab Legion was the most efficient army but they hastened to point out that such an army was of no value to an Arab state because its operations would be controlled from London and not by its Arab chiefs.[20]

The British not only pressed the Arabs to accept the truce but also advised the Israelis to re-establish contact with Abdullah. Hector McNeil, the minister of state at the Foreign Office, told Dr Nahum Goldmann that they were encouraging Abdullah to get ready for a settlement with Israel.[21] The more urgent task was to bring the fighting to an end. Abdullah needed no convincing of the gravity of the military situation. He assured Christopher Pirie-Gordon, first secretary in the British Legation in Amman, that he was doing all he could. This consisted of sending a telegram to his prime minister in Aley regularly every hour urging him to insist on the acceptance of the truce. He sent an extra one in Pirie-Gordon's presence as a makeweight and sign of good faith.

Despite Iraqi and Syrian opposition, on July 18 the Political Committee decided to accept the truce. Since the military reports did not encourage the continuation of fighting, the motives for this opposition must have been largely political. In any case, it had no practical effects because the following day the fighting ceased on all fronts. To the embattled Transjordanian forces the truce arrived just in time. They

[20] Brig. Glubb, 'The Trans-Jordan Situation', 12 Aug. 1948, FO 371/68822, PRO.
[21] DFPI, i. 336–8.

had maintained their positions in the Old City, Latrun, and Ramallah but they could not have continued to do so as their ammunition was almost exhausted. Besides, the troops were needed at home to deal with the influx of refugees, anti-British protests, and the indignation of thwarted patriotism sparked off by the fall of Lydda and Ramle.[22] Israel's position improved immeasurably as a result of the ten days' fighting; she seized the initiative and was to retain it until the end of the war (see Map 8).

Recriminations and reforms

The Arab coalition was torn by discord and mutual recriminations after the guns fell silent. The line that the Arab Legion was being prevented from using its full strength against the Jews, both through the treachery of the British officers and the withholding of supplies by the British government, was actively propagated by the Syrian and Iraqi authorities and by Azzam Pasha. Iraqi army officers operating in Transjordan were particularly hostile to both the British and the Arab Legion.[23]

Iraqi politicians joined in the general condemnation of Abdullah for the failure of the campaign in Palestine and for acceptance of the truce. The Iraqi Parliament sent a delegation to the front to investigate and report on the causes of the disaster. The delegation headed for Amman on July 28 and was received by King Abdullah soon after its arrival. The king described his country's desperate plight and claimed that it had been let down by the other Arab states and by the Arab League. As for the Palestine Arabs, he felt that they had not done enough to defend themselves and that it was therefore their own fault that they had ended up as refugees like the Hashemites before them. 'The Arabs', he said, 'made a mistake in sending their armies to Palestine without preparing them for war against the Jews and they did not heed my advice that we should settle this matter without war.' Muhammad Kubbah, the leader of the Iraqi Independence Party, challenged the royal version of events. He revealed that he had seen the telegram that the king had sent to the Iraqi prime minister urging him to despatch his army to Palestine and threatening to intervene unilaterally if the other Arab governments delayed sending their armies. Looking embarrassed and then angry, Abdullah admitted that he had done this but returned to the charge that the Arab governments did not send sufficient forces to confront the powerful Jewish army. When Kubbah remarked that his country had sent all the forces requested by the Arab League's Military

[22] Pirie-Gordon to Burrows, 25 July 1948, FO 371/68822, PRO; Iraq, *Report on the Palestine Problem*.
[23] Kirkbride to FO, 6 Aug. 1948, FO 371/68830, PRO.

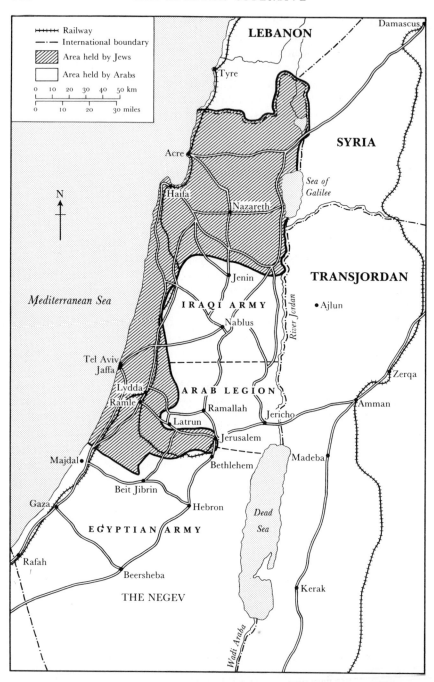

MAP 8 Situation at the beginning of the second truce

Committee, the king retorted that the committee had made a wrong estimate of what the situation required.[24]

The Iraqis accorded prime responsibility for the failure to prosecute the war against the Jews more vigorously to Glubb. They believed that King Abdullah had no real control over the operations of the Arab Legion and that Glubb was playing a double game in pretending to serve the Arabs but secretly working to impose on them London's policy of partition. The suspicion about Glubb and the other British officers accounted for the virtual breakdown of relations between the two Hashemite armies and for the Iraqi branch jealously guarding its freedom of action. Glubb explained to one member of the Iraqi parliamentary delegation that in his view they could not destroy the Jewish state by force because the Jews enjoyed superior resources, international support, and commitment to their cause. On the other hand the Jewish state was surrounded by Arab states on all fronts and it could not survive in the long run if denied a regional outlet for her economy. It followed that the best Arab strategy for dealing with the Zionist danger was economic blockade and containment.[25] To the suspicious Iraqis, however, this sounded like an excuse for running away from the fight.

Glubb was even suspected of collaboration with the enemy, and the surrender of Lydda and Ramle was widely attributed to a secret deal between him and the Zionists. On one occasion during their tour of the front, the Iraqi Parliamentarians, led by the regent, visited Colonel Goldie at his headquarters in Ramallah. Just before they entered the tent, the regent's ADC whispered in Goldie's ear to watch what he said about liaison with the Jews. During the subsequent discussion, the parliamentarians questioned Goldie about any form of liaison between the Arab Legion and the Jews. Goldie realized that what they were really looking for was evidence that Glubb Pasha had indeed betrayed the Arab cause and that any revelations about his own meeting with the Haganah officers would be political dynamite. In the face of persistent probing, Goldie therefore remained persistently evasive. There were a number of tense moments but he managed not to trip up.[26]

In the first week in August talks were held in Amman between Iraqi ministers and King Abdullah on the subject of withdrawing the British officers and placing the two Hashemite armies under a unified command. It was rumoured that the purpose of the talks was to break British control over the Arab Legion by replacing the British subsidy with an Iraqi subsidy and requiring all the British officers of the Arab

[24] Muhammad Mahdi Kubbah, *Memoirs* (Arab.) (Beirut: Dar al-Talia, 1965), 261, 267 f.
[25] Ibid. 262, 270.
[26] Interview with Col. Desmond Goldie.

Legion to take long leave or to resign. The withdrawal of the British personnel, it was said, would remove the brakes which had hitherto checked the effectiveness of the Arab Legion and would enable that force to operate under higher Iraqi command, free from any foreign interference. Abdullah, however, lost interest in the idea when it was made clear to him that Iraq was in no position to help Transjordan financially. The upshot of the discussions was that both sides adhered in principle to a unified operational command but decided that their armies would act as independent units. In short, the earlier arrangement which had left each force free to act as it saw fit remained undisturbed.[27]

Following the loss of Lydda and Ramle, King Abdullah and his ministers did consider removing the British officers from positions of executive authority and retaining their services in the form of a military mission. So as not to offend Britain, it was thought best to adopt the alternative of forming a separate Ministry of Defence and of concentrating all authority in the hands of the minister, thus reducing the chief of staff to the position of adviser. Until that time the normal practice had been for the prime minister also to hold the defence portfolio. A new ministry was duly formed under Fawzi el-Mulki as defence minister, and Glubb was granted a month's leave in England.

During Glubb's absence a reaction set in and the hostility towards the British officers began to dissipate. Nevertheless, the Council of Ministers persisted in their desire to exercise closer control over the actions of the Arab Legion than they had done hitherto. Kirkbride felt that this desire was only natural and indeed welcomed the change. The free hand exercised by Glubb meant that the British government was blamed for any failure or unpopular action taken by the Legion. Under the new arrangement, the Council of Ministers could not avoid responsibility in the eyes of the Arab world for the actions of their troops.[28]

Before his departure, Abdullah had given Glubb a letter to convey to the British foreign secretary. 'The Jewish question,' wrote Abdullah, 'which has given both you and us so much trouble, will not be solved through the Arab League. All concerned must understand and appreciate the dangers inherent in this problem and seek for a remedy. I think that we have reached at least a partial understanding with you on this subject, according to the information submitted to me by my Prime Minister, who actually met Your Excellency and discussed this problem.' This gentle reminder of Bevin's complicity in the Transjordanian design to partition Palestine was followed by the claim that behind the

[27] Kirkbride to Bevin, 24 Aug. 1948, FO 371/68376, PRO.
[28] Kirkbride to Bevin, 25 Sept. 1948, FO 371/68832, PRO.

Jewish movement lay a wider Soviet design and a request for material assistance to help Transjordan resist Soviet expansion. The letter was brief but it promised that Glubb Pasha would explain to Bevin 'all the activities which our jealous Arab rivals have engaged in against us, with even more alacrity than our enemies the Jews'.[29]

During his month-long stay in England, Glubb Pasha did indeed elaborate on the activities of Transjordan's Arab rivals and painted in the process a most alarming picture of the political situation, of the state of the Arab Legion, and of the British influence there. In his first comprehensive report, Glubb claimed that the more extreme members of the Arab League, aided and abetted by Azzam Pasha, were straining every nerve in propaganda against Transjordan in the hope of destroying her once and for all and dividing up her territory. Nothing less than the continued existence of the kingdom lay in the balance.

Transjordan herself was presented by Glubb as the victim of circumstances beyond her control:

The original Trans-Jordan plan was based on the supposition that, at the end of the British Mandate, the Jews would proclaim a Jewish state within the boundaries laid down by the UNO partition scheme. The Arab areas of Palestine would remain vacant, except possibly for bands of irregulars. The Arab Legion would march in and occupy these areas, pending a decision on their final disposal. There would be no conflict between the Arab Legion and the Jewish forces. The proposed occupation was to be no more than a police operation. The British Government were aware of this plan.

It was the fiasco of the Arab Liberation Army and the tragedy of the Arab refugees that made the intervention of the Arab armies inevitable, claimed Glubb. Transjordan still hoped to occupy the hill areas of Hebron, Ramallah, and Nablus without serious fighting. But as a result of Jewish manœuvres, the whole of the Arab Legion became engaged in the Jerusalem operations. Meanwhile the operations of the Arab armies were obviously ineffective. The Iraqi, Syrian, and Lebanese armies had scarcely succeeded in crossing the frontier. The Egyptian army caused the Jews some anxiety at first, but after fifteen days of operations the Egyptians took up a static position on the coast, north of Majdal. As a result, the real struggle of the war became more and more a duel between the Arab Legion and the Jewish forces for possession of Jerusalem.

Again and again Glubb returned to his central point:

The Trans-Jordan Government had never intended to involve itself in any serious military operations at all, and it was fully aware from the first that partition was inevitable. I missed no opportunity to inform them that Trans-

[29] FO to Amman, 21 Aug. 1948, FO 800/477, PRO.

Jordan had not sufficient resources to wage war on the Jewish state and the Prime Minister assured me frequently that he understood this.

Transjordan's friendship and loyalty to Great Britain was considered by Glubb the principal reason for the suspicion and hatred with which she was viewed by the politicians of certain other Arab countries. In the first month of fighting in Palestine, tiny Transjordan, with a total population of 500,000, had done more than any other to fight the Jews; more than Egypt, which was 36 times bigger in population and revenue, more than Iraq which was 10 times as large, and more than Syria, which was 8 times as strong. The conclusion was said to be only too obvious: a treaty with Britain had resulted in making the weakest Arab country into militarily the most effective.

At the end of the mandate, Azzam Pasha gave the Transjordanian prime minister £250,000 out of a central fund of several million pounds set up by the Arab League and promised a further £500,000. At the end, however, Azzam refused to pay the balance on the grounds that Transjordan had betrayed the Arab cause by her subservience to Great Britain. As a result, Transjordan was some £500,000 in debt. The British subsidy of £500,000 for the July–September quarter was first withheld, then released after the truce, but the whole amount was written off against outstanding bills. Unless extra cash was provided to pay for the Arab Legion for August, September, and October, warned Glubb, the force would disband and the Arab front would collapse.

Nor would this be the end of the matter. The crushing of the Arab Legion in Palestine would expose the flank and communications of the Iraqi army and necessitate a hasty withdrawal. Transjordan would be invaded by some 12,000 Arab soldiers of doubtful loyalty and discipline, and collapse into anarchy would ensue. After a period of anarchy, the country would probably be divided between Syria, Iraq, and Saudi Arabia. The collapse of Transjordan, concluded Glubb, would inflict irreparable damage on the policy of Anglo-Arab friendship and allow the Jews to get the whole of Palestine: 'If we hang on a little longer, Trans-Jordan may receive a substantial increase in territory, which will make her a more valuable ally. If we abandon her now and she collapses, the solution to the Palestine problem itself will be rendered more difficult.'[30]

A week later, on August 19, Glubb circulated in Whitehall another long and alarmist report on the precariousness of Transjordan's position and the threat of renewed Jewish aggression. During the previous fifteen days, claimed Glubb, the Jews had been constantly advancing, seizing fresh territory and attacking one or other of the

---

[30] Brig. Glubb, 'The Trans-Jordan Situation', 12 Aug. 1948, FO 371/68822, PRO.

Arab Legion's positions. They were defying the UN observers and playing power politics as crudely as the Russians on a smaller scale. The Jewish attempt to occupy the Government House ridge, south of Jerusalem, signalled to Glubb that they might try to capture the whole of Jerusalem by cutting off the road to Transjordan east of the city. Should they succeed in reaching the Jerusalem–Jericho road, the Arab Legion would either have to evacuate Palestine or risk being cut off. The Transjordanian government, whose ideas about strategy were said by Glubb to be 'peculiar', had already made it clear to him that it would not sanction evacuation, and would prefer the whole Arab Legion to be cut off and destroyed in Palestine.

The Iraqi army, too, would be cut off should the Jews reach Jericho, and this would either mean a disorganized and demoralized retreat into Transjordan by 12,000 undisciplined Iraqi soldiers or that the Iraqi army would be surrounded and destroyed in Palestine. This could cause a revolution in Iraq, and probably result in a republican regime allied to Russia.

The effect on British prestige would be disastrous, argued Glubb, if fighting in Palestine were to recommence and Transjordan were to collapse. Britain's only friend in the Middle East would be the first to disappear. Transjordan did not have the resources to take on the Jewish state single-handed while the other Arab states looked on. For example, she had no aircraft and virtually no anti-aircraft defence, while the Jews were believed to possess some five squadrons of aircraft with which they could destroy Amman in a couple of days. Moreover, there were now nearly 400,000 destitute Arab refugees, half of them in Transjordan or being supported by her. A further Jewish offensive might produce another 300,000 Arab refugees, and it would take many years and millions of pounds to resettle these wretched people. To supply the Arab Legion with ammunition was therefore no longer enough, though it was badly needed; only strong diplomatic action to prevent the Jews recommencing the fighting could save Transjordan. Economic sanctions, Glubb believed, would quickly be fatal to the Jewish state because it depended entirely on trade and supplies from overseas and on funds from America. But, he said, he had the impression that the Security Council would in practice never take action against the Jews; the time had therefore come to face the likelihood of an Arab collapse in Palestine due to Jewish infringement of the truce, leading probably to the downfall of Transjordan and revolution in Iraq.

Before Glubb left Amman, King Abdullah asked him to enquire in London whether and how Great Britain would carry out her treaty obligation to defend Transjordan in the event of the Arab Legion being overwhelmed in Palestine and the Jews reaching the Jordan River. Glubb's recommendations were that the Security Council issue a strong warning to both sides before adjourning; that four Dakota loads of ammunition be flown by the RAF to Amman; and that the British minister be instructed to assure the government there that Britain would fulfil her obligations should Transjordan be attacked.[31]

The chiefs of staff were not oblivious to the repercussions that a military reverse in Transjordan could have on Britain's whole position in the Middle East. Before Glubb's arrival in London they had received a report from Sir Alec Kirkbride in which he registered his 'growing conviction that if a disaster overtakes Trans-Jordan whilst we are witholding supplies and ammunition, we might as well abandon the present policy of building defensive alliances in the Middle East'.[32] These sentiments coincided all too closely with the forebodings of the chiefs of staff. They felt that it was not only the goodwill of the Arab states but of the whole Muslim world that was at stake. In their report to the minister of defence, A. V. Alexander, they pointed out that the treaty with Transjordan seemed to be unequivocal and that if Israel attacked Transjordan, Britain would be bound to be at war with the Jews. They suggested that a clear statement to this effect might forestall such an attack. They also emphasized the urgency of sending the necessary equipment and ammunition to RAF stations in Transjordan and Iraq. A more tentative suggestion made by the chiefs of staff was that Britain should offer to guarantee the frontiers of the Arab states generally against Jewish aggression.[33]

Bevin was not prepared to go as far as the chiefs of staff in responding to the urgent pleas for help from King Abdullah, Sir Alec Kirkbride, and Glubb Pasha. As foreign secretary he had to consider the implications of any help in the light of Britain's position at the United Nations and her relations with the United States. And he tended to take rather personally the charges that Britain had let down her Arab allies. Bevin gave Glubb a personal interview but the latter, according to Kirkbride's recollections, got no satisfaction from the occasion: 'Mr Bevin indulged in a long tirade on the subject of the behaviour of the Arabs who had, he said, rewarded his many attempts to assist them with abuse and ingratitude; he admitted that the Jordanians were not as bad as some of the others but could not give them preferential treatment. He did not send a written reply to the King's letter.'[34]

[31] Note by Glubb Pasha, 19 Aug. 1948, FO 371/68822, PRO.

[32] Kirkbride to FO, 6 Aug. 1948, FO 371/68830, PRO.

[33] Copy of a minute dated 12 Aug. 1948, to the minister of defence from the secretary, Chiefs of Staff Committee, FO 371/68822; A. V. Alexander to Ernest Bevin, 13 Aug. 1948, FO 371/68830, PRO.

[34] Kirkbride, *From the Wings*, 53.

There is no reason to doubt that at his meeting with Glubb, Bevin gave vent to his despair of the Arabs and that the general atmosphere was distinctly less cordial than the one which prevailed during the February meeting to which Glubb had accompanied Abul Huda. But Bevin's contemporary report to Kirkbride is a rather more accurate guide to the meeting that took place in the foreign secretary's private flat on August 19.

Bevin read the two memoranda by Glubb and at their meeting he gave him a non-committal but friendly letter to take back to King Abdullah. Whereas the king had referred to a 'partial understanding', Bevin reminded his emissary that 'we had never urged the Trans-jordan Government to take action in Palestine. They had told us beforehand that they intended to do this and we had mentioned the difficulties that might arise for us with the United Nations. We had not even been told beforehand that the Arab Legion would go into Jerusalem.'

As regards help, Bevin said that it would be too provocative to move war material into the RAF base in Amman but they could keep aircraft and the necessary supplies ready in the Canal Zone so that material could be moved quickly if necessary. Secondly, Bevin gave an assurance that the subsidy to the Arab Legion would continue to be paid to meet recurring expenditure and a solution will be found to the problem of the accumulated debts. Glubb said that this appeared to be satisfactory.

In addition to these two lines of action, Bevin emphasized the efforts he was making to enlighten the US government and public opinion on the aggressiveness of the Jews. It was important, therefore, that the forces under Glubb's command should continue to adopt a non-provocative attitude and that maximum publicity should be given to any infringement of the truce by the Jews. Glubb emphasized the need for speed in sending assistance as the Legion could only hold out for a few days if fighting was resumed.

Finally, Glubb said, King Abdullah had also requested him to ask what Britain would do if the Jews, after resuming hostilities, reached the Jordan? Bevin replied that this question ought not to be asked: 'We had our treaty and we would not go back on it. We would not abandon Transjordan or give up Transjordan territory. But Transjordan must not rely on the treaty or this assurance to create an incident.' Glubb said there was no danger of this; the only risk was an Irgun attack on the Arab Legion.

Bevin instructed Kirkbride to inform King Abdullah very confidentially of the gist of this conversation and add that, in their discussions with the Americans on the Palestine situation, they were carefully bearing in mind Transjordan's interests. He was expected to make the king see that Britain continued 'to attach considerable importance to the existence and integrity of Transjordan, to the maintenance and development of our close relations with Transjordan and to the continued existence of the Arab Legion as an effective fighting force in close relations with the British Army'.[35]

Glubb thus had every reason to be satisfied with the meeting and with the generally sympathetic hearing he was accorded in Whitehall. When he went to see Field-Marshal Montgomery, the Chief of the Imperial General Staff, the latter said he hoped they would give Transjordan a guarantee that they would go to her help if she was attacked and that they would inform the Jews that this assurance had been given. While Glubb was naturally all in favour of such an assurance, he was strongly against the idea of informing the Jews that it had been given. He felt that this would make it more difficult for the Jews to accept the absorption of Arab Palestine into Transjordan and would also be likely to make the Jews think that they could occupy the whole of Palestine with impunity provided they did not actually threaten Transjordanian territory. Glubb's view was confidentially relayed back to Bevin so when the latter saw Montgomery, he was able to discourage him from pursuing this idea and to urge him to concentrate on ensuring readiness to carry out Britain's treaty obligations.[36] Glubb may not have been as good a soldier as Montgomery, but he was immeasurably more subtle as a politician. For a man on holiday, at any rate, he had accomplished a great deal during his visit to England.

One of Glubb's achievements lay in steering British thinking on the future of Palestine in a direction favourable to King Abdullah. If in the final settlement in Palestine Britain left the fate of the Arab areas to be decided by the Arabs themselves, he pointed out to Bernard Burrows, this was unlikely to result in a large part going to Transjordan and the rest to Egypt or other Arab states. A more likely result, given Transjordan's unpopularity, would be the setting up of a separate Arab state, presumably under the influence of the mufti. The disadvantages of a separate Arab state under the mufti, minuted the head of the Eastern Department afterwards, needed no elaboration, but he elaborated them all the same: 'It would be a hotbed of ineffectual Arab fanaticism and after causing maximum disturbances to our relations with the Arabs would very likely fall in the end under Jewish influence and be finally absorbed in the Jewish state, thereby increasing the area

[35] Bevin to Kirkbride, 21 Aug. 1948, FO 800/477, PRO.
[36] Minute by Burrows, 25 Aug. 1948, and Minute by Bevin, 26 Aug. 1948, FO 371/68822, PRO.

of possible Russian influence and excluding the possibility of our obtaining strategic requirements in any part of Palestine.'[37]

Bevin acted on the advice of his Foreign Office officials and obtained the Cabinet's approval for advising the UN mediator that the setting up of a separate Arab state on the territory occupied by the Arab states in Palestine was unlikely to provide a permanent solution and that this territory should therefore be incorporated in Transjordan, subject to frontier modifications that might be desired by the Egyptian government. Bevin told the Cabinet that any attempt to make further progress through direct discussions between the Arabs and Jews themselves would fail and that the only hope lay in the imposition of a settlement by the United Nations. The Cabinet decided that if agreement could be reached with the US government and with the mediator on the scheme proposed by Bevin, Britain's influence should be used to obtain support for it from the other members of the United Nations.[38]

The implication of this decision was that the mediator should not try to mediate between the parties to the Palestine dispute but should use the UN's authority instead to impose on them a solution devised by the Anglo-Saxon Powers. But no one in the Cabinet challenged this curious Foreign Office conception of the mediator's role.

The Foreign Office found itself competing with the Israeli representative in Washington for the ear of the State Department on the question of procedure. Whereas the Foreign Office pressed the view that only an externally imposed solution could settle the Palestine problem, Eliahu Epstein persuaded Robert Lovett, the under-secretary of State, that the best chance of reaching a settlement in Palestine would be if the Israelis and Arabs could get together themselves, independently of the mediator. Epstein suggested to Lovett that if only King Abdullah and one or two of the more moderate Israeli leaders could meet quietly, it should not be difficult for them to come to terms. Lovett was impressed by what Epstein told him, and he himself became increasingly convinced that the best course for the United States and the United Kingdom to adopt was to make a determined effort to stage a meeting between the Arabs and the Israelis in the near future. Lovett thought that King Abdullah ought to take the lead because he was the only Arab leader who could be relied upon to take a sensible and constructive view of things, and if some agreement emerged out of such a meeting, the frontiers between the Jewish and Arab states should then be guaranteed by the United Nations.[39]

[37] B. A. B. Burrows, 'Transjordan', 17 Aug. 1948, FO 371/68822, PRO.
[38] Memorandum by the secretary of state for foreign affairs, 'Palestine', CP (48)207, 24 Aug. 1948, CAB 129/29; and CM 57(48)4, 26 Aug. 1948, PRO.
[39] F. R. Hoyer Millar (Washington) to Michael Wright, 27 Aug. 1948, FO 371/68584, PRO.

The Foreign Office reacted very strongly against the suggestion that Transjordan should enter into direct negotiations with the provisional government of Israel. The Foreign Office believed that if Transjordan were to do this, it would lose the last vestige of respect accorded to it by the other Arab states and the net result might be the disappearance from the scene of the most moderate and co-operative Arab League state along with the Arab Legion.[40]

Support for the British approach came from Tawfiq Abul Huda, who expressed the hope that the United Nations would make a final decision on Palestine without any prior consultation of the Arab states. Concerted international pressure involving Britain and America, he argued, would make it easier for the Arab leaders to abandon their earlier stands. 'It would be dangerous', underlined Kirkbride, 'to suggest bilateral negotiations between Transjordan and the Jews to King Abdullah. He is already flirting with ideas of this kind but both I and the Prime Minister, with whom I discussed the tendency some time ago, feel that he is not really in a strong enough position to ride out the storm which such action would cause in the Arab world.'[41]

[40] *FRUS 1948*, v. 1343.   [41] Kirkbride to FO, 31 Aug. 1948, FO 371/68822, PRO.

10

LULL IN THE STORM

The renewal of Israeli contact with Abdullah

During the lull in the storm that followed the ten days' whirlwind, King Abdullah kept flirting with the idea of bilateral negotiations with Israel even though he got no encouragement from either his ministers or his British friends. He was reported to be in good spirits following the cessation of hostilities, and the prospect of a large kingdom seemed to agree with him.[1] Though it did not go as planned, the war had served its basic purpose in enabling him to occupy the central areas of Arab Palestine. Not only was there nothing further to be gained from an appeal to arms, but such an appeal could jeopardize both his territorial gains and his army, the mainstay of his regime and his only defence against his Arab opponents. Accordingly, the king shifted his attention from the military to the political arena. He now desired a restoration of peace and understanding with the Israelis and he was ready for the resumption of direct contact with them.

For the Israeli leaders, too, the centre of gravity began to shift from war to politics as they picked their way through the maze of negotiations, trying to keep clear of all the pitfalls. They regarded the truce as a thinly disguised continuation of the war since it did not permit them to demobilize the population under arms, thus imposing an unbearable economic burden. To them an indefinite truce was equivalent to a death sentence to be executed at the convenience of the Arabs. Prompt and direct negotiations with the Arab states were, from their point of view, the only practicable way out of the impasse.[2] The Israeli leaders remained deeply suspicious of the British and therefore anxious to exclude them as far as possible from any peace negotiations. Count Bernadotte was viewed as Britain's poodle, hence the attempts to undermine his credibility, isolate him, and bypass him. In a major speech before the Provisional State Council on July 22, Prime Minister Ben-Gurion declared that the time had come for a solution of the Palestinian problem by direct negotiations and not through the good offices of the mediator. Foreign Minister Shertok, who had marked the establishment of the State of Israel by adopting the Hebrew name

---

[1] *FRUS 1948*, v. 1237 f.   [2] Ibid. 1338 f.

Sharett, cunningly used the mediator's good offices to convey to the Arab governments an invitation to hold direct talks.[3]

Apart from limiting British influence there were two other advantages that the Israelis expected to realize through direct talks. First, the obvious disunity in the Arab camp gave Israel considerable room for manœuvre. The Arabs had marched into Palestine together but as they sustained blows and military reverses, each country looked increasingly to her own needs. Within ten days the position of the Arab states changed fundamentally, from being the attacker to being attacked. Each country was licking its wounds and was in no position and in no mood to help the others or subordinate her interests to the common cause. Under these circumstances anyone looking for cracks in the wall of Arab unity could easily find them. Israel, with the memory of her military victories still fresh in everybody's mind, was well placed to play off the Arab states against one another. Secondly, it was a propitious time to engage in exploratory talks because the positions of both sides were still rather fluid. The Arab demands on borders and refugees had not crystallized yet, nor had Israel's response to these demands. The Israeli aim was therefore to seize the diplomatic initiative, to establish direct contact with Arab leaders, to sound out opinion, and to exploit opportunities.

Elias Sasson, Israel's greatest-ever practitioner of the art of Oriental diplomacy and now head of the Middle East Department in the Israeli Foreign Ministry, was sent to Paris in early July in order to set the process in motion. Two Arabic-speaking assistants, Shmuel Divon and Tuvia Arazi, accompanied him to Paris to set up a base for their diplomatic and intelligence operations. His deputy, Yaacov Shimoni, stayed at home to run the department and help co-ordinate the activities of the Paris-based unit with local efforts to initiate talks with local Arab figures.

Sasson set himself the task of contacting as many Arab representatives as possible in Paris, both official and unofficial, in order to exchange views about ways and means of settling the Arab–Israeli conflict. These conversations were conducted in the most general terms and rarely progressed to the 'brass tacks' level. Sasson's brief was to emphasize Israel's readiness to conclude close alliances with her neighbours and establish mutually beneficial economic relations. He contacted, for example, several prominent Egyptians whose attitude was not unfriendly but who could not contribute anything concrete. Sasson also wrote personally to Riad al-Sulh, the prime minister of Lebanon, to Lutfi al-Haffar, the prominent Nationalist Party politician in Syria, and many others, telling each he knew him to be a dis-

[3] *DFPI*, i. 409 f.

tinguished Arab personality and he would like to renew his acquaintance.[4] Lutfi al-Haffar took the letters he received to Prime Minister Mardam and President Quwatli, who decided to ignore them. So there was no Syrian response to Sasson's overtures.[5]

Sasson was not constrained to pursue any particular political orientation; either Egyptian, or Syrian or Hashemite or specifically Transjordanian. He was left a free hand to follow his hunches and contact anyone he chose to. 'There was no agenda for negotiations', remarked Shimoni. 'Sasson's role, and Sasson's forte, lay in maintaining contact, in serving as a sounding board and communicating ideas. He was like an octopus with a thousand tentacles looking for catch. And we were very catholic in those days. We had contact with the Sudanese, with Egypt, with Azzam and, indirectly, with Quwatli and Mardam. We even had contact with the Iraqis. It was a process of probing and exploration on the part of both sides; an endless chain of forging links with just about anybody.'[6] 'We had no orientation, neither Egyptian nor Transjordanian,' commented another Israeli official 'we were prepared to talk to anyone who came along. The term orientation in the Zionist context is a misnomer. It is used to cover up something which is much more practical and self-serving. Abdullah was ready, we went with him. Had the Egyptians been ready we would have gone with them.'[7]

Yet it was not entirely fortuitous that Sasson reserved much of his skill and energy for the task of restoring the severed link with King Abdullah. Nor is it accidental that of all Sasson's efforts this was the one that was most quickly crowned with success. The two sides had reached agreement on the partition of Palestine in November 1947 and despite all the subsequent misunderstandings and the war, the basis for that agreement had not entirely disappeared. The king was not responsible for severing the link with the Zionists. At his last meeting with Golda Meir he expressed his readiness to meet with them even if they found themselves at war. The personal element was very important in Abdullah's relationship with his environment. He was a cautious man who never put all his eggs in one basket. Towards Sasson his attitude was one of great respect and trust based on long-standing acquaintance. A letter from Sasson had considerable weight in Abdullah's eyes. Of all the Israeli diplomats Sasson was the only one who knew how to approach Abdullah and how to win his co-operation.[8]

Sasson wrote to Dr Shawkat as-Sati, the king's personal physician and confidant, and invited him to talks in Paris. Instead of Dr Sati, the

[4] Ibid. 453, 533; *FRUS 1948*, v. 1347, 1376. [5] Interview with Salma Mardam-Bey.
[6] Interview with Yaacov Shimoni. [7] Interview with Gershon Avner.
[8] Interview with Moshe Sasson.

Transjordanian minister in London, Amir Abdul Majid Haidar, arrived in Paris, saying he had been sent by the king 'to exchange views and examine the possibilities for an understanding'. The first meeting, on August 3, was friendly and lasted four hours. Haidar wanted to know Israel's final aim and her attitude to Bernadotte, to the refugee problem, and to the annexation of Arab Palestine to Transjordan.[9]

Since Haidar promised to send a copy of Israel's reply to the king, Sharett cabled Sasson detailed guidelines and answers. Sasson was to preface his answer by saying that Transjordan's aggression caused them to revise their whole attitude to the king, leading to serious doubts as to whether it would not be preferable for Arab Palestine to stand alone. Nevertheless, in view of their past friendship, they were prepared to make a renewed attempt to reach an understanding, but the fact that aggression had been committed would naturally influence their attitude. They had no confidence in Bernadotte and preferred direct dealings to his mediation. More specifically, Sasson was to propose a solution based on the UN partition plan with substantial changes in Israel's favour, the balance to be joined to Transjordan; the resettlement of the refugees in the enlarged kingdom with the king's political assistance and Israeli financial support; an economic alliance that would benefit Transjordan; Israeli assistance in getting an American development loan for the king and in securing Transjordan's recognition by the United States and admission to the United Nations. The king could have an unspecified part of Jerusalem, with the Israelis keeping new Jerusalem and the corridor to Tel Aviv, while the Old City would be administered jointly with an international umpire.[10]

Abdullah did not wait to hear the outcome of the Paris talks before embarking on an initiative of his own. The Belgian consul-general in Jerusalem, Jean Nieuwenhuys, had sent the king his greetings for the fast of Ramadan and concluded with a hope for peace. Abdullah seized on this last sentence of the letter to ask Nieuwenhuys to visit him urgently. During the visit, on August 8, the king referred several times to 'my friend Shertok' and asked the consul to propose to him that their representatives should meet informally in Cyprus. Regarding the refugees, the king said he would keep all the mufti's supporters in Transjordan and asked that Israel should readmit the others. Sharett asked the consul to tell Abdullah that they agreed to meet but preferred Paris to Cyprus. When no word came back from Amman, Sharett suspected that the British had got wind of the king's move and advised him not to carry it through.[11]

In fact the Belgian consul did not convey Sharett's reply until August 27 when he saw the king in Amman. Also present on this occasion was

[9] DFPI, i. 453.   [10] Ibid. 490.   [11] Ibid. 533; FRUS 1948, v. 1375-7.

Abdel Ghani al-Karmi, who had frequently served as a secret emissary between the court and the Jewish Agency. The king said he had stopped the London–Paris talks because of press leaks but that he would send another representative to meet Sasson in the near future. He was hopeful of positive results despite the fact that Sharett had to contend with the right-wing extremists while he himself had to contend with the Arab League. If agreement was reached, said Abdullah, he would be prepared to go ahead without the League.[12]

At his next visit to the palace, on September 9, the Belgian consul, at Sharett's behest, assured the king that the leak to the press had occurred in Tel Aviv and that Sasson was completely innocent. The king stated that Fawzi el-Mulki, the minister of defence, and Said al-Mufti, the minister of trade, would proceed to Paris as observers to the General Assembly and would be available for working out a peace settlement with Sasson. To enhance his prestige in the Arab League, the king requested that Israel readmit the refugees from Lydda and Ramle, whose distress was particularly acute, but if a peace programme including this measure of repatriation was to be rejected by the League, he would go ahead regardless. He reported that he was taking steps to check the increase in Husayni activity in Palestine by sending contingents to the affected areas. He pressed the consul to revisit him in Irbid after seeing Sharett.

Sensing Abdullah's impatience, Sharett resorted to the usual diplomatic ploy of feigning indifference. He told the consul to say that he was in a very cautious mood and that with reports that the Arab armies in Palestine had doubled their strength during the truce, Israel would have to strengthen her positions along the entire front and could not possibly spare the troops to deal with the massive repatriation of the people of the two towns. Sharett said they would treat any Transjordanian proposals on their merits but urged Abdullah to start thinking seriously about the resettlement of the bulk of the refugees in her zone, and hoped that Israel might prevail on the United States to give him a loan for this purpose.[13]

Nieuwenhuys visited Abdullah in Irbid on September 14 to convey Sharett's comments. The king said that the Egyptian and Iraqi armies had received scant reinforcement. The Legion had received more substantial reinforcements but the Israelis had no need to worry as it was firmly in hand. He again insisted on the readmission of the non-Husaynis to Lydda and Ramle as a gesture that would enhance his prestige, defeat the intrigues of Nuqrashi and the mufti, deal a blow to the League as a whole, and serve as a basis for a population exchange between Palestine and Transjordan. Sharett told the consul that

[12] *DFPI*, i. 563.   [13] Ibid. 576 f.

repatriation of refugees, even partial, was out of the question for the present but he would formulate his reply within a couple of days so that the thread would not snap.[14] In short, Sharett had correctly identified the refugee problem as the most critical and burning issue in Israeli–Transjordanian relations, but he was stalling in the hope that a solution would emerge without any substantial Israeli concessions.

Sharett's stand reflected a rapidly evolving Israeli consensus against permitting any Arab refugees to return to their homes.[15] The new official line was that as long as the war continued no refugees would be allowed to return, and that after the war Israel would consider schemes for a solution but only within the framework of a comprehensive peace settlement. Sasson was one of the very few officials who dared challenge the official line against repatriation. He was moved not so much by humanitarian concern for the plight of the refugees but by an enlightened conception of Israel's self-interest, and above all her interest in peaceful coexistence with her neighbours. Sasson urged his colleagues to reconsider whether it would not be worth exploiting the refugee problem to finish the war, win over Arab public opinion, establish contacts with Arab statesmen, remove Bernadotte and his British and American supporters, and modify the country's borders so that they could turn their attention to solving the country's internal problems.[16]

Sasson pointed out that Israeli propaganda on the refugee question was counter-productive. The intention behind it was to turn the refugees and their anger against the Arab leaders whereas Israel's true interest lay in promoting the absorption of these refugees in the Arab countries. The only Arab leader who could be counted on to adopt a reasonable and co-operative attitude was Abdullah. Logic suggested, therefore, that Israel's effort should be directed not at undermining him but at making him popular with the refugees so that he in turn would be able to negotiate the fate of the refugees without fear from his rivals and appear as the saviour of the Palestine Arabs, not as a traitor to the Palestine cause.[17]

From his isolated outpost in the French capital, Sasson fired off a barrage of angry letters at his colleagues. The indiscretion of the officials in Tel Aviv in revealing to the press that secret peace talks were under way, he charged, had aborted his contact with Amir Abdul Majid Haidar. In vain Sasson waited for the two Transjordanian ministers to contact him and, for a while it looked as if he had lost the

[14] *DFPI*, i. 611.

[15] Benny Morris, 'The Crystallization of Israeli Policy Against a Return of the Arab Refugees, April–December, 1948', *Studies in Zionism* 6/1 (1985).

[16] Sasson's letter from Paris, 13 Aug. 1948, 2453/2, ISA.

[17] Sasson's letter from Paris, 20 Aug. 1948, 2453/2, ISA.

thread to Amman altogether. But it was on the broad questions of policy towards the Arab world that Sasson found himself most out of accord with the official line. He urged his colleagues at home not to remain within the confines of a parochial and blinkered view on such questions as the future of the refugees and the renewal of the war but to widen their horizons and impress on the policymakers the need for a broader international perspective. In a letter to his deputy, Sasson recalled that he himself had asserted, when the war started, that they could not subdue the Arabs by force alone. He continued:

If the war is renewed, I have no doubt that it would be possible for us to capture Tulkarem, Nablus and more. It would also be possible for us to strike blows at the armies of Egypt, Syria, etc. But we can only move the Arabs from one place to another and that is all. The tension will not subside. Tranquillity will not prevail and the peace will not come any nearer. And the question is: do we want this? I regret that these days I am not near you or near the leadership because I would not have been deterred from swimming against the current for the common good.[18]

Shimoni denied that there was any substantive difference between Sasson and the other officials in the Middle East Department except on the refugee question. They too were of the opinion that if hostilities recommenced Israel would score victories and capture further territories but this would not be sufficient to compel the Arabs to accept a settlement. What might lead to a settlement, in the department's view, was either progress in the secret explorations that Sasson had embarked on, or a dictate by the United Nations and the Great Powers, or an internal uprising in one of the Arab states that would divert attention away from the Palestine conflict.

Efforts to create such a diversion revolved round Syria and were given a boost by the establishment of a contact with Zeid al-Atrash, the tribal chief from Jebel Druze in south-east Syria. Like his older brother Sultan al-Atrash, Zeid was a supporter of Abdullah and of the Greater Syria scheme and had played a part in the revolt that started in Jebel Druze in 1925 and developed into a national uprising. Shimoni and his colleagues were encouraged to think that 'a link-up with the potential rebel forces in Syria and above all, of course, with the Druze, to create a major diversion and insert a poisoned dagger in the back of the Arab unity that is fighting us—is one of the ways which might help to bring about the desired solution'. An alliance with the Druze and with other forces in Syria and Lebanon would obviously involve a major financial investment as well as concrete help and co-operation from the IDF. The foreign minister, however, told his subordinates that in view of the

[18] *DFPI*, i. 566 f.

government's weak financial position a major plan of this kind was out of the question. Nevertheless, he gave them permission to continue to explore possibilities for action on a more modest scale. Apart from the moves to activate the Druze of Jebel Druze, efforts were to continue to encourage the defection of further Druze and Circassian units from the Syrian army to the Israeli side. Here the Druze and Circassian units already serving in the IDF were to provide the connecting link.

Shimoni also informed his boss that there would be a chance to renew the contact with Transjordan through emissaries who were leaving from the Beisan area. At first Shimoni was doubtful about this prospect because he did not want to get in the way of Sasson's operations. But Sharett ruled that it was important to try and win over Muhammad Zubeiti not for the purpose of conducting parallel negotiations or shifting the centre of gravity from Paris to Tel Aviv but solely in order to be able to steer the king in the right direction and monitor his actions and his thoughts.[19]

Count Bernadotte's last will and testament

Count Bernadotte was aware of the efforts being made by the Israelis to dispense with his mediation and establish direct contact with the Arabs. But he also had Azzam Pasha's assurance that all the members of the Arab League took the view that it would be a mistake to open direct negotiations with the Jews and that any discussions on a proposal for a final settlement should be conducted through the offices of the United Nations mediator.[20] During the summer of 1948, Bernadotte continued to hold the centre of the stage and he stepped up his activities in search of a settlement. Yet even members of his own staff could not help wondering whether he was really equal to the task. 'The Count gives me the impression', recorded one of them in his diary, 'of a man who is lost in a labyrinth, who yet continues walking with great speed and decision as if he knew exactly where he is going.'[21]

Having had his first set of suggestions rejected by all local parties to the Palestine dispute, Bernadotte increasingly looked to the Great Powers for guidance and support. He was not eager to offer suggestions until he was assured that the British and American governments were in agreement with him. He realized that the Israelis would make exorbitant demands and that the Arabs would refuse to countenance officially the existence of a Jewish state. Nevertheless, he felt that if the

[19] Shimoni to Sasson, 16 Sept. 1948, 2570/11, ISA.
[20] Bernadotte, *To Jerusalem*, 229 f.
[21] Pablo de Azcarate, *Mission in Palestine 1948–1952* (Washington DC: Middle East Institute, 1966), 94.

two governments lined up behind him, both Israelis and Arabs would move protestingly towards an eventual settlement.[22]

Discussions between the Foreign Office and the State Department in the course of August and early September revealed a remarkable measure of agreement on the outlines of a settlement. The main feature of this consensus, as of Bernadotte's tentative ideas, was the partition of Palestine into two geographically compact territories instead of the enclaves, corridors and complicated lines recommended by the General Assembly in November 1947. This involved the inclusion of the whole of the Galilee in the Jewish state in exchange for the allocation of the Negev to the Arabs.[23]

The gap between what the British, the Americans, and the Swedish mediator considered an equitable settlement and what the Arabs and Israelis were prepared to agree to remained unbridgeable. Nearly all the Arab politicians consulted by the mediator said they would not be coerced by the United Nations into recognizing Israel or making peace with her. Nuqrashi Pasha said that he realized that the hope of preventing the emergence of an independent Jewish state had been crushed but the Arabs would nevertheless continue to regard Palestine as Arab territory and the Jews as rebels, and in his view the wisest course would be to constitute the Arab part of Palestine as a separate and independent state supported by the Arab League. Nuqrashi did not wish to see Palestine united with Transjordan because that would upset the balance of power in the Arab world. Nor could he agree to the partition of Arab Palestine among a number of Arab countries because that would only be grist to the mill of those who claimed that Egypt had entered the war in order to make territorial conquests. Only the Transjordanian prime minister shared the mediator's view that there was no getting away from the fact that the Jewish state existed and would continue to exist, and that the best solution would be the partition of Palestine.[24]

At his meeting with the Israeli foreign minister, Berndotte outlined three theoretical possibilities for the future of the Arab part of Palestine: a separate state; annexation to Transjordan; and a division of the territory between the neighbouring states. Sharett said that his government would probably prefer the creation of a separate Arab state, while the breaking up of the territory into fragments would be the worst eventuality which they would in all probability even fight to prevent. He did not exclude the possibility of annexation to Transjordan, seeing

---

[22] *FRUS 1948*, v. 1308–10.

[23] Historical Memorandum on the Situation in Palestine Since 1945, 15 Jan. 1949, CAB 129/32, PRO.

[24] Bernadotte, *To Jerusalem*, 196, 201 f., 231 f.

that the latter was at least administratively, if not financially, a going concern, while Arab Palestine was, in Metternich's phrase about Italy, merely a geographical expression. It was not a political entity and had no leadership. Still, efforts might be made to find out whether a group of people could not be welded together to serve as a centre for a separate state. While the Israelis would not fight to prevent the joining of Arab Palestine with Transjordan, said Sharett, they were very much disillusioned with King Abdullah's misguided truculence, and anyhow a smaller and a weaker neighbour was preferable to a bigger and stronger one. Transjordan and Iraq belonged to the same dynasty and might, in the course of time, be united together under a common crown. The prospect of having an Iraqi empire right on their doorstep was not one they could relish.[25]

The Americans, like Bernadotte, felt that the State of Israel should have boundaries that would make it more homogeneous and well-integrated than the hour-glass frontiers drawn on the map of the November 29 resolution. They wondered whether a settlement between Israel and Transjordan could be worked out which would materially simplify the boundary problem by allowing Israel to expand into the fertile area of the Galilee in return for relinquishing a large portion of the desert land of the Negev to her eastern neighbour. Jerusalem, the Americans thought, should be an international enclave, but they were prepared to consider any other arrangement satisfactory to Israel and the Arab states provided the safety and access to the Holy Places were guaranteed. Finally, the Americans urged Israel to consider some constructive measures for alleviating the distress of the Arab refugees. James McDonald, the special representative of the United States in Israel, was asked to make it clear to Ben-Gurion and Sharett that although tentative and in the nature of 'trying on for size', these suggestions were offered in an earnest desire to assist Israel in becoming a permanent force for the maintenance of peace and economic development of the Middle East. If the provisional government of Israel could show any constructive response to these suggestions, the Americans would commend them to the mediator and also to the British government which could be expected to exert considerable pressure on the Arab governments.[26]

Ben-Gurion's response was definitely negative but also inquisitive. He wanted to know the reason behind the suggestion for taking away from Israel the desert that she alone was prepared to develop and giving it to Transjordan which already had enormous uninhabited areas of desert land. He also asked what was meant by the 'fertile'

[25] Bernadotte, To Jerusalem, 208–12; DFPI, i. 501–6.
[26] FRUS 1948, v. 1366–9; DFPI, i. 570 f.

portion of 'occupied' west Galilee, stating that all the Galilee could be made fertile by Jewish effort. Regarding Jerusalem Ben-Gurion conceded that the US suggestions admitted some flexibility but wondered whether they envisaged a Jewish corridor to the city, which he declared to be absolutely vital. On the Arab refugees he was willing to consider constructive proposals but offered no plan of his own. Ben-Gurion observed that the people of Israel had a right to all of western Palestine but that personally, if given the choice, he would choose a small area in order to get a Jewish–Arab peace rather than the entire area without Arab consent. Finally, Ben-Gurion expressed surprise that the American government proposed to mediate between Israel and the mediator and the British government. There was no dispute, he said, between Israel and the mediator. Consequently, if the US government wished to mediate, she should mediate directly between Israel and the Arabs.[27]

Sharett informed McDonald at a separate meeting that they had a favourable though tentative response from Transjordan to their feeler and that they also had an approach from King Abdullah on his own initiative. But to Sharett it appeared that the king's anxiety to explore peace bilaterally was curbed by the British who sought to achieve through the indefinite second truce what they had failed to achieve through war, namely, a reduction of Israel's territory and sovereignty.[28]

Despite all the objections raised by Arabs and Israelis to their suggestions, the mediator, the State Department, and the Foreign Office remained convinced that the solution they favoured could be enforced. The Foreign Office remained strongly wedded to a solution based on the present 'lines of force'. Sir Hugh Dow, the consul-general in Jerusalem, was one of the very few officials who saw through this spurious realism. The main obstacle to a settlement based on the lines of force and worked out by the United Nations, he observed, was the conviction that in no circumstances would the United Nations despatch an adequate force to compel respect for their decisions. This conviction was held by both Jews and Arabs, and though it elated one and depressed the other, in each case it had the effect of encouraging the more extreme elements. Whereas the assembly resolution of November 29 was at least accepted by one party, neither party accepted the mediator's proposals which the Foreign Office now endorsed as the new basis for a settlement:

The Jews are frankly expansionist and refuse to put forward any terms, for fear they should ask for less than changing circumstances and the inefficiency of the United Nations may enable them to grab. The Arabs see little hope of practical

---

[27] *FRUS 1948*, v. 1384–6; Ben-Gurion's diary, 8 Sept. 1948. [28] *DFPI*, i. 587 f.

help, either from us or from the United Nations, and in consequence the 'in for a penny, in for a pound' school of thought tends to prevail.

In one of the earlier chapters of *Don Quixote*, it is related that the knight, before setting out on his adventures, made for himself a helmet of pasteboard, and in order to test its strength, gave it several good blows with his broadsword, and thereby demolished his whole month's labour. 'The facility with which it was dissolved liked him nothing' (I am quoting as nearly as I can remember from Pierce Motteux's translation) 'whereupon he fashioned it anew, placing within it certain iron bars in so cunning and artificial a manner, that he rested content both with the solidity of his handiwork and with the excellence of his invention; and *without exposing it to the further hazard of a blow*, held it in estimation for a most excellent beaver.'

Dow did not wish to press the analogy between Count Bernadotte and Don Quixote too far but he hoped that the unfavourable reception given to the count's first proposals by both Jew and Arab would not lead him to suppose that his next would necessarily be better or that it could be produced at Lake Success without first ascertaining whether it was likely to be acceptable in the Middle East. Both Nuqrashi Pasha and Moshe Sharett expressed to the mediator their preference for an Arab Palestinian state rather than either of the two other solutions put to them. Dow hoped that the mediator would perceive the ulterior motive behind this specious agreement: 'Egypt does not want any other Arab state to increase in relative power and importance, and an Arab Palestinian state would be a hopeless proposition and render the next step in Jewish expansion a very easy one. And it would, of course, play directly into the hands of the Mufti.'[29]

Dow's penetrating observations did not command the attention they deserved in London. The attention of Bevin and his advisers was focused on the problem of getting the Arabs to agree among themselves on the disposal of the Arab areas of Palestine. This rather than the Arab refusal to accept the permanence of a Jewish state or the lack of trust in the efficacy of the United Nations was viewed in London as the chief obstacle to a Palestine settlement. Various ideas were therefore circulated round the British legations in the Middle East on action that Transjordan might take to lessen Arab opposition to its acquisition of this territory. One idea was that King Abdullah should renounce his claims to the Hijaz. Another idea was that he should issue a public disclaimer of any hostile intention towards Syria and possibly even renounce altogether his Greater Syria scheme.[30]

The response to these ideas was not encouraging. From the British Middle East Office in Cairo it was pointed out that Abdullah's

[29] Dow to Burrows, 23 Aug. 1948, FO 371/68584, PRO.
[30] FO to Amman, 3 Sept. 1948, FO 371/68861, PRO.

difficulties with the other Arab states derived not merely from his particular disputes with Ibn Saud and Syria but also from the not wholly unfounded suspicion that he would be prepared to do a deal over Palestine behind their backs. Those, like Azzam Pasha, who felt passionately about the Palestine problem were always likely to distil poison into the minds of other Arabs about Abdullah's political probity. It could therefore be no easy task to persuade the rest of the Arab states to agree to Transjordan being territorially enlarged as a result of the Palestine crisis.[31] British diplomats in Damascus doubted whether any action by King Abdullah could allay fears of his future intentions towards Syria. They predicted that any increase of his territory or importance would be resented by the Syrians, and the British government would be blamed for it.[32]

Sir Alec Kirkbride was likewise convinced that no amount of political manœuvering could secure Arab approval for the incorporation in Transjordan of the Arab part of Palestine. The Transjordanian authorities were under no illusion on this subject but given international approval, they were prepared to disregard any reactions which their expansion was liable to cause in the rest of the Arab world. The only suggestion which Abul Huda could make for decreasing jealous opposition was to arrange for both Egypt and Syria to receive parts of Palestine also.[33]

The prime minister and the king were determined to avoid for as long as they could any commitment on the subject of Bernadotte's emergent proposals because anything they said was immediately misrepresented and used against them. The attempt by the Lebanese prime minister to provoke Abdullah into making an announcement which could only commit Transjordan to refusing the plan or alternatively damn the king for accepting it was typical. Kirkbride's own view was that nothing said or done by the Transjordanian authorities would affect the attitude of the other Arab governments regarding Palestine in the slightest, and that in the circumstances it was best for them to say nothing and be able later to acquiesce in a position by the United Nations which they were in no position to oppose.[34]

The officials in London feared that US recognition of Transjordan before the Arabs had acquiesced to Bernadotte's proposals would greatly weaken Transjordan's already shaky position in the eyes of its Arab neighbours, who would be quick to allege that it was evidence of a deal by which the United States paid Transjordan with recognition for

[31] BMEO to FO, 9 Sept. 1948, FO 371/68861, PRO.
[32] Dundas (Damascus) to FO, 7 Sept. 1948, FO 371/68861, PRO.
[33] Kirkbride to FO, 8 Sept. 1948, FO 371/68861, PRO.
[34] Kirkbride to Bevin, 8 Sept. 1948, FO 816/130, PRO.

selling out the Arab cause in Palestine. The Foreign Office officials had no doubt that the Arab press and public would roundly denounce any proposals put forward by Bernadotte even though they believed that the 'acquiescence' of the Arab states could be secured eventually. However, the vigour of these denunciations, they warned the American ambassador to London, would be greatly increased if a local scapegoat wearing the horns of perfidy were available. The United Nations had the advantage of being 'an intangible villain, but "Rabbi" Abdullah, upon whom we will have to rely so heavily at a later stage, is already on the spot and would be in an even worse one if he were to appear prior to UN action as party to [a] "deal" '. If Transjordan was to be useful in achieving a lasting settlement, it was essential in the Foreign Office view that Abdullah should seem just as outraged as the other Arab leaders with whom it was expedient that he should display every sign of solidarity. In essence, the Foreign Office view was that the timing of US *de jure* recognition of both Transjordan and the provisional government of Israel should be decided on the basis of progress actually made with regard to Bernadotte's proposals.[35]

Bernadotte himself was at his headquarters in Rhodes working frantically on the proposals he was due to submit to the General Assembly. On September 13, Sir John Troutbeck, the director of Britain's Middle Eastern Office in Cairo, and Robert McClintock of the State Department arrived secretly in Rhodes to confer with Bernadotte. Previously there had been complete identity of views that the best solution of the Palestine problem would be along the lines of the mediator's previous proposals minus the idea of union between the two states and including some form of international responsibility for Jerusalem. But the contacts were kept secret because the British officials felt that the proposals would have a better chance of success if they carried the 'made in Sweden' label.[36]

The conversations on the island were devoted more to the perfection of Bernadotte's first draft of the conclusions than to matters of substance, on which all three were in agreement. McClintock did suggest that Israel should be given a token salient in the Negev by projecting Israeli territory south to the Beersheba–Gaza road. Troutbeck, however, wanted to draw Israel's border much further north, along the Majdal–Faluja line which was then occupied by Egyptian forces. Bernadotte firmly supported the British position with the argument that strict justice demanded that the Jews, who were to receive the whole of the Galilee, should not have even a token holding in the Negev.[37] McClintock drew attention to the mystical attachment of the Jews to the Negev. While he himself was willing to recommend to the

[35] *FRUS 1948*, v. 1383 f.   [36] Ibid. 1266–71, 1371–5.   [37] Ibid. 1398–1401.

State Department that they should support the mediator's suggestion to give the whole of the Negev to the Arabs, he thought it quite possible that the White House would intervene in defence of the Jewish claim.[38]

On September 16, just before the opening of the General Assembly in Paris, Bernadotte submitted his report to the secretary-general of the United Nations, Trygve Lie. Bernadotte's premises were that the 1947 UN partition plan was no longer workable; that the Jewish state was a 'living, solidly entrenched and vigorous reality', and that the Arab dream of a unitary Arab state was, therefore, no longer realistic. His principal recommendations were to give the whole of the Galilee to the Jews, the whole of the Negev to the Arabs, to attach all the Arab parts of Palestine to Transjordan, to accord Jerusalem a special status under UN supervision, and to ensure the right of the Arab refugees to return to their homes, with adequate compensation for any who might choose not to return.[39]

The day after Bernadotte issued his report, four Stern Gang terrorists ambushed his car in Jerusalem and murdered him. It was a senseless and utterly superfluous act of political violence. The intention behind it was to change the course of history by signalling to the outside world that the Israeli people would not allow any foreigners to dictate their borders and to compel the Israeli government to display greater resolution in asserting Israel's rights. The outside world, however, was shocked by this brutal manifestation of Zionist fanaticism, and the failure of the provisional government of Israel to apprehend the suspects dealt a blow to its authority and credibility abroad. Yitzhak (Yizernitzky) Shamir, one of the chief architects of the assassination, remained at large (at the time of writing he is Israel's prime minister). Yehoshua Cohen, widely believed to have been the man who pulled the trigger, became a personal friend of Ben-Gurion following the latter's retreat to Kibbutz Sde Boker in the Negev. At the time, the cold-blooded murder of the man of peace made it considerably more difficult for the Israeli government to stave off the attempt to deprive the country of the Negev. Bernadotte became a martyr in the cause of peace, a UN soldier who had given his life in the service of international morality. Bernadotte's report, which in the normal course of events would have been the subject of bargaining and modifications, acquired the quality of a sacred political testament that had to be honoured as it stood and carried out to the letter.

Following a pre-agreed strategy, George Marshall and Ernest Bevin issued statements establishing the positions of their respective govern-

---

[38] Troutbeck to Bevin, 18 Sept. 1948, FO 371/68587, PRO.
[39] Progress Report of the United Nations Mediator on Palestine, 16 September 1948, Official Record of the General Assembly, Third Session, Supplement no. 11 A/648.

ments firmly behind the Bernadotte plan as a whole.[40] Marshall recommended that the General Assembly in Paris accept the proposals contained in the final report 'in their entirety as the best possible basis for bringing peace to a distracted land'.[41]

Bevin believed that if a prompt declaration in favour of Bernadotte's proposals were made by the British government, the Arab states would be less likely to oppose them. On the other hand the text of his speech had been drafted with great trepidation because it would 'once and for all put His Majesty's Government flatly on record as favouring partition as a permanent solution for Palestine and thus burn His Majesty's Government's boats with the Arabs'.[42] In the House of Commons, Bevin singled out for praise Bernadotte's proposal that the Arab parts of Palestine should be incorporated in Transjordan. The British government had always considered that the Arab parts of Palestine by themselves, being an infertile area, would not form a viable state, and Bevin accordingly stated his belief that 'the United Nations should avoid the risk of creating a state which could not support itself and should endorse the Mediator's arguments in this matter'.[43]

In Paris, Hector McNeil summoned Abba (Aubrey) Eban, Israel's representative to the United Nations, and told him in Bevin's name that the British government not only supported the settlement advocated by the mediator but that it would demand the strongest resolution of the Security Council against any side that tried to set aside an assembly recommendation by military force. He added that acceptance of a settlement along these lines would be immediately followed by British *de jure* recognition of Israel and advice to other powers to act similarly. Ben-Gurion viewed McNeil's statement as important and worrying, yet he went ahead with the issuing of an official statement rejecting the proposals of the mediator.[44] Sharett went to Paris to present Israel's case before the General Assembly and to direct the diplomatic campaign for retaining the Negev as part of the Jewish state.[45]

There was no need for Britian to exert any pressure on Abdullah to secure his acquiescence in the settlement advocated by the late mediator. On the contrary, Britain felt she had to restrain Abdullah from playing his hand too forcibly. Her own critics had long been saying that the end of Britain's policy was to enlarge the territory of her satellite, Transjordan, so that she might continue to exercise paramount influence in an area which was strategically important to

---

[40] *FRUS 1948*, v. 1409–12.   [41] Ibid. 1415 f.   [42] Ibid. 1410.
[43] *Parliamentary Debates* (Commons), 22 Sept. 1948, col. 899.
[44] *DFPI*, i. 624–7; Ben-Gurion's diary, 23 Sept. 1948.
[45] Sharett, *At the Gate of the Nations*, 296.

herself. Such suspicions were likely to be fanned if Britain became too blatant in her advocacy of the enlargement of Transjordan, or if Abdullah appeared too eager to fall in with Bernadotte's wishes.[46] Kirkbride impressed upon the king that as Transjordan was a beneficiary, he should not complicate Britain's task by making any statement on the subject until it became clear how the other Arab states were reacting.[47]

On this occasion Abdullah was all too painfully aware of the delicacy of his position. As he explained to Wells Stabler, the American vice-consul in Jerusalem, he was surrounded by hostile elements in Syria, Lebanon, Egypt, and to a certain degree in Iraq who were seeking to destroy him and who criticized every step he made which they considered not in concert with Arab League's decisions. There, as an Arab leader, he was obliged to concur in any decisions made by a majority of the Arab leaders. So far the strength of the Arab Legion had served as a deterrent to any overt conspiracy. Nevertheless, Abdullah feared that any forthright acceptance of the mediator's plan would make his position untenable and that in the storm that such acceptance would cause, he might lose all he had struggled for. There could be no doubt that the king generally favoured Bernadotte's conclusions since he was the principal beneficiary. It could therefore be assumed that Transjordan would be among the first, if not the first, to urge acquiescence by the Arab states to a UN-imposed solution based on the mediator's conclusions.[48]

None of the other Arab states was prepared to accept or acquiesce in a settlement based on Bernadotte's report. Azzam Pasha said flatly that the report was unacceptable to the Arabs. When asked whether a guarantee of international frontiers would not constitute a gain for the Arabs, he responded that guarantee of the frontiers of a state not recognized by the Arabs was of no interest. In any case, UN guarantees meant nothing since the Zionists were defying the UN and would continue to do so. Azzam said he could understand how ambition swayed Abdullah as the tool of the British but he could not understand the attitude of Britain or the United States. Both maintained that they backed the report in the interest of peace and out of friendship for the Arabs. Yet peace was impossible under Bernadotte's plan. The Arabs, he asserted, would continue to resist. If Britain and the United States wished to impose the plan on the Arabs, they would have to send men, planes, and battleships. In no other way could Bernadotte's plan be enforced.[49]

[46] BMEO to FO, 23 Sept. 1948, FO 371/68861, PRO.
[47] Kirkbride to FO, 23 Sept. 1948, FO 816/129, PRO.
[48] FRUS 1948, v. 1419 f.   [49] Ibid. 1422 f.

The British delegation in Paris continued to do their utmost to persuade the General Assembly to endorse Bernadotte's plan. They were faced, however, not only by the determined opposition of both Arabs and Jews, but also, after Truman's re-election, by the withdrawal of the US government from the position it had previously taken on the territorial aspects of a peace settlement for Palestine. While recognizing that there should be some compensation to the Arabs for the territory which the Jews had occupied over and above that awarded to them in November 1947, the White House declined to support any resolution involving modification of the November frontiers without Jewish consent.[50] As McClintock had warned, the White House was quite capable of intervening to keep the Negev in Jewish hands. Once again the pro-Jewish White House had pulled the rug from under the feet of the pro-Arab State Department. In the end the Assembly's action was confined to the appointment, on December 11, of a Conciliation Commission for Palestine, consisting of the representatives of the United States, France, and Turkey. Britain's elaborate diplomatic strategy for making the Negev part of Abdullah's kingdom was soundly defeated by Arab defiance, unexpectedly effective Jewish resistance, and the peculiarities of the American electoral process.

The All-Palestine government

Britain's efforts to turn the United Nations into executor of Bernadotte's last will and testament aroused Arab hostility towards her and the other principal beneficiary—King Abdullah. Britain's selective emphasis on Bernadotte's recommendation for the merger of the Arab part of Palestine with Transjordan rather than on his statement that the disposition of the Arab part might be left to the Arab states was regarded as evidence of her desire to enlarge her own sphere of influence. Many Arab leaders, including some of her friends, became convinced that it was her policy to create an equilibrium between Jews and Arabs in order to bolster her own position in the Middle East. Abdullah's loyalty to Britain was increasingly equated with disloyalty to the Arab cause.

A second major cause for Arab disillusionment with Abdullah was the knowledge that he had been in contact wth Jewish leaders and that he would be prepared to compromise the Arab claim to the whole of Palestine as long as he could acquire part of Palestine for himself. The international debate over Bernadotte's proposals was thus accompanied by a noticeable increase in the tension between the Arabs

[50] Historical Memorandum on the Situation in Palestine Since 1945. 15 Jan. 1949, CAB 129/32, pt. 1, CP (49)10, PRO.

themselves. 'The internecine struggles of the Arabs', reported Glubb, 'are more in the minds of the Arab politicians than the struggle against the Jews. Azzam Pasha, the Mufti and the Syrian Government would sooner see the Jews get the whole of Palestine than that King Abdullah should benefit.'[51]

To thwart Abdullah's ambition, the other members of the Arab League, led by Egypt, began to manoeuvre for the creation of an Arab government for Palestine. This idea was at the top of the agenda for the meeting of the Arab League's Political Committee which opened in Alexandria on September 6 and lasted ten days. Transjordan was represented by its defence minister, Fawzi el-Mulki and the minister of the interior, Said al-Mufti. Before their departure for Alexandria, Mulki and Mufti were instructed to oppose any move for resuming hostilities in Palestine and any change from the existing arrangement whereby each Arab army was responsible for the administration of that part of Palestine which it occupied. Transjordan had no objection in principle to the formation of a Palestine Arab Army but no units of that army would be permitted to be stationed or to operate in areas of Palestine occupied by the Arab Legion. If any member of the committee was to attack Transjordan, as was the case at the last meeting, her representatives were to withdraw.[52]

Though no open attack was made on Transjordan, the Political Committee decided to approve the establishment of an Arab Government of Palestine. The motives for this decision were diverse and contradictory but, in more than one way, they were antagonistic to Transjordan. The desire to placate Arab public opinion, critical of the governments for failing to protect the Palestinians, was one consideration. Another was the determination to safeguard the Arab claim to sovereignty over the whole of Palestine by providing an alternative to international recognition of Israel and by preventing any Arab government from recognizing the Jewish state or taking over Arab areas. In addition, there was a desire to demonstrate the Arab world's commitment to continue the fight against the Jewish state. But at the same time, the decision to form an Arab Government of Palestine and the attempt to create armed forces under its control furnished the members of the Arab League with the means for divesting themselves of direct responsibility for the prosecution of the war and of withdrawing their armies from Palestine with some protection against popular outcry.[53] Whatever the long-term future of the proposed Arab Government of Palestine, its immediate purpose, as conceived by its Egyptian

[51] Glubb to Burrows, Secret and Personal, 22 Sept. 1948, FO 371/68861, PRO.
[52] Kirkbride to Burrows, 6 Sept. 1948, FO 371/68822, PRO.
[53] Evans (Beirut) to FO, 21 Sept. 1948, FO 371/68376, PRO.

sponsors, was to provide a focal point of opposition to Abdullah and serve as an instrument for frustrating his ambition to federate the Arab regions with Transjordan.

In view of the conflict between the Arab League's plan and the British plan of greater Transjordan, the Foreign Office made an attempt to abort the former. Abdullah was reminded that Britain was working for a solution to the Palestine problem that would favour his country and that he could help in this process by doing everything to prevent the proclamation of an Arab Government of Palestine.[54] Other Arab leaders were warned that Britain would regard any attempt to set up such a government as ill-timed and likely to serve the interests of the mufti. The claim by such a government to the whole of Palestine, it was added, would inevitably precipitate a claim by the Jewish government to the whole of Palestine and possibly Transjordan as well. In other words it would force the Jewish authorities to adopt the extreme programme of the Revisionists, which they had not done hitherto.[55]

Disregarding Britain's warning, the Arab League, on September 22, announced the formation of an All-Palestine government with its seat in Gaza. Word was sent round to the supporters of the mufti to rally in Gaza and Egyptian troops were sent to Bethlehem to distribute small arms to anti-Hashemite elements. The new administration was headed by Ahmad Hilmi Pasha, who had recently been appointed by Abdullah as military governor of Jerusalem. Hilmi's Cabinet consisted largely of followers of the mufti but it also included a number of prominent Palestinians who had previously supported Abdullah.

On September 30, a Palestinian National Council, with seventy-five representatives, convened in Gaza. Hajj Amin al-Husayni, returning to Palestine after an absence of eleven years, was elected president, while Ahmad Hilmi was confirmed as prime minister. On the following day a declaration of independence was issued for an independent, sovereign, and democratic state with borders defined as 'Syria and Lebanon in the North, Syria and Transjordan in the East, the Mediterranean in the West and Egypt in the South'.[56]

The contrast between the pretensions of the All-Palestine government and its capability reduced it to the level of a farce. It claimed jurisdiction over the whole of Palestine yet it had no civil service, no money, and no army of its own. Even in the small enclave round the town of Gaza its writ ran only by the grace of the Egyptian authorities. Taking advantage of the new government's dependence on them for funds and protection, the Egyptian paymasters manipulated it to

---

[54] FO to Amman, 19 Sept. 1948, FO 371/68861, PRO.
[55] FO to Cairo and BMEO, 19 Sept. 1948, FO 371/68861, PRO.
[56] *Al-Ahram*, 3 Oct. 1948.

undermine Abdullah's claim to represent the Palestinian Arabs in the Arab League and in international forums. Ostensibly the embryo for an independent Palestinian state, the new government, from the moment of its inception, was thus reduced to the unhappy role of a shuttlecock in the ongoing power struggle between Cairo and Amman.

Despite the weakness and geographical isolation of the All-Palestine government, Abdullah took the challenge very seriously. When the government was proclaimed he refused to recognize it and announced that it would not be permitted to operate in any of the areas occupied by the Arab Legion. He also took steps to formalize his authority over these areas and to organize his own Palestinian supporters in opposition to the government in Gaza. On the very same day that the Palestinian National Council issued its declaration of independence in Gaza, the 'First Palestinian Congress' convened in Amman, its several thousand participants swearing allegiance to the Hashemite monarch. The Amman Congress denounced the formation of the Gaza government as being contrary to the wishes and interests of the Arabs and resolved that no Arab government should be set up for Palestine until the entire country had been liberated.

Popular support for the high sounding but largely illusory All-Palestine government was never extensive and it began to dwindle after the two rival congresses had been held. Many of the Arab towns and villages in Palestine sent delegations to Amman to pledge their loyalty to the king and to give him power of attorney to solve the Palestinian problem as he saw fit. In some cases these delegations were the result of local political initiative; in others it was the Transjordanian military governors who helped in collecting the signatures and dispatching the delegations to Amman.[57] The Transjordanian regime also used bribery to induce the supporters of the mufti's government to transfer their loyalty to King Abdullah. Even members of that government gradually moved to Amman in response to royal gestures of pardon or to take up offers of lucrative positions.[58]

Initially, the formation of the All-Palestine government revived the mufti's forces known as the Holy War Army (al-Jihad al-Muqaddas). They carried out attacks on UN observers and Israeli troops designed to embroil the Arab Legion in fighting and gave the impression of attempting to create disturbances in the areas occupied by Transjordan especially in and around Jerusalem. Glubb Pasha and King Abdullah feared that these subversive activities would endanger their own control in Arab Palestine and they decided to nip in the bud the growth of this army.

[57] Nevo, *Abdullah and the Arabs of Palestine*, 100–10.
[58] Avi Plascov, *The Palestinian Refugees in Jordan, 1948–1957* (London: Frank Cass, 1981), 8 f.

Hebron had been the scene of very acrimonious disputes between the Transjordanian and the Egyptian forces. The Transjordanians hoisted their own flag over the police station and prevented the Muslim Brothers, who volunteered to fight for the Palestinians alongside the Egyptian army, from putting up their own flag, claiming that the Arab Legion was responsible for the entire region. The dispute between the two sides spread to the local population which became divided into two camps. Glubb exploited this dispute in order to discredit Egypt and the Muslim Brothers.[59] Towards the end of September he wrote to Abdullah al-Tall that he was concerned about the activities of the Holy War Army in Hebron because these activities aroused hostility towards Transjordan and sympathy for Egypt. Accordingly, with the king's agreement, Glubb instructed Tall: (a) to confiscate the arms of the Holy War fighters in Jerusalem and Hebron; (b) to draw public attention to the value of having the protection of the Arab Legion and the sympathy of King Abdullah and thereby erode the popularity of the Egyptian forces; and (c) to spread rumours that the departure of the Egyptian forces from Palestine was imminent and that the fate of the country was bound up with the future of Transjordan.[60]

The king himself had on several occasions since June 1948 expressed to Tall the intention of disbanding the Holy War units and seizing their arms. Tall was opposed to this plot for a number of reasons. First, the Jerusalem area was in a state of war with the Jews. Secondly, they needed every man who could bear arms for the defence of the Holy City. Thirdly, the Holy War Army consisted of Palestinians who had defended their country before the entry of the Arab armies. How could they be demobilized and disarmed when the Arab states had failed to save their country? Fourthly, there was the need for co-operation between all the armed forces in Palestine against the common enemy. Last but not least, Tall was absolutely convinced that the originator of this idea was Glubb Pasha, unable to see weapons in the hands of any Palestinian Arab not under his command.[61]

Glubb's diary entry for October 3 reveals that he indeed regarded the Holy War Army as a potential threat rather than a potential asset:

The position of Transjordan is extremely awkward. We are still in action against the Jews, the Jerusalem truce is only partially effective, and we have daily casualties in killed and wounded. Yet behind our front line, the Mufti's emissaries are raising armed forces, which are drilling and training, but not taking part in holding the line. Now that the Arab League has declared a number of the Mufti's henchmen to be the sole legal Government of All-

[59] Kamil Ismail al-Sharif, *The Muslim Brotherhood in the Palestine War* (Aras.), (Cairo: Dar al Kitab al-Arabi, 1951).
[60] Tall, *The Palestine Tragedy*, ch. 11.   [61] Ibid.

Palestine, his retainers in the Jerusalem area have become distinctly hostile to us . . . Our situation is more like Alice in Wonderland—or perhaps Dante's *Inferno*—than real life.[62]

Since the mufti's men were not only menacingly positioned across the Arab Legion's communications but also started actively canvassing for the All-Palestine government, the Transjordanian government decided to act. On October 3, Glubb received a written order from the minister of defence, laying down that all armed bodies operating in the areas controlled by the Arab Legion were either to be under its orders or to be disbanded.[63] Glubb carried out this order promptly and ruthlessly. Because his Arab officers were likely to balk at carrying out such an unpatriotic task, he sent British officers to surround and forcibly disarm the various units of the Holy War Army. The operation brought the Arabs to the brink of internecine war when they were supposed to be co-operating against the common enemy. But it effectively neutralized the military power of Abdullah's Palestinian rivals and checked the growth of public sentiment in favour of an autonomous Palestine state.

Outside Palestine the Gaza government was largely unsuccessful in its efforts to gain international recognition as the sole legitimate representative of the Palestinian people. London, of course, had no intention of recognizing 'this so-called government', and most other members of the United Nations followed the British example and British advice in ignoring it. Among the Arab League members, Egypt was predictably the first to grant formal recognition. Iraq's position was particularly crucial because it held the northern half of central Palestine. Iraqi co-operation with the Egyptian-sponsored body would have made Transjordan's position very difficult. Abdullah called the regent in Baghdad to ensure that this did not happen but was not given a clear reply.[64] Iraq eventually recognized the All-Palestine government and, three days later, Syria, Lebanon, and Saudi Arabia followed suit.

Israel was content to see the rift develop inside the Arab League but prudently refrained from voicing any opinion for or against the All-Palestine government. The Israeli position regarding the future of the Arab part of Palestine was fluid and ambivalent. In his address to the Provisional State Council, on September 23, Sharett described this part as a 'geographical expression' rather than a political entity. He could detect no process of integration round one political centre which could

---

[62] Glubb, *A Soldier with the Arabs*, 192.   [63] Ibid.

[64] *FRUS 1948*, v. 1447; Kirkbride to FO, 25 Sept. 1948, FO 371/68641, PRO; Abdullah, *My Memoirs Completed*, 11 f.

provide the foundation for an independent regime. One candidate for ruling over this geographical area was the Transjordanian government. Sharett described Transjordan as a country with a governmental apparatus that was quite developed by local standards, enjoying British support, but also possessing intentions of its own that did not always coincide with Britain's intentions. The desire manifested by Transjordan to reach agreement with the Jewish side was cited by Sharett as an example of this yearning for independence. He added that this desire was not in accordance with British advice but essentially contrary to it. This phenomenon, Sharett believed, reflected Transjordan's struggle to liberate herself from the humiliating status of being Britain's tool, and to attain a measure of independence and self-respect.

The other candidate for ruling the Arab part of Palestine was the mufti who, through the provisional government in Gaza, was trying to establish for himself a forward position in one corner of the country. Sharett described this government as utterly dependent on the attitude of the Arab states since it had no international status, no control over territory, and no effectively organized army. In principle, said Sharett, he and his colleagues preferred a separate government in the Arab part of Palestine to a merger with Transjordan. Such a government would be dependent on Israel, it would preserve the unity of western Palestine, and it would be a barrier to Iraqi penetration. Annexation to Transjordan, on the other hand, carried the risk, in the event of a Transjordanian–Iraqi merger, of a large and powerful Arab neighbour bearing down on Israel. Nor was Transjordan's alliance with Britain a recommendation for allowing her to expand. Yet, if these things were stated in public, it would be inferred that Israel favoured the rule of the mufti over western Palestine. On the other hand, a clear statement of opposition to the All-Palestine government would be taken to imply Israeli support for the annexation of the Arab part to Transjordan. For the time being, concluded Sharett, it was best not to say anything but to follow events with a vigilant eye and be prepared to act, when the opportunity arose, to further Israel's own interests.[65]

Israel's official posture of neutrality at the declaratory level as between the option of an independent Palestinian state and annexation to Transjordan was merely a diplomatic ploy to conceal her real preference. As Yaacov Shimoni, the deputy head of the Middle East Department at the Foreign Ministry, explained, there are two separate points here both of which must be understood very clearly:

If we talked about a Palestinian Arab state, we most emphatically did not

---

[65] Sharett, *At the Gate of the Nations*, 307–9.

mean the government in Gaza. That one was totally disqualified in our eyes for a number of reasons. First of all this was a so-called government. It was not a real government. This was a government under Egyptian occupation with no authority or even a leg to stand on. Furthermore, it was a government with no control over the principal part of Arab Palestine but only over one remote corner of it. We did not see it as related at all to the problem or question of a Palestinian state. It was not a Palestinian state. Thirdly, this was a state which was established by our sworn enemies, and the most extreme among them: the Husaynis, the leaders of the Arab gangs, etc. It was certainly not to these men that Sharett referred if he talked about a Palestinian state. Fourthly, Sharett knew that we had agreed with Abdullah that he will take and annex the Arab part of Palestine and Sharett could not support this ludicrous, impotent, and abortive attempt made by the Egyptians against Abdullah. This attempt had nothing to do with us. It was a tactical move by Abdullah's enemies to interject something against his creeping annexation. At that time there was no annexation. Formal annexation only occurred in April 1950. But he had started taking and preparing for annexation. So they tried, without any success, to build a countervailing force.

The second point is that at that time Sharett and our men knew what the powerful State of Israel has forgotten in recent years. He understood the meaning of diplomacy and knew how to conduct it. Sharett was definitely aware that publicly we were obliged to accept the Palestinian Arab state and could not say that we are opposed to the establishment of such a state. In the first place we had accepted the UN resolution which included a Palestinian Arab state. And secondly, this was the right, fair, and decent course and we were obliged to agree to it. The fact that below the surface, behind the curtain, by diplomatic efforts we reached an agreement with Abdullah—an agreement which had not been uncovered but was kept secret at that time—was entirely legitimate but we did not have to talk about it. Sharett knew that our official line must be in favour of a Palestinian state if the Palestinians could create it. We could not create it for them. But if they could create it, certainly, by all means, we would agree. The fact that he made a deal with Abdullah on the side to prevent the creation of such a state, that is diplomacy, that is alright. Sharett behaved in accordance with the rules of diplomacy and politics that are accepted throughout the world.[66]

Israeli war plans and 'missed opportunities'

The rivalries among the Arab states that gave rise to the so-called All-Palestine government complicated Israel's diplomacy but simplified its strategy. David Ben-Gurion, the man in charge of Israel's strategy, was anxious to exploit the divisions and fissures in the enemy camp in order to extend Israel's gains. He had his own internal difficulties with the right-wing and militantly nationalistic branch of the Zionist

[66] Interview with Yaacov Shimoni.

movement. The Revisionists laid a claim to the entire territory held under the original British mandate, including Transjordan, but they were serious about liberating the whole Land of Israel which stretched from the Mediterranean Sea to the Jordan River. The Irgun, under the leadership of Menachem Begin, brought a ship loaded with arms, the *Altalena*, during the truce, in open defiance of the provisional government. Even after the *Altalena* was sunk by troops loyal to the government in an incident that brought the country to the brink of civil war, the Irgun and Stern Gang units in Jerusalem continued to pursue independent policies in a city over which Jewish sovereignty had not been officially proclaimed. They rejected the truce and planned to fight on in order to establish a 'Free Judaea' outside the State of Israel. The assassination of Count Bernadotte by members of the Stern Gang calling themselves the Fatherland Front forced the government to crack down on the dissident organizations. Although these dissidents complied with the government order to surrender their arms and join the IDF rather than risk bloodshed, Ben-Gurion knew that there was widespread support in the IDF and in the country for proclaiming Jewish sovereignty over Jerusalem.[67]

Internal pressures were not the only factor in leading Ben-Gurion to adopt a more aggressive strategy. He had long been critical of the second truce for the unbearable political and financial burdens it entailed. He saw it as a British device for breaking the will of the new state and undermining its international standing. 'Our most dangerous enemy now', he observed, 'is a truce without an end. It places a question mark over the existence of the state in the consciousness of the world, it places UN officials over us, and it enables the Arabs to prepare and choose their own time for an offensive against us.'[68] Bernadotte's report hovered over Israel's head like Damocles' sword. Jerusalem and the Negev were the most vulnerable targets. Military force, in Ben-Gurion's view, would be decisive in settling the borders of the Jewish state and the future of Jerusalem. Unlike Sharett he was not content to wait on events and limit Israel's struggle against the unlimited truce and Bernadotte's plan to a diplomatic campaign at the United Nations.

In a speech before the Provisional State Council on September 27, Ben-Gurion clarified some of the basic assumptions on which his strategy was based:

First of all, we are in the midst of a combined political and military campaign, and we should not consider one phase without taking the other into consideration. Neither will be decisive on its own. Secondly, two groups of interests are involved: those of the Arabs and Jews of the Middle East on the one hand, and

---

[67] Shlomo Nakdimon, *Altalena* (Heb.) (Jerusalem: Edanim, 1978), 358–419.
[68] Ben-Gurion's diary, 3 Aug. 1948.

those of the Great Powers on the other. If only the interests of the Jews and Arabs were involved, the military factor would be decisive. The Arabs believed that their military strength would settle the issue, but they were wrong. They lost the military struggle. Indeed, were military factors in the Middle East to determine the outcome, then we could speak in terms not only of the November 29 resolution, but perhaps also of the Biltmore Program [for a Jewish commonwealth over the whole of Palestine]. But developments in the Middle East will not be decisive on their own. The larger world arena, with friendly and hostile forces, is also involved. In the present period, *our military position is stronger than our political position*, for not all the Great Powers are supporting us. Therefore, it seems to me, we cannot depend solely on the political struggle. At the same time, the military struggle *alone*, even if it develops to our advantage, will not be decisive; there are forces in the world that will see to it that it is not decisive.

Theoretically, Ben-Gurion saw three possible means for solving the Palestine problem: an agreement between Jews and Arabs, a UN decision, or a military decision in a struggle between Jews and Arabs. There was scarcely any chance of an agreement between Jews and Arabs at that time. The UN, while ready to concede more than the Arabs, was unlikely to adopt a resolution, and even more unlikely to enforce a resolution, that would meet Israel's requirements with respect to the Galilee, the road to Jerusalem, Jerusalem, and the Negev. If Israel did not take measures herself to make territorial adjustments, or at least the most vital ones, they would not be made at all. The conclusion from all this was clear: 'we cannot depend solely on political activity, or on political decisions, even if the decisions are desirable from our point of view. We must be ready to exploit the military factor whenever and wherever necesary.'[69]

In the undoctored Hebrew version of his speech, Ben-Gurion gives a less nuanced and more frank assessment of the outcome of a military contest in Palestine:

In my view, it is not unlikely that, in the event of a military decision, we would succeed in capturing the roads to the Negev, Eilat, and the Dead Sea, and secure the Negev in our hands; in enlarging the corridor to Jerusalem from the north and the south; in liberating the rest of New Jerusalem (Shaikh Jarrah, and the university area and Hadassah); in capturing the Old City; in seizing the entire central and western Galilee; and in enlarging the frontiers of the state in a number of other directions.[70]

The blowing up of the pumping station near Latrun that had helped to bring water from Rosh Ha'ayin to Jerusalem provided an excuse for

[69] David Ben-Gurion, *Israel: A Personal History* (Tel Aviv: Sabra Books, 1972), 272–5. Emphasis in the original.
[70] Ben-Gurion, *When Israel Fought in Battle*, 267.

action. The Israelis laid a second pipeline not dependent upon the Latrun pumping station, but this did not justify its destruction. Under the terms of the truce neither side had the right to carry out hostile acts. Knowing that the IDF had grown stronger, Ben-Gurion concluded that they should react militarily to this open violation of the truce by the Arab Legion, the alleged purpose of which was to make the Jews of Jerusalem die of thirst.[71] Ironically, it was nationalistic elements inside the Arab Legion who committed this act in order to subvert the growing co-operation they suspected between Tel Aviv and Amman. The violation of the truce occurred not on orders from Amman but on the initiative of the officers of the 2nd Regiment stationed in Latrun. According to Abdullah al-Tall's account, when these officers heard that Glubb Pasha had granted Bernadotte's request to permit the supply of water to the Jews of Jerusalem, they decided unanimously to blow up the pumping station in Latrun. On the night of August 12, volunteers from the 2nd Regiment carried explosives and blew up the station, thereby discontinuing the supply of water to Jerusalem.

Five days later, Lieut.-Col. Moshe Dayan, who had been selected by Ben-Gurion to replace David Shaltiel as military commander of Jerusalem, ordered an attack to capture Government House. Had it succeeded, this operation would have helped the IDF to encircle the Old City as a prelude to its capture. But Tall's Arab Legion units, assisted by some Holy War Army fighters, repelled the attack and dashed the hopes of the energetic new commander.[72]

On September 24, local Arab fighters, apparently with the encouragement of Arab Legion officers, attacked and captured an IDF position in Modiin but were later dislodged by a counter-attack. Ben-Gurion wanted to use the incident as a pretext for launching a major offensive on the eastern front. He called a meeting of the General Staff and suggested that they storm Latrun and then push on to Ramallah, Jericho, and the Dead Sea, as well as moving south of Jerusalem to capture Bethlehem and the Hebron region. Yigael Yadin said that it would take some time to prepare for an attack on Latrun and questioned the feasibility of the proposed plan. The General Staff backed Yadin in opposing a frontal attack to storm Latrun and put forward instead an alternative plan for attacking the Iraqi forces in the northern part of the West Bank.[73]

The old differences between the military experts and the prime minister thus reasserted themselves because of his continuing obsession with Jerusalem. They were agreed on the need for seizing the initiative but they could not agree on a target. The prime minister was convinced

---

[71] Ben-Gurion, *Israel: A Personal History*, 269.   [72] Tall, *The Palestine Tragedy*, ch. 10.
[73] Ben-Gurion's diary, 24 Sept. 1948.

that the road to Jerusalem would not be secure unless they captured Latrun. The military experts, having made five abortive and costly attempts against their own better judgement, were extremely reluctant to attempt another frontal attack on the fortress of Latrun, preferring the strategy of the indirect approach. Their plan was to attack the Iraqi army in the Triangle from the direction of Jenin and from the north simultaneously.[74] And they could have probably captured the whole of the West Bank by sending a column down from Beisan to move along the Jordan River, cut off the lines of communication of the Hashemite armies, and link up with Jerusalem from the north.

Despite the reservations of the military experts, Ben-Gurion brought his plan for attacking the Arab Legion before the Cabinet on September 26. As he recalled,

The plan was to destroy the Legion's fortified positions in Latrun and to proceed to the point where the Jordan flowed into the Dead Sea, south of Ramallah, and to capture the whole of Jerusalem and the southern pocket containing Bethlehem and Hebron where some hundred thousand Arabs lived . . . I assumed that most of the Arabs of Jerusalem, Bethlehem, and Hebron would run away, like the Arabs of Lydda, Jaffa, Haifa, Tiberias, and Safed, and that we would control the entire breadth of the country up to the Jordan and that all of the western part of the Dead Sea would be in our hands . . . I confess that in those days I did not attach any decisive weight to the decisions of the General Assembly except those concerning the Old City of Jerusalem where the holy places of the Christian and the Muslim worlds are located but that did not require Arab rule, and they would have been content with international supervision, and that is what I proposed to the Cabinet.[75]

At the meeting, which was attended by all thirteen members of the Cabinet, Ben-Gurion proposed that they give the General Staff an order to prepare a plan of action for capturing Latrun and contingency plans in case this operation should touch off hostilities throughout the country. Jerusalem's fate, he stated, would not be settled inside Jerusalem itself but outside, in Latrun. Latrun was stuck like a bone in their throat, and it was imperative to remove it and secure the road to Jerusalem. Much blood had been shed in the earlier attempts to take Latrun but their failures in the past did not mean that the task was impossible. There was a definite possibility, continued Ben-Gurion, that the United Nations would call on Israel to cease fire and withdraw but verbal or written protests could be shrugged off. It was also possible, though less likely, that an attempt would be made to restrain Israel by military force. If an American–European force was despatched, Israel would be compelled to retreat, but Ben-Gurion did

[74] Interview with Gen. Yigael Yadin.
[75] Ben-Gurion to Dr S. Gross, *Haaretz*, 23 Mar. 1962, quoted in Bar-Zohar, *Ben-Gurion*, ii. 823.

not expect the United Nations to back up its protests by force. And in any case it was not a disgrace to submit to force. A third possibility, of the renewal of the war on all fronts, was not unwelcome to Ben-Gurion for it would have provided the IDF with the opportunity to capture the whole of the Galilee, break the Egyptian blockade of the Negev, defeat the Iraqi forces in the Triangle and move the border further east to the mountains of Samaria, and widen the corridor to Jerusalem.[76]

The Cabinet debate was very heated, with the majority of the ministers, including Ben-Gurion's party colleagues, opposing his proposal. Those who opposed it emphasized the fact that the recent assassination of Count Bernadotte had stirred up enmity towards Israel and they feared that, in such an atmosphere, a fresh military initiative would undermine their country's international position. There was also concern about the reaction of the General Assembly which was scheduled to discuss the Bernadotte plan at its next meeting in Paris. Strong objections were voiced against a military campaign that involved a violation of the truce and the frustration of the mediator's plan while Israel had his blood on her hands. David Remez, who was the minister of communications and transportation, thought that to murder Bernadotte and to rebel against UN decisions would be going too far and that it could unleash a violent Arab reaction both in the field and in Paris. He reminded his colleagues that they had called their army the Israel Defence Forces because they saw it as precisely that—a *defence* force. For his part, he thought that the IDF should remain a defence force and the war a defensive war. Another Mapai representative, Eliezer Kaplan, disputed the desirability of a general conflagration at a time when they were planning to wage a diplomatic campaign in Paris. If forced to they would enter a military campaign, but they must not be the ones to start it. Sharett was opposed to a general offensive which he would find difficult to justify but he did not specifically rule out an attack on Latrun that could be presented as a response to Transjordanian provocations. As he had to leave before the end of the meeting, he handed the Cabinet secretary, Zeev Sharef, a note stating he wished to vote against any action that was bound to be seen as provocation on their part.[77]

The proposal was eventually defeated by seven votes against six. When Sharef reported the vote to Sharett, the latter remarked that had he known that this would be the outcome he would have voted differently. Sharef brought this remark to Ben-Gurion's attention but the prime minister did not choose to exercise his right to call another vote on his proposal at the next Cabinet meeting. He asked Sharef to

---

[76] Bar-Zohar, *Ben-Gurion*, 823 f.; Protocol of Cabinet Meeting, 26 Sept. 1948.

[77] Protocol of Cabinet meeting, 26 Sept. 1948; Ben-Gurion, *Israel: A Personal History*, 269.

contact Yadin and instruct him to recall immediately the IDF unit that had set off from the south of the Dead Sea on the way to the Transjordanian-held north whence it was due to proceed to Jerusalem via Jericho.[78] In his diary Ben-Gurion recorded how every minister voted, adding caustically: 'Fortunately for us, it was not this lot who had to vote on and carry out most of the operations we launched this year.'[79]

In later years Ben-Gurion described this vote as the greatest missed opportunity of the 1948 war. He lamented the decision of his own Cabinet as a cause for 'mourning for generations to come' because it left Transjordan in possession of the Judaean mountains, of the roads to Jerusalem, and of the Old City itself. He presented himself as the bold and far-sighted statesman intent on enlarging the borders of his country but, being also a democratic leader, had no choice but to bow to the will of the pusillanimous and misguided majority. That Ben-Gurion's plan was bold and far-reaching cannot be doubted. The defeat of the Legion would have forced the Iraqi army to retreat behind the Jordan and to leave the whole of the West Bank in Israeli hands. But for Israel to undertake such a plan would have struck at the very heart of the accord with Abdullah and would have left no possible basis for future co-operation between the two countries. So clearly there was much more at stake, strategically and politically, than Israeli possession of Latrun.

But if there was indeed so much at stake, and if the Cabinet was guilty of a major strategic and political blunder, why did Ben-Gurion not mobilize Sharett and their party colleagues in order to reverse this decision? And why did he put his plan to a vote in the Cabinet in the first place when, by his own admission, most of the military operations of 1948 had been launched without reference to the Cabinet? And what is one to make of his insistence on a frontal attack on Latrun only two days after the General Staff had advised him that this would be tantamount to knocking their heads against a brick wall when plans for an indirect approach from the north were in existence?

The answer must surely be that Ben-Gurion himself had second thoughts, not least about the timing, and that he was not fully committed to carrying through his original plan to its logical conclusion. Fear of Britain was the only logical explanation Zeev Sharef could offer for Ben-Gurion's failure to keep up the pressure for the adoption of his proposal to attack the Arab Legion. It was Ben-Gurion, after all, who had laid down the rule that Israel should not go to war against the army of a foreign power.[80] Yigael Yadin also underlined Ben-Gurion's

[78] Interview with Zeev Sharef. [79] Ben-Gurion's diary, 26 Sept. 1948.
[80] Interview with Zeev Sharef.

sensitivity to the attitudes of the Great Powers and thought that Britain's support for Abdullah may have subtly influenced Ben-Gurion's calculations.[81] Moshe Carmel formed the more definite impression that Ben-Gurion was not afraid of Transjordan but only of Britain, and that it was for this reason that he opposed the General Staff's plan:

Towards the end of the war, from about October onwards, our forces were perfectly capable of reaching the Jordan and staying there. We were riding high while the Arabs were beaten. There would not have been any problem about moving our forces to the Jordan and taking up positions there. The army of course wanted to do that. From a military point of view it was obvious that the Jordan river represented the best line of defence. The army wanted to reach the Jordan first, before the start of the negotiations to draw the permanent borders. Ben-Gurion, however, had inhibitions in this matter. He did not agree to our plan. As far as I can remember his main argument was that Jordan had an alliance with Britain and such a move on our part could draw us into a conflict with Britain and it was even possible that Britain would send forces to fight us. Ben-Gurion had a conception that we should fight the Arabs alone and not get involved in fighting with the regular armies of Western powers.[82]

The decision against attempting to capture the southern part of the West Bank has to be seen against the background of the psychological climate of the time. Israel had accepted the partition plan and in the course of the fighting had acquired additional territory. There was no strong or pervasive sense among politicians that she must have the whole of western Palestine. Ben-Gurion's subsequent attribution of faint-heartedness to his Cabinet colleagues is therefore as unjustified as his account of his own role is misleading. If the decision has to be seen in terms of heroes and cowards then Ben-Gurion himself must be counted among the cowards. It was his own highly exaggerated fears of British military intervention that was chiefly responsible for letting the matter rest after only one inconclusive vote in the Cabinet.

The reservations voiced by Ben-Gurion's contemporaries against his plan appear amply justified in retrospect. His plan was unsound from both the military and the political point of view; it was ill timed and it carried the risk of incalculable damage to the international position of the new state. In short, the plan had very little to recommend it and those who voted against it showed a better understanding of the international political repercussions of military action than did its author.

The Cabinet decision did not reflect a contest between heroes and cowards but varying degrees of caution and different appraisals of the

---

[81] Interview with Gen. Yigael Yadin.   [82] Interview with Gen. Moshe Carmel.

wisdom of initiating a war against Transjordan. Israel found herself in the position of a person who goes to lift a heavy weight and discovers that it is as light as a feather. The weak resistance of the Arabs permitted Israel, almost compelled her, to advance faster and further than she had planned to go. The question then arose as to whether it would be best to extend her territory all the way to the Jordan River, and on this question there were different approaches. There were those who realized the military advantages of having more depth and more room for manœuvre. And there were those who were content with the existing borders because they contained a much smaller Arab population. Ben-Gurion's assumption that the Arabs of the West Bank would run away was almost certainly mistaken, as events in Galilee were soon to show. The high mobilization ratio of Israeli society left the economy denuded of vital manpower. Under these circumstances further territorial expansion would have placed additional strain on Israel's limited financial, economic, and manpower resources. So quite apart from the damage to relations with Transjordan and adverse international reactions, there were sound domestic reasons against attempting to capture the West Bank. The decision not to capture either part or all of the West Bank thus made very good sense in the prevailing circumstances.[83]

The tactics that led to this decision are less important. So untypical was it of Ben-Gurion to bow to the will of the majority when he was convinced that he was in the right that some observers have concluded that he deliberately brought his plan before the Cabinet in the knowledge that it would be defeated and in order to have it on the record that he was in favour. In this particular instance, however, this cynical explanation is not warranted by the facts. The most that can be claimed is that the Cabinet decision provided a convenient way out once Ben-Gurion had realized the folly of his own proposal. Ben-Gurion was certainly conscious of his place in Jewish history and anxious to go down as an audacious and far-sighted leader. Consequently, when there were inglorious decisions to be made, as in this instance, it suited him well to have it on record that he was restrained or overruled by the majority of his ministers and that it was therefore they, not he, who were guilty of failing to grasp a historic opportunity.

[83] Interview with Yehoshua Palmon.

11

THE WAR AGAINST EGYPT

Israeli war plans and Egyptian peace feelers

After the defeat of his plan for an operation against the Arab Legion in the Jerusalem–Hebron area, Ben-Gurion showed growing interest in the idea of a military offensive against the Egyptian forces in the Negev. The situation in the Negev was worrying. A 15,000-strong Egyptian force was deployed in two heavily fortified defensive lines running from Rafah to Isdud along the Mediterranean coast and north-eastward from El Auja in the south through Beersheba and the hills of Hebron to Bethlehem. Below the Egyptian front line, which stretched in a wide arc from Rafah to the outskirts of Jerusalem, there were twenty-six Israeli settlements in the northern part of the Negev. The Israeli lines of communication from north to south thus crossed with Egyptian lines from west to east. Under the terms of the second truce, the UN mediator prescribed that the cross-roads west of Faluja be used in six-hour shifts: by the Israelis to send supplies south to their isolated settlements and by the Egyptians to move convoys east. The Egyptians, however, placed the Israeli settlements under siege by preventing the passage of Israeli convoys through their territory. Beyond the immediate problem of supplying the settlements loomed the much greater danger that lack of effective control over the Negev would be used, as Bernadotte had proposed in his last testament, for detaching the Negev altogether from the State of Israel.

Yigael Yadin as chief of operations and some other members of the General Staff had all along regarded Egypt, not Transjordan, as the principal enemy and were now strongly in favour of a large-scale operation to expel the Egyptian invaders from the Negev. Persuading Ben-Gurion to give top priority to a campaign in the south proved easier than Yadin expected. Yigal Allon, who was well aware of Ben-Gurion's obsession with Jerusalem, suggested a two-stage plan of action to the prime minister when the latter visited him at his headquarters in Southern Command on October 5. The objective of the first stage was to force a way through the Egyptian lines to the besieged settlements in the Negev and bring about the collapse of the Egyptian front. Once this was achieved, part of the striking force would branch off to capture Hebron and Bethlehem, cut off the Jerusalem–Jericho road, and link up with the Israeli enclave in Mount Scopus.[1]

Allon's plan won Ben-Gurion's whole-hearted approval, although this time Ben-Gurion considered it necessary to enlist the support of his party colleagues before presenting the new proposal to the Cabinet. Egyptian violations of the UN-decreed truce provided the pretext for the proposed Israeli offensive in the Negev, but the basic motive behind the offensive was in fact to establish effective control over the Negev before the UN could decree that Israel should not have it. Time was therefore a crucial consideration.

Ben-Gurion opened the General Staff meeting on October 6 by asking an innocuous enough question: if a fight breaks out in the south between Israel and Egypt, and if it is assumed that Transjordan and Iraq do not intervene, how large a force would be needed to defeat swiftly the Egyptian invaders and improve the position around Jerusalem without clashing with the Legion or the Iraqis? Allon, the youthful and assertive commander of the Palmach, unfolded his plan, and it formed the basis of the ensuing discussion. Yadin, suspecting that Ben-Gurion still hoped to shift the centre of gravity from the Negev to Jerusalem, raised objections. He doubted whether a fight could take place with Egypt without the other Arab countries intervening. There was no possibility, he said, of reaching the Mount Scopus enclave from the south without clashing with the Arab Legion. He admitted that it would be easier to defend the corridor to Jerusalem from the south, but added that by the same token it would be easier for the Legion to attack the corridor from the north. If the 8th Brigade was pressed into action against Egypt, the central front would be dangerously exposed. Transjordan and Iraq would then attack in the centre of the country along a 50-kilometre front, which could not be defended without mounting an attack on the entire Triangle. Some of the front commanders also doubted the wisdom of approaching Jerusalem from the south. Moshe Carmel thought that their first priority should be to break the strength of the Iraqi army and he was confident that, with the 8th Brigade in reserve, they could capture the whole Triangle. Ben-Gurion, however, remained unconvinced by this military logic. He disliked the idea of a war on two fronts and feared that an unprovoked attack on the Hashemite armies would lead to intervention by their British ally. He pointed out to the assembled generals that relations between Egypt and other Arab states were very tense and that it was

<hr>

[1] Ben-Gurion's diary, 5 Oct. 1948; interview with Yigael Yadin; Yeroham Cohen, *By Light and in Darkness* (Heb.) (Tel Aviv: Amikam, 1969), 168–70.

unlikely, therefore, that a battle with Egypt would bring about fighting on all the fronts.[2]

On the afternoon of the same day, the Cabinet met to discuss Ben-Gurion's proposal to force open the road to the Negev. Ben-Gurion described the serious situation that had developed in the south as a result of the Egyptian blockade and his plan for breaking the siege. It was possible, he observed, that the fighting would spread to the other fronts, though not likely in view of the worsening relations between Egypt and Abdullah. Abdullah did not recognize the government established by the Egyptians in the Gaza Strip since it consisted of supporters of the mufti. Nevertheless, Arab rivalry could conceivably be overcome by a decision of the Arab League—for example, that all the Arab armies must fight. If the fighting remained confined to the south, continued Ben-Gurion, they would be able to gain control of the entire Negev as far as the Dead Sea and thence down to the Red Sea. It might also be possible to capture Hebron and Bethlehem and improve the Israeli position round Jerusalem if Arab forces did not come down from the north. The government endorsed the plan subject to approval by Foreign Minister Sharett who had departed in the meantime for the General Assembly session in Paris. The date for the operation was fixed for October 14.[3] In his diary Ben-Gurion recorded: 'We took in the Cabinet today the most serious decision since we decided to proclaim the establishment of the state.' Even after the decision was taken, Ben-Gurion remained troubled by the uncertainty surrounding the reaction of the other Arab states. Contrary to what he had said to both his generals and his ministers, he concluded on a pessimistic note: 'Had it not been for the Iraqis, it would have been possible to assume that Abdullah will not intervene if we do not harm him, but it is difficult to assume that the Iraqis will not react immediately and drag Abdullah with them.'[4]

On the following day, October 7, Ben-Gurion reverted to his more optimistic forecast of Arab reactions. At a meeting with the chief of staff and chief of operations, he said that two factors had to be taken into consideration. First, the fighting would probably not last more than four or five days—seven days at the very most—for the Security Council would intervene immediately. Second, it was reasonable to assume that under these circumstances the Iraqis and Transjordanians would not have time to intervene. Abdullah was at odds with the Egyptians, and the others would not intervene unless the Egyptians asked them to do so. Even if there were such an Egyptian request, the fighting might be halted by the Security Council before they had a

[2] Ben-Gurion's diary, 6 Oct. 1948; id., *Israel: A Personal History*, 275 f.
[3] Id., *Israel: A Personal History*, 276–8.   [4] Id., diary, 6 Oct. 1948.

chance to weigh in. From these assumptions Ben-Gurion drew two
operational conclusions. First, the largest possible force had to be
concentrated in the south so that a great deal might be accomplished in
a very short time, even if this did not include the destruction of the
entire Egyptian army. Second, they had to hasten to capture the
railway station in the south and clear the southern sector of Jerusalem
of enemy forces. He therefore suggested that another brigade from the
north be sent south. Yadin objected strongly, considering it certain that
once fighting broke out in the south the war would start again along all
the other fronts. Nevertheless, additional men, supplies, and weapons
immediately began streaming south.[5] At a meeting on October 10,
Ben-Gurion informed the Cabinet that Sharett had approved the plan
and that all the necessary preparations were being made so that the
operation could commence at the appointed hour. By a fortunate
coincidence, the Egyptians had stepped up their operations in the south
and were opening fire from time to time.[6] What the prime minister
omitted to mention was that he had also had word from Sharett about
an Egyptian peace feeler.

The Egyptian peace feeler was the product of Elias Sasson's
assiduous letter writing and indefatigable efforts in search of an
understanding with the ruling classes of the Arab countries. In the case
of Egypt, disillusion in political circles with the war in Palestine
ensured that Sasson's persistent pleas for a political settlement did not
fall on deaf ears. The usually well informed weekly *Akhbar el-Yom*
reported on August 14 that some Egyptian statesmen considered a
unitary Jewish–Arab state in Palestine to be more dangerous than the
Jewish state. This was one of the first open indications of the tendency
in Egyptian political circles to distance themselves from the oft-
repeated and uncompromising opposition to any form of partition.

Differences of opinion persisted, however, between the government
and the royal court. King Farouk, it should be remembered, had
decided personally to go to war in May 1948 against strong opposition
from the government and the army. Dynastic ambitions and the desire
to limit Abdullah's territorial gains featured prominently in the decision to intervene. Now, however, Farouk was looking for a way out of
a war in which the Egyptian army had not distinguished itself. The
government headed by Mahmud Nuqrashi realized that the existence
of the State of Israel would have to be accepted sooner or later but it was
not ready to say so publicly yet. Nor could it accept any portion of
Palestine without betraying the declared purpose of the intervention
which was to secure Palestine for the Palestinians. King Farouk, on the
other hand, was interested in acquiring a portion of Arab Palestine

[5] Id., *Israel: A Personal History*, 279 f.   [6] Ibid. 280.

either in exchange for acquiescing in the Bernadotte plan or even by means of a bilateral deal with the Zionist enemy.

Kamal Riad, a representative of the Egyptian court, called on Sasson in his Paris hotel on September 21. He had been sent very suddenly by order of King Farouk to examine the possibility of a separate settlement between Egypt and Israel. The basic conflict between the ambitions and the outlook of the Egyptians and Transjordanians that had surfaced during the recent Arab League meeting in Alexandria apparently persuaded the king and his supporters that Egypt's good required an independent foreign policy, outside the framework of the Arab League. Riad did not deny that the Egyptian government maintained the mufti and supported his political plans. But it had no illusions about the effectiveness of this move, which had been taken, he claimed, not to upset Israel but to settle accounts with the Hashemite bloc, whose superiority over all the other Arab armies had been demonstrated in the course of the war with Israel. If this bloc was to acquire the Arab part of Palestine and the Negev, it would be able to threaten Egypt's independence—a situation that would have been inconceivable a few months previously. At the end of the meeting Riad asked whether Israel would be interested in a separate agreement with Egypt. In his view the time was ripe but the basis for such an agreement should be proposed by Israel, not by Egypt, and that was the purpose of his visit.[7]

An elated Sasson immediately set about drafting in French a fourteen-point peace treaty on the basis of general guidelines he had received from Sharett previously. The draft peace treaty declared that 'Egypt considers the establishment of the State of Israel as a *fait accompli*' and undertook to withdraw its troops from all parts of Palestine. Israel, for its part, undertook not to occupy the evacuated areas and to accept the decision of the Palestinian Arabs about their future whether they were to decide to establish an independent state in the Arab part of Palestine or to seek to be annexed by one or other of the neighbouring Arab states. Israel further agreed to join the Arab League if its name could be changed to the Oriental League.[8]

The draft treaty was transmitted to Riad who, after informing the court and consulting three political and military advisers of the Egyptian delegation to the United Nations, submitted written 'elucidations and observations'. During Riad's next meeting with Sasson, on October 2, it emerged more clearly that the Egyptians were thinking seriously about the annexation of the southern part of Palestine to Egypt. This area was allegedly needed for two reasons: so that in the event of an armed clash with Israel they would be able to fight on

---

[7] *DFPI*, i. 632–4.   [8] Ibid. 634–6.

Palestinian land and not on their own territory, and, secondly, to prevent the annexation of this area to Transjordan and its conversion into a British base. It was for this reason, explained Riad, that the Egyptian government supported the All-Palestine government. He requested detailed assurances to dispel the triple Egyptian fear generated by the establishment of the State of Israel—of territorial expansion, economic domination, and communist infiltration.

Sharett sent a copy of all this important material, including his own reply to the points raised in the Egyptian paper, to the director-general of the Foreign Ministry, Walter Eytan. Sharett noted that implicit in the Egyptian paper there was recognition of Israel, agreement not to subvert it, to evacuate Israel territory, not to demand the return of the refugees, and to consider changing the name of the Arab League to the Oriental League. Much more explicit was the Egyptian desire to annex the coastal strip and a strip of territory in the south and in the Negev. Sharett refrained from giving a clear-cut reply on this sensitive point. He tried to steer a middle course between an irreversible commitment and a complete rejection that might scuttle the negotiations. For him this was the crucial point on which largely hinged the possibility of talking to the Egyptians in defiance of both the British and the Transjordanians. Sharett was inclined to give a qualified agreement because this was the only real reward they could offer Egypt, all the talk about economic co-operation being empty rhetoric. He instructed that the whole matter be brought before Ben-Gurion urgently.[9]

The senior officials in the Foreign Ministry—Walter Eytan, Reuven Shiloah, and Leo Cohen—all looked favourably on the talks with Egypt.[10] The prime minister, however, did not seem to appreciate this diversion from the task of preparing for the war against Egypt. His rejection of the Egyptian request, at any rate, was emphatic and uncompromising. He cabled Sharett to say that although he appreciated the importance of friendly relations with Egypt and the continuation of the negotiations, they should under no circumstances agree to the annexation of the coastal strip by Egypt. Egypt, he wrote, was Israel's only large and densely populated neighbour and it was good that desert should separate them. Annexation of the coastal strip by Egypt would also create a dangerous precedent for the annexation of the Galilee by Lebanon. The scheme would also antagonize Britain and Abdullah unnecessarily. If Egypt was genuinely interested in excluding Abdullah and the British from central Palestine and the Negev, she should co-operate with Israel in creating an independent Arab state in Palestine which would join them as a member of an Oriental League. For Ben-Gurion this was the end of the matter. He had no positive

[9] Ibid. ii. 21–9.   [10] Ben-Gurion's diary, 8 Oct. 1948.

suggestions for furthering the negotiations with the representative of the Egyptian court. Instead he urged Sharett to give his observations on the government decision of October 6 regarding the offensive in the south.[11]

It seems that Ben-Gurion did not take the Egyptian peace feeler seriously because he did not even report it to the Cabinet. He may have also feared that this indication that the royal court was open to the idea of peaceful coexistence with Israel might lead some of the hesitant members of his Cabinet to reconsider their support for the imminent war against Egypt. At the Cabinet meeting on September 26 there had been some discussion of grand strategy, something which Ben-Gurion usually preferred to keep in his own hands. Mordechai Bentov, a representative of the left-wing Mapam, asserted that military operations should be planned by defining first the political aim and not the other way round because war after all was policy pursued by other means. Bentov thought it wrong to allow purely military considerations to dictate their war strategy—attacking Egypt first if that was easier or Abdullah first if that was easier. Political considerations ought to be paramount and if the fighting was renewed the objective should be to bring part of the Arab coalition to the conference table. To this end some forward planning was called for. The government had to ask itself whether its orientation was on seeking to co-operate with Egypt, which was anti-British, against Abdullah, or, conversely, on seeking a point of contact with Abdullah against Egypt.[12]

Bentov touched on a fundamental point which Ben-Gurion did not wish to bring out into the open: the existence of two latent orientations within the Zionist camp, one on Egypt and one on the Hashemites. Bentov was not alone in perceiving the basis for co-operation between Israel and Egypt. It was generally recognized that Egypt was both the main enemy and the main partner for peace. An understanding with any Arab party was to be welcomed, but Egypt was the key to peaceful coexistence between the Arab world and Israel. The territorial dispute between Egypt and Israel was not nearly as serious as the conflict with Transjordan over central Palestine. And the fact that the Egyptians, like the Israelis, aspired to full independence and the ending of British presence on their soil provided another important basis for co-operation that Israel did not share with Transjordan.

On the other hand, there were some questions, notably the Palestinian question, where Israeli interests coincided more closely with those of Transjordan than they did with those of Egypt. Towards the end of 1948 an alliance developed, as witnessed by the All-Palestine government, between the Egyptian government and the Palestinians of

[11] *DFPI*, ii. 44.   [12] Protocol of Cabinet Meeting, 26 Sept. 1948.

the mufti. Correspondingly, on Palestinian matters, it became easier for Israel to co-operate with Abdullah because he worked with Israel's friends among the Palestinians whilst his enemies collaborated with the Egyptians. On Palestinian matters, therefore, Israel had no common language with Egypt.[13]

There was one other consideration which worked against an agreement with Egypt, namely, the effect that such an agreement could have on Israel's relations with Abdullah. This consideration must have appeared more relevant to Ben-Gurion when the first signals were received that an agreement with Egypt might be possible. As one of his advisers explained in connection with the Egyptian peace initiative of September 1948:

If we were going to make peace, then it had to be with Transjordan. Why? Because Transjordan dominated the centre of the country—from the north, the south, and opposite Tel Aviv. The position was that if you made peace with Egypt, it would place you in bad odour with Abdullah. Perhaps the Egyptians wanted peace with Israel in order to gain a free hand to strike at Abdullah, who had achieved much more with his policy of annexation than they did with the government of Ahmad Hilmi. Our calculation was that by making peace with a mouse, we would enrage a lion. In Palestine, at any rate, Egypt was small. For peace with her we would have had to pay with land at a time when there was a pretty substantial Arab bloc sitting in Judaea and Samaria.

Not until 1952 did either Ben-Gurion or Sharett waver in their conviction that the important bloc with which it was worthwhile to make peace was the Hashemite bloc which included Iraq. When we talked with Abdullah, we knew that this included Iraq. Until 1952 we looked to the Hashemites first and foremost. In 1952, following the revolution in Egypt, we said to ourselves that now we have an ideologically compatible partner. But when the relationship with Egypt did not work, we returned to our original orientation and persisted in it until the Hashemite force was decimated by the Iraqi revolution in 1958.[14]

The interesting fact about these two orientations is that they were hardly ever discussed openly, let alone clearly articulated. Ben-Gurion did not encourage a free debate of these big issues, preferring to concentrate on the conduct of the war with as little interference as possible from his ministers or party colleagues. Political power in a sense consists of being able to determine the agenda of the national debate, of deciding what are the big issues and what are the non-issues. And it was a mark of Ben-Gurion's success in manipulating the political agenda that no serious debate took place in 1948 on whether Israel ought to have a Hashemite or an Egyptian orientation—not in the provisional government, not in the Provisional State Council, and not in the Political Committee of Mapai.[15]

[13] Interview with Yaacov Shimoni.   [14] Interview with Yehoshua Palmon.
[15] I am grateful to Professor Dan Horowitz for this point.

Ben-Gurion himself was inclined to favour an agreement with Abdullah, but he was not firmly or unswervingly committed to a Hashemite orientiation. Sharett, by contrast, was much more open to the possibility of an agreement with Egypt. It was Sharett who cultivated the link with Abdullah before the war, during the war, and after the war. These efforts were rooted in the knowledge that under existing circumstances Abdullah was the only Arab head of state who acknowledged Israel's right to independence and was prepared to live with her in peace. Yet all along, Sharett recognized that ultimately it was Egypt that held the key to Israel's acceptance or rejection by the rest of the Arab world. That is why he took so seriously the tentative Egyptian peace feeler of September 1948.

The talks in Paris between Elias Sasson and Kamal Riad were fraught with uncertainties, not least in view of the rivalry between the government and the court in Cairo. They were in the nature of preliminary reconnaissance rather than substantive peace negotiations, a beginning rather than a breakthrough. Sharett's approach to these talks was realistic. His main concern was to maintain the dialogue with Egypt. Ben-Gurion, on the other hand, wrote them off from the very start. He may have been right in thinking that nothing of substance would come out of these talks. But he surely owed his Cabinet colleagues at least a report on what had taken place so that they could review their decision to go to war against Egypt on the basis of all the relevant information.

No such report was made to the Cabinet by Ben-Gurion or anyone else. Preparations for the offensive in the south, named Operation Yoav, continued without interruption. 'The first and essential objective of this large operation', in the words of the official history of the War of Independence, 'was to cure the Negev once and for all of the "disease" of being cut off. By contrast to previous operations, the objective this time was not to be content with blasting a corridor and holding on to it, but to destroy the Egyptian forces. The estimate was that the destruction of the enemy would in itself yield control over the territory.'

Capability to carry out this operation depended to a large extent on how large a force could be allocated to it, and the answer to this question depended, *inter alia*, on the answer to another question: what would the other Arab armies do during the IDF operation against the Egyptians? 'From information we possessed about the friction between the Arab states—friction which increased as their successes on the battlefield diminished—there was room for supposing that they would stand aside and not intervene; but military planning has to take into account the worst possible scenario. It was therefore decided, after prolonged discussions, to keep sufficient forces on the other fronts too.'[16]

On October 15, following a pre-arranged plan, a military supply convoy put to the test Israel's right of passage to the settlements in the northern Negev. The plan was to draw Egyptian fire on the convoy and thereby to implicate Egypt in a violation of the agreement worked out by the UN mediator. But on this occasion, for whatever reason, the Egyptians failed to rise to the bait and held their fire. Undeterred by this deplorable show of Egyptian passivity, the Israeli soldiers fired on one of their own trucks and immobilized it. UN observers were promptly called to the scene and, seeing the bullet-ridden truck, declared the Egyptian forces guilty of breaking the cease-fire.[17]

This ruling gave Israel the pretext she needed for launching a general offensive along the entire front. The fighting lasted seven days, ending when the Security Council's cease-fire resolution entered into force. At the end of this fighting, the road to the Negev was open, Israel extended its control to Beersheba and beyond, the Egyptians suffered heavy losses and an Egyptian brigade was trapped in the Faluja enclave inside the new Israeli front line (see Map 9).

Arab discord over the future of Palestine

In his polemical and frequently inaccurate account of the tragedy of Palestine, Abdullah al-Tall makes the claim that King Abdullah knew and approved in advance the Israeli plan to go to war with Egypt. According to Tall, Abdel Ghani al-Karmi, an official of the royal court who enjoyed the king's trust, was sent to Paris specifically for the purpose of maintaining contact with the Israeli delegation to the General Assembly. The other participants in these talks were the Transjordanian ministers to Paris and London. The Jewish delegation was headed by the king's 'old friend', Elias Sasson. The talks lasted six weeks, through which period the king and his government received regular reports from Paris. From Paris came the first hint about the possibility of a Jewish attack on the Egyptians in the Negev. And from Amman was conveyed the promise to Paris that Transjordan would adopt a neutral stand and would not intervene in the war against the Jews. Tall's account is based on what Karmi allegedly told him in private after the event.[18] No evidence can be found in any Israeli sources to corroborate this charge of a deliberate war plot against Egypt.

Yet, as we have just seen, the Israelis were oblivious neither to the

---

[16] *History of the War of Independence* (Heb.) (IDF History Branch: Maarahot, 1959), 295.
[17] Interview with Col. Mordechai Bar-On.   [18] Tall, *The Palestine Tragedy*, 263.

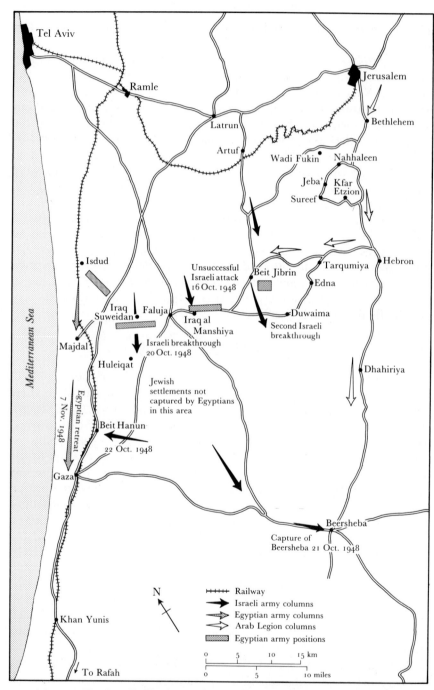

Tel Aviv

Ramle

Latrun

Artuf

Wadi Fukin

Nahhaleen

Jerusalem

Bethlehem

Jeba'

Kfar
Etzion

Sureef

Isdud

Unsuccessful
Israeli attack
16 Oct. 1948

Beit Jibrin

Tarqumiya

Hebron

Edna

Mediterranean Sea

Iraq
Suweidan

Faluja

Iraq al
Manshiya

Duwaima

Second Israeli
breakthrough

Majdal

Israeli breakthrough
20 Oct. 1948

Dhahiriya

Huleiqat

Egyptian retreat
7 Nov. 1948

Jewish
settlements not
captured by Egyptians
in this area

Beit Hanun

22 Oct. 1948

Gaza

Beersheba

Capture of
Beersheba 21 Oct. 1948

N

Railway

Israeli army columns

Egyptian army columns

Arab Legion columns

Egyptian army positions

0   5   10   15 km

0   5   10 miles

Khan Yunis

To Rafah

MAP 9   The Israeli offensive against the Egyptian army, 15 October 1948

tension between Transjordan and Egypt nor to the strategic luxury it might yield of a war only on one front. Abba Eban, the Israeli representative to the United Nations, told a British delegate that the Israeli government had recently held conversations with the representatives of Egypt and Transjordan but they had come to the conclusion that relations between the two countries were like those of enemies on the brink of war and he could not see how they could come to any agreement.[19]

Rising tension between Transjordan and Egypt led Glubb Pasha to radically revise his views on the future of the Negev. During his visit to London, he advised everybody that the best solution would be to give Beersheba and Gaza to Egypt, and Hebron, Ramallah, and Nablus to Transjordan. He made this recommendation under the influence of what he had heard from the prime minister and the defence minister, whose policy was to co-operate with Egypt. The Egyptians, however, it now appeared to Glubb, could not be trusted to co-operate with them, and in consequence he became critical of Tawfiq Abul Huda's desire to buy off the Egyptians. 'I am now inclined to think', Glubb confessed in a secret and personal letter to Kirkbride, 'that both Tawfiq and Fauzi spend too much time in the Arab League. Their thought is almost entirely formed by what Azzam, Nokrashi or Jamil Mardam will say about them in the Political Committee and they are more influenced by this than by public opinion.'

A two-day visit to Palestine persuaded Glubb that the majority of Palestinians tended to regard union with Transjordan as the least unpleasant of all possible solutions, but on condition that Transjordan took the whole of Arab Palestine. He found widespread opposition among the Palestinians against any further partition of the Arab areas of Palestine after the formation of the Jewish State. Under these circumstances any scheme of partition between Egypt and Transjordan could only strengthen the cause of the mufti and his party. In short, Glubb now felt that he had advised the British government wrongly and he asked Kirkbride to inform them of his modified views. He realized that the other Arabs might object if Transjordan tried to enforce the annexation of the whole of Arab Palestine, but felt that they could weather the storm as they had done in the past.[20]

Arab politics generally were at a very low ebb, and Arab leaders almost without exception appeared to be prepared for purely local ends to sacrifice Arab interests in Palestine. The Lebanese, the Syrians, and the Saudis did not care much what happened to the Arab parts of

---

[19] From the UK delegation to Paris to the FO, 29 Sept. 1948, FO 371/68588, PRO.
[20] Glubb to Kirkbride, 29 Sept. 1948, FO 816/129; Kirkbride to FO, 30 Sept. 1948, FO 371/68642, PRO.

Palestine provided they did not go to Abdullah. Abdullah's stock slumped partly because he was suspected of being only too ready to do a direct deal with the Jews but partly because it became fashionable in Arab League circles to denigrate him as being generally untrustworthy. Abdullah's role in the saving of Jerusalem and his army's brave stand at Latrun had been forgotten amidst a deliberate campaign by the Arab leaders to turn him into a scapegoat for the failure of their Palestine policy. Riad al-Sulh, the Lebanese prime minister, expressed a horror of King Abdullah and played a leading role in pressing the Political Committee to give its blessing to the All-Palestine government. He seemed prepared to go to any length, including a slanderous exposure of Abdullah, rather than retreat.[21] Even the regent of Iraq joined in the general campaign of vilification against his uncle; his criticisms were heartily reciprocated, and the relationship between them became so sour that they could no longer have a sensible discussion about Palestine.[22]

The Iraq government did not help matters by recognizing the Gaza government and encouraging the mufti to extend his influence to the rest of Palestine while withholding support from his numerous opponents. In order to get Iraqi support for the Palestinian Arab government, Jamal Husayni, the vice-president of the Arab Higher Committee, on a visit to Baghdad, promised that the mufti would be kept out and that, if Palestine were saved for the Arabs, its throne would be offered to King Abdullah.[23] Shortly afterwards the regent lunched with Abdullah in Amman but the matter was not thrashed out. There was no serious discussion of Palestine, and Abdullah, who was usually criticized by his nephew for talking too much, only threw out a word now and then to keep the conversation going.[24]

The Iraqi prime minister, Muzahem al-Pachachi, felt unable to declare open antagonism towards the mufti and considered that Abdullah would be better advised to go slowly.[25] Whilst in Amman on his way back to Iraq from Egypt, Pachachi, with the tacit support of the regent, did his utmost to induce King Abdullah to agree to recognize 'temporarily' the All-Palestine government, using the argument that the government would fail and Arab Palestine would be bound to come to Transjordan ultimately. The king countered that recognition would merely implement the partition of Palestine before it was known what the United Nations was going to decide.[26]

[21] Beirut to FO, 10 Oct. 1948, FO 371/68862; Beirut to FO, 9 Oct. 1948, FO 371/68642, PRO.
[22] Kirkbride to FO, 2 Oct. 1948, FO 371/68642, PRO.
[23] Sir H. Mack (Baghdad) to FO, 30 Sept. 1948, FO 371/68642, PRO.
[24] Mack to FO, 13 Oct. 1948, FO 371/68643, PRO.
[25] Chapman Andrews (Cairo) to FO, 2 Oct. 1948, FO 371/68642, PRO.
[26] Kirkbride to FO, 12 Oct. 1948, FO 371/68642, PRO.

Sir Henry Mack was perturbed by the strength of the criticism of Abdullah that the prime minister and the regent constantly expressed to him. And it was Mack who was given the task by the Foreign Office of educating them about the dangers of going along with Egypt in encouraging the mufti to extend his influence in Palestine. To the regent in particular it was pointed out that any growth of the mufti's influence would necessarily be dangerous to the Hashemite house. The regent was told, in what amounted to a rebuke, that he could not sit back and allow attacks on the position of King Abdullah without any danger to himself. Whatever the regent's own views in the matter, the British view was that a strong and enlarged Transjordan was in the interest of the maintenance of stability in Iraq and of the position of the regent and the royal family.[27]

So overwhelming was the Arab resistance to Transjordan's enlargement, that the British argument that a weak Palestinian government would enable the Jews to gain control over the whole country made no impression. A major stumbling block in the way of the British policy of using the Bernadotte plan to secure the lion's share of Palestine for Abdullah, was thus Arab opposition to frontier adjustments that would reduce Arab Palestine to nothing. Paradoxically, as one British official observed, 'although the primary Arab objection to the Bernadotte plan is that its acceptance would involve partition, there are clear signs that, in their hearts, all but the most rabid fanatics, like Hajj Amin, realise that the existence of the State of Israel will have to be accepted sooner or later'. What the Arabs could never agree upon was the partition of Arab Palestine. Preventing the expansion of Abdullah's kingdom was one of the few goals behind which they could all rally:

Various reasons can be assigned for this attitude—jealousy of Transjordan, antipathy to King Abdullah, mistrust of his reliability in an anti-Zionist sense, disbelief in the suitability of the Transjordan administration to the parts of Palestine to be taken over, fear of an extension of British influence—none of them objections having any foundation on a statesmanlike appreciation of the facts.[28]

Statesmanlike or not, these were the attitudes that militated against any Arab agreement on the division of Palestine and especially one between King Abdullah and King Farouk on a common approach to the Negev. Britain had urged Abdullah to make a direct approach to Farouk and try to reach a prior agreement with him on the division of the Arab areas while the UN was considering the Bernadotte plan.[29] Abdullah however disagreed with this suggestion for two reasons. The

[27] FO to Baghdad, 28 Sept. 1948, FO 371/68641, PRO.
[28] Minute by K. C. Buss, 11 Oct. 1948, FO 371/68642, PRO.
[29] FO to Amman, 28 Sept. 1948, FO 371/68641, PRO.

first was that Egypt would immediately use the *démarche* against him, producing the usual accusations that he was accepting partition, betraying the Arab cause, and bargaining away the rights of the Palestine Arabs to decide their own future. The second was that Egypt had sponsored the new All-Palestine government in order to be able to control Palestine indirectly while publicly announcing that Egypt had no territorial ambitions and had acted throughout solely in the interests of the Palestine Arabs.[30]

Accusations of bad faith flying in the opposite direction made a further dent in the prospects of mediation. Egyptian diplomats urged Britain to abandon the idea that it might be possible for Transjordan to be given the Negev. Abdullah, it was alleged, was not capable of administering it, and his army could not be relied on. The British were told that if Abdullah came to an agreement with them whereby the Negev would be ceded to Transjordan, he would be branded as a traitor by all the Arab states and his action would probably result in a war between Egypt and Transjordan.[31]

Ibn Saud was incensed with Britain not so much for supporting Bernadotte's conclusions of agreeing to a Zionist state but for going even further in the advocacy of a Greater Transjordan. Ibn Saud had always suspected that there was a secret understanding between Britain and Abdullah with the object of enlarging the dominions of the latter. The Saudi monarch did not object to Egypt having the Negev but made it clear that he would never agree to Abdullah having it, and that if Britain persisted she would forfeit his friendship.[32]

Abdullah's position in the Arab world was not helped by the mismanagement which characterized his handling of the Palestinian population who came under his control. For the most part the Arabs of Palestine evinced little desire to be incorporated in Transjordan. The most sophisticated among them saw little attraction in the political despotism of Transjordan, dependent as it was on the volatile temper of the king. They were also aware of the economic non-viability of Transjordan and realized that Arab Palestine and Transjordan together would be even less of a going concern. Hence their opposition to Transjordanian rule and insistence on a unitary state.[33] From being a hero a few months previously for heeding their calls and going to the rescue, Abdullah had sunk almost to the level of a pariah among his brother Arabs.

So bitter was the enmity and jealousy of the surrounding Arab

[30] Kirkbride to FO, 2 Oct. 1948, FO 371/68642, PRO.
[31] Clutton to Burrows, 24 Sept. 1948, FO 371/68589, PRO.
[32] Chapman Andrews (Cairo) to FO, 29 Sept. 1948, FO 371/68642, PRO.
[33] Beaumont (Jerusalem) to FO, 30 Sept. 1948, FO 371/68642, PRO.

countries and the apparent dislike of Palestinians for Transjordanian rule that Abdullah thought they might give rise to internecine violence and his government felt compelled to reconsider their membership of the Arab League and their co-operation with the Arab powers in Palestine. Tawfiq Abul Huda mentioned the alternatives of leaving the Arab League and withdrawing the Arab Legion from Palestine or of merely withdrawing the Legion and staying in the League. He was inclined to think that as all the Arabs were opposing Transjordan and the United Nations was unable to enforce a decision favouring Transjordan, it would be best to write off the Palestine adventure and get the Arab Legion back lest it become embroiled in a military disaster. He was also worried by the fact that the only military formation left in Transjordan was the Iraqi army, which could get out of hand if things went badly.[34]

Awareness that the withdrawal of the Arab Legion would lead to the defeat of the other Arab armies and the occupation of the whole of Palestine by the Jewish forces prompted the British to urge Abdullah to refrain from doing anything precipitate in the way of breaking the Arab front and to assure him that they would stand by the Anglo-Transjordanian treaty even in the unlikely event of Transjordan being attacked by another Arab state.[35] At the same time the British were forced to recognize that by their outspoken insistence on giving the Arab areas to Transjordan they were spoiling their relations with the other Arabs. Some British representatives argued that 'the key to the situation in the Arab world lies in Egypt. It may be a poor key but it is the only one there is.'[36]

Doubts were cast on the wisdom of basing Britain's policy in Palestine and in the Middle East generally to such a large extent on maintaining the stability of Transjordan. 'It is sometimes suggested', reported the head of the Eastern Department to the Minister in Amman, 'that we are putting all our eggs into one basket and leaning too heavily on one individual, and a very old one at that.'[37] This suggestion, replied Kirkbride, was not unjustified, 'but what else are we to do when the other baskets available seem to be so unwilling to accommodate our eggs? So long as the other Arab states continue to protest their friendship for Great Britain and, at the same time, consistently disregard our advice and, in some cases, frustrate our policy, it seems worthwhile taking some trouble to keep Transjordan alive and on our side.' As for the eventuality of the king's death,

[34] Kirkbride to FO, 4 Oct. 1948, FO 371/68862, PRO.
[35] Bevin to Kirkbride, 11 Oct. 1948, FO 816/130, PRO.
[36] BMEO to FO, 8 Oct. 1948, FO 371/68642, PRO.
[37] Burrows to Kirkbride, Secret and Personal, 8 Oct. 1948, FO 371/68364, PRO.

Kirkbride felt that it would certainly leave a gap but he was not pessimistic about Transjordan's ability to survive the loss.[38]

Transjordan and the Israeli–Egyptian war

Abdullah's own attitude towards Israel was somewhat paradoxical during this delicate phase in his relations with the Arab League. On the one hand, he feared a major Israeli offensive which the Arab armies were in no position to contain. On the other hand, an Israeli offensive could be of some benefit if directed solely against the Egyptian forces in the south. Recognition of the All-Palestine government by Egypt and the other members of the Arab League placed both Israel and Transjordan in a peculiar position. Abdullah watched the activities of the Egyptian army closely, believing them to be related to the formation of the puppet government in Gaza. As the American representative reported from Tel Aviv, there was a good chance that if war resumed in the south Abdullah might stand by and let the Israeli army maul the Egyptian forces in order to eliminate both the Gaza government and the potential Egyptian menace to his territory. The Israelis estimated that they could defeat the Egyptians soundly, provided Abdullah held his Legion back. This unhappy situation could also open up an avenue for a political settlement between Israel and Transjordan.[39]

Glubb Pasha had few qualms about reaping the political benefits of an Egyptian defeat at the hands of the Israelis. As we have seen, Abdullah al-Tall went as far as to claim that the Israelis had actually informed Amman of their intention to attack Egypt, and Amman responded by promising not to intervene if the war in the south were resumed. According to Tall, Glubb visited Jerusalem on October 12, gathered all the Arab and British officers, gave them a lecture on the history of the Palestine problem, and warned them not to open fire so as not to upset the truce because that would put the Arab Legion in an awkward position, not least as ammunition was in short supply. The timing and content of this talk led Tall to suspect that his British commander knew in advance of the impending Israeli attack against the Egyptian army.[40] No firm evidence, however, is adduced to substantiate the charge of high-level Transjordanian involvement in a war plot against an allied Arab army.

Yet, whether or not there had been any collusion, Glubb could barely conceal his excitement when the Israeli offensive opened on October 15. In a letter he wrote to Col. Desmond Goldie, the commander of the

---

[38] Kirkbride to Burrows, Secret and Personal, 21 Oct. 1948, FO 371/68364, PRO.
[39] *FRUS 1948*, v. 1476 f.
[40] Tall, *The Palestine Tragedy*, ch. 13.

1st Brigade, Glubb gave his frank assessment of the significance of this development and of the political and military dividends it could be made to yield for their side. Interestingly, the responsibility for starting this war is laid by Glubb at the door of the mufti:

The Mufti's government in Gaza wanted to increase its prestige by starting a fight. For the past week, supported by the Egyptians, the Mufti's irregulars have been shooting at the Jews. The Jews have now got cross and are going to see them off.

Secondly, the Jews are going to try at U.N.O. to get both Galilee *and* the Negeb. The Mufti and the Gyppies [*sic*] have given them just the chance they wanted. They can now break through to Beersheba and occupy both the Negeb and Galilee. How are U.N.O. going to get them out? It looks as if the Gaza government have given the Jews *just* the chance they wanted.

Now if the Jews break through to Gaza and Beersheba, the Egyptians in Hebron will be cut off. We don't want the Jews to capture Hebron too. If we step in and occupy Hebron, we shall have no further political complications in the Hebron area! We shall appear as saviours, to rescue Hebron from the Jews when the Egyptians have run away.

This Jewish offensive may have good and bad sides. It may finally knock out the Gaza government and give the gyppies a lesson. On the other hand, it will make the Jews even more arrogant, and if they knock out the Egyptians, they may turn on us.

Anyway, if we do send someone to Hebron, I don't think we can send the 8th Regiment! This may well mean business, and not be a mere political demonstration . . . Presumably the gyppies cut off in Hebron would co-operate for what they are worth!

I don't see how we could let the Jews occupy Hebron if we could prevent it. At the same time, if the Jews are going to have a private war with the Egyptians and the Gaza Government, we do not want to get involved. The gyppies and the Gaza Government are almost as hostile to us as the Jews!

The situation therefore is a bit delicate. I wonder whether it would be worth while mentioning it very privately to the top U.N.O. man? I imagine that U.N.O. will not want the Jews to occupy Hebron either. If so, perhaps we could send a regiment to Hebron and U.N.O. at the same time drop a hint to the Jews not to go to Hebron. We want to save Hebron, but we do not want to break the truce. However, if you do talk to U.N.O., do not let *anyone* else know you have done so.[41]

Small wonder that the recipient of this letter came to regard his commanding officer as a politician first and foremost, as a man whose love and aptitude for politics far outstripped his knowledge of the technical aspects of warfare.[42] Obliquely 'the pasha' rebutted this

---

[41] Glubb to Goldie, 16 Oct. 1948, 1800 hours, Papers of Col. Desmond Goldie. Emphasis in the original.
[42] Interview with Col. Desmond Goldie.

charge in his memoirs by arguing that the 1948 Arab–Israeli war was not covered by the normal rules of strategy:

It is an axiom of war that the object of all military operations is to destroy the enemy's forces. Once this task has been accomplished, the victor can dictate such terms as he wishes. The seizure or evacuation of territory is irrelevant, except in so far as it assists or hampers the main objective—namely, the destruction of the enemy's forces . . .

But the war in Palestine was different, because there was no chance of it being fought to a finish. It was not a straight military war, but a combination of politics and war. Standing, as it were, on the touch-line were the Great Powers, all immensely stronger than the combatants. They were almost certain to intervene and stop the fighting in a few days. Moreover, the United Nations showed a lamentable tendency to acquiesce in every *fait accompli*. The only thing that really interested them was to stop the fighting, and in order to do so, they were prepared to acquiesce in everything that had happened. This was indeed a comfortable creed for petty conquerors. The art was obviously to seize whatever territory you could, and then, when the Security Council ordered you to cease fighting, to obey with protestations of devotion. It was certainly safe to assume that you would be able to keep what you had snatched.[43]

This admirably lucid exposition of the peculiar rules that governed the Palestine war says as much about the author's strategy as it does about the conduct of the Israeli 'petty conquerors'. While undoubtedly proceeding with *faits accomplis*, the Israelis could at least claim that they were expelling the Egyptian invaders from territory that had been allocated to them by the United Nations. No such claim could be used to justify Glubb's action in snatching Hebron from the hands of the Egyptians.

The Israeli *blitzkrieg* of October 15 pulverized the Egyptian front and cut off the Egyptian forces in Hebron and Bethlehem from the rest of the army that was retreating southwards into Sinai. Two courses of action were considered in Amman when the magnitude of the Egyptian defeat had become apparent. One was to initiate a diversionary attack in the Jerusalem or Latrun areas in order to draw Israeli forces away from the south. The other was to send reinforcements round the east side of Jerusalem down to Bethlehem and Hebron and thereby secure this area against a possible Israeli advance.

Glubb preferred the second course of action but some of his Arab subordinates in Jerusalem pre-empted by launching an attack on October 18. The purpose of this local attack instigated by Abdullah al-Tall was to deceive the Israelis into thinking that the Arab Legion had embarked on a major offensive in Jerusalem and force them to divert

[43] Glubb, *A Soldier with the Arabs*, 199.

some of their forces from the Negev to Jerusalem. Though Glubb was told that the enemy started the fight, his intelligence service informed him of the deliberate provocation on the part of the 6th Regiment and of the immediate counter-attack launched by the Israelis. On October 20 Glubb convened the officers serving in Jerusalem and warned them not to provoke the Israelis and not to listen to the advice of certain individuals, meaning Abdullah al-Tall. The officers chose this very individual to present their complaints to the minister of defence and to urge the deployment of the Transjordanian and Iraqi units held in reserve to launch a major operation in Jerusalem. On hearing this advice the minister simply smiled and told Tall to relax because the Jews would simply not attack the Legion and that their best course was to leave the matter to the discretion of their king.[44]

The action of the hotheads of the Legion's 6th Regiment came near to overturning the restraint that by now had been built into the strategy of the top policymakers on both sides. For Ben-Gurion acceded to the request of Lieut.-Col. Moshe Dayan to send two battalions on the night of October 19 to capture the Beit Jala ridge, south of Jerusalem, overlooking Bethlehem and the road to Hebron. Dayan, whose strongest suit was politics rather than military organization and planning, botched the operation, and his men retreated from Beit Jala in some disarray at the first sign of resistance from local snipers. Yigael Yadin, the IDF chief of operations, has singled out this episode as conclusive proof that Ben-Gurion was not bound by any understanding, whether explicit or implicit, with King Abdullah. Though the action was an operational failure, argued Yadin, the most significant fact about it was that it had been explicitly authorized by Ben-Gurion. The capture of Beit Jala, Yadin continued, would have inescapably led to the capture of Bethlehem and Hebron, and that in turn would have rendered it impossible to partition Palestine because it would have deprived Abdullah of a full and important third of the territory he wanted. All this only went to prove, in Yadin's view, that Ben-Gurion had no political conception of restricting military operations against the Arab Legion, at least not at this stage, and that he had no agreement of any kind with King Abdullah.[45]

The weakness of Yadin's case stems from the fact that Dayan had not been given a free hand but restricted to one specific objective—Beit Jala—and given only one day for carrying out the operation. Moreover, when Dayan pressed to be given another chance to capture the villages south of Jerusalem all the way to Beit Jala and put their inhabitants to flight, and a majority on the General Staff supported this plan, Ben-Gurion ruled against it. The reasons given by Ben-Gurion for this

[44] Tall, *The Tragedy of Palestine*, 413 f.   [45] Interview with Gen. Yigael Yadin.

negative decision were predominantly political in character and amounted to unmistakable restraint in relation to the Arab Legion:

1) such an operation after a truce has been declared will create a bad impression in the world, 2) if we do succeed in capturing the place—we would have to cede it under UN pressure—and it would not be worth the life of even one man, 3) harm to Beit Jala (and Bethlehem) will annoy the Christian world, 4) we have no interest at present in provoking the Legion which did not help the Egyptians, 5) this attack is liable to draw the Legion and the Iraqis into the battle—and to counteract the impression of Egyptian isolation and of a rift in the League, 6) such an attack would make it more difficult to hold the position that we are not going to withdraw from the points we have seized.[46]

Similar considerations prompted Ben-Gurion to veto Yigal Allon's plan to extend the gains made in the first stage of Operation Yoav by sending a force to capture or at least encircle Hebron and advance towards Jerusalem from the south. That such an expedition was feasible from the military point of view, no one doubted. Ben-Gurion and his army commanders also knew, from monitoring enemy radio communications, that the Arab Legion units in the Jerusalem area were under clear instructions not to intervene on the side of the Egyptians.[47] So small were those units that even if they had been ordered to intervene, they would have been no match for the Palmach fighters who were champing at the bit. So the only conceivable reason for the veto of an exceptionally promising military plan is that there were overriding political considerations, chief among which was Ben-Gurion's desire to preserve Transjordan's neutrality in the war between Israel and Egypt. And there can be little doubt that by pulling back his forces from Mount Hebron, Ben-Gurion helped indirectly to reinforce Abdullah's and Glubb's inclination to stay out of the 'private war' between the Israelis and the Egyptians.

Having overcome the little local difficulty he had with the officers of the 6th Regiment in the Old City of Jerusalem, Glubb proceeded, on October 21, to send reinforcements to hold Beit Jala and Bethlehem and a hastily improvised column, consisting of two companies of infantry and a squadron of armoured cars, to Hebron. The thinking behind this move, as he explained in another long letter to Colonel Goldie, was a compound of military, political, and economic calculations:

If the enemy were to take Bethlehem and Beit Jala, our troops in the south would be cut off.

Kirkbride also sent for me today and told me that he thought that for

---

[46] Ben-Gurion's diary, 22 Oct. 1948.   [47] Ben-Gurion's diary, 23 Oct. 1948.

political and economic reasons, it was essential not to let the Jews take Bethlehem or Hebron.

Politically we should have another Lydda and Ramla, especially as the King ordered me to send a Regiment there two days ago! It would again be me who had betrayed the Arab cause.

Economically it would mean another 50,000 to 100,000 refugees. Would you therefore please send the armoured cars . . . It looks from the news as tho' the Jews will accept a cease fire in another two or three days, so that they can get the maximum advantage of their victory first.

It is really essential to hold Bethlehem and if possible Hebron for those three days. Please arrange accordingly even if you have to send a company from 8th Regiment or anywhere else, or weaken your front temporarily.[48]

Small as was the force sent into Hebron, in belated compliance with the king's orders, it was adequate to the task of seizing effective control of the area from the hands of the Egyptian soldiers who rejoined the main body of their army in Sinai by way of Aqaba or Amman. Thus, by the time the UN order to cease fire became effective, on October 22, Hebron had been absorbed into the Transjordanian sphere of occupation and any Israeli move to capture it carried the risk not only of international condemnation but the flare up of the entire Transjordanian–Iraqi front.

To forestall such a move, Abdullah asked Wells Stabler, an American member of the Truce Commission, to request his government to inform the Jewish authorities that he had been forced by circumstances to take part in hostilities and that he was now ready to come to some reasonable settlement in regard to Palestine. In his report to the State Department, Stabler listed the points that the king urged him to convey to the Jews:

1. Prior to May 14 he had favored partition and had informally undertaken with Jews to occupy Arab areas of Palestine only, provided Jews remained in their areas.
2. Massacre at Deir Yassin and other provocations had incited all Arabs including himself, and he had entered war with serious intent which he still holds. Arab Legion alone among Arab armies still strong.
3. However he now desires restoration peace and understanding with Jews with whom he believes he could have close relations. He realizes Jews and Arabs can only live peacefully in separate areas with defined boundaries.
4. Palestine question now under jurisdiction and discussion UNGA [UN General Assembly] and all parties must contribute to finding solution in that body.
5. In meantime he hopes Jews will appreciate his sincere desire find solution and refrain from attacking Arab Legion and area occupied by them. Such attacks merely incite further animosity and delay settlement.

[48] Glubb to Goldie, 21 Oct. 1948, Papers of Col. Desmond Goldie.

6.   On his side King has given strict orders Arab Legion must respect truce
and must not attack unless attacked. He believes his orders are being
obeyed.

[7.] King said except for contact with Jews through Prince Abdel Majid
Haidar, Transjordan Minister to London, and Sasson of Israeli Foreign
Office, he had not requested anybody previously to convey his views to
Jews.[49]

The king did not even mention this *démarche* to his own prime minister
or the British minister both of whom considered the suggestion
premature and hoped that the British government would decline to act
as a go-between if the US government should seek its advice or,
alternatively, ignore the message altogether.[50]

Abdullah could not be certain that the Americans would transmit his
message, or, if they did, that the Israelis would take the bait of separate
negotiations and refrain from attacking his forces in the Judaean
mountains round Hebron. So later in the day he phoned the regent of
Iraq and said he wished to discuss with him defence against Jewish
aggression, a possibility he feared would occur as soon as the Jews had
polished off the Egyptians. Abdullah invited the regent, and through
him the prime ministers of Egypt and Syria, to urgent consultations
in Amman. On hearing of the conversation, Sir Henry Mack, the
British ambassador in Baghdad, told Abd al-Illah that he was glad
to hear that Abdullah laid the emphasis on defence and advised him
to adopt the line of complete solidarity with his uncle at the forthcoming meeting. Mack also urged that there should be no question of
anything more than defence on Iraq's part. Abd al-Illah agreed and
said that indeed nothing more was possible in the absence of arms,
equipment, and ammunition. He also confessed that he feared not
just a Jewish attack but also the Iraqi army. The latter, if attacked,
could not hold out for long and were liable to run riot in the event of
being forced to withdraw before a Jewish advance through lack of
ammunition. Abd al-Illah therefore renewed his appeal for equipment
and ammunition.[51]

The regent, the prime ministers of Egypt and Syria, and their
military advisers arrived in Amman on October 23 but nothing was
achieved in their two-day summit meeting. The discussions sound like
a scene from *Alice in Wonderland*. At the first meeting Nuqrashi Pasha
took the wind out of everybody's sails by saying that the situation in the
Egyptian Army was excellent and that it was moving forward to further

[49] *FRUS 1948*, v. 1501 f.
[50] Kirkbride to FO, 23 Oct. 1948, FO 371/68643, PRO.
[51] Sir H. Mack to FO, 22 Oct. 1948, FO 371/68689, PRO.

victories. This was rather a surprise because Azzam Pasha had previously issued an appeal for help to all the members of the Arab League in the name of Nuqrashi and his defence minister. At the second meeting, which included the military chiefs, the Egyptian premier totally reversed his position by tabling a complaint that no one had come to the assistance of the Egyptian forces when they were attacked and demanding that plans should be made to ensure that this unfortunate occurrence was not repeated. The Syrian premier, Jamil Mardam, then produced an offer to capture Nazareth and Safed if the Iraqis would move up to Afuleh. This offer left everyone speechless once more, but it did enable the Iraqis to decline on the grounds that they could play a more useful role by taking over the Latrun area from the Arab Legion and so freeing Legion units to move to Hebron and Bethlehem and fill the gap there. The meeting ended without any decision being taken on any subject at all.[52]

The Israelis were in a buoyant mood as a result of their victory over the Egyptian army, and the spectacle of Arab disunity only added to their joy. The new mood was reflected by Gideon Rafael in a letter to another Israeli diplomat suggesting that 'the rift between Egypt and Transjordan is now so deep that Abdullah and his British wire-pullers prefer an Israeli victory over Egypt than Egyptian occupation even of a small portion of the Negev . . . We are now not engaged at all with Abdullah and have our full freedom of movement. I personally feel that Abdullah has missed the bus for getting an overall understanding with us, and therefore we have to look for other forces in the Middle East which are less dependent on Great Britain.'[53]

A day after this assessment was penned, Dean Rusk of the State Department conveyed Abdullah's six-point message offering separate peace talks to the youthful and ebullient Abba Eban who had recently been appointed Israeli ambassador to Washington while continuing to serve as representative to the UN.[54] But before this message could reach Tel Aviv, Moshe Sharett ordered Elias Sasson, who was still in Paris, to make a protest to Abdullah about Arab Legion interference with Israeli food supplies to the enclave on Mount Scopus and counsel him to learn from the Egyptian experience and show reasonableness in time rather than repent uselessly later. The king was to be told that so far the Israelis had left the Arab Legion alone but unless the convoys to Mount Scopus were allowed to operate regularly, they would be constrained to take effective and comprehensive action.[55] Sasson made

[52] Kirkbride to FO, 25 Oct. 1948, FO 371/68689, PRO. See also Abdullah, *My Memoirs Completed*, 23–5.

[53] G. Rafael to A. Lourie, 25 Oct. 1948, *DFPI*, ii. 93–5.

[54] Eban to Sharett, 26 Oct. 1948, ibid. 102.

[55] Sharett to Eban, 26 Oct. 1948, ibid. 103.

these points, though not so bluntly, in a telegram to Abul Huda, concluding with the hope that the Transjordanian authorities would take the necessary measures in order to maintain quiet in the Holy City and facilitate the efforts of those seeking a peaceful solution. The reply from Amman stated that the agreement reached in the presence of the UN observers was still in force and that the Arab Legion was under standing orders to observe it.[56] The next day, to the surprise of the UN observers in Jerusalem, Israeli convoys were allowed unrestricted passage, and the local commander of the Arab Legion waived his earlier demand for the withdrawal of the Israeli 'policemen' who had remained on Mount Scopus under the terms of the original agreement.

Nevertheless, the Israelis' response to the American offer to mediate between Abdullah and themselves remained non-committal. Rusk was informed that Israel's general policy was to refrain from attacking the Arab Legion so long as the Legion did not start. The problem, however, was complicated by the Iraqis who, under the same command, allegedly kept attacking at various points. Rusk was asked whether Abdullah's undertaking applied to the Iraqis as well.[57] Eban also showed Rusk the exchange of telegrams between Elias Sasson and Amman. In Eban's view this exchange illustrated the value of direct contact between the parties; the possibility of effective action if the UN mediator's services were dispensed with; and the necessity of direct negotiations in working for a settlement.[58]

In Amman, however, it was far from clear whether the Israeli telegram was intended to further a peaceful settlement or provide an excuse for an offensive action against the Arab Legion.[59] This tiny army was dangerously overstretched following the collapse of the Egyptian front and the Iraqi army's refusal to extend its front to take over Latrun and thereby release Legion units for the defence of Hebron. Meanwhile, the Israelis had reduced the Syrian army to impotence in the north, knocked Qawukji's Arab Liberation Army out of the fight, and, not content with banishing the Lebanese army from the Galilee, chased it across the frontier and captured fourteen villages in southern Lebanon. Thus, by the end of the month, the tide had changed very dramatically and menacingly against the Arabs.

Kirkbride received a letter from King Abdullah asking him to draw Bevin's attention to the critical situation of the Arab Legion following the recent military developments in the south. Abdullah claimed that although it was fully extended before, the Arab Legion had been

[56] E. Sasson to Tawfiq Abul Huda, 28 Oct. 1948, *DFPI*, ii. 109 f.
[57] Eytan to Eban, 29 Oct. 1948, ibid. 113.
[58] Eban to Eytan, 1 Nov. 1948, ibid. 118.
[59] Kirkbride to Bevin, 1 Nov. 1948, FO 816/132, PRO.

compelled to send detachments into the Hebron district to prevent panic among the local population, which would have resulted in a new wave of refugees that Transjordan simply would not have been in a position to cope with. Abdullah also pointed out that with nothing but ammunition for small arms the Arab Legion would be unable to deal with a Jewish attack in force, and that if the Arab Legion broke, the whole Arab front in Palestine would collapse and Transjordan would be overwhelmed by a flood of refugees and disbanded soldiery. He therefore begged once again that Bevin reconsider the decision to withhold supplies of arms and ammunition from the Arab Legion. He also asked, with less insistence, that Transjordan might be given financial assistance in the form of a loan from Great Britain to meet the cost of creating and operating an administration in the Arab areas of Palestine.[60]

Abdullah also convened a special meeting of his Council of Ministers, on the night of November 2, to discuss the position of the Arab Legion in Palestine. Glubb Pasha was asked to report and gave the opinion that, after the withdrawal of the Egyptian forces, the Arab Legion would be unable to maintain its positions if attacked by the Jewish forces. He added that, in his view, the supply of artillery and mortar ammunition would not alter that fact as the preponderance of strength on the Jewish side was now too great. The meeting also felt that in their present state of nerves, the Iraqi forces would do nothing to assist the Arab Legion if the latter came under attack.

As a result of this meeting, the prime minister went to see Kirkbride to put through him a question to Bevin. Abul Huda prefaced his question with an oblique reference to the secret understanding he had reached with the secretary of state in London prior to the outbreak of the war. The Arab Legion, Abul Huda stated, was stationed only in areas of Palestine allocated by the United Nations to the Arabs and in the Arab quarters of Jerusalem. It had no intention of doing more than defending itself. Under these conditions, if attacked by Jewish forces, would the provisions of Article 3 of the Anglo-Transjordanian Treaty of Alliance apply and the United Kingdom come to Transjordan's aid? He went on to say that if the reply was that the treaty only applied to the defence of Transjordan's territory, the Transjordanian government would have to consider the alternatives of withdrawing the Arab Legion from Palestine or of negotiating with the Jews. He added that the final choice would have to rest with King Abdullah.[61]

Bevin was alarmed by the reports of the military situation in Palestine. It was not just the partition scheme that he had so carefully

---

[60] Kirkbride to Bevin, 30 Oct. 1948, FO 816/132, PRO.
[61] Kirkbride to FO, 3 Nov. 1948, FO 371/68822, PRO.

worked out, but Transjordan, the Arab Legion, and the credibility of Britain's commitment to her allies that were all in danger of collapsing under the hammer blows of the Israeli army. Bevin left the American secretary of state, George Marshall, in no doubt about the gravity of the situation and the danger of war between Britain and the Jewish state:

With the defeats inflicted upon the Egyptian Army and the present position of the Jewish forces, Abdullah's Arab Legion might become exposed to annihilating attacks on the part of the Jews. Bevin said he was under great pressure to let Abdullah obtain at least some arms in order to permit the Arab Legion to survive. He dwelt in some length on the importance of the Arab Legion as the only disciplined Arab force for the implementation of any Palestine partition solution. He made it quite plain that Great Britain could not stand by and see Transjordan and the Arab Legion placed in a position where it would be unable to defend itself against possible Jewish attack. He went so far as to state categorically that if the Israel forces should attack Transjordan proper at any time, the treaty of assistance with Great Britain would be immediately operative.[62]

Though Bevin was actively considering British military intervention in Palestine, he carefully refrained from making any definite promises to the king and prime minister of Transjordan. In his reply Bevin mentioned some practical measures that were under consideration such as the sending of a sloop to Aqaba and the despatch of war materials to Amman to be held by the RAF pending further instructions. He also repeated the assurance of British readiness to help, under the terms of the treaty, in the event of an attack on Transjordan's territory. But he could give no assurance that British troops would be sent into Palestine to repel a Jewish attack on the Arab Legion, if one were to take place.[63] This latter contingency was not covered by the treaty, nor had it been addressed by Bevin and Abul Huda at their secret meeting in London because at that time both parties to the collusion had expected a peaceful, not a violent, partition of Palestine.

The upshot was that the king and his ministers could not be sure what the British reaction would be if the Israelis chose to round up their victories in the south and the north of Palestine with an attack on the Arab Legion. The practical steps mentioned by Bevin were too puny and too grudging and his reply to the key question regarding help in Palestine was too evasive to deflect the king from pursuing the alternative of negotiating with the enemy.

[62]   *FRUS 1948*, v. 1521.
[63]   FO to Amman, 6 Nov. 1948, FO 371/68822, PRO.

12

A FAREWELL TO ARMS

Thoughts about peace talks

The weakness of the Arab Legion and the prospect of its annihilation in renewed fighting in Palestine gave Abdullah a powerful incentive to negotiate with the Israelis. The road to negotiations, however, was strewn with pitfalls and obstacles. So while proceeding along this road, Abdullah could not afford to ignore the views of his own government, the obligations imposed by membership of the Arab League, the feelings of the Palestinians, or the advice of Great Britain. Unilateral action by Abdullah in opening talks with the Israelis could bring down on Transjordan the wrath of the Arab world and even lead to her expulsion from the Arab League.

Since the king started talking openly about negotiations with the Jews, the prime minister felt he had to point out that if these negotiations became necessary, it would not be possible for the Council of Ministers he headed to undertake the task. This attitude, Abul Huda emphasized, was not due to the belief that the policy of negotiations would necessarily be wrong but to personal reluctance, in view of their past statements on Palestine, to change their grounds so drastically. However, he went on to say that he was aware of Abdullah's contacts with the Jews, and that while a few weeks previously he would have asked that they should cease, he now felt that they might be useful; he even offered to send a telegram to Transjordan's minister in London, Abdul Majid Haidar, instructing him to stay in touch with Elias Sasson in Paris, and this telegram was in fact despatched.[1]

Although Abul Huda was prepared to resign so that a new government could undertake negotiations, and even made it clear that he and his colleagues would remain neutral and not hamper the work of their successors, the king felt that nothing would be achieved by such resignations unless the other Arab governments resigned at the same time.

Palestinian opinion had shifted perceptibly in favour of merging the Arab parts of Palestine with Transjordan, partly as a result of disillusionment with the Arab governments. The misfortunes of the Egyptian

[1] Kirkbride to FO, 3 and 8 Nov. 1948, FO 371/68822, PRO.

army in the Negev and the hasty withdrawal of the Egyptian-backed All-Palestine government from Gaza diminished such slender dominion as that government had succeeded in establishing over the Arabs of Palestine. The political trimmers in Palestine concluded that the prospects of an independent Arab state were receding, while union with Transjordan appeared more probable and perhaps more profitable. Among the more educated Palestinians the dislike and mistrust of Abdullah persisted. Musa Alami, for example, doubted whether any Palestinian whose mind rose above petty politics would find scope in a unified kingdom since Abdullah intended to treat Arab Palestine not as the second element of a dual monarchy, as in the Austro–Hungarian Empire, but as a straight colony to be administered from Amman. The upshot, however, was to present Abdullah with an opportunity of rehabilitating himself with the Arabs of Palestine. The logic of events had spoken in favour of the king's realism as opposed to the bombastic self-deception of the other Arab countries.[2] A number of delegations of Arabs from Palestine approached the king requesting that he undertake negotiations. Some even said that if he would not negotiate with the Jews, they would.

On October 3 Abdullah sent a personal message to King Farouk informing him of the desire of many Palestine Arabs to end the war and reach a settlement and of his belief that the matter should be seriously considered. Abdullah added that he could not take such a step on his own and therefore wished to consult with his colleagues. No reply was received and this was a cause for disappointment to Abdullah and concern among his advisers that the message might be used to embarrass Transjordan.

Three days later the Arab League Political Committee met in Cairo. Transjordan's delegation had received instructions to explore, without committing itself, the attitude of the other members towards a settlement in Palestine. Once in Cairo, however, the delegation followed the lead of the other members in reconsidering the question of a unified command for the Arab armies operating in Palestine. Abdullah received a telegram from the delegation requesting him to send two senior Arab Legion officers. He was annoyed by the disregard shown for his instructions but none the less sent two officers to Cairo.[3] Meanwhile, to combat rumours that Amman was contemplating separate negotiations with the enemy, the Transjordanian delegation issued the following communiqué in Cairo:

The policy of the Transjordanian government has always been, and will continue to be, in complete harmony with the policy of the Arab states on the

[2] Beaumont (Jerusalem) to FO, 29 Oct. 1948, and 12 Nov. 1948, FO 371/68643, PRO.
[3] *FRUS 1948*, v. 1564 f.

question of Palestine and past events have proved that the Transjordanian Kingdom has consistently adhered to this principle. The Arab armies entered Palestine to restore peace and liberate her people from the aggressions and atrocities of the Zionist gangs. Because of this, the government of Transjordan must of necessity condemn any such fabricated reports that it intends to conclude a separate peace with the Zionists.[4]

The Zionists for their part were in no particular hurry to enter negotiations and under no pressure to make any concessions. Whereas the cockiness displayed by the Arabs before the Negev offensive had given way to a willingness to face facts and seek an end to the conflict, the Israelis, in the words of one British observer, were 'cock-a-hoop'. Militarily they could do whatever they wished, and there was a great deal more that some of their leaders still wished to achieve.

Ben-Gurion was sufficiently emboldened by the capture of Galilee and the banishing of the Lebanese army and Qawukji's irregulars to start making plans for rolling back the Hashemite armies across the Jordan. His plan was to start with the Triangle by applying pressure on Jenin and Tulkarem and then, if Nablus could be captured, to proceed from there to Ramallah. He was at one with the IDF commanders in preferring the strategy of the indirect approach to frontal attacks on the positions of the Hashemite armies. His orders were to prepare for a two-pronged attack on the Iraqi army in the Triangle, from the north and the east, and then move south to engage the Arab Legion. Some pitched battles were fought between the IDF and the Iraqi army, and interception of a message from the Iraqi chief of staff to Baghdad provided precise information on the vulnerability of the Iraqi army's flanks.

'What next?' was the question posed by Yigael Yadin in a top-level military consultation on October 31. Ben-Gurion replied that they had to wait a few days to assess the likely reaction of the UN General Assembly then in session in Paris. Yet, it was not the UN but Bevin who was viewed by Ben-Gurion as Israel's most sinister enemy and the chief manipulator of the Arab armies: 'If Bevin could act on the basis of rationality alone, without anti-Semitic emotions, he would have been bound to conclude that the Arab army is worthless, that we are now the only military power in the Middle East, and hence that he has either to find immediate and effective means to destroy us or to accept us as an important power. But it is not clear whether he can reach a clear-cut conclusion.' In the meantime Ben-Gurion favoured action to liquidate the Egyptian force encircled at Faluja but without too blatant a violation of the truce. Provided nothing serious happened in Paris, Ben-Gurion planned by the end of the week to deploy four brigades to attack Jenin, Umm al-Fahem, Tulkarem, Beit Nabala, and Tubas. His final

[4] *Al Ahram*, 7 Nov. 1948.

observation was also the most revealing about the high stakes for which he was now playing: 'If we reach Nablus, Ramallah will fall by itself and Jerusalem will be liberated, the Legion will flee to Transjordan and the whole country will be in our hands.'[5]

Something serious did happen in Paris on November 4: the Security Council passed a resolution calling on the combatants in the Negev to withdraw their forces to the lines of October 14 and threatened to take unspecified further measures if either party failed to comply. Eager as he was for further conquests, Ben-Gurion re-evaluated his policy in the light of this vague threat of international action. In a further meeting with Yadin and the chief of staff, he explained that the stand of the Security Council, and America's tendency to follow the British Foreign Office, raised doubts in his mind concerning the planned campaign in the Triangle. From a military point of view he still considered that the best way to capture Jerusalem was by launching a concerted attack on the Triangle from the north, the east, and the west. He realized, however, that

in order for this operation to succeed and bring the desired result in Jerusalem—the flight of the Legion—the time available to us must be unlimited. This is doubtful and we may possibly have to stop the operation after a short time, when the Legion may have received help from the Iraqis for intensified pressure on Jerusalem. For this reason it seems to me necessary to ascertain whether it might not be possible in a shorter time to act in the area around Jerusalem—in the direction of Ramallah on the one hand and in the direction of Bethlehem on the other.[6]

International pressure thus helped to switch Ben-Gurion's support from the big plan for capturing the northern Triangle and Jerusalem to a smaller plan for enlarging the territory held by Israel in and around Jerusalem.

Ben-Gurion presented the dilemma to the Security Committee of the provisional government in the form of a hypothetical question: assuming they were going to resort to military action against the Triangle, which alternative would they prefer, the northern one or the southern one? Yitzhak Gruenbaum, the minister of the interior, who had lost his son in the battle for Jerusalem, was afraid to take action against the Triangle because that would constitute the greatest blow against Britain. He suggested that they seize only Hebron, Bethlehem, and the railway station in Jerusalem and leave Shaikh Jarrah and Latrun alone. Ben-Gurion pointed out that a war on Hebron meant a war on the Arab Legion, that the Legion would extend the war to its entire front and this, from the British point of view, would be the hardest and

[5] Ben-Gurion's diary, 30 and 31 Oct. 1948.   [6] Ibid. 8 Nov. 1948.

most dangerous blow. Eliezer Kaplan, the minister of finance and a leading dove in Mapai and in the Cabinet, doubted whether they could take any action at all without stretching the line too far. But if they were going to act, he preferred the northern plan because a blow against the Iraqis would finish off the last dangerous enemy and lead Abdullah to make peace with Israel.[7]

At the end of November, Ben-Gurion summed up the lessons he had drawn from the previous year's experience and the fundamentals of his own policy in what he termed 'non-military remarks' to the General Staff and the field commanders:

It has been said that war is the extension of policy by other means. This is not always true. Our war, initially, was a defence against an attempt to destroy us. In essence it has remained so until the present day but since the first truce (11 June 48) our military action has contained a kind of political act. This is true to some extent of the ten days' war, and even more so of the campaign in the south and the sixty hours of the Galilee. A debate was due to take place in the Assembly and there was a necessity to change *the facts*, so that the fate of the Negev and the Galilee will not depend exclusively on the outcome of these deliberations. And the operation in the Negev necessitated the operation in the Galilee, because with the Negev in our hands there was a political danger to the Galilee. There is another objective: Jerusalem, which means the corridor (Latrun, the railway station, Batir), Shaikh Jarrah, and the environs of Jerusalem to the north and south—and the Old City. The Galilee was decided by virtue of the military operation and is almost settled from the political point of view too. In the Negev the military position will be largely, if not wholly, decisive. The fate of Old Jerusalem will be decided not by military force but by political–religious considerations. And whether we are allowed to operate in other areas will depend on many circumstances.

A final 'non-military remark' by the Israeli war leader related to the prospective end of the war. Whether or not the war was renewed, he said, would depend not on truce resolutions or paper agreements but on the historic reality.

What is our reality: the Arab nations have been beaten by us. Will they forget that swiftly? 700,000 men have beaten 30 million. Will they forget this insult? It has to be assumed that they have a sense of honour. We shall make efforts for peace—but for peace two sides are required. Is there any certainty that they will not want to have their revenge on us? Let us recognize the truth: we won not because our army is a performer of miracles but because the Arab army is rotten. Is this rot bound to persist? Is an Arab Mustafa Kemal not possible?[8]

The reference to Mustafa Kemal Ataturk, the founder and first president of the Turkish Republic, was highly revealing. For having led the nationalist struggle against both the Ottoman sultan and the Allies

---

[7] Ibid. 11 Nov. 1948.　　[8] Ibid. 27 Nov. 1948.

and achieved Turkey's independence after the First World War, Ataturk embarked on an ambitious programme of transforming the country into a modern, Westernized, secular state. He not only had an enduring impact on the evolution of Turkish society and politics but became a model for leaders of many developing countries. Ben-Gurion's greatest fear was that Arab society would undergo a similar transformation under a leader inspired by the ideas of Kemalism. By a curious touch of historic irony, at the very moment when Ben-Gurion was articulating this fear, surrounded by Israeli troops in the enclave of Faluja, there was a young brigade major who would later emerge as an Arab Mustafa Kemal—Gamal Abdul Nasser.[9]

Ben-Gurion drew two main conclusions from his analysis of contemporary Arab society and his expectations of the thirst for revenge that would grow out of the Arab defeat in Palestine: first, that Israel's peace efforts would encounter strong psychological and emotional resistance and, second, that even after the termination of hostilities Israel would have to maintain a large and effective defence force.

To a far greater extent than Ben-Gurion, Moshe Sharett saw war as the extension of policy by other means. Whereas the former attached overriding importance to the military factor in Israeli–Arab relations, the latter, in a true Clausewitzian fashion, insisted that military policy must be subordinated to a clear and well-defined political purpose. The two men had worked very effectively in double-harness during the early stage of the war, but now that military ascendancy had widened the scope for political choice, differences between them began to emerge just below the surface. The most significant difference concerned the use of force against the Arab Legion and the future of the West Bank.

If the prime minister's idea was to spur the Cabinet on to order the capture of the Triangle, Sharett demanded that three factors be taken into consideration: (a) it would preclude the option of an Arab state in western Palestine, or even a rump state for annexation to Transjordan, and this would stretch to the absolute limit the departure from the UN partition resolution of 29 November 1947; (b) it would facilitate immeasurably the pressure of the Western powers on Israel to concede the Negev; and (c) it would give the problem of the Arab refugees catastrophic proportions.[10]

Differences at the top greatly complicated the task of the officials responsible for the implementation of Israel's Middle Eastern policy. The conflicting pulls and the consequent confusion were laid bare by

---

[9] For Nasser's own reflections on that experience see 'Nasser's Memoirs of the First Palestine War', translated and annotated by Walid Khalidi, *Journal of Palestine Studies*, 2/2 (1973), 3–32.

[10] Comments by the foreign minister on the Research Department's survey of 31 Oct. 1948, 2451/1, ISA.

Yaacov Shimoni, the deputy head of the Middle East Department at the Foreign Ministry, in a letter to his boss, Elias Sasson, who continued to maintain the contact with various Arab quarters from Paris. Shimoni began by recalling that Moshe Sharett had ordered them to encourage the inhabitants of the Arab part of Palestine to form an independent government of their own or to rebel against the extremist Arab line by concluding a pact with Israel. A number of emissaries were accordingly sent to the Arab parts, and especially to the Triangle, and their reports painted a rosy picture. According to these reports, the Arabs of Palestine had despaired of the Arab League, the Arab countries, the Arab armies, the mufti, the Gaza government, and Abdullah. They craved for peace and were ready to start talks to see if a basis could be found for understanding and co-operation with Israel. A number of prominent people offered their services as go-betweens in bringing the rest of the Palestinian leadership to peace talks with Israel. These reports gave rise to a welter of reactions and considerations, some of them contradictory, at the receiving end:

What shall we ask of them: an open Palestinian government? With Abdullah? Against Abdullah? A government-in-exile with us? An underground? An uprising and rebellion? Preparation of the ground for our conquest? And what about the borders—a problem that is bound to surface and come up in every discussion of this kind? And in the meantime our army is in any case doing its duty from the military point of view and is creating important and surprising political facts, without taking into account our own political thoughts, which are becoming more out-dated day by day. For what happened yesterday in the Galilee and the day before yesterday in the Negev, is liable to happen tomorrow in Hebron and the day after tomorrow in the Triangle. And BG [Ben Gurion] altogether treats with severe scepticism, almost dismissively, such political plans and one has the impression that he seeks to solve most of the problems by military means, in such a way that no political negotiations and no political action would be of any value.

In a discussion with Sharett, Shimoni expressed the opinion that the Palestinians could not seriously be expected to form an open government in defiance of the entire Arab world, or alternatively to go underground, and, consequently the most realistic suggestion that Israel could make to them was to reach an understanding with one of the Arab states and co-operate with Israel in reaching an agreement with that state. As far as the Triangle was concerned, the obvious party was Abdullah, although other considerations called for steering the main effort towards a settlement with Egypt. In relation to any agreement with Abdullah, Sharett voiced the fear that if Iraq were to swallow up Transjordan following the annexation of Arab Palestine to Transjordan, Iraq would be sitting right on Israel's border. Shimoni disputed this argument for the same reason that he disputed Ben-Gurion's argument against the annexation of Gaza to Egypt. There was only one way to prevent the annexation of Gaza: Israeli conquest. If Israel did not conquer, then it was only to be expected that Egypt would take her bit and Abdullah would take his bit of Palestine. Moreover, the practical possibility for creating an independent Palestinian state diminished with every successive Israeli conquest. Yet, while accepting these arguments, Sharett still valued the tactical advantage of the threat to help in establishing such a state for future negotiations either with Abdullah or with Egypt. It was clear that if the Israeli intention in approaching the Palestinian leaders was to get a tactical advantage and a bargaining asset for herself, without any intention of remaining faithful to the independence of Arab Palestine, her approach to the whole matter ought to be different. No firm conclusion was reached on this occasion on how to proceed. Sharett simply promised to give further thought to this problem and to consult with the other policymakers.[11]

By this time, however, Ben-Gurion's scepticism had hardened into outright opposition against any plan for organizing the West Bank into a separate political entity. He gave very short shrift to Ezra Danin, a leading expert on Palestinian affairs, to judge from the latter's account to Sasson:

I met with DBG, again telling him of our thinking about attempts to put out feelers, about the advisability or not of establishing a government dependent on Abdullah or completely independent. I also told him of our thinking about Syria and about the fact that most of its army, and a sizeable proportion of the heads of its administration are from the country's ethnic minorities. To this he replied tersely: 'We will not embark on any new adventures. The Arabs of the Land of Israel are left with just one role: flight.' With that he rose and terminated the conversation. I merely wished to share with you my gratification over the encouragement we get here.[12]

Peace overtures

Just as the attempt got under way at the Foreign Ministry in Tel Aviv to resolve the contradictions in Israel's Arab policy, Elias Sasson was approached in Paris with a message from the Egyptian royal court. The messenger was Kamal Riad who had once before approached Sasson with peace feelers, prior to the launching of Operation Yoav. Now he contacted Sasson again on behalf of the court to say that Egypt was

[11] Shimoni to Sasson, 2 Nov. 1948, *DFPI*, ii. 126 f.

[12] Danin to Sasson, 24 Oct. 1948, 2570/11, ISA. Quoted in Amikam Nachmani, 'Middle East Listening Post: Eliyahu Sasson and the Israeli Legation in Turkey, 1949–1952', *Studies in Zionism* 6/2 (1985), 278.

prepared to sign a fully-fledged armistice with Israel which would remain in force until a final political settlement was reached. Egypt's conditions for signing the armistice agreement were that Israel would withdraw from all captured areas in the south that were not within the boundaries of the State of Israel, and would agree in advance that the entire coastal strip from Israel to Rafah, including Gaza, as well as the inland strip from Rafah south-east along the border, would remain in Egyptian hands. On the other hand Riad was confident that Egypt would agree not to budge in the event of renewed warfare between Israel and any other Arab state. Although Transjordan was not mentioned by name, it was clear enough from the context that provided the price was right Egypt was now prepared to sell out her erstwhile ally. Transjordan, after all, had been first to abandon Egypt to Israel's tender mercies during Operation Yoav. Egyptian neutrality in a war between Israel and Transjordan would thus simply even the score. Secondly, Riad was confident that a way would be found to recognize Israel *de facto*. He explained that the proposed armistice negotiations would be military in character and conducted by military men but, if successful, they might be followed by political talks. He also offered to arrange for Sasson a meeting with Mahmud Fawzi, Egypt's delegate to the United Nations, so that Fawzi would confirm the offer officially.[13]

A special meeting of the Israeli Cabinet was convened to discuss the Egyptian peace feelers, and Sasson was authorized to meet Fawzi in order to give the talks a more official and binding character. The Egyptians were to be told that the government of Israel was not favourably disposed to the annexation of the Gaza area by Egypt because it feared Egyptian expansionism and believed that the future of Gaza should not be decided upon until there was some decision on the future of the Arab section of Palestine; but that it would probably agree to Egyptian control of the desert area from Rafah south-eastwards, which under the November 1947 resolution was to be part of the Arab state.

Within the Cabinet there was a dispute in progress on whether to initiate peace talks with Egypt first or with Transjordan first. News of the Egyptian peace overture momentarily boosted the position of the 'Egypt firsters'. Mapam, the left-wing party which counted among its members some of the ablest field commanders, favoured Egypt, claiming that Abdullah was a British puppet and Egypt the only independent Arab country. Mapai, the ruling party, tended to prefer Abdullah on the grounds that he was more reliable and realistic.[14]

[13] Sharett to members of the Cabinet, 4 Nov. 1948, 2425/7, ISA.
[14] *FRUS 1948*, v. 1558; Ben-Gurion, *Israel: A Personal History*, 293–6.

Sharett, number two in the Mapai hierarchy, was uncertain as to whether the decisive element in Egyptian policy was opposition to Israel, which might lead to compromise with Britain and Abdullah, or resistance to British bases in the Negev, leading to compromise with Israel.[15]

Before any progress could be made in settling Israel's official order of priorities, increasingly clear signals were received from King Abdullah via Paris about his desire to restore co-operation and enter into negotiations with Israel. On November 9, Abdul Majid Haidar, Transjordan's minister in London, visited Sasson in Paris bearing a message from the king. Firstly, His Majesty hoped that the Israeli side appreciated the arrangements that had been made for free passage through the area held by the Arab Legion to Mount Scopus. Secondly, he assumed that with the advent of winter, the Burma Road (which had been hastily constructed during the first truce to carry supplies to Jerusalem) would become impassable, and that if the Israelis were therefore to request free passage along the main road in Latrun, the request would be granted. Thirdly, he was worried by the situation in Jerusalem, where the Israeli troops were being aggressive, and he suggested that both sides issue orders to cease firing. Fourthly, he urged restraint on the Iraqi front, where Israeli aggression was liable to provoke attacks. Fifthly, he resented the slanderous attacks made on him by Kol Israel (the Israel Broadcasting Service) which undercut his efforts to bring public opinion around to conciliation and he urged that Kol Israel should neither attack nor compliment him. Finally, the king did not object to Israel negotiating with Egypt but, on the contrary, thought this would pave the way to an understanding between Transjordan and Israel, provided his interests were safeguarded. He was definitely against Egyptian annexation of Gaza, which he claimed as his outlet to the sea. Sasson reassured Haidar on this point and then wrote to him to say that Moshe Sharett was most satisfied when he heard about their conversations.[16]

The next day another royal emissary visited Sasson in Paris: Abdel Ghani al-Karmi, King Abdullah's private secretary, who had frequently carried messages in the past between his master and the Jewish Agency. Those who had met him remembered him as an amiable and loquacious individual, perpetually short of money and prone to exaggerate his own importance and the value of the services he could render. His anti-British sentiments went down well enough with the Israelis but his partiality to alcohol raised some doubts about his reliability as the conveyor of sensitive messages. Absent-minded though he was,

[15] *DFPI*, ii. 141–3.
[16] Sharett to Eytan, 9 Nov. 1948, *DFPI*, ii. 155; Sasson to Haidar, 10 Nov. 1948, 2453/2, ISA.

Karmi rarely forgot his hip flask of whisky, and his Israeli hosts generously provided water for his favourite tipple.

Karmi told Sasson that Abdullah was under pressure, from the public as well as the government, to terminate the war and save what could still be saved from the Arab parts of Palestine. But the British would not allow him to begin immediate, official, and direct negotiations so long as the Israelis had not agreed to concede a part of the Negev to meet the strategic needs of the British Empire. The Iraqis, too, wanted to end the war so that they could withdraw part of their army before the onset of winter. It appeared that the Israeli army had struck terror into Arab hearts, and the Iraqis preferred to leave Palestine before it could get the chance to demonstrate its superiority over them too.

Karmi had come to Paris in connection with some land deals, but the king had instructed him to begin negotiations for a final solution to the Palestine problem. He even brought a signed letter from the king to Abdul Majid Haidar, indicating Transjordan's maximum and minimum demands and empowering the two of them—Haidar and Karmi—to start negotiations immediately. Karmi was reluctant to give details of these demands until he had spoken to Haidar, except to say that the king was pressing for the return of the people of Lydda and Ramle to their homes; but not all of them, only the 'good' ones among them, that is to say, those who were loyal to him and accepted the creation of the State of Israel.

Karmi related that the relations between Tawfiq Abul Huda, Fawzi el-Mulki and the king were rather strained. The prime minister and the minister of defence showed themselves to be cowardly and vulnerable to threats from the Husaynis. More than once they had tried to persuade Abdullah to recognize the Gaza government and to extend military and political support to Egypt; they even tried to influence him through the British. When they failed, they made efforts to organize demonstrations of solidarity with Egypt in Amman and other cities. In Karmi's estimate, these two ministers would not stay in power much longer.

Like Haidar on the previous day, Karmi conveyed the king's request that Kol Israel cease its attacks on him, attacks which he considered harmful to the common cause. Instead, Karmi recommended, propaganda about British intrigues regarding the Negev should be stepped up, stressing the threat they carried for Arab independence in Iraq, Transjordan, and Egypt. He also suggested directing special broadcasts at the refugees to prove to them that the Arab states were delaying their salvation and bargaining at their expense. Such broadcasts, according to Karmi, could lead to an uprising of refugees and the downfall of the political bosses of the Arab world: Jamil Mardam, Mahmud Nuqrashi, Riad al-Sulh, and others.[17]

The two messages from Abdullah arrived just when the generals were lobbying Ben-Gurion for a massive attack to liquidate the Egyptian enclave in Faluja. Ben-Gurion was in favour of such an attack, not least because it could release some of the IDF units now tied down in the south for a future operation in the Triangle. But Moshe Sharett strongly opposed the plan because it entailed a flagrant violation of the truce on top of Israel's refusal to return to the lines of October 14. Ben-Gurion therefore sent Yigael Yadin to Paris to co-ordinate Sharett's political action there with the military action planned at home. Sharett was persuaded to give his consent to a military operation in the south but he persevered in his opposition to any action on the eastern front. So the plan to capture the Triangle had to be shelved, at least for the time being.[18]

Ben-Gurion now felt able to respond to the royal overture from Amman. He favoured negotiations with Transjordan and agreed to an immediate cease-fire in Jerusalem. He was not interested in the offer of free passage through Latrun because the Burma Road was adequate, but he was definitely interested in acquiring Latrun against territorial compensation elsewhere. He favoured a general straightening of the lines, with the Arabs shifting eastward on the central front in return for Israeli movement westward in the Hebron area. His first reaction was strongly against ceding Gaza to the Egyptians, preferring to give it to Abdullah after it was captured. But he had not made up his mind yet on the method of communication between Gaza and the rest of Abdullah's territory.[19]

By this time, however, British influence was being brought to bear to dissuade King Abdullah from embarking too precipitately on separate peace negotiations with Israel. On November 12 the attention of the British Cabinet was drawn to Israeli violations of the truce in Palestine and it was agreed that steps should be taken to ensure that Britain could carry out her treaty obligations to Transjordan if the latter was attacked. On the other hand, there was great reluctance to consider the despatch of British troops to support the Transjordanian forces operating in Palestine. It was recalled that when it was decided to withdraw from Palestine, the general understanding had been that British troops would not be called on again to operate there except as part of a United Nations force engaged in carrying out an international

---

[17] Sasson to Shimoni, 10 Nov. 1948, *DFPI*, ii. 161–3.

[18] Sharett to Eytan, 21 Nov. 1948, and Yadin to Ben-Gurion, 12 Nov. 1948, 182/3, ISA; Ben-Gurion's diary, 10, 13, 14, and 18 Nov. 1948; interview with Gen. Yigael Yadin.

[19] Ben-Gurion's diary, 21 Nov. 1948; Shiloah to Sharett, 20 Nov. 1948, *DFPI*, ii. 209 f.

settlement and it was felt that there should be no departure from that policy.

In the course of the discussion the suggestion was made that the best means of securing a settlement might be to encourage direct negotiations between Israel and Transjordan. The general view of the ministers, however, was that this would be a blow to the prestige of the United Nations. Moreover, it was argued that the great discrepancy in the military strength of the two sides would preclude the possibility of equitable negotiations. In the circumstances, it was thought that the right course was to give full support to the efforts of the Security Council to achieve a settlement.[20] Prime Minister Attlee summoned the American ambassador, Lewis Douglas, to Chequers to inform him of the Cabinet's conclusions, to underline the dangers of further Israeli advances, and to state that Britain was determined to uphold her treaty obligations to Transjordan because otherwise the whole British and perhaps Western position in the Middle East might be lost.[21]

Sir Orme Sargent, the permanent under-secretary at the Foreign Office, specifically invoked the lessons of Munich when discussing with Douglas the prospects of Israeli–Arab negotiations. Sir Orme's 'personal view' was that to enjoin negotiations would be tantamount to holding the ring and telling the contestants, between whom military equilibrium had been destroyed by the preponderance of Israeli arms, to thrash out their problems in their own way. He expressed the belief that such an action would amount to a cowardly avoidance of responsibility. He feared that another Munich would be in the making if the powers were to ask the United Kingdom to tell Abdullah that if he should refuse to settle with Israel, the Anglo-Transjordanian Treaty would no longer be operative. To sell Abdullah down the river for the sake of a spurious peace, easy consciences, and the greater good would in Sir Orme's view, be a re-enaction of the Czech tragedy.[22] The Americans rejected this historical analogy casting Israel in the unlikely role of Hitlerite Germany and Transjordan in that of Czechoslovakia. They had no intention of putting pressure on Transjordan or turning her into the victim of a Near-Eastern Munich, but they saw no reason why they and the United Kingdom should not consult with the parties to try and bring about a meeting of minds. In essence, the Israelis wanted direct negotiations and no Bernadotte plan, while the British wanted the Bernadotte plan and no negotiations between the parties. The US policy was to try to bridge the gap between these two extreme positions.[23]

The British held out the Bernadotte plan to dissuade Transjordan

[20] CM 71(48)1, 11 Nov. 1948, PRO. [21] *FRUS 1948*, v. 1585–9.
[22] Ibid. 1602 f. [23] Ibid. 1621–3.

from entering into negotiations and indirectly sided with Abul Huda against King Abdullah on this question. Abul Huda was disturbed to learn that Abdel Ghani al-Karmi had discussed the possible terms of a settlement with Sasson. Considering that the talks with the Israeli representative in Paris had gone too far, Abul Hada sent a telegram to Haidar instructing him to restrain Karmi, and he also asked the king to recall his personal emissary.[24]

Abdullah himself was upset by a defiant speech that Moshe Sharett made on November 15 before a committee of the United Nations. In this speech Sharett stated that the provisional government of Israel refused to relinquish the Negev; would never accept loss of its share in the Dead Sea; was uncompromisingly opposed to being debarred from the Gulf of Aqaba; demanded the permanent inclusion in Israel of new Jerusalem; and claimed all of the Galilee.

So while the general tendency in Amman was to back-pedal, Kirkbride was sure that the king, who was a great believer in re-insurance, would maintain contact with the Jews either against the wish of his prime minister or without his knowledge. He also felt certain that Haidar's visit to the Foreign Office had been made on Abdullah's instructions and not on those of the prime minister. In view of the prime minister's attitude, Kirkbride's advice was not to encourage further talks with the Jews for the time being, not even for the purpose of discovering what the Jews had in mind.[25]

Accordingly, when Haidar called at the Foreign Office again, he was informed that Britain was about to circulate a resolution for the adoption of the Bernadotte plan in the United Nations Political Committee. He was asked to wait a little to see the results of this initiative and told that further discussions by him with the Jews at that stage could only cause confusion and misunderstanding.[26]

In the light of the British manœuvres to delay negotiations, it seemed all the more important to the Israelis to preserve the direct channel of communication with Amman. Elias Sasson wrote to Tawfiq Abul Huda on November 10 expressing Israeli readiness to co-operate in preventing hostilities in Jerusalem and asking that the local commander of the Arab Legion should establish direct contact with the Israeli commander. Sasson also asked that steps should be taken to control the Arab irregulars who were causing all the trouble. The necessary orders were sent to the Arab Legion in Jerusalem and every precaution was taken not to give the Israelis an excuse to attack.[27] A

[24] Kirkbride to FO, 17 Nov. 1948, FO 371/68862, PRO.
[25] Kirkbride to FO, 18 Nov. 1948, FO 371/68862, PRO.
[26] FO to Amman, 19 Nov. 1948, FO 371/68862, PRO.
[27] Kirkbride to Bevin, 13 Nov. 1948, FO 816/133, PRO.

week later Sasson sent Abul Huda a telegram dealing with the protection of the Rutenberg works by the Arab Legion during the approaching flood period of the Yarmuk River. Abul Huda replied that the Transjordanian government was continuing to ensure the passage of Israeli convoys to Mount Scopus and at Bab el Wad but could not offer much assistance in relation to the Palestine Electric Corporation because Naharayim was the responsibility of the Iraqi army.[28] Sasson's next message referred to rumours that the Arab Legion was planning an offensive in Jerusalem and expressed the hope that these rumours were not true. The prime minister replied that unless attacked, the Arab Legion would not take the initiative in breaking the truce.[29]

Towards the end of November, the Jews formed the impression (as Nahum Goldmann, the moderate American Jewish leader, told Hector McNeil) that Abdullah wanted to negotiate but was prevented from doing so by the British. McNeil denied that Abdullah was under any pressure from Britain not to enter into negotiations. Neither Egypt nor Transjordan, opined McNeil, could open negotiations in the face of opposition from the other Arab states. At this point Goldmann inadvertently gave the game away by saying that he knew that the Egyptians and Abdullah would fall out in any joint negotiations because each of them had separately tried to bind the Israeli government to agreeing that they should have Gaza. It was therefore clear that the Israelis had been discussing this major point of substance with both the Egyptians and Abdullah. Goldmann declined to say what the Jews expected to get in the Negev and merely referred to Ben-Gurion's recent declaration that 'we could win much with our arms but we are prepared to take less if we can have peace'.[30]

Ben-Gurion said this in an interview with Kenneth Bilby, who had prominently reported in the *New York Herald Tribune* Abdullah's determination to end the war and to begin peace talks. When Bilby had finished giving a firsthand account of his meeting with the ruler of Transjordan, Ben-Gurion said slowly:

I believe in Abdullah's sincerity. I think he really wants peace. Now if he will just translate his words into action. We are willing to meet him halfway. For the sake of peace we'll take less, even though we might get more.

Abdullah has always gotten on well with some of our people. Shertok was friendly with him. I remember once they even played 'Hatikvah' (the Jewish national anthem) in a theatre in Amman when a group of us were visiting there. We've always been willing to talk with Abdullah and we are now.[31]

28 Secretary of the government of Jordan to E. Sasson (Paris), 21 Nov. 1948, *DFPI*, ii. 213 f.
29 Kirkbride to FO, 23 Nov. 1948, FO 371/68690, PRO.
30 Minister of state to FO, 24 Nov. 1948, FO 371/68671, PRO.
31 Kenneth W. Bilby, *New Star in the Near East* (New York: Doubleday, 1951), 58.

A 'sincere and absolute cease-fire' in Jerusalem

Jerusalem, the most explosive flashpoint along the entire Israeli-Transjordanian front, provided the starting point for talks between the two sides. Ben-Gurion was ready to offer a real cease-fire in Jerusalem as the bait to draw Abdullah into comprehensive peace negotiations. This represented a reversal of Ben-Gurion's earlier strategy of bringing the whole of Jerusalem under Israeli sovereignty. From September onwards there was no doubt that the IDF's superiority over all the Arab armies placed this goal within Israel's reach, and all Ben-Gurion's military plans had this as their ultimate goal. But by the end of November Ben-Gurion had quietly set aside this goal in favour of the much more limited objective of dividing up Jerusalem with the Arab opponent who had the best credentials for becoming a partner in peace.

Signs of a more conciliatory attitude on the part of the Israeli authorities had the effect of allaying, without eliminating entirely, Abdullah's fear of an all-out offensive in Jerusalem. When Glubb Pasha asked him his opinion on the Jewish advances for a 'real ceasefire' in Jerusalem, the king, with a twinkle in his eye, invoked a Turkish proverb: 'If you meet a bear when crossing a rotten bridge, call her "dear Auntie"!'[32]

There was a certain similarity in the way that Abdullah and Ben-Gurion approached the talks on the future of Jerusalem. Neither could admit to his own followers or partners that the real purpose of the talks was to reach a compromise with the enemy. Both presented the talks as relating merely to truce matters while personally directing them from behind the scenes on account of their broader political implications. Both worked through young and assertive army officers whose direct manner masked considerable political deviousness.

The king was represented by Abdullah al-Tall, whom he had promoted from major to lieutenant-colonel for the part he played in the battle for Jerusalem and later appointed him as governor of the city. Since Tall had established a reputation for himself as a radical Arab nationalist and an outspoken critic of British control over the Arab Legion, he was an unlikely choice for such a sensitive political mission. Yet the king must have reckoned that he could control the young officer and use him to reduce to a minimum British influence over the talks.

Tall's opposite number in the talks was Lieut.-Col. Moshe Dayan, who had impressed Ben-Gurion during the war as a tough and aggressive combat officer. By his own account Dayan ascribed little importance to the idea of negotiations with the Arabs on assuming the command of the Jerusalem. He planned for and expected military

---

[32] Glubb, *A Soldier with the Arabs*, 213.

decisions. He viewed the problems through fortified posts and trenches and their solution through fire and assault. But when the cease-fire had put an end to the fighting, the struggle passed from the battlefield to the negotiating table and he became deeply involved in political work that brought him into direct contact with the prime minister.[33] Although Dayan was no more successful as a military planner and organizer than his predecessor, he was a more astute and skilful politician. And it was Dayan's skills as a politician and negotiator that the prime minister exploited to the full in furthering his new aims of reconciliation and partnership with Transjordan.

The lines held in Jerusalem on the eve of the talks were extremely awkward for both sides, with enclaves, bulges, and criss-crossing lines of communication. The fighting had cut the city into two, but the line of demarcation was unnatural and troublesome. Israel held the western part of the city, with an enclave in Mount Scopus. Israel also controlled part of the Jerusalem–Bethlehem road, forcing the Transjordanians to use a longer, secondary route. Transjordan held the eastern half—the Old City, including the Wailing Wall, the Temple compound, and the Jewish Quarter—and the Latrun salient, midway between Jerusalem and Tel Aviv.

The first meeting between the two military governors of Jerusalem was held in Government House, the former residence of the British high commissioner, on November 29, in the presence of United Nations observers and the three-man Consular Truce Commission. Tall found his opposite number unexpectedly friendly and forthcoming, and tentative agreement was reached on a cease-fire extending from Beit Jala and Bethlehem in the south to Ramallah in the north and Latrun in the west. On the following day, a formal agreement was signed for 'an absolute and sincere cease-fire' covering the entire Jerusalem area and reaffirming the earlier agreement for the supply of the Israeli enclave in Mount Scopus (see Map 10).

On Dayan's initiative, a direct telephone line was established between the two commanders, ostensibly for dealing with local incidents and smoothing misunderstandings but basically for eliminating third-pary intervention. Since both sides aspired to direct control in Jerusalem, the bypassing of the UN observers, whose main task was to supervise the cease-fire, helped to clear the decks for the eventual partition of the Holy City between Israel and Transjordan.

A number of subjects were raised in the course of the meeting. Tall offered free passage along the Latrun–Jerusalem road, without UN supervision or passes, if the Israelis in return would allow free movement along the Latrun–Ramallah road. Secondly, in exchange for

[33] Moshe Dayan, *Story of My Life* (London: Weidenfeld and Nicolson, 1976), 96 f.

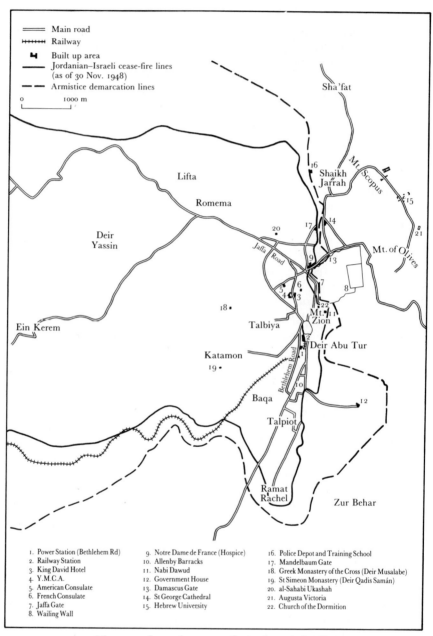

Key legend (top left):
- Main road
- Railway
- Built up area
- Jordanian–Israeli cease-fire lines (as of 30 Nov. 1948)
- Armistice demarcation lines

0   1000 m

Map labels:
Sha'fat, Lifta, Romema, Shaikh Jarrah, Mt Scopus, Mt of Olives, Deir Yassin, Jaffa Road, Ein Kerem, Talbiya, Mt Zion, Deir Abu Tur, Katamon, Bethlehem Road, Baqa, Talpiot, Ramat Rachel, Zur Behar

1. Power Station (Bethlehem Rd)
2. Railway Station
3. King David Hotel
4. Y.M.C.A.
5. American Consulate
6. French Consulate
7. Jaffa Gate
8. Wailing Wall
9. Notre Dame de France (Hospice)
10. Allenby Barracks
11. Nabi Dawud
12. Government House
13. Damascus Gate
14. St George Cathedral
15. Hebrew University
16. Police Depot and Training School
17. Mandelbaum Gate
18. Greek Monastery of the Cross (Deir Musalabe)
19. St Simeon Monastery (Deir Qadis Samán)
20. al-Sahabi Ukashah
21. Augusta Victoria
22. Church of the Dormition

MAP 10   Jerusalem cease-fire and armistice lines

restoring the supply of electricity to the Old City, he was willing to grant the Jews free access to the Holy Places. Thirdly, he proposed that the Jews would be permitted to return to their homes in the Jewish Quarter of the Old City if the Arabs could return to their homes in Katamon in the south of the city. Dayan raised the question of the convoys to Mount Scopus and the railway line to Jerusalem. Regarding Latrun, he expressed an interest not in the right of passage but complete evacuation of the Arab Legion. Tall replied that he must consult the king on this matter and a time was fixed for the next meeting.[34]

William Burdett, the American consul-general in Jerusalem, felt that the atmosphere during the meeting was indicative of a definite desire on the part of both parties to terminate the fighting in Jerusalem. Both commanders advanced practical suggestions for achieving this objective. Dayan's statement about broadening the accord was particularly significant since he was acting on instructions from his government. In contrast to previous meetings, the cease-fire was approached as a first step to lasting peace rather than in an effort to obtain tactical advantage prior to the resumption of fighting.[35]

After the cease-fire agreement had been signed, Ben-Gurion suggested that at the next meeting Dayan should take Tall aside to discuss the railway line and Shaikh Jarrah, through which lay the road to Mount Scopus and Latrun. If arrangements could be worked out, wrote Ben-Gurion in his diary, 'the Jerusalem question will be solved'.[36] This was indeed indicative of a fundamental change of attitude, but it remained to be seen whether arrangements could be worked out peacefully. In a report to his colleagues on Mapai's Central Committee, Ben-Gurion defined the minimum requirements for rendering secure the economy and communications of Jerusalem: Israel's possession of the area between the old road and the new road, and of the entire railway line; the removal of the Arab Legion garrison from Latrun, free access to the university on Mount Scopus, and a solution to the problem of the Old City. Some of these problems, said Ben-Gurion, might be solved amicably, but there was no certainty that all of them could be solved without resort to war. Israel was capable of carrying out a military operation to expel the Arabs from Latrun, to capture the last railway station in Batir, and to capture the northern part of the city, all the way up to the university. But the debate on the Israeli truce violations in the Security Council had begun, and Ben-

---

[34] Dayan, *Story of My Life*, 100–2; *DFPI*, ii. 250; Ben-Gurion's diary, 29 Nov. 1948; id., Report to the Foreign Affairs Committee of the Provisional State Council, 30 Nov. 1948, 2392/12, ISA.

[35] *FRUS 1948*, v. 1634 f.

[36] Ben-Gurion's diary, 29 Nov. 1948.

Gurion feared UN sanctions and hostile actions on the part of Britain in the guise of enforcing UN resolutions.[37]

Elias Sasson, who had originated the idea of direct negotiations between the military commanders in Jerusalem, regarded the cease-fire agreement as a good omen. In a telegram to Transjordan's prime minister he wrote: 'We welcome the agreement signed recently by our respective commanders in Jerusalem. I hope that just as we overcame the difficulties involved in reaching this agreement, we will likewise resort to logic and reason in order to find a way to reach a general and enduring peace.'[38]

Abul Huda, however, preferred to proceed with caution and with due regard to the attitude of the other Arab states. The Jews were showing a real desire for an accord with Transjordan, but he did not think that the time had come to meet as governments to consider political matters. Having always felt 'safe' as regards the king, the Jews were now evidently trying to involve the government. Abul Huda thought that Abdullah's contact with the Jews through personal emissaries might prove useful when the time came for direct negotiations. If they became known in the meantime, they could be repudiated by the government. The publicity surrounding the talks in Government House was not harmful because they dealt only with truce matters. But if the king chose to undertake negotiations, Abul Huda had no intention of standing in his way and was always ready to resign and make way for a government of negotiation.[39]

Rather than change his government, Abdullah preferred to empower Tall to shift the talks from the strictly military to the political plane. At a meeting on December 5 held in the Armenian Monastery in the Old City, Tall stated that he had been authorized by the king to offer a partial withdrawal of troops from Latrun and their replacement by a mixed Arab–Jewish police force in exchange for permission to a small number of refugees to return to Lydda and Ramle. Tall also asked that the cease-fire covering Jerusalem should be extended to the entire front between the Arab Legion and the Israeli army. Dayan replied that he had not been authorized to do this, but a gentlemen's agreement was reached to extend the ceasefire for the ten days until they were to meet again. In response to Dayan's earlier suggestion for reopening the Tel Aviv–Jerusalem railway line, Tall agreed but wanted in return permission to use the road from Bethlehem to Jerusalem up to the Jaffa Gate. These proposals fell short of what Ben-Gurion had defined as Israel's minimal requirements. He considered Latrun not as a question

---

[37] Protocol of Central Committee Meeting, 30 Nov. 1948, Labour Party Archive, Beit Berl.
[38] Sasson (Paris) to Eytan, 2 Dec. 1948, 182/2, ISA.
[39] *FRUS 1948*, v. 1641 f.

of traffic arrangements but of the division of territory. Basically he was opposed to partial arrangements and the reply he gave Dayan to transmit to the king via Tall was that they would not continue discussions merely on the basis of the truce. They were ready to negotiate the conditions for a real peace with a political representative and only in such negotiations would they find solutions to the specific problems of supplying electricity to Jerusalem, opening the railway line, the road to Bethlehem and so on.[40]

For Abdullah, peace negotiations with Israel posed not so much a question of principle but a problem of timing. He needed Israel's agreement, whether formal or tacit, for his plan to annex the Arab parts of Palestine. The second Palestinian Congress, held in Jericho on December 1, was an important landmark on the road to annexation. It was attended by some 3,000 delegates including the mayors of Hebron, Bethlehem, and Ramallah, military governors of all the districts controlled by the Arab Legion in Palestine, notables from Transjordan, Syria, and Lebanon, and former supporters of the mufti. The promoters of the congress had been encouraged and assisted by the king and government of Transjordan. Their original idea was that this second Palestinian Congress would pass resolutions pressing for an urgent settlement of the Palestine problem and so strengthen their hand if they undertook direct or indirect negotiations with the Israelis. In the event, the congress did indeed proclaim the union of Palestine and Transjordan and acknowledged Abdullah as the king of the united country. But it went astray, through the influence of some radical delegates, in calling on the Arab states to complete the task of liberating Palestine. At Abdullah's insistence, a drafting committee reformulated the resolutions. The new resolutions expressed no confidence in the Arab Higher Committee or the Gaza government, called for the union of Transjordan and Palestine under the Hashemite crown, and gave Abdullah power of attorney to solve the Palestinian problem to the best of his ability and as swiftly as possible. These resolutions were ratified by the government of Transjordan on December 7 and by the Parliament in Amman on December 13.[41]

The Jericho Congress constituted a turning point in the evolution of Abdullah's attitude towards negotiations with the Zionist state. Prior to the congress, Abdullah had been deterred by the failure of the Arab world to accord legitimacy to political talks with Israel aiming at a final settlement; after the congress there were increasing signs that Transjordan was ready for a separate deal with Israel even at the price of

[40] *DFPI*, ii. 226; Ben-Gurion's diary, 5 and 9 Dec. 1948; Dayan, *Story of My Life*, 104 f.

[41] Kirkbride to FO, 9 Dec. 1948, FO 371/68643, PRO; and Nevo, 'Abdullah and the Arabs of Palestine'.

creating a rift within the Arab League. The decline in Egypt's political standing following her military defeat no doubt made it easier for Abdullah to choose between the two unwelcome alternatives of isolation in the Arab world and the loss of territories he had occupied in Palestine. He chose the former as the lesser of the two evils in order to preserve most of his gains in Palestine.[42]

Another reason for beginning peace talks as soon as possible was the unfolding of Operation Lot. At the end of November, Jewish forces which had been pushing eastwards and southwards from Beersheba set up a post between the Dead Sea and the Red Sea and sent patrols into Transjordan. The operation was designed to remove the siege on Sdom, at the southern tip of the Dead Sea, where the works of the Palestine Potash Corporation were located, and to prevent the Arab Legion from penetrating across the northern part of Wadi Araba or into the Judaean desert from Hebron. Britain drew the attention of the Security Council to these incursions and to her own obligation under the terms of the Anglo-Transjordanian Treaty. But since there was nothing that Britain could do immediately to preserve the territorial integrity of her ally, it was not surprising that Abdullah tried a diplomatic approach. At their meeting on December 5, Tall suggested to Dayan recognition of the mandatory Transjordan–Palestine frontier as the border between their two states up to Husub and a cease-fire arrangement down to Eilat or stabilization of the existing lines along the entire front. Dayan promised to look into this matter and orders were subsequently issued to all IDF units to observe the cease-fire not just in Jerusalem but along the entire front with the Arab Legion.[43]

Talks with Transjordan and the second offensive against Egypt

A new stage in the talks between Israel and Transjordan began with the return of Elias Sasson from Paris. Sasson, who had been first to suggest direct talks between the two military governors, saw more clearly than anyone else the potential for moving beyond the discussion of technical issues to full-scale peace negotiations. He had always been a great believer in direct contact with Arab leaders and in bypassing third parties in general and the United Nations in particular. He was also one of the leading proponents of the tacit alliance with Transjordan. Upon his return home, he gave Ben-Gurion a comprehensive report on

[42] Uri Bar-Joseph, 'The Relations Between Israel and Transjordan: November 1947–April 1949', MA thesis (Hebrew University of Jerusalem, 1982), 163 f.

[43] Kirkbride, *From the Wings*, ch. 6; FO to UK delegation to UN General Assembly (Paris), 4 Dec. 1948, FO 371/68643, PRO; *DFPI*, ii. 266; Meir Pail, 'The Zionist–Israeli Strategy on the Jerusalem Question in the War of Independence', *Chapters in the History of Jerusalem in Modern Times* (Heb.) (Jerusalem: Yad Ben Zvi, 1976).

the various talks and contacts he had in Paris and on the political situation in the Arab world. Sasson argued that their aim should be to terminate hostilities and hasten the departure of the Arab armies from Palestine. At a recent meeting in London, Sasson had asked Abdul Majid Haidar and Abdel Ghani al-Karmi whether Transjordan would evict the other Arab forces from Palestine herself or, in the event of agreement with the Jews, prefer the latter to undertake the task. He pressed in particular for the denial of Transjordanian territory to the Iraqis, adding that the Iraqi army could be defeated without difficulty by the Israeli forces and that the talks between Israeli and Transjordanian representatives should continue whatever happened elsewhere. To secure Abdullah's co-operation in expelling the other Arab forces from Palestine and reaching a final settlement, Sasson was in favour of giving him Gaza as a free port.[44]

On December 10 Sasson wrote a letter to King Abdullah to announce that he had returned from Paris for a brief visit and was anxious to meet someone close to the king to discuss matters of mutual interest. The letter was handed by Dayan to Tall for delivery to the palace at Shuneh. Tall called Dayan on their direct telephone line the following day to say that he wanted to meet the author of the letter in order to give him Abdullah's reply. With Dayan's help, Sasson and Abdullah al-Tall met in no man's land and conversed in Arabic for nearly half an hour. After conveying Abdullah's warm regards, the young officer stated that His Majesty was ready to start peace talks but wanted to wait ten days to see if he could persuade the other Arab rulers to join in the talks. If they refused, he would go ahead on his own. He wanted to be sure that the Israelis were serious about opening separate negotiations with him and he planned to raise the following subjects: Jaffa, Lydda, Ramle, Beisan, Jerusalem, and the Negev. Sasson replied that the king was free to raise any subject he wanted and that they were willing to wait ten days, but that what they wanted to discuss was not a truce but an official armistice. Sasson also wanted to know whether Abdullah would maintain his neutrality in the event of a clash between Israel and one of the other Arab countries, Iraq for example. Tall stated that as far as he knew the Iraqi army was also interested in a cease-fire, and that the king had told him that the Iraqis knew and approved of his contacts with the Israelis.

Tall was given advance notice that Dayan had been instructed to say at the meeting with the UN observers that Israel saw no point in continuing these talks without the official agreement of Transjordan to begin armistice and peace talks. Tall suggested cancelling the meeting scheduled for the following day with the UN observers, but Dayan

[44] Ben-Gurion's diary, 9 Dec. 1948; Kirkbride to FO, 9 Dec. 1948, FO 371/68862, PRO.

preferred to have the meeting and say his piece. Tall said that the king was aware of Sasson's talks with other Arab parties and that he requested that these talks should not be taken too far so as not to complicate matters unduly. The meeting ended with Tall's promise to return with Abdullah's answer to the idea of starting either armistice or peace talks.[45]

Colonel Tall made a full report to the King and on December 13 called Sasson to convey the following message: first, the king agreed to a general armistice and to peace talks but; secondly, he needed a week in order to consult the regent of Iraq and in order to find out whether Abul Huda would undertake the task himself or make way for a braver man; thirdly, he urged that Sasson should remain in the country for a week to await his final reply, which promised to be satisfactory; and, finally, he was curious to have Sasson's views on the steps that were being taken by Transjordan to implement the resolutions of the Jericho Congress.

Sasson dictated his reply and a number of additional points which Tall took down in writing to present to the king:

1. If the king was determined to implement the Jericho resolutions, the Israelis had no objection and Sasson thought this ought to be done swiftly in order to present both friends and opponents with a *fait accompli*.

2. When the king proceeded with implementing the Jericho resolutions, he should make no mention of the Jewish side either for good or for ill. He could simply state that he was taking steps to save what could be saved and to restore peace and happiness to the people of Palestine.

3. In carrying out the Jericho resolutions, it would be undesirable for the king to stake a final position regarding the fate of Jerusalem, old or new. The United Nations had passed a resolution a few days previously regarding the internationalization of Jerusalem but Sasson considered that such a fate would not be in the interest of either Jews or Arabs. It was preferable, he thought, to work together for a solution that would satisfy both sides. (Here Tall interjected to say: 'will you agree to the partition of Jerusalem between you and us? Wouldn't that be the ideal solution?' Sasson replied that the subject should be reserved for negotiation and that in the meantime the king should not say anything so as to avoid further complications.)

4. Sasson advised the king to consent to a general armistice before proceeding to implement the Jericho resolutions. Such a move would enable him to withdraw his troops from Palestine and employ them on

---

[45] Ben-Gurion's diary, 12 Dec. 1948; *DFPI*, vol. iii, *Armistice Negotiations with the Arab States, December 1948–July 1949* (Jerusalem: Israel State Archives, 1983), 229 f.

other fronts—the Egyptian or Syrian, for instance. If the current circumstances in the Arab world did not permit him to proclaim an official armistice, a secret armistice agreement could be signed. (Here Tall interrupted again to ask whether Sasson really thought that Syria or Egypt were about to attack Transjordan. Anything was possible, replied Sasson, and Transjordan had to be prepared for every eventuality.)

5. Sasson advised the king to act expeditiously in securing the withdrawal of the Iraqi forces from Palestine, and especially from the Triangle and their replacement with Transjordanian forces. If he did so, the Israelis could assure him that they would respect the current lines in the Triangle until the end of the peace negotiations. But if the Iraqi forces remained in their present positions, it was not impossible that the Israelis would clash with them and try to evict them by force. (At this point Tall interjected for the third time to reiterate the king's request to refrain from a clash with the Iraqis and leave it to him to talk to the regent. 'What will be Transjordan's attitude in the event of renewed hostilities between us and the Egyptians in the south?' enquired Sasson. 'Hit the Egyptians as much as you can. Our attitude would be absolutely neutral', was Tall's prompt and devastatingly frank response.)

6. Sasson advised the king to make efforts to obtain the withdrawal of Egyptian forces from the south of Jerusalem and Hebron so as to save himself from the difficulties and political trouble that their presence was liable to cause.

7. Sasson advised the king to avoid, as far as possible, foreign mediation for the settlement of matters between themselves and to opt, as they did, for direct negotiations.

8. If the king acceded to the last seven points, Sasson could promise him the services of the Zionist propaganda machine, locally and internationally, in mobilizing the support of the enlightened world for the implementation of the Jericho resolutions and in weakening the resistance of his opponents.

At the end of the conversation, Tall asked Sasson once again not to stray too far in his talks with the other Arab states. Sasson himself reported to his superiors that in advising Abdullah to make haste in carrying out the resolutions of the Jericho Congress he intended to encourage the king to face up to any rift or conflict that might develop inside the Arab League and to create the impression that he could rely on Israel's friendship.[46]

[46] Telephone conversation, E. Sasson–A. al-Tall, Jerusalem, 13 Dec. 1948, *DFPI*, iii. 331–3; Tall, *The Palestine Tragedy*, 443 f.

Abdullah was indeed heartened by this message and wrote his comments and observations on the message for transmission to Sasson:

1. This is a good suggestion.
2. This is our long-standing plan.
3. Old Jerusalem for the Arabs and new Jerusalem for the Jews. The question be postponed for negotiations.
4. I approve this secretly on condition that it applies to the Iraqi front.
5. For discussion with the regent of Iraq.
6. It is possible after we have settled the problems between us and Egypt and the Arab League.
7. For secret discussion with the pasha (Dr Shawkat as-Sati) and he will inform you of my opinion.
8. Yes.[47]

Sasson was now convinced that negotiations with Abdullah were the most promising avenue for bringing about a termination of hostilities. Inside the army, however, there was reluctance to make concessions to Abdullah and considerable pressure for further military operations to gain more land before the war came to an end. General Yadin and Colonel Dayan felt that Sasson had gone too far during his talks with Abdullah al-Tall in signalling Israel's tacit agreement to the annexation of the Arab parts of Palestine by Transjordan.[48]

Ben-Gurion was not ready to come down decisively on one side or the other. At a meeting of senior officials at the prime minister's office in Tel Aviv on December 18, Sasson spoke in favour of opening peace negotiations with Abdullah. Ben-Gurion stressed that while two further military operations, in the Negev and in the Triangle, were under consideration, the primary aim now was peace and he warned against being flushed with victory. He added:

Immigration demands that there be an end to war. Our future need is peace and friendship with the Arabs. Therefore I am in favour of talks with Abdullah, although I doubt whether the British will let him make peace with us. But we should make it clear at the beginning of the talks that apart from the truce there is no agreement between us and the talks would have to be conducted without any prior commitments. To the annexation of parts of Palestine to Transjordan we cannot agree easily for the following reasons: (1) Israel security: an Arab state in Western Palestine would be less dangerous than a state linked to Transjordan, and maybe tomorrow to Iraq. (2) Why should we annoy the Russians unnecessarily. (3) Why should we do it—in contrast to all the Arab states. This does not mean that we would not agree under any circumstances—but only as one element in a comprehensive settlement. There is the Jerusalem question: Latrun, Shaikh Jarrah, and the Old City. We cannot agree to the return of the Arabs to Katamon. On his side he [Abdullah] would raise the questions of Lydda, Ramle, Jaffa. The great

[47] Tall, *The Palestine Tragedy*, 445.　　[48] Ben-Gurion's diary, 16 Dec. 1948.

problem would be the Triangle. It would be difficult to acquiesce in the narrowness of our strip of territory in Samaria and I do not believe that this can be changed by peaceful means.[49]

Ben Gurion spoke in a similar vein at a Cabinet meeting on December 17 devoted to discussing the campaign in Negev, the possibility of military action in the Triangle, the political status of Jerusalem, and the relations with Abdullah. In his opening statement, he emphasized that, apart from the two operations that lay ahead, they should devote all their efforts to making peace or at least ending the war. For many years to come security would remain the central question and this could not be guaranteed by military power alone. Security entailed mass immigration and settlement on the land in addition to acquiring sophisticated weapons. 'The only solution, perhaps, is Abdullah.' In the debate ministers expressed very diverse views. Some ministers were opposed to military action altogether while others questioned the logic of directing it against the Egyptians rather than Abdullah. Ben-Gurion summed up the discussion with the following policy guidelines: 'For the time being we do not change the status of Jerusalem, we carry out the operation in the Negev, we enter into talks with Abdullah. If the talks reach a turning point, the matter would be brought before the Cabinet, and the Cabinet will decide on changes.'[50]

The decision to renew the offensive against the Egyptians while opening peace talks with Abdullah fitted in with Ben-Gurion's tactical preference for fighting only one opponent at a time. Yet opening peace talks with Abdullah did not rule out the resort to force. On the contrary, as Sasson reported to Sharett, it seemed that Ben-Gurion had some military plan he wanted to carry out before the start of serious official talks with the king. That is why he refused to agree even for merely tactical reasons to Abdullah's scheme for annexing Arab Palestine.[51] And that is why he instructed Dayan to insist on peace negotiations in his talks with Tall and to settle for nothing less. Dayan told Tall that unless Transjordan was prepared to talk business there was no point in continuing the contacts, and the Israeli government would in fact be compelled to break them off. He said Israel was anxious to negotiate but, if the Arabs refused, would consider herself free to take any action she wished and was in the fortunate position of being willing and able to engage in both war or peace talks. Tall said that he would have to refer back to his superiors; then Dayan telephoned him three times pressing for an answer most insistently.[52]

---

[49] Ibid. 18 Dec. 1948.   [50] Ibid. 19 Dec. 1948; *DFPI*, iii. 333.

[51] *DFPI*, ii. 306 f.

[52] Ben-Gurion's diary, 21 Dec. 1948; *FRUS 1948*, v. 1662 f.; Kirkbride to FO, 14 Dec. 1948, FO 371/68691, PRO.

The ball was now firmly back in Transjordan's court. Abdullah's game of playing for time, of protecting his position in the Arab world by not embarking formally on peace negotiations with the enemy, had been rudely interrupted by what amounted to an ultimatum from the Israeli side. And the inevitable consequence of meeting Israel's demands was to exacerbate the antagonism between Abdullah and his Arab partners.

Egypt's reaction to the Jericho Congress destroyed any chance there might have been of a common front with Transjordan in the matter of negotiating a settlement. Egypt, followed by Syria, Saudi Arabia, and Yemen, bitterly denounced Transjordan for pursuing an independent policy in Palestine. The Arab League seemed to be falling apart, its individual members placing their individual interests over those of the Arab world as a whole and hastening to save what they could from the debris. Lebanon as well as Egypt and Transjordan offered to conclude a non-aggression pact with the Israelis. Furthermore, each of the three made it perfectly clear that she was willing and anxious to sign such an agreement even though Israel might continue to attack other Arab forces. Their only interest was to get out of a situation which had taken a disastrous turn for the Arabs and which could only lead to further military defeats and, quite possibly, internal disturbances at home. In Amman the ostrich-like policy of the Arab states caused general resentment and widened the circle of politicians who were ready to countenance an independent line. Abul Huda certainly changed his tune. Previously he had maintained that he could not have anything to do with negotiations as his policy was based on unity with the Arab states. Now he decided to remain in office and even informed the UN representative in Amman that he was willing to consider an armistice plan and suggested that the Israelis should submit an armistice plan in writing for consideration by the Transjordanian government.[53]

The tendency to take an independent line gave rise to some differences between King Abdullah and his British advisers since London still hoped to maintain some kind of pressure on the new Jewish state. Ironically, Abdullah was suspected of being ready to come to terms with the Jews even on the basis of giving up any claim to the southern Negev, an area which London had sought strenuously to have assigned to Transjordan. As for the Arab parts of Palestine, Foreign Office advice to Abdullah was not to announce their annexation but wait for a more propitious time to carry out the merger. Meanwhile, the British thought that Abdullah should play for time and keep open the discussions that had begun with the Jewish representations, that he should ascertain their intentions and prepare the ground for the final

[53] *FRUS 1948*, v. 1647 f. 1667 f., 1674.

settlement that would give him at least the greater part of Arab Palestine but without making any binding commitments or risking total isolation from the Arab world.

Another reason given by the British to Abdullah for stalling related to the Israeli elections that were scheduled for January 1949. Mapai leaders were claiming privately that a settlement should be made before the elections because this would help the moderates to win. To the British, however, it seemed that no final settlement involving Israeli concessions could be made before the elections because any party making such concessions would be vulnerable to extremist attacks and criticism. This was a reference to the ultra-nationalist Herut party led by Menachem Begin that was agitating for the 'liberation' of the entire Land of Israel all the way to the Jordan River. Consequently, it was felt that Abdullah's object should be to keep the Jews in play until after the elections and the arrival of the Palestine Conciliation Commission appointed by the United Nations.[54]

When the Truce Commission called on Col. Dayan to suggest secret armistice negotiations as a means to breaking the deadlock between Transjordan and Israel, he replied that his government had been ready to negotiate armistice and peace either publicly or secretly but that after a promising start Tall had received new orders and held up the progress of the talks. Dayan believed that King Abdullah, after sponsoring the Jericho Congress and reaching the point of direct talks with the provisional government of Israel, had stopped short because of adverse Arab reactions. Recalling that Abdullah was known to be a wily fox, Dayan attributed to him the order to stall and also accused the British of discouraging him from proceeding with the talks. He stressed that his government would brook no delaying tactics and implied that it would resume hostilities if the stalemate continued. There was no doubt at all that the Israelis could quickly terminate the war by pushing to the Jordan River, thereby ending the drain that prolonged mobilization placed on their economy.[55]

When Israel did resume hostilities on December 22, it was not against Transjordan but against Egypt. The objective of Operation Horev was to complete the destruction of the Egyptian forces, to drive them out of Palestine, and compel the Egyptian government to negotiate an armistice. Conflicts between the Arab states and poor coordination between their armies in Palestine gave Israel the strategic freedom to choose the timing and place of this second offensive. Egypt appealed to her Arab allies for help but her appeals fell on deaf ears.

---

[54] Minute by Hector McNeil, 15 Dec. 1948, FO 371/68862; FO to Amman, 16 Dec. 1948, FO 371/68644, PRO.
[55] *FRUS 1948*, v. 1687 f.

Lebanon, Saudi Arabia, and the Yemen all promised assistance but failed to honour their promises. The Iraqis shelled a few Israeli villages near their front line as a token of solidarity with their embattled ally. King Abdullah did not even bother to reply. Without exception the Arab states were either afraid to intervene or did not wish to intervene. The Israeli troops surged forward, expelled the Egyptians from the south-eastern flank of the Negev, brought strong pressure to bear on the Gaza Strip, but failed to liquidate the Egyptian enclave in Faluja. In the course of the fighting, a column commanded by Gen. Yigal Allon penetrated into Sinai, attacked Abu Ageila, and reached the outskirts of El Arish.[56]

At this point Britain intervened by presenting an ultimatum to Israel, under the terms of the 1936 Anglo-Egyptian treaty, to withdraw her troops from Egypt's territory. The ultimatum was communicated by the Americans together with a severe warning from President Truman. Under this combined Anglo-American pressure, Ben-Gurion caved in and issued the order recalling the Israeli force from El Arish. On 4 January 1949 Egypt announced her readiness to begin armistice negotiations and on January 7 the UN-decreed cease-fire went into force, marking the formal end of the first Arab–Israeli war. A few hours before the cease-fire took effect, an incident occurred which brought Israel to the verge of that nightmare of Israeli strategists—a war with Britain. When RAF planes flew a reconnaissance mission from the Suez Canal zone to check whether the Israeli troops had really pulled back across the international border, five of them were shot down by Israeli planes. The British government demanded an explanation and compensation and sent reinforcements to Aqaba in response to a call for protection from King Abdullah who invoked the Anglo-Transjordanian Treaty. But this time President Truman came out strongly against Attlee and Bevin, as did the British media and Parliament, for taking perilous and needless risks in the Middle East.[57]

Operation Horev ended without fully attaining its aim: the Egyptian enemy remained in the Gaza Strip and in the enclave at Faluja. Pressure from the United Nations and the Great Powers forced Israel to call off the operation and thereby also reduced her bargaining power in the forthcoming armistice negotiations. But the operation was successful in compelling Egypt, the strongest Arab state with the best claim to lead the others, to open negotiations with the State of Israel and thus to bring the war to an end.

---

[56] IDF, *History of the War of Independence*, 345–63; Edgar O'Ballance, *The Arab–Israeli War, 1948* (London: Faber and Faber, 1956), 198–203.

[57] James McDonald, *My Mission in Israel, 1948–1951* (New York: Simon and Schuster, 1951), ch. 12; Ben-Gurion's diary, 31 Dec. 1948; 3, 7, and 8 Jan. 1949.

Another consequence of the second Israeli offensive against Egypt, and of Transjordan's strict neutrality from the beginning to the end of that offensive, was to exacerbate inter-Arab suspicions and recriminations and all but destroy the possibility of a co-ordinated diplomatic effort to end the war. Abdullah's readiness to come to terms with Israel and his refusal to break the truce by sending the Arab Legion to help the Egyptian army in the Negev raised not just wrath but the possibility of reprisals from that quarter. Relations between the two Arab monarchs reached their lowest ebb on December 24 when an unidentified aircraft dropped six large bombs near Abdullah's winter residence at Shuneh. No damage or casualties were caused but two bomb fragments were found which bore the message 'From King Farouk to M. Shertok' in Arabic characters. Abdullah was infuriated by this attack and by the insinuation that the Israeli foreign minister was a frequent visitor to Shuneh. But there was some evidence to suggest that the air raid had been carried out by an Israeli plane with bombs captured from the Egyptians, probably with the objective of deepening discord among the Arabs and ensuring that King Abdullah would remain neutral to the end in the war against Egypt: Dayan had called Tall on the morning of the raid to say that Israel had reliable intelligence that the Egyptians were planning to attack from the air the Arab Legion and other Arab armies and pretend that these attacks were carried out by the Israelis so as to drag the other Arabs into the fighting. In retrospect, this accurate forecast may have pointed to Israeli authorship of the insulting message delivered by so unconventional a method to Shuneh.[58]

Relations between Iraq and Transjordan were also strained as a result of the latter's refusal to go to the aid of Egypt and readiness to come to terms with the Israelis. The cease-fire agreement covering Jerusalem, and its extension to cover the entire Arab Legion–IDF front, left the Iraqi front dangerously exposed. Iraq's prime minister therefore sought an assurance that the Iraqi forces in Palestine could count on the intervention of the Arab Legion in the event of an Israeli attack. King Abdullah replied on December 15 that the Iraqi army was the apple of his eye and that he would not excuse himself or anybody else who tried to harm it. Abul Huda also replied in the name of the government to say that they would help as far as they could. But it was made clear that no help would be forthcoming if the Iraqis themselves were to recommence hostilities.[59]

Renewed fighting on the central front was not a purely theoretical

[58] Kirkbride to FO, 25 and 28 Dec., and Sir Ronald Campbell (Cairo) to FO, 28 Dec. 1948, FO 371/68377, PRO; Tall, *The Palestine Tragedy*, 299 f.

[59] Juburi *The Palestine Misfortune*, 325–8.

possibility. There was considerable tension along the northern sector of this front with occasional outbursts of fire from the Iraqi positions. To Gen. Shlomo Shamir who came to report on these incidents Ben-Gurion said that they must exercise restraint, that they must not allow themselves to be drawn into fighting in the Triangle against their own decision, but that after the operation in the south was completed they would reconsider the possibility of attacking in the Triangle. This, said Ben-Gurion gravely, would be the final and the most dangerous stage of the war for it would carry the risk of British intervention.[60]

Precisely how far Britain ought to go in supporting Abdullah was the subject of a lively debate among British Arabists. Sir Alec Kirkbride maintained that the other Arab rulers were no better than Abdullah, that time was running out, and that Britain should nail her flag to Abdullah's mast and disregard the protest of his Arab opponents. Britain's representatives in Egypt, on the other hand, argued that if Britain identified herself too closely with Abdullah's policy and ambitions, the result would be to disrupt Arab unity, play into the hands of the extremists, and weaken the Arab bargaining position *vis-à-vis* Israel. By supporting Transjordan in a separate peace with Israel, Sir Ronald Campbell conceded, Britain might gain a *partial* Judaeo-Arab peace but he feared that the end result would be to prevent a *general* Judaeo-Arab settlement. Would it not be better, he asked, to discourage unilateral action by Transjordan and work for joint, peaceful action between Transjordan and Egypt? Kirkbride retorted that the policy of all the Arab governments other than Transjordan was to prevent or delay any official settlement of the Palestine problem in the hope that future events might provide them with an opportunity of turning the tables on the Jews. Transjordan, on the other hand, could not afford to let the matter drift, whatever the reactions of the other Arab states might be. When the other Arab states talked of Transjordan co-operating with them they meant that Transjordan should do nothing, and Kirkbride thought it would be absurd to urge the Transjordanian authorities to follow such a policy.

The policy formulated in London on the basis of these conflicting views from British legations in the Middle East was to strengthen Abdullah's hand by moving additional equipment and supplies to Amman and placing a unit of land forces on alert in Aqaba. These measures, it was hoped, would enable him to spin out things, resist Jewish pressure, and negotiate an armistice rather than a final settlement.[61]

---

[60] Ben-Gurion's diary, 28 Dec. 1948.
[61] BMEO to FO, 20 and 31 Dec., Campbell to FO, 21 Dec., Kirkbride to FO, 28 and 29 Dec., FO to Amman, 30 and 31 Dec. 1948, FO 371/68644, PRO.

Shiloah, Dayan, and al-Tall

Ben-Gurion, having decided that peace was now the basic objective, remained uncertain as to the best means of attaining it. He believed that of all the Arab rulers Abdullah was the only one who would dare to defy internal opposition and Arab public opinion and come out in favour of peace with Israel; but he was also convinced that even if Abdullah could be squared, Britain would not allow him to conclude a separate peace agreement with Israel.[62] Ben-Gurion was also sceptical about the possibility of gaining possession of the routes to Jerusalem and broadening Israel's narrow waistline by peaceful means. 'After all', he wrote in his diary, 'the most natural border is the Jordan.' If the West Bank had to stay in Arab hands, Ben-Gurion was not sure whether its annexation to Transjordan would be the best solution because that would bolster Britain's position in the Middle East and antagonize the Soviets, who regarded Transjordan as a client state of the British Empire. For a mere armistice agreement, at any rate, Ben-Gurion was not prepared to give up the option of extending Israel's border to the Jordan by military action; only real peace was worth the sacrifice. Significantly, when Ben-Gurion decided to put Abdullah to the test and compel him to choose either peace or war, it was not the gentle and accommodating Sasson who was sent to deliver the 'ultimatum' but two hardliners—Moshe Dayan and Reuven Shiloah.

Reuven Shiloah was destined to play a vital part in developing the relationship between the Zionist movement and King Abdullah. Born in Jerusalem in 1909, Shiloah had specialized in Oriental studies in Baghdad and later served as a liaison officer between the Jewish Agency and the British administration in Palestine. During the Second World War he had liaised with the Allied forces in the Middle East and helped Moshe Sharett to organize the recruitment of Jewish volunteers for the British army, to send agents into Nazi-occupied Europe and to prepare plans for guerrilla warfare in the event of a Nazi invasion of Palestine. With the establishment of the State of Israel, Shiloah was appointed as political adviser to the foreign minister. Shiloah disliked the Anglo-Saxon clique at the Foreign Ministry both because he felt that they placed form and ceremony above substance and because they had little knowledge of the Middle East. The Foreign Ministry was rather small and tightly knit in those days whereas Shiloah was a loner and an independent political operator. Much of his work was shrouded in mystery and even to Sharett he did not always report all his clandestine activities. Shiloah's colleagues regarded him as a strange

[62] Protocol of Mapai's Central Committee, 11 Nov. 1948, Labour Party Archive, Beit Berl; Ben-Gurion's diary, 22 Dec. 1948.

character because he used to take large quantities of stimulants in order to keep himself alert and dynamic and sleeping tablets in order to sleep, and ended up ruining his health. But most of them also recognized that he had a brilliant and fertile political mind and tactical virtuosity in the conduct of negotiations.

Although Shiloah remained very closed to Sharett at the personal level, in his outlook on the Arab world he was closer to Ben-Gurion and the senior members of the defence establishment. With his background in intelligence, Shiloah was one of the few Zionist officials who combined a profound grasp of the country's security problems with a natural talent for diplomacy. And it was this ability to see problems simultaneously from the diplomatic and military angle that carried Shiloah into the inner circle of policymaking and made him an indispensable co-ordinator between the diplomatic and the security agencies of the new state.[63]

Shiloah was accompanied by Moshe Dayan, a close personal friend, to his first meeting with Abdullah al-Tall and Dr Shawkat as-Sati. The meeting took place in no-man's land in Jerusalem on December 25. Dr Sati noted with disappointment the absence of Elias Sasson, to whom his monarch had sent warm personal greetings. Abdullah, declared Dr Sati, wanted peace with all his heart and ardently hoped that the cease-fire in Jerusalem would last. Shiloah replied that his government, too, wanted peace, but that it did not believe that a mere truce could lead to peace. Dr Sati said that he was ready to start negotiations for an armistice but that in view of the king's delicate position in the Arab world it would be desirable to keep these negotiations secret. Shiloah rejected the offer, saying that the Israelis were now interested only in negotiating peace and if it was not to be peace, it would be war. If the Israelis showed willingness to discuss the return of Jaffa, Lydda, and Ramle to the Arabs, observed Dr Sati, Abdullah's position would become stronger and it would become easier for him to make peace. Shiloah said he would report the king's request to his government, but that since all the problems were interrelated it was a mistake on the king's part to single out this question. What they should do is to have proper meetings in a conference room, with maps, to discuss all the questions. Before parting Shiloah asked whether the British were aware of the discussions in Jerusalem, and both Shawkat and Tall promised an early reply.[64]

After seeing King Abdullah, Tall called Dayan to say that the king had entrusted him and Dr Sati with preparing a peace plan and representing him at the talks. When their proposal was completed the

[63] Interviews with Mrs Betty Shiloah, Walter Eytan, and Moshe Sasson.
[64] *DFPI*, iii. 334–6; *FRUS 1948*, v. 1699–702.

king would present it to the government; if the government rejected it, he would replace the government. Tall proposed that they should meet alternately in Arab and Jewish buildings rather than standing in no-man's land, that they should wear civilian clothes, and bring with them papers and maps. On hearing the news Ben-Gurion drew up a list of issues for discussion: the border in Wadi Araba, restoration of the potash works on the south of the Dead Sea, Jerusalem, Shaikh Jarrah, the Old City, the railway line, Latrun, the borders in the Triangle, annexation of the West Bank or the creation of an independent state, the Etzion bloc, compensation, Naharayim, and the release of prisoners.[65]

To discuss in more detail the forthcoming peace talks, a group of officials convened in Ben-Gurion's office on December 30. The participants at this preparatory meeting were Walter Eytan, Elias Sasson, Reuven Shiloah, David Horowitz, and Shabtai Rosenne of the Foreign Ministry, Col. Moshe Dayan, and Gen. Yaacov Dori, the ailing chief of staff. The deliberations revealed a great deal about the motives, aims, tactics, and strategy that lay behind the initiation of peace talks with Transjordan.

Elias Sasson gave a comprehensive survey of the situation in the Arab countries, underlining that internal instability in the wake of failure in Palestine could end up by making the regimes in these countries more dependent on foreign powers. Two very different courses were outlined by Sasson in the light of this situation. They could take the line that a Jewish state had been established and that it was capable of continuing the war until it had repelled Egypt, Transjordan, Iraq, and Syria and consolidated her borders. Though located in the East, they could say that they were a Western state with no interest in developing any economic or political links with the East. This was one possible course. But there was another, whose starting point was that Israel could not turn her back on the Arab world, primitive and in need of development though it was, because she herself was part of the East and if she wanted to be strong, the Arab world had to be strong and if she wanted to be free of foreign influence she had to help the Arabs to rid themselves of foreign influence.

Sasson himself was not only driven by logic to prefer the second course but also feared that the opportunity would be missed unless they acted promptly. The objective as he saw it was not to drive the Arabs into Britain's arms, and the key was that stable country called Transjordan. In concrete policy terms this meant encouraging the early annexation of the remaining Arab parts of Palestine to Transjordan while striving at the same time to engage in peace talks

[65] Ben-Gurion's diary, 29 Dec. 1948.

with the other Arab states. By seeking to confirm the annexation to the Arab parts of Palestine and opposing the Greater Syria scheme, a basis could be established for the talks with Syria. Whereas hostilities could be terminated immediately, peace would take a great deal of time and effort, said Sasson. He therefore suggested proceeding in stages: to end the war, to develop *de facto* relations, and eventually to establish formal links with the Arab states.

A further reason given by Sasson for favouring the annexation of the rump of Arab Palestine to Transjordan was that it would facilitate the settlement of the Palestinian refugee problem. There were around 200,000 refugees on the east and west banks of the Jordan and if agreement on their resettlement could be reached with Transjordan, the refugees in Syria and elsewhere would give up hope of returning to their homes and become more amenable to other solutions.

Ben-Gurion wondered whether annexation of the Arab part to Abdullah's kingdom and prevention of his entry into Syria by means of an Israeli–Syrian pact would not lead either to Abdullah's annexation of Iraq or Iraq's annexation of Transjordan, the upshot in either case being one large state stretching from the Soviet border to Nablus. Sasson replied that Abdullah's kingdom would not be able to survive without Israeli support and that in Iraq there was deadlock between those politicians who looked to the Soviet Union and the politicians in power who looked to the West. As long as Abdullah was alive, said Sasson, union between Iraq and Transjordan was out of the question. And Abdullah was utterly dependent on Britain because the entire budget of Transjordan did not exceed £700,000–£800,000 whereas the British subsidy amounted to £2.5 million.

David Horowitz, the director-general of the Ministry of Finance and a prominent moderate, elaborated on the reasons for Abdullah's dependence on Britain. He was dependent because he had no hinterland, no industry, no large cities, and just a small bedouin population that could not constitute a state. With the annexation of the Arab territories, argued Horowitz, the situation would grow worse because Abdullah would be getting the hilly part of Palestine, with no industry, not much arable land, limited possibilities for taxation, and the added burden of maintaining the municipal services set up under the British mandate. As Abdullah grew poorer, he would also become more dependent on Israel, especially as a market for wheat, vegetables, and fruit. To maintain stability in his own kingdom, Abdullah would need Israeli help. The standard of living was low, there were no political parties and no democracy, and all this, explained Horowitz, stemmed from the country's still being at a pre-capitalist stage. In Israel, on the other hand, population, national revenue, and industrialization (and with them the country's military potential), were likely to grow at such a pace as to rule out the possibility of Transjordan ever catching up.

General Yadin interrupted these learned disquisitions to say that the question of the border was paramount in any approach to Abdullah and that it was unlikely that even their minimal requirements could be achieved by diplomatic negotiations. Minimal requirements, as defined by Yadin, included Israeli possession of Wadi Ara, Umm al-Fahem, Tulkarem, Kalkilya, and a border along the first mountain ridge. And Yadin thought that they should not waste time in elaborate negotiations but present their demands to Abdullah and insist on an unequivocal 'yes' or 'no'. If they could not get what they wanted by such 'diplomatic' means, they should seek a military solution. He went even further and suggested that they should not talk to Abdullah at all until after they had extended their line further east into the Triangle. The way to play the game was to provoke the Iraqis, take the Triangle from them, and pretend that all this had nothing to do with Abdullah. Here Sasson interrupted to complain that Yadin was ruining his entire conception because for him annexation of the West Bank to Transjordan was the key.

Ben-Gurion did not come out decisively in favour of either the political solution urged by Sasson or the military solution urged by Yadin. His own contribution to the debate consisted of pointing out, firstly, that Abdullah could not agree in advance the border demanded by Yadin even though he might be compelled to accept it later and, secondly, that it was convenient to drag out the talks with Transjordan until the operation in the Negev had been completed.[66]

The second meeting between Shiloah, Dayan, and Colonel Tall went rather well though they did not get down to substantive talks. Shiloah suggested that both sides should bring formal letters of accreditation from their governments and that a summary should be written down at the end of every session. He insisted on confining the talks to the areas held by the Arab Legion and listed the points of interest to the provisional government of Israel. For the second time he tried to find out whether the British were being informed but again met with evasion. Tall indicated that the king was thinking about the division of Jerusalem and the division of the Negev and listed several other points of interest. All these subjects were listed as the agenda for the next secret meeting to be held in Jewish Jerusalem on 5 January 1949.[67]

Another consultation was held in the prime minister's office in preparation for this meeting. Ben-Gurion succinctly recorded in his diary: 'Sasson proved that the key to peace with the Arab world [is] our agreement to the annexation of the Arab part by Abdullah and the

[66] DFPI, ii. 320–31; Ben-Gurion's diary, 30 Dec. 1948.   [67] DFPI, iii. 336–9.

prevention of "Greater Syria". He does not see the difficulties of the agreement with Abdullah (territorial questions) and its dangers (British penetration).'[68]

The detailed guidelines given by Ben-Gurion, following a discussion with Sharett, to Shiloah and Dayan for their third meeting with Colonel Tall were intended to keep all Israel's options open. They were to continue the talks, even if they were unproductive, for as long as the fighting with the Egyptians continued in the south. Secondly, they were not to commit Israel on the annexation of the West Bank by Transjordan, but nor were they to express opposition to it. They were to explain the international difficulties, express sympathy, and say that their government had not reached a final decision. Thirdly, they were to insist that the eastern border of the Negev should remain as it had been during the mandatory period—up to and including Eilat in the south. Fourthly, they could mention the possibility of offering Transjordan rights in Gaza with access to it through Israeli territory. Lastly, they were to reject the king's requests regarding Ramle and Jaffa and leave open the question of an Arab return to Lydda but not to enter into any discussions concerning the Negev.[69]

To the third meeting Shiloah and Dayan brought a letter of accreditation signed by the prime minister and the foreign minister; Tall brought a letter written in King Abdullah's own hand. After the exchange of letters Tall reported that the king did not view these talks as armistice talks following a war; he did not treat what had happened in the last few months as a war but as a *fatna*, an unfortunate quarrel. He recalled the talks that they had held before this unfortunate quarrel and during it, in Paris, and regarded the present talks as a direct continuation of the long-standing contact between them. Shiloah replied that they too recalled this link but that they could not disregard what had happened in the meantime, and whether it was termed war or an unfortunate quarrel, the fact was that they had been attacked, that blood had been spilt, and that a certain military and political reality had emerged.

When Tall outlined Abdullah's specific proposals, it became clear just how wide was the gulf separating the two sides. In the Negev the king wanted a strip of land connecting his country with Egypt. He assumed that Israel's main interest in the Negev was oil, and he was agreeable that Israel should have the oil region south-west of the Dead Sea. Tall was told that this assumption was utterly mistaken and that Israel's interest in the Negev included access to the Dead Sea, an outlet to the Red Sea, land, and settlement. In response to a question about the reasons for the king's interest in the Negev, Tall mentioned three

[68] Ben-Gurion's diary, 2 Jan. 1949.   [69] Ibid. 4 Jan. 1949; Dayan, *Story of My Life*, 105.

reasons: access to Egypt, the 100,000 bedouins living there, and strategic needs. He laughed when asked whether he meant Transjordan's strategic interests or those of the king's allies, remarking only that if agreement was reached it would be the Israelis who would become the king's allies.

Abdullah's conception of the division of Jerusalem was that he should have the Old City, Katamon, the German Colony, and all the quarters in the south of the city while the Jews kept the rest. He also wanted to include in the Arab part Talpiot and Kibbutz Ramat Rachel, in exchange for the Arab suburbs of Lifta and Romema that were already in Israeli hands. International rule was to be confined to a road passing between the Arab and Jewish parts and including the King David Hotel and the YMCA. Dayan said that this entire approach was out of touch with reality: since Katamon, Lifta, Romema, and the other suburbs in the south of the city were in Israel's possession, what Tall was proposing was to take areas that were in Israel's possession and offer in return other areas that were also in her possession. He proposed instead that areas in the south of the city might be exchanged for Shaikh Jarrah to link Israel with the Hebrew University. Tall replied that this was out of the question because it would drive a wedge between Arab Jerusalem and Ramallah. Shiloah and Dayan stressed that world opinion would be satisfied with nothing less than international super-vision of the Old City and enquired as to the status of the Jewish Quarter under the king's plan. Tall replied that they were prepared to hand it over to Israel and provide access to it. At this point the talks were ended and it was agreed to resume them a week later. Before taking his leave Tall said that the British knew about the talks and that they were in favour of a peaceful solution but that they were not kept informed of the details and they were not the ones who had put forward those conditions.[70]

Shiloah and Dayan reported back to Ben-Gurion and said that there was obviously no point in going on with the talks. 'We must probe every possibility of achieving peace', he said. 'We need it probably more than the Jordanians—though no doubt they are losing more than a little, becoming more and more subservient to the British.' A subsequent report of a flare up of fighting with the Iraqis near Kfar Saba found Ben-Gurion in a cautious mood. He ordered that the utmost restraint be exercised on the eastern front and saw to it that a senior officer was sent to ensure that this order was obeyed.[71]

Developments on the southern front deeply worried Ben-Gurion. He thought that the British reconnaissance flights, the shooting down of

[70] DFPI, iii. 340–2; Dayan, Story of My Life, 106; Ben-Gurion's diary, 6 Jan. 1949.
[71] Dayan, Story of My Life, 106; Ben-Gurion's diary, 7 Jan. 1949.

the British planes over Egyptian territory, and Egyptian violations of the cease-fire were all connected in some sinister fashion. Egypt's eventual disengagement was not enough to dissipate Ben-Gurion's suspicions of British plots. On January 9, he was apprised by Yadin that there was information from Transjordan and Iraq pointing to an Anglo-Hashemite plan to conquer the Negev. Apart from the landing of British forces in Aqaba, there were naval manoeuvres, RAF reinforcements, and advice to British subjects to leave Israel. Whatever Britain's intentions might have been—a show of force, intimidation, or the preparation for a fight—Ben-Gurion felt that it would be a grave mistake to provoke Egypt. Rather, since Egypt was not working hand-in-hand with Britain, and since it was extremely important for Israel to keep it that way, Ben-Gurion endeavoured to start armistice talks with Egypt, to break up the Arab front, to weaken Britain's influence in the Middle East, and to deny Bevin ammunition for his campaign to discredit Israel in Washington.

The Iraqis took the initiative in sending a message to Ben-Gurion, relayed via Tall and Dayan, to say that it was the Israeli troops who had provoked the clashes near Kfar Saba and that in any case they had no intention of starting a war. King Abdullah and his advisers wanted time to consider the outcome of the last meeting with the Israeli representatives, and another meeting was fixed for January 14. While on the phone, Dayan decided to say to Tall what he thought of his earlier proposals and to express his personal view that if there were no change in Transjordan's approach, they would bring about war, not peace.[72]

In a conversation with an American official in Amman, Glubb Pasha said that progress in the talks with Israel was too slow due mainly to the fact that Abul Huda was not supposed to be informed in the matter. Since the government was not officially involved, it was difficult to present concrete suggestions. In Glubb's view, unless both parties ceased fencing and started discussing definitively what each one wanted and what each was prepared to give, the talks themselves might end in failure. Glubb thought that the Israeli–Egyptian agreement to start armistice talks under UN auspices could make it easier for the king to bring the current Transjordanian–Israeli talks into the open. His hope was that Israel would not use these talks to play one Arab state against another.[73]

Ben-Gurion was not ready to stop fencing and clung to his view that Britain was the chief obstacle to success in the talks between Israel and

[72] Ben-Gurion's diary, 7 and 9 Jan. 1949; Dayan, *Story of My Life*, 106.
[73] *FRUS 1949*, vol. vi, *The Near East, South Asia, and Africa* (Washington, DC: US Government Printing Office, 1977), 631 f.

the Arabs. The Americans were exerting influence to restrain Bevin yet Ben-Gurion feared that if Israel defied security council resolutions, Bevin would take drastic measures and start re-arming the Arabs. Moshe Sharett wanted to prepare a peace plan for the forthcoming talks with Egypt in Rhodes. But Ben-Gurion thought that it would be sufficient to declare their general desire for peace and wait for the other side to state its terms first. He was inclined to agree with Sharett that it would be preferable to let Egypt rather than Abdullah take Gaza, because giving Abdullah Gaza and a corridor leading to it would not only antagonize the Egyptians but enable Bevin to re-enter Palestine through the back door. He could not agree, however, with Sharett's suggestion that they should undertake in advance to permit food supplies to the Egyptian brigade in Faluja, arguing that they had already demonstrated their goodwill by withdrawing from El Arish.[74]

On the evening of January 12, Chief of Staff Yaacov Dori brought Ben-Gurion copies of three telegrams. The first was from the Egyptian HQ to the Egyptian commander in Hebron instructing him to prevent passage by Arab Legion troops to Hebron even if it meant war. The second was from the Egyptian commander to his HQ reporting that he had started mining the road to Beersheba and asking for anti-tank weapons to enable him to deal with the Legion. The third was from Transjordan's HQ, placing its front-line units on alert. From all this intelligence Ben-Gurion concluded that there was a combined Anglo–Transjordanian plan to attack Israel in the Negev and that the Egyptians were so estranged from the British that they were prepared to go to war against Transjordan to prevent her from capturing the part of the Negev that Egypt herself had lost to Israel while Transjordan stayed on the side-lines. It was certainly not too soon now to start talking to the Egyptians in Rhodes.[75]

As Glubb had predicted, the armistice talks between Israel and Egypt, which opened officially on January 13 in Rhodes, gave King Abdullah the impetus to get down to the real business of peace-making. On that very day, a day before they were due to meet again at the Mandelbaum Gate, Tall called Dayan to say that the king was inviting them to come and talk with him at his palace in Shuneh so that he could personally demonstrate his sincere desire for peace.[76]

The end of the war

The final stage of the Arab–Israeli war was thus marked by renewed co-operation, both tacit and explicit, between Transjordan and Israel.

[74] Ben-Gurion's diary, 11 Jan. 1949.   [75] Ibid. 12 Jan. 1949.
[76] Ibid. 13 Jan. 1949; Dayan, *Story of My Life*, 106.

There were a number of ingredients that characterized this renewed co-operation. First, on the Transjordanian side, Abdullah consolidated his rule in the areas of Palestine captured by the Arab Legion. This process reached its climax with the Jericho Congress which opened the road to eventual annexation. Second, in order to secure his rule over the West Bank, Abdullah intensified his contacts with the Israeli side, concluded a cease-fire agreement to cover Jerusalem, and initiated peace talks that would make it more difficult for Israel to initiate hostilities. Third, while Abdullah was consolidating his rule over the West Bank, the Israelis carried out a series of military operations which destroyed the power of King Farouk, his chief rival in the Negev, thereby enhancing Abdullah's position in the Arab world as well as in Palestine. Israel's military operations also forced the mufti's All-Palestine government to flee to Cairo, thereby facilitating Abdullah's task of mobilizing Palestinian support for the merger of the West Bank with Transjordan. Fourth, because the king recognized that Israel's expulsion of the Egyptian army from the southern part of Palestine would rebound to his advantage, he ordered his army not to join in the fighting; by not lifting a finger to help the Egyptians, he made an important contribution to the Israeli victory in the Negev. Fifth, the destruction of Egyptian power in the Negev ironically enabled the Israelis to concentrate most of their military power against their secret ally to the east. The Israeli ultimatum of 'either peace or war' was the direct result of the collapse of the Egyptian army. Finally, the Israeli leadership was inclined to forego at this stage further strategic conquests on the eastern front, but this self-restraint was contingent on continuing co-operation on the part of the Hashemite king. Failure to realize a number of minimal strategic objectives was liable to tip the balance in favour of exploiting the new balance of forces to Israel's advantage.[77]

Although Israel's territorial achievements at the end of the war greatly surpassed even the wildest expectations of May 1948, some important groups in Israel considered it an unfinished war—unfinished in the sense that the military balance of forces would have enabled Israel to take the whole of mandatory Palestine up to the Jordan River. In other words, it was political choice rather than military necessity that brought the war to an end.

Another sense in which the war was unfinished was its failure to settle once and for all Israel's place in the Middle East. This was closely connected with another question, namely, the fate of the Arab part of Palestine. Partition, as formulated by the international community in the UN resolution of November 1947 and accepted, at least formally,

[77] Bar-Joseph, *The Relations Between Israel and Transjordan*, 169 f.

by Israel, involved the creation of two new states, one Jewish and one Arab. Throughout the second half of 1948 various plans were considered by the Israeli policymakers for helping to organize the Arab part of Palestine into an independent unit. Foreign Minister Sharett was particularly instrumental in keeping this option open and at times seemed to genuinely favour it. On August 8, for example, he formulated policy guidelines which called for the initiation of talks 'with various Palestinian groups on the establishment of self-rule for the Arab part of Western Palestine. While the possibility of annexation to Transjordan was not ruled out, all the emphasis was to be placed on Israel's preference for the creation of an independent Arab state in western Palestine.[78] One of the reasons for Sharett's own preference for an independent Arab state alongside Israel was that this solution was closer in spirit to the UN partition plan than the alternative of annexation to Transjordan. Sharett saw the UN plan as a basic point of reference because he wanted to facilitate Israel's acceptance into the comity of nations. One of the principal reasons for Sharett's support for the military operations in the Negev and resistance to seizing the West Bank by force was that the former was included in the boundaries of the Jewish state whereas the latter was not.[79] By the end of the war, however, and with the emergence of Transjordan as a serious partner for peace talks, Sharett's 'Palestinian option' became a tactical lever and a bargaining card rather than an operational goal of Israel's foreign policy.

With the elimination of the Palestinian option as a serious contender, two other options were open to Israel with regard to the future of the West Bank: to seize all of it by force, or to seek to realize Israel's minimal strategic objectives through diplomatic negotiations with Transjordan. With the benefit of hindsight it is possible to discern two rival schools of thought, based on their preference for force or diplomacy for finishing the 1948 war.

The first school advocated the exploitation of Israel's military superiority in order to expel all five Arab armies from western Palestine. Virtually all the generals in the High Command supported this activist approach, the military logic of which was not easy to fault. This approach also found adherents across the entire political spectrum, especially on the extreme left (Mapam and the Communists) and on the extreme right (Herut and the smaller offshoots of the Revisionist movement). On the long-term future of western Palestine, however, there was no consensus. The disciples of the left, with some notable exceptions, supported either the creation of an independent Palestinian

[78] *DFPI*, i. 498.
[79] Foreign minister's meeting with newspaper editors, 17 Jan. 1949, 2446/14, ISA.

state or the conversion of Israel into a binational state based on political equality between Jews and Arabs, whereas those of the right trumpeted the idea of a large Jewish state across the entire length and breadth of Palestine, or the Land of Israel as they preferred to call it, with its Arab citizens permanently relegated to a minority status with limited autonomy in educational, cultural, and religious matters.

The other school, which actually directed Israel's strategy, was less activist. This school was not so clear-cut in its aims nor did it develop a coherent doctrine on how the war should be terminated. Among its supporters were most of the leaders of Mapai, the centrist parties, and the religious parties. The spokesman of this school was Moshe Sharett but its real leader was David Ben-Gurion, though the latter frequently cloaked his real position with uncompromisingly activist rhetoric. The question posed by subscribers to this school of thought was roughly as follows: what would happen to the state of Israel if she sent her army to banish all five invading armies and to take over the whole of western Palestine? The answer was that despite the impressive military victory, a Jewish community of about 650,000 people would find itself in charge of a Palestinian population of about a million concentrated largely in the hilly area between the Jenin–Nablus–Tulkarem Triangle in the north and Hebron in the south. The nationalist political leadership which this population had supported since the 1920s had acted with uncompromising hostility to the Zionist enterprise, employing violence, guerrilla warfare, and even terror. If Israel decided to impose its sovereignty and its rule over this population, the result, it was assumed, would be permanent unrest and rebelliousness.

Looking at the Jewish side of the great divide, the subscribers to this school further reflected that this small community which had suffered 6,000 casualties in the war for independence was now duty-bound to absorb immigration from the survivors of the Holocaust in Europe (around 300,000) and the Arab countries (another 300,000). Other priorities included economic reconstruction, the building of industry, settlement of the land, education, housing, and related tasks that lay at the heart of practical Zionism. If Israel became immersed, at the end of a long and exhausting war, in military government and a prolonged struggle against a million Palestinians, would she really be able to fulfil her Zionist mission?

Turning their attention to the Arab circle around Palestine, the members of this school noted that to the east they had a relatively powerful neighbour—Transjordan. It was true that Transjordan had joined in the invasion in order to take a share of the spoils at the expense of Palestinian and Israeli independence, but like the other invaders she had failed. The rulers of Transjordan, and particularly King Abdullah, were now displaying commendable pragmatism and willingness to come to terms with Israel on the basis of the new status quo. On the other hand, this Hashemite regime regarded the mufti, the Arab Higher Committee, and Palestinian nationalism as enemy forces with whom no compromise was possible. It made sense, therefore, to leave it to this regime to deal with the rebellious Palestinians provided a political arrangement could be worked out between Transjordan and Israel based on *de facto* recognition. From the Zionist point of view, it was argued, this would be the best settlement and it would be worth striving for it even if it involved the division of Jerusalem between the two countries. For if Israel were to expel the Arab Legion and capture the whole of Jerusalem there was the danger that the international community would compel her to accept the internationalization of the city. In other words, partition was preferable to internationalization.

In strategic terms, the political analysis outlined above called for the expulsion of all the regular Arab armies from western Palestine except for the Arab Legion. And that is what the Israeli army actually achieved in the final phase of the war.

The withdrawal from El Arish and leaving the Gaza Strip in the hands of Egypt when the armistice talks began provoked a bitter controversy between the leaders of the activist and of the moderate schools. The activists were undoubtedly right in claiming that the IDF's superiority and international support would have enabled Israel to complete the expulsion of the Egyptian army from the borders of Palestine. Finishing the war in such a way would have made it much easier for the Ben-Gurion–Sharett school, the most realistic school at the time, to manœuvre Abdullah into a peace settlement by offering him the choice between sovereignty over Gaza and a free passage to it in addition to the Triangle, East Jerusalem, and Hebron, or, in the absence of peace, the conquest of all these places by the IDF and the ejection of both the Hashemite armies from western Palestine. Without the possibility of offering Gaza, the objective capability to bring Abdullah to a peace settlement with Israel was significantly reduced.[80]

Meir Pail, the military historian who analysed these rival conceptions and recognized the realism that governed Ben-Gurion's approach, was nevertheless critical of Ben-Gurion for the way in which he terminated the war or rather for his failure to terminate it satisfactorily. It was the old charge of the unfinished war pressed with an original argument:

Ben-Gurion did have a conception for ending the war, but it was incomplete. This shows that he was not a great statesman, unlike Stalin who towards the

---

[80] Meir Pail, 'Political Constraints on Military Moves' (Heb.), *Davar* 30 Apr. 1979.

end of the Second World War developed and imposed a firm political conception on the post-war order in Eastern Europe. The Hashemite conception was the most realistic conception at the end of the War of Independence. But in order to realize it it was necessary first to complete the defeat of Egypt. Only if the Egyptians had been forced back to their side of the border with Palestine would it have been possible to do business with Abdullah—either peace with concessions from him or else the capture of the entire West Bank by Israel.[81]

Failure to capture Gaza and use it as the bait to lure Abdullah into a separate peace agreement was not the only flaw in Ben-Gurion's strategy for bringing about the termination of hostilities. His entire attitude towards the Arab world was ambivalent and contradictory. Most fundamental was the political contradiction between Ben-Gurion's socialist convictions and his choice of Transjordan, one of the most economially backward and politically reactionary kingdoms in the Arab world, as Israel's principal partner in laying the foundations for the post-war order in the Middle East. A Hashemite orientation in foreign policy, however compelling the security arguments for its adoption, was at odds with the ideology of socialism and egalitarianism practised at home. Nor could Ben-Gurion's avowed anti-imperialism be easily reconciled on the ideological plane with the partnership he sought to cultivate with Abdullah, the closest ally and most dependent client of the British Empire in the Middle East.

Ben-Gurion's attitude towards the progressive forces in the Arab world was highly ambivalent, combining fear of potential power in the long-term with a residual hope that co-operation with them might yet be possible. Typical of this ambivalence was his reaction to the emergence of the Ba'ath or Renaissance Party on the West Bank during the period of transition from war to peace. After summarizing the platform of this party in his diary—Arab unity, freedom from imperialism, individual liberty, modernization, and a relentless fight against the Jewish state—Ben-Gurion adds ominously:

This is the road for the Arabs, and all the time I fear that an Arab leader would rise to lead the Arabs along this road. They ignore the internal and external obstacles and *the time* required to attain Arab unity. And woe betide us if we fail to exploit *this time* in order to grow, to entrench ourselves, to acquire a position in the world, to move closer to the Arab world, and to prove to people of this kind that the Arabs' road to unity, freedom, and progress lies not in war with us but in alliance. The question is whether our people will understand this adequately and in the available time . . .[82]

[81]　Interview with Meir Pail.
[82]　Ben-Gurion's diary, 29 Jan. 1949 (emphasis in the original).

Another question to which this highly revealing diary entry gives rise is whether Ben-Gurion himself was aware of the contradiction between his hope for an understanding with the progressive forces in the Arab world and the actual road he chose of collaboration with Abdullah. The emphasis on the time dimension suggested that he was. At this stage, the new forces spurred on by the Arab military defeat were not yet dominant, so the emphasis had to be on reaching a *modus vivendi* with the existing ruling classes and governments of the Arab countries. And if the quickest way to achieve this was through collaboration with Abdullah, then the end justified the means.[83]

[83] Bar-Joseph, *The Relations Between Israel and Transjordan*, 181 f.

13

NEGOTIATING THE ARMISTICE AGREEMENT

Rhodes

Armistice negotiations between Israel and the neighbouring Arab states got under way with the help of the UN acting mediator, Dr Ralph Bunche, on the island of Rhodes in January 1949. Israel negotiated bilaterally with each of the neighbouring Arab states, beginning with Egypt, and concluded a separate armistice agreement with each of them. The roll-call was impressive: the agreement between Israel and Egypt was signed on February 24; between Israel and Lebanon on March 23; between Israel and Transjordan on April 3; between Israel and Syria on July 20. Each set of negotiations had a distinctive character, conditioned by the specific military and political circumstances peculiar to that front and, in no small measure, by the personalities of the negotiators. What all the negotiations had in common was that they were held on the basis of the Security Council resolution of 16 November 1948, and under the auspices of the United Nations.[1]

The Arab states were going through a very difficult and frustrating period. They had learnt the hard way that it is easier to get into a war than to get out of it and they were unable to close ranks against the common foe and the bitter consequences of defeat. Defeat on the battlefield led to mutual recriminations and all but shattered co-operation within the Arab League on the Palestine question. Disunity was compounded by rumours of secret exchanges and secret meetings between some Arab governments and Israel and by the general disillusion with the Western Powers and the United Nations. Far from presenting a united front, the Arab governments dealt with Israel independently from positions of terrible weakness, and the selfish manner in which they pursued their national interests was utterly at odds with the commitment they still professed to the cause of Palestine.

Israel emerged from the War of Independence economically

---

[1] In this chapter I rely heavily on the volume of official Israeli documents relating to the armistice negotiations and on the editor's excellent introduction to this volume, *Documents on the Foreign Policy of Israel*, vol. iii, *Armistice Negotiations with the Arab States, December 1948–July 1949*, ed. Yemima Rosenthal (Jerusalem: Israel State Archives, 1983). (Henceforth, *DFPI*, iii.)

exhausted, but with superior organization and morale, a tremendous sense of achievement, and a confident outlook on the future that formed a solid foundation for the development of parliamentary democracy. The first general election for the 120-member Knesset or Parliament was held on January 25. Mapai won some 36 per cent of the votes, the left-wing Mapam 15 per cent, the United Religious Party 12 per cent, the right-wing Herut Party 11.5 per cent, the General Zionists 5 per cent, the Progressive Party 4 per cent, the Communists 3.5 per cent, and the Sephardim 3.5 per cent, the rest of the votes being divided among a number of smaller parties. Following the elections, David Ben-Gurion formed a coalition government consisting of Mapai, the Religious, the Progressive, and the Sephardi parties. The three senior posts remained unchanged, with Ben-Gurion as prime minister and minister of defence, Moshe Sharett as foreign minister and Eliezer Kaplan as finance minister. Mapai thus retained a virtual monopoly in the defence and foreign affairs sphere and it succeeded in excluding the extreme left and extreme right from power.

The election results also had some influence on the country's external orientation. With strong international support from Russia and continuing dependence on arms and immigrants from Eastern Europe, the prospects for extending communist influence in the Jewish state were thought to be considerable. But the swing to the left did not materialize. There was strong American influence pulling the other way and there were also strong trading and economic links with the United Kingdom and Western Europe. Formally, the new government subscribed to a policy of non-alignment but in practice it looked increasingly to America for economic, military, and political support.

The Israeli government saw Britain, long after its departure from Palestine, as still all-powerful and irreconcilably hostile. Britain was the invisible enemy standing behind the Arabs and encouraging them to continue their resistance to Israel. It was widely believed that Britain had deliberately provoked the RAF incident as part of her war of nerves against Israel and in order to demonstrate to the Arabs that if the armistice talks failed, she would be prepared to lend all out support for a renewed Arab war effort. Even when the talks got under way in Rhodes, the Israeli leaders were seriously concerned with the danger of British military involvement and British moves to reactivate the Transjordanian or the Iraqi fronts. Ben-Gurion in particular was certain that London was weaving dark plots to maim or even strangle Israel, and his hatred of Bevin knew no limits. Years later, during a visit to England, he sought out Bevin's burial place and stamped on the grave.[2]

---

[2] Ben-Gurion's diary, 11, 12, and 16 Jan. 1949; Bar-Zohar, *Ben-Gurion*, iii. 872 f.

Bevin himself gave a rather different account of British aims in a memorandum to the Cabinet:

We have not opposed the creation of a Jewish state and, by supporting the Bernadotte proposals, we recognized that the existence of such a state was an accomplished fact. Our policy has been based on the desire that the state would be set up as soon as possible in reasonably homogeneous territory and in such a way as not to cause a continuation of chaos in the Middle East, i.e., we have sought a settlement including the existence of a Jewish state in which the Arabs could reasonably acquiesce and which they will not bend all their energies to undo. We have made it clear that we will recognize and establish normal relations with the Jewish state as soon as it is properly set up with defined frontiers.[3]

This was undoubtedly the best possible construction that could be placed on Britain's policy towards Palestine, yet it does faithfully convey the essential pragmatism of that policy. Britain's aim was not to sabotage the armistice talks, but to keep up the pressure on Israel and redress the balance in favour of the Arabs. The guiding line for Britain was to make the most of a bad case and to safeguard as far as possible her own vital interests in the area.

American influence was brought to bear to end the war of nerves waged by Britain against Israel. The British were urged to close the RAF incident, to take positive steps to liquidate hostilities in the Middle East, and to abstain from hindering Israel's negotiations with Egypt. A significant shift had taken place in America's attitude to Israel, making the former increasingly wary of being manœuvred into underwriting Britain's position in the area. The American joint chiefs of staff had come to view Israel as an independent state and a military power in the Middle East second only to Turkey. It was hoped that the United States, as a result of its support of Israel, might gain strategic advantage in the Middle East that would offset the effects of the decline of British power in that area.[4] Too close an association with Britain was liable to cause friction and loss of influence in Israel. Some sort of a balance had thus come into being by the time the armistice talks began, with Britain backing the Arabs and America backing Israel.

The formal talks were held on the island of Rhodes, which had the merit of being neutral and isolated yet within easy reach of all the Middle Eastern capitals. Over the proceedings presided Dr Ralph Bunche, the distinguished member of the United Nations Secretariat

---

[3] 'Palestine', memorandum by the secretary of state for foreign affairs, 15 Jan. 1949, CP (49) 10, PRO.

[4] Kenneth W. Condit, *The History of the Joint Chiefs of Staff*, vol. ii, *1947–1949* (Washington, DC: Historical Division, Joint Secretariat, Joint Chiefs of Staff, 1976), 108 f. Record Group 218, Records of the United States Joint Chiefs of Staff, NA.

who had been Count Bernadotte's principal assistant. One wing of the spacious Hotel des Roses was used by Dr Bunche and his staff as their headquarters and living accommodation. The other wing was reserved for the Israeli and Egyptian delegations, with the former occupying one floor and the latter the floor immediately above. It was a perfect setting for negotiations and informal contacts, with all the participants gathered under one roof.

Dr Ralph Bunche, with his impressive range of skills and talents, proved to be a perfect mediator. A black American and a former professor of government at Harvard University, he was bright, articulate, and immensely resourceful. Unlike Count Bernadotte he was also a realist who not only preached but also practised the doctrine of 'one thing at a time'. After Egypt had broken the ice, Transjordan and Lebanon informed Bunche that they too were ready to join in the negotiations, but he replied that they would have to wait until the agreement between Israel and Egypt had been concluded. No one grasped more clearly than he that separate negotiations between Israel and each of the Arab states were the condition for success. As a draftsman and a conjurer of compromise formulas, Bunche had a talent that verged on genius. When the parties had reached an understanding, he could record it in clear and incisive prose. Difficult issues on which no agreement could be reached he would circumvent with vague formulations which each party could interpret in its own way.

Personal charm and a sense of humour were also great assets to Bunche in carrying out his duty as a mediator. But he knew when to be gentle and mollifying, when to be firm and uncompromising and when it paid to be hectoring and intimidating. Dr Walter Eytan, the head of the Israeli delegation, relates that Bunche had the pleasant notion of ordering from a local manufacturer two sets of the decorated ceramic plates for which Rhodes is famous. Each member of the two delegations and of his own staff was to receive such a plate, inscribed 'Rhodes Armistice Talks 1949' as a memento. At one point they floundered in what seemed insuperable difficulties. Dr Bunche took them to his room and opened a chest of drawers. 'Have a look at these lovely plates!' he said. 'If you reach agreement, each of you will get one to take home—if you don't I'll break them over your heads!'[5]

The negotiations between Israel and Egypt lasted six weeks. The advantage enjoyed by Israel by virtue of her victory in the war and military control over most the Negev was offset to some extent by the force of the UN resolutions that worked in Egypt's favour. The main

---

[5] Walter Eytan, *The First Ten Years: A Diplomatic History of Israel* (London: Weidenfeld and Nicolson, 1958), 27–31. See also Saadia Touval, *The Peace Brokers: Mediators in the Arab-Israeli Conflict, 1948–1979* (Princeton: University Press, 1982), ch. 3.

bones of contention were the Gaza Strip, Beersheba, Bir Asluj, El Auja, the armistice demarcation line, and the level of forces in the northern Negev. On some of these issues the Israeli delegation was internally divided, the military representatives led by General Yadin feeling that the government's position was too accommodating and the Foreign Ministry representatives led by Dr Eytan warning that the government's line was not flexible enough. Parallel to the military talks there were informal discussions between the Egyptian political advisers and Elias Sasson in which mutual trust was swiftly established and thorny problems found their solution. These talks went well beyond the technical issues relating to the armistice and dealt with broader political questions such as Israel's relations with Egypt and the other Arab states.

On February 24 the armistice agreement formally terminating the state of belligerency between Israel and Egypt was signed. Both sides had to move a long way from their opening position to make this agreement possible. Israel had to agree to Egyptian military presence in the Gaza Strip, to the release of the Egyptian brigade from Faluja, and to the demilitarization of El Auja. Despite these concessions, the agreement carried significant gains for the Israeli side. On the military plane it secured Israel's control over the northern Negev and left her freedom of action to capture the southern Negev. On the political plane, it strengthened Israel's international position and helped to establish her credentials for membership of the United Nations. The conclusion of an armistice with the largest of the Arab states paved the way to similar agreements with the other Arab states and gave rise to the hope—soon to be dashed—that armistice would lead to a peace settlement. It was because of these gains that Ben-Gurion regarded the signature of the agreement as the greatest event in a year of momentous events, after the establishment of the State of Israel and the IDF's victories on the battlefield.[6]

On the day the armistice agreement was signed, Elias Sasson summarized for Sharett the main points of his discussions with Abdel Monem Mostafa and Omar Lutfi, the political advisers to the Egyptian delegation. The Egyptians repeatedly stressed that for their country the military armistice was only the first step towards political peace and that Israel's observance of the agreement would therefore constitute an important test of her future intentions. Secondly, the Egyptians expressed the hope that the negotiations with Transjordan would deal only with the military problems. They did not rule out the annexation of the Arab part of Palestine to Transjordan, but they appeared to prefer the setting up of an independent Palestinian state with an

[6] *DFPI*, vol. iii, pp. xi–xviii.

indigenous leadership associated neither with the Husaynis or with Abdullah. No clear conception was advanced by the Egyptians on the future of the coastal strip round Gaza. Sasson gained the impression that they would have been glad to be rid of it altogether but were reluctant to hand it over either to Israel or to Abdullah. They were certainly receptive to Sasson's idea of demilitarizing the area with a joint Israeli–Egyptian guarantee of its security and internal autonomy for its inhabitants. On all these problems, the Egyptians invited constructive suggestions from Israel as a basis for future peace talks. Their main aim was to find an honourable way out of the Palestine imbroglio and they were therefore ready to explore any reasonable proposals.[7] And they hoped that Sasson would participate in all the armistice negotiations in Rhodes, continuing with the Lebanese and the Syrians the same role that he had performed so successfully with Egypt: building confidence in Arab hearts about Israel's good intentions.

Negotiations between Israel and Lebanon began on March 1 and lasted three weeks. In secret talks with Sasson the Lebanese had intimated that they could not be the first Arab state to negotiate directly with Israel but they expected to be the second one. The talks were held in Ras al Naqura, alternately in the customs house behind the Lebanese line and the police station on the Israeli side. The footpath linking the two buildings passed through a minefield but offered a magnificent view of the Mediterranean. The atmosphere was much more relaxed and informal than in Rhodes, with the UN chairman, Henri Vigier, nicknamed 'the French fox', playing a much less active role than Ralph Bunche. Privately the Lebanese said to the Israeli delegates that they were not really Arabs and that they had been dragged into the Palestine adventure against their will.

When the talks began, the Israeli army was occupying a narrow strip of Lebanese territory containing fourteen villages. It soon became clear that there was no fundamental problem as both sides expected that the international border would become the armistice line and that with the signature of the armistice agreement the Israeli army would withdraw from Lebanese territory. The negotiations nevertheless took three weeks to complete because Israel tried to make her withdrawal conditional on Syrian withdrawal from Lebanese territory and, much more importantly, from points that the Syrian army still held in Israel, along the Jordan River and on the east bank of the Sea of Galilee. The Israeli argument was that her entire northern border from Ras al Naqura to the Sea of Galilee constituted one geographical unit and that the principle of withdrawal to the international border should apply to all of it.

---

[7] Sasson to Sharett, 24 Feb. 1949, *DFPI*, iii. 271–3.

The rejection of this condition provoked bitter arguments between Israel's soldiers and diplomats. Lt.-Col. Mordechai Makleff, the chief of the Israeli delegation, refused to give way and protested that Sasson was too preoccupied with developing personal relations, speaking Arabic, and sending regards to his many Lebanese friends and that he did not understand how to negotiate with a powerful army behind him. To Ben-Gurion Makleff said that in twelve hours the Israeli army could reach Beirut and in seventy-two hours they could set up a Mapai government in Lebanon for him.[8] Ben-Gurion had his own pet scheme for annexing the area up to the Litani River and turning the rest of Lebanon into a Maronite state, but on this occasion he apparently made no reference to it. General Yadin complained to Dr Eytan that the Foreign Ministry did not understand the problems of the northern border and failed to grasp that the military problems were of paramount importance compared with the political ones.[9]

The UN observers also rejected the Israeli conditions; Bunche applied heavy pressure, threatening to blame Israel for the failure of the talks. In the end a high-level decision was taken to abandon the attempt at linkage between Israeli withdrawal from Lebanon and Syrian withdrawal from Israel. Ben-Gurion felt that an armistice agreement with Lebanon would strengthen Israel's international position, place her in a better position to negotiate with Transjordan, and facilitate a military operation in the Triangle should one become necessary. He also thought that it was in principle undesirable to link one Arab country with another, preferring to deal with each one separately.[10] Accordingly, he ordered that the armistice agreement with Lebanon be signed and the fourteen villages evacuated even though all Israel's conditions and proposals for minor border changes had been rejected.

Prelude to the Israel–Transjordan armistice talks

The armistice negotiations between Israel and Transjordan were dissimilar in almost every respect to the preceding negotiations with Egypt and Lebanon and the negotiations with Syria that were to follow. The character of these negotiations was decisively shaped by the unique features of the Transjordan front, by Iraqi control over part of the front, and by the special political relationship between King Abdullah and the Zionist movement.

[8] Interview with Mordechai Makleff, second meeting, 12 Oct. 1975 and third meeting, 16 Oct. 1975, Oral History Project, the Leonard Davis Institute of International Relations, the Hebrew University of Jerusalem. I am grateful to Mrs Makleff for giving me permission to see the transcripts of the interviews with her late husband.

[9] Yadin to Eytan, 11 Mar. 1949, *DFPI*, iii. 309.

[10] Ben-Gurion's diary, 15 Mar. 1949.

The Transjordanian front consisted of long and tortuous lines dissecting Arab and Jewish population centres. The northern part was held by the Iraqi army while some points in the south were held by Egyptian units. In Jerusalem the front line divided the city into two halves separating the two populations (see Map 11). Intertwined with the barbed wire was the heart and core of the Arab–Israeli conflict.

The truce lines at the end of the fighting diverged considerably from the UN partition lines, shaping a new military reality in Palestine: the western Galilee, Lydda, Ramle, Jaffa, parts of southern Judaea and the northern Negev, including Beersheba, all of which had been assigned to the Arab state, were now under Israeli control. The Gaza Strip was cut off from central Palestine and was held by the Egyptian army. Only in Samaria had the Iraqi army succeeded in capturing a small piece of territory that had been assigned to the Jewish state.

Two major military matters complicated the armistice negotiations between Israel and Transjordan: the Negev and the Iraqi front. The future of the southern Negev was a bone of contention between Israel and Transjordan. Transjordan, with very active British support, sought to incorporate this area in its domain, while Israeli leaders saw it as a vital part of their country and hoped to give effect to their claim by political means.

The question of the Iraqi front was rather more complicated. The truce line in this sector of the front left only a narrow Israeli corridor in the coastal plain, with the Iraqis holding Wadi Ara and the chain of hills overlooking Israeli territory to the east. From a security point of view, this line, which extended across part of the Hadera–Afuleh road, was extremely vulnerable. Consequently, ever since the fighting had come to an end, the Israelis had been looking for ways of changing the line. Various plans for military action had been considered but all were shelved on account of more urgent military operations in the Negev. Yet the defence experts held to their assessment that military action offered the only solution and repeated their fears that negotiations with King Abdullah would jeopardize Israel's military option.

During the preliminary armistice talks with King Abdullah's representatives in late December 1948 no substantive agreement of any kind had been reached because the starting points of the two sides were very different: the king wanted a settlement based on a combination of the UN partition plan with the Bernadotte plan while Israel maintained that the existing situation be taken as the basic foundation for the settlement.[11]

These preliminary talks were overtaken by the inauguration of the

[11] *DFPI*, iii. 20–4.

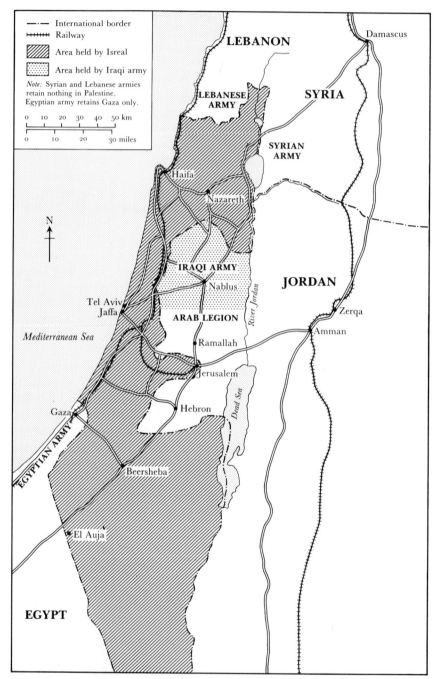

LEBANON

Damascus

SYRIA

**LEBANESE
ARMY**

**SYRIAN
ARMY**

N

Haifa

Nazareth

IRAQI ARMY

JORDAN

Nablus

Tel Aviv
Jaffa

ARAB LEGION

River Jordan

Zerqa

Amman

Mediterranean Sea

Ramallah

Jerusalem

Dead Sea

Gaza

Hebron

EGYPTIAN ARMY

Beersheba

El Auja

EGYPT

MAP 11   Situation at time of signing Rhodes armistice

Israeli–Egyptian armistice negotiations in Rhodes. Not wanting to be left out in the cold, Abdullah issued an invitation for further talks to pave the way for official negotiations. Elias Sasson was recalled from Rhodes and on January 16 he and Moshe Dayan, disguised in foreign uniforms, were driven by Col. Abdullah al-Tall to the winter palace at Shuneh. This meeting did not yield any tangible results but it enabled the king to convey to the Zionist leaders his sincere desire for peace talks and it provided them with some useful clues as to his thinking. He declared that he had no use for the Arab League, that he was determined to act alone, and that the fate of Palestine was a matter for discussion only between Israel and Transjordan. The British, he said, knew of his intentions and they not only raised no objections but were pressing him to begin armistice talks in Rhodes. In connection with the Israeli–Egyptian armistice talks Abdullah expressed the hope that the Egyptians would be made to withdraw altogether from Palestine. Sasson replied that he himself had just come from Rhodes, that the talks there were of a military nature, and that it was possible that the Egyptians would stay in Gaza. On hearing this the king grew rather anxious and urged his visitors in the strongest possible terms not to give Gaza to Egypt. He himself needed it as an outlet to the Mediterranean. 'Take it yourselves,' he said excitedly, 'give it to the devil, but do not let Egypt have it!' Before leaving the palace, Dr Shawkat as-Sati, the king's faithful physician, took Sasson on one side and told him to buy al-Tall and then everything would be all right.[12]

The subtle hint was well received by Sasson, who saw in Abdullah al-Tall a potentially valuable figure in furthering the Zionist cause on account of his senior position in the Arab Legion and his closeness to King Abdullah. It was with some difficulty, however, that Sasson persuaded Dayan to hand Tall what amounted to a bribe in return for help in securing the release of the 700 Israeli prisoners, most of them from the Etzion bloc and the Jewish Quarter of the Old City, held by the Arab Legion. An opportunity arose two weeks later when King Abdullah invited Sasson and 'the one-eye' for another talk and a sumptuous meal. On the way to the palace Sasson concentrated on winning Tall over. He said that if the king should agree to the release of the Israeli prisoners, he hoped that buses could be provided without delay to transport them to Israel and that the Israelis would meet the expenses, whatever they came to. Tall remarked that it would be more convenient if payment could be made in British currency. At this point Sasson signalled to Dayan who handed over the money. After pocketing the money Tall added that there was no need to trouble His Majesty

---

[12] Sharett to Elath, 18 Jan. 1949, *DFPI*, iii. 343 f.; Ben-Gurion's diary, 16 and 17 Jan. 1949; Dayan, *Story of My Life*, 107 f.; Tall, *The Palestine Tragedy*, 460–2.

with the operational and logistical details as he himself would make all the necessary arrangements.[13]

King Abdullah and Dr as-Sati received the party graciously in the palace. The king began the meeting by stating that all the Arab governments, Transjordan included, had decided to send representatives for armistice talks in Rhodes but he himself preferred to negotiate separately and favoured prior agreement between Tall and Dayan as well as direct contact during the negotiations. Sasson then raised the question of the Iraqi front and Iraqi representation in Rhodes. The king replied that he was unable to force Iraq to withdraw its army from Palestine, but that he would strive to remove the Iraqis from the border zones and replace them with Transjordanian police and that he himself would assume responsibility for the remaining Iraqi troops. While expressing sympathy for the king's predicament, Sasson made it clear that they would raise the matter in Rhodes and insist on total Iraqi evacuation. The king was determined to start negotiations for a peace treaty immediately after the conclusion of the armistice. This would be done publicly, not in secret, in Jerusalem, without UN involvement, and with an opening ceremony at his palace in Shuneh. Iraq, Saudi Arabia, and Yemen had already given their consent, he claimed, to the opening of political talks with Israel, Lebanon's reply was expected to be positive, while Syria and Egypt would have no choice but to agree. Britain, he continued, was in full accord with his line but had advised him to insist in the peace negotiations on two points which he was unable to divulge. Sasson assumed that these points related to the southern Negev and pressed for freedom of movement to Eilat as part of the armistice. Abdullah was non-committal, holding out a vague prospect of an amicable arrangement in the future.

Towards the end of the conference, the king inquired about the progress of the Israeli–Egyptian armistice talks. He expressed the insistent hope that Israel would not allow the Egyptians to stay in any part of Palestine. When Sasson pointed out that Egyptian police forces might be allowed to stay in Gaza to ensure internal security until the final peace settlement, he retorted that the Egyptians had no business being in Gaza any more than the Syrians in north Galilee. The ejection of the Egyptian troops from Gaza would serve to liquidate Egypt's conquest and the mufti's government. During this part of the talk, the king begged to inform Ben-Gurion that Transjordan saw Gaza as her only outlet to the Mediterranean. He realized the difficulty of recovering Jaffa and therefore counted on Israeli sympathy for his needs in Gaza. To keep this hope alive, Sasson said that Ben-

[13] Shmuel Segev, article on Eliahu Sasson, *Maariv*, 22 Oct. 1978; interview with Moshe Sasson.

Gurion constantly bore in mind Transjordan's interest in Gaza and that it was very probable that a satisfactory arrangement could be worked out.

During dinner the conversation turned on events in the various capitals of the world. The king was pleased that the Israeli elections had disclosed such slight communist strength, adding that Transjordan had no need for elections as he ruled and Parliament carried out his will. There were endless expressions of goodwill and the king sent his respects to President Chaim Weizmann, David Ben-Gurion, and Moshe Sharett. Against Golda Meir, however, he had nursed ill-feelings ever since their last meeting before the war. According to his version, by presenting him with a choice between submitting to an ultimatum delivered by a woman and going to war, she had forced him to join with the other Arab states in the invasion of Israel. When he was told that Golda Meir had been posted as Israel's minister in Moscow, he remarked with a twinkle in his eye: *Halooha hoonak, halooha hoonak!* (leave her there, leave her there).[14]

Sasson was so well versed in Arab customs that he did not feel out of place in the entourage of the royal court. One of the rules was to meander at leisure over pleasant irrelevancies before getting down to brass tacks. King Abdullah played chess, wrote poetry, and his spoken Arabic was elegant, even ornate. Whenever a visitor came to the court he enjoyed displaying his wisdom and wit by posing riddles to his advisers on Arab literature and history. Another rule of etiquette required them to pretend that they did not know the answers so that the king could answer the questions himself.

Moshe Dayan, whose command of Arabic was inadequate and who was mystified by this elaborate protocol, lost his patience and started nudging his colleague to come to the point. Sasson ignored Dayan's elbow and after midnight whispered in his ear: 'When I get up to go, follow me.' Dayan was dumbfounded by this failure to even mention the subject they had been instructed to press. Sasson, accompanied by the king, walked towards the door, and when they reached the door the king embraced him. At this point Sasson slid his hand under the king's silk sash. Abdullah gasped because bedouin tradition dictated that if a man placed his hand under the sash of a shaikh, the shaikh had to grant his wish. Sasson's victim raised both his hands in a gesture of surrender and said: 'Ya Elias, please ask what is possible.' Dayan looked on incredulously, wondering whether Sasson had taken leave of his senses. When Sasson pleaded for the release of the 700 prisoners of war, the

---

[14] Sasson to Sharett, 1 Feb. 1949, *DFPI*, iii. 344–7; Sharett to Eban, 2 Feb. 1949, 2453/2, ISA; Ben-Gurion's diary, 1 Feb. 1949; Dayan, *Story of My Life*, 107 f.; Tall, *The Palestine Tragedy*, 464 f., 504.

king turned to al-Tall and asked for his opinion. Al-Tall replied that some of the prisoners were women and children and nothing but a burden for the Arab Legion. He also assured the king that the British would have no objection to the freeing of the prisoners. *Taib!* (good), said Abdullah. 'Let them go and may they be blessed.' On hearing these words, Sasson removed his hand from the king's sash and the two men embraced. Most of the prisoners were released the next day.[15]

Abdullah also contacted the Iraqi regent and arranged to meet him for a discussion on Palestine on February 2 at 'H3', the last pumping station of the Iraqi Petroleum Company on the Iraqi side of the border with Transjordan. The royal party from Amman included Fawzi el-Mulki, the Defence Minister. From Baghdad came Abd al-Illah, Prime Minister Nuri al-Said, Defence Minister Shakir al-Wadi, and the chief of staff, Salih Saib al-Juburi. Abdullah's first request was that the Iraqi forces should hand over their first line of defence to the Arab Legion in order to put an end to the clashes between the Iraqis and the Zionists. He also asked to be given permission to negotiate an armistice with the Zionists on behalf of Iraq. Nuri agreed to start withdrawing the Iraqi troops gradually but he was evasive about empowering Abdullah to represent Iraq in the armistice talks. While raising no objection to Abdullah accepting Bunche's invitation to start armistice talks at once, Nuri stated that Iraq would reply to this invitation by saying that she would follow the arrangements to be agreed by the other four states.

The Iraqis found Abdullah anxious to declare himself as early as possible king of Arab Palestine and to start negotiations for a final settlement. They urged him to defer both declaration and negotiations in the hope of getting a united Arab front for the negotiations. Abdullah did not tell them of his contacts with the Jews. They guessed that there had been such contacts since he informed them that the Jews were asking him for an assurance that Iraqi forces would not attack.

Abdullah's second request was that Transjordan be allowed to set up a civil administration in the parts of Samaria occupied by the Iraqi army. Realizing that this request was part of Abdullah's policy of creeping annexation, Wadi and Juburi said that this area was unsettled and insisted on keeping it in Iraqi hands. Despite this understanding at H3, Abdullah and his government subsequently sent numerous letters pressing for the creation of a Transjordanian civil administration and the appointment of district commissioners for Nablus, Jenin, and Tulkarem. The letters claimed that the Palestinian leaders themselves favoured a union with Transjordan, but the suspicious Iraqis doubted

<hr>

[15] Shmuel Segev, *Maariv*, 22 Oct. 1978; Kurzman, *Genesis 1948*, 690–2.

this claim and pledged to respect the wishes of the Palestinian majority.[16]

Although Abdullah had nothing very new or important to report as a result of the meeting at H3, he sent his doctor to the Israelis with a long message. Dr as-Sati and Colonel Tall met in Jerusalem with Moshe Dayan and Yaacov Shimoni, Sasson's deputy, who had been and remained a fervent supporter of the secret alliance with Transjordan. The message covered familiar ground and was couched in very general terms. Basically it outlined an armistice based on the existing lines but envisaged Israeli concessions on Lydda and Ramle and implied Transjordanian retention of the southern tip of the Negev. The message also said that Abdullah would be responsible for the Iraqi front, without indicating whether he had obtained power of attorney or whether the Iraqi forces were going to withdraw. At the end of the meeting Dayan therefore suggested that if the king wanted to proceed quickly to official talks, he should provide a map showing the exact front-line in the southern Negev and a letter from the Iraqi government authorizing him to negotiate in its name.[17]

Whether deliberate or unintentional, Abdullah's vagueness caused the Israeli leaders not to take him seriously. They suspected that these contacts were merely a public relations exercise as Abdullah was not master of the situation in relation either to Britain or to his own government. For some time Ben-Gurion had been having doubts about the practical utility of these exchanges. Abdullah reminded him, he said, of the loquacious Zionist politician and journalist Nahum Sokolov: 'he speaks pleasantly but without a grasp of the issues and without authority'.[18] On the other hand, Israel was in no hurry to begin armistice talks with Transjordan. Only by military action, it was felt, could she secure an outlet to the Red Sea and foil British designs. The tactic adopted by the Israelis, therefore, was to go slow on the talks with Abdullah and to expedite the negotiations with Egypt.[19] At Rhodes, Gen. Yigael Yadin and Lt.-Col. Yitzhak Rabin were already planning what was soon to become known as Operation Uvda (*Fait Accompli*) to extend Israel's control over the Negev down to Eilat. Yadin privately informed Gen. Seif el-Din, the head of the Egyptian delegation, that Israel would only agree to the demilitarization of El Auja on condition that the reduced forces zone would extend to the Beersheba–Eilat line and not apply to the triangle east of that line. Seif el-Din understood

[16] Tall, *The Tragedy of Palestine*, 465 f.; Juburi, *The Palestine Misfortune*, 368–71; Trevelyan (Baghdad) to FO, 4 Feb. 1949, FO 371/75331, PRO.
[17] Shimoni to Ben-Gurion and Sharett, 14 Feb. 1949, and Sharett to Eytan, 15 Feb. 1949, *DFPI*, iii. 349–54; Ben-Gurion's diary, 14 Feb. 1949.
[18] Ben-Gurion's diary, 26 Jan. 1949.
[19] Sharett to Eytan and Sasson, 15 Feb. 1949, *DFPI*, iii. 353 f.

perfectly that this arrangement was directed against Transjordan, and only after he agreed to it did Ben-Gurion authorize Yadin to sign the armistice agreement with Egypt.[20]

Operation Fait Accompli

The official armistice talks between Israel and Transjordan opened in Rhodes under the chairmanship of Dr Ralph Bunche on March 4. The head of the Israeli delegation was Reuven Shiloah. The other members of the delegation were Lt.-Col. Moshe Dayan, Lt.-Col. Dan Laner, and the legal adviser of the Foreign Ministry, Shabtai Rosenne. After a while, Yaacov Shimoni also joined the delegation. Two other Israeli officers, Yehoshafat Harkabi and Shaul Ramati, were attached to the delegation but without becoming official members.

The Israeli delegation went to Rhodes with a set of clear and detailed instructions approved by the Cabinet. Israel's position had already been presented in the preliminary talks but it was now elaborated and defined much more precisely. The principal guidelines were the moving of the front-line in the Iraqi sector in Samaria eastward; adjustment of the front-line south-east of Wadi Ara so that the entire Afuleh–Hadera road would be under Israeli control; evacuation of the Latrun salient; fixing the international border as the armistice line in the Araba; in Jerusalem—free access to Mount Scopus, to the cemetery in Mount Olives, and to the Wailing Wall; use of the railway line to Jerusalem; free access to Naharayim and the reopening of the electricity-generating station; resumption of the water supply to the Dead Sea potash works and free movement in the Dead Sea for its sailing vessels, as well as transport of its produce in Israeli vehicles to Jerusalem. The delegation was instructed not to agree to any reciprocal concessions, whether in territorial exchange or the return of the refugees, without express orders, as well as to ensure the inclusion of a clause in the armistice agreement clarifying that Israel's signature did not constitute recognition of Transjordanian sovereignty over territories west of the Jordan.[21]

The Transjordanian delegation to Rhodes was headed by Col. Ahmed Sidki el-Jundi and included Lt.-Col. Muhammad al-Ma'ayita, Capt. Ali Abu Nuwar, Maj. Radi Hindawi, and the legal adviser, Riad al-Mufleh. These men were all East Bankers with very little understanding of land values, water resources, or conditions in the villages on the West Bank. Tawfiq Abul Huda had resisted the inclusion of Palestinians in the delegation with the argument that the talks were of a

[20] Interview with Gen. Yigael Yadin.   [21] *DFPI*, vol. iii, pp. xxiii f., 358–60.

military nature and it was not proper to raise political claims until the final settlement had been reached.[22]

In Rhodes it soon became clear that these relatively low-ranking army officers lacked the authority to decide on major issues and were unequal to the task of conducting complex armistice negotiations. They looked helpless and lost and kept referring every minor question back to their capital. So inferior were these East Bankers to all the other Arab negotiating teams as to give rise to the suspicion that they had deliberately been chosen to ensure that no serious negotiations took place in Rhodes and that everything was referred back to Amman where British representatives could have their say.[23] King Abdullah after all was an autocratic ruler who believed in keeping a close watch on developments and keeping political decisions firmly in his own hands. Now that he was facing one of the most critical decisions of his career, it was all the more important that he personally should remain in charge. It was not long before Abdullah indicated that he could not rely on his delegation to negotiate on his behalf and that he wanted to conduct the negotiations himself, privately and secretly at his winter palace at Shuneh. The tragicomic talks in Rhodes were to provide an official façade while the real bargaining was being carried on elsewhere. Only the king's closest confidants were to know; the rest of the world was to go on watching the puppet show in Rhodes.[24]

The show lasted a month and was divided into four phases: 4–11 March, 12–18 March, 18–23 March, and 24 March–3 April.

The opening session in Rhodes raised a storm in a teacup. It had been agreed with Bunche beforehand that he would formally present the leaders to one another, but when he came into the conference room Colonel Jundi was already seated and he declined to stand up and shake hands with Shiloah. It soon transpired that there had been no malevolent intent but a simple misunderstanding. Yet Sharett pompously cabled Shiloah: 'Notify Bunche that if the Jordanians continue to behave in this boorish manner, we shall stop the negotiations and announce that they will be renewed only after we are satisfied that they have learned the elementary lessons in civilized deportment.'[25]

The first phase of the deliberations on the armistice lines was immediately plunged into a crisis by the unfolding of Operation *Fait Accompli*. This operation, designed to capture the southern Negev, was conducted, in accordance with Ben-Gurion's precept of one war at a time, between 5 and 10 March. Ben-Gurion was afraid of upsetting the armistice agreement with Egypt, afraid of wrecking the armistice talks

[22] Majali, *My Memoirs*, 90.
[24] Eytan, *The First Ten Years*, 38.
[23] Ben-Gurion's diary, 7 Mar. 1949.
[25] Dayan, *Story of My Life*, 109 f.

with Transjordan, afraid of provoking all-out war with the Arab Legion, and, above all, afraid of a direct clash with the British forces stationed in Aqaba. Strict central control and severe political constraints were accordingly maintained throughout the operation. The plan was that two brigades would depart from Beersheba towards Eilat in a pincer movement, one going through the middle of the Negev mountains and the other through Wadi Araba along the border with Transjordan. The order to the brigade commanders was not to engage in any fighting and in the event of encountering enemy forces, to break off contact. Yigal Allon's creative interpretation of this order from HQ, for the benefit of his two brigade commanders, was that they should defend themselves all the way to Eilat! The first brigade did not encounter any enemy forces but the second brigade came across Arab Legion units who tried to block its advance. The most serious clash occurred in Gharandal. The Arab Legion also took up positions in Ras al-Naqb, near the Egyptian–Israeli border and near Umm Rashrash (Eilat). But on orders from Glubb Pasha these positions were evacuated during the night between 9 and 10 March, and on that day the Israeli brigades reached Eilat.[26] (See Map 12.)

Amman made frantic attempts to halt the Israeli advance by diplomatic means, through an official complaint submitted to Bunche, a personal message addressed by Abdullah to Sharett, and through the British government. The latter communicated the Transjordanian protests to the Israeli government and even threatened to open fire on the IDF forces if they attacked the British forces stationed in Aqaba or crossed the border in that area. Abdullah's message of March 8 warned that the IDF forces were liable to clash with his units at any moment and begged Israel to refrain from further advance towards Aqaba pending a settlement in Rhodes. It also pointed to the contradiction between Sasson's nice letter from Paris and Israel's military actions and asked for an explanation. Sharett replied that he did not understand His Majesty's concern and assured him that Israel's forces had not crossed and had no intention of crossing the border. If the king ordered the Arab Legion to refrain from crossing the border into Israel, no clash would occur. Sharett ended with the hope that the armistice negotiations would be successfully concluded, based on the territorial integrity of both parties.[27]

Sasson was not surprised to learn that the king felt that the behaviour of the IDF contradicted his promises. The king, Sasson explained to Sharett, was under the impression that when the time came it would not be difficult for the two 'friends' to find a common language; he did

---

[26] Ben-Gurion's diary, 3 and 11 Mar. 1949; Cohen, *By Light and in Darkness*, 257–69.
[27] *DFPI*, iii. 372 f.

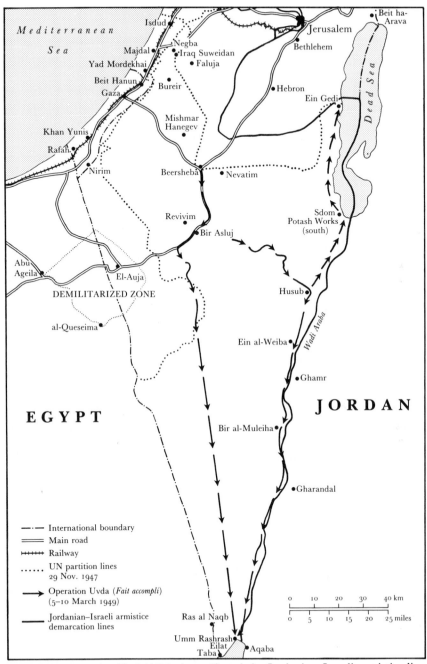

MAP 12   Operation Uvda (*Fait Accompli*) and the Jordanian–Israeli armistice line
(south)

not realize that the negotiations with Transjordan would be more difficult and complex than with any of the other Arab countries. At times he forgets his 'allies' and their intrigues. Sasson's advice was to treat the king fairly, to be patient with him, and to explain things to him in the language of friends seeking the common good and not in the language of politicians insisting only on their own interests. This was what they themselves had led Abdullah to expect in the past and Sasson had no doubt that continuing to behave in this gentlemanly fashion was a sure way of attaining their objectives.[28]

Although Abdullah was clearly disturbed by the new patterns of Israeli behaviour, he did not break off the talks. The Israelis' tactic of delaying signature of the cease-fire agreement until they had completed their advance to the Gulf of Aqaba had worked. Operation *Fait Accompli* had indeed created new facts which neither the UN nor Transjordan nor Britain had the power to change. On March 11, a general cease-fire agreement between Israel and Transjordan was signed in Rhodes. UN observers were sent to the Araba region and shortly thereafter certified the location of the Israeli positions in the southern Negev.

Nor was this the only example of the coercive diplomacy practised by Israel during the armistice talks. The ripples created by the Aqaba affair had not died down before the Israeli leaders once again spoke to Abdullah in the language of politicians with a victorious army behind them. The second phase of the armistice talks was confined essentially to the Transjordanian front since the position of the Iraqi front remained unclear. The Iraqis refused to send representatives to Rhodes or to let the Transjordanians negotiate on their behalf. It was a question of principle for them, as well as one of national honour and prestige, not to enter into any negotiations with the Zionists and not to recognize the Zionist state. The Iraqis did agree, on March 10, that the Arab Legion should take over their forward positions and that the hand-over should be completed within 15 days, freeing the Iraqi army to return home with its honour and commitment to the Palestine cause intact. But the Transjordanian government seemed hesitant about taking over the Iraqi front stage by stage and Glubb Pasha seemed to be dragging his feet. Glubb had never favoured replacing the Iraqi army in the Triangle for fear that his own little army would become too thinly stretched. He would have preferred the Iraqis to sign an armistice agreement like all the other Arab countries and to stay put and he regretted that Abdullah had asked the Iraqis to retire quietly from the field in favour of the Arab Legion. These prevarications gave rise to the suspicion, forcefully expressed to General Juburi by Fadal al-Jamali,

---

[28] Sasson to Sharett, 10 Mar. 1949, *DFPI*, iii. 377 f.

the new prime minister, that there was a Transjordanian–Zionist plot afoot to force Iraq into negotiations with the Zionists.[29]

In Amman there were also fears that the radical pro-Palestinian elements in the Iraqi army might get out of hand and turn against the Transjordanian regime for its failure to stand fast against the enemy. Having to conduct military operations under severe political constraints had a frustrating and a radicalizing effect on the Iraqi army. Regardless of rank, many Iraqi officers were of the opinion that they were capable of accomplishing the mission for which they had been sent to Palestine but that they were being made to fight with one hand tied behind their backs as a result of political interference from above. Some of the younger Iraqi officers, their political conciousness heightened by the experience at the front, indeed began to talk among themselves about the need to get rid of the British and to replace the regimes subservient to the British in Baghdad and Amman.[30] Some of these officers were also under the influence of the Egyptians and the Syrians but General Juburi knew of nothing to indicate that there was an actual plan to overthrow either the Transjordanian or the Iraqi branches of the Hashemite monarchy.[31]

However, on one occasion when Colonel Goldie was in temporary charge of the Arab Legion, he received a message from Glubb saying that their allies, which could only mean the Iraqis, were plotting something, such as a sudden rush with armoured cars to Amman. Glubb did not believe that there was a serious threat but suggested that Goldie might take some precautions. After consultation with Sir Alec Kirkbride, Goldie moved a battalion to guard the entrance to Amman. It was a false alarm but one which was symptomatic of mutual mistrust between the British and the Transjordanians on the one hand and the Iraqis on the other and of the prevalent fear that the Iraqis would stab their allies in the back.[32]

In the more serene setting of the Hotel des Roses, the negotiations dealt with the Israeli demands for including the Latrun salient on their side of the line, for free access to Mount Scopus, for reactivating the railway to Jerusalem, and with the Transjordanian demand for free access to Bethlehem. But in the protracted deliberations on these subjects, Bunche was unable to induce the two delegations to soften their stand. He tried to break the deadlock with a compromise proposal

[29] Juburi, *The Palestine Misfortune*, 372–6.
[30] 'Historical Memories of the Revolution of July 14, 1958,' *Aafaq Arabiya* (Baghdad), 1985; G. C. Littler, acting consul general, Basra, to the chargé d'Affaires, British embassy, Baghdad, 26 Aug. 1948, FO 371/68451, PRO.
[31] Mouayad al-Windawi's interview with Salih Saib al-Juburi, Baghdad, 12 Sept. 1986. I am grateful to Mr al-Windawi for conducting this interview on my behalf.
[32] Interview with Col. Desmond Goldie.

of his own which called for the demilitarization of Jerusalem, and joint supervision, with UN participation, of the contested roads and railway. Both sides rejected this proposal. The Israeli delegates regarded it as a ploy to take advantage of the dispute between the parties in order to put into effect the UN resolutions on Jerusalem. They concluded that it would be preferable to deal with Jerusalem and its environs in direct talks outside Rhodes and to sign an armistice agreement based on the lines of the 'sincere truce' that Dayan had previously concluded with al-Tall. The Transjordanians concurred and this item was consequently removed from the agenda. The discussions now turned to the reduction and deployment of forces and other military matters.[33]

Upon completion of Operation *Fait Accompli*, the Israelis received intelligence that the Iraqi army had agreed to hand over its forward positions to the Arab Legion. King Abdullah had assumed all along that Israel would welcome the transfer. It was Elias Sasson who had first urged him to take over the Iraqi positions. But now Israel seized on the proposed transfer as a convenient excuse to press for the modifications she had long desired in the Sharon and Wadi Ara lines. In the General Staff, plans for capturing the Triangle, or the whole of the West Bank, including the Old City of Jerusalem, were under constant discussion. The generals were convinced that the strategic value of controlling central Palestine up to the Jordan far outweighed any temporary inconvenience and diplomatic embarrassment that another military operation would entail. Three brigades were moved to the central front and preparations for military action began in earnest.[34]

At this point, however, Israel's political leaders paused to consider the possible consequences and international repercussions. They feared that an operation, such as the one insistently advocated by General Allon for taking over the whole West Bank in three days, might sway world public opinion against Israel and against Israeli membership of the United Nations, as well as aggravating the already enormous Arab refugee problem. They were much less ready, therefore, to tempt fate in the Triangle than they had been in the Negev. Ben-Gurion felt that with Israel still in the dock over its advance to Aqaba, it would be a mistake to launch another major military operation. He was especially reluctant to push Britain too far and to risk her re-entry into Palestine and a possible clash with the IDF. Bevin, he assumed, was looking for an opportunity to take revenge on Israel for the humiliating defeats inflicted on him in El Arish and in Eilat, and a premature move could provide him with just the opportunity he was looking for.[35] The

[33] *DFPI*, vol. iii, pp. xxiv f.   [34] Interviews with Gen. Yigael Yadin and Moshe Carmel.
[35] Ben-Gurion's diary, 14 Mar. 1949.

question was how to obtain the vital piece of territory without fighting for it.

In the end it was decided to use the preparations for what was code-named Operation Shin-Tav-Shin as an instrument of coercive diplomacy. The three brigades were ostentatiously shuffled around in broad daylight as part of the new war of nerves being waged against Transjordan. The Israeli government protested to Bunche that the contemplated redeployment of forces on the Iraqi front would be a violation of the existing truce and that it reserved all its rights. Israel was now in fact claiming that she had no less of a right to occupy the positions to be vacated by the Iraqi army than the Arab Legion. And the well-publicized manœuvres near the Iraqi front were designed to leave no doubt in Abdullah's mind that if Israel failed to secure these positions by diplomacy, she would take them by force.[36]

With constant reports of fresh Israeli advances, the stone-walling in Rhodes, the Iraqis beginning to pull back, and the 11,000-strong Arab Legion facing an army ten times bigger, Abdullah's anxiety grew too deep to contain. On March 14, he sent an urgent message to Foreign Minister Sharett: 'It is reported that you have declared that an Israeli army unit has reached the shore of the Gulf of Aqaba in territory considered to be included in Palestine. That, I know, is correct. It is further reported that in your declaration you went on to say that any part of Palestine which is evacuated by the Iraqi army will be captured by Israeli forces to ensure defence stability. Is this true?'

On the next day, Walter Eytan sent a reply in the name of the Israeli government:

Foreign Minister Sharett is abroad and I am acting in his place. I have the honor to thank you in his name for your kind letter, which was received yesterday. As to the evacuation of Iraqi forces from the areas they now hold and their replacement by Arab Legion forces, we have already notified the UN acting Mediator that we regard this step as a flagrant violation of the truce and we shall not recognize it so long as our agreement has not been secured. However, we have no intention of capturing this territory nor threatening its Arab inhabitants, since it is our wish to reach a peace agreement in this area too. It is our view that a discussion of this matter falls outside the purview of the armistice talks at Rhodes, but we are prepared to recall Colonel Moshe Dayan from Rhodes for a talk with the King's representative in Jerusalem on the arrangements acceptable to both parties for the territory to be evacuated by the Iraqi forces. We shall be grateful to Your Majesty if you would let us know if it is your wish that we invite Colonel Dayan for such a talk in Jerusalem. We are convinced that this will be agreeable to you, for you, no less than we, would prefer a solution by peaceful means.[37]

[36] Interview with Gen. Yigael Yadin.
[37] *DFPI*, iii. 417 f.; Dayan, *Story of My Life*, 111 f.; Tall, *The Palestine Tragedy*, 451–4.

Abdullah agreed and Dayan said goodbye to the Hotel des Roses and to the butterflies in the woods to return to dark-of-night talks in the no-man's-land of Mandelbaum, the gentleman whose name and war-ravaged house between the Transjordan and Israeli lines had entered history as a unique gate of Jerusalem. When Dayan met Abdullah al-Tall on March 18, he felt no need for lengthy preliminaries or for gentle treading around the subject. He told Tall directly that Israel wanted the Wadi Ara defile and the heights overlooking the narrow coastal plain. Tall replied that in his view such a concession was not possible both because of the stand of the Iraqi army and because of public opinion at home. In that case, said Dayan, there were two alternatives: either the Transjordanians would not replace the Iraqis at all, or they would reach an agreement with Israel which would be implemented gradually to avoid publicity. Tall favoured a secret agreement but reserved the final decision for the king.

On the following day the king sent the following message to Walter Eytan: 'I know you will agree with me on the question of our taking over the Iraqi sector of the front, since this arises out of the talks I had with Mr Sasson and Col. Dayan. I myself talked to the Iraqis when I met them at the border and persuaded them that I would take over the entire front. If you and Dayan could meet me, I hope the results would be what we all desire.'

Dayan asked the General Staff for an interpreter who spoke good literary Arabic and for a map and promised that in talking to the king they would not 'ask for a mountain in order to settle for a mouse' in the manner of Oriental hagglers but would tell him what they want and stand by it. Maj. Yehoshafat Harkabi ('Fati'), a staff officer who was to become the Director of Military Intelligence and later a leading expert on the Arab–Israeli conflict, accompanied Dayan to the meeting at Shuneh as the interpreter. 'The meeting did not last long', wrote Dayan in his memoirs. 'We greeted, dined, explained and departed at 10 p.m., leaving the King to digest our proposals—which were just, though by no means modest—and to consult with his ministers.'[38]

For Harkabi, whose Arabic was fully equal to the occasion, this was the first meeting with an Arab potentate and it made a strong impression on him. What surprised him most was the ease with which Abdullah seemed prepared to grant Israel's demands. The huge stumbling-block he had expected turned out to be scarcely a pebble. From the mature vantage point of some thirty-five years after the event, Harkabi has conceded that the Israeli approach was crude and little more than a series of improvisations directed at seizing every possible extra bit of land. In fairness, he added, it may have been felt that

---

[38] Dayan, *Story of My Life*, 112 f.

favourable conditions would enhance the prospects of peace. The aim was to secure as favourable an armistice agreement as possible because it was believed that the terms of the final peace settlement would closely correspond to those of the temporary armistice agreement. This was in line with the basic Zionist conception that peace is not a goal in its own right but a function of the prevailing conditions. Hence the dynamic approach to negotiations, hence the preoccupation, verging on obsession, to do everything possible to gain more land and to improve Israel's strategic conditions.

Harkabi had nothing but praise for the way in which the 34-year-old Dayan presented Israel's demands for Wadi Ara and the ridge south-east of it. 'With the Iraqis', said Dayan, 'we are there as enemies. With you we shall be there as friends.' Not understanding precisely what was involved, Abdullah turned to Colonel Tall to ask for his opinion. *Ma'akul?* he asked—Is it reasonable? *Ma'akul*, replied Tall. And thus was reached the basic understanding that was eventually translated into detailed provisions in the armistice agreement. In his memoirs Abdullah al-Tall presents himself as the fervent supporter of Palestinian nationalism, as the only man who tried, and failed, to rescue the king from the clutches of the wily and rapacious Jews. But Harkabi testifies that at the meeting itself Tall was helpful and instrumental in promoting the accord.[39]

No doubt the British communication telling Abdullah that Great Britain did not regard her treaty obligations as extending to anything that might happen outside the borders of Transjordan itself also helped to place the king in a receptive frame of mind, as did the growing impatience of the Iraqis. In any case, the main point that emerged from the meeting was that he was willing, in return for Israel's consent to the Arab Legion replacing the Iraqis, to give her Wadi Ara, the ridge to the south-east of it, and the first line of hills on the north-west side of the Wadi. By agreeing specifically that Tulkarem and Kalkilya with their large civilian population would not be involved and would remain purely Arab areas, Dayan made it easier for the king to yield on the territory that was strategically vital for Israel. The king wanted the agreement to be kept secret and to include a cause for face-saving purposes in case the agreement ever leaked out, to the effect that Israel had handed over to Transjordan comparable areas elsewhere. He also preferred the agreement to be implemented in stages over a period of four to six months. Dayan indicated that in general the ideas propounded by the king seemed sound, and it was arranged that the following day Tall would obtain the consent of Glubb and also fly to

<hr />

[39] Interview with Yehoshafat Harkabi. For Tall's highly distorted account of the meeting, see *The Palestine Tragedy*, 454.

Beirut to inform the prime minister and the foreign minister of the king's tentative decision. Tall was to give Dayan the final word of approval by 6 p.m. on March 21, after consulting all these parties.[40]

Various meetings were hastily arranged with ministers, officials, and military commanders in Amman to discuss the latest developments. Although the strip to be surrendered included some of the richest land still in the possession of the Arabs, it was assumed that the object of the Israeli demand was strategic rather than economic. The sparing of Tulkarem and Kalkilya was greeted with a sigh of relief. Glubb calculated that the total area demanded by Israel was some 400 square kilometres, whereas the whole area defended by the Arab Legion and the Iraqi army amounted to some 6,000 square kilometres. The area to be ceded, therefore, represented just over 6 per cent of the whole. In response to the letter from the prime minister, Glubb replied that if the Israeli demands were rejected and hostilities were renewed, the Arab Legion would not be able to hold the line after the Iraqis had gone. Moreover, if war recommenced, the Israelis might well seize more territory than they had asked for. At the most, 2,000 Transjordanian troops could be mustered to replace the 10,000 Iraqi soldiers, and as the latter proposed to withdraw forthwith regardless of what everybody else did, the Transjordanian government had no choice but to accept the Israeli terms. There was some loose talk from junior officers about fighting on, but the leaders knew that the game was lost and the forfeits had to be paid.

It was finally suggested by the prime minister and agreed by the king that a special ministerial committee should be appointed to conduct direct and secret negotiations with Israel while the shadow boxing continued in Rhodes. Falah al-Madadha, who was minister of justice and acting defence minister, was appointed as head of the delegation. Abdullah's advice was to accept the Jewish demands and reach agreement with them whatever the cost so that they might settle the Palestine problem once and for all. 'We have many strategic positions in the mountains in Tubas and Jericho', he added. 'What can we lose if we give them some hills to protect their lands!' When Tall intervened to suggest that something should be asked in return for those hills, the king's anger was only deflected by Education Minister Muhammad Amin Shanqiti who said: 'The Arabs in Palestine have fled their villages, left their homes to the Jews and His Majesty—may God prolong his life—is now their only protector, so there is no room for arrogant self-exaltation. It is best to negotiate with the Jews, whatever the cost.'

During lunch Abdullah was in a maudlin and self-pitying mood. 'I

[40] Eytan to Sharett, 23 Mar. 1949, *DFPI*, iii. 468–70; and Ben-Gurion's diary, 20 Mar. 1949.

am ready to give up my throne before renewing battle with the Jews,' he mused. 'But the question is, who would assume power after I had gone? In the name of God, I love Transjordan and its people, not out of personal interest, as the country is poor. If I left the country, I wouldn't have enough money to pay for even a single dinner.' After lunch he ordered Tall to invite the *jama'a* (by which word he meant the Jews)—to dinner![41]

Carrying out the royal order, Tall informed Dayan that everyone on his side was willing to sign an agreement on the basis that had been outlined two evenings earlier at Shuneh and asked that an Israeli delegation appear in the no-man's land near the Mandelbaum Gate at 7 p.m. on the evening of March 22.

Three nights at Shuneh

The Israeli delegation consisted of Walter Eytan, Yigael Yadin, Moshe Dayan, and Yehoshafat Harkabi. Before the meeting Yadin prepared a map with three lines representing Israel's maximum, minimum, and intermediate demands and obtained Ben-Gurion's approval and instructions.[42] The arrangement was that the party should set out from Jerusalem after dark and return before dawn so as to minimize the chances of anyone seeing them cross the lines—a jumbled mass of debris and half-destroyed houses, with minefields on either side. The party had to pick its way through several hundred yards of this dangerous shambles in pitch darkness, stumbling over planks, twisted iron, and cement blocks until it came to a clearing on the other side. There Colonel Tall stood waiting with a car in which he conveyed the party across the Allenby Bridge and other heavily guarded checkpoints to Shuneh. For Eytan this was a journey into unknown country, and enemy country at that, but he was the king's guest and had no qualms. Soon after crossing the river, they reached Shuneh, where the winter palace struck him as not so palatial after all. It was a reasonably comfortable country house with a very large oil painting, curiously enough, of the Battle of Trafalgar, a gift to King Abdullah from King George V.[43]

Abdullah received the party with exquisite courtesy. In attendance were Falah al-Madadha, Hussein Siraj, the under-secretary of state for foreign affairs, and Abdullah Tall. Some of the *dramatis personae* were away in Beirut at a meeting with the UN's Palestine Conciliation

---

[41] Glubb, *A Soldier with the Arabs*, 233–7; Musa and Madi, *History of Jordan in the Twentieth Century*, 530; Tall, *The Palestine Tragedy*, 499–501.

[42] Interview with Gen. Yigael Yadin.

[43] Walter Eytan, 'Three Nights at Shuneh', *Midstream* (Nov. 1980), 52–6.

Commission. The king opened the proceedings with a long speech, studded with many Arabic sayings, such as, 'your neighbour who is near is dearer to you than your brother who is far away', and similar words of proverbial wisdom. After Eytan had made a suitably courteous reply, the king retired and the two delegations got down to business.

They talked for six hours, although the atmosphere was not friendly as the Israelis took a very strong line. With the help of a map Yadin presented Israel's demands for territorial adjustments in the 60-kilometre-long front line held by the Iraqis (see Map 13). A cursory look at the new line drawn by Yadin revealed the unexpected depth of the area demanded by Israel. Within the area in question there were several Arab villages, and the Transjordanian delegates were concerned about their future. A long discussion ensued about the size of the area, the fate of its inhabitants, and the possibility of reciprocal Israeli concessions. By 1 a.m., however, the two sides had agreed on a line and on a draft text for the agreement.

It was finally arranged that the map and the draft should be taken to Amman for the king's final approval, as according to Tall the Hashemite ruler had never realized that he would have to give up so much territory. The line finally agreed upon apparently left some thirty villages, including a number of large ones, in Israel's area, and Tall thought that the king might be rather appalled when he saw this. Tall was to telephone by 2 p.m. the next day to inform the delegation of the king's acceptance or rejection of the scheme, but they made it clear that they would negotiate no further and it was now a question of take it or leave it. Tall duly telephoned at the appointed hour to report that the king agreed and invited the delegation that evening to Shuneh to feast and sign the agreement.[44]

What Yadin had presented was an ultimatum: nothing more and nothing less. He left no room for doubt that unless the agreement was signed within twenty-four hours, Israel would take that whole area, and possibly more, by force. Abdullah had to pay a price, a very heavy price, but once again he felt that he had no alternative.[45] To the American chargé in Amman, Wells Stabler, Abdullah confessed that he felt that if he refused to sign the agreement, Israel would recommence hostilities and the whole area might be lost. It would in fact be better to sacrifice another fifteen villages with an additional estimated 15,000 refugees than to lose what little was left of Arab Palestine. On the other hand, if he did sign the agreement and then an armistice, it might be difficult for the Israelis to make further excessive demands.

[44] Eytan to Sharett, 23 Mar. 1949, *DFPI*, iii. 468–70; Tall, *The Palestine Tragedy*, ch. 16; *FRUS 1949*, vi. 859–61.
[45] Interview with Anwar Nuseiba.

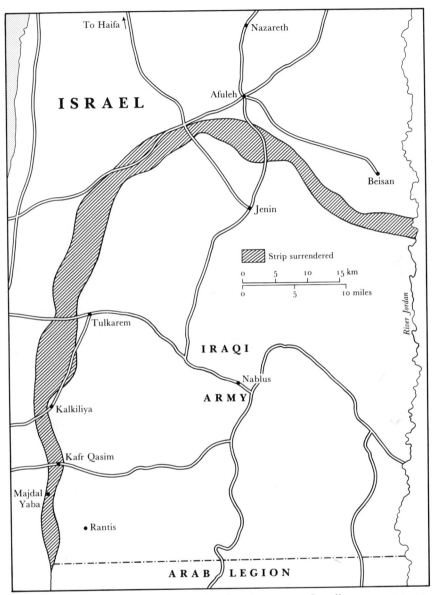

MAP 13 Strip of territory surrendered to Israel, to secure Israeli agreement to an armistice on the Iraqi front

Stabler, whose sympathies were entirely on the king's side, only wished it were possible to believe that the Israelis would present no further demands. In a cable to Secretary of State George Marshall, Stabler described the Israeli demands and the 24-hour ultimatum as being in the nature of blackmail, adding for good measure that it appeared to be rank injustice for the United States government to stand by while Israel was forcing Transjordan into such an agreement at gun-point.[46]

On the evening of March 23, the same Israeli delegation proceeded by the same route to Shuneh to meet a much larger team than on the previous night. The team that the king had now assembled included a large ministerial component, several members of the royal court, and a British officer, Lt.-Col. Charles Coaker, who served as Glubb's chief of staff and head of the Survey Department. The king had invited Glubb himself to attend but the latter had apparently excused himself, saying he did not want to see the Jews' faces. It suited the Israelis not to see Glubb's face either because they did not want it said in the Arab world that this agreement was the product of British–Zionist collusion.[47]

Walter Eytan felt that he could write a small book about this experience, about the queerness of passing through Jericho and over the Allenby Bridge, about sitting down at the king's table with a British officer, and similarly unusual impressions. In his report to Sharett, Eytan gave a vivid account of the general atmosphere, of the principal personalities, and of the strange proceedings of that very memorable evening:

The king, who appeared to be in excellent health apart from an affliction of the bladder which makes him take "Urodonal" and run out to the lavatory every quarter hour or so, is surrounded by the most extraordinary types. His Acting Prime Minister, whose name is something like Said Pasha Mufti, is to all appearances mentally deficient, though this does not prevent him from being at the same time Minister of the Interior and Acting Minister for Foreign Affairs. Our friend of the previous night, Falah Pasha el Madadha, who is Minister of Justice and Acting Minister of Defence, had little notion of what the whole thing was about, and signed the agreement, which was in English, without understanding a single word of what the document contained, though I presume it had been conveyed to him that it was good thing for the King. Abdullah Tall, who is an outstanding figure in that crowd, maintained an attitude of utter cynicism throughout the proceedings, though he helped actively to get the agreement concluded. He seems to be wholly disillusioned— about the Arabs, about the British, and about everything else—and speaks about the King, even in the King's presence, in a way which can only be described as contemptuous. As, however, he appears at the same time to feel some affection for the King and to be sincerely anxious to safeguard his

[46] *FRUS 1949*, vi. 859–62.   [47] Interview with Gen. Yigael Yadin.

interests, I can only assume that there are things in the Arab character which I simply do not understand.

We reached Shuneh at about 8.00 p.m., bringing the King a present consisting of two silver candlesticks and a badly printed *Tanach* [Bible] encased in a heavy silver binding. In return I received a murderous looking dagger. We stood around in the drawing room smoking, while someone kept a lookout for the King's approach—the signal for putting out cigarettes quickly. The sight of His Excellency, the Minister of Justice and Acting Minister of Defence trying like a schoolboy to conceal a cigarette which he did not have time to put out was one I shall not quickly forget. After we had been introduced and said a few polite things, the King led us in to dinner, at which I sat on his right and Yadin on his left. The dinner was excellent, as we had all expected. Conversation was a little difficult, but whenever it failed the King put things right by extending his hands and grasping Yadin and me by the arm, apparently as a silent gesture of friendship. After dinner we all went back into the reception room, the King sat down at one end with the Acting Prime Minister sitting opposite and the rest of us grouped in between. The King then started a long speech about friendship between our two countries, the past (including Deir Yassin), the future (naturally not so specific), his relations with Britain and the United States, as well as many other things, including what he thought of the Mufti and solicitous inquiries after the health of Mr. Ben-Gurion, Mr. Sharett, Mrs. Myerson ('Saida Golda'), Mr. Sasson and Mr. Rutenberg. In the end, after the King had gone (saying he usually went to bed at nine o'clock—it was by this time nearly eleven), we got down to business. The agreement was finally signed at 2.00 a.m., as were the maps which go with it, and we left Shuneh at 2.30 a.m., reaching Tel Aviv just over three hours later.

A copy of the agreement itself is attached to this letter. I have already told you by cable of how the new line runs and the only additional thing worth saying about it is that Glubb's Chief of Staff helped to draw it and finally signed the maps together with the members of the Transjordan Delegation. At first, when Abdullah Tall told us on the way to Shuneh that a British officer would be present, we raised objections, but Abdullah Tall said that the members of the delegation and the various Ministers at Shuneh had no more idea of map-reading than the King had, and that it was essential for a military man to be present and see to this side of things. As all the good Transjordanian officers were away at Rhodes, they had asked Lt.-Col. Coaker to help them. In the end both Yadin and Dayan thought it was a good thing that this officer was present and certified the line, as this would make it impossible for the Transjordanians afterwards to say that we had tricked them. Col. Coaker's presence means, of course, that the British know about the arrangement and presumably give it their blessing. . .

In a sense, this agreement is too good to be true, and I shall not believe in its reality completely until I see what happens when the time comes for it to be implemented. It gives us in respect of territory—nearly all of it highly strategic—far more than we should ever have contemplated taking by military action.

In conclusion I should like to emphasise once again the need for secrecy. We have guaranteed, under Article 11, not to publish the agreement, and it is obviously in our interest to get its provisions implemented before they become generally known in the Arab world, where they would be sure to produce an outcry, perhaps on a scale that might make their execution impossible.[48]

Yadin's most vivid memory was of King Abdullah's extraordinarily long opening speech, giving his version of the events that had led to that bizarre gathering. Though addressed to the Israeli delegation, much of this speech was really directed at the king's own advisers and took the form of a reprimand for their having failed to heed his warning that the Arabs, a weak and backward people, had no chance of defeating the Jews who were a united and advanced people. In a nutshell, Abdullah claimed that he had always wanted peace and that it was the other Arab rulers and his own advisers who had pushed Transjordan into war. The British, he stated, had misled him from start to finish and had even supplied him with shells stuffed with sawdust instead of gunpowder. Turning pointedly to his advisers, he said:

I now want to tell you a story in the presence of our guests. As you know and they know, I am a bedouin and there is an ancient bedouin saying that I first heard from my father and it goes as follows: if you are fleeing from your enemy, with your tent and all your possessions loaded on your horse, and you see that the enemy is getting closer, you have two alternatives: either to fall into your enemy's hands with all your goods or to throw to him parcels as you continue to flee. And I want you to know that I have invited our Israeli friends in order to throw parcels to them![49]

At a certain moment in this long and devastatingly frank speech, when the king explained how heavy were the sacrifices he was being called upon to make, Dayan could not restrain himself and told him that the three military members of their delegation—Yadin, Harkabi, and himself—had each lost a younger brother in this war—a war which they had not wanted and which would not have broken out if the Arab states, Transjordan included, had not attacked them. The time to have talked about concessions and compromise was before the war, in order to prevent it. Now one had to bear the consequences and pay the price.[50]

Nevertheless, the Israelis did make some minor concessions which made it easier for the Transjordanians to sign the agreement. Yadin's original line was slightly redrawn and an article was inserted into the agreement, to save Transjordan's face in the Arab world, stating that

[48] Eytan to Sharett, 24 Mar. 1949, 64/1, ISA.
[49] Interview with Gen. Yigael Yadin. For another account of Abdullah's opening speech see Tall, *The Palestine Tragedy*, 513.
[50] Dayan, *Story of My Life*, 113.

Israel, for its part, made similar changes for the benefit of 'the Hashemite Kingdom of Jordan'. Another article safeguarded the rights of the inhabitants of the villages to be surrendered to Israel. Thirdly, Israel undertook to pay Transjordan the cost of building 20 kilometres of first-class road in compensation for the road between Tulkarem and Kalkilya. The agreement laid down a timetable for the transfer of the territories over a period of some four months (see Appendix 1) and incorporated a map signed by the representatives of Israel and the Arab Legion indicating the new line.

The king reappeared when the agreement was signed. Seeing sad, tired faces all around him, he gave an order to a servant who returned with a bunch of roses. With a weary but sincere smile, Abdullah gave each of the Israelis a rose as he blessed their homeward journey, saying: 'Tonight we have ended the war and brought the peace.'[51]

Although the agreement was signed on March 23 it required the ratification of Transjordan's prime minister who was still in Beirut. The final date for its ratification was therefore set for March 30, with the delay giving Abdullah more time to consider its implications, to elicit the views of Britain and the United States, and possibly even to secure their intervention to stop the agreement being ratified and to take steps to protect Transjordan for reneging on the agreement and against further military threats from Israel.

It was in fact Sir Alec Kirkbride who had suggested using the prime minister's absence in order to gain time. Kirkbride hoped to achieve two things: first, to alert the British government to the gravity of the situation and, secondly, to urge Abdullah to appeal personally to President Truman to exert pressure on the Israelis to modify their position. In order to convey to London the strength of his own feeling, Kirkbride described the last meeting at Shuneh as taking place in circumstances 'strongly reminiscent of Hitler and the late Czech President'. However, it seems that Kirkbride was more alarmed than the Transjordanians themselves by the terms of the proposed agreement, and his appeal to the Foreign Office yielded nothing more substantial than a note to the State Department stating that the proposed deal would endanger Transjordan's internal security as well as her position in the Arab world. Abdullah's direct appeal to President Truman for help was equally unproductive. All it elicited was a general statement about the disfavour with which America would view any attempt to violate the provisions of the secret agreement. Both Kirkbride and Stabler were greatly disappointed with what they saw as the apathetic attitude of their respective governments. Unfortunately for the king, they could not offer any practical alternative to the ratification

[51] Ibid. 114.

of the secret agreement, nor could they guarantee any external support for a policy of defiance.[52]

The king reported on the disappointing results of his appeal to Britain and the United States to a special meeting of the Council of Ministers in Shuneh on March 26. He then turned to Glubb and questioned him about the extent of the Arab Legion's preparedness for renewed warfare. Glubb replied that the army was very small and that it only had ammunition for two or three days of fighting. Tawfiq Abul Huda, who had returned from Beirut, was critical of Britain for leaving Transjordan in the lurch, and the council resolved to invite the Israelis to another meeting and to accept their demands but amend some of the terms of the secret agreement.[53]

Following the council meeting, Tall informed Harkabi that the prime minister approved the agreement in principle but that the king would like them to come again to Shuneh to discuss a number of points that had arisen. He stated specifically that instead of the provisions of the agreement remaining secret, the king now wished them to be included in the general armistice agreement being negotiated in Rhodes, that the timetable which governed the handing over of territory in the original agreement might now be deleted and all the territory handed over as soon as the Iraqis evacuated it, and that certain changes would be suggested in the border. Harkabi replied that they were willing to come to Shuneh, but only on condition that no changes in the border were proposed or discussed. This condition was accepted and they duly proceeded to Shuneh on the evening of March 30. The party consisted of the same four who had gone on the two previous occasions, together with Reuven Shiloah whom it was thought wise to take because Colonel Jundi, the head of the Transjordan delegation at Rhodes, was going to be there, and because in any case the provisions of the secret agreement were now to be incorporated in the general armistice agreement which Shiloah was negotiating at Rhodes.

On arrival at Shuneh they found that with the exception of Abdullah Tall and Colonel Coaker, all the participants on the Transjordanian side had been changed so they were now faced with new and much tougher, shrewder, and more experienced characters. The protagonists on this occasion were Prime Minister Tawfiq Abul Huda, Defence Minister Fawzi el-Mulki and Hamad Farhan, the secretary to the Cabinet. This represented a distinct rise in level as far as both personal

---

[52] Pappé, 'British Policy towards the Middle East, 1948–51' 309–11; *FRUS 1949*, vi. 871–3, 878 f.; Glubb, *A Soldier with the Arabs*, 237; Musa and Madi, *History of Jordan in the Twentieth Century*, 531 f.

[53] Tall, *The Palestine Tragedy*, ch. 16.

rank and individual ability were concerned. The king on this occasion did not go to bed when the actual proceedings began, but stayed up until four o'clock in the morning, in the company of a ravishing black-haired shaikh, sitting on the terrace of his house, until he was sure that the agreement had been reached and that he could safely see his visitors off the premises.

Abul Huda opened the proceedings with a long speech aimed at placing the current negotiations in the context of the original accord between the two sides on the partition of Palestine. 'Transjordan', he said, 'was pushed into a war which we strenuously tried to avoid. The only serious clash between our forces and yours, however, occurred in the Old City of Jerusalem. Other than that, we kept our forces within the boundaries of Arab Palestine. And this was according to the policy which both of us agreed on. We are very anxious to reach a final and permanent settlement with you.'[54]

The negotiations centred on the disposition of the villages and towns in and around the strip of land 5 kilometres deep and 60 kilometres long that under the secret agreement was due to be handed to Israel. Eytan was amazed that the king had yielded so readily on Wadi Ara when he must have realized that he could have demanded a very high price in return. But during the conversation on this occasion, he began to understand, or thought he understood, Abdullah's approach. In the whole of the Wadi Ara area there was not a single Arab town or even a major village. There were six or seven small villages, of which the largest was Umm al-Fahem, and others called Ara, Arara, and other names unknown in the Arab world. King Abdullah had no great interest in these villages, and the road that the Iraqis had cut led from nowhere to nowhere as far as *he* was concerned. So he was not losing anything, and it would pay to make Israel a gesture.

It was quite a different story when they came to discuss the fate of and future of the three Arab towns, the names of all of which were very well-known: Tulkarem and Kalkilya in the Triangle, and Beit Jibrin in the south, near Hebron. The cease-fire had left the first two in the hands of the Iraqi army and the last in Israel's hands. The Israelis were interested in obtaining Tulkarem and Kalkilya, while the king was equally anxious to secure possession of Beit Jibrin. The king had one reason and one reason only for refusing to withdraw the Legion from the two northern towns (at any rate there was only one reason he gave, and Eytan did not doubt his sincerity): he could not allow it to be said throughout the world that he, an Arab king, had surrendered Tulkarem and Kalkilya into the hands of the Jews. Ara and Arara were not important because no one had heard of them, but these were cities

<hr/>

[54] Eytan to Sharett, 3 Apr. 1949, *DFPI*, iii. 498–500; Tall, *The Palestine Tragedy*, 531.

with familiar names so it was impossible for him to hand them over. The Israelis, for their part, were unwilling to yield Beit Jibrin. Their reasons had to do more with security than prestige—to hand it over would have meant redrawing the lines in the Hebron region in a way that could imperil their lines of communication between Jerusalem and Beersheba. Their refusal was made easier by the king's own refusal on Tulkarem and Kalkilya. So the three towns remained in the hands of those who held them at the end of the fighting, and this particular match ended in a draw.[55]

The other match, more vigorously contested between Mulki and Yadin, was over the future of the villages. Mulki and Abul Huda buttressed their case for improving the terms that had already been accepted by their faint-hearted colleagues with two powerful arguments. In the first place, they argued, the king did not really understand the implications of the secret agreement, and the surrender of the villages could bring about his downfall. Secondly, the surrender of the villages to Israel could set in train another wave of some 40,000 refugees and was therefore out of the question. Abul Huda left before the hard bargaining began, saying there was no need for his personal involvement in the technical details. The king, however, now wearing a long white night gown, said he would not go to sleep until the business had been completed. Mulki pleaded with him to go to sleep, saying there was no need to worry and that they would finish the business in the end, however long it took. Yadin explained to Mulki that Israel was not interested in the villages but only in the lands that the villagers used for farming and that it would be inconceivable for the villages to be on the Transjordanian side of the border while their lands were on the Israeli side. Mulki's reply was: 'General Yadin, the world does not know about lands; the world knows the name of villages. I don't care a damn about the lands; but give back some of the villages.' Although he saw the strength of the argument, Yadin stood his ground and refused to let Transjordan have even a single village. The only concession made by Yadin was to keep his troops out of the villages so as not to frighten their inhabitants, and it was a very minor concession since his only concern was with obtaining the strategically important high ground.[56]

In the end the new line remained unaltered in spite of the determined efforts made by the Transjordanians, supported by the king's most winning smiles. It was to be incorporated into the Rhodes Agreement (see Map 14) with the help of Colonel Jundi and Reuven Shiloah who were both present, though for the most part as silent observers, throughout the proceedings. Article 4 was amended to read: 'Israel, for its part, has made similar changes for the benefit of the Hashemite

[55] Eytan, 'Three Nights at Shuneh', 54.   [56] Interview with Gen. Yigael Yadin.

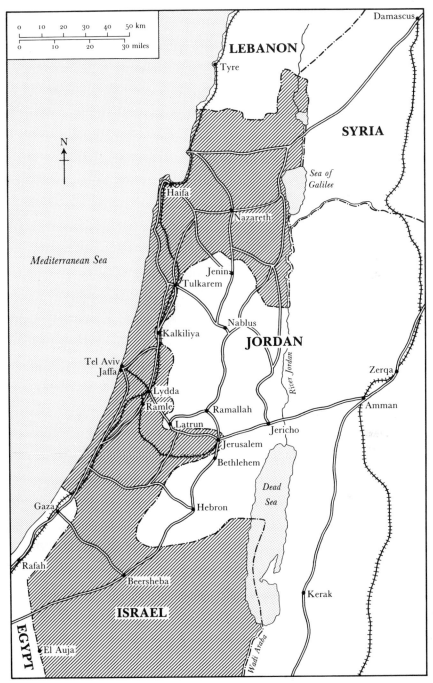

MAP 14   The Jordanian–Israeli armistice demarcation line

Jordan Kingdom in the Hebron area, as delineated in blue ink in the map annexed thereto.' No such change was actually effected and this article was merely a fig leaf to cover Transjordan's nakedness. To Article 8 was added the stipulation that neither Israeli nor Transjordanian forces were to enter or to be stationed in the villages to be evacuated by the Iraqis, and a local Arab police was to be organized there for internal security purposes. As already noted, Yadin felt able to make this concession because he was not interested in the villages anyway, but concerned only to place his men at strategic points in the hills. Finally it was resolved that both parties should keep the fact of the direct meetings at Shuneh and the existence of these two agreements absolutely secret, though the content of these agreements was to be made public once the armistice was concluded at Rhodes. (For the text of the agreement, see Appendix 2.)

The bargaining and drafting went on until 4 o'clock in the morning. As there was no English typewriter in the palace, the agreement was written by hand. The Israelis kept the copy written by Eytan, the Transjordanians that written by Shiloah. Throughout the proceedings, coffee, orange juice, chocolates, and cigarettes were handed round at intervals to fortify the negotiators; they were much appreciated by the Israelis as on this occasion Fawzi Mulki, ably supported by Hamad Farhan, proved to be a tough customer.[57]

When Moshe Sharett had heard of the original agreement concluded at Shuneh on March 23, he could hardly believe his ears, acclaiming it as 'a tremendous diplomatic victory'. So at the end of the report to Sharett on the cosmetic changes made to that agreement during the long night of March 30, Eytan added a little piece by way of a personal reaction, a piece which as far as he was concerned qualified somewhat the foreign minister's accolade. The upright and humane director-general of the Israeli Foreign Ministry, moulded in the best tradition of the British civil service, clearly had a sense of guilt arising out of the agreement, both towards the Transjordanians who had been so moderate and reasonable all along, and towards the Palestinian victims of the cynical deal that he himself had so ably helped to clinch between the Hashemites and the Zionists:

I do not know how Shiloah and Dayan felt about this, but certainly Yadin and I had qualms, and if you like moral scruples, about what we were doing. Although the Transjordanians had agreed that there would be no further discussion of the new line, we discovered soon after we got to Shuneh that they in fact wanted to change the line to the extent of leaving on their side of it the largest villages in the area to be evacuated by the Iraqis—for example Umm al-Fahm, Baqa Gharbiya and Taibiya. We resisted this claim for all we were

[57] Eytan to Sharett, 3 Apr. 1949, *DFPI*, iii. 498–500.

worth, and resisted it successfully. But both Yadin and I were acutely conscious of the Transjordanians' right to take up the position they did. We were, after all, discussing the future of villages which were wholly Arab in population and situated in territory under Arab control. They were not villages we possessed, but villages we would possess if the deal between us and the Transjordanians went through. In spite of all guarantees and fine phrases, it was as clear to the Transjordanians as to us that the people of these villages were likely to become refugees as soon as the Iraqis withdrew, and possibly even before. . . . The people who are letting these Arab villagers down are of course the Transjordanians, but that does not make it any more agreeable for us. We are partners to this deal, and it is we and not the Transjordanians who will be blamed for its results.[58]

There was a final twist to the drama that featured so much discord as well as collaboration between the Zionists and the Hashemites during the three long nights at Shuneh. On the third and longest night, after the agreement was signed and the king was finally free to retire to his bedroom, Abdullah Tall, who had been hovering around in the palace, came forward to drive the Israeli party back to Jerusalem. Once they were in the car, Tall began by saying that he hoped to be the first Transjordanian officer to enter Syria, and that in any case, he was due to go to Damascus in a day or two to carry King Abdullah's good wishes to Col. Husni Zaim, the Syrian chief of staff who had overthrown the regime headed by President Shukri al-Quwatli in a bloodless coup on March 30. Tall asked what Israel's attitude would be if the king marched on Damascus, hinting that Israel's air force might play a useful part. Nothing would be easier than to paint Israel's aircraft with the colours and markings of Transjordan. If they were interested, he would be able to let them know in two or three days whether Abdullah intended to carry out his plan. The plan provided for the unification of Syria and Transjordan under a single government whose seat would be in Damascus. The king would rule from Damascus, while his elder son Talal would remain in Amman as the prince of Transjordan. Tall hoped that the Israelis would not take advantage of Abdullah while he was engaged with the bulk of his forces elsewhere, and asked point blank what their attitude would be, to which they replied that they should not interfere. Tall believed that even if marching into Syria meant killing fellow Arabs, the king would not hesitate. He was anxious to rid himself of the British, and the overthrow of the regime in Damascus provided a golden opportunity.[59]

Needless to say, Abdullah Tall makes no mention of this conversation in his lengthy and convoluted account of the tragedy of Palestine and of the part played by the Hashemite king and his British masters in

[58] Ibid. [59] Ibid.; Eytan, 'Three Nights at Shuneh', 55 f.

engineering this tragedy. What Tall does say on the subject of Colonel Zaim's *coup d'état*, is that it was a hopeful sign for the plot that he himself had been hatching, together with other patriotic officers and young Palestinian nationalists, for a military coup in Transjordan. Tall's case for overthrowing the regime in Amman was allegedly based on the inactivity of the Arab Legion during the war on Egypt and on the contacts with the Zionists, going back to Elias Sasson's letter of 8 December 1948. According to Tall's account, he had succeeded in turning to his own advantage the goodwill mission on which the king had sent him to Damascus by enlisting Zaim's, and Egypt's, support for the cause of the revolution he was planning to carry out at home.[60]

Whether Tall's real purpose in going to Damascus was to blaze the trail for a Greater Syria under the Hashemite monarchy, as he told the Israelis, or to seek the support of the new military regime there for the overthrow of this monarchy, as he was later to claim in his memoirs, is difficult to say. What can be established with reasonable certainty on the basis of the documentary record is that no Israeli help, aerial or otherwise, was forthcoming for the plan to exploit the fall of the civilian regime in Syria in order to bring the country under the Hashemite crown. When Ben-Gurion learnt of Tall's request he rejected it instantly, telling Eytan it was out of the question.[61]

The Zionist leaders, of course, were well aware of Abdullah's long-standing scheme to make himself the ruler of Greater Syria. They knew about his family history, his thwarted dynastic ambitions, and his longing to break out of Britain's tutelage. They knew of his dream to make Damascus his capital and his feeling that Amman was no substitute—a spring-board at best. Not only did they understand all this but they also professed themselves to be sympathetic and support-ive. No doubt Abdullah's preoccupation with bringing Syria into his domain suited and was exploited by the Zionists as a means of diverting him from the equally burning preoccupation with bringing Palestine into his domain. Nevertheless, the Jewish Agency had always led the amir of Transjordan to believe that it looked with favour on his ambition to conquer Syria, and this was indeed one of the props of the unwritten alliance between the two sides. The Agency did not pledge its active support for the realization of this particular ambition, but it did promise not to stand in his way.[62] An appeal by Abdullah to Israel to lend him military support for the long-awaited march on Damascus was therefore not as bizarre as it might seem at first sight.

But in the general confusion that followed the overthrow of the parliamentary system in Syria, there was little chance, as the nocturnal

---

[60] Tall, *The Palestine Tragedy*, ch. 19.   [61] Interview with Walter Eytan.
[62] Interview with Yaacov Shimoni.

passengers in Tall's car had predicted, that their government would wish to extend anything more than passive support for the king's plan. Zaim's coup was the curtain-raiser for a comedy of errors in which everybody suspected everybody else of being the new military dictator's secret backer. The British and the French were the most widely suspected of being the villains of the piece. In fact, it would appear that it was the American CIA that had helped Zaim to plan and execute his coup.[63] In the course of his chequered career, when he lived as an exile in Paris for his sins of embezzlement, this brave and capable soldier had also come in contact with Tuvia Arazi, one of Elias Sasson's assistants, and he did not emerge any poorer as a result of this acquaintance.[64] But all the intelligence that reached Ben-Gurion after the coup pointed to British involvement designed to remove from power the anti-British President Quwatli and Prime Minister Khalid al-Azm. Gen. Edward Spears was specifically mentioned as the chief British instigator of the coup. So Ben-Gurion mistakenly chalked up the change of regime as another victory for his great enemy, Ernest Bevin, writing in his diary: 'So in Iraq—Nuri [al-Said], in Transjordan—Abdullah, in Syria—Spears and Zaim. Bevin rules the Middle East . . .'[65] Given this perspective on the events in Damascus, Ben-Gurion understandably had no desire to become embroiled in plots by one British Middle Eastern puppet against another.

The Israeli–Jordanian armistice agreement

The fourth and final phase in the negotiations between Israel and Transjordan started with the initial approval of the agreement with Abdullah and ended with the signature of the general armistice agreement (see Appendix 3) in Rhodes on April 3. Officially Bunche had not been notified about the direct talks that had been taking place between the two parties elsewhere, but he knew that such talks were taking place and he patiently awaited their outcome. Meanwhile, the representatives on the warm and hospitable Greek island discussed minor technical matters such as the reduction of forces and their distribution in the various sectors. Disagreements on these matters did not constitute a serious obstacle to the successful conclusion of the talks. When Colonel Jundi and Reuven Shiloah flew back to Rhodes with the approved maps and told Bunche that their countries were ready to sign an armistice agreement, he was surprised but delighted.

---

[63] Miles Copeland, *The Game of Nations* (London: Weidenfeld and Nicolson, 1969), 42; Patrick Seale, *The Struggle for Syria* (London: Oxford University Press, 1965), ch. 5.

[64] Avi Shlaim, 'Husni Zaim and the Plan to Resettle Palestinian Refugees in Syria', *Journal of Palestine Studies* 15/4 (1986), 68–80.

[65] Ben-Gurion's diary, 3 Apr. 1949.

All that remained for him to do was to dress up the provisions of the agreement in the appropriate legal phraseology and to place them within a formal UN framework which was faithfully copied from the Israeli–Egyptian armistice agreement. In a more festive mood, he also presided over the final session at which the agreement was signed.

The signing of the general armistice agreement represented an important landmark in the history of Transjordan and in the development of the relations between Transjordan and the State of Israel. The agreement was signed in the name of the Hashemite Kingdom of Jordan. It was the first time that this title was used officially. Palestine and Transjordan gave way to Israel and the Hashemite Kingdom of Jordan, and the official nomenclature reflected the new reality. The name Palestine disappeared, at least from the map. Arab Palestine, or what remained of it, was officially designated as West Jordan, or more colloquially as the West Bank, while former Transjordan was known from now on as East Jordan or the East Bank. In a very real sense, therefore, the ceremony over which the distinguished representative of the United Nations presided with such abundant charm and good humour marked not only the birth of a new phase in the relations between the Hashemite Kingdom of Jordan and the State of Israel but also the official demise of Arab Palestine.

The general armistice agreement itself delineated, with the aid of maps signed by the two sides, what was officially called the armistice demarcation line but to all intents and purposes became the border between the two countries until 1967. In the Araba, between the Dead Sea and the Gulf of Aqaba, the armistice line coincided with the international border; on the Iraqi front, it corresponded to the agreement with Abdullah; in the Jerusalem sector to the 'sincere truce' agreement of 30 November 1948; and in the Jerusalem–Hebron–Dead Sea sector it essentially followed the cease-fire line of 18 July 1948.

The agreement did not tackle the complex problems of Jerusalem, Bethlehem, Latrun, and the economic enterprises on the Dead Sea and in Naharayim. But under Article 8, it was agreed to set up a joint committee, without UN representatives, to deal with all these and other questions on which, in Dr Bunche's optimistic phrase, there was agreement in principle. In the event, however, except for the resumption of the railway service to and from Jerusalem, these questions remained unresolved throughout the eighteen years during which the armistice between Israel and Jordan remained in force.

The agreement did not formally signify Israeli recognition of the annexation of the West Bank to Jordan. It was explicitly stated in Article 2 that the provisions of this agreement would in no way prejudice the rights, claims, and position of either party in the ultimate peaceful settlement of the Palestine question. In other words, the armistice demarcation lines were only temporary lines, dictated by military considerations, without prejudice to future territorial settlements. Like the agreements with Egypt and Lebanon, as the identical preamble made clear, the armistice agreement between Israel and Jordan was not a final peace settlement but a provisional measure designed to facilitate the transition from the truce to a permanent peace in Palestine.

Despite its shortcomings, the armistice agreement with Jordan represented a major victory for Israeli diplomacy. Considerable territorial and strategic gains in the Wadi Ara area had been secured without any further bloodshed and without endangering Israel's position in the international arena. The whole of the Little Triangle, as this area was popularly called, to differentiate it from the Big Triangle that stretched from Nablus to Jenin and Tulkarem, was added to the territory of the state of Israel. The newly born state had achieved its objectives through a highly effective combination of diplomatic moves with limited military moves. Through Operation *Fait Accompli*, which was limited in scope and conducted under strict political constraints, Israel had extended her border down the Gulf of Aqaba. By resorting to military threats during the negotiations for redrawing the line in the Triangle, Israel had achieved a much improved line of defence in the centre of the country which was also its soft underbelly. Only in the Jerusalem sector were the Israeli objectives not achieved through negotiation and the temporary armistice arrangements became frozen. But at the time when the decision to postpone the resolution of this set of problems to a later stage was taken, a peace settlement with Jordan looked not only attainable but almost the inevitable next step.

For King Abdullah, too, despite all the concessions he had to make, the agreement represented a major diplomatic triumph. Another military confrontation with the large and battle-hardened Israeli army might have wiped out all his territorial gains in Palestine and even cost him his throne if the Arab Legion were crippled in the process. Abdullah bought an armistice agreement with parcels of land taken from under the feet of the Iraqi army and then used this agreement to get the troublesome Iraqis to go home quietly. Moreover, by concluding the agreement, he secured *de facto* if not *de jure* Israeli recognition of his control of Palestinian territory not formerly his. In one diplomatic swoop he had restored the special relations that he had always had with the Zionist movement and at the same time quashed the hopes of other Arab quarters of setting up a separate state in Arab Palestine.

After Jordan came Syria's turn to negotiate an armistice with Israel. Of all the Arab countries, Syria proved the toughest nut to crack. The negotiations were the most protracted, lasting nearly four months, and the most difficult. In the course of the fighting the Syrians had entrenched themselves on the Israeli side of the international border and the attempts to push them back across the Jordan were unsuccessful. The course of the negotiations was also affected by Husni Zaim's coup, which set the pattern for military intervention in Arab politics and for the overthrow of the old order which was held responsible for the loss of Palestine. Although Zaim had promised his co-conspirators a fight to the finish against Zionism, once he had captured power he made a determined effort to come to terms with Israel. He offered to meet Ben-Gurion face to face in order to conclude a peace settlement. Zaim wanted to skip the armistice talks altogether and proceed directly to the conclusion of a peace, with an exchange of ambassadors, open borders, and normal economic relations. As an additional incentive, Zaim offered, in the context of an overall settlement, to settle 300,000 Palestinian refugees, nearly half the total number, in Syria. But since he was offering a separate peace agreement, Zaim wanted a modification of the border to give Syria half of the Sea of Galilee. Ben-Gurion declined to meet Zaim and insisted that before Israel would discuss peace and co-operation, Syria must withdraw her forces from Israel's territory and sign an armistice agreement based on the previous international border. It was on this basis that Syria did eventually sign the armistice agreement on July 20. Three weeks later Husni Zaim was overthrown.[66]

With the conclusion of the agreement between Israel and Syria on July 20, the Rhodes armistice negotiations were completed. The first Arab–Israeli war was officially over (see Map 15).

Public opinion and the armistice

Bitter controversies about the armistice agreements, however, continued on both sides of the new border. In Israel, the government was subjected to criticism from the public, the press, and the opposition for what was alleged to be defeatism and appeasement. The public was in a more hawkish mood than the government. Having emerged victorious from a long and cruel war which took such a heavy toll in human lives, the Israeli public was in no mood for making concessions. Some 6,000 Israelis had died in the war, or 1 per cent of the total population. The rational pragmatism that guided Ben-Gurion's government through the negotiations was not widely enough appreciated amid the clamour for total victory, the liberation of the West Bank, and the imposition of Israel's terms for peace on the enemy.

[66] Shlaim, 'Husni Zaim', 72–80.

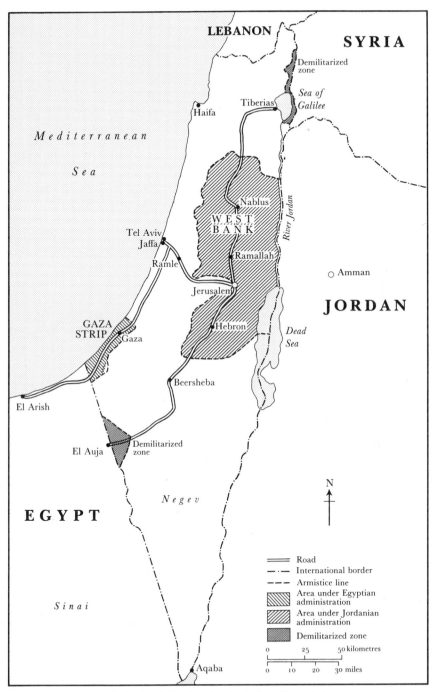

MAP 15   Palestine following the Arab–Israeli armistices, 1949

In the Knesset the government came under fire from both left and right for its armistice with Jordan, though it won a vote of confidence at the end of the debate. Ben-Gurion's opponents charged that the armistice was tantamount to recognizing the incorporation of the West Bank and the Old City of Jerusalem into Abdullah's kingdom. The right-wing Herut party, formed after the dissolution of the Irgun by Menachem Begin and his fellow Revisionist Zionists, rejected the partition of Palestine and especially its western part. Begin had already invoked the spectre of Munich following the agreement with Egypt and warned that the partition of western Palestine would divide not only the land but the soul of the Jewish people. In the Knesset, Begin demanded that the armistice with Jordan be made a test of confidence in the government. Ben-Gurion replied that it was preferable to have a Jewish state without the whole of the Land of Israel than to have the whole land without the Jewish state. A Jewish state, he argued, was not possible over the whole Land of Israel or even in its western part if that state was also to be democratic because the number of Arabs there exceeded the number of Jews. Did they want a democratic state of Israel in part of the land or a Jewish state over the whole of the land and the expulsion of its Arab inhabitants? asked Ben-Gurion. For his part, he wanted a democratic Jewish state even if it did not extend over the entire Land of Israel.

Ben-Gurion's left-wing opponents, the Communists and Mapam, charged him with having opened up Israel to Anglo-American influence. If Abdullah were allowed to annex the Big Triangle, said Mapam members, Israel might as well invite back the British. Ben-Gurion retorted that possibly Transjordan was a puppet of Britain, but Israel seemed to have its own puppet parties serving outside interests—a clear reference to the Soviet Union.

Mapam's opposition to the agreement with Abdullah stemmed not only from its anti-imperialist stance but also from a curious blend of military activism, a streak of territorial expansionism, and a commitment to Jewish–Arab coexistence. Half-heartedly, the party advocated the capture of the West Bank and the creation there of an independent Palestinian state under the leadership of 'progressive elements' who would make peace with Israel. It even suggested mobilizing Palestinian fighters and supporting them in their struggle to establish their own state. This suggestion was countered by Ben-Gurion by observing that it was not Israel's responsibility to create a state for the Arabs of Palestine. 'We are not contractors for the building of an independent Arab state', he said sarcastically. 'We believe this is a matter for the Arabs themselves.'[67]

[67] Tom Segev, *1949: The First Israelis* (Heb.) (Jerusalem: Domino Press, 1984), 34 f., 50 f.

Although in his heart of hearts Ben-Gurion aspired to a Jewish state over the whole Land of Israel, he regarded that as a task for future generations. In the circumstances of 1949, with the need to consolidate the country's international position and the overriding imperative of absorbing immigration on a large scale, he regarded the armistice agreements as a tremendous achievement and a very promising beginning in the quest for security. He was fully prepared to make peace on the basis of the new territorial status quo, he was encouraged by the signs that some Arab leaders accepted the new reality, and he was hopeful that the armistice agreements would pave the way to peace.[68] Initially at least, Ben-Gurion accepted the armistice agreements in their entirety. He was a purist in this respect. He saw the agreements as marking the definite end of the war and he expected them to be honoured to the letter by both sides.

Nor was there any serious difference of opinion between the Foreign Ministry and the defence establishment on the subject of the armistice agreements. Some members of the latter believed that Israel had not exploited her military advantage to the full, that by maintaining the pressure on the Arab countries she could have compelled them to conclude peace agreements instead of a mere armistice, and that, in Yigal Allon's phrase, 'Israel had won the war but lost the peace.' But this was very much a minority view. The predominant view of the Israeli Establishment—the Cabinet, the Foreign Ministry, and the defence establishment—was that the armistice agreements represented a very positive step towards peace and that peace indeed was just round the corner.

King Abdullah also came in for some criticism for his part in the negotiation of the armistice agreement with Israel, though the full extent of his personal involvement was not known at the time. Nuri al-Said, Iraq's prime minister, regarded the Israeli demand for areas that were purely Arab as a ploy to discredit Great Britain, King Abdullah, Glubb Pasha, and Transjordan and to spoil their relations with the other Arab countries. Accordingly, he sent a telegram to Amman urging Abul Huda to stick to the existing line and to refuse to budge. This advice was not well received in Amman. It was felt that Iraq's own refusal to negotiate had landed Transjordan in the situation in which they had to make either the best agreement they could or to run a very definite risk that a new Israeli attack would be launched against both the Transjordanian and Iraqi positions.[69]

Iraq's military leaders regarded the agreement with the Zionists

[68] Interview with Isser Harel.
[69] Sir H. Mack (Baghdad) to FO, 19 Mar. 1949, and FO to Baghdad, 30 Mar. 1949, FO 371/75387, PRO.

both as a betrayal of the Palestinian Arabs and as a perfidious act that placed their own forces in mortal danger. The Iraqis were convinced that the Zionists saw this agreement as a means of getting the Arab Legion out of the war as a prelude to mounting an offensive to force the Iraqi army to leave Palestine unconditionally. Various messengers were sent and various arguments were used to dissuade Abdullah from signing the agreement and his refusal to listen only confirmed the impression that he was acting out of selfish motives and left behind a legacy of suspicion.[70]

The most scathing criticism and the strongest resentment was expressed by the Palestinians who were uprooted from their villages as a result of the agreement that Abdullah concluded with the Zionists. 'Lamentations, biblical in colour and intensity, with women beating themselves and refugees starting to stream along the road from the Plain of Sharon' was how one eye-witness described the latest developments in Arab Palestine.

Under the terms of the armistice 70,000 acres of land in the plain went to the Israelis. With it went the only means of livelihood and the hopes of thousands of Arab *fellaheen*, because the new line cut them off in their villages in the foothills of Samaria from their land and crops in the plains below. The new line cut houses and schools in half and severed the only railway line at various places. At Bir Siki it gave the village to the Israelis and the village school to the Arabs. At Zeita it left the Arab village without any wells, and in other regions it cut off entire villages from the only roads out of them.[71]

The villagers of the Little Triangle who had defended their homes during the entire period of the conflict saw no possible justification for the surrender of their lands at the end of the conflict. They begged the Iraqis to stay and they sent a delegation to Baghdad to plead their case. The clause permitting the villagers to remain and stating that Israeli troops would not enter the villages was scoffed at. It was pointed out that similar pledges to the villagers of Faluja had been broken and that once the Egyptians had withdrawn the villagers were ejected from their homes by physical violence. And it was feared that once the Iraqis withdrew, the great majority of the villagers in the Little Triangle would be forced to leave and would end up as refugees.[72]

The Hashemite regime's failure to consult the villagers whose homes, properties, and livelihood were most directly affected by the agreement with Israel gave rise to bitter recriminations. It was openly stated that in his haste to conclude an immediate peace and obtain a title to the Arab areas in Palestine, King Abdullah paid no heed to the

[70] Juburi, *The Palestine Misfortune*, 377–80.   [71] *Daily Telegraph*, 11 May 1949.
[72] *FRUS 1949*, vi. 900–2.

wishes or rights of the Palestine Arabs. Amidst widespread protest and unrest, those whose lands were trapped on the Israeli side of the border in the Tulkarem and Jenin areas formed a committee to challenge the king's decision. A delegation of mayors also went to see the king in April 1949 to press him to arrange for free passage for the land owners. They challenged the accuracy of the maps that had supposedly been agreed upon by pointing to discrepancies that were liable to seal the fate of thousands of acres and hundreds of people.[73] But all the protests, arguments, and pleas were to no avail. Even if he had wanted to, the Hashemite king could not go back on the agreement that he himself had concluded with the representatives of the State of Israel. And as Walter Eytan had foreseen and the Palestinians had suspected, despite all the fine phrases and the guarantees written into the agreement, many of the inhabitants of the areas ceded by the Jordanians to Israel became refugees soon after the withdrawal of the Iraqi army.

[73] Plascov, *The Palestinian Refugees in Jordan*, 14 f.

14

THE STERILE ARMISTICE

Arab and Israeli stock-taking

One of the distinguishing characteristics of the armistice agreements signed at Rhodes was their temporary character. They were tailored to meet the needs of a brief transition period. It was taken for granted on the Israeli side that as soon as the armistice agreements had been concluded, peace talks would get under way with all the neighbouring states. It never occurred to the Israeli negotiators that they were designing a permanent regime. Otherwise they would not have been likely to agree to the restrictive clauses and unnatural demarcation lines that were written into the agreements. They believed that what they had agreed to was a further provisional measure to facilitate the transition from the present truce to a permanent peace in Palestine and that was precisely what the preambles stated. Cease-fire, truce, armistice, and peace were seen as a progression, with the armistice serving as the prelude to permanent and contractual peace treaties.[1]

It is possible that at the time of the Rhodes conference, this expectation was not confined to the Israeli side but was shared, albeit with little or no enthusiasm, by the ruling classes or at least the rulers of the Arab states concerned: King Farouk, King Abdullah, Husni Zaim, and Riad al-Sulh. But soon after the Rhodes conference was over, Arab political activists and the Arab press started saying that this was only a truce, that the conflict continued, and that the Arab world would never agree to the existence of Israel. After the end of the Palestine war, there was a general tension in all the Arab countries, a feeling which might be described as bordering on nervous breakdown. This came about as a result of the acute sense of frustration at the failure of Arab diplomacy and arms in the war with Israel and the fear of future Israeli aggression.

The sense of humiliation and outrage, the deeply felt hatred of Israel, and the widespread fear of Israeli expansionism placed formidable obstacles on the road to reconciliation with the new state. Arab rulers could not remain impervious to the strong popular undercurrents of hostility towards Israel and Zionism. Half-hearted leanings towards accommodation with the new force were largely drowned by the

[1] Interview with Yehoshafat Harkabi.

clamour for revenge. The armistice agreements had been signed under
the impact of military defeat, continuing military threat, pressure from
the UN and the Great Powers, and division inside the Arab camp. But
there was not the same urgency about making peace as there had been
about ending the fighting and the bloodshed. It was possible to live in a
state of no war and no peace. Under the impact of strong popular
resistance, the Arab leaders began to regret what was widely described
as their 'surrender' to the Zionists at Rhodes. And the charges of
surrender were accompanied by calls from various political quarters for
closing ranks, mobilizing all the Arab resources, and taking up arms in
a second round against Israel.[2]

Of all the Arab leaders, King Abdullah, as usual, was least affected
by the powerful currents of belligerence that were sweeping through the
Arab world in the wake of the Palestine defeat. From his vantage point
there were powerful countervailing reasons for seeking peace with
Israel. As a result of the war and the new armistice demarcation lines
Jordan was cut off from the Mediterranean, and through peace with
Israel Abdullah hoped to gain an outlet to the outside world. Peace
with Israel was also necessary in order to enable Abdullah to consolidate his hold over the territories he had acquired in the course of the
Palestine war. A second round against Israel would have provided her
with the pretext to expand and could probably end with the destruction
of the Arab Legion. In short, in Abdullah's view, the prosperity, the
security, and the expansion of his kingdom all required a final peace
settlement with Israel.

Abdullah believed when the armistice agreement was signed that it
would lead to a comprehensive peace with Israel and he pursued this
interest vigorously and involved some of his ministers. But it was not
easy. For one thing, as Israel grew in strength, so did her appetite for
land and lack of readiness for compromise.[3] And this time Abdullah
could not count on either British or American support for any attempt
to reach a separate agreement with Israel. Both the British and the
Americans suspected, on the basis of recent experience, that if Abdullah was to embark on separate negotiations, he would be vulnerable to
strong Israeli pressures and threats and might end up by losing more
territory. Their aim was to explore the possibilities of a comprehensive
peace settlement through the Palestine Conciliation Commission
(PCC) that had been appointed by the United Nations for this purpose and they accordingly advised the king not to forge too far ahead
with separate talks until the commission's own attitude was clearer.

[2] Arab Threats to Renew the War Against Israel, March–April 1949, 6 May 1949, and
Supplement, 25 May 1949, 2447/3, ISA.
[3] Interview with Anwar Nuseiba.

Abdullah was in favour of the Arab states being asked to send representatives to a joint meeting with the PCC though he had no illusions about the chances of agreement. If the other Arab states declined to work through the PCC or tried and achieved nothing, Jordan would still be able to carry on direct negotiations with Israel and they would be less able to criticize her for doing so.[4]

The king's first minister had no independent policy of his own on the conduct of relations with Israel. Cautious and risk-averse by nature, he preferred to tread a middle course between Abdullah's policy of peace at almost any price and the equally determined opposition to peace with Israel that was surging up in the Arab world, including Jordan. As a Palestinian, Tawfiq Abul Huda was particularly sensitive to his reputation inside and outside Jordan—a reputation that could only be tarnished through too close an identification with the king's policy. On being asked by Sir Alec Kirkbride whether he was clear as to how the armistice was to be converted into a peace settlement, he replied that the best method would be a direct settlement between Jordan and Israel to which the PCC would give their blessing.[5] As the questioner once observed, in a classic British understatement, 'the difficulties of getting King Abdullah and his Ministers to take into account considerations other than their own troubles are not slight'.[6]

The Israeli leaders had their own reasons for wanting to convert the armistice with Jordan into a final peace settlement. Such a settlement would not only break the circle of enmity round Israel's borders but might also encourage other Arab states to follow in Jordan's footsteps. Apart from these foreign policy considerations, social and economic problems made it necessary and urgent to start demobilizing and to cut down drastically on defence spending. But at the same time there were domestic political constraints on the government's ability to pursue a constructive peace policy. The internal struggle for power between centre parties making up the coalition with Mapai at their head and the opposition on the extreme left and the extreme right curtailed the freedom of action available to the former. So as not to lose ground in popular esteem to Menachem Begin's rumbustiously chauvinistic Herut party, the government had to appear as no less staunch in its defence of the national interest. The effects of this internal struggle for power on Israel's policy towards her neighbours and the great powers were very well explained in a report of the American National Security Council:

[4] Kirkbride to Burrows, 22 Feb. 1949, FO 371/75348; minute by B. A. B. Burrows, FO 371/75349, PRO.
[5] Kirkbride to Burrows, 6 Apr. 1949, FO 371/75349, PRO.
[6] Kirkbride to FO, 12 Mar. 1949, FO 800/477, PRO.

The present Government of Israel is intensely nationalistic in character, and maintains an internal policy of compromise dictated by the necessity of reconciling the demands of its extremist elements with the more moderate tendencies of the government party. The necessity of maintaining this internal balance makes it difficult for Israel's leaders to meet external demands for compromise with respect to relinquishment of territory and readmission of refugees which are essential to final settlement in Palestine. It also results in further increasing Israel's isolation among the neighbouring Arab states and in reinforcing the charges of intransigence and expansionism which have been levelled against Israel. In addition Israel endeavours to pursue a neutral course in its relations with East and West. This position of neutrality is motivated by the desire to obtain further assistance from the United States, and to retain the diplomatic support of the Soviet bloc, to obtain military material therefrom, and to facilitate immigration to Israel of Jews from Eastern Europe. In view of the delicate nature of Israel's internal political equilibrium, the government will be subjected to increasing pressures from political radical and extremist groups to the extent that it makes concessions to the Arab states or otherwise follows policies contrary to the views of these groups.[7]

In addition to the political constraints, potent psychological factors impeded the process of bargaining and accommodation with the enemy. Foremost among these was what might be termed the Holocaust syndrome—the tendency to view the Arab threat in the light of the destruction of central Europe's Jewry by the Nazis during the Second World War and the consequent determination to base Israel's security not on the goodwill of outsiders or paper guarantees but on her own strength, on defensible borders, and on military deterrence. As one left-wing soldier–politician remarked:

From 1948 until today, there has been a conceptual blackout on the part of our leaders on the question of how to turn Israel into a living tissue and part of this region. There is a Diaspora complex, and a Holocaust complex and a complex that the Arabs want to destroy us, and as a result there is a conceptual barrier against taking political initiatives. The central question is how Israel should manœuvre herself into becoming a normal state in the Middle East? And on this question there is despair from the beginning. The security consideration became paramount after the 'war of survival' of 1948.[8]

Security considerations were indeed paramount in the thinking and planning devoted to Israel's post-war relations with her neighbours. Intensive consultations were held in Tel Aviv with experts from the Foreign Ministry, the IDF, and the Treasury to formulate the strategy and tactics that should guide Israel's representative in the forthcoming

[7] Report by the National Security Council on United States Policy Towards Israel and the Arab states, 17 October 1949, in *FRUS 1949*, vi. 1430–40.
[8] Interview with Meir Pail.

talks with the PCC and the Arabs at Lausanne and the talks with the Jordanians in the Special Committee set up under Article 8 of the armistice agreement. Four meetings were held between April 12 and 22, with both the foreign minister and the prime minister attending the last meeting. At the first meeting Ben-Gurion defined the bringing in of immigrants to expand the country's population as the top priority in the years to come. Borders, he said, were never absolute and there was always the possibility of changing them later, and at that particular juncture immigration was more urgent and vital than anything else. It was within Israel's power, he observed, to capture the Triangle, the entire Galilee, and the Golan Heights, but such conquests would not strengthen Israel as much as would the doubling of her population. The fate of the state depended on immigration because without immigration there could be no settlement of the land, and only settlement constituted true conquest. In foreign policy Ben-Gurion wanted to support the independence of the Arab countries and to squeeze out the foreign powers so as to expand the scope for Israeli influence in the region.

There was some debate on the orientation that Israel should adopt given the division of the Arab world into a Hashemite bloc headed by Jordan and an anti-Hashemite bloc headed by Egypt. Reuven Shiloah came out against either a pro-Hashemite orientation or an anti-Hashemite orientation, proposing instead an Israeli orientation of living in peace with all the Arabs. Elias Sasson, on the other hand, was for opposing the Hashemite bloc in the matter of Greater Syria because, as he saw it, Jordan and Syria, with Britain's backing, would constitute a serious danger to Israel's security. Yaacov Shimoni thought there was no contradiction between the two positions provided a clear distinction was made between policy and tactics. He himself supported Shiloah's stand for neutrality between the rival Arab blocs but he also saw the value, without wishing to openly join, of the opponents of Greater Syria. Abdullah, he said, could annex the Arab parts of Palestine with or without Israel's consent so it was best for Israel not to take sides openly but to use the annexation as the bait to induce Abdullah to give up his Greater Syria scheme. All those present were united in their opposition to Greater Syria. Most of them were also for withholding formal consent for the annexation of the West Bank in order to retain a means of putting pressure on Abdullah to abandon his wider regional ambition.

The key question in the debate thus related to the future of the West Bank. Since the polar alternatives of formal consent to annexation by Jordan and capturing the area for Israel by military force were equally unacceptable, a consensus emerged in favour of an intermediate course: accepting the annexation *de facto* without recognizing it *de jure* and exacting the highest price possible for this acceptance. Israel was not to sign any document recognizing the annexation of parts of Palestine or Jerusalem to Jordan, but this axiom did not rule out *ad hoc* arrangements with Jordan.

A second major issue in the deliberations was the future of the Gaza Strip. Here two distinctly different approaches emerged. One, put forward by Sasson, called for giving the entire coastal strip around Gaza to Abdullah in order to divert him from the pursuit of Greater Syria. Abdullah, according to this view, had to have access to the Mediterranean sea and he was likely to persist with Greater Syria until he attained such access. If, on the other hand, his need for an outlet was met through Gaza, it would weaken his will and his efforts to reach Syria. The road linking Jordan with Gaza would be at Israel's mercy and could be severed at any time and this would increase King Abdullah's dependence on Israel. Another argument adduced in favour of this policy was that it would preclude Abdullah from gaining the coastal strip through direct negotiations and an understanding with Egypt that would be to Israel's detriment and lessen his dependence on her.

The other approach was elaborated by Reuven Shiloah, who pointed out that Abdullah's interest in Greater Syria transcended his need for an outlet to the sea and could therefore not be deflected by giving him such an outlet at Gaza. Nearly all the other participants sided with Shiloah in this debate. They were against giving the Gaza Strip to Jordan and for an attempt to work out some sort of an arrangement with Egypt: either by handing it over to Israel, or by an Egyptian–Israeli condominium, or, failing all else, by maintaining the status quo without formal annexation to Egypt.

Jerusalem was a third major issue on the agenda. Colonel Dayan, who had been designated as the Israeli representative to the Special Committee called for by Article 8 of the Israeli–Jordanian armistice agreement, reported that the Jordanians were in no hurry to appoint their representatives or to negotiate further arrangements for Jerusalem because they knew that Israel would not concede anything. In his view only the IDF could compel the Jordanians to carry out the obligations they had assumed by signing the armistice. The solution to the Jerusalem problem lay either in partition with Jordan or, as Dayan preferred, in leaving the line of demarcation deliberately fluid so that in the long run the entire city might be swallowed up by Israel.

Previously Israel's position had been that it should get new Jerusalem, Jordan should get the Arab quarters, while the Old City should be placed under international supervision. There was a shift of opinion, however, in favour of trying to take over the whole city, with special rights for Muslims and Christians over the Holy Places in the Old City, and for using the partition suggestion to undermine internationalization as the first step towards that ultimate end. Though Ben-Gurion did not initiate this shift in policy, he did not resist it either.

Resistance to the change in policy came from the foreign minister. Sharett pointed out that their position at the United Nations would be greatly eased if they could go there armed with a prior understanding with Abdullah. To illustrate his point about the risks involved in UN arbitration, Sharett quoted the Arab proverb about the two cats who found a block of cheese and asked the monkey to divide it between them. The monkey divided the cheese into two unequal parts and kept cutting slices for himself to equalize the parts. When the cats, realizing that they might lose all the cheese, said they were satisfied with the division and asked the monkey to stop, he replied: 'You may be satisfied but justice is not satisfied.'

The question, said Sharett, was whether they were willing to accept the division of Jerusalem into a Jewish part and an Arab part. If not, they would have to capture the Old City by force and reveal themselves in the most unfavourable light as aggressors. To his way of thinking this was out of the question. They had to be realistic, and realism could only mean seeking a joint solution with Abdullah. Sharett understood Dayan's motives for refusing to agree officially to the annexation of parts of Jerusalem by Abdullah. Whatever the juridical position, Sharett argued, in practice there was no real alternative to an agreement on the partition of Jerusalem with Abdullah.

Ben-Gurion declared himself to be in agreement with Sharett on the question of Jerusalem though he did not heed the latter's warning about the dangers of being drunk with victory. Whereas Sharett was groping for diplomatic solutions involving bargaining and accommodation with Abdullah, Ben-Gurion expected all the concessions to come from the other side. There were two questions, he said, in which they required Abdullah's co-operation, questions affecting only Israel and Jordan and no one else:

One is the northern part of Jerusalem, the link to Mount Scopus. It is vital that all the territory up to Mount Scopus should be in our hands. Maybe this can be achieved by an exchange or by some other means. If there is war, we shall capture it by force. Second, the entire western bank of the Dead Sea should be ours. Abdullah, from his point of view, finds it difficult, justifiably, to surrender territory if it involves surrendering a settlement. In this territory there is no Arab settlement. It is a desolate land which does not belong to him and which he does not deserve. Half of the Dead Sea belongs to him, but all the western part up to the Jordan must be ours. And if Abdullah has an interest in reaching a compromise with us, then this is not all that impossible. We must accept the existing position as it is. If we get concessions, well and good; if we don't—we are preparing ourselves.[9]

It would be a mistake to think that Ben-Gurion took such a hard line on the forthcoming talks with Jordan because he was peculiarly hostile towards this country. On the contrary, he explicitly stated that Israel and Jordan had common interests and that it was desirable to reach an understanding with Jordan, even for a limited period. But he was simply not prepared to contemplate substantive Israeli concessions in order to achieve an agreement when he had at his disposal such a devastatingly effective means as the IDF for dictating his terms to the other side.

On April 15, after the first of these four high-level meetings, Sasson, Eytan, and Dayan went to see King Abdullah at his winter palace at their request. The Israeli attitude on this occasion was more friendly and reasonable than during the previous meetings to conclude the armistice. The Israelis agreed that areas governed by Article 6 of the armistice agreement should remain intact and that the villagers would be given free passage back and forth to the Arab lines.

King Abdullah stated that the Jordanian delegation to the meeting of the PCC at Lausanne would be headed by Fawzi el-Mulki and that it would include four to six Palestinian notables. By including so many Palestinians in the delegation, the king evidently intended to demonstrate the extent of Palestinian support for himself personally and for the merger of the West Bank with Jordan. However, he doubted whether an accord could be reached at Lausanne and wanted to settle all matters privately with the Israelis as he had done during the armistice negotiations at Rhodes. He foresaw that his delegation would be isolated at Lausanne, he feared that his neighbours were likely to ditch him there, and he was therefore anxious to secure in advance the support of the Israeli delegation. He said that Jordan would be prepared to accept a peace agreement at Lausanne regardless of the attitude of the other Arab states and he invited the Israelis to return a few days later to work out the details with his prime minister.

The Israelis asked what his general requirements would be and he said he still wanted a port on the Mediterranean, a solution to the refugee problem, and the unfreezing of Arab financial assets in Israel. Asked to give more details about the port, he said that it should be either in the vicinity of Gaza with access via Beersheba or at Acre with access through Nazareth. This seemed to take his visitors aback. They

---

[9] Protocols of consultations held on 12, 19, and 22 Apr. 1949, 2441/7, ISA.

said that it would obviously cut Israel in two and suggested instead full transit facilities to and through Haifa. The king jokingly countered by offering them transit facilities to Aqaba if Jordan took over Beersheba and also offered to be helpful in connection with the Dead Sea and the Palestine Electric Corporation's concessions at Naharayim. They pointed out that the Israeli government had been attacked already for having given such good terms to Jordan. The king answered that he had been attacked universally for having accepted those terms.

The visitors also asked whether the Anglo-Transjordanian Treaty would apply to Arab Palestine if this area was taken over by Jordan. The king replied evasively that it was not the Arab part of Palestine but the Syrian part that interested him, but the British were stopping him. The Syrians, he said, did not like the British, and he did not want to take the British with him wherever he went, especially not to Syria. Moreover, information had reached him that the Turks had cast their eyes on northern Syria and he wanted to prevent that by taking Syria himself. From his answer the Israelis inferred that in return for agreeing to Jordan's annexation of Arab Palestine, they could obtain an official commitment that the treaty with Britain would not apply to this area.

Finally, Abdullah promised to instruct his government to appoint representatives to the Special Committee called for by the armistice agreement and to commence talks soon.[10]

The Special Committee

The Jordanian representatives to the Special Committee were duly named. They were Col. Ahmed Sidki el-Jundi and Capt. Ali Abu Nuwar who had represented their country at the Rhodes talks and had just been appointed to the Israeli–Jordanian Mixed Armistice Commission (MAC). This MAC had been set up under the Israeli–Jordanian armistice agreement and functioned alongside the other MACs set up by the armistice agreements with Egypt, Lebanon, and Syria. These agreements included various provisions for no-man's land, demilitarized zones, and the limitation of forces in border areas. The latter gave rise to interminable disputes, especially in Jerusalem and on the Syrian front. The agreements also established the four MACs, each of which consisted of two Israeli representatives, two Arab representatives, and a United Nations officer serving as chairman. In

---

[10] Report by E. Sasson at the consultation held on 19 Apr. 1949, 2441/7, ISA; Eytan to Sharett, 16 Apr. 1949, 2451/3, ISA; *FRUS 1949*, vi. 922; Kirkbride to FO, 16 Apr. 1949, FO 371/75349, PRO.

the first period following the signing of the armistice agreements, the MACs dealt mainly with the implementation of the decisions regarding such matters as the exchange of prisoners of war, the reduction and withdrawal of military forces, and the drawing of the demarcation lines. But their basic function was to supervise the armistice—to investigate complaints, to rectify violations, and to settle disputes. Since the votes of the Israeli and Arab representatives cancelled out, it was usually the UN chairman who made the decisions and was left to try and enforce them as best he could. The result was to inflame innumerable trivial matters into international disputes, as was the case with the poor Jewish family whose outside lavatory was only yards away from an Arab Legion post and whose attempt to build another lavatory apparently contravened the armistice agreement. But there were also instances of co-operation within the framework of the MACs, as for example, when Israeli and Jordanian search parties were despatched to separate the barbed wire and retrieve the false teeth of a nun who had inadvertently dropped them when leaning across her nunnery window. The Israel–Jordan MAC was kept busier than its three counterparts because of the relatively long border it had to supervise, and because of the manifold and acute problems of this border which separated not just armies but living communities and in some cases families.

Only the Israeli–Jordanian armistice agreement included a provision for the creation, in addition to the MAC, of a Special Committee composed of two representatives of each party 'for the purpose of formulating agreed plans and arrangements designed to enlarge the scope of this Agreement and effect improvements in its implementation'. The Special Committee could consider any matter submitted to it by one of the parties. But it was specifically enjoined to formulate agreed plans and arrangements on the following questions regarding which the text of Article 8 misleadingly claimed that an agreement in principle already existed: free movement of traffic on vital roads, including the Bethlehem and Latrun–Jerusalem roads, resumption of the normal functioning of the cultural and humanitarian institutions on Mount Scopus and the free access to them; free access to the Holy Places and the use of the cemetery on the Mount of Olives; resumption of the operation of the Latrun pumping station; provision of electricity for the Old City, and resumption of the operation of the railway to Jerusalem.

There was a considerable overlap between the functions of the Special Committee and those of the Israel–Jordanian MAC. All that the Armistice Agreement had to say on this subject was that the former would have exclusive competence over such matters as might be referred to it and that the plans it agreed might be supervised by the MAC. The key difference, however, was that the MAC was chaired by a UN officer from the United Nations Truce Supervisory Organization (UNTSO), whereas the Special Committee was not. It provided a channel for direct negotiation between the parties without the intervention of any third party. Israel had long shown the desire to settle the problem of Jerusalem directly with Jordan, and the Special Committee provided a convenient means of doing so without taking into account the UN interest in the city. It was also thought that without outside assistance Jordan would accede more rapidly and generously to Israeli demands. Hence the pressure exerted on Abdullah to appoint his representatives to this committee.

Dashing, one-eyed Colonel Dayan was appointed as Israel's chief representative to both committees and quickly carved out a major role for himself in policymaking as well as in the day-to-day conduct of Israeli–Jordanian relations. A special relationship developed between the young officer and the ageing prime minister, and the fact that Dayan received his orders from Ben-Gurion and reported to Ben-Gurion directly enabled him to accumulate power and influence out of all proportion to his rank. Sharett, who was capable of standing on his dignity, made no attempt in this case to fend off prime ministerial encroachment on his prerogatives. What Sharett and his men found much more difficult to tolerate were the arrogance, the aggressive approach, and the blatant expansionism of the prime minister's protégé.

Dayan was far from satisfied with the armistice demarcation lines and was particularly outspoken in arguing that the line with Jordan— the one he himself had negotiated—was unsatisfactory and could not possibly serve as the final border. Once the Arabs showed themselves reluctant to move beyond the armistice to peace and started reneging on some of the obligations they had incurred under the armistice agreements, Dayan emerged as the most uncompromising advocate of the use of force to secure Israel's interests regardless. Dayan began to propound the view that the War of Independence was not finished, that Israel's borders had to be enlarged, and that it was within Israel's power to enlarge them. He did not openly advocate going to war to seize more territory. Rather, he claimed that if war broke out, and his analysis of the Arab position left no room for doubt that a war would indeed break out, then he was for exploiting it to enlarge Israel's borders. For Dayan expansionism was not just an answer to specific problems but a general worldview, a philosophy of life—a Zionist philosophy of life that measured achievements principally in territorial terms. 'The existential mission of the state of Israel', as one of Dayan's colleagues put it, 'led us to be demanding and acquisitive, and mindful of the value of every square metre of land.'[11]

Dayan's detractors, and they included virtually the entire staff of the Foreign Ministry, maintained that this Zionist impulse to acquire more and more land and the reliance on force as the final arbiter did not serve well the interests of the State of Israel. Gershon Avner, the Oxford-educated protégé of Sharett, who headed the Western Europe Department of the Foreign Ministry, spoke with some vehemence about Dayan's short-sightedness and about the nefarious influence he had on Israel's relations with the Arabs. Dayan's saying 'if only the men of the Foreign Ministry were like the tanks of the IDF, all Israel's international problems would be solved', was quoted by Avner as an example of Dayan's political immaturity. 'Dayan's claim is idiotic. A tank can be destroyed by a direct hit, but a diplomat cannot be destroyed by a punch. Diplomacy is not like boxing; it is brain against brain.'

Israel's diplomats looked aghast at the heavy-handed, devious, and plainly unscrupulous methods employed by Dayan and his fellow officers in the conduct of armistice affairs. Here Avner had to concede that Dayan's approach was a manifestation of, rather than an aberration from, Zionist norms:

Cleverness, *shatara* [an Arabic word meaning shrewdness or cunning], is an inseparable part of the Zionist approach. If they want to get something, and there is a straight way and a crooked way of getting it, they always take the crooked way. This is not a trait that the Oriental Jews brought to Israel. It was here from the beginning. As early as 1949 we had an argument with Ben-Gurion's men—about our attitude to the armistice agreements. They always pushed to lie, to deceive, to resort to tricks. I am not opposed to lies in principle. A diplomat is a person who lies for his country. But why lie when there is nothing vital at stake? Yet, Ben-Gurion's men wanted to lie in any case, even if it was unnecessary and brought no advantage.

There was general disappointment when it transpired that the Arabs had signed but were not living up to their obligations, that the armistice agreements were being used as an instrument to continue the conflict. Nevertheless, Sharett took the view that it was undesirable to employ underhand methods in armistice affairs unless there was something really vital at stake.

When the first signs that the Jordanians were not going to honour Article 8 appeared, there was a debate on how we should react. Dayan took the line that we too should disregard the agreement, that we should resort to deception and use any means and any ploy that would serve to advance our interests. Sharett did not accept this approach. Later, Dayan also suggested the use of force but in the end Ben-Gurion himself rejected this suggestion.[12]

Three meetings of the Special Committee were held towards the end of

[11] Interview with Yehoshafat Harkabi.   [12] Interview with Gershon Avner.

April, from all of which UN observers were excluded at Dayan's insistence. Three major items were on the agenda: the withdrawal of military forces, the division of no-man's land, and the physical demarcation of the new lines by a barbed-wire fence. The map that Dayan took to these meetings was the one he and Col. Abdullah al-Tall had signed on 30 November 1948 in connection with the 'sincere and absolute cease-fire' for Jerusalem. On that occasion they had used a 1:20,000-scale map, Dayan tracing his front line in red while Tall traced his in green. They used soft wax pencils and the lines they drew on the map were 2–3 millimetres thick, or 40–60 metres on the ground. The line covered houses and even entire streets, and with the passage of time the wax 'sweated'.[13] And as the line on the map spread, so did the demands of the amateurish, but far from naïve, one-eyed cartographer.

The most contentious question proved to be the division of no-man's land, which included parts of the railway line and Government House, the former residence of the British high commissioner that had been built on the Hill of Evil Counsel with its magnificent view of the Old City to the north, Bethlehem to the south, and the Dead Sea to the East. Dayan offered to remove the railway from the agenda, pretending that a decision had been made to build a new line entirely within the Israeli side, but the Jordanian representatives obtained their king's consent for giving Israel a 200-metre strip in the south of Jerusalem through which the railway line ran. So the whole of the railway passed into Israeli hands, to Ben-Gurion's surprise and satisfaction since nothing was requested in return.

Initially, the Jordanian representatives also agreed in principal to the division of Government House which served as the headquarters of UNTSO. But fierce international protest and the arguments of Abdullah al-Tall against giving the lion's share of this strategically important position to the Israelis persuaded the king to retract his agreement, and the Government House compound remained under the flag of the United Nations.

The Jordanians were prepared to evacuate not just the village of Latrun but the entire salient with the road that passed below and the pumping station in return for Israeli withdrawal from certain villages to the north-east of Latrun. Dayan considered the demand to be excessive and since what he did offer was unacceptable, the question remained unresolved.

Mount Scopus was of even greater importance to Israel than Latrun because the Hebrew University and the Hadassah Hospital were there and because it was the highest point in north Jerusalem and as such a key strategic point, overlooking the roads from Ramallah and from

---

[13] Uzi Narkiss, *The Liberation of Jerusalem* (Heb.) (Tel Aviv: Am Oved, 1977), 24 f.

Jericho as well as the Old City. The Jordanians were prepared in principle to offer Israel free access to the Mount Scopus enclave but they balked at Dayan's demand for allowing Israel to build a new road on which she would be able to transport troops, tanks, and artillery. So no agreement was reached. Nor was there agreement on other radical proposals for exchanging Jordanian-held land for Arab quarters that had been captured by Israel in the course of the fighting. The Jordanian delegates announced that they were proceeding to Lausanne and proposed that the Special Committee suspend its work until their return. This was badly received by the Israelis who said that they would not discuss peace with Jordan at Lausanne unless Jordan conformed to the armistice agreement and continued the Special Committee talks.

The first attempt to implement such decisions as had been reached on the division of no-man's land met with stormy protest and violent resistance from the hapless inhabitants. The suburb of Beit Safafa in southern Jerusalem was doomed to be severed in the middle, the northern half close to the railway line going to Israel and the southern half remaining in Jordan. When a group of Israeli and Jordanian soldiers tried to put up a barbed-wire fence through the village, the angry villagers prevented them from completing the job. Dayan's solution was to carry out the division swiftly and ruthlessly. He notified the Jordanians that if they did not co-operate in enforcing the division, his soldiers would do it alone, by force if necessary. The next day, May 2, at 9 a.m., a new Jordanian delegation appeared with disciplined officers who firmly resumed the demarcation work and erected the barbed-wire fence. The village of Zur Bahar, with its dominating hillside position in south Jerusalem, also passed into Israel's hands.[14]

Sharett's visit to Shuneh

Moshe Sharett fully recognized that Israel was no less responsible than Jordan for the failure to forge ahead with the solution of outstanding problems through the Special Committee. There was a difference, he explained to the Knesset Foreign Affairs Committee, between Jordan and the other Arab states. With Egypt, Lebanon, and Syria, Israel's interest lay in concluding swiftly a final peace settlement which would bring stability and permit mutually advantageous trading relations. This was not the case with Jordan. Here Israel's best interest lay in withholding for the time being formal recognition of Jordanian annexation of parts of Palestine and Jerusalem and concentrating instead on

---

[14] Ibid. 25–31; Ben-Gurion's diary, 23 and 28 Apr. 1949; *DFPI*, ii. 591, 602, 608; *FRUS 1949*, vi. 895 f., 919 f., 960 f., 978; Dayan, *Story of My Life*, 115 f.; Tall, *The Palestine Tragedy*, ch. 17.

the solution of specific problems through the broadening of the armistice agreement and through a series of special agreements. The snag with this tactic, Sharett admitted, was that just as they themselves were saying to the Arab states that if they wanted a solution to the refugee problem they must make peace with Israel, so Abdullah could say to them that if they wanted a solution to various problems, they must enter into peace negotiations.[15]

This was precisely what Abdullah did claim three days later, on May 5, when Sharett, accompanied by Lieutenant-Colonel Dayan and Major Harkabi, visited Shuneh. The king received the visitors who had been brought by Abdullah al-Tall in his car with two other Arab Legion cars serving as a guard of honour in the presence of Tawfiq Abul Huda. He began by expressing his pleasure that Sharett was meeting him and his prime minister together for the first time. Sharett replied that for him too this was a historic meeting, coming after a long break in their personal contact, and that the presence of the prime minister only enhanced its importance. Round the dinner table there were about ten people. Nothing of political significance was discussed during the dinner except when the king turned to Sharett and asked in a whisper what would become of the Gaza Strip and whether the Egyptians intended to stay there. Sharett replied that Egypt's intentions had not been made clear yet. At the business part of the meeting there were only five men: the three Israelis, the king and his prime minister.

The king and the prime minister opened the discussion by referring to the new dispute that had arisen over the line to which the Arab Legion was supposed to withdraw in the Little Triangle. Apparently there was a discrepancy in the maps of the two sides concerning this line. Colonel Dayan proposed that Israeli forces move into the undisputed area and the whole problem be cleared up within a week by the Special Committee. King Abdullah seemed very troubled by the new complication and mentioned several times the unrest in the villages concerned. Sharett promised that immediately upon their return orders would be issued to their forces in the Little Triangle.

Reassured, the king proceeded to deliver a lecture on the necessity for peace and the need to prepare public opinion for peace. Sharett replied, somewhat disingenuously, that they too were anxious for peace, hence the importance that they attached to the resolution of outstanding problems. They were disappointed, he said, that the work of the Special Committee had been interrupted before it could complete its task. They too were having problems with public opinion, and the interruption of

[15] Sharett's speech before the Foreign Affairs Committee of the Knesset, 2 May 1949, 2392/12, ISA.

the committee's work caused much anger and was not conducive to a spirit of conciliation.

The king politely inquired whether they intended to deal only with practical problems and whether they did not think that more general negotiations should commence, leading to a comprehensive peace settlement. Sharett replied that they must proceed gradually. The armistice agreement had laid the foundations, now they had to build the walls by resolving the outstanding problems and eventually they would build the roof with an overall agreement.

The prime minister now begged to speak frankly. It seemed to him that Sharett proposed to discuss only those issues from which Israel stood to gain. Sharett replied that, on the contrary, their final objective was peace but it was necessary to proceed gradually towards that destination. There were questions on the agenda of the Special Committee and there were questions on the agenda of the Lausanne conference. It would be only logical to proceed stage by stage, to work through the agenda of the Special Committee and then to move on to the discussions in Lausanne, yet they would be prepared to carry on talks in Lausanne and Jerusalem simultaneously. His only concern was that problems of co-ordination between the Arab delegates to Lausanne would hold up consideration of the practical problems that need not wait until the final settlement.

Here the prime minister declared very firmly that they did not consider themselves bound by the position of the other Arab delegates and that they were prepared to conclude a peace agreement with Israel for the sake of their own country even if others were opposed.

Sharett stated that he was glad to hear this declaration, and that Israel, for her part, intended to conduct not multilateral negotiations but separate negotiations with each country, discussing only those matters that directly concerned the particular negotiating partner. On Jerusalem, declared Sharett, they would not enter negotiations with Egypt, Lebanon, or Syria, but only with the king. They did not concede any rights to the other Arab states over Jerusalem, except those that went with membership of the United Nations. Towards King Abdullah, on the other hand, their position was entirely different because both he and they were in Jerusalem and they therefore had to negotiate. Abdullah could not conceal his delight with this definition of the Israeli position. His face lit up and he looked at his prime minister as if to say: 'Did you hear that?!'

The prime minister then inquired whether Israel would agree to the 1947 UN partition resolution as the basis for the final settlement, or whether she intended to negotiate only on the basis of the existing situation. Sharett replied that the Arabs had never accepted the partition resolution and therefore it was now part of history; negotiations could proceed only on the basis of existing facts. The prime minister, feeling that Sharett had adopted a somewhat superior attitude, retorted angrily that in that case there was no point to any negotiations between the Arabs and Israel at all and there could be no peace.

Calmly, Sharett expounded the view that the UN partition plan was no longer relevant because it rested on a series of assumptions that had not materialized. The first assumption was that it would be achieved by peaceful means. The second assumption was that the Arab part of Palestine would be constituted into an independent state. The third assumption was that the two sides would be prepared to form an economic union. All these assumptions were shattered. A war had broken out, Israel had defended herself, and a completely new situation had arisen. It was not possible to turn the wheel back. Sharett did not agree that negotiations would be pointless. The Arab world, he said, could not possibly want to leave things as they were because that would mean anarchy; it needed to stabilize the situation and to forge a lasting peace.

The king intervened to say that he too, like the Israelis, had entered the war against his will. The prime minister went further and said that in fact there had not been a war, and the king added that throughout the period of military operations his forces had not crossed the borders of the Jewish state as defined by the UN resolution. In truth, he said, the only place where their respective forces had clashed was Jerusalem, and there it was the Israelis who had provoked the fight.

The prime minister returned to the charge that Israel was behaving selfishly and trying to make gains without giving anything in return. Sharett replied that the solution to all the problems before the Special Committee rested on reciprocity: free access to Mount Scopus in return for free access from the Old City to Bethlehem; Jordanian withdrawal from Latrun in return for Israeli withdrawal from some villages. As for the questions reserved for the Lausanne talks, there too agreement would be to the advantage of both sides. Jordan and Israel had jointly issued the concessions to the Palestine Potash Company on the Dead Sea and the Palestine Electric Corporation in Naharayim and both countries were the losers as a result of the failure to resume operations.

Several times the king raised the question of Gaza, stressing how important it was for him to have a foothold on the coast. Sharett said that Israel could accommodate his needs through the port of Haifa. The king said this would not be enough, that territorial control was essential, and that he reserved the right to raise the matter again at the Lausanne talks.

The king also expressed his concern over the refugee problem. Sharett said they knew that America intended to devote large sums of money to the settlement of the refugees in the Arab countries and that Israel would work to increase Jordan's share of this money so that refugee resettlement might be turned into a springboard for the economic development of His Majesty's country. His Majesty did not respond. Sharett expounded on the benefits that could accrue to both countries from joint irrigation schemes that would exploit the waters of the River Jordan. Both the king and prime minister were taken aback and said they thought that the time had not yet come for considering such projects.

Sharett therefore turned the conversation to the situation in Syria following Husni Zaim's *coup d'état* and mentioned the desirability of working out a common position in relation to Syria. Sharett was trying to find out whether there was any basis for the impression that Sasson had brought back from his last visit to Shuneh, namely that if the King could obtain Damascus, he would not insist on the annexation of Arab Palestine. But the prime minister was careful not to give anything away, saying casually that they were waiting to see the results of the Syrian elections. What about Syria's future, persisted Sharett. Did they think Syria should remain in her existing borders? Now the king perked up and announced self-importantly: 'If you are referring to the idea of Greater Syria, this idea is one of the principles of the Arab Revolt that I have been serving all along.' Thus ended the discussion on the Syrian question.

Towards the end of the meeting, which lasted three hours, the Israelis returned to the subject of the Special Committee and pressed for the resumption of its work. The king readily agreed but the prime minister was more reserved, pointing out that the formation of the new government would be completed during the following week and that this matter would have to be brought before it.

Another discussion took place on the final peace settlement. Sharett concluded by saying that although detailed guidelines had already been issued to their delegation to the Lausanne talks, as a result of this important meeting he would repeat the guidelines more firmly and instruct his delegation to spare no effort in trying to reach an accord with the king's delegation on all the outstanding issues.

It was midnight. Although the meeting had made little progress, it ended on a friendly note. The king breathed a sigh of relief and sent his visitors on their way home.[16]

On the long journey home, across the Allenby Bridge and Jericho,

---

[16] Moshe Sharett, 'A Meeting with King Abdullah, 5 May 1949', 2408/13, ISA; *FRUS 1949*, vi. 980–2.

the Israelis continued to spar among themselves. Dayan relates this episode in his memoirs in a manner calculated to draw attention to Sharett's pedantic nature. Apart from Sharett's pedantry, this trivial argument also illustrates Dayan's own cynical pragmatism and crudely utilitarian approach to the conduct of relations between states.

Towards Moshe Sharett he [Abdullah] was well disposed—at first. Sharett spoke a polished Arabic and was meticulously mannered and appropriately reverent in the presence of royalty. But at one of our meetings, a rather unsuccessful one—it was a hot night, we dripped sweat, and there were many mosquitos on the wing—Sharett corrected the king when he mentioned in passing that China had not been a member of the League of Nations. A king never errs and Abdullah stood by his statement. Sharett, like a demonstratively patient kindergarten teacher with a backward child, kept saying, 'But Your Majesty you are wrong, China *did* belong to the League.' Of course, that was the end of *that* meeting—and of the royal regard for Sharett. In the car on our drive back, I asked Sharett what the devil it mattered what the king thought about China and the League. Sharett turned on me with some heat: 'But China *was* a member of the League of Nations!'[17]

To the historian, the most interesting aspect of the meeting at Shuneh was the debate on the origins of the 1948 war and on the continuing relevance or otherwise of the UN partition resolution of 29 November 1947. It would have been difficult to challenge Abdullah's version of events and Sharett made no attempt to do so. Abdullah said he had not wanted to go to war but a series of events beginning with Deir Yassin and ending with the Jewish breach of the cease-fire in Jerusalem had forced him to take action. Abul Huda had not wanted to go to war either and remained faithful throughout to the limited strategy for which he had obtained Britain's secret endorsement. It was Israeli attempts to capture the Old City that brought about the clash between the Arab Legion and the Haganah. Even during the war, the Jordanians continued to pursue a limited strategy and at no point tried to force their way across the frontiers of the Jewish state. By implication Abdullah was now claiming that it was not he but the Jews who had gone back on the secret understanding they had reached on the partition of Palestine.

The other point made by Abul Huda was that Jordan had not rejected the UN partition resolution but had accepted it all along, at least as far as the creation of a Jewish state was concerned, and was therefore not being inconsistent in demanding that this resolution should serve as the basis for peace negotiations. Abul Huda told Sharett that he had no right to talk to him as he would to the Egyptians

[17] Dayan, *Story of My Life*, 108 f. Emphasis in the original.

or the others because he had not wanted war but had it forced upon him. Since Jordan did not initiate the war against Israel, she was not responsible for the consequences. Implicitly both Abdullah and Abul Huda seemed to be saying that there had been a special relationship in the past based on the agreement to partition Palestine, that they wanted to preserve this special relationship, and that this fact should be taken into account in the forthcoming peace talks.

There was another point of interest about this meeting relevant to the question of peace. Israeli spokesmen had always claimed, in 1949 and subsequently, that they sought with all their hearts a just and lasting peace, but that the Arabs remained adamant in their rejection of Israel's right to exist. This may have been true in the case of some Arab countries; it was emphatically not true in the case of Jordan. What the meeting at Shuneh, as well as Sharett's address to the Knesset Foreign Affairs Committee, reveal is that in this case all the pressure to move swiftly forwards towards comprehensive peace came from Jordan; it was Israel that was holding back.

Any doubt on this score is dispelled by the text of Sharett's talk to the heads of departments at his ministry on May 25:

The situation between us and Transjordan several weeks ago was as follows: Transjordan said—we are ready for peace *immediately*. We said—of course, we too want peace, but we cannot run, we have to walk. The foundations have already been laid in the armistice agreement. The walls are the agreements on Latrun, Mount Scopus, the railway etc., and then of course we shall put the roof. To this Transjordan replied: you only want to gain advantages from the process and then you will desert us. No, first we must establish peace. To this we replied again: it is not possible to run, we must learn to walk first.'[18]

Deadlock in the Special Committee

The reconstruction of the Jordanian government proceeded in an atmosphere of mounting popular discontent directed against its policy of accommodation with Israel. With more than a dash of hyperbole, Abdullah al-Tall described the rage experienced by the Palestinians at seeing their motherland consumed by wolves, with their Arab rulers serving the prey piece by piece to the mouths of the hungry wolves. This spectacle intensified their quest for revenge. When the king ordered the government to resign, they thought he was removing from power the treacherous government headed by Tawfiq Abul Huda. But their joy was short-lived for Abul Huda stayed on as prime minister and simply added to his old Cabinet three Palestinian public figures who,

[18] Foreign Minister's talk at the meeting of heads of departments, 25 May 1949, 2447/3, ISA.

according to Tall, had devoted their lives to the service of the British in Palestine.[19]

Of the three new ministers, only Ruhi Abdul Hadi, who became minister of foreign affairs, was known for his pro-British and his pro-Hashemite leanings. The other two were not old supporters of Abdullah, and their appointment signalled that he understood that if he was to have the support of his Palestinian subjects he could no longer confine his favours to the small and subservient clique of East Bank politicians. Khulusi Khayri, minister of agriculture and commerce, and Musa Nasir, minister of communications, were progressive Palestinians, reared in the half-light of the British democratic tradition and intent on reforming the Jordanian political system into a British-style constitutional monarchy.[20]

One of the new Cabinet's first acts was to appoint Abdullah al-Tall and Hamad Farhan, with Ahmad Khalil as legal adviser, as Jordan's representatives to the Special Committee. When the Special Committee renewed its work in mid-May, the Israelis wished to discuss only two points—the Latrun salient and access to Mount Scopus. In return for the salient and access to Mount Scopus, the Israelis were willing to give only the use of the Bethlehem road. The Jordanian representatives said they would agree to both points only if Israel returned the Arab quarters in new Jerusalem. But the Israelis refused to consider any proposals relating to Jerusalem itself.[21]

Dayan reported to Ben-Gurion that Farhan and Tall were very bitter, claiming that only the Jews benefited from the agreements made in the past. The anger of the inhabitants of Tulkarem and Kalkilya also affected them and made them more inflexible in the negotiations. Dayan consoled his chief with the thought that he had one means of exerting pressure: according to the latest map, the village of Latrun and Deir Ayub were in no-man's land and it was therefore permissible to fire on the inhabitants if they did not get out. At the same time Dayan admitted to Ben-Gurion that the Legionnaires were behaving very fairly, keeping to agreements even if they were against them and careful to tell the truth when they gave evidence before a UN committee, even if it pointed against them.[22]

The prospects of agreement in the Special Committee disappeared as the Jordanians stiffened their position and stepped up their demands. This was due not just to the pressure of public opinion but also to the belief that the armistice agreement would restrain Israel from renewing

[19] Tall, *The Tragedy of Palestine*, 398 f.

[20] Ann Dearden, *Jordan* (London: Robert Hale, 1958), 79 f.

[21] *FRUS 1949*, vi. 1039–41; Harkabi to Eytan, 15 May 1949, 2442/7, ISA; Tall, *The Tragedy of Palestine*, 402.

[22] Ben-Gurion's diary, 16 May 1949.

hostilities to attain her ends. Moreover, the government had reached the conclusion that it would be preferable to leave all the negotiations to the Lausanne conference, and the king apparently concurred in this policy following Sharett's disappointing response to his plea for peace. Dayan asserted privately that he was gloomier about the prospects of continuing peace in Jerusalem than at any time since he had assumed command the previous August. He advised the Israeli government to request the United Nations to return the Jewish sections of Mount Scopus to complete Israeli control under the terms of the agreement signed in July 1948 for UN protection on Mount Scopus 'until hostilities end'. He further proposed to inform Jordan bluntly that Israel intended to have free access by agreement or otherwise. He felt that Jordan was bound by Article 8 of the armistice agreement to grant free access and that refusal to do so would justify strong Israeli measures.[23]

The atmosphere surrounding the Special Committee talks was much the same as that which had characterized the armistice negotiations. The Israelis were presenting strong and irrevocable demands as well as stipulating what the Jordanians should agree to receive in return, while at the same time indicating that if their demands were not satisfied, they would obtain them by other means. Very little was offered to Jordan by way of positive inducements. The Israelis, for example, seemed intent on providing electricity for the Old City and on giving the Jordanians free use of the Bethlehem road. They did not appear interested in the fact that the Jordanians had no particular desire for either. The unabating storm of criticism from the Palestine Arabs, however, made the king and his ministers less amenable to further attempts at blackmail and intimidation. Most of them preferred the Israelis to make their threats good by force rather than meekly submit to the threat of force. The only possibility of reaching agreement, they insisted, would be for Israel to curb her voracious territorial appetite and to show some signs of willingness to negotiate in the genuine meaning of this term.[24]

From May 29 until August 8, while the Lausanne conference was in progress, the Special Committee remained suspended. During this period Dayan's patience seemed to be exhausted and he resorted increasingly to unilateral action which envenomed Israel's relations with the Arabs and brought her into open conflict with the United Nations. On June 6, in an effort to enforce the division of the Government House compound, Israeli soldiers entered the neutral area that had remained under the UN flag, erected a barbed-wire fence, installed machine-gun posts, and laid a minefield. This action brought forth

[23] FRUS 1949, vi. 1039–41.   [24] Ibid. 1049–51.

such an intemperate letter of protest from the chairman of the Israeli–Jordanian MAC that it later had to be withdrawn on orders from above.[25]

Within the MACs, with the exception of the Lebanese one, Israel became embroiled in a growing number of disputes, and the UN chairmen usually upheld Arab complaints of Israeli breaches of the armistice. The villagers of Wadi Fukin, on the border between Israel and Jordan near Hebron, were forced across the border and were not allowed to go back to their homes in Israel despite the ruling of the MAC.

Israel's treatment of Baqa el Gharbiya, an Arab village at the northern end of the Little Triangle—the border area ceded to Jordan—constituted the first major test case of her attitude to the armistice. In this village there were 1,500 Palestinian refugees in addition to its permanent residents when it was handed over by the Arab Legion to Israel under the armistice agreement. Article 6 of the agreement guaranteed the full rights of residence, property, and freedom to all the inhabitants of this and the other villages in the Little Triangle. Notwithstanding this solemn undertaking, an argument arose between Ben-Gurion's men and Sharett's men on whether Israel ought to treat the Arab residents she acquired with the new territory ruthlessly or humanely. Ben-Gurion himself was altogether oblivious to the human tragedy of the Arabs of Palestine, placing his pragmatic conception of the national interest above those of any individuals or minority groups. 'Land which has Arabs on it and land which has no Arabs on it are two completely different kinds of land', he said to his party colleagues, who were left in no doubt that his own concern was with land, not with people.[26] With his advisers he discussed more directly the treatment to be meted out to the Arabs of the Little Triangle. The discussion went as follows:

BEN-GURION: Do we want the Arabs on the part handed over by Abdullah to leave the place or to stay?
ELIAHU [ELIAS] SASSON: It would be better if they stay and there are several reasons for this.
ZALMAN LIFSHITZ: I think it would be better if they left.
BEN-GURION: I want to think further about this matter.[27]

By early August the Foreign Ministry point of view represented by Sasson must have been overruled, for Israeli soldiers ruthlessly expelled all the refugees and several of the regular inhabitants of Baqa

[25] The Government House Affair, 9 June 1949, 2453/2, ISA.
[26] Segev, *1949: The First Israelis*, 42.
[27] Political Consultation, 12 Apr. 1949, 2441/7, ISA.

el Gharbiya across the armistice line into Jordan. In a report to the
Prime Minister's Office and to the foreign minister, Colonel Dayan, the
staff officer for Mixed Armistice Commissions, explained the IDF
tactics in this matter in the past and in the future.

There is a fear that even if we are justified in all the reasons we gave against the
return of the refugees of Baqa, the question will be put to the vote and be
decided by a majority of the chairman and the Arab delegates—against us.
Therefore, we are seeing to the spread of rumours among the Arab refugees to
say that whoever is returned to Israel will not enjoy the help of the Red Cross
and also, since his return would be against the wishes of the government of
Israel, there is no chance that one day he would have back his land. We hope
accordingly that even if it is decided that we should take back the refugees, the
majority would refuse to return.[28]

At the meeting of the MAC to consider the Jordanian complaint, Israel
took the position that she would not permit the return of any of the
expelled Arabs except as part of a general solution to the refugee
problem. In a personal conversation with Capt. Ali Abu Nuwar, the
Jordan representative, in the presence of the MAC's chairman, Col.
Samuel Ballentine of the United States Marine Corps, Dayan said that
Nuwar could bring the question to the vote and force Israel to
repatriate the expellees but 'they would regret it if they returned'.
Although Israel's position was in direct violation of the armistice
agreement, General Riley advised Ballentine to refrain from exercising
his casting vote since the UN would be powerless to ensure that the
Arabs who decided to return would receive fair treatment. Ballentine
accordingly proposed that the question be removed from the agenda of
the MAC and referred to a civilian intergovernmental committee. In
the meantime Israel magnanimously agreed to take back thirty people
who were able to prove that they had been residents of the village.
General Riley considered this typical of Israel's tactic of negotiating by
threat and of her disregard for the authority of the United Nations.[29]

The men concerned with Israel's image abroad as a newcomer into
the community of nations were no less troubled by the tactics of the
IDF's staff officer for armistice affairs than was General Riley. Their
main concern was not that these heavy-handed tactics were bound to
stir resentment and antagonism on the part of its victims but that
subversion of the armistice regime would undermine Israel's international position and play into the hands of her enemies. Walter Eytan
expressed sentiments that were widely shared in the Foreign Ministry
when he wrote to Sharett:

---

[28] Lt.-Col. Moshe Dayan to the foreign minister, 11 Aug. 1949, 2431/6, ISA.
[29] *FRUS 1949*, vi. 1314; Harkabi to Abba Eban, Israel's Representative at the UN, The
Situation in the Mixed Armistice Commissions, 17 Oct. 1949, 64/2, ISA.

For some time now I have been very concerned about the increasingly acute crises in three out of the four Mixed Armistice Commissions. Most of these crises developed as a result of unilateral action on our part, for example, actions in Baqa el Gharbiya and Wadi Fukin. These affairs gave the other side concerned the opportunity to present complaints against us. In most cases the facts compelled the chairman to identify with the Arab point of view and the result: we achieved nothing. We only succeeded in arousing general anger and in creating the impression that the Armistice Agreements are not being properly observed and that their existence is in danger.

I do not know who decides on the steps that we take in these matters. Who, for example, decided that it was necessary to expel the inhabitants of Wadi Fukin and to destroy some of their houses? Did those responsible for these deeds seek the opinion of the Foreign Ministry about the political conse-quences that these actions were liable to bring about? It is true that we may be able to produce legal rationalizations for most of these actions, but the accumulation of a can of worms of this kind is bound, in the end, to work against us.[30]

The affair of Baqa el Gharbiya crystallized the different views of the diplomats and the soldiers on the armistice and on the treatment of the Arabs inside Israel's borders. It was the first blatant manifestation of 'cruel Zionism' in the aftermath of war and it provoked the first open confrontation between Ben-Gurion's men and Sharett's men on the all-important question of how Israel's Arabs should be treated. Ezra Danin, Reuven Shiloah, Yehoshafat Harkabi, and Moshe Dayan saw in the expulsion an Israeli achievement and maintained that this was how Israel ought to act in the future. Sharett's men saw the affair as a political blow to Israel and warned against the use of deliberate provocations in order to bring about the expulsion of the Arabs. Sharett's men were not necessarily in favour of conceding what the Arabs demanded. But they were against the use of such underhand methods. Ben-Gurion's men wanted to manufacture pretexts for expel-ling the Arabs from the border areas as Dayan had done from Lydda and Ramle. The big difference was that the expulsion of the inhabitants of Lydda and Ramle took place during the war whereas now it was after the war, after the establishment of the state, and after the signature of the armistice agreements. What lent poignancy to the debate was the observation of Chaim Weizmann the veteran Zionist leader and the first president of the State of Israel—that it would be by her treatment of the Arabs that the Zionist movement would be judged.[31]

Physical coercion to expel Arabs from Arab land was now piled on top of the diplomatic coercion by which this land had been acquired in the first place. Walter Eytan's misgivings at the time the armistice

[30] Eytan to Sharett, 11 Sept. 1949, 64/2, ISA.   [31] Interview with Gershon Avner.

agreement was signed—that despite all the promises and the fine phrases, the Arabs of the Little Triangle would be molested and maltreated—were now seen to have been fully justified. Yet there can be little doubt that Dayan's strong-arm tactics were in conformity with Ben-Gurion's wish to turn land which had Arabs on it into land that had no Arabs on it.

Inevitably, there was a political price to pay for this strategy and tactics in terms of Israel's relations with Jordan. No progress was made in the Special Committee following the renewal of its meetings. The new Jordanian delegates were less well disposed towards Israel than their predecessors had been and there was no longer any question of unrequited concessions. The railway remained the only matter to have been successfully handled by the Special Committee, before and after its adjournment. On all other matters the Special Committee was unable to formulate any agreed plans. The new Jordanian delegates, while maintaining that they still agreed in principle to free access to Mount Scopus, were unable to reach agreement with the Israelis on how free access might be worked out. Since Mount Scopus was such a strategic location, overlooking the Old City and most of the main arteries leading to Arab Jerusalem from Jordan-controlled territory, the Jordanians were not willing to give the Israelis complete freedom of passage without any form of control.

Israel approached the negotiations with a minimum plan and a maximum plan. The minimum plan was to obtain free and unrestricted passage to Mount Scopus without having to submit to inspection. In return, Israel offered free passage along the Jerusalem–Bethlehem road. The Jordanian delegates pointed out that what Israel stood to gain under this plan was immeasurably more valuable than what she was offering in return. The maximum plan called for territorial contiguity between Israel and Mount Scopus, entailing Jordanian withdrawal from Shaikh Jarrah and Wadi Joz. Under this plan there would have been a complete reversal of positions with Jordan becoming dependent on Israel for access to Nablus. The plan would have also put an end to the special status of Mount Scopus as an area under UN protection. For this plan Israel was prepared to consider limited territorial compensation in the south of Jerusalem but once again she hoped to acquire much more than she was prepared to give away.

What was important to the Jordanians was the return of certain Arab quarters held by the Israelis, and they were determined to make use of the Mount Scopus situation as a bargaining point for their demands. There was nothing in Article 8 which required the Jordanians to accept any plans and arrangements for free access to Mount Scopus unless they agreed to them. And in the atmosphere of suspicion and ill-will that marked the second phase of the Special Committee meetings, they did not agree to any of the plans proposed by Israel.[32]

Dayan had definite ideas on what should be done to break the diplomatic stalemate and he presented his ideas verbally to Ben-Gurion and followed them up with written memoranda. On September 29, in a memorandum to the chief of staff, Dayan proposed military action to capture Mount Scopus:

> True, Mount Scopus is on the other side of the Arab line, but at the time when we recognized this line it was agreed that there would be free passage to Mount Scopus. Our recognition of the line was conditional on an opening in this line for free movement by us to Mount Scopus. If they do not permit that, our recognition of the line expires. Graphically, one can say that we recognized this wall on condition that there would be a door in it for us; if the door is closed, we do not recognize the wall and we shall break through it.

Without control of Mount Scopus, continued Dayan, their military position in Jerusalem would remain vulnerable. Moreover, with the passage of time the armistice lines would harden into permanent borders. Unless Israel acted quickly to enforce her rights, the decision reached at Rhodes would be worthless. After all, it was not up to the Arabs but up to Israel to give tangible expression to her rights, and her failure to do so, in Dayan's view, amounted to a surrender of those rights.[33]

Ben-Gurion asked Dayan whether the military action he proposed would not bring about a renewal of the war. Dayan confidently predicted that it would not. In his estimate even if it came to an open military clash and the use of force to break open a corridor to Mount Scopus, it would remain an isolated episode and not touch off general hostilities. Moreover, argued Dayan, it was probable that a show of force by Israel would induce the Jordanians to fulfil the terms of the agreement, as they had done with the division of no-man's land in southern Jerusalem.

Ben-Gurion did not accept Dayan's proposal. Although he was convinced that the plan could be executed, he did not sanction the use of force. His main reason was that the time had come for concentrating on the tasks of peace: the care and rehabilitation of immigrants, the settlement of the land, and the injection of life into the desert regions. The Land of Israel, Ben-Gurion said, would not remain theirs solely through war and the power of the army. For Ben-Gurion the book of war was closed—for the time being at least.[34]

---

[32] Sharett's speech before the Foreign Affairs Committee of the Knesset, 2 May 1949, 2392/12, ISA; *FRUS 1949*, vi. 1405–7.

[33] Lt.-Col. Moshe Dayan to the chief of staff, 22 Sept. 1949, 2436/5, ISA; Dayan, *Story of My Life*, 117 f.   [34] Dayan, *Story of My Life*, 118; Ben-Gurion's diary, 28 Sept. 1949.

15

THE LAUSANNE CONFERENCE

The three-headed monster

The task of translating the armistice agreements into peace was assigned by the United Nations to a Palestine Conciliation Commission. Failure of the earlier UN attempt at political mediation, during the second half of 1948, did not augur well for the new attempt. Count Bernadotte's proposals were unacceptable to Israel even as a basis for discussion, and the Arab representatives had roundly dismissed them as unjust, unlawful, and unworkable. Nevertheless, at the end of the debate on the mediator's proposals, the General Assembly, on 11 December 1948, passed a resolution setting up a Conciliation Commission, composed of American, French, and Turkish representatives and instructing it to assist the governments concerned to achieve a final settlement of all questions outstanding between them. The brave word 'peace' did not appear in the resolution for fear of offending Arab susceptibilities, but peace was the unmistakable aim. Two additional tasks were specifically assigned to the PCC: to draw up a scheme for a permanent international regime for Jerusalem and to facilitate the repatriation, resettlement, and economic and social rehabilitation of the refugees.

The PCC marked an important turning-point, for the worse, in the evolution of Arab–Israeli relations. The fundamental challenge was to continue the process begun by Dr Ralph Bunche at Rhodes, to convert the armistice agreements into a lasting peace. Yet, even before the last of these agreements was signed, this process began to falter and was soon to be reversed. The PCC was unable to arrest the deterioration in Arab–Israeli relations, let alone settle all the outstanding questions between them. And while it presided over a potential turning point in the history of the Middle East, history failed to turn. During the first year of its existence the PCC spent hundreds of hours in discussions, held one major international conference at Lausanne, and generated thousands of reports, letters, and cables—but success persistently eluded it. It went round and round in circles and in the end utterly failed to bridge the gulf between Arabs and Israelis on any of the major issues. Judged by its results, the commission's attempt at conciliation was an exercise in futility.

What are the reasons for this unmitigated failure? First of all there are the weaknesses and shortcomings of the commission itself. Instead of a single UN mediator with the full authority of the world organization behind him, authority was divided among the three powers who appointed representatives to the commission. Consequently, national interests frequently took precedence over the requirements of conciliation by what was quickly dubbed the three-headed monster. The Turkish member, Hussein Yalchin, was an elderly politician, no longer capable of sustained work and in no hurry to get results, who had published a series of articles calling for a military alliance between his country and the Arab states in blithe disregard for the need to preserve at least a semblance of impartiality as between Arabs and Israelis. The French member, Claude de Boisanger, was a career diplomat who was not only imbued with the traditional French suspicion of British designs in the Middle East but actively worked behind the scenes to limit British influence by encouraging the Israelis to resist the claim of Britain's client, Abdullah, to eastern Palestine. The American member, Mark Ethridge, was the publisher of a Louisville newspaper who was appointed by Harry Truman as a reward for his political services during the 1948 presidential elections. Though forceful and energetic and in a great hurry to get results, Ethridge was handicapped in carrying out his international assignment by the continuing tug of war at home between the pro-Israeli White House and the pro-Arab State Department.

Power politics within the PCC could perhaps have been held in check by an exceptionally forceful secretary. But the man chosen was Dr Pablo de Azcarate, who had served on the staff of Bernadotte and Bunche but had neither the inclination nor the force of personality to assume a commanding position. As one American confidentially wrote:

Azcarate is a charming man with a wealth of experience, but he is a routinist, timid and lacking in the capacity to take initiative. A triple-headed organization such as the PCC is by its very nature inhibited from strong affirmative action unless the secretary is a dynamic individual willing and able to lead. The very least, therefore, that should be done is to replace Azcarate by someone who has the qualities which Bunche demonstrated so strikingly when he was on the Secretariat of UNSCOP.[1]

A second reason, and in the official Israeli view the fundamental reason, for the failure of this attempt at conciliation derived from allowing the Arab representatives to appear as one body in talks with

[1] James McDonald to George McGhee, 16 Nov. 1950, James G. McDonald Papers, Columbia University, New York. On the personalities and attitudes of members of the commission, see also David P. Forsythe, *United Nations Peacemaking: The Conciliation Commission for Palestine* (Baltimore: The Johns Hopkins University Press, 1972), 37–9; Touval, *The Peace Brokers*, ch. 4.

the commission and, worse still, to shirk any direct negotiations, whether multilateral or bilateral, with the Israeli representatives. Whereas Bunche had been insistent on separate and direct negotiations between Israel and each of the Arab states concerned, the commission insisted neither on separation between the various Arab delegations nor on face to face meetings between each of them and the Israeli delegation. According to Dr Walter Eytan, who headed the Israeli delegation to the Lausanne conference, this was the commission's first and most fatal error:

The appearance of the Arabs as a single party inevitably made them, individually and thus collectively, more intransigent. The representatives of Egypt, Jordan, Lebanon and Syria never met the PCC except in a body. The Commission not only tolerated this arrangement but encouraged it. The result was, naturally, that any Arab representative who may have had relatively moderate views on a given subject was intimidated. He would not dare to express in the presence of three colleagues from the other Arab countries any opinion that these might consider weak or treasonable, even if his opinion was sincerely held and might well have been discussed if he were meeting representatives of Israel, or even the Conciliation Commission, alone. In that way the Commission pushed the Arabs along the path of extremism, from which, spurred also by other forces, they have never since looked back.[2]

This officially propagated and widely accepted account of why the PCC failed to produce a settlement of the Palestine dispute has been subjected to a withering critique by another Israeli diplomat, Gershon Avner, who also represented his country at the Lausanne conference. According to Avner the failure of the Lausanne conference was essentially a political failure rather than one of diplomatic technique:

The explanation that the conference failed because the Arab representatives appeared together rather than separately is childish. It is based on the assumption that if one meets the Arab delegations separately they would not be extreme and on the further assumption that whatever is agreed bilaterally will not become known to the other Arabs. But in reality it is inconceivable that two sides to a conflict would want a settlement and only a problem of method would prevent them from reaching it.

And there was no real chance of reaching a peace agreement at Lausanne. The Arabs signed the armistice agreements because they had an urgent need to do so. The IDF was on the offensive on all fronts and only by means of armistice agreements could it be stopped. If the Arabs have to sign, they will sign. Signing a document is not binding. They are not Swedes. If on the following day it does not suit them, they will disregard it. At the time when the armistice agreements were signed the Arabs had no intention of making peace. They had a pressing interest in putting an end to the fighting and it was for this

---

[2] Eytan, *The First Ten Years*, 50.

reason, and only for this reason, that they signed the armistice agreements. It was not until 1949 that the Arabs understood that they were beaten and began to recognize the scale of the disaster. Previously they had been confident that the Jews would be beaten and that they would take their property. They had set out to protect the Palestinians and now the Palestinians were crushed and trampled underfoot. And now the Arabs were shocked by the contrast between the expectations they had in the first half of 1948 and what actually happened in the second half of that year. So from a psychological point of view they were not ready to make peace with Israel.

On our side there was a great mistake in the evaluations preceding the Lausanne conference. We were drunk with victory. We had no doubt whatever that we were going forward to peace agreements. Moreover, we could also base ourselves on the texts of the armistice agreements which stated explicitly that this is only a stage in the transition to peace. We did not understand that the Arabs had no intention of making peace with us.

The assumption at the base of the accepted version is that there were some Arab states who wanted to make peace with Israel but were afraid of the others. But this was not so. They were all extreme in their demands. Eytan spent much time with Fawzi Mulki in an attempt to reach a separate agreement. He repeatedly asked whether the Jordanians really wanted peace and Mulki kept replying that they did but he had a long list of demands. The demands of the various Arab delegations were uniform: the borders of the UN partition plan, the internationalization of Jerusalem, and the return of the refugees. If you talked to Abdullah he would say my view is such and such but the Arab position is different. At Lausanne the Arabs established and maintained a united front.

Our expectations were totally unrealistic. They were predicated on the armistice agreements. It is not that there were opportunities and we missed them; there was no chance whatever of reaching a peace agreement. I cannot prove it but I believe that even if we had accepted all the Arab demands, they would have still been unwilling to sign a peace agreement with us. It is important to distinguish between a failure of method and a political failure that is rendered inevitable by mistaken political estimates.

The explanation that the Lausanne conference failed because the Arab delegations were allowed to appear as one party was invented for propaganda purposes and is devoid of any basis in reality. When the Commission failed we immediately wanted to pin the blame on the Arabs and it was convenient to say that we had gone there with sincere intentions of striving for peace and only because the Arab states adopted the position of the extremists it was impossible to attain it. This is not an explanation but a propaganda gambit, and a successful one.[3]

Gershon Avner spoils a good case by over stating it. He is helpful in pinpointing the gaps in the Israeli-inspired version but he is too sweeping and categorical in his dismissal of this version. Just because the Israeli version is self-serving does not mean that it is completely

---

[3] Interview with Gershon Avner.

invalid. The procedure adopted by the PCC and its effect of welding the Arabs into one party was not the basic cause for the failure of the Lausanne conference, but it was nevertheless a contributory cause.

The basic cause behind the PCC's failure to promote a settlement was that the Israeli and Arab positions were so far apart and so inflexible that the gap between them was unbridgeable. Israel's leaders yearned for peace and acceptance by their neighbours, but not at any price. The armistice agreements lent international legitimacy to the borders of the new state, consolidated its security, and provided a sound basis for economic development, immigrant absorption, and settlement. There was a school of thought, of which Abba Eban was the most articulate spokesman, which said that the armistice agreements met all Israel's needs, that she did not need anything else, and that by appearing too anxious to attain peace Israel would only encourage the Arabs to demand a price for it. Moshe Sharett recognized that from a tactical point of view it would be a mistake to dwell constantly on Israel's need for peace lest the Arabs interpret it as a sign of weakness, but in the long run he felt that Israel could not live in splendid isolation, nor could she afford to forgo the manifold economic benefits that only true peace could bring. Ben-Gurion, on the other hand, was persuaded by Eban's argument that the armistice agreements were perfectly adequate, that by seeming to be in a hurry to get peace Israel would give rise to Arab expectations for concessions on borders, on refugees, or on both, and that it would therefore be better to wait a few years because there would always be opportunities to talk to Arab leaders. In an interview with Kenneth Bilby, the correspondent of the *Herald Tribune*, Ben-Gurion succinctly summed up his position: 'I am prepared to get up in the middle of the night in order to sign a peace agreement—but I am not in a hurry and I can wait ten years. We are under no pressure whatsoever.'[4]

In practical policy terms this position meant that while Israel was interested in peace, she was not prepared to pay a price for it. Ben-Gurion's instructions to the Israeli delegation on the eve of the Lausanne conference was to negotiate peace on the basis of the existing armistice demarcation lines. There was no willingness on his part to make or even to consider any significant territorial concessions for the sake of peace. As far as the refugees were concerned the question was not whether to allow them to return before or after the conclusion of a peace settlement but whether to allow them to return at all. By April 1949 the government had formulated a very clear answer; its line was not to allow the return of the refugees. This policy was not openly proclaimed so as not to give the impression that Israel was blocking

[4] Ben-Gurion's diary, 14 and 18 July 1949.

peace and so as not to antagonize the Arabs before the negotiations began. Instead, the Israeli leaders sought refuge in evasive formulas. While remaining obstinately opposed to wholesale repatriation, on political, economic, social, and security grounds, they declared their willingness to discuss the repatriation and the resettlement of the refugees within the framework of comprehensive peace negotiations. Government policy thus left the Israeli delegation with very little latitude to negotiate on the refugee question. Whether a more flexible line could have led to a different outcome is, of course, impossible to tell. It is interesting to note, however, that one Israeli scholar, who has written what remains the most scholarly and objective study of the Arab refugee problem, considers that had Israel, in March–May 1949, accepted the right of the refugees to return to their homes and lands, the subsequent history of the region might have taken a different course.[5]

The Arab leaders, because of weakness and internal instability and because of the serious loss of prestige and legitimacy that accompanied their recent defeat in Palestine, were for the most part either unwilling or unable to conclude a peace settlement with Israel. All the Arab countries were in a state of considerable turmoil, with Syria still in the throes of the military coup staged by Col. Husni Zaim. Other Arab rulers, to maintain their precarious hold over power, engaged in appeasement of the masses whose hatred of the Zionists and of the Western powers soared to new heights in the wake of military defeat. This internal tension and nervousness in the Arab countries made it difficult for their leaders to pursue a prudent and practical foreign policy or to respond positively to international initiatives designed to pacify and stabilize the region.

On the pressing question of how to respond to the challenge posed by the creation of a Jewish state in their midst there was no uniform answer; in fact, looking at the political debates that were taking place at that time in Egypt, Jordan, Iraq, Syria, and Lebanon, three broad schools of thought may be discerned. The first called for an early attack on Israel with the aim of wiping it off the map before it had time to consolidate itself militarily, economically, and internationally. The fact that the Arab states had been defeated in the first round should not, according to this view, delay or deflect the proposed attack, since that defeat was linked to various internal and external factors which had nothing to do with Israel although they had worked in Israel's favour.

The second school of thought also maintained that the good of the Arab world required an attack on Israel to wipe her off the map but considered that a number of years should be allowed to pass in order to

---

[5] Rony E. Gabbay, *A Political Study of the Arab-Jewish Conflict: The Arab Refugee Problem* (Geneva: Librairie E. Droz, 1959), 273.

ensure victory in the second round. The interlude was necessary for settling the internal disputes of the Arab world; for organizing properly its military power; for improving relations with the Western powers; for developing the natural resources of the Middle East and improving social and economic conditions; and above all for furthering the process of unity and for extending it to include Turkey, Iran, and Pakistan.

The third school of thought, which claimed to be more pragmatic and realistic, said that the Arab world must strive above all to limit as far as possible the borders and the Jewish population of Israel in order to forestall any future territorial expansion at the expense of her neighbours or economic domination of the markets of the East, and in order to keep her a weak state, dependent on her neighbours, and incapable of adopting a separate foreign policy. In the second place this school called on the Arabs to refrain as far as possible from recognizing or co-operating with Israel in order to be able to examine more closely this 'foreign entity' with its political intentions and racist tendencies and in order to keep it for a long time in a state of military tension and social and economic instability in the hope that it would collapse by itself. If Israel proved able to withstand all these pressures over a number of years and changed into a Middle Eastern state that genuinely had the interests of the people of the region at heart, then, according to the third school, would come the time to compromise with her and accept her.

It is not easy to say precisely which of the Arab states or which of the Arab leaders subscribed to the first, second, and third schools of thought. All three approaches featured in the public debate and all three strategies were being considered by the politicians of all countries—Egyptian or Iraqi, Jordanian or Saudi Arabian, Syrian or Lebanese. All three approaches together informed the backdrop to the talks between the Arab leaders themselves and between them and the West. All three approaches formed the united and rather extreme position adopted by the Arab delegations at Lausanne and thus hindered progress in the work of the PCC.[6]

Iraq, Saudi Arabia, and Yemen declined the PCC's invitation to send representatives to the Lausanne conference. Nuri al-Said considered it necessary to involve Ibn Saud in the talks with the PCC, as no other Arab leader had the authority to accept the partition of Palestine and ensure its acceptance by his people. Since all the other Arab leaders and governments had compromised themselves by making promises which they were unable to fulfil, argued Nuri, they could not accept partition without the lead being given by Ibn Saud. The latter, however, had no interest and was under no pressure to take the lead in

[6] Sasson to Sharett, 27 Sept. 1949, 2403/12, ISA.

coming to terms with the Zionist enemy and accepting a partition that was most likely to benefit his greatest Arab enemy, King Abdullah. Nuri was equally unrealistic in holding that the Arabs should negotiate with the Conciliation Commission only if four principles were agreed in advance: (a) the whole of the city of Jerusalem should come under the administration of the Palestine Arabs; (b) disarmament of the Jews, who would be allowed to maintain a police force only for internal security, (c) all the Arab refugees should be allowed to return to their homes (otherwise the Jews of Iraq, of whom there were over 150,000, would be sent to Palestine), and (d) the port of Haifa and the end of the Iraqi oil pipeline should be placed under international control. Both King Abdullah and the Egyptians pointed out that these conditions had no chance of being accepted, and in the end the Iraqis decided not to participate in the Lausanne talks at all.[7]

At this stage, before the signature of the armistice agreement, the Jordanians hoped that the PCC would help to bring about a settlement between themselves and Israel and even questioned the need for a general peace conference. At a meeting with the commission on February 11, in the winter palace at Shuneh, Tawfiq Abul Huda hinted at the possibility of bilateral negotiations between his country and the State of Israel but the commission did not think it prudent to take the hint, at least until it had sounded out the other Arab governments. After years of fruitless attempts at conciliation it is easy to say that the commission should have seized the chance offered by the Jordanian prime minister and concentrated its efforts on obtaining a separate peace between Israel and Jordan. But at the time the commission had no real cause to think that it would fail in its attempt at general conciliation. Moreover, since its mandate from the General Assembly referred to all the states concerned in the Palestine conflict, the commission would have had difficulty in justifying a decision to limit its efforts to two of these states before attempting general conciliation. Lastly, and in Pablo de Azcarate's opinion this was the decisive argument in favour of the attitude adopted by the commission, the least gesture on its part favouring the conclusion of a separate peace between Israel and Jordan would have immediately ruined whatever possibility existed of negotiating with the rest of the Arab states, and this without any certainty of a positive result in the limited field of relations between Jordan and Israel.

Dr de Azcarate also suspected that this idea of direct negotiations between Israel and Jordan was a kind of bait which the government of Israel dangled before the eyes of the commission, seeking to paralyse its activities by suggesting that any inopportune interference on its part

[7]   Mack to FO, 15 Jan. 1949; Note by Sir H. Mack, 19 Jan. 1949, FO 371/75330, PRO.

might cause the negotiations to fail. And on more than one occasion he had the impression that some members of the Secretariat of the United Nations were won over by this effort to represent the PCC as little less than an obstacle to peace in Palestine. In reality, there was only one firm supporter of direct negotiations and a separate peace with Israel in the Kingdom of Jordan, and that was King Abdullah. And the king himself realized that he could not overcome strong opposition to his policy from some of the active political elements in the state.[8]

Anatomy of failure

The Lausanne conference opened on 27 April 1949 and lasted until September 15. Whereas at Rhodes the Israeli and Arab delegates as well as Dr Bunche and his staff had been housed together under the same roof, in Switzerland all the Arab delegations were put up at the Lausanne Palace at one end of the town, while the Israeli delegation and the commission were accommodated at the Hotel Beau Rivage by the lake at the other end of town. To describe the proceedings of those five months as a conference is to stretch a point since the delegations of Israel and the Arab states never met officially even once; it was the PCC that conferred and corresponded with each side separately.

The gulf separating the two sides was evident from the very outset. The Arabs, with the exception of Jordan, were not prepared to enter into general peace negotiations until a solution to the refugee problem had been found. Israel was not prepared to negotiate on any point separately, outside the framework of general peace negotiations. The Arabs maintained that the refugee problem must be settled first, while Israel wished the territorial problem to be settled first. This was the first and most formidable stumbling block on the road to negotiations that the PCC was called upon to remove.

In its efforts to remove this stumbling block, the PCC registered one notable success when it got the two sides to sign separately, on May 12, identical documents, accepting the UN partition plan of 29 November 1947, as a basis for discussion with the commission. But the success was very short-lived. The Arabs signed the famous Lausanne Protocol because it appeared to commit Israel to acceptance of the partition frontiers—those frontiers that they themselves had waged, and lost, a war to destroy. Their earlier position, which was to discuss only the refugee problem and not a territorial settlement, was now reversed. Walter Eytan signed the Lausanne Protocol because at that time Israel's application for membership of the UN was under consideration and he believed that signing would improve her chances of being

---

[8] Azcarate, *Mission in Palestine*, 142 f.

accepted, and also because the protocol was merely *a* basis for discussions with the commission, not *the* basis.

Eytan signed the Lausanne Protocol, which he later described as a sham, without being authorized to do so; he did so because he was certain that no risk was involved. Members of the government, and especially the prime minister, were shocked to learn that Israel suddenly accepted the partition plan and they called Eytan to account. Their anxieties were allayed when Eytan explained that the protocol bound neither side to anything except to begin discussions. The exchange of views with the commission was to bear on certain territorial adjustments. 'Adjustment' was an elastic word. It could mean adjustment in any direction—increase or decrease. The Arabs could put forward the UN partition plan as a basis for discussion if they wanted to, but Israel was free to present any plan of her choice as an alternative. Three days after signing the protocol Eytan indeed declared that the Arab states had no territorial rights to any part of Palestine, demanded the withdrawal of their forces and suggested a plebiscite to decide the future of the Arab areas. These propositions dispelled not only Israeli fears but also Arab hopes while the commission, shattered and confused, was forced back to square one.[9]

To break the deadlock, the American member of the commission, Mark Ethridge, persuaded the Israelis to take all the refugees in the Gaza Strip (occupied in the war by Egypt), in return for the ownership of the strip itself. The Israeli government hoped to gain a number of very important advantages from accepting this proposal: additional territory; extending the coastal strip down to Rafah; having the desert as the border between Egypt and Israel; removal of the threat to the security of Tel Aviv and the southern Negev; and forestalling the danger that Jordan and Britain would become entrenched on Israel's western as well as eastern flanks in the event of the strip going to Abdullah.[10] In May 1949, when the government took the decision to offer to incorporate the Gaza Strip in Israel, it was estimated that the entire population of the Strip, residents and refugees, was about 180,000. It therefore came as something of a shock when the experts discovered shortly afterwards that the correct number was 310,000, of whom 230,000 were refugees.

Horrified by the prospect that Israel's Arab population would rise to half a million if the Gaza scheme was realized, Sharett immediately backtracked. He ordered his representatives not to raise the subject of

[9] Azcarate, *Mission in Palestine*, 150 f.; Eytan to Sharett, 9 May 1949, 2447/6; Eytan to Raday, 12, 14, and 15 May 1949, 2447/1, ISA; Eytan, *The First Ten Years*, 57–9; Forsythe, *United Nations Peacemaking*, 50–2; interview with Gershon Avner.

[10] Sharett to the Knesset Defence and Foreign Affairs Committee, 1 Aug. 1949, 2451/13, ISA.

the strip so as not to give the Arabs an opening to stipulate conditions, but to wait until they raised it so that Israel could lay down the conditions. And the condition he had in mind for Israel's annexation of the Gaza Strip was that its population would be in the region of 150,000.[11] Ben-Gurion, who was more obstinate than Sharett in his opposition to the return of the refugees, had a more open mind as far as the Gaza scheme was concerned. Though he doubted that the Egyptians would agree to let them have the Gaza Strip, Ben-Gurion did not share Sharett's concern because:

1) The coast of Gaza is of singular importance, 2) the land is good, and it is possible to establish fishing villages, so that it would have economic as well as security value, 3) we would avoid having the Egyptians as neighbours at this place—such neighbourhood could become a serious military danger in the future, by land and even more so by sea, 4) we would prevent the entry of Abdullah, which is liable to bring the British back, and which is bound to lead to a territorial dispute: if Abdullah rules Gaza, he (or his successor) would be bound to demand a corridor.[12]

The Americans saw in the Gaza scheme a real possibility for a breakthrough since the number of the refugees there was greater than the 200,000 they had been urging Israel to take back. They urged the Egyptians to give serious consideration to the original and informal Israeli offer, but the Egyptians nevertheless turned it down. Despite the heavy economic burden it placed upon them, the Egyptians preferred to remain in occupation of the Gaza Strip rather than hand it over either to Abdullah or to Israel. They were reluctant to lay themselves bare to the charge of trading land for refugees and perhaps they feared that they would end up with the refugees anyway, and lose the strip into the bargain.[13]

President Truman personally intervened in an effort to save the Lausanne talks. In a note addressed to Ben-Gurion on May 28, Truman expressed serious disappointment with the position taken up by Israel at Lausanne with respect to a territorial settlement and to the question of Palestinian refugees and threatened that, unless there was a positive change, the United States would have to reconsider its attitude to Israel. Even when presented with this exceptionally strong note from the leader of the most powerful country in the world—a country on whose goodwill Israel was crucially dependent—Ben-Gurion refused to budge. To James McDonald, who handed him the note, Ben-Gurion

[11] Sharett to Sasson, 2 June 1949, 2451/13, Id., 28 July 1949, 2442/8, ISA; Sharett at Mapai's Secretariat, 28 July 1949, 24/49, Labour Party Archive.

[12] Ben-Gurion's diary, 26 June 1949.

[13] George McGhee, *Envoy to the Middle World: Adventures in Diplomacy* (New York: Harper and Row, 1983), 36.

said off-the-record but with great passion: 'The United States is a powerful country; Israel is a small and weak one. We can be crushed, but we will not commit suicide.'[14]

James McDonald was passionately devoted to the Zionist cause and it was for this reason that he had been appointed by President Truman as America's special representative and then ambassador to Israel. As the only political appointee in the Near Eastern Affairs Bureau he enjoyed direct access to the president and he used that access to counteract what he saw as the repeated attempts by the State Department's pro-Arab career officers to get Truman to approve steps and policies which contradicted his essential position vis-à-vis Israel.[15] The Israelis were not slow to appreciate the possibilities of using their friends at the White House or friends with access to the White House in order to undercut State Department initiatives. In this instance, George McGhee, the recently appointed co-ordinator for Palestine refugee affairs at the State Department, recommended the holding up of the remainder of the $100-million Export–Import Bank of Washington loan to Israel, which was $49 million, to put pressure on Israel to take at least 200,000 refugees. Armed with what he thought was White House approval for his plan, McGhee broke the news to the Israeli ambassador over lunch. The ambassador looked at him straight in the eye and said that he would not get away with this move. Within an hour of his return to his office McGhee received a message from the White House that the president wished to dissociate himself from any withholding of the Export–Import Bank loan. 'I knew of the President's sympathy for Israel', commented McGhee ruefully, 'but I never before realized how swiftly the supporters of Israel could act if challenged.'[16]

To deflect the ever increasing international, and especially American, pressure from itself to the Arabs, the Israeli government reconsidered its policy and tactics on the question of the refugees and authorized the Israeli delegation at Lausanne to announce, on July 31, that Israel would be prepared to repatriate 100,000 refugees as part of a comprehensive settlement to the Middle East conflict. This figure included the 25,000 who had already returned to Israel as part of a scheme for the reunion of families and it represented the absolute limit of Israel's contribution. This offer was not only conditional on the agreement of the Arab states to resettle all the remaining Arab refugees in their countries and on the conclusion of a permanent peace settlement but it also left the Israeli government the freedom to determine

[14] FRUS 1949, vi. 1072–5; McDonald, My Mission in Israel, 181–4; Ben-Gurion's diary, 29 May 1949.
[15] McDonald, My Mission in Israel, 186–8.
[16] McGhee, Envoy to the Middle World, 36 f.

what categories of refugees to take back, the timetable for their repatriation, and the places where they would be resettled. In substance this offer represented a retreat from the Gaza scheme, which involved more than twice as many refugees. Yet, because the ground had not been prepared for this announcement, there was a storm of protest from inside Mapai, from nearly all the parties in the Knesset, and from the public at large. The government was angrily denounced for giving in to 'imperialist pressures'; Ben-Gurion, who had been far from enthusiastic about this idea, left it to Sharett to beat a hasty retreat. Unless the Arabs hastened to accept the offer and to take it upon themselves to resettle the remaining refugees, declared the embattled Sharett, the government would be forced to withdraw the offer. Several months later, the Israeli government, 'tired of holding out its hand', withdrew the offer.

The PCC considered the Israeli figure not only unacceptable but so far removed from what it thought reasonable that it did not even communicate it officially to the Arab delegations. These delegations none the less let Israel off the hook by declining her offer and making a counter-proposal involving nearly total repatriation. Any offer made by Israel was suspect in their eyes. One suspicion was that Israel would choose the balance of the 100,000 from among those who owned property and who would go back, sell their land and other assets, and clear out of the country with the proceeds. Yet, from a tactical point of view, they would have done better to accept the Israeli proposal, if only to call Israel's bluff, for the Israeli offer to take back 100,000 refugees had been dictated not by a genuine change of heart but by tactical considerations and its rejection by the Arabs temporarily improved Israel's position *vis-à-vis* the commission and the Great Powers.[17]

No one saw more clearly than Elias Sasson, the only Oriental Jew of senior rank in the Foreign Ministry, that Israel's obstinate defence of the status quo barred the way to an understanding with the Arabs and doomed the Lausanne conference to failure. His colleagues of European extraction treated him with some reserve and even condescension because culturally and temperamentally he resembled an Arab, or rather the Israeli diplomats' stereotype of an Arab, while politically he was considered somewhat unreliable on acount of his excessively moderate views. When the question arose as to whether

[17] Azcarate, *Mission in Palestine*, 151 f.; Don Peretz, *Israel and the Palestine Arabs* (Washington, DC: The Middle East Institute, 1958), 43–50; Brief by the Foreign Minister for the Delegation at Lausanne, 27 July 1949, 2446/6; Shiloah to Sharett, 3 July 1949, 2451/13; Sharett to the Knesset Defence and Foreign Affairs Committee, 1 Aug. 1949, 2451/13; Sharett to Shiloah, 2 Aug. 1949, 2442/8; Sharett to Shiloah and Sasson, 7 Aug. 1949, 2447/5; Sharett to Shiloah, 10 Aug. 1949, 2442/8; Sharett to Dr M. Eliash (London), 10 Aug. 1949, 2412/26, ISA; Ben-Gurion's diary, 1 Aug. 1949; interview with Gershon Avner; interview with Anwar Nuseiba.

Sasson, as the head of the Foreign Ministry's Middle Eastern Department, should be placed at the head of the Israeli delegation to the Lausanne talks, his colleagues were opposed. 'Reuven [Shiloah] and I', wrote Walter Eytan to Sharett, 'are definitely against Elias being the head of the delegation as a whole. We see his role as that of the ideal liaison officer between our delegation and the Arabs, making contacts, speaking soft words into Arab ears, formulating difficult matters in a way which may make it easier for the Arabs to swallow them, etc., etc.—precisely the task which he discharged so excellently at Rhodes.'[18]

Not even Sasson's silver tongue, however, could make Israel's tune music to Arab ears at Lausanne. At the end of the first phase of the talks, Sasson wrote to his subordinate, Ziama Divon, about his personal disappointment and frustration; in an even more savagely frank vein, about the absurdity of Israel's position; about the incompetence and uselessness of the PCC; and about the selfishness and rivalries of the Arab states, all of which combined to produce the impasse at Lausanne and frustrate any possibility of a constructive solution to the refugee problem.

You have no idea how sorry I am that I came to Lausanne. The town, it is true, is very beautiful. The hotel at which we are staying—Beau Rivage—is really magnificent. So is the weather and so on. But, as you know, we did not come here to enjoy the beauty of the town or to admire its illustrious buildings or famous mountains. We came here for a particular purpose, for one and only one purpose, which is to obtain peace with the Arab states. But we have been here for two months and we have not advanced one step towards this desired and exalted goal and there are no chances of progress in the future even if we decide to stay at Lausanne for another several months. Every day that passes strengthens the feeling and the belief among us, the Arabs, and the Conciliation Commission that the Lausanne talks are sterile and doomed to end in failure. Nor is this surprising:

Firstly, the Jews think they can achieve peace without any price, maximal or minimal. They want to achieve (a) Arab surrender of all the areas occupied today by Israel; (b) Arab agreement to absorb all the refugees in the neighbouring countries; (c) Arab agreement to border adjustment in the centre, the south and the Jerusalem area to Israel's exclusive advantage; (d) the relinquishment by the Arabs of their assets and property in Israel in exchange for compensation which would be evaluated by the Jews alone and which would be paid, if at all, over a number of years after the attainment of peace; (e) de facto and de jure recognition by the Arabs of the state of Israel and its new frontiers; (f) Arab agreement to the immediate establishment of diplomatic and economic relations between their countries and Israel, etc., etc. . . .

[18] Eytan to Sharett, 10 Apr. 1949, 2447/2, ISA.

Secondly, the Arabs do understand that Israel has become a fact etc., but they ask themselves: if these are her conditions, what obliges them to hasten and recognize her? Egypt argues, for example, that her recognition of Israel would strengthen not only Israel but her two Hashemite neighbours, the near one—Transjordan, and the far one—Iraq, and upset thereby the balance of power in the Arab world, to the detriment of at least four Arab states: Saudi Arabia, Syria, Egypt, and Lebanon. The situation could have been entirely different had it been possible to create an independent Arab state in the other part of Palestine. But the factor that is blocking that today is Israel. By her current position and current demands Israel is making the second part of Palestine unsuitable for all but one thing—annexation to one of the neighbouring states, namely, Transjordan. Hence, in Egypt's view, her one and only way out of this entanglement is: not to come to terms with Israel, not to recognize Israel and to prolong the present situation for some time on the assumption that in the meantime she would succeed in strengthening herself militarily, economically, and scientifically and withstand any separate threat, Israeli, Transjordaian, and Iraqi, or any joint threat of these three forces together.

This is only one example out of dozens that I hear from the head of the Egyptian delegations, Abdel Monem Mostafa, every time I meet him and try to press him to change his position. Nor is this more than one example out of dozens that I hear from the Lebanese or the Palestinians who serve as advisers to the Syrian delegation. And the truth has to be said: from the angle of Egypt's interest, it is difficult to dispute this or similar points of view, especially as the relations between Iraq and Syria or Transjordan and Syria are going from bad to worse every day and one discovers, little by little or in large doses, the British intrigues that lie behind the entanglements.

As for the Conciliation Commission, all its efforts and modes of operation add oil to the fire. Abdel Monem Mostafa said to me once: 'Even if Egypt wanted to agree to Israel's demand about withdrawal to the political boundary of the mandate period, America would not let her. American policy is not in favour of such withdrawal without compensation.' And the Lebanese delegate, Mohamed Ali Hamade, once told me the same thing about the fate of western Galilee: 'The French are encouraging Syria and Lebanon to insist firmly on the detachment of the Galilee from Israel and its annexation to one of them.' In the light of this situation it appears that the UN should be asked to appoint a new 'conciliation commission' to conciliate between the members of the Conciliation Commission themselves so that they might be able to free themselves from the policy of their governments and to devote themselves in all seriousness to the task they took upon themselves which is: the attainment of peace between Israel and the Arab states.

As for the refugees—they are the scapegoats, so no one takes any notice of them. No one listens to their demands, explanations, and suggestions. On the other hand all the parties use this problem towards ends that are practically unrelated to the aspirations of the refugees themselves.

For example: all the Arab states demand the return of the refugees to their places whereas in practice not one of them—except Lebanon—is interested in this. Transjordan and Syria want to hold on to their refugees in order to enjoy

American or international aid and thus to become strong states that can support themselves in every way and are capable of threatening others. Egypt wishes to leave the refugee problem open and pending for a number of years in order to prevent stability in Transjordan and Israel and so that she herself could grow stronger in the meantime and occupy again her appropriate place in the Arab world, and also in order to be able to bargain at their expense with America and Britain. The truth of the matter is that the refugee problem is not pressing on Egypt at all. All the refugees under her rule are concentrated in the Gaza area and are being supported for the time being by international agencies. If these refugees die or live, if their number increases or decreases, makes absolutely no difference to her. As a backward, feudal, and over-populated state, she is used to such phenomena as poverty, indigence, mortality, etc.

And it is not just the Arab states who pay no attention to the explanations of the refugees and their suggestions; we too are not listening to their words and plans. And it is not because we are not interested in these, but because we have resolved not to receive them back in our country, come what may. I do not deny that I was and remain one of the movers and supporters of this resolution. I do not regret and I am not ashamed of this. The absorption of the refugees in the Arab states and not in the state of Israel is, in my opinion, the best guarantee for turning any peace that may be achieved between Israel and the Arab states into a genuine and lasting peace. But this position of ours should not in my opinion stop us from using the refugees towards a certain practical action that would be of benefit to them as well as to us.[19]

Secret talks with Jordan

Sasson's devastatingly honest critique of the attitudes of Israel, the Arabs, and the PCC during the first phase of the Lausanne conference also reveals, incidentally, that some face to face meetings did take place between the Israeli and Arab delegates. What was said at these secret meetings is infinitely more interesting and more instructive than the turgid proceedings of the PCC at its formal and separate meetings with the two sides. In fact, one of the few positive results of this singularly futile international conference was the cover it provided for direct contacts between the principal protagonists themselves. Most of the Arab delegates were not averse to direct contact with the representatives of the Zionist state, but they took elaborate precautions, such as meeting outside Lausanne and at night, in order to avoid detection by members of the other delegations and because these trysts made nonsense of their refusal to hold direct negotiations with Israel under the commission's auspices.[20] Elias Sasson himself initiated and conducted most of these clandestine discussions, though other Israeli

---

[19] Sasson to Divon, 16 June 1949, 2447/2, ISA.
[20] Eytan, *The First Ten Years*, 51 f.

officials were also involved. Thanks to their punctilious reporting of every contact to their minister and thanks to the twenty-two numbered letters that Sasson sent Sharett from Lausanne during August and early September, we have a fairly comprehensive if one-sided record of what transpired at these secret, largely nocturnal meetings. The meetings were held concurrently but for simplicity's sake we shall look first at the meetings with Jordan, then with Egypt, and finally with representatives of the refugees.

It was probably no accident but a reflection of the special relationship that the first direct contact that the Israelis made was with the Jordanians. On May 3, Sasson went to Vevey to meet Fawzi el-Mulki, the minister of defence and head of the Jordanian delegation, and Riad al-Mufleh, who had participated in the armistice negotiations at Rhodes and in the work of the Israeli–Jordanian Mixed Armistice Commission in Jerusalem. When Sasson got in touch with Mulki on the phone, Mulki was perfectly prepared to meet him, but not in Lausanne. They therefore picked on the Hotel Trois Couronnes at Vevey as a likely sounding place and the meeting was duly held. There was nothing of very great interest to report about the content of this conversation, whose importance lay in the fact that it was the first direct contact with an Arab delegation.[21]

Before the end of the month Sasson sent a message to King Abdullah asserting that the Lausanne talks were a complete failure and requesting Jordan to enter into separate talks, parallel to the Lausanne discussions, in Jerusalem. The king was not inclined to accede to this request in view of what had happened when separate talks last took place between Israel and Jordan without the presence of a third party, but he was anxious about the possibility of an Israeli attack on his country if the request were refused. He confided his fears to Sir Alec Kirkbride and to Wells Stabler, the American chargé in Amman. Both the British and the Americans assured him that the Lausanne talks had by no means failed and urged him not to take any action likely to undermine those talks. The British planned to release the munitions held by them at Amman in the event of an Israeli attack on the Arab Legion and a decision was taken against holding separate talks as long as the Lausanne conference was in progress.[22]

Sasson became rather pessimistic about the practical effect of private talks with the Arabs, but Eytan was determined to have a real go at the Arabs himself. He met Mulki by chance one night and sat drinking with him and his two companions for an hour or so. The fastidious Eytan, who had lost none of the airs and graces of an Oxford don during the

[21] Eytan to Sharett, 3 May 1949, 2441/1, ISA.
[22] FRUS 1949, vi. 1056 f., 1077 f., 1082 f.

years he had spent in the Middle East, found Mulki a bit crude in manner but very jolly and was greatly encouraged by Mulki's positive response to his suggestion for a personal meeting.[23]

At their second meeting, on June 22, Eytan outlined to Mulki Israel's tentative proposals for peace. First and most important was the proposal to divide up Palestine between Jordan and Israel only. In other words, Lebanon, Syria, and Egypt would be stuck with the old frontiers. Second, Israel and Jordan would each recognize the right of the other to keep what they held. Third, Israel might agree to give Gaza to Jordan if the latter could persuade Egypt to cede it. Fourth, Israel would not give up western Galilee nor pay any territorial compensation for it. Fifth, Israel agreed to discuss with Jordan frontier adjustment elsewhere in their mutual interest. Finally, as a gesture in the event of peace being established, Israel would make some contribution towards solving the refugee problem. Mulki said he would cable the king and arranged a further meeting. Though Mulki was non-committal at this stage, Eytan received the impression that Jordan was anxious to make peace but that she would try to trade area for refugees. In other words, the more land Israel let her have, the fewer refugees she would insist on Israel taking back and vice versa.[24]

Mulki himself was in a truculent mood, fed by the conviction that none of the Arab states could afford to make any further concessions beyond those they had already made in agreeing to the armistice lines without risking the fall of their governments. The Arabs wanted peace, he privately told Mark Ethridge, on a basis they regarded as decent, that is, one that would not overthrow their governments. Jordan's attitude had hardened following the experience in the Triangle and in the Jerusalem area. Mulki felt that by their excessive gun-point demands, the Jews, while pretending to want friendship with Abdullah, had actually lowered his prestige to a point where he could no longer help them in peacemaking. This feeling, said Mulki, was shared by all of Abdullah's advisers and even by the king himself and was responsible for the failure of the Special Committee in Jerusalem and for the king's refusal to approve separate negotiations with the Israelis. Unless the Jews made some concessions by which Jordan could restore some of her prestige, Mulki doubted whether peace could come and he personally was determined not to sign such a peace. 'All the King can do is dismiss me', he exclaimed, 'I will not face the wrath of the people of Transjordan and the Arab world by signing away more than we have already given. The Jews have been too clever.'[25]

Mulki had a series of conversations with Eytan, at the end of which

---

[23] Eytan to Sharett, 13 June 1949, 2441/1, ISA.
[24] Id., 21 June 1949, 2435/2, ISA.   [25] FRUS 1949, vi. 1071 f.

Eytan felt that the time had come to give his superiors a picture of the situation. Eytan summarized the Jordanian position, as presented to him by Mulki, under eleven heads:

1. Jordan wanted peace and was prepared to make a greater effort than any other state to get it.

2. Jordan found it extremely difficult to make a separate peace. The king's popularity and influence went down to near zero after the armistice agreement and he was not in a position to stick his neck out any further. At the beginning of the year he had been at the height of his popularity internally and of his influence externally and could do what he liked. Now he was branded as a traitor and had to watch his step.

3. Accordingly, Jordan wanted to make peace jointly with all the other Arab states. If, however, the PCC and the rest of the Arabs were to follow a course not leading to an early settlement, and if Israel were willing to help Jordan by offering honourable terms, then Jordan would take the initiative in trying to induce the other Arab states to come to an agreement on the basis of these terms. Should this attempt fail and Jordan remain satisfied that Israel's terms represented a worthwhile offer, then Jordan would be willing to go ahead in common understanding with the people of Palestine.

4. Mulki believed that it was in Israel's interest too to arrive at a settlement with all the Arab states together, and not just with a single one. This, of course, would make things much easier for Jordan.

5. It was the declared policy of Jordan to assimilate to herself (i.e. to annex) the Arab parts of Palestine, and Jordan believed this to be in accordance with the wishes of the Arabs of Palestine. If, however, it became evident that the pursuit of this policy stood in the way of peace, then Jordan would leave the decision to the Arabs of Palestine themselves and not force them in any way. The desire for peace, in other words, transcended the desire for additional territory—'a few mountains more' to use Mulki's phrase.

6. Jordan was ready to settle with Israel on any terms compatible with the UN resolution of 11 December 1948. Jordan held that refugees and territory were inextricably linked and stood in a direct relationship to one another. The more refugees Israel took, the less territory she would need to give up; the more territory she gave up, the fewer refugees she would need to take.

7. Jordan understood that Israel would be unwilling to take up all the refugees or to give up all the territory she held beyond the November 29 lines; and Jordan would not insist on the complete acceptance by Israel of both these UN resolutions. The king had always been in favour of accepting the November 29 partition plan and he was in favour of doing

so still. How many refugees Israel would take and how much territory she would cede was a matter for negotiation bearing in mind the direct relationship between the two matters. A little more here or a little less there would not stand in the way of peace between the two countries.

8. If Jordan, under the terms of a peace agreement with Israel, annexed the Arab part of Palestine, the Anglo-Transjordanian Treaty would not apply west of the Jordan, and the peace agreement could contain a provision to this effect.

9. If everything else was settled, there would be no trouble about reaching a satisfactory understanding on Jerusalem that would take full account of Israel's interests and needs.

10. Jordan conceived of three types of refugee rehabilitation: (a) repatriation to Israel; (b) repatriation to, or resettlement in, territory to be ceded by Israel; (c) resettlement in the Arab countries.
If Israel did her share under (a) and ceded enough territory to make possible some tangible measure of resettlement under (b), then Jordan would be prepared to accept that the Arab states, including herself, had a responsibility under (c)—which might, under these circumstances, even amount to the lion's share.

11. As Israel would clearly not take all the refugees, the question arose as how to select the refugees for repatriation. Would it be according to their place of origin or present whereabouts? Was preference to be given to town-dwellers or to country folk? On these questions Jordan, or at any rate Mulki, had clear-cut notions: preference should be given to property owners. If a man owns land or a house, he has something to attach him to his place of origin. An orange grove near Kfar Saba or a house in Jaffa represent an asset on which the owner's whole economic existence is based. If he loses it, he is himself lost. On the other hand, a penniless peasant is the same everywhere; it makes no difference to him whether he ploughs a field in Israel or Jordan. For this reason, according to the Jordanian idea, property owners had a prior claim to repatriation, and Mulki added that he was sure that they were also the most desirable and stable element from Israel's point of view. Taking the matter a little further, and assuming that not all the property owners could be repatriated, Mulki distinguished between people owning land and people owning houses, giving prior claim to the former, on the grounds that land is indestructible and establishes an inalienable right whereas a house might or might not exist, and therefore an owner's attachment to it might or might not be real.

Eytan's impression was that Mulki would have been perfectly satisfied if nobody except the landowners were repatriated. This led Eytan to observe how true the Arab ruling class was to itself: 'The leopard does not change his spots.'[26] Eytan gave a clear and accurate picture of what was going through the Jordanian mind but it was a foregone conclusion that these expectations, flexible and moderate though they were, could not be reconciled with Israel's twin notions of a territorial settlement and a solution to the refugee problem.

King Abdullah himself seemed to be losing interest in the Palestine problem. He was uninformed about and uninterested in the negotiations at Lausanne. A temporary spell of indifferent health was probably responsible for the 67-year old monarch's listlessness. Even Greater Syria was seldom mentioned and the only thing that struck any spark in him was the supply of ammunition to the Arab Legion. He complained feverishly to a British diplomat about his government, which he described as 'worse than the Jews', but he lacked the energy either to galvanize it as he used to do or even to change it for another.[27]

The head of the government, Tawfiq Abul Huda, took up the question of the arms embargo with the minister of state at the Foreign Office, Hector McNeil, while on holiday in Britain in July 1949. Abul Huda stated that Jordan's intentions were defensive rather than aggressive, but his country was under the constant threat of aggression from Israel. The fact that his country was seriously short of arms and ammunition, owing to Britain's strict observance of the arms embargo, argued Abul Huda, meant not only that Israeli aggression was much more likely, but that the Israelis could bring much heavier pressure to bear on Jordan in the negotiations on the demarcation of the armistice lines than they would have been able to do if Jordan had been in a position to fight. He said that the Israelis were trying to use this fact as a lever to force Jordan into direct negotiations at which they would impose stiffer terms, but that the Jordanian government continued to hold out for negotiations through the United Nations Conciliation Commission. He added that if the Israelis succeeded in imposing an unfair settlement by using their military superiority, there would be a resulting lack of balance between Jew and Arab in the Middle East which would lead to a permanent threat to its stability. McNeil could not hold out much hope that the arms embargo would be lifted, and Jordan was consequently left in a weak bargaining position.[28]

Despite this weak bargaining position, or perhaps because of it, Mulki adopted an uncompromisingly nationalistic line at Lausanne and went further than even the Egyptians in his verbal attacks on Israel. Sasson was anxious to meet him privately in order to mollify him

[26] Eytan to Sharett, 1 July 1949, 2441/1, ISA.
[27] Letter to Burrows, 12 July 1949, reproduced in Nasir al-Din Nashashibi, *Who Killed King Abdullah?* (Arab.) (Kuwait: Manshurat al-Anba, 1980), 182.
[28] Ibid. 179. Reproduction of the draft Record of a Conversation Between the Minister of State and the prime minister of Jordan on July 20.

and persuade him to mend his ways but Mulki was evasive, saying he needed a few days in order to obtain the king's permission. Sasson thought it would help if Sharett sent the king a message through Dayan, urging him to give his permission. But Sharett did not consider it advisable to make another attempt to get closer to Jordan, especially if it involved another appeal to the king. Every appeal of this kind, said Sharett, placed Israel under some obligation, and 'after we have caused the king so many bitter disappointments, I do not wish to add new ones'.[29]

When Mulki tried to bring the Lausanne talks to an end, however, Sasson could contain himself no longer. The heads of the Egyptian, Syrian, and Lebanese delegations wished to continue the Lausanne talks and urged their governments not to do anything and not to support any decisions by the Political Committee of the Arab League that would jeopardize the talks. Only Mulki dissented from this position and demanded that the Arabs suspend the talks with the Conciliation Commission and take their case to the UN General Assembly due to convene in New York in September. According to Sasson's Lebanese informant, Mulki's insistence on going to the General Assembly was based on the belief that, with the support of America and Britain, the assembly would abandon the idea of an independent state in the Arab parts of Palestine and call for the joining of these parts to Jordan, thereby giving Jordan an official recognition of her conquests in Palestine that would make her less dependent on the favours of Israel or the Arab states. Sasson also learnt that Mulki was to leave Lausanne for London in order to join his king there for the talks with the British government. Sasson therefore sent a letter to his old friend in London, the Hashemite prince Abdul Majid Haidar, asking him to convey his regards to His Majesty, to point out to him that he was still awaiting Mulki's reply, and to explain the need for direct talks between the parties concerned in order to facilitate the work of the Conciliation Commission.[30] This letter, too, remained unanswered. The Jordanians—king, ministers, and diplomats—were all agreed at this point that there was nothing to be gained from embarking on separate talks with Israel and a great deal to be lost.

By the time Abdullah arrived in London in August 1949, a definite shift in his favour had taken place in Britain's policy, a shift that had crystallized in the previous month at a conference of Britain's representatives to the Middle East convened by Ernest Bevin. The possibility of

---

[29] Sasson to Sharett, 5 Aug. 1949, 2442/6; Sharett to Shiloah and Sasson, 7 Aug. 1949, 2447/5, ISA.

[30] Sasson to Prince Abdul Majid Haidar, 13 Aug. 1949, 2453/2; Sasson to Sharett, 14 Aug. 1949, 2447/5, ISA.

Israeli aggression against Jordan weighed heavily on the minds of the participants. Sir Alec Kirkbride made it clear that King Abdullah had been personally anxious to come to agreement with Israel and in fact it was Britain's restraining influence that had prevented him from doing so. Sir Knox Helm, the minister at Tel Aviv, was convinced that Israel had no aggressive intentions and referred to the fact that immigration was diminishing. He added, however, that the delay in the incorporation of Arab Palestine in Jordan was an invitation to Israel to expand. Sir Hugh Dow, the consul-general in Jerusalem, agreed with this view and pointed out that the non-application of the Anglo-Transjordanian Treaty to this area was an encouragement to the Israelis to advance. Sir John Troutbeck conceded that in their hearts the Jordanian and other Arab governments wished to conclude peace with Israel but were afraid of breaking the Arab front and stressed the danger of Britain's incurring general Arab resentment if she encouraged any one state to act independently. Moreover, British endorsement of a permanent settlement between Jordan and Israel, argued Troutbeck, would be viewed by the Egyptians as appeasement of militant Zionism. In the end, however, the arguments of Kirkbride, Knox, and Dow in favour of a 'Jordan first' approach carried the day. Bevin held firmly to his opinion that 'the Arab part of Palestine should be annexed to the Kingdom of Jordan' and he expressed the hope that the settlement of the Palestine problem would clear the way for their military plans for the Middle East.[31]

During the royal visit to London, King Abdullah was given assurances by the Foreign Office that Britain still supported the union of the Arab part of Palestine with his kingdom. In Whitehall's view the union would make an Israeli attack less rather than more likely, would have the added merit of countering the trend towards independence among the Palestinians, and would provide a basis for solving the Palestine problem without waiting for a comprehensive settlement. Since, however, it was still hoped that America might put pressure on Israel to make territorial concessions in the Negev, in accordance with the principle of territorial compensation to which the Americans continued to adhere, Abdullah was advised to hold off for a while longer.[32]

A message from King Farouk

One of the reasons for the Israeli policymakers' unwillingness to offer far-reaching concessions in order to entice Jordan into separate talks

[31] Minutes of the Middle East Conference 21–28 July 1949, FO 371/75072, PRO; Louis, *The British Empire in the Middle East*, 578–80.

[32] Wilson, 'King Abdullah of Jordan', 356 f.

was the residual feeling that a peace settlement with Egypt ought to come first. Many of Israel's politicians, officials, and military commanders subscribed to what might be termed the 'Egypt first' school of thought, to distinguish it from the 'Jordan first' school. The 'Egypt first' school of thought was based on a number of premises, all of which required a policy that gave Egypt precedence over Jordan in Israel's quest for a peace settlement. First, Egypt was the most powerful and influential of the Arab states. Second, the territorial claims of Egypt and Israel were not fundamentally irreconcilable. Third, both countries had a common interest in gaining complete freedom from foreign rule and in expelling Britain from the Middle East. Fourth, there was at least the possibility of a joint policy of resisting Jordan's claim to the West Bank, whereas a settlement with Abdullah recognizing his rule over the West Bank was bound to antagonize Egypt. Fifth, there was practically no chance that the other Arab states would follow a Jordanian lead to make peace with Israel and a very good chance that they would follow an Egyptian lead. Egypt, after all, had taken the lead in signing an armistice agreement with Israel at Rhodes, and the understanding that had been reached on that occasion augured well for the future of Israeli–Egyptian relations. In short, the road to peace between Israel and her neighbours lay through Cairo.

The Egyptian policymakers, for their part, were also looking for a way out of the Palestine impasse. At Lausanne the Egyptian delegates were friendly and co-operative. King Farouk asked the head of his delegation, Abdel Monem Mostafa, to tell the Jews at Lausanne that his government was for peace and stability in the Middle East but they would rather not be pressed to sign peace treaties because that was not possible in the light of the internal conditions then prevailing in Egypt and in the entire Arab world. In all the talks that Mostafa had in Cairo after the first phase of the Lausanne conference, the prime minister, the foreign minister, Egypt's ambassadors to the Arab states, and Azzam Pasha all agreed with King Farouk's view that it was essential to find the path of compromise and an honourable way out. But all of them suspected the Israelis of being partial toward the Hashemites and of having reached secret political and military agreements with Abdullah, with the knowledge and encouragement of the British. Despite these suspicions, Mostafa himself wanted to continue to work in Lausanne as if there were no General Assembly and thought it best to avoid new contests between Israeli and Arab representatives in international forums in Lake Success, Geneva, or other places.[33]

Parallel to the message conveyed through Egypt's official representative, King Farouk went through a private channel to convey a similar

---

[33] Sasson to Sharett, 1 Aug. 1949, 2447/13, ISA.

message to Elias Sasson personally. The bearer of the second message from Cairo was Sylvester Sicurel, a prominent Jewish merchant headed for America on a business trip. A few days before his departure, he was summoned to an urgent meeting at the royal court by Karim Sabt, King Farouk's public relations adviser. Karim Sabt told Sicurel that the king had heard about his trip and wanted to transmit through him a message to one Jewish Zionist named Elias Sasson who was either in Paris or at Lausanne. Sabt added that this Sasson was known in Egypt and in the Arab world as a friend of the Arabs who was searching for ways to bring about peace between his nation and the Arab nations. The message was about the situation of the Jewish community in Egypt and it was intended to prepare the ground for an understanding between Egypt and Israel. The king wanted Sasson to be informed that his government had done everything in its power in order to improve the conditions of Egypt's Jews, to restore their freedom, and to gradually free the detainees and their property. In addition, the Egyptian government had decided to review seriously the situation that had been created in Palestine. On the other hand, the king requested that Israel's radio and newspapers should stop their attacks on him, on his government and his people, and that Israel should use her influence to put an end to the attacks on Egypt in the Western, and especially American, media. If Sicurel could not find Sasson, he was asked to look for another responsible Zionist and to transmit through him this message to the government of Israel.[34]

Sicurel did find Sasson in Lausanne, and Sasson prevailed on him to send a telegram to the royal court, followed by a long letter, to say that he had met the man and conveyed the message, that the man was sure that his government would regard this message as a true earnest of Egypt's desire for peace, and that he (i.e. Sasson) was ready to meet in secret with any emissary who might be sent to discuss the improvement of relations between their two countries and to further the cause of peace in the Middle East.[35]

While the Egyptian delegation continued to behave in a helpful and positive manner at Lausanne, the Israelis were outraged to discover the full extent of Egypt's territorial claims in Palestine, not least in view of the repeated public declarations that Egypt had no territorial ambitions of her own in Palestine and had only intervened to uphold the rights of the Palestinian Arabs. Mostafa did not deny that at the time of the Rhodes talks he had told the Israelis that his country had no territorial ambitions in Palestine but, he explained, the lessons of the 1948 war compelled Egypt to think about her security. A number of

---

[34] Id., 31 July 1949, 2447/13, ISA.
[35] Id., 3 Aug. 1949, 2447/13, ISA.

military experts had been consulted by the Egyptian government, and they all allegedly advised her to hold on to the Gaza Strip, to extend the area of the strip in the south and in the north, to extend Egypt's border to the Dead Sea in a line that would include Majdal and Beersheba, and to attach to Egypt the southern Negev. Although Sasson and Shiloah realized that this was Egypt's opening bid, and as such it was deliberately pitched high, they refused to consider these claims or to put forward alternative proposals for a territorial compromise.[36]

Towards the end of August, there was a marked change for the worse in Egypt's attitude towards Israel. On August 21, Sasson and Shiloah spent seven hours in the company of Mostafa in a small village near Lausanne. The meeting yielded no positive results but, on the contrary, only exposed the distance separating the positions and the outlooks of the two sides. Mostafa stated that the new Egyptian policy had two aims: first, the creation of a wedge between Egypt and Israel and between Egypt and Jordan by turning the entire Negev into Palestinian Arab territory; and second, the gradual improvement of the political and economic relations between Egypt and Israel. Mostafa added that the conversion of the Negev into a wedge would assist in settling a large number of refugees in Palestine itself and that it would make the Arab parts of Palestine suitable for independence and thereby prevent Jordan from annexing the Triangle and preserve the status quo in the Arab world.

Mostafa believed that all the refugees from Egypt and the Gaza Strip, whose number he estimated to be 260,000, could be settled in the northern Negev, and that if the need arose, it might be possible to transfer refugees from other areas there as well. The project could be carried out with American financial assistance. By making the entire Negev an Arab area and joining it with the Triangle it would be possible to implement the UN resolution of 29 November 1949 about the creation of an independent Arab state in part of Palestine. While such a state would initially require international and Arab capital, Mostafa estimated that after a number of years it would become self-supporting.

Sasson and Shiloah observed that the partition plan had assigned most of the Negev to Israel. Mostafa replied that he knew that, but it was obvious that Israel would not give up the Galilee which according to the partition plan was Arab. When told that Israel could not be expected to yield even one square foot of the Negev, the Egyptian retorted that in that case there was no basis for an understanding between Israel and Egypt and it would be best to bring the whole matter before the General Assembly. He added that if the General

[36] Sasson to Sharett, 4 Aug. 1949, 2447/13, ISA.

Assembly should decide in favour of Israel, Egypt would comply, terminate her claims, evacuate the Gaza Strip, and return to her international border, but then not only would there be no basis for understanding peace, and co-operation between Israel and Egypt, but there would be a strong chance that the war between the two countries would be resumed.

Getting more and more worked up, the senior Egyptian diplomat continued with some vehemence. 'You must understand', he said, 'that Egypt does not want a common border with Israel. Egypt would have been glad if Israel had not been established. She did everything in order to prevent her establishment. Egypt is convinced that the state of Israel, alien in every way to the Arabs . . . would inevitably be a source of disputes, complications and instability in the Middle East.' Mostafa blurted out that in his talks with the Americans he had stressed that in order to regain the confidence of the Arab world and bring lasting stability to the Middle East, America had to ensure that the State of Israel would not be large, nor powerful, nor overpopulated with Jews. Egypt, he explained to them, would not feel secure if on her border in the Negev there were to be three or four million Jews, all educated, all enterprising, all imbued with the spirit of self-sacrifice.

When Sasson and Shiloah tried to explain that their country posed no threat to Egypt, militarily, socially, or economically, Mostafa replied that only the future could prove that, and in the meantime Egypt had to prepare for the worst possibilities. The Israelis made it clear that if the General Assembly ruled against them on the question of the Negev, they would defy the Assembly and dig in because the Negev was so vital to them. Mostafa dejectedly remarked that they could do as they pleased. This argument about the Negev did not allow the Israelis to broach other problems. When they tried to do so, Mostafa said it would be pointless. When they suggested a further meeting, he said he was ready to meet them at any time but if that was their position, it would be better to talk about other matters and not about politics.[37]

The sudden change in the Egyptian attitude to Israel was thought by Sasson to be the consequence of internal political changes. When the Lausanne talks were renewed, King Farouk faced great difficulties at home and abroad. At home he was supported by a government that did not represent the people, did not enjoy popular support, and had to rule by force. Abroad he was in conflict with the Hashemite bloc and with Britain. In the course of August, however, the situation changed radically. At home, Farouk got a coalition government representing all the main political tendencies in the country and seeking to arrange free parliamentary elections. Abroad, his relations wth the Hashemites and

[37] Id., 21 Aug. 1949, 2447/13, ISA.

the British steadily improved. In this changed political constellation Farouk had no reason to hasten to settle the conflict with Israel. He considered it opportune to pose again as a national hero and to stand at the head of those Arab statesmen who advocated boycotting Israel and waging a cold war against her.[38]

Domestic political calculations undoubtedly played a part in bringing about the sudden shift in Egypt's attitude against a settlement with Israel, just as they had influenced the earlier change announced in Farouk's message to Sasson. Domestic issues influence the politics of all states and Farouk's Egypt was no exception. Yet it would be a mistake to think that the evolution of Egypt's policy was unaffected by Israel's own behaviour and terms for a settlement. It was to become an often-repeated Israeli charge that the quest for peace was frustrated at Lausanne by Arab intransigence and Arab refusal to recognize Israel's right to exist. What Mostafa's lecture to Sasson and Shiloah showed, and in this respect there was no fundamental difference between Egypt and the other Arab states, was that in 1949 the Arabs did recognize Israel's right to exist, they were willing to meet face to face to negotiate peace, they had their conditions for making peace with Israel, and Israel rejected those conditions because they were incompatible not with her survival as an independent state but with her determination to keep all the territory she held and to resist the repatriation of the refugees.

[38]   Sasson to Sharett, 29 Aug. 1949, 2447/13, ISA.

16

ISRAEL'S PALESTINIAN OPTION

The Palestinian delegations at Lausanne

At Lausanne members of the Israeli delegation held talks not only with the official delegations of Egypt, Jordan, Syria, and Lebanon but also with the representatives of various groups of Palestinian refugees. The proliferation of groups who claimed to represent the refugees before the PCC reflected the confusion, the disarray, and the bitter rivalries that beset the Palestinian community in the aftermath of the Palestine disaster. Just before the conference in Beirut, the Arab Higher Committee approached the PCC and asked to be recognized as representing the whole of Arab Palestine. This initiative was frowned upon by the Arab states and particularly by Jordan, which threatened to stay away from the Beirut conference if the mufti participated in it. When the PCC withheld recognition, it was the Arab Higher Committee which stayed away. Yet it did send one solitary representative to the first phase of the Lausanne talks, to be joined by two more four months later.

The other body with a serious claim to represent the Palestinian refugees was the Ramallah Refugee Office headed by Muhammad Nimer al-Hawari, who played an active role in both the Beirut and the Lausanne conferences. This body, elected by the refugees from Jordan and the Arab part of Palestine, marked the attempt of the refugees to take charge of their own affairs.

The first General Refugee Congress was held in Ramallah on 17 March 1949, and was attended by some 500 delegates. It was at this Congress that Hawari was elected president, with Yahya Hamuda and Aziz Shehadah as his deputies. And it was from this congress that they received the authority to negotiate on behalf of the refugees in all matters concerning them.[1]

Hawari himself had been the commander of the Najjada, the paramilitary organization formed in 1946 in opposition to the Husaynis. Hawari's strong anti-Husayni leanings provided a basis for sporadic collaboration between him and the Haganah but his organization did not play an important role in the 1947–8 war. Under his

---

[1] Plascov, *The Palestinian Refugees in Jordan*, 20 f.

leadership, the Ramallah Refugee Office openly collaborated with the Israeli authorities, providing, for example, in a report to Behor Shitreet, the minister of police and minorities, one of the earliest estimates of the number and location of Palestinian refugees. According to Hawari's figures, there were 14,000 refugees in Egypt, 200,000 in Gaza, 50,000 in the Hebron district, 15,000 in the Bethlehem district, 20,000 in Jerusalem, 40,000 in Jericho, 72,000 in Ramallah, 100,000 in Nablus, 70,000 in Jordan, 80,000 in Syria, 100,000 in Lebanon, and 5,000 in Iraq, making a total of 750,000 refugees. Ben-Gurion calculated that, excluding Gaza, there were 297,000 refugees in Arab Palestine and 199,000 in the neighbouring Arab states. Some of these figures appeared to him to be inflated but they give some idea of the scale of the problem, and the important point to note here is that Hawari collaborated with Israel in his search for a solution to the refugee problem before, during, and after the Lausanne conference.[2]

Apart from Husayni and anti-Husayni factions, there was a third Palestinian delegation at Lausanne, representing the wealthier class of refugees—the land owners, the orange grove owners, the property owners, and the business men. The PCC was baffled by the arrival of these successive groups of uninvited representatives, while the official Arab delegations were dismayed. Ironically, it was only with the Israeli delegation that the second and third groups succeeded in establishing friendly contact at Lausanne. Yet, the only concrete result of these contacts was that the Israeli government accepted, in principle, a limited and conditional unfreezing of the blocked accounts which the Arab refugees had left behind. From the political point of view, these contacts were a cul-de-sac.

Did Israel have a Palestinian option for the settlement of the Middle East conflict at the time of the Lausanne conference? If so, why was this option not exercised? One Israeli scholar, Ilan Pappé, has advanced the thesis that at this critical juncture, when everything was in a state of flux and Israel was consequently in a strong position to shape the new political and territorial order in the Middle East, Israeli diplomacy was paralysed by an inner conflict between the advocates of this option and the advocates of the Hashemite option. According to this thesis, Moshe Sharett espoused a Palestinian option (a partitioning of the country into Palestinian and Jewish states), while other leading figures in the Yishuv, with Ben-Gurion at their head, advocated a Hashemite option (partitioning the country between the Hashemite kingdom and Israel). While Ben-Gurion, so the argument runs, prejudged the Lausanne conference a waste of time, preferring immediate bilateral talks with Jordan, Sharett devised an alternative to the Hashemite option:

[2] Ben-Gurion's diary, 29 May 1949 and 20 Jan. 1950.

He hoped to use it in negotiations with the Palestinian delegates at Lausanne to establish an independent Palestinian state on the West Bank. The foreign minister's support for Israel–Palestinian negotiations therefore originated in his conscious preference for an Israel–Palestinian agreement to an Israel–Jordan one. By adopting such an attitude, Sharett undermined the Jewish–Hashemite understanding and clashed with Ben-Gurion, who regarded this understanding as a corner-stone of Israeli policy.[3]

A careful examination of the available evidence, however, fails to disclose any fundamental difference over policy, let alone a clash, between the two Zionist leaders. On the contrary, this evidence points to a remarkable consensus on the part of the prime minister, the foreign minister, and their government colleagues on the need to base the settlement on the existing territorial status quo, and that of course inclined them towards an understanding with Jordan. Sharett was not an advocate of an independent Palestinian state except as a public relations exercise and as a tactical ploy in the negotiations with Jordan. As early as 15 June 1948, Sharett had written to Nahum Goldmann:

The most spectacular event in the contemporary history of Palestine—more spectacular in a sense than the creation of the Jewish state—is the wholesale evacuation of its Arab population which has swept with it also thousands of Arabs from areas threatened and/or occupied by us outside our boundaries. I doubt whether there are 100,000 Arabs in Israel today. The reversion to *status quo ante* is unthinkable. The opportunities which the present position opens up for a lasting and radical solution of the most vexing problem of the Jewish State are so far-reaching as to take one's breath away. Even if a certain backwash is unavoidable, we must make the most of the momentous chance with which history has presented us so swiftly and so unexpectedly.[4]

Sharett's subordinates in the Middle East Department predicted that the refugees would somehow get over their displacement and settle down to a new life in the host countries: 'Those with the highest capacity for survival and adjustment will manage by a process of natural selection while the rest would be crushed. Some of them would die and most of them would turn into human dust and the waste of society, and join the most impoverished classes in the Arab countries.'[5]

In as much as the idea of a Palestinian state had any appeal to Sharett, it was not as a solution to the refugee problem but as a complement to an accord with Egypt. The Egyptians had given every indication at the time when the armistice agreement was concluded that they were looking for a political solution to the Palestine problem

---

[3] Ilan Pappé, 'Moshe Sharett, David Ben-Gurion and the "Palestinian Option", 1948–1956', *Studies in Zionism* 7/1 (1987), 77–96.

[4] *DFPI*, i. 162–4.

[5] The Palestinian Refugee Problem, 2444/19, ISA.

that would permit them to make peace with Israel and return home without loss of face. The trouble, as Sharett privately confided at the time, was that Sasson had only one record to play and it was beginning to show signs of wear. Progress was held up by the lack of a clear Israeli position on the principal questions: the future of Arab Palestine, the fate of the Gaza Strip, and the attitude towards the two vital blocs within the Arab League. Yet, while clearly grasping Israel's responsibility for the lack of progress, Sharett had no constructive suggestions to make. All he could say was that the transition from wartime diplomacy to peacetime diplomacy must not be precipitate, and that Israeli diplomacy had to be patient. Sharett admitted that on the main question posed by Egypt, regarding the future of the Arab part of Palestine: 'We are in dire straits; we cannot state categorically that there is a prospect for forging an independent Arab state because in doing so we would take upon ourselves a responsibility that we cannot bear or even pretend to; on the other hand we must not bind ourselves with Egypt to the conclusion that the annexation of this part to Transjordan is inescapable. So there is no alternative but to spin out things and refrain from giving a clear-cut answer.'[6]

The truth of the matter is that neither Sharett nor any other prominent Israeli leader genuinely desired the establishment of an independent Palestinian state in the spring of 1949. A Palestinian solution entailed Palestinian independence and Palestinian statehood and pressure on Israel to return to the borders of the 1947 partition resolution. Israel's leaders considered that the 1947 borders would not permit them to live under conditions of tolerable security; they therefore preferred a solution with Jordan based on the 1949 borders.[7] There was, it is true, a tendency to resist the merger of the West Bank with the East Bank for fear that a larger and stronger Jordanian kingdom would expose Israel to hostile Iraqi and British activities. But the general feeling was that in the long run Abdullah, of all the Arab leaders, offered the best prospect for attaining peaceful coexistence, and in this respect there was no fundamental difference between Ben-Gurion and Sharett. On the future of the West Bank neither of them had very clear ideas, and the result was not a conflict of orientations but a tendency to improvise, to muddle along, and to trail behind events.

There was nothing in the guidelines given to the Israeli delegation for the Lausanne conference to indicate any possibility of official support for the creation of an independent Palestinian state. Indeed, on arrival at Lausanne, Walter Eytan became troubled by the official reticence on this issue and implored his superiors to make up their minds:

[6] Sharett to Eytan, 15 Mar. 1949, 174/2, ISA.
[7] Interview with Gideon Rafael.

We, or rather you, will soon have to decide what is to be Israel's attitude about the Arab parts of Palestine. The Arab delegations here are at one another's throats, and fierce quarrels take place between them until late in the night. One of the main subjects at issue between them is the fate and future of Arab Palestine. The Transjordanians, of course, insist on annexation while the Egyptians, supported by Syria and (in absentia) by Saudi Arabia, demand the creation of an independent Palestine state. I beg you to take an early opportunity of sitting down with B. G. and hammering out for us a really clear line on this central issue . . . I have a feeling that if we had a clear line one way or the other we could, such is the confusion in men's minds, get our way.

Sharett's reply was as swift as it was short 'If we support [an] independent Arab State, we shall have struggle [to] avoid November 29th partition. Would love to have best of both worlds but think it [a] bit risky to try.'[8]

If it was too risky to allow large-scale repatriation of refugees or to experiment with an independent Arab state, there was still a possibility of a settlement with the privileged group of property-owning refugees. Their representatives impressed upon the Arab governments the urgency of coming to terms with Israel, since any delay in reaching a settlement was contrary to their interests, and they took the initiative in approaching the Israeli delegation at Lausanne. All the Israeli officials, however, were of one mind in thinking that nothing of political value could come out of negotiating with the representatives of the propertied refugees. Gideon Rafael, who conducted these negotiations, was in favour of easing the plight of these refugees by unfreezing their blocked accounts, by releasing their property, by helping with their resettlement in the Arab countries, through development projects, and through the creation of an international agency to deal with the refugees—but not through the creation of a Palestinian state.[9] Even if Israel had wanted to, there was no possibility, according to Gershon Avner, to use these refugees as a political lever:

When we met them at Lausanne they talked only about property and the reunion of families. The talks revolved round the bank accounts. They had left the jewellery of their wives in a safe deposit box in Barclays Bank in Jerusalem, for example, and they wanted it back. They had abandoned their orange groves and the fruit-picking season had arrived and they wanted to be allowed to go back to pick their fruit or to be compensated for their lost property. They did not ask anything of Gideon Rafael except the safe deposit boxes and the orange groves. They did not talk at all about the future of the country or about its borders and the talks were devoid of any political meaning. They themselves did not advance any proposal for a political settlement. They sat like

---

[8] Eytan to Sharett, 3 May 1949, and Sharett to Eytan, 4 May 1949, 2447/1, ISA.
[9] Interview with Gideon Rafael.

sheep in front of Gideon Rafael. They were subservient. They said: 'We are pulverized refugees, we are finished as a nation, we lost everything, the Arab states betrayed us, give us back our property.' We agreed but there were technical difficulties in carrying out this agreement. In their flight they frequently forgot to take with them their papers and the keys to their safe deposit boxes.

They had one other request: the reunion of families. Many families were split up, dispersed, and lost contact. There were many requests to rejoin their relatives or to locate their relatives and enable them to rejoin their families. They said they were not conducting negotiations with us because they were refugees, but begged us to permit the reunion of families.[10]

Some of the representatives of the refugees with property, like Said Bidas and Francis Jalad, did venture into political discussions. They told Elias Sasson of their anger at the Arab states who were scheming to divide up the Arab parts of Palestine between themselves, and at the Conciliation Commission for not pressing the Arab states to make peace. And they suggested that Israel should declare either that she accepted in principle the UN resolution of 11 December 1948 if the Arab states agreed to peace talks, or that she was willing to conduct direct negotiations with the representatives of the refugees regarding their property and their other problems. A declaration of this kind, they claimed, would turn the tables on the Arab states as well as on the Conciliation Commission and further the interests of Israel and the refugees.[11] The Israelis, however, remained unconvinced. Ben-Gurion noted in his diary: 'Some of the rich refugees supposedly support Israel and want to hold direct talks with the Israeli government—we have no interest in creating a new force. These men are motivated by greed. They now appear as if they were opposed to the Arab states. One cannot rely on this opposition.'[12]

From co-operation to collaboration

The five-man delegation headed by Muhammad Nimer al-Hawari representing the refugees of Palestine and Transjordan fared no better in its efforts to induce the Arab states to reach a quick settlement with Israel. It also failed to modify the Israeli stand on the refugee question, though not for lack of trying. In his book entitled *The Secret of the Catastrophe*, Hawari makes reference to this aspect of the activities of his delegation at Lausanne:

We have had with the Israeli delegation many meetings and negotiations on which we reported to the official Arab delegations in Lausanne and also to the

---

[10] Interview with Gershon Avner.   [11] Sasson to Sharett, 5 June 1949, 2772/5, ISA.
[12] Ben-Gurion's diary, 6 June 1949.

Higher Refugee Council. We conducted correspondence with Israeli ministers and we informed the Arab delegations of this correspondence also.[13]

The response of the Israeli leaders was not encouraging. They were not averse to having discussions with these Palestinian representatives but they regarded the conflict not as an Israeli–Palestinian one but as an Israeli–Arab one and they preferred to deal with it at the inter-state level. They also knew that the representatives of the refugees had neither power nor authority, and they had no intention of changing this state of affairs. This attitude was politely but firmly conveyed in a letter sent to the refugees by Behor Shitreet, Israel's minister of police and minorities:

We would like very much the Arab refugee problem to find its solution, but that unfortunately cannot be done with the refugees themselves, since they are divided among themselves and are following the policy of the country where they live. Let us suppose that we are successful in our endeavours to come to terms with you, who will guarantee us that our agreement would be honoured by the different Arab countries? What will be the attitude of the Arab Higher Committee? Surely it would reject any such dealings, and what will be your position if you decide to continue in your peaceful intentions in open defiance of the Arab delegates?[14]

These questions were also posed to the Palestinians at Lausanne verbally. Moshe Sasson, a junior official in the department headed by his father, recalled the questions and the answers in this unproductive dialogue:

Our central thesis was: 'In whose name are you speaking? If we reach an agreement with you, what value would it have? What would you do with it?' The Palestinians at Lausanne replied: 'We will go to the Arab rulers to ask for their support.' We said: 'In that case you should obtain the consent of the Arab rulers for negotiating with us in advance or speak to the Arab delegates here in Lausanne'.[15]

Despite this basically negative official stance, Elias Sasson succeeded in exploring a wide range of possibilities for political co-operation with Hawari. Hawari's essential purpose in going to Lausanne was to press for a solution to the refugee problem. Sasson persuaded him to put pressure on the Arab states to make peace with Israel. At their very first meeting Sasson sounded Hawari out on the idea of setting up an Arab state in the Triangle. Hawari did not reject the idea, but he argued that the population of the Triangle would not be able to sustain it economically or politically because they lacked the necessary means; however,

[13] Muhammad Nimer al-Hawari, *The Secret of the Catastophe* (Arab.) (Nazareth, 1955), 376.
[14] Ibid. 384.
[15] Interview with Moshe Sasson.

he took it upon himself to raise the matter with the Conciliation Commission.[16]

Subsequently, after Sasson had promised Hawari financial support and a permit to return to his home in Israeli-occupied territory, he agreed to serve Israel. One of the early ideas to emerge from the discussions between them was to get the Palestinian delegation to demand of the PCC and the Arab and Israeli delegations that they steer clear of the refugee problem to allow the Palestinian delegation time to visit Israel and hold direct talks with the Israeli government. With this ploy Sasson hoped to force the Arab delegations to leave the refugee problem on one side and to discuss the question of borders first. Hawari and his colleagues were willing to work along these lines. They believed that they could thwart Jordan's ambitions and force the other Arab states to end their involvement in the affairs of Palestine by turning the Triangle into an autonomous region linked to Israel.[17]

Sharett poured cold water on this plan. He reminded Sasson that Hawari had received money from them in the past and that that investment had borne no fruit. He also thought that any prestige that would accrue to Israel from a visit by a Palestinian delegation would quickly give way to bitterness and anger when it left empty-handed. Moreover, during its visit the delegation would discover how many abandoned Arab villages there were and how much of their land remained unsettled. To be of any real value, concluded Sharett, Hawari should be used to advance the Syrian project for settling 250,000 refugees in al-Jezira and to direct towards Israel a serious group of Palestinians ready to set up a political authority in the Triangle.[18]

Hawari and his delegation repeated their offer to visit Israel and hold direct talks with the government there. They claimed that if an agreement was reached they would be able to influence most of the refugees and the Palestinian inhabitants to demand the merger of the remainder of Palestine with Israel. Sasson pressed for a decision as Hawari and his colleagues intended to leave Lausanne unless there were some signs of progress.[19]

Ben-Gurion therefore convened a meeting of his advisers to review their options in relation to Jordan. Moshe Sharett came out in favour of peace negotiations with Jordan, involving Israeli recognition of Jordan's annexation of the West Bank and some arrangements concerning Gaza and Jerusalem. One of the advantages of an accord with

[16] Sasson to Sharett, 4 May 1949, 2442/5, ISA.
[17] Id., 8 May 1949, 2442/5, ISA.
[18] Sharett to Sasson, 10 May 1949, 2442/7, ISA.
[19] Sasson to Sharett, 2 June 1949, 2442/5, ISA.

Jordan, Sharett argued, was the obliteration of the borders of 29 November 1947. Another adviser thought the greatest danger lay in the formation of a united refugee front; if an accord with Jordan could prevent such a front, he was all for it. Moshe Dayan, on the other hand, was opposed to a settlement with Jordan and argued that although the Jordanians needed Gaza as an outlet to the sea and were trying to secure it with the help of Egypt and Britain, they realized that without Israel's consent they could not have it. Dayan's principal argument against a settlement with Jordan, however, was that the armistice line in the south was unacceptable: the whole of the 'southern triangle', encompassing Bethlehem and Hebron, was 'unnatural'; there was no access to Transjordan because the Dead Sea protruded into the area, so for the Jordanians too the armistice line did not constitute a natural border. In other words Dayan was not only opposed to granting Jordan access to the sea at Gaza; he was even opposed to a settlement based on the existing territorial status quo, without concessions to Jordan. Presumably the only natural border as far as Dayan was concerned was the River Jordan. Although Dayan did not explicitly propose Israeli expansion to the Jordan in the 'southern triangle', that was the logic behind his argument. And it was a military logic that did not fail to impress Ben-Gurion, at least momentarily. As he wrote in his diary,

The only alternative to an agreement with Transjordan is an autonomous state of Nablus linked to the state of Israel or part of it. An agreement with Transjordan, apart from all the other difficulties, carries the danger that after Abdullah's death, this would become the most forward hostile salient inside our country. An agreement with Abdullah would involve three difficulties: the border in the Triangle, Jerusalem, and the Dead Sea. Under no circumstances could we agree to give up the western shore of the Dead Sea.[20]

The shift of opinion on the West Bank in favour of union with Israel increased the leverage enjoyed by Israel in dealing with Abdullah. Several factors combined to make this an attractive option for the Palestinians: awareness of Israel's military superiority; the failure of the Jordanian government to protect their interests against Israel; the failure of Abdullah to give them a say in determining their own fate; dislike of the narrow and autocratic nature of the Jordanian regime; Jordan's backwardness and the expectation that Israel would provide more favourable economic opportunities, especially higher priced markets for agricultural goods; and last but not least, the possibility that such a union would permit the return of large numbers of refugees to both Arab Palestine and the areas under Israeli control.[21]

Reports about the changing attitudes of the Arabs of Palestine

---

[20] Ben-Gurion's diary, 8 June 1949. [21] *FRUS 1949*, vi. 999 f.

reached Israel from various quarters. One of the most striking reports came from Revd Garland Evans Hopkins, a pro-Arab American priest who was trying to co-ordinate Catholic and Protestant policies on Palestine. Hopkins had been on a tour of the Arab states and had spoken with Palestine Arabs everywhere, including the refugee camps in the Triangle, Transjordan, and Gaza. He was amazed to discover, as he told Walter Eytan, that 90 per cent of them wanted autonomy in the Arab parts of Palestine, those parts to be loosely federated to Israel. They were willing for Israel to manage their foreign affairs and their economic affairs as long as in their own parts of the country they could have autonomy. Hopkins suggested that a plebiscite should be held as this would show beyond the shadow of doubt that the Palestinian Arabs wanted no part of Abdullah or the Egyptians, but autonomy linked with Israel. He said that if the ballot paper, for the sake of simplicity, bore on it two names, Abdullah and Ben-Gurion, there was no doubt that 90 per cent of the Palestinian Arabs would vote for Ben-Gurion. Even if a few timid souls, under military pressure, voted for Abdullah in the Triangle and for the Egyptians in Gaza, there would still remain an overwhelming majority for Israel. This report confirmed and reinforced what the refugees' delegation had been telling Elias Sasson.[22]

Ben-Gurion was surprised and intrigued to learn of the extent of his popularity among the Arabs of Palestine. The irony that he who had been such a deadly opponent of the Palestinian national movement and the leader who was ultimately responsible for the expulsion of so many Palestinians from their homes during the fighting was now preferred by those same people to an Arab ruler who was a descendant of the Prophet Muhammad, seems to have escaped Ben-Gurion. Characteristically, his mind focused on the advantages that could be squeezed out of this new situation. It was Sharett who had to point out to him the constraints that would continue to operate even if Revd Hopkins's report was accurate: since Abdullah had effective control of the West Bank and Egypt and Syria were not prepared to go to war with him, how could Israel prevent him from annexing this territory unless she herself was prepared to fight him? Ben-Gurion's only answer was to suggest that they sent one of their experts to check the report. If the report turned out to be true, Ben-Gurion insisted that the whole situation would be radically changed: Israel would have to assume additional responsibilities but the Jerusalem problem would be solved, Britain would be kept out of Western Palestine, and all sorts of possibilities would open up.[23]

Elias Sasson thought that both Sharett and Ben-Gurion were har-

[22] Eytan to Sharett, 13 June 1949, 2441/1, ISA.
[23] Ben-Gurion's diary, 19 June 1949.

bouring illusions, so he laid down very clearly what he himself, on the basis of extensive talks with the Arabs at Lausanne, considered to be the minimal conditions for peace:

1. Agreement to Jordan's annexation of the Triangle with only minor border adjustments.
2. Waiving of all claims to the Gaza and Rafah areas and agreement to their merger with either Egypt or Jordan.
3. In the event of the merger of these areas with Jordan, agreement to a corridor that would connect the Jordanian kingdom with Gaza.
4. Agreement to the division of Jerusalem between Israel and Jordan with international supervision of the Holy Places.
5. Agreement to border adjustments with Syria.
6. Agreement to take back about 100,000 refugees from various places.
7. Agreement to compensate refugees with property who settle elsewhere.

None of these conditions, emphasized Sasson, would jeopardize Israel's existence or check her development. Full peace based on these conditions would be viewed as a major achievement and win Israel the sympathy of the entire world. On the other hand, the prospects for a separate peace with Jordan or any other country without substantial concessions were remote. Jordan could leave Lausanne with the approval of the Arab and the Western worlds for her demands and she would no longer need Israel's consent. Sasson therefore called for a fresh evaluation of Israel's interests and a decision on what was preferable: immediate peace or the continuation of the conflict that would mean another few years of boycott, isolation, the severance of relations, instability, strong external pressure on Israel, and possibly even military hostilities.[24]

Sharett accepted Sasson's first, second, fourth, and seventh conditions; he rejected the third and fifth. He was prepared to consider Jordanian access to Gaza but not a corridor under Jordanian sovereignty that would divide Israel in two and serve as a bridge between two British bases. As far as repatriation was concerned, Sharett thought it best not to be committed to any specific number and to take back as few refugees as possible.[25]

It was at this point that Sasson fired off his angry letter about the deadlock at Lausanne in which he reserved his severest strictures for his own country. The thrust of Sasson's argument was that if Israel were

[24] Sasson to Ben-Gurion and Sharett, 13 June 1949, 2442/5, ISA.
[25] Sharett to Sasson, 15 June 1949, 2442/7, ISA.

not prepared to pay the price for peace with the neighbouring Arab states, she should at least try to get the refugees on her side, but a decision had to be made one way or the other. Sasson thought that the proposal of the refugees' delegation for a union between the Arab parts of Palestine—the Triangle, the districts of Hebron and Gaza, and Jerusalem—was worth considering in this context. This proposal was conditional on Israel's agreement to absorb some of the refugees, around 100,000 within her borders and, secondly, to grant administrative autonomy to the Arab areas that would come under her control. Apart from these two basic conditions there was a third condition of a practical nature, namely, that Israel would commit herself to aid the refugees in their struggle until victory was achieved. This meant diplomatic support in appearing before the General Assembly and demanding the withdrawal of all the Arab forces from Palestine and direct negotiation between Palestinians and Jews to settle the whole problem. It meant helping the refugees to organize themselves into armed gangs to harass the occupational regimes whether they were Egyptian, Syrian, or Jordanian. And it meant promising the rebels and insurgents asylum in Israel in the event of their struggle ending in failure. Though this plan seemed adventurous, Sasson considered that it had a good chance of meeting with success. In any case, it was the only means he could think of for clearing the Arab armies out of Palestine, for removing foreign influence, for extending Israel's borders, for solving the refugee problem in a manner that would not be too onerous for Israel, and for inducing the Arab states to enter into a genuine and lasting peace with Israel.[26]

The double game

As so often in the past, Sasson's recommendations proved too radical for Israel's policymakers. They had simply not made up their minds on the future of Arab Palestine. This policy vacuum moved Walter Eytan to propose a blatantly Machiavellian strategy to Sharett in a letter from Lausanne dated June 17. Eytan took three facts as axiomatic: '1. Abdullah wants to annex the Triangle. 2. The Palestine Arabs don't want him to do anything of the sort. 3. We would prefer a weak independent state as our neighbour.' Under these circumstances, continued Eytan, it would be in their interest to foster an anti-Jordanian movement in the Triangle. All their experts said that nothing would be easier, because the population were waiting to be stirred up, even if they did not accept Hopkins's optimistic estimate of a 90 per cent majority for Ben-Gurion. By fostering anti-Abdullah

[26] Sasson to Divon, 16 June 1949, 2447/2, ISA.

sentiments in the Triangle, Sharett would be able, when the time came, to take his choice between

1. Seeing the thing through and establishing an independent state. Egypt and Syria will probably help you in this in the Triangle, and France and others will stand by you as well.

2. Or, instead of seeing the thing through to independence, you may at any time you like use the anti-Abdullah feeling to squeeze concessions out of Abdullah as the price of your agreement to annexation. At the moment, Abdullah is not particularly interested in talking to us, as he feels he can get what he wants through the PCC or the Egyptians or Britain or even the USA. But put him under the pressure of anti-Abdullah movements in the Triangle, and then you can get things out of him as easily as we got Wadi Ara, etc. under pressure of a different kind.

But the main thing is for the Government to decide. It almost looks as if the good old days, in which we could only stand to gain by being neither for nor against annexation, have pased. Could we not restore them by fomenting anti-Abdullaism among the Palestine Arabs and refugees? Please let me have your views.[27]

Sharett's views, though compressed into a telegram, were highly revealing and every bit as Machiavellian. He was ready to talk business to the Palestinians and had instructed Dayan to put out feelers. Sharett stressed that he had always favoured a separate state both on its merits and as a tactic to be used against the king. But in the final analysis the question was who would fight to expel the Arab Legion from Palestine, and Sharett was convinced that it should not be the Israeli army even if 90 per cent of the population voted for Ben-Gurion. Nevertheless, Sharett favoured the idea of a plebiscite both as a means of pressure on Abdullah and so that he would not take annexation for granted as far as Israel and the Arabs were concerned. Sharett also favoured stirring-up tactics and revealed that the military were already active in the Latrun sector where, despite terror from the Legion, villagers were signing *mazbatas* or petitions for inclusion in Israel. Rather unconvincingly, Sharett added that they must beware of the risk involved in letting these people down.[28]

The PCC had already been informed that the general view of the Israeli government was that the future of the Arab regions of Palestine should be left to the inhabitants to decide and that the principles of political independence for those areas should be conceded and supported. Before a legitimate authority or administration could be established, Eytan told the PCC, the people living in those districts had the right to be consulted concerning the form of that authority and that

[27] Eytan to Sharett, 14 June 1949, 2451/2, ISA.
[28] Sharett to Eytan, 19 June 1949, 2453/2, ISA.

administration. As Mark Ethridge observed, Eytan had in effect asked the commission to organize a plebiscite. On June 19, pursuing this duplicitous tactic a step further, Eytan wrote to Dr Azcarate, the secretary of the PCC: 'My delegation, which believes that it is expedient, just and practicable to carry out a plebiscite of this kind, will be glad to co-operate with the Commission in giving the matter further study.'[29]

No one at Lausanne was deceived by Israel's diplomatic manœuvres, and the Israeli diplomats themselves grew tired of dissembling. The principal difficulty at Lausanne, Gideon Rafael confided to Abba Eban, was the constant improvisation that stemmed from the absence of a clear line. Peace could not be attained by purely tactical expedients. Not only was there need for grand strategy, but the ultimate target had to be determined in advance. Israel's presentation of her case before the PCC, added Rafael, lacked credibility and undermined the confidence that must form the basis of any negotiation. Nowhere was this lack of credibility more glaring than in the talks with Jordan:

It would appear that the central problem between us and the Jordanians is not Eilat or Gaza but our agreement to recognize the annexation of the eastern part of Palestine to Transjordan. If we had the courage to take this step, of course with appropriate camouflage like a plebiscite for example, in my view we would be able to reach a basic agreement with Abdullah.

In the negotiations with Transjordan it was revealed once again that we value the tactic more than the target. On the one hand we are looking for a way to come to an arrangement with them, and on the other hand we believe in the illusion that through a plesbiscite it would be possible to secure the setting up of an independent Arab state or even the joining of this part to the state of Israel. Even in the Middle East there is a limit to the double-game and I think that the time has come to adopt a straight line.[30]

Moshe Sharett evidently did not think that the time had come to define the target and adopt a straight line leading to it. His guidelines to the Israeli delegation for the second phase of the Lausanne talks elevated to a new peak the double-game that he had been playing all along:

One should refrain for the time being from commitment to a peace covenant that entails our agreement to extending the sovereignty of the Jordanian kingdom west of the Jordan. Possible ferment in that region against annexation as well as the uncertain future of the kingdom given Syria's and Iraq's expansionist aims that are directed at swallowing it, necessitate considerable reserve and moderation on our part regarding the future of western Palestine. In the event of the delegation seeing no escape from entering into such

---

[29] Eytan to Azcarate, 19 June 1949, 2451/2, ISA.
[30] Rafael to Eban, 8 July 1949, 71/19, ISA.

negotiations, it will be necessary to hold a special consultation. In the meantime one should continue to explore the possibilities of creating an autonomous region in the Arab part of Palestine that would be linked to Israel, and to intensify the ferment in that direction.[31]

These guidelines hardly support the view of Sharett as the apostle of a Palestinian option who did not recoil even from a clash with Ben-Gurion in his fight against the Hashemite option. Indeed, during the critical period in Israeli–Arab relations spanned by the Lausanne conference, both leaders exhibited a strikingly similar tendency to hover, to flounder, to improvise and, above all, to have their cake and eat it. Ben-Gurion was no less mistrustful of the Palestinians who were now tilting towards a union with Israel than he was of King Abdullah.

One should not rely too much on the mood of the Arabs who prefer a link with Israel to annexation by Transjordan, but one should not scoff at this possibility—if it exists. Because here there is a solution to Jerusalem. I do not much regret that we did not capture the Triangle (this is a 'mixed blessing')—but I greatly regret that we did not capture Jerusalem—up to Kalia and beyond. A link with the Triangle—if it is possible—gives us Jerusalem to the Jordan and the Dead Sea. It is true that there is an Arab Legion—but this is not an absolute handicap. If the Arabs are serious in their resistance to Abdullah and Egypt too—this obstacle can be overcome.[32]

This is hardly the diary entry of a man who is unswervingly committed to the Hashemite option, nor does it suggest irremovable opposition to the Palestinian option. Rather it suggests protracted vacillation between the Hashemite and the Palestinian options or, more precisely, an attempt to realize the benefits of the latter without paying any price or running any risk.

The plan for a Palestinian state

The growing co-operation between Israel and the Hawari group was threatened by the arrival in Lausanne, in early August, of two representatives of the All-Palestine government—Raja al-Husayni, the minister of finance and Yussuf Dahayon, the minister of information—followed by two representatives of the refugees from the Gaza Strip, Rashad Shawwa and Musa al-Surani. Initially Hawari thought that the purpose of these men coming to Lausanne was to serve as advisers to the Egyptian delegation and to frustrate any agreement, whether official or tacit, between the Arab delegations and Israel.[33] When the

[31] Foreign Minister's Guidelines to the Delegation at Lausanne, 25 July 1949, 2446/6, ISA.
[32] Ben-Gurion's diary, 26 June 1949.
[33] Sasson to Sharett, 11 Aug. 1949, 2447/5, ISA.

mufti's men claimed to speak in the name of the Arabs of Palestine as the representatives of the Arab Higher Committee and the Gaza government, however, an open clash between them and Hawari's group became inevitable.[34]

The growing co-operation between the Ramallah Refugee Office and Israel implicitly challenged King Abdullah's claim to represent the Palestine Arabs as well as threatening the secret hope he still entertained of Israeli recognition for his annexation of the West Bank. To ward off this challenge to his authority, the king began to show the iron fist behind the velvet glove. His government dispersed Hawari's organization, closed down his offices in Ramallah, arrested some of his colleagues, impeded the departure of others for Lausanne, and prohibited the forwarding of funds to any of the organization's leaders abroad. In addition, the government issued an order forbidding anyone enjoying Jordanian nationality or protection from having contact with the Jews on pain of death. To cap it all, the Arab delegations at Lausanne closed their doors to Hawari, claiming that he had dealings with the Israeli delegation and that he was serving its interest for money.

At the start of the final phase of the Lausanne talks, Sasson found Hawari in a mood of gloom and doom. First, Sasson gave Hawari a few hundred francs and sent him to pay his bill at the hotel and the restaurant, thus making him a 'free man'. Second, Sasson dictated a threatening letter for Hawari to send to Fawzi el-Mulki, the head of the Jordanian delegation at Lausanne. The letter said that if Mulki did not intervene immediately with his government to cancel all the measures taken against the refugee organization and its branches in Jordan, Hawari would be compelled to ask for the intervention of the PCC and also to hold a press conference that would embarrass the Jordanian and other Arab delegations. Third, Sasson urged Hawari to contact the representatives of the refugees with property, Shukri al-Taji and Said Bidas, and invite them to return to Lausanne and form with him a new delegation that would demand to represent the Palestinian refugees at the Lausanne talks.

Hawari did exactly what he was told to do. The first to respond was Mulki, who sent several telegrams to Amman. A week later Hawari received letters from his friends in Transjordan saying that their organization had been allowed to resume its work and that there was some improvement in the attitude of the Jordanian authorities towards them. Ten days later Taji and Bidas turned up at Lausanne; the Arab delegations ended their boycott and once again started consulting Hawari and listening to what he had to say. Hawari and his colleagues

---

[34] Sasson to Sharett, 17 Aug. 1949, 2441/2, ISA.

were saying, to anyone who cared to listen, not only that Israel's existing borders should be recognized but that she should be given additional territory to enable her to absorb a larger number of Palestinian refugees. This position was elaborated in various letters sent by Hawari to his friends and acquaintances in the Arab countries, to the Arab press, to Azzam Pasha at the Arab League, and to radio stations around the world. In all these letters Hawari called for realism and urged the Arab states to recognize the new facts that had emerged in Palestine and to come to terms with Israel.[35]

Hawari had one long talk with Amir Mansour, the defence minister of Saudi Arabia who was passing through Switzerland. At the end of the talk the amir asked for a written memorandum that he could pass on to his father, King Ibn Saud, and to the Saudi government. The memorandum was duly prepared by Hawari, with some help from Sasson. It spoke of the inflexibility of the Arab delegations at Lausanne and of the territorial ambitions of their governments and explained that there was no alternative to facing the facts in Palestine and co-operating with Israel, for the sake of the refugees and for the sake of stability in the entire Middle East.

Hawari also replied to a questionnaire addressed by the PCC in an attempt to identify some common ground between the parties. First Hawari demanded the repatriation of all the refugees who wanted to return and were prepared to live in peace. But he also appealed to the commission to give serious consideration to the contribution that Israel could make towards a comprehensive solution to the refugee problem. In the second part of his reply, Hawari argued that Israel's territory should not be reduced so that she would be able to absorb a larger number of refugees and so that these refugees would be able to live comfortably and become loyal Israeli subjects. As head of the refugees' delegation, Hawari could not go further in his reply without being seen as a traitor by the Arab delegations and by the Arabs who sent him. As it was, the reply aroused the wrath of the Arab delegations and attempts were made to prevent its communication to the Conciliation Commission.[36]

Hawari's activities brought him into renewed conflict not just with the Arab delegations but, more directly with the mufti's men at Lausanne. Taji and Bidas sided with Hawari in this conflict. Together they put pressure on the PCC to recognize them as the spokesmen for all the refugees and to allow them to attend its meeting with the Arabs

[35] Ibid. Shukri al-Taji had acted as a front-man for the Jewish National Fund in its efforts to lease land in Transjordan in 1936. See Kamal T. Nimri, 'Abdullah Ibn al-Hussain: A Study in Arab Political Leadership', Ph.D. thesis (University of London, 1977), 255.

[36] Sasson to Sharett, 29 Aug. 1949, 2441/2, ISA.

and Israelis as observers. And with the help of the rich refugees, Hawari's group gradually gained the upper hand in this internal Palestinian struggle for power.[37]

In view of the uniform replies of the Arab delegations to the PCC's memorandum on the territorial question and the fear that Abdullah would secure Britain's support for the annexation of the West Bank during his visit to London, it was deemed necessary to accompany Hawari's activities at Lausanne with a campaign to mobilize Palestinian resistance to a merger with Jordan and to the continuing interference of the Arab states in their affairs. An elaborate plan of action was evolved during discussions between Sasson and Hawari. The plan called for the creation of a political authority-in-exile, consisting of five to seven men, to represent the refugees. These representatives were to receive full and irrevocable powers of attorney from the refugees in Lebanon, Syria, Jordan, and Egypt. Under Israel's guidance these representatives were to operate in Europe, in America, and in Palestine. In Palestine the purpose was to whip up local opposition to Jordan through radio broadcasts and by other means, whereas in Europe and America it was to mount a propaganda effort, to send memoranda to international organizations, and to educate Western leaders about the urgent necessity for peace. All three groups of representatives had to co-ordinate their work. Israel, for her part, had to promise advisers, funds to meet the expenses of the proposed political authority, and asylum for its members in Israel.[38] In essence, this was a proposal for the creation of a Palestinian puppet government-in-exile with Israel as the exclusive puppeteer.

Sasson's report on the plan he had worked out with Hawari crossed with a report he received of a meeting that had taken place in Lydda between Shmuel Divon and Yehoshua Palmon and Daoud Dajani. Daoud Dajani had served as an informer to the Haganah in the past, being motivated by a deep personal grudge against the Husaynis from a belief that they were responsible for the murder of his brother, and was related to Omar Dajani, code-named 'the orphan' who had also collaborated and received money from the Jewish Agency (albeit at a higher political level, given his association with King Abdullah and his extensive Arab and international contacts). According to Daoud, Omar was organizing a movement for the independence of the Arab part of Palestine and was planning to appear in its name at the next annual meeting of the General Assembly. Omar was allegedly in contact with Ahmad Shukairy, a former member of the Arab Higher Committee and a future chairman of the Palestine Liberation

[37] Sasson to Sharett, 17 Aug. 1949, 2441/2, ISA.
[38] Sasson to Divon, 1 Sept. 1949, 2442/6, ISA.

Organization. Daoud offered to travel to Cyprus to meet Omar and work out a joint plan of action. The Israelis replied that they would be willing to receive a representative delegation of Palestinians that would include Ahmad Shukairy. Daoud also reported that there was no confidence in King Abdullah in the Triangle and bitterness was universal. On the other hand there was no organized initiative towards the achievement of full independence. Hawari's organization was virtually non-existent, and it was being rumoured that Hawari himself had collected money from the refugees and gone abroad on holiday.[39]

Sasson was worried by this report and warned his colleagues not to place any trust in Ahmad Shukairy and not to involve him in any action. At Lausanne, Shukairy had apparently worked for the mufti and only became friendly with the refugee delegations in order to spy on them. Nor was Omar Dajani to be entrusted with any political role because, 'though bold and courageous, his expenses are high and he is inconstant and childish in his political outlook'. Sasson's advice was to bring him back to Palestine and harness him to work at a broadcasting station under close Israeli supervision. Hawari's organization was held out as the most serious in the Arab world, and Sasson warned against giving any encouragement to Daoud and Omar Dajani who wanted to destroy it in order to build their own power base over its ruins. Having personally gone over the correspondence and plans of Hawari's organization, Sasson was persuaded that it was the only organization that Israel could rely on and work through.[40]

At his next meeting with Hawari, on September 2, Sasson got down to business. In the end Hawari agreed to carry out the joint plan but he had a number of conditions, chief of which was that the basis for co-operation between his side and Israel would be resistance to the annexation of Arab Palestine and the creation of a Palestinian state, even if only a small one. The idea of a state, Hawari now argued, would attract many supporters and undermine the territorial claims of the Arab states. Secondly, Hawari wanted an assurance that Israel would not abandon them in the middle of the road but continue to back them even if the struggle for independence turned into a rebellion. Thirdly, Israel had to promise that in the event of the Arab states resorting to detention, imprisonment, and repression she would give asylum to those persecuted, even if their number exceeded a thousand. Fourthly, Israel would have to provide guidance and meet the expenses of the organization in Europe and America. Fifthly, Hawari requested that Israel should not oppose his organization's rapprochement with Ibn

---

[39] Divon to the Israeli Delegation (Lausanne), 1 Sept. 1949, 2442/8, ISA; interview with Yehoshua Palmon.

[40] Sasson to Divon and Palmon, 2 Sept. 1949, 2442/6, ISA.

Saud, which was designed to win moral support for its operations in the Arab world. Finally, Hawari, having evidently shaken off his earlier gloom and despair, pressed for a meeting in Paris of all those concerned so that they could get down to work as early as possible.[41]

Two days later Moshe Sharett gave his agreement in principle to the Sasson–Hawari plan. Yet, while giving the go ahead to this 'experiment', as he called it, Sharett pointed to two contradictions inherent in the plan. First Hawari advocated an independent regime for the Triangle without even pretending to represent the population of the Triangle but only the refugees who were dispersed in the neighbouring countries. Secondly, by aiming at a rift between the refugees and the Arab states, the plan contradicted Israel's aim of resettling the refugees in the Arab countries, an aim that could not be realized without the cooperation of the governments of these countries.[42]

Sasson was glad to receive the go-ahead, but his reply to Sharett's critical observations revealed that he himself was playing the kind of double-game with Hawari that the foreign minister was intent on playing with King Abdullah. Sasson conceded that Hawari and his colleagues represented refugees but saw no reason why refugees should not adopt the slogan of independence and thought that such a slogan would bring them many supporters and sympathizers in the East and in the West, would cause political ferment on the West Bank, and aggravate inter-Arab conflicts and complications. Hawari's stand could help Israel's delegations to the PCC and to the UN in rebutting the demands of the Arab states for Palestinian and Israeli territory. It could also relieve British and American pressure on Israel and encourage these powers to try and solve the refugee problem by resettlement in the neighbouring Arab countries. Thus, concluded Sasson, new facts would be created that would ensure the annexation of the Triangle (presumably to Israel), and hence its compatibility with Israel's intentions.[43] In other words, the plan for a Palestinian government-in-exile was not intended to pave the way to the creation of an independent Palestinian state but, on the contrary, to the annexation of what was left of Arab Palestine either to Israel or to Transjordan as part of a deal with Israel.

Of all the brave talk about a Palestinian government-in-exile, of a struggle for independence, of a separate state or a mini-state, nothing was put into action. Hawari had neither the personal qualities and stature, nor power base, nor the popular following required to lead an effective campaign for independence. His reputation as a collabora-

---

[41] Sasson to Divon and Palmon, 3 Sept. 1949, 2442/6, ISA.
[42] Sharett to Sasson, 5 Sept. 1949, 2442/8, ISA.
[43] Sasson to Sharett, 6 Sept. 1949, 2442/6, ISA.

tionist destroyed any credibility he might have enjoyed with the Palestinian community. His organization continued to co-operate with the Israeli authorities on practical matters such as the reunion of families, the resettlement of refugees, and the restitution of property but it carried very little political weight. Hawari himself remained in close touch with the Israelis and was once suggested by Ben-Gurion as the possible leader for an Arab party inside Israel. But when his political usefulness had been exhausted, Hawari, who was a lawyer by training, was allowed to settle down in Nazareth and was appointed a judge.

Was there any real possibility of establishing a separate state in Arab Palestine at the time of the Lausanne conference or was the whole idea a mere phantom, a figment of Sasson's fertile imagination? Sir Alec Kirkbride for one had no doubt at all that the idea was a non-starter, 'a manifest absurdity'. Asked by American visitors what would be the attitude of the Arabs of Palestine to this proposal and what were the chances of such a state surviving, Kirkbride replied that

the Arabs of Palestine were probably prepared for any folly and, in view of their disunion, there might be some who would favour the creation of a separate Arab state. The creation of such a state from the sorry remnant of the hill country which remained of Arab Palestine with a settled population of 400,000 persons plus more than 400,000 refugees would be a manifest absurdity. Such a state could not exist, except perhaps as a satellite of Israel. That might, of course, be the Israeli plan.[44]

Kirkbride was not far off the mark. On their own, in the aftermath of the Palestine disaster, the Palestinians could not create a viable state, let alone an independent state. Only in co-operation with Israel and, in the final analysis, only if Israel were prepared to use her own army to expel the Arab Legion from the West Bank could such a state be formed, but then it could have been nothing more than a satellite.

In retrospect, the surprising fact is not that Israel did not go through with the plan for a separate Palestinian state but, in view of her close association with Abdullah in the past, that this idea should have received any serious consideration at all. One Israeli scholar has persuasively argued that the willingness of so many Israeli policymakers to contemplate the creation of an autonomous Palestinian Arab region or even a separate Palestinian state alongside Israel stemmed from the fear that Israeli consent to Jordanian Hashemite rule might lead to the return of the Iraqi army to the West Bank, arouse the opposition of the Arab states who were hostile to the Hashemites, and present Israel as a country whose actions were contrary to the

---

[44] Kirkbride to M. R. Wright, 17 May 1949, FO 371/75287, PRO.

resolutions of the United Nations and the position of the Soviet Union. Above all, the Israeli government feared the application of the Anglo-Transjordanian Treaty in the event of the West Bank being annexed to the Hashemite Kingdom of Jordan.[45]

In other words, Israel's motives for favouring, or pretending to favour, a separate Palestinian state were negative rather than positive in nature: it was to ward off a greater evil. Whether the Israeli leaders genuinely favoured such a state is open to doubt, to say the least. The slogan of an independent Palestinian state was a useful weapon in Israel's diplomatic armoury, especially in the effort to discredit the other Arab states and to confuse the PCC. Sharett, who is portrayed by Ilan Pappé as the chief proponent of the Palestinian option in Israel's foreign policy, emerges as the originator of the tactic of using the slogan of Palestinian independence to Israel's own advantage. At first Sharett feared that Israeli sponsorship of Palestinian independence would backfire in the form of international pressure on her to retreat to the borders of the 1947 partition plan. By early May, however, he instructed Eytan to encourage and certainly not oppose the idea that the PCC should hold a plebiscite as this would 'take time and cause complications', and to 'pull strings discreetly for a separate Arab state' as the fear of reversion to the borders of 29 November 1947 was by then 'utterly unreal'.[46] If this was the real attitude of the man who is supposed to have been the most consistent and dedicated advocate of the Palestinian option, then the whole thesis about a conflict of orientations among Israel's leaders can be safely discarded.

Israel's official line, at any rate, was to endorse the principle of Palestinian statehood and to do nothing about it except for scoring points off the Arabs. 'Israel had endorsed the plan for the creation of an independent Arab state in Palestine', Eytan declared before the PCC, 'but it could not agree that the neighbouring Arab states were entitled to profit from the failure of the Palestine Arabs to establish that State. The Arab states had no right to secure territorial expansion through the absence of a legitimate authority in the area when they had themselves, through the hostilities begun by them, prevented the establishment of that authority.'[47]

While the two sides continued to spar, the Conciliation Commission was reduced to acting as a post office, transmitting suggestions between the two sides, all of which proved unacceptable. While Israel continued

---

[45] Avraham Sella, *From Contacts to Negotiations: The Relations of the Jewish Agency and State of Israel with King Abdullah, 1946–1950* (Heb.) (Tel Aviv University: Shiloah Institute, 1986), 39.

[46] Sharett to Eytan, 10 May 1949, 2453/2, ISA.

[47] Summary Record of a Meeting Between the Conciliation Commission and the Delegation of Israel, 9 June 1949, 2477/6, ISA.

to insist on an overall settlement, the Arabs continued to talk about the refugees. Neither side was prepared to make the concessions that would have made a settlement possible. In the end, the commission had to concede defeat. Although its official and increasingly indolent life was extended by many more years, it never recovered from the failure of the Lausanne conference.

The Israeli leaders shed no tears over the failure of the Lausanne conference. It was a cardinal tenet of Israeli diplomacy that no foreign mediation, however neutral and objective it might be, was capable of working out a settlement; and the dispute could be settled only by direct negotiations between the parties. Apart from this opposition in principle to third party involvement, the composition of the PCC aroused Israeli suspicions. Ben-Gurion had no confidence in the PCC. A man like Bunche, he once said, might have had a chance of succeeding in the task of conciliation because he was dedicated to the cause and cared only about peace, whereas the members of the Commission were influenced by the wishes of their governments.[48] Sharett similarly considered the PCC to be harmful because it obscured Arab unwillingness to settle; because it served as an instrument for Great Power interference in the affairs of the Middle East; and because it cast a negative light on Israel by demanding concessions in the name of compromise that Israel was unwilling to make. 'Any bad compromise that is laid at the foundation of a permanent peace settlement can become for us a cause for weeping for generations to come',[49] wrote Sharett to Abba Eban, the propagator of the view that the armistice agreements had already given Israel everything she needed. To the possibility of a good compromise that might have been the source of rejoicing for generations to come Sharett made no reference, presumably because he thought the price was not worth paying.

From the very start, Israel was wary of embarking on detailed negotiations with the neighbouring countries, believing that the commission's invitation to come to Lausanne would simultaneously deprive them of individual freedom of manœuvre and force them to toe the extremist and intransigent pan-Arab line. As a UN body, the PCC posed a direct threat to Israel's interests in Jerusalem since its terms of reference required it to work out a plan for implementing the UN decision to internationalize the Holy City. Here Israel's interests coincided with those of Abdullah and provided a powerful incentive for bypassing the PCC and seeking to reach a bilateral accord. Israel not only preferred direct negotiations to third party mediation, she also preferred to negotiate with each Arab party separately and thereby enhance her own leverage. It is therefore probably no exaggeration to

[48] Ben-Gurion's diary, 18 July 1949.   [49] Sharett to Eban, 26 Sept. 1949, 2447/1, ISA.

say, as one Israeli scholar has done, that Israel consciously and deliberately set out to bring the talks at Lausanne to an impasse while exploiting the encounter to develop contacts and a preliminary understanding towards separate negotiations with several Arab states, notably Egypt and Jordan.[50]

[50] Sella, *From Contacts to Negotiations*, 42.

17

THE ELUSIVE PEACE TREATY

The resumption of direct talks

The failure of the Lausanne conference opened the way to the resumption of direct talks between Israel and the Arab states. Israel publicly declared her readiness to enter into peace negotiations with any of the surrounding Arab countries. Privately, messages were sent to the royal courts in Cairo and Amman, carrying invitations to parley. No response was received from Egypt, and the only positive response to this informal invitation came from King Abdullah. Direct negotiations between Israel and Jordan therefore got under way in November 1949 and continued intermittently until the king's death in July 1951. They proceeded in fits and starts, were beset by endless problems and suffered many setbacks, but they also represented one of the high water marks of Israeli–Jordanian co-operation.

Overlapping interests in the economic, security, and political spheres laid the foundations for the peculiarly intimate co-operation between these two countries and lent some urgency to their mutual quest for a final peace settlement.

Both countries were in the throes of an acute economic crisis as a direct result of the long and exhausting war they had fought. Jordan's sterling balance had been swept away by the costs of war and occupation and by an extremely adverse balance of trade. Her exports to Europe could not go by the traditional route of Haifa's port. Using Beirut meant an additional land haul of 190 kilometres, while using Aqaba involved paying Suez Canal dues. Greater Transjordan, with its largely destitute or impoverished population, was thought to have no economic future unless the frontier with Israel was opened for trade and normal economic relations. Israel, too, needed an open border if she was to have local markets for her goods and save on transport costs. She depended on Jordan to circumvent the Arab economic boycott, and she depended on Jordanian goodwill for the reactivation of the economic enterprises in the Dead Sea and in Naharayim. With her meagre resources Israel could ill afford to maintain a large standing army and meet the challenge of absorbing mass immigration. Economic development was now a very high priority, and an open border with Jordan would have served as a means to that end.

The security interests of Israel and Jordan were equally vital and closely interdependent. The border between them was long and unnatural, cutting across communities and giving rise to problems of unparalleled scope and complexity. A continuing state of war along this border was likely to absorb the attention, the energies, the manpower, and the scarce financial resources of both sides. A state of peace, on the other hand, would have greatly eased all the problems associated with policing this border and would have freed both societies to concentrate on the more constructive tasks of nation-building and economic development. Yet the interdependence of the two countries in the security sphere was not complete for they also had some divergent interests. The Israelis were reluctant to agree to the annexation of the West Bank by Abdullah because of their ingrained conviction that Jordan was Britain in disguise and that annexation would therefore mean the return of Britain to Palestine by the kitchen door. On the other hand, Jordan was a weaker and less important state than Egypt and therefore offered a better prospect of ultimate Israeli dominance. For Abdullah, by contrast, it was Israel's proven military strength that enhanced her value as a potential ally. An alliance with Israel, while narrowing his diplomatic options, could widen the strategic room for manœuvre he enjoyed *vis-à-vis* his Arab rivals and possibly even permit the realization of his Greater Syria scheme at some future date. On the other hand, if things went badly for Jordan and she herself became the target of military aggression from one of her Arab rivals, then it would have been useful to at least have the option of falling back on the alliance with Israel. In other words, a peace treaty with Israel would have resolved Jordan's immediate security dilemma as well as insuring the Jordanian branch of the Hashemite dynasty against future threats from its Arab opponents.

While in the security sphere the interests of Israel and Jordan were partly convergent and partly divergent, in the political sphere they had one overriding interest in common: the suppression of Palestinian nationalism. Even though the Palestinian national movement had only recently sustained the most catastrophic disaster of its entire history, there was always the prospect, however remote, that it would recover and stage a comeback. Even though the leader of that movement, Hajj Amin al-Husayni, was utterly discredited and politically impotent, he was alive and well and living in Cairo and it would have been rash to write him off completely. Even though the idea of an independent Palestinian state seemed so far fetched as to verge on fantasy, there was no guarantee that this would always be the case. Abdullah for his part wanted to give no hostages to fortune. He was determined to proclaim the annexation of the West Bank. His determination was strengthened by the moves to unite Syria with Iraq following the overthrow of Husni Zaim because such a union would have diminished the prospect for the fulfilment of Abdullah's own plan for Greater Syria. He was also getting old and wanted to see his kingdom enlarged before his death. Although Abdullah did not need Israel's formal consent to the annexation of the West Bank, he was very anxious to secure her agreement.

Israel tried to exact as much as she could in exchange for her agreement, but her leaders had their own reasons for favouring the extension of Abdullah's rule over the part of Palestine that was occupied by his troops. They feared that the Palestinian problem would rekindle the Arab–Israeli conflict; they wanted the Palestinian problem to go away, and since it showed no sign of going away of its own accord, they were content to try and sweep it under Abdullah's carpet.

Abdullah now had the support of the leading Western powers for his plan to proclaim the annexation of the West Bank and to enter into direct negotiations with Israel. Previously both Britain and America had advised him not to enter into separate negotiations with Israel but to wait and see what might be produced by the Palestine Conciliation Commission. Since the commission produced nothing, they withdrew their objections and conceded the need for direct bilateral negotiations between Israel and the Arabs.

British policy towards Israel underwent a significant change during the summer of 1949, leading to *de jure* recognition and the exchange of ambassadors. There were two major reasons for this. Firstly, the British policymakers recognized that Israel was the strongest military power in the Middle East and concluded that her co-operation would be essential to the success of any scheme for the containment of Soviet advances into this area. Secondly, they discovered that the Anglo-Transjordanian Treaty would apply to the West Bank if this area was to be formally annexed to Jordan and that they themselves would be obliged to come to the rescue of Jordan in the event of an Israeli attack. Yet the mighty British Empire no longer had the troops necessary for intervention in a land war in Palestine, to say nothing of the political will for intervention in such a war. The conclusion was obvious: a Jordanian–Israeli settlement was required in order to reduce to a minimum the likelihood of war. Accordingly British reservations about separate Jordanian–Israeli negotiations gave way to a qualified endorsement. The British did not openly encourage Abdullah to make peace with Israel, but they did not stand in his way either. They approved the idea of direct talks but cautioned Abdullah not to proceed too far or too fast and to take into account the opposition to peace in his own country and in the Arab world. At the same time the

British lent their unqualified support to Abdullah's plan to annex the West Bank.[1]

The British also persuaded the Americans, following the failure of third-party mediation, to look favourably on the attempt by Jordan and Israel to engage in bilateral talks and to waive their objection to the annexation of Arab Palestine by Jordan. A delegation from the Foreign Office led by Michael Wright went to Washington in the middle of November 1949 to hold talks with the State Department experts on the Middle East. Wright argued that the Middle East was the key to the overall struggle between the West and the Soviet Union. If Western influence was to be removed from the Middle East, the Soviet Union would fill the vacuum and this would prejudice the future of Europe and pave the way for communist domination in Africa. King Abdullah was held out as one of the most reliable allies of the West in the struggle against communism and the Americans agreed in principle to the incorporation of Arab Palestine into Jordan though they still had some reservations about the timing.[2]

Later in the month a conference of the American chiefs of mission to the Middle East was held in Istanbul under the chairmanship of George McGhee. The general aim of American policy was said to be to minimize the dislocations created by the Arab–Israeli war and the problem of the Arab refugees and to promote economic stability, security, and peace. And one of the conclusions reached at the conference was to agree to encourage direct negotiations between Israel and the Arab states and to agree to the merger of Arab Palestine with Jordan, if accompanied by appropriate steps to ensure representation of the Palestinians in the Jordanian legislature.[3]

A favourable international climate thus existed for the annexation of Arab Palestine and for the initiation of peace talks with Israel. But there was also one major obstacle to progress on both fronts: Arab opposition. In the aftermath of the Palestine defeat, it would have been extremely difficult, if not impossible, to gain public support or the acquiescence of the Arab League to a settlement with Israel. Abdullah habitually overestimated his own power and underestimated the strength and seriousness of the opposition to his peace policy with Israel. In conversation with American representatives he voiced his contempt for the stalling and obstructive attitude of the other members of the Arab League and reserved the right to decide when and how to

---

[1] Policy Towards Israel, Bevin to Troutbeck, 20 May 1949, FO 371/75056; 'Middle East Policy', note by the secretary of state for foreign affairs, 25 Aug. 1949, CP (49) 183, CAB 129/36; minute by B. A. B. Burrows, 16 Nov. 1949, FO 371/75344, PRO.

[2] Record of Discussion Between Mr Michael Wright and Members of the State Department, 14 Nov. 1949, FO 371/75355, PRO; McGhee, *Envoy to the Middle World*, 54–8.

[3] McGhee, *Envoy to the Middle World*, 84–6; *New York Times*, 30 Nov. 1949.

negotiate with Israel.[4] But with the passage of time the king's weakness and isolation became more and more apparent, as did the determination of the political forces that were arraigned against him.

A visit from Abdullah's old acquaintance, Moshe Novomeysky, the founder and director of the Palestine Potash Company, paved the way to the resumption of contact at the official level. Novomeysky had always found the amir of Transjordan friendly and co-operative and, in welcome distinction from other Arab leaders, hostile neither to Jews as people nor to Zionism. Abdullah often told Novomeysky that he had inherited this attitude of friendliness from his father who did not consider respect for Jews to be a derogation from Islam. When Abdullah visited London in August 1949, Novomeysky called on him in the Hyde Park Hotel to ask for his assistance in restoring the fresh water supply to the chemical works at the southern tip of the Dead Sea. Abdullah turned to the possibility of peace between Jordan and Israel, particularly seeking conditions that would satisfy Arab sentiment. He told Novomeysky that if he should wish to see him when back in Palestine, he need only write. In November Novomeysky did write to Abdullah requesting an interview; he received an invitation by return to meet him for dinner at Shuneh.

The talk in the winter palace at Shuneh was a very long one, and it was only in the small hours that Novomeysky returned home. The principal subject of Abdullah's interest was not the construction of a new water canal, but the possibility of real peace and the conditions on which it might be concluded.[5] Novomeysky suggested that the Israeli authorities would probably agree to the return of some of the Arab quarters in Jerusalem in exchange for Jordanian co-operation in the restoration of water supply to his chemical works. Bearing in mind the lesson of the armistice negotiations, the king replied that he could not agree to piecemeal suggestions of this kind but would assent to a general settlement which would recover sufficient territory to enable him to meet the criticism which a separate peace with Israel would arouse. Novomeysky suggested that Samir Rifai, the minister of the court, who was doing the translation, should meet an Israeli spokesman and discuss the matter as the king's personal representative. The king agreed.

Sir Alec Kirkbride who was given the king's version of this conversation doubted whether the Israelis would agree to the king's terms but thought it would be useful for Samir Rifai to hear what they had to say, especially as he was in no position to commit the Jordanian government. Kirkbride reminded the king of the unsatisfactory outcome of the last negotiations and counselled extreme caution. But he made no

[4] *FRUS 1949*, vi. 1483–6.   [5] Novomeysky, *Given to Salt*, 30 f.

attempt to discourage him from undertaking exploratory talks.[6] A series of talks were held at Shuneh during the autumn of 1949 between Rifai and Reuven Shiloah of the Israeli Foreign Ministry. Rifai reported the gist of these talks to Kirkbride, who was neither disappointed nor surprised at their lack of concrete results. In his recollections of this period, aptly called *From the Wings*, Kirkbride gives the following gloss on these high-level talks:

> The visitor used to travel down from Jerusalem in a car sent by the King, dine at the royal table with the Prime Minister and then retire with the latter to an ante-chamber for discussions which seemed to be interminable. King Abdullah used to stay up for as long as he could keep his eyes open in the hope that some positive result might emerge. The exchange usually terminated at about three o'clock on the morning after which Shiloah went back across the lines. I marvelled at the amount of time the two participants managed to take up with their discussions.[7]

During the week following Novomeysky's visit, three letters arrived from Israel in rapid succession. One was from Novomeysky himself to Samir Rifai, saying he had delivered the king's message to Ben-Gurion and Sharett and that they were both anxious to discuss a settlement with Jordan. One was from Dr Walter Eytan to King Abdullah, expressing the readiness of the Israeli government to come to a settlement on a friendly basis with Jordan, and stating that Elias Sasson and Reuven Shiloah had been accredited as the representatives of Israel and would present themselves at the time and place chosen by the king. One was from Sasson to Samir expressing deep satisfaction that there were prospects of permanent peace and the hope that talks should begin as soon as possible. Samir responded by inviting the Israelis to a preliminary talk at Shuneh on Sunday evening, November 27.[8]

The first phase, consisting of exploratory talks, lasted two months, from the end of November 1949 until the end of January 1950. The enthusiasm with which Israel embarked on the talks and the desire to produce an agreement with Jordan in time for the opening of the annual meeting of the General Assembly were tempered by a recognition of the price that would have to be paid for success. Foreign Minister Sharett estimated at the outset that they could reach a separate agreement with Jordan if they were prepared to make substantial concessions. But given the range and complexity of the issues concerned, he also estimated that there was no chance whatever of producing such an agreement before the meeting of the General Assembly. 'This will be a

[6] Kirkbride to FO, 11 Nov. 1949; and FO to Amman, 17 Nov. 1949, FO 371/75344, PRO.
[7] Kirkbride, *From the Wings*, 112.
[8] Kirkbride to FO, 23 Nov. 1949, FO 371/75344, PRO.

protracted, exhausting and complicated affair', he predicted. 'One of the serious complications is connected with the indirect but real participation of the British in these negotiations. In general, this is not a matter for a quick fix. *It will require a great deal of time and a great deal of patience.*'[9]

The Israeli government's latitude for making concessions was restricted by various domestic considerations. It was known that the government was reluctant to extend official recognition to the annexation of the West Bank by Jordan and that it did not want to go down in history as the body that officially waived the claim to any part of the Land of Israel.[10] There was also opposition from the left-wing parties, Mapam and the Communists, to negotiations with Jordan because they regarded King Abdullah as a British puppet, and from the nationalist Herut party, which claimed Israeli sovereignty over all of Palestine.

The prime minister appears to have shared both the suspicion felt by the left for Abdullah and his British masters and the unease felt by the right about compromising Israel's claim to the whole area of Mandatory Palestine. But as a pragmatic statesman he recognized that no agreement was possible without some Israeli concessions. On November 26, the day before the first meeting at Shuneh was due to take place, Ben-Gurion gathered his advisers for a consultation. They included Golda Meir, Walter Eytan, Elias Sasson, and Reuven Shiloah, all of whom had first-hand experience of negotiations with the ruler of Jordan. Ben-Gurion posed the question: what did they stand to gain from a peace agreement with Jordan apart from peace? Sasson replied that all the Arab states were afraid to be the first to make peace with Israel and that a peace agreement with Jordan could therefore open the road to peace with Egypt, Lebanon, and possibly other states as well. Shiloah replied that a peace agreement with Jordan would break the deadlock, split the Arab camp, yield economic advantage, and permit shipping from Eilat. Mrs Meir thought that Abdullah was negotiating on behalf of the British and that great vigilance was therefore called for, especially regarding the Negev. The implications of a peace agreement with Abdullah for the Israeli–Egyptian armistice agreement were also discussed. Ben-Gurion stressed that they must make it clear to Abdullah that they could not spoil their relations with Egypt by agreeing to the replacement of Egyptian control over the Gaza Strip by Jordanian control without first obtaining Egypt's consent. Ben-Gurion was also opposed to a joint port in Eilat but he

[9] Sharett to Dr A. Katzenelson (Israeli delegation to the UN), 4 Nov. 1949, 87/11, ISA. Emphasis in the original.
[10] *Haaretz*, 7 Nov. 1949.

anticipated that the hardest problem to resolve would be Jerusalem. As far as tactics were concerned, he was in favour of going directly to the point and putting the cards on the table in order to find out whether an agreement was possible or not. The guidelines agreed upon at this meeting consisted of numerous demands and very few concessions. The guidelines were

1. To demand the Jewish Quarter in the Old City right up to the Wailing Wall.
2. A territorial link with Mount Scopus.
3. Latrun.
4. The western bank of the Dead Sea including the north-western corner.
5. The inclusion of Naharayim in Israel and compensation in the south.
6. Mutual border adjustments in other places.
7. Recognition of the annexation of the Gaza Strip after Egypt had given her consent.
8. Free passage to Gaza, but not a corridor.
9. A free area in Haifa and passage to it.
10. A Jordanian undertaking not to allow British bases west of the Jordan.
11. A Jordanian proclamation that the Treaty with Britain would not apply west of the Jordan.
12. Cancellation of the Treaty in the event of a union between Jordan and another country.
13. An agreement on shipping from Eilat.
14. The passage to Gaza and Haifa to be restricted to civilians only, with weapons for the police requiring Israeli approval in each instance.[11]

Five nights at Shuneh

Armed with this detailed brief, Shiloah and Sasson set off for Shuneh on November 27 for the first in a series of exploratory talks. The royal host's face lit up when he saw Sasson, but he was disappointed to learn that this genial Oriental Jew, who had done so much for the cause of Arab–Jewish understanding, was about to desert them to take up his new post as Israel's first minister in Ankara. The king opened the discussion with his by now familiar lecture about having been drawn into the war against his will, about the failure of the Arab world to carry out its duties in war and in peace, and about his intention to save the situation in peacetime just as he had done in wartime. After a quarter of an hour of genial generalities, the king delegated matters to Samir Rifai with his blessings and retired.

Samir described in realistic terms the situation of the two sides. He

[11] Consultation for Negotiation with Jordan, 26 Nov. 1949, 64/2, İSA; and Ben-Gurion's diary, 26 Nov. 1949.

conceded that Israel had power and the ability to get assistance from the United States, but the challenges facing Israel were enormous and she was surrounded by a hostile Arab world whose hatred was inflamed by its defeat on the battlefield. Despite immigration the Jews would always remain a minority and hence their most vital interest was peace. Notwithstanding all the Arab rhetoric, Jordan recognized Israel as an existing reality and her interest too lay in peace. But to enable His Majesty to make peace, this peace had to be honourable and capable of being presented to the Arab world as an achievement. His Majesty was ready to pursue an independent policy but this policy must not detract from his dignity. On the basis of an honourable peace they were prepared to talk, and Samir proposed a three-point agenda dealing with political matters, economic matters, and the problems of the refugees.

The Israelis said that the Anglo-Transjordanian Treaty should also be an item on the agenda and asked whether this treaty would extend to Arab Palestine in the event of annexation by Jordan. Samir replied that it would naturally apply to the whole Hashemite Kingdom of Jordan, whereupon the Israelis indicated that they might have further to say on this subject later.

Addressing the first item on his agenda, the question of a territorial settlement, Samir distinguished between practical proposals and unrealistic demands such as Jordan's old claim for the restoration of Lydda, Ramle, and Jaffa. Even if it were possible to get the UN to reaffirm its partition plan of November 1947, the Jordanians knew that this plan had no chance of being realized. They did not want to make life hard for geography students and were therefore thinking of more logical arrangements. Here Samir mentioned that Jordan considered access to the Mediterranean at Gaza of vital importance and that they needed a territorial link to it, and that meant the Negev. Samir argued that for Israel the Negev was just a question of prestige, since it was desert land of no economic or settlement value. If Israel thought she had a real need of access to the Red Sea, Jordan would be prepared to grant access to Aqaba in return for free access to Haifa. Moreover, with the exception of Jordan, the entire Arab world was hoping for revenge, and it would be better for Israel not to have a common border with Egypt. The Israeli wedge in the Negev disrupted the territorial continuity of the Arab world from Casablanca to Afghanistan. The removal of this wedge was the kind of achievement with which His Majesty could appear before the Arab world. If agreement could be reached on this vital matter, none of the other problems would be an obstacle to peace, not even Jerusalem. As Novomeysky had been told, the way forward lay not in *ad hoc* solutions to specific problems but in tackling the central question, after which everything would fall into place.

The Israelis explained that for them the Negev was much more than a question of prestige and that its surrender was out of the question. While they agreed that an outlet to the sea was vital to Jordan, and that Jordan could have Gaza provided Egypt raised no objections, the settlement could not be based on any Israeli territorial concessions in the Negev. Discussion of this question was left to another meeting, but Samir stated frankly that he saw no prospect for a settlement without territorial continuity. He said he could not be indifferent to the terms of the settlement because when the negotiations were completed he would assume power and it would be his responsibility to defend in the Arab world the peace settlement with the Jews.

At about 11 p.m. the king returned to the lounge to check on progress before going to bed. Samir surveyed briefly and accurately the position of the two sides, and Abdullah was relieved to hear that another meeting had been arranged for December 1. As they were standing around the king said that his father had neglected to consolidate his position in the Hijaz and had ended by losing his throne because of his preoccupation with Palestine. He did not wish to repeat his father's mistakes and was determined to put his own affairs in order. As his main enemies he listed first Egypt and then Iraq. He was looking, he said, not towards Arab unity but towards Islamic unity with Pakistan, Hindustan, and Iran. The king then took his leave by kissing Samir and shaking hands with the Israelis.[12]

The same Israeli representatives met Samir Rifai for the second time at Shuneh on December 1. The discussion, which lasted longer than the first one, could not be said to have carried the matter much forward but a number of interesting points emerged.

The visitors started by saying that their superiors had come to the conclusion that it would not be possible for Israel to cede any territory as part of the settlement with Jordan. Samir pointed out that the statement was irreconcilable with their earlier admission of Jordan's right of access to the sea. They replied that there were many precedents which could be found for solving a problem of this kind without territorial surrender. Samir said that if they had in mind free zones, rights of transit, or other such devices, he could say immediately that that was not what he meant by the term access to the sea. Jordan must have access to the Mediterranean through territory under its own sovereignty. They answered that this was going to be very difficult and

[12] The Meeting with King Abdullah at Shuneh on 27 Nov. 1949, 29 Nov. 1949, 64/2, ISA; Ben-Gurion's diary, 28 Nov. 1949; Kirkbride to FO, 29 Nov. 1949, FO 371/75344, PRO; FRUS 1949, vi. 1512–18.

repeated their inability to give up territory. Samir said that in that case there did not seem to be any point in continuing the talks as this Jordanian claim was basic to any settlement.

Samir's readiness to stop the talks took the visitors aback and after consultation in Hebrew they asked Samir what scheme he had in mind for reaching the sea. After ascertaining that their claim to the Negev stemmed principally from the need for a reserve of land capable of development, Samir said that what he proposed was partition of the Negev, Israel to take the fertile northern part and Jordan to take the southern part which could not be cultivated in any way. That solution would give Jordan its two principal needs, access to the sea and a common frontier with Egypt. Sasson said that there were other factors to be taken into consideration, one of which was that without this living space expansionist thoughts might creep into Israel's head. A long argument ensued leading to no conclusion about the Negev.

The Israelis then said that they had three other points to raise. With regard to Jerusalem both parties were opposed to internationalization and thought that partition was the best solution. Samir said that he was not ready to tackle this complicated question in detail, but that if Jordan's basic demands were satisfied, he would not anticipate difficulty in reaching agreement over Jerusalem. Shiloah indicated that free access to the Wailing Wall would gratify certain religious elements and secure their support against other groups who were opposed to concessions to Jordan in the south. Samir said he would bear this point in mind.

The second point was that of resuming the operations of the potash works in the Dead Sea and the Palestine Electric Corporation in Naharayim. Samir said that Jordan could not make so valuable a concession except as part of a general settlement. He also referred to the potential value to Israel of the resumption of trade generally in the context of a general settlement.

Thirdly, the visitors brought up the question of the Anglo-Transjordanian Treaty and asked whether it would be possible for Britain to keep bases only east of the River Jordan. The distances were such as to be of little practical difference in modern war but the question was one of psychology, and it would be much easier for Israel to recognize the union of eastern Palestine with Jordan if there could be some arrangement whereby British bases would not be established on Palestinian territory. Such an arrangement would also help the Israeli government to make concessions to Jordan on other points. Shiloah said that he did not want an answer right away but asked Samir to bear the point in mind. When Samir did not respond, the Israelis remarked that they assumed that Jordan's insistence on the Negev to be prompted by British strategical considerations. Samir denied this and, to reinforce this point, offered as an alternative to accept a piece of territory stretching from Hebron through Faluja to Majdal, or from Jenin to Nazareth and Acre in the north.

Samir asked finally that they should obtain from their superiors a clear answer to his question as to how it was possible to reconcile recognition of Jordan's right of access to the sea with refusal to cede territory. The answer would show whether it was any use meeting again. They promised to send a message saying whether they considered further talks likely to be useful. The atmosphere throughout was courteous, in fact almost amicable.

King Abdullah employed his usual tactic of staying in the background, letting his aide do the bidding so that he himself could play the mediator and intervene if the talks got stuck. On this occasion he 'swore by his father's grave and other convicing oaths' that the British had never told him to demand the Negev; that all they had said was to make peace with Israel. He envisaged one or two more preliminary talks to establish a basis for agreement, after which he said he would change the government, make Samir prime minister, and openly start official peace negotiations.[13]

Ben-Gurion consulted his military advisers about the question posed by Samir, and they all preferred giving Jordan access to the sea in the north to access in the south. Gen. Yigael Yadin, the chief of staff, was even prepared to exchange Eilat for a Jordanian-held part of Jerusalem. Ben-Gurion did not agree. He realized that there could be no Israeli shipping through the Red Sea without Egypt's agreement but he felt that peace with Jordan would improve Israel's prospects of attaining peace with Egypt.[14] In talks with American representatives, Ben-Gurion insisted that Egypt was the key to Israel's relations with the rest of the Arab world, that peace with Egypt would mean peace and stability throughout the Middle East, and emphatically gave priority to peace with Egypt over peace with Jordan. But he had no incentives to offer, not even a face-saving device, to entice Egypt to agree to direct negotiations. On the contrary, he said that Gaza was now wanted by Abdullah and hence could not be a bargaining point between Egypt and Israel. Other Israeli leaders, too, believed that if only they could settle with Egypt, the danger of a 'second round' would be removed. They had put out feelers to the Egyptian court through Col. Ismail Sherine, King Farouk's brother-in-law, but no answer was received. The Israelis therefore asked for an American initiative to

---

[13] Eytan to Sharett, 2 Dec. 1949, 2339/14, ISA; Kirkbride to FO, 3 Dec. 1949, FO 371/75344, PRO; *FRUS 1949*, vi. 1518–20.

[14] Ben-Gurion's diary, 3 Dec. 1949.

bring the two parties together and for their part were careful in the negotiations with Jordan not to agree to anything that might further alienate Egypt.[15]

Just as the Israelis tried to prompt America to play a more active role, Egypt tried to prompt Britain. After a pause to enable King Farouk to consider the matter, Colonel Sherine had a conversation with the British ambassador to Cairo, Sir Ronald Campbell, regarding the possibility of Israeli–Egyptian negotiations. Sherine said that Egypt would be ready to discuss a political settlement with Israel if, but only if, a British or American guarantee could be given that the Israelis would withdraw from the Gulf of Aqaba. He envisaged an Israeli withdrawal from the southern Negev, preferably up to the southern end of the Dead Sea, thus giving Egypt and Jordan a common frontier. Egypt would retain the Gaza Strip and extend it south and east as far as Aqaba and Beersheba. Sherine also asked that Britain should restrain Jordan from reaching any agreement with Israel that did not stipulate Israeli withdrawal from the Aqaba coast and for an early intimation of the British government's thinking.

The British thought that a settlement between Israel and Egypt would be most desirable, not least because it would remove all the restrictions on Suez Canal traffic, but they feared that if the Egyptians and the Jordanians negotiated together or at the same time, there would be a danger that they might double-cross each other. The conclusion was that it would be better for Jordan to continue to talk alone for the moment and for Egypt to join only if the talks reached a deadlock or a successful conclusion.[16]

A third meeting at Shuneh on December 8 between the two Israelis and Samir Rifai was rather stormy. The principal bone of contention continued to be Jordan's demand for access to the Mediterranean. The Israelis offered to give Jordan 'jurisdiction' over a corridor and cited as a precedent the American–Panamanian agreement giving America the right of access to Colon. Samir turned down the offer flatly. The Israelis argued that they could not give Jordan sovereignty over the corridor as this would split their country in half, to which Samir replied that there was no question of splitting the country in half since Jordan desired the southern Negev as well.

The tension was eased by the call to dinner during which an Arab Legion orchestra played in the background. Muhammad Amin Shanqiti, the minister of education, elevated the conversation to a

---

[15] Ibid. 4 Dec. 1949; M. S. Comay. Minute of a Conversation with Mr James McDonald, 6 Dec. 1949, 64/2, ISA; Sir O. Franks (Washington) to FO, 8 Dec. 1949, FO 371/75344, PRO; *FRUS 1949*, vi. 1521 f., 1528 f.
[16] FO to Washington, 22 Dec. 1949, FO 371/75344, PRO.

theological plane by asking whether the *Hadith*, the tradition of the Prophet and his Companions, permitted Muslims to eat eggs as well as chickens or only chickens. The king then raised a more contemporary philosophical question: whether the purpose of the UN was to ease the relations between states or whether, to the contrary, it only complicated them. When the meal was over, the visitors returned to the lounge but on hearing the orchestra play the Jordanian national anthem, the diminutive monarch rushed out to salute.

There was an unproductive discussion about the problems of Jerusalem, Naharayim, and the Dead Sea, after which Samir reverted to his original suggestion that the southern Negev be given to Jordan. This time Shiloah reminded Samir rather pointedly that the whole of the Negev was in their hands while the Gaza Strip was occupied by Egypt; that they were going out of their way to be accommodating; and that if Jordan rejected their offer, they would be more inclined to take the logical course of coming to terms with Egypt. To remove any illusions, he also pointed out that they were happy with the existing situation, that they were in no hurry to make peace, and that negotiations could only proceed on the basis of 'give and take'. Somewhat startled, Samir observed that what Jordan wanted was also peace but it had to be a peace that the king could defend before the Arab world.

At this point the king came in and Samir gave him an accurate survey of the proceedings. Abdullah responded by saying that Shiloah was right, Palestine had been under British rule for thirty years; the Jews had prepared for the struggle prudently, expelled the British, and ended up with more territory than they had expected; the Arabs of Palestine had failed to grasp what was happening and behaved like cowards; the Arab countries had pushed him into war and then run away: the Egyptians and Syrians had been beaten, Lebanon was not worth mentioning, while the despicable Iraqis had sat in Gesher for a couple of days and then returned to Amman to breathe down his neck. There were only two sides that had held their own, that did not tangle with or beat one another, and it was for them to make the peace. He himself was thinking about his children and his visitors' children, but they had to understand his position and help them. What he asked was that Shiloah and Sasson go to their 'wise men'—Weizmann, Ben-Gurion, and Sharett—and urge them to grant his needs so as not to push him into the hands of the Arabs for he was standing at the crossroads, faced with the choice between joining Arab solidarity or shattering it.

The king and Samir had an exchange in Turkish, almost in a whisper, not realizing that Sasson spoke this language as well as Arabic. Abdullah urged Samir to agree to the Israeli proposal because a corridor under Jordanian jurisdiction represented a concession. What will happen, he asked, when Sasson, who was the only one fighting for them, leaves? Samir said he preferred to wait, and forecast that the Israelis would give in in the end. Abdullah's reply was that currently the Israelis were eager for peace but their eagerness might not last. Samir repeated that they were in a difficult situation, they needed peace and were therefore bound to soften their stand. And if there was no peace, persisted the king, what would he say to Abul Huda, who knew about the contact with the Israelis and had warned against it, and what would he say to the British, the Americans, and the Turks who were all pressing him to settle? Samir ended the exchange by saying that he could not carry through such a settlement and that the king would have to find someone else. It was with obvious reluctance that Samir gave in to the king's demand that a further meeting be arranged.[17]

The breakthrough in the negotiations was achieved in the fourth meeting at Shuneh, which lasted from seven in the evening until three in the morning on December 13. A resolution by the UN General Assembly to place Jerusalem under an international regime spurred both sides to overcome their differences and move forward quickly to partition Jerusalem between themselves before the UN could give effect to its decision. At the meeting Shiloah, Sasson, and Rifai, in the presence of the king, began to draft the written basis for an agreement. Since Samir was wary of the term 'peace treaty', it was called a 'paper' on which were inscribed the 'Principles of a Territorial Settlement' (see Appendix 4).

The first principle was the partition of Jerusalem, with Jordan giving Israel sovereignty over the Jewish Quarter in the Old City up to the Wailing Wall and secure access to Mount Scopus and Israel conceding to Jordan a stretch of land up to the Bethlehem road. Secondly, Jordan agreed to hand over to Israeli sovereignty the entire western shore of the Dead Sea up to and including the northern potash works. Thirdly, the principle of mutual frontier adjustments was accepted subject to the military and agricultural needs of both sides. Fourthly, and most importantly, in recognition of Jordan's vital need for access to the Mediterranean, Israel was to grant her a corridor from Hebron through Beit Jibrin to the Gaza coast. This corridor was to be under full Jordanian sovereignty and to form an inseparable part of Jordan's territory, but there were three conditions: Israel would enjoy free crossing at several points; Jordan would maintain no army and erect no military installations; and the Anglo-Transjordanian Treaty would not apply to the corridor. No agreement was reached on the meaning of the

[17] The Third Meeting at Shuneh, 8 Dec. 1949, 64/2, ISA; *FRUS 1949*, vi. 1540 f.

term 'Gaza', and the written document said that Jordan understood by Gaza the coast between Majdal and the Egyptian line while Israel understood the Egyptian-held strip. This meant that the Israeli government would have to decide whether it was willing to give Abdullah a strip of coast south of Majdal on the secret understanding that he would give it back if and when he got Gaza proper from the Egyptians.

Other matters discussed were the application of the Anglo-Transjordanian Treaty west of the Jordan River and Israeli access to Naharayim, on both of which agreement was in sight. Abdullah wanted to meet Ben-Gurion in person, and tentative plans were discussed for a royal visit to the Jewish part of the city the following week. Walter Eytan optimistically reported to Moshe Sharett, who was leading the struggle against internationalization at the UN in New York, that it was most likely that the agreement would be initialled before the end of the month.[18]

The document constituted a major breakthrough on two key questions: Jerusalem and access to the sea under Jordanian sovereignty. It did not amount to a peace treaty or even a draft peace treaty but an incomplete set of principles, a rough and ready basis for further negotiations. Detailed provisions on the implementation of these principles had to be worked out, and two sticking points were already apparent: the width and precise location of the corridor and the meaning of the term Gaza. Nevertheless, the log-jam had been broken and the climate in which the talks took place dramatically improved. Shiloah and Sasson added to the drama by presenting the offer of a corridor as evidence of Israel's good faith and adding that it was decided upon by Ben-Gurion in appreciation of the king's conciliatory attitude, and in the face of serious opposition, especially from the military. When Abdullah heard the offer he expressed so much pleasure that it seemed he believed a final agreement was at hand.[19]

Sharett hailed the written document as a 'tremendous achievement'. Though conceding sovereignty over the corridor was an extremely bitter pill to swallow and internally could prove a stumbling block, he assumed it was inescapable and heartily congratulated Shiloah and Sasson on their success.[20]

Moshe Dayan, who was preparing at that time to replace Sasson in

[18] Eytan to Sharett, 14 Dec. 1949, 2453/2, ISA. For the full text of the 'Principles of a Territorial Settlement', see Moshe Dayan *Milestones: An Autobiography* (Heb.) (Jerusalem: Edanim Publishers, 1976), 89 f. Only a summary appears in the English edition of this autobiography. There are two factual misrepresentations in Dayan's account: the meeting in question took place on 13 Dec., not 17 Dec., and it was not he who represented Israel at this meeting alongside Shiloah but Sasson. Nor did Dayan attend the next meeting, on 23 Dec. It was characteristic of Dayan to claim for himself credit that was due to others.

[19] *FRUS 1949*, vi. 1545-7.

[20] Sharett to Eytan, 14 Dec. 1949, 2453/2, ISA.

the negotiations, stated in his memoirs that he did not know whether the Israeli government would ratify this agreement: 'Ben-Gurion did not reject it, but he wrinkled his nose when he read it.'[21] Ben-Gurion's diary bears no trace of any reservation that he might have had about the agreed principles. What the diary does suggest is that it was the young colonel who wrinkled his nose and, whether deliberately or unwittingly, helped to sabotage the agreement. It was in a consultation with his military advisers on December 15 about the negotiations with Abdullah that Ben-Gurion learnt from Dayan that the Egyptians had given their verbal agreement to a division of no-man's land north of Gaza that would give Israel another 10 kilometres along the coast. Although streams ran through this area, making it an important source of water for irrigation, Ben-Gurion was against backing out of the negotiations with Jordan because of the intrinsic importance of an Israeli–Jordanian agreement, because of its importance in opening the road to an agreement with Egypt, and because of the need to stand shoulder to shoulder with Abdullah in the campaign against the internationalization of Jerusalem.

It was the military who expressed doubts about Abdullah's claim to the territory adjoining the Bethlehem road. Dayan proposed that Israel's link to the Jewish Quarter in the Old City should be through the Dung Gate rather than the Zion Gate and, if need be, Abdullah could be given territory south of Mount Zion. It was agreed (a) to inform Abdullah that his 'new claim' to Israeli territory on the Mediterranean coast was unacceptable, (b) that the next meeting be postponed until after December 21, (c) that if the Egyptians signed the agreement, it might be possible to give Abdullah the new area, (d) to assign to Dayan and two other officers the task of tracing the route of the corridor from Jordan to the sea, (e) to ask them to examine alternative routes of access to the Old City, (f) to offer Abdullah the same kind of access to Bethlehem that he was offering them to Mount Scopus.[22] Thus, before the ink was dry on the document that gave rise to so much hope, the Israelis began to renege on their promises. What Shiloah and Sasson had given with one hand, Dayan and his fellow officers clawed back with the other. An offer presented as proof of Israel's good faith was virtually overnight turned into a demonstration of her bad faith.

The guidelines given by Ben-Gurion to Shiloah and Sasson did not augur well for the prospects of success at the fifth meeting at Shuneh on December 23. These guidelines laid all the emphasis on Israel's demands and failed to take adequate account of Jordan's needs.[23]

---

[21] Dayan, *Story of my Life*, 114 f.   [22] Ben-Gurion's diary, 14 and 15 Dec. 1949.
[23] Ibid. 22 Dec. 1949.

Ben-Gurion had clearly not learnt that negotiations consist of more than one-sided insistence on advantages that had not been achieved by war and stubborn refusal to take into account the arguments of the other party. If he seriously thought that the Jordanians would agree to initial an agreement on this unilaterally modified basis and issue a joint statement on the opening of official peace negotiations, he was simply deluding himself. At any rate, he took the trouble to sign a letter certifying that 'His Excellency Mr Eliahu Sasson, Minister Plenipotentiary and Envoy Extraordinary of Israel to Ankara and His Excellency Mr Reuven Shiloah, Counsellor for Special Affairs, Ministry for Foreign Affairs, have been granted full powers, as Plenipotentiaries of the Government of Israel, to negotiate, conclude and sign, subject to ratification, a Treaty of Peace, Friendship and Boundaries with the Plenipotentiaries of the Government of His Majesty the King of the Hashemite Jordan Kingdom.'[24] Unfortunately this bombastic phraseology could not compensate for the poverty of Israel's diplomatic approach, any more than calling Sasson Envoy Extraordinary could turn him into a magician capable of performing diplomatic miracles. Ben-Gurion could have saved his breath to cool his porridge, to use a Scottish expression.

Samir Rifai opened the meeting by asking Shiloah and Rifai what formula had been devised to satisfy Jordan's claim for access to the Mediterranean. Shiloah replied that after much consideration the Israeli government decided that it could not give Jordan a sea front of more than three kilometres just north of the Egyptian–Israeli line and possibly three additional kilometres if the no-man's land were to be divided between Egypt and Israel. Jordan would be allowed full sovereignty over a corridor from Hebron to this point on the coast, whose width was to be between 50 and 100 metres. However, should Jordan later obtain the Gaza Strip from Egypt—and Israel was to support Jordan's claim—Jordan would have to return the coastal area obtained from Israel. Shiloah admitted that this point by the sea consisted of rough country covered with sand dunes and that it would be of little economic value, but he thought it would satisfy Jordan's political ambition.

To this proposal Samir replied that access to the sea was important to Jordan purely from the economic standpoint and that the Israeli offer was therefore worthless. He could not think of a corridor in terms of metres but only of kilometres; Jordan had to obtain a substantial amount of territory to justify a peace settlement with Israel to the Arab world, and there was no point in continuing the negotiations if Israel

---

[24] Jerusalem, 22 Dec. 1949, 2453/2, ISA.

did not recognize the validity of these arguments. At this point King Abdullah injected a conciliatory note, but an ill-considered comment by Sasson stiffened his attitude. Sasson said that even if Israel made peace with Jordan, she would have to maintain a large army in view of the potential threat from the other Arab states, and substantial concessions could not be made to Jordan except as part of an overall settlement of the Arab–Israeli conflict. The king became indignant and expressed surprise that so little importance should be attached to an agreement with his country.

In the end it was decided that negotiations should continue, though Samir was of the opinion that the time had come to inform the Jordan government of the progress made so far and let it decide whether an adequate basis existed for the initiation of formal discussions or whether the matter should be dropped. It was also tentatively agreed, at the king's suggestion, that Samir should discuss the situation with Ben-Gurion in Jerusalem.[25]

Such an egregious failure only a week after the dramatic breakthrough called for an explanation, and the Israelis were quick to point an accusing finger at Britain. Moshe Dayan, for example, wrote that when they returned to the king to continue the negotiations on the 'Principles of a Territorial Settlement', he informed them that his friend Sir Alec Kirkbride did not agree that Jordan should enter into such a treaty with Israel while the other Arab states had not done so. The king therefore asked them to regard the 'paper' as cancelled.[26] This explanation is fatuous; not even Dayan himself believed it at the time. In the first place, Dayan was not present either at the meeting on December 13 at which the paper was drafted or at the meeting on December 23 which resulted in deadlock. Pretending that he was already calls into question Dayan's honesty. Even more damning is the fact that there was no mention of Britain in Dayan's contemporary second-hand account of the Shuneh meeting to the American consul at Jerusalem; he advanced two factors, neither of which involved Britain. One was Abdullah's inability to find a prime minister willing to sign an agreement with Israel. The other was Abdullah's preoccupation with the move for union between Iraq and Syria and the rekindling of his interest in Greater Syria that led him to postpone any action regarding peace with Israel.[27]

There was probably an element of truth in both of these explanations. Other constructions put on the Jordanian stand by Sharett was that they wanted a broad belt on which to settle some of the Gaza refugees and cut Israel in two; that this was a bargaining move from

[25] *FRUS 1949*, vi. 1558–60, 1561 f. [26] Dayan, *Story of my Life*, 114 f.
[27] *FRUS 1949*, vi. 1560 f.

which they would retreat if Israel stood firm; and that this was an attempt to discredit the whole idea of a corridor with a view to forcing Israel back to their original solution based on cession of the southern Negev.[28] Ben-Gurion tended to believe that the last explanation was the right one; he instructed the foreign ministry to inform Abdullah in writing that his conception of a corridor in the Negev was utterly unacceptable, and that if he wanted to continue the talks he would have to come forward with a new proposal.[29]

Samir Rifai represented this latest Israeli move as an indefinite postponement of the negotiations. He felt that the time had come for him to withdraw and permit the government to continue, if it desired, on an official basis. He counselled the king to be patient and avoid any rash action. Tawfiq Abul Huda's position was that he would not criticize an agreement with the Israelis provided he himself was not a party to it.[30] That left Samir as the only serious contender for the job of prime minister, and he could only improve his chances by obtaining for the king a satisfactory agreement with Israel. However, he preferred to retain his comfortable post as minister of court which gave him a strong position with the king and enabled him to engage and keep *au courant* of palace intrigue rather than assume the heavy responsibilities of the prime ministership.[31]

The Israelis were not much more successul in using the talks with Jordan as a lever for getting a British promise not to extend the Anglo-Transjordanian Treaty to King Abdullah's new domain. The Israeli argument was that Arab Palestine was of little use to the British militarily, and that they could well afford to waive the extension of the treaty so as to make it politically easier for Israel to come to terms with Jordan. Walter Eytan put the question directly to Sir Knox Helm, an independent-minded and quick-tempered Scot who was appointed as Britain's diplomatic representative to Israel following the *de facto* recognition and rapidly gained the confidence and trust of the suspicious Israelis. Helm was sure that his government would not want the treaty to stand between Israel and Jordan and that such an act of voluntary renunciation could be a decisive contribution to the cause of peace, but he also foresaw the technical difficulty of making the treaty apply to only part of the territory of one of the signatories.[32] On December 26, Helm delivered the following written reply:

I am to make it clear to Mr. Eytan that the question of the extension of the

[28] Sharett to Eban, 29 Dec. 1949, 2329/14, ISA.
[29] Ben-Gurion's diary, 24 and 27 Dec. 1949.
[30] *FRUS 1950*, v. 691 f.
[31] *FRUS 1949*, vi. 1562.
[32] Eytan to Sharett, 15 Dec. 1949, 2453/2, ISA.

Anglo-Jordan Treaty to areas of Arab Palestine is a matter for decision by His Majesty's Government and the Jordan Government alone.

I am at the same time to say that Israel has nothing to fear from Britain unless indeed she were to embark on aggression against her neighbours.

I am also to indicate that it is not the intention of His Majesty's Government to establish bases or to station forces in Arab Palestine west of the River Jordan in time of peace. Action which might take place between the United Kingdom and Jordan in the event of war or the imminent threat of war is, of course, another matter.[33]

Ben-Gurion described this official reply as 'tough' and saw in it a clear threat that Israel would have the British to contend with if she provoked Jordan or any other country and an indication that Britain meant to retain the right to establish military bases in Arab Palestine whenever it suited her.[34] Like most high-ranking Israelis, Ben-Gurion believed that the British strategical map of the Middle East showed the Negev in Arab hands and that Britain had not abandoned the hope of getting a portion of the Negev away from Israel. A more perceptive analysis of the thinking that lay behind the official note was given by Michael Comay, the head of the British Commonwealth Department in the Foreign Ministry. Comay acted as the devil's advocate and tried to see the matter through British eyes:

Neither the British nor the Transjordanians appear to believe that Israel will remain satisfied with its present frontiers, or that an attempt will not sooner or later be made to extend those frontiers at least to the River Jordan. Insofar as the treaty guarantees the territorial integrity of Transjordan, such a guarantee would be regarded as doubly necessary for an annexed Triangle. It would be argued that the extension of the Treaty would serve as a red light to Israel, whereas a waiver would serve as a green light. It is for this reason, I suggest, that Helm's statement not merely retains the right to take action in the event of war or a threat thereof, but couples this with a plain warning to Israel not to embark on aggression against her neighbours.

It was on account of this persistent British fear of Israeli aggression, concluded Comay, that further British concessions on the applications of the treaty were improbable.[35]

As 1949 turned into 1950, the prospects as seen from Tel Aviv of a breakthrough in the talks with Jordan, or of limiting the British commitment to Abdullah so as to reduce the risks of a settlement with him, must have looked rather bleak.

---

[33] M. S. Comay to Dr M. Eliash (London), 26 Dec. 1949, 2412/26, ISA.

[34] Ben-Gurion's diary, 28 Dec. 1949.

[35] M. S. Comay, 'Note on Extension of Anglo-Transjordan Treaty to Western Palestine', 2 Feb. 1950, 2408/12, ISA.

Two unholy alliances and the Holy City

One chink of light amid the general gloom was the question of Jerusalem, which provided a powerful impetus to Israeli–Jordanian co-operation. Historically, Jerusalem was both a major bone of contention and a major prize in the rivalry between the Hashemites and the Zionist movement. The threat of internationalization looming ever more ominously over the international sky towards the end of 1949 helped to transform this rivalry into one of active collaboration. Differences over boundaries and rights of access were dwarfed by the overriding imperative of resisting the imposition of an international regime over the city. Differences in the quest for a comprehensive political settlement had to be set aside in order to ward off the imminent threat of the UN moving in on them. A new basis thus began to emerge for the renewal of the unholy alliance between the Hashemites and the Zionists, and by an ironic twist it concerned the fate of the Holy City.

Jerusalem was of immense religious, political, and strategic signifi-cance to both sides. Whoever ruled Jerusalem was likely to rule ultimately all of Palestine. For Abdullah, Jerusalem was a coveted prize and the hub of a new empire. He derived great personal satisfaction from being able to worship at the Dome of the Rock where his ancestor, the Prophet, began his journey to heaven and at the Mosque of Omar where his father was buried. Being guardian of the Old City, the third holiest shrine of Islam, also enhanced his stature throughout the Muslim world. And having Jerusalem as his capital would have provided a noble setting for the Hashemite throne in contrast to the shoddy and lack-lustre Amman which was used by the Ottomans to settle Circassians in the nineteenth century and could not even boast of a glorious past. Politically, Abdullah needed to control Jerusalem, the traditional stronghold of the Husaynis, in order to nip in the bud any attempt by the Palestinian nationalists to shake off his rule and form a state of their own under the leadership of the mufti. Strategically, a strongpoint in Jerusalem, such as that provided by the walled city, was as essential for the defence of Jordan's eastern flank against an Israeli attack as having an unbroken line from Jericho to Jerusalem was to preserving Abdullah's suzerainty over the rest of Arab Palestine.

Israel similarly coveted Jerusalem for its biblical and religious associations. Israel's spiritual heritage and historical greatness were intimately associated with this ancient city. Relinquishing Jerusalem would have therefore struck at the very heart of Israel's national aspirations and unique international mission. From being 'a light unto the nations' it would have been reduced to the level of just another Levantine state along the Mediterranean coast. No less intimately involved with Jerusalem was the security of the Jewish state. Jewish Jerusalem endowed the state with strategic depth, a wedge into Arab Palestine and, with the surrounding hills, an extremely effective bulwark against attack on the coastal plain.

When it became clear that the provisions of the UN resolution of 1947 for turning Jerusalem into a *corpus separatum* were not going to be put into effect, the Palestine Conciliation Commission was asked to prepare a new plan for the internationalization of the city and to present it to the autumn 1949 session of the General Assembly. The PCC was faced with the fact that the Jewish and Arab parts of Jerusalem were being administered to all intents and purposes as though they were part of Israeli and Jordanian occupied territory respectively. They took account of this situation in the plan which they presented to the assembly. The assembly rejected this compromise plan and on 9 December 1949 voted by a large majority for a resolution which called for treating Jerusalem as a separate entity under UN rule.

The vote in favour of full internationalization was the offspring of an unholy alliance between three international groups: the Soviet bloc, the Vatican and the Catholic countries, especially of Latin America, and the Islamic and Arab states (with the exception of Turkey and Jordan). The Arab states that had rejected the original UN partition resolution lock, stock, and barrel now became enthusiastic proponents of a UN regime for the city. This reversal had as much to do with undercutting Abdullah as it did with depriving the Israelis of their part of the city. Abdullah certainly regarded the move as an assault on his position in Jerusalem by his fellow members of the Arab League and he did not therefore flinch from joining hands with Israel in the fight against internationalization. *In extremis amici.*

Israel, too, received the UN vote with dismay and regarded it as an assault on her position in Jerusalem. Ever since the guns had fallen silent in Jerusalem towards the end of 1948, both Israel and Jordan had been in favour of partition with, at the very most, special international arrangements for the Holy Places. The passing of this resolution spurred on both parties to present the UN with *faits accomplis*. Sharett, who had led Israel's diplomatic campaign against internationalization in New York, took the defeat rather badly and offered Ben-Gurion his resignation, but the prime minister reacted more robustly and persuaded the foreign minister not to resign.

To the UN resolution Ben-Gurion reacted with Churchillian defiance, in deeds as well as words. From the podium of the Knesset he announced the decision to move the government offices from Tel Aviv to Jerusalem, and no time was lost between the announcement of this decision and its implementation. By Ben-Gurion's own account this was one of the most difficult and fateful decisions he was ever called upon to make, for it involved not just defiance of the UN but a confrontation with the Catholic, Soviet, and Arab worlds. It was a campaign, he declared in one of his speeches, in which Israel, perhaps for the first time in her history, was pitted against the entire world.

Ben-Gurion saw the imposition of an international regime in Jerusalem in apocalyptic terms. On the one hand it would have placed 100,000 Jews outside the boundaries of the State of Israel, and on the other it would have injected international intrigues and rivalries into the political life of a country that was already polarized between a pro-Soviet and a pro-Western orientation. The growth of Jewish Jerusalem would be arrested if not reversed, and the process could lead to ruin and the first victory of the Arab people against Israel. Moreover, the loss of Jerusalem would only be a beginning. It would be followed by international pressure to take back the refugees and to place other religious places under international supervision; the end result would be loss of independence and anarchy.

These dangers, observed Ben-Gurion in his diary, could only be fended off by making a stand from the very start on the question of Jerusalem. Jerusalem was the all-important test case. If Israel defeated the UN resolution, the question of borders would be solved and the pressure to repatriate refugees would cease: 'Our success in Jerusalem solves all the international problems around the state of Israel.' As for the chances of success, Ben-Gurion estimated them to be quite good because Israel had allies, and the attitude of these allies was influenced by her own actions. First and foremost there was Abdullah:

It is true that he is a prisoner in Britain's hands, but in relation to the other Arab states (whose independence is also dubious) he is a factor, sometimes a decisive one. He destroys Arab unity and can possibly pull behind him our most despicable enemy among the Arab peoples—Iraq. And if Abdullah himself has no weight, there is weight to those who stand behind him—the British. It is an irony of history, but it is a fact, and to a certain extent we must exploit every fact to our advantage: in this dispute with the UN, Britain is our ally, implicitly, without the need to talk to us. She will stand behind Abdullah and, willy-nilly, behind us . . . There is also the help of Abdullah, and since he sits in Jerusalem, we must not belittle this help, and the talks that are being conducted with him now are of great help.

The decision to transfer the government offices to Jerusalem met with strong opposition from inside Ben-Gurion's party. At a meeting of the Mapai members of the Knesset, the move was resisted on the grounds that it would isolate Israel, instigate international sanctions against her, provoke the hostility of the Christian world, and so forth. Ben-Gurion's remarks, as recapitulated in his diary, were extremely revealing of the inner mood in which he embarked on this campaign against the world:

I said that I know our comrades and their fears, and I know myself, and I can say that none of them can approach me in his cowardice. I am the greatest coward, even though I am sometimes afraid of other things, that the comrades are not afraid of or pay no attention to. I do not always express all my 'fears' because I am afraid that I might frighten too much our comrades and the movement, and out of 'fear' I am in favour of defying the UN resolution, immediately and with deeds. I can see the danger that the comrades who are opposed to my line see, but I see graver dangers in their line, and the road is in any case full of pitfalls, and the decision is for resistance to the UN resolution.[36]

Ten years later Ben-Gurion was asked why he had thought Israel could get away with acting so defiantly against the wishes of the UN. His reply highlighted the centrality of the alliance with Abdullah to his political strategy:

I knew we had an ally—Transjordan. If they were permitted to hold on to Jerusalem, why weren't we? Transjordan would permit no one to get them out of Jerusalem; consequently no one would dare to remove us. I would have done it without this, but it was a great reinforcement. I knew that nothing bad would happen to us. I was sure that the UN warning was mere words and of no importance.[37]

A letter was sent to King Abdullah in the middle of January 1950 proposing discussions regarding Jerusalem in view of the mandate given to the Trusteeship Council and the possibility of international action to implement the UN resolution. The king responded favourably and asked his minister of court to arrange a meeting. Samir Rifai declined, saying the time had come for the government to consider the matter and, if appropriate, to participate in the discussions on a formal basis. The government debated the matter and chose Defence Minister Fawzi el-Mulki, a veteran of the armistice negotiations and the Lausanne conference, to accompany Samir to the talks with the Israelis. A second phase in the talks between Israel and Jordan thus began at the end of January. Although it revolved round the problems connected with Jerusalem, the Israelis still hoped that it would lead to a comprehensive settlement. In the event it lasted less than a month.[38]

Shiloah and Dayan represented Israel at the meeting in Shuneh on 24 January 1950; the king was absent due to a light attack of flu. The Israelis stated at the outset that their fundamental aim was an overall peace and this aim dictated their specific approach to the Jerusalem

---

[36] Ben-Gurion's diary, 14 Dec. 1949.   [37] Bar-Zohar, *Ben-Gurion*, ii, 892.
[38] *FRUS 1950*, v. 703 f.; Ben-Gurion's diary, 24 Jan. 1950.

problem. They were forced, however, to drop the general issues in favour of a more limited objective—permanent arrangements for the future of Jerusalem. Here, too, an impasse was reached because the Jordanians demanded the restoration of the Arab quarters in the New City (Talbiya, Katamon, Greek Colony, and Baqa) and offered only limited concessions in return. They asked how far Israel would go in defying the UN and what might their country expect from an agreement. Shiloah replied that Israel would leave the UN before giving up Jerusalem, and Dayan added that they would consider rectification of the present armistice line but only on a 'metre for metre' principle. Samir said that this approach was unacceptable and reverted to the principles of December 13. No progress was made except for an agreement to meet again a week later with maps and detailed proposals.[39]

The next meeting was held on January 30. Khulusi Khayri, a Palestinian from Ramallah and a minister in the government, was included in the Jordanian delegation—a sign of the growth of Palestinian influence in Jordanian politics that accompanied the creeping annexation of the West Bank. The Jordanian delegation proposed to discuss the partition of Jerusalem on the basis of a map proposed by a British chief justice in Palestine, Sir William Fitzgerald, in 1945, but this was dismissed out of hand by the Israelis as an approach that ignored reality and tried to turn the wheel of history back as if the war had not taken place. Only the existing reality, insisted the Israelis, could serve as a starting point for mutual adjustments leading to an effective settlement.

Khulusi Khayri lived up to his reputation as a militant nationalist and an opponent of the king by his uncompromising insistence on the restoration of all the Arab quarters of Jerusalem. Dayan's response was equally crisp and forthright. The king intervened in a vain attempt to move the discussion to the broader questions of a general settlement. He said that Khulusi and his people had been responsible for the war and their duty now was to find a way out.

Dayan said that a permanent solution to the problem of Jerusalem could be approached by one of three alternative routes. First, there could be a radical solution involving the exchange of all the Arab quarters in south Jerusalem for a comparable area in the north that would link the New City with Mount Scopus. Second, there could be financial compensation for the Arab quarters that remained in Israel's possession. Third, there could be minor rectification of the present armistice lines on the basis of 'plot for plot and access for access'. Dayan

---

[39] The Sixth Meeting at Shuneh, 23 Jan. 1950, 2453/2, ISA; Ben-Gurion's diary, 25 Jan. 1950; *FRUS 1950*, v. 703 f.

stressed that whatever the approach, an irreducible condition would be the handing over of the Jewish Quarter and secure access to Mount Scopus. No Israeli government, he explained, could sign a final peace agreement that left the holiest place in the biblical heritage of the Jews under foreign occupation and only a few hundred metres from its border.

The Jordanians ruled out the radical solution because it would have left the strategically important Nablus road in Israeli hands. Mulki showed a paper prepared by unnamed advisers, presumably senior British officers in the Arab Legion, arguing that this road was indispensable not merely for the protection of Jerusalem but for the defence of the entire West Bank. Samir therefore wondered whether Israel would agree to a negotiating formula that would combine the last two approaches. The Israelis did not think so but arranged to return after further consultations with their superiors. Once again, they began their homeward journey at 3 o'clock in the morning.[40]

In the days after this meeting, reports began to reach the Israeli leaders about conflicting currents of opinion on the subject of peace with Israel in Jordan and in Arab Palestine. After a long absence, Abdel Ghani Karmi returned to Jerusalem to report that agreement was a long way off: the king and Samir wanted to settle but the government would not go along with a settlement that did not restore Arab property. The Palestinian Arabs went further in demanding a complete restitution of all their property. As for Jerusalem, it was apparently Sir Alec Kirkbride who suggested the Fitzgerald plan as an opening gambit from which retreat was always possible. General Riley, the UN observer, reported that a greed for money had been aroused; the prospect of receiving financial compensation had excited some Arabs but the difficulties ahead were still considerable.[41]

The next meeting, on February 3, took place in the house of the Israeli commissioner for Jerusalem. The absence of the Palestinian minister was taken to indicate a desire on the part of Samir and Mulki to make progress. Yet they attended the meeting with conflicting instructions. From the king the order was to make no move serving to break off negotiations and make no final commitment without having consulted him. From the government the order was to offer a guarantee of free access to Mount Scopus, the Wailing Wall, and the Jewish Quarter, but no surrender of territory. When Mulki presented this offer, the Israelis ridiculed it as going no further than Article 8 of the armistice agreement and falling short of the rights Israel would enjoy

<hr/>

[40] The Seventh Meeting at Shuneh, 30 Jan. 1950, 2453/2, ISA; Ben-Gurion's diary, 31 Jan. 1950; *FRUS 1950*, v. 716–18.

[41] Ben-Gurion's diary, 2 Feb. 1950.

under the Garreau plan that was being considered by the UN Trusteeship Council at the time. Dayan thanked the Jordanian government for
its generosity and explained that this would be the end of the talks
unless it changed its position. Mulki agreed to consult further with his
government and Samir explored hypothetically the limits of Israeli
compensation in the event of the government agreeing to surrender
territory.[42]

At the next meeting of the Jordanian Cabinet there was unanimous
refusal to concede territory to the Israelis in the Old City. The prime
minister and his colleagues seriously considered the Garreau plan as a
means of reaching a settlement over Jerusalem without making direct
concessions to Israel and told the king that they were ready to resign
over this issue. The king pretended to Kirkbride that he had never
favoured the admission of the Israelis into the Old City. Having formed
a common front to fight internationalization, both sides were now using
the threat of internationalization in order to extort better terms. Abul
Huda even suspected that Israel was less interested in an agreement
with Jordan than in giving the UN the impression that agreement was
virtually reached so that active consideration of the Garreau plan
might be postponed and the General Assembly's resolution might
ultimately be rescinded.[43] This guess was not far off the mark.[44]

In any case, the negotiations for an accord on Jerusalem were no
more successful than the earlier talks intended to lead to a comprehensive settlement, and a third stage now began with a more modest aim of
concluding a non-aggression pact.

Non-aggression pact

On February 17 Shiloah and Dayan visited, at their request, the king
and his minister of court at Shuneh to reopen discussions on a
comprehensive agreement. The government was not represented at
this meeting but its decision of the previous week cast a long shadow
over the proceedings. As Samir explained to the visitors at the outset,
the government was in a truculent mood, and even if an agreement
could be devised to meet Israel's minimal demands there was no
prospect that the present government would ratify it and little prospect
of finding a more pliant government to replace it. After the meal, the
king again left Samir and his visitors alone to define their irreducible
demands and see if the gulf between them could be bridged. Samir

[42] The Eighth Meeting, 3 Feb. 1949, 2453/3, ISA; Ben-Gurion's diary, 5 Feb. 1950; *FRUS 1950*,
v. 727–30.

[43] *FRUS 1950*, v. 741 f.

[44] Ben-Gurion's diary, 29 Jan. 1950; Rafael to Eytan, 3 and 10 Feb. 1950, 2447/6; telephone
conversation between Mr Eban and the Foreign Minister, 16 Feb. 1950, 2441/21, ISA.

stated that a coastal strip between Majdal and Gaza to serve as a port and a 2-kilometre wide corridor under Jordan sovereignty was a *sine qua non* for a settlement. The Israelis said it was impossible to meet these demands. At this point the king came in for a few minutes, learnt the gist of the discussion, urged the participants to pursue it until they reached either consensus or deadlock, whereupon he would rejoin them and suggest a new idea to get them out of the straits.

The discussion continued for over an hour but the chasm could not be bridged. Around eleven the king reappeared and Samir reported to him that although both sides wanted peace they were unable to overcome the differences separating them.

The king now made his well-timed and dramatic intervention. He opened by saying that although he was greatly distressed at the failure of his efforts to mediate between the two sides he did not despair and he was sure that in the end the two neighbouring peoples would succeed in establishing peaceful relations between themselves. It was apparent that they had not yet overcome the feelings of bitterness and mutual mistrust that were the inevitable consequences of war and bloodshed. In order for the two sides to be able to see things objectively, a transition phase was needed from war to peace. A mere armistice was manifestly inadequate and it was necessary therefore to make temporary arrangements for a period of several years—arrangements that without pretending to be a final solution of all the difficult problems, would foster reconciliation and a better climate between the two sides. Both sides were demanding concessions of one another. In the prevailing atmosphere these concessions could be seen to signify surrender and even treason. But were the atmosphere to change, each nation would view these concessions in a different light. Consequently, the king proposed that instead of signing a final peace agreement, they should sign a non-aggression pact valid for five years.

The Israelis were greatly encouraged by the new proposal and in view of its importance requested it in writing. Since Samir seemed evasive, the king dictated the proposal to Shiloah. The main elements in the proposal were the conclusion of a non-aggression pact between Israel and Jordan for five years, based on the existing borders as demarcated in the armistice agreement; guarantees to the UN that Israel and Jordan would honour the Holy Places; special compensation to the inhabitants of Jerusalem for their property; negotiations to renew the commercial relations between the two countries and a free zone for Jordan at Haifa; permission to all Arab property owners to return to Israel or send a lawyer to dispose of their property; and the appointment of mixed committees to work out the details of the final settlement.

Finally, the king reserved his right in connection with the territorial modifications and a port on the Mediterranean under Jordanian sovereignty that had been agreed in principle at previous meetings. Most of all, he begged to be told whether the Israeli government could see its way to making any concession on the Arab quarters in Jerusalem so he could decide whether to recommend to his government to yield on the Jewish Quarter in the Old City.[45] Although he did not say so, the king must have wanted desperately to recover some of the Arab quarters, or even just one quarter, in order to be able to demonstrate to the Palestinian Arabs, who constituted two-thirds of the population of his enlarged kingdom, that he had achieved something for them.[46]

The skill and ingenuity with which the king navigated the negotiations out of the straits and thereby saved them from certain shipwreck were remarkable. His analysis of the emotional and psychological impediments that barred the way to a settlement was masterly, as was the gradualist strategy he outlined for overcoming them and effecting the transition from war to peace. The meeting showed how subtle and constructive the king's personal brand of statecraft could be and highlighted some of the qualities that enabled him to excel in negotiations: patience, empathy for the other side, foresight, the ability to keep short-term and long-term goals simultaneously in mind, and the combination of a firm purpose with flexible tactics. It also provided a striking demonstration of the realism and the positive spirit that had been the hallmark of his approach to relations with the Zionist movement over the previous three decades.

The Israelis took heart from the latest turn in the negotiations and welcomed the king's new terms as a great contribution to the common cause. A few days after the meeting, Shiloah informed Samir through a special messenger that the government of Israel had considered the proposal and empowered him and Dayan to proceed with negotiations on this basis. The messenger returned to announce in Samir's name that if Israel was not willing to come forward with new concessions, there would be no point in meeting again. Suspecting a ploy on Samir's part to sabotage the talks, Shiloah wrote directly to Abdullah to say that the Israeli government accepted in principle the proposal that he had dictated and asked him to name the time and place for the next meeting. The messenger returned with an invitation from the king to a meeting at Shuneh on the following day, February 24.

On arrival at Shuneh the Israeli delegation was met not just by the king and Samir but also by Fawzi el-Mulki, who had learnt about the

---

[45] Ninth Meeting Between Israel and Jordan, held at Shuneh, 17 Feb. 1950, 2408/13, ISA.
[46] *Haaretz*, 21 Feb. 1950.

new proposal only that morning. Samir's tortuous explanation of the 'misunderstanding' that had occurred only aroused the king's wrath and confirmed the Israelis in their suspicion that his intention had been to derail the talks. Shiloah confirmed the Israeli government's agreement in principle to the king's five-year non-aggression proposal and the delegation's authority to discuss it in detail.

During the meal Abdullah was in an ebullient and confident mood. He said that his mind was made up not to go back on his word, and if his present government resisted he would get a new government that would carry out his policy.

After a pleasant dinner there followed three hours of more dicussion at which the king was an active participant. He suggested that Shiloah read out the text of his proposal so that Fawzi would understand it, and so they could then go through it item by item in order to make his personal text more precise. After the revision and amendment had been completed, Abdullah summoned the mayor of Amman, who had been present at the dinner, and instructed him and Mulki to make fair copies of the text, one for each delegation. These copies were duly produced, whereupon the king turned to Samir and Mulki first and Shiloah and Dayan next and told them to initial both copies, adding with a smile: 'You will sign and I shall serve as a witness.' Samir and Mulki looked embarrassed and tried to explain to Abdullah that there was no need for a signature. But he insisted and, reluctantly, they initialled the agreed set of principles. The king showed much joy and hailed the signature as a turning-point in the negotiations. It was agreed that, after consulation with their respective governments, the two delegations would bring draft agreements based on the written directive to the next meeting at which they would compare them with a view to working out one unified text for the agreement.[47]

Four days later a further meeting took place at Shuneh at which Jordan was represented by Fawzi el-Mulki and Jamal Toukan, a Palestinian Arab who was the administrator of Jerusalem, while Samir attended as 'observer' for the king. Both sides presented draft agreements based on the recently initialled document. The Israeli draft was excessively long and legalistic, with annexes and joint declarations that were rather verbose even by Oriental standards. The draft defined in detail those points that were advantageous to Israel, glossing over the concessions to Jordan in a rather vague manner.

For all its faults, the Israeli draft at least addressed all the points in the agreed document. That much could not be said for the Jordanian draft. The latter 'removed all the meat from the agreed statement'. It substituted 'modification of armistice' for 'non-aggression pact', made

[47] Tenth Meeting at Shuneh, 24 Feb. 1950, 2408/13, ISA; *FRUS 1950*, v. 757 f.

no reference to the provision for five years, and omitted any mention of 'freedom of commerce and trade'. On the other hand it emphasized the right to a corridor, an outlet to the sea, a free port at Haifa, and a committee to study these questions.

After the presentation of the two drafts there followed three hours of vigorous argument during which Mulki was the chief Jordanian spokesman while Toukan mostly remained silent. The Israelis made it plain that the Jordanian draft was deficient in many critical respects and that they had no intention of signing a second edition of the armistice agreement, much less an inferior edition of that agreement. They explained that they had already lowered their original expectations of a final peace treaty as a result of the king's persuasive argument concerning the need for a gradual transition from war to peace. The Jordanian draft, it was argued, represented not progress but retrogression in that it omitted two elements—a five year non-aggression pact and normal economic relations—that were central to the king's proposal and on the strength of which it was accepted by the Israeli government.

Mulki answered rather lamely that the Jordanian draft was also intended as an interim step towards peace but it was thought preferable not to place a time limit on the renewed commitment not to resort to force. As for the second element, it had to be omitted for fear of breaking the Arab League boycott, but he could give a faithful assurance that the intention was to establish normal economic relations with Israel at the earliest possible moment.

At midnight Shiloah said that there was no point in repeating themselves, and that to prevent misunderstanding he would leave a note for the king explaining the impasse. To this the Jordanians strongly objected and insisted on waking His Majesty. On being woken up from his slumbers, His Majesty, who had not seen the Jordanian draft, flew into a rage, saying he evidently had more influence with the Israelis than he did with his government. This outburst of royal fury had a terrific impact, and his criticism of the Jordanian draft was so forthright that the visitors present felt a bit embarrassed. His plan, he stated, was the result of considerable thought, and he intended to adhere to it. Then he described Jordan's difficulties and the suffering of both countries due to loss of trade. The only alternative to agreement was war, and Jordan was in no position to resume the war. After telling his ministers, in effect, to sign or resign, and to choose between war and peace, the king 'commanded' both parties to come back on Friday. For the first time he laid down that there was no possibility of delay and that the position must be clarified. He appealed to Israel to take account of Jordan's difficulties in revising its draft. Shiloah replied that his was not a bargaining draft but he left himself room for manœuvre by remarking that it was not the Ten Commandments either.[48]

Sir Alec Kirkbride was in favour of continuing the efforts to reach agreement. In his report to the Foreign Office he upheld the Jordanian government's acceptance in principle of a non-aggression pact as the most important step towards a settlement taken so far and a reversal of the earlier position that they would never conduct peace negotiations with Israel. But when Kirkbride saw Abul Huda after the stormy meeting, the prime minister was 'green with anger' and said he could not accept the Israel draft and that he saw no point in trying to come to an agreement with tricksters like the Jews. Kirkbride tried to calm him down, saying that all negotiations require time and patience. But Abul Huda submitted his resignation, retracting it only after Samir Rifai had tried and failed to form another Cabinet and the king had promised to hold his horses until after the April elections.[49]

One of the reasons that compelled the king to slow down the pace was the violent propaganda launched against his policy of peace with Israel from the capitals of the Arab world. Col. Abdullah al-Tall, who was implicated in a plot to overthrow King Abdullah and fell out with Glubb Pasha over his demand for rapid promotion, went into political exile in Egypt towards the end of January 1950. Tall now released to the press photostat copies of letters confided to his safe keeping by Abdullah that exposed the secret contacts between the court and the Israelis before and during the armistice negotiations. In interviews to the press, Tall also alleged that British officers in the Arab Legion had prevented their units from fighting, to help the Jews, and denounced Abdullah as a lackey of the British and the Zionists and a traitor to the Arab cause. Outdoing Tall, one Egyptian newspaper claimed to have found secret documents proving that King Abdullah and Glubb Pasha had sold the plans of invasion of the Arab armies to the Zionists. Tall orchestrated a campaign demanding that the Arab League send a court of inquiry to Amman to investigate the treachery of the Jordanian authorities and of the Arab Legion.[50]

Towards the end of February, leaks also began to appear in the press about the talks that were then in progress between Jordan and Israel. The *New York Times* carried on its front page a report that a five-year non-aggression pact had been brought to the Cabinet by Sharett and that the treaty proposals were being studied at the same time by the

---

[48] Israeli–Jordanian Talks, 28 Feb. 1950, 2408/13; Sharett to Eban, 5 Mar. 1950, 2453/3, ISA; *FRUS 1950*, v. 773–5.

[49] *FRUS 1950*, 773 f.; Kirkbride to FO, 2 Mar. 1950, FO 371/82178, PRO.

[50] Glubb, *A Soldier with the Arabs*, 255–7; P. J. Vatikiotis, *Politics and the Military in Jordan: A Study of the Arab Legion, 1921–1957* (London: Frank Cass, 1967), 99–108.

Jordanian government.[51] Radio Damascus broadcast that an agreement had been signed by Abdullah and Ben-Gurion on board ship in the Gulf of Aqaba in the presence of representatives from Britain and the United States.[52]

These rumours had the effect of stiffening the resistance of Abul Huda's government to the continuation of the talks with Israel. The opposition centred around the Palestinian members of the Cabinet and was sustained by public opinion on the East Bank as well as the West Bank. Cabinet members may have also been influenced by threats of personal violence if they approved a settlement with Israel. Samir Rifai's failure to form an alternative Cabinet was thus seen as a major setback for the king and a victory for the diehard Palestinian elements both in and out of the Cabinet.

The king remained unruffled and sent Israel a message saying: 'Abdullah, son of Husayn, does not break his word.'[53] Israel, however, watched the trend of events with dismay; the Israelis attached the greatest importance to Abdullah's success because it was hoped that this would remove the key log in the jam which still prevented peace in the Middle East. Suggestions that Israel should get America and Britain to put pressure on the king met with a terse reply from Sharett: 'King needs no persuasion but Ministers ready to sign and damn consequences.'[54] The real doubts in Sharett's mind concerned not the king's sincerity but his ability to overcome the opposition he faced at home and the pressure on him from all the Arab countries, which in the case of Syria took the form of a threat to close the border with Jordan, and in the case of Egypt and Iraq, to cut off food exports to Jordan. This is why Sharett appealed to the Americans to place themselves behind the king with an official but secret assurance of moral support and economic assistance in the event of sanctions being applied against Jordan. All that the State Department would approve, however, was discreet encouragement through its minister in Amman to the king and his ministers to continue the talks.[55]

The British position was a mystery to Sharett. His impression was that they were in favour of the negotiations but afraid of swimming alone with Abdullah against the current of Arab opinion. Their answer was therefore to sit on the fence and wait upon events: if the king triumphed they would claim some of the credit for his success; if not, he alone would bear the bitter consequences of defeat while their hands

[51] *New York Times*, 1 Mar. 1950.
[52] Palestine Telegraphic Agency, News Summary for 15 Mar. 1950, 2408/13, ISA.
[53] *FRUS 1950*, v. 777 f., 783.
[54] Sharett to Eban, 5 Mar. 1950, 2453/3, ISA.
[55] Sharett to Sasson, 19 Mar. 1950, 2408/13, ISA; *FRUS 1950*, v. 781–4, 787 f.

would remain clean.[56] This guess, like most Israeli assessments of British intentions during this period, was wide of the mark. In fact there was a striking similarity in the way that Abdullah's predicament was viewed from London and from Jerusalem and British officials played a much more constructive role in supporting Abdullah's peace efforts than the Israelis ever gave them credit for.

Among British officials the leading advocate of a Jordanian–Israeli settlement was Sir Knox Helm, the minister in Tel Aviv. Helm impressed on the Foreign Office his judgement that a strong Israel at peace with her Arab neighbours offered the best prospect for pursuing Anglo-American interests in the Middle East. It followed that the Arab refusal to make peace with Israel was dangerous to Anglo-American interests, whereas Abdullah's courage in facing realities was worthy of encouragement and support. This unorthodox outlook on the part of a British diplomat made a great impression on James McDonald, President Truman's fervently pro-Zionist envoy to Tel Aviv. Helm was able and objective, reported McDonald—with no Palestine background to confuse his judgment.[57]

Shiloah kept Helm informed of the progress of the negotiations with Jordan. In retrospect Helm felt that in 1950 an opportunity had been missed, and that if Ernest Bevin had been in good health he would have taken up these negotiations and pushed them through. The man mainly responsible for putting the brakes on had been Alec Kirkbride. Not that Kirkbride had been opposed in principle, but he thought that it would be better to complete the annexation of the West Bank and to get the parliamentary elections out of the way before proceeding to an agreement with Israel. In Helm's judgement, however, these things not only failed to improve the chances of a settlement; they actually diminished them. Kirkbride himself apparently told Helm at the end of 1950 that they had missed the boat.[58]

Yet it is unlikely that a more resolute Anglo-American intervention could have tipped the scales in favour of a settlement, if only because it could have so easily been represented as interference by outside powers in Jordan's affairs. In any case, the balance tipped the other way with Abul Huda's return to power. He was now in a much stronger position to resist the pressure from the royal court to conclude the non-aggression pact with Israel.

The next meeting took place at Shuneh on March 7. It was the twelfth meeting since direct contact was resumed in November 1949

[56] Sharett to Sasson, 19 Mar. 1950, 2408/13, ISA.

[57] *FRUS 1950*, v. 783; McDonald, *My Mission in Israel*, 213 f.

[58] Interview with Sir Knox Helm, 29 Oct. 1958, Monroe Papers; Elath to Eytan, Visit to Sir Knox and Lady Helm, 13 Feb. 1955, 93.03/47/9, ISA.

and it was doomed to be the last in this particular round of talks. Israel was represented by Shiloah and Dayan, who had recently been promoted from colonel to major-general. Jordan was represented by the king, Fawzi el-Mulki, and Said al-Mufti, the minister of interior in Abul Huda's reconstituted Cabinet. The meeting was short. The king, looking solemn, opened by saying that he had hoped that at this meeting they would be able to reap the fruit of their joint labour by concluding an agreement, but to his great regret luck was not on their side. Many obstacles, both internal and external, had been put in his way, forcing him to slow down. This slowing down meant the suspension of the talks rather than a rupture, and it was his duty to stress that this time there were no differences of opinion between himself and his government on the elements of the agreement.

Mulki then read out a *note verbale*, saying that the Jordan government accepted the king's plan as the basis for a settlement. However, owing to rumours and lies circulating in Jordan and since there were elections in progress, it was decided not to press ahead with the negotiations but ask for their adjournment. He concluded with the hope that these negotiations would be resumed at the earliest possible moment and that they would be 'animated by the same spirit and objectives as the conferences to date'.[59]

The suspension of the talks represented a draw in the tug of war between the government and the royal court. The contest was not ended but merely suspended, with neither party enjoying or claiming a clear victory for its policy. The government conceded in principle the need for negotiations and a pact with the enemy, and this decision was formally conveyed to Israel. On the other hand, the court agreed not to force the issue and not to proceed with the implementation of a settlement until after the elections, lest it be said that on the question most crucial to the future of the union—relations with Israel—a definite policy had already been laid down on the eve of the elections. Within this broad question no aspect was more sensitive than that of normalizing economic relations with Israel, for just as for Israel this represented the greatest prize on account of its political and symbolic significance, so for the government party in Jordan, it represented the greatest danger to its position *vis-à-vis* its own people and the rest of the Arab world.[60]

The Israelis experienced disappointment verging on despair—so much attempted and so little achieved. Yet they did not blame the king for the failure of their joint efforts and hoped that he would live to fight

---

[59] Twelfth Meeting Between Israel and Jordan, 3 Mar. 1950, 2453/2, ISA; *FRUS 1950*, v. 796 f.
[60] Meeting of the Foreign Minister with Newspaper Editors, 9 Mar. 1950, 2453/3, ISA.

another day. Elias Sasson, the architect of the Israeli–Jordanian rapprochement and now Israel's minister to Ankara, felt the disappointment more acutely than most. But it was Sharett's analysis of the events of the last few months that was most revealing, for it placed the Israeli–Jordanian negotiations in the much broader context of the relations between the Jewish state and the Arab world as a whole. He had no doubt whatever, as he wrote to Sasson,

that during the days of crisis that occurred in the negotiations, the Circassian village called Amman served as a focal point for a head-on confrontation between the two trends that operate in the Middle East in relation to our problem—on the one hand the trend for reconciliation with the State of Israel and the drawing of advantage from its existence, and on the other hand the trend of non-recognition of the reality of Israel, the continuation of the boycott of her today, and mental and practical preparation for renewed war against her tomorrow and the day after tomorrow.

Sharett went on to pay a tribute to the courage and steadfastness of the man who epitomized the first school of thought:

Given the consolidation of the forces that rose against him at home and abroad, I consider that the king held his own, morally and politically, to an extent that deserves respect. He did not surrender, he did not reverse his position, he did not cancel his previous resolutions. On the contrary, he brought Abul Huda's Cabinet to an explicit endorsement of the policy of settlement, and even to an official undertaking to renew the negotiations 'in the same spirit and for the same objectives'. Of course these declarations and undertakings are now suspended in the air, in that their implementation has been postponed to an unspecified date and is contingent on the election results which no one can guess in advance. Nevertheless, the stage we have reached, after the retreat and the delay, must be seen as a positive station on the road to negotiation when compared with our starting point at the beginning.[61]

No doubt King Abdullah would have been flattered by these comments on his own conduct in the face of adversity, just as he would have shared Sharett's judgement that, despite the setbacks, some progress had been made along the long and arduous road to peace between their respective countries. It was a fitting epitaph on a chapter in Israeli–Jordanian negotiations that had begun in November 1949 with the search for a comprehensive settlement, been diverted in search of a specific accord on Jerusalem, was reactivated by Abdullah's proposal of a five-year non-aggression pact in mid-February 1950, and ended inconclusively in early March.

[61] Sharett to Sasson, 19 Mar. 1950, 2408/13, ISA.

18

ANNEXATION AND NEGOTIATION

Tug of war in the Arab League

Following the suspension of the Jordanian–Israeli talks, the crisis in the relations between the Arab League and Jordan reached its climax. The long-standing conflict between the Hashemites and their Arab opponents, and more particularly between Jordan and Egypt, now crystallized round two burning issues: the question of a separate peace with Israel and the annexation of Arab Palestine by Jordan. Discord over these two issues within the Arab League was nothing new, but the crisis in the spring of 1950 was so acute that it threatened, for the first time, the very existence of this five-year old organization for Arab unity.

King Abdullah did not relax his efforts to bring about an accommodation with Israel. He kept faith with his Israeli partners, showing by deeds as well as words his determination to carry the talks to a successful conclusion. During the lead-up to the elections scheduled to take place on the West Bank and the East Bank on April 11, an energetic campaign was conducted through the pro-Hashemite press and radio in favour of an understanding and a settlement with Israel. Of the newspapers, *Filastin* systematically preached for a settlement with Israel, *Al-Sariya*, *Al-Jill al-Jadid*, and *Al-Hadaf* either openly or indirectly supported the position of the king and only *Al-Shaab* was opposed to peace. The radio propagated Abdullah's point of view, explained the rationale behind it, and dwelt in a critical vein on the mistakes and misfortunes of Arab policy towards Palestine over the previous thirty years.

The king also rallied political support behind the policy of peace with Israel. Most of the officials in the royal court supported his policy, notably Abd al-Rahman Khalifa, the head of the Diwan, Ghazi Raji, the secretary for Arab affairs, Munawar Shahr, Hashem al-Dhabassi, Abdel Ghani al-Karmi, and others. Most of the mayors, on both banks of the Jordan, also supported the king's policy, and some took it upon themselves to explain to the inhabitants of their towns the benefits that could be expected to come with peace. Prominent among them were Sulayman Tuqan (Nablus), Shaikh Muhammad Ali al-Jabari

(Hebron), Haza al-Majali (Amman), and Dlaywan al-Majali (Kerak). The Arab Legion and the police were overwhelmingly loyal to the king, but the Palestinian police force contained pockets of malcontents who could not be relied to stand by him in times of need. Among the organized political groups, the ruling party, Hisb al-Akhrar wa-Alnahda, supported the king's position on peace with Israel.

The political forces opposed to peace with Israel were diverse and badly organized, yet their collective influence was considerable. Hisb al-Baath, the largest opposition party, was weak and divided, with the majority of its leaders, like Khulusi Khayri, irreconcilably opposed to peace, while a minority made up of Musa Alami and his associates came under the influence of the royal court. Jumiyat al-Umul, a smaller party with socialist leanings, was also divided internally, with the majority of its members opposing peace with Israel. Supporters of the internationalization of Jerusalem, though not organized as a party, were influential in shaping public opinion in Jordan and abroad. The majority were Christians, some with property in Jerusalem that they hoped to repossess. Their interest in internationalization turned them against the king, but they were not irreconcilably opposed to Jordanian–Israeli peace provided their property could be restored to them. Finally there were the mufti's men, the sworn enemies of the Hashemites and of the Jews. A number of public figures received letters from the mufti's men threatening them with death if they lent a hand to a Jordanian–Israeli peace. Emil al-Ghuri operated this propaganda machine from Beirut and sent leaflets to Jordan. Although the mufti's men were few and not well organized, their threats of violence were taken seriously and court officials were worried that they would get material support from Egypt and Saudi Arabia.[1] These opposition groups gained the upper hand in the struggle against the royal party for the hearts and minds of the ruling classes and of the Jordanian and Palestinian masses with the approach of the general elections.

Internal opposition to the king's foreign policy was further incited and deepened by externally directed attacks. Rumours in early March about his negotiations with the Jews led the other Arab states to exert pressure on him, on his government, and on his representatives in Middle East capitals. A violent campaign was launched to expel Jordan from the Arab League and to impose an economic boycott against her. The Syrian prime minister threatened to close the border with Jordan. The Saudi foreign minister threatened to include Jordan

---

[1] Moshe Sasson, 'The Attitude of Various Forces in the Jordanian Public to the Possibility of Peace with Israel', 22 Mar. 1950, 2408/13, ISA. See also Ammon Cohen, *Political Parties in the West Bank under the Jordanian Regime, 1949–1967* (Ithaca: Cornell University Press, 1982); Aqil Hayder Hasan Abidi, *Jordan: A Political Study, 1948–1957* (London: Asia Publishing House, 1965), ch. 3.

within the wall separating Israel from the Arab world. The Jordanian minister to Saudi Arabia, Muhammad Fahmi Hachem, fled into exile in Egypt in protest against the secret peace negotiations which he said King Abdullah was carrying on with Israel. As a Palestinian, Hachem bitterly resented what he called a plot against his native country on the part of Abdullah and the Zionists. Hachem also alleged that Abdullah had said to him that his mission was to annex to Jordan the Arab part of Palestine, to realize the Greater Syria project, and to occupy the Hijaz, and that he wanted Hachem to concentrate all his efforts on the last objective of uniting the Hijaz with Jordan.[2]

The strongest opposition to Abdullah's negotiations with Israel and annexation of the Arab part of Palestine came from Egypt. Although the Egyptians had persistently declined to negotiate with Israel themselves, they were not prepared to leave Abdullah to do so because any concessions Israel made to him would diminish the chance of concessions to Egypt if negotiations between Egypt and Israel were to take place in the future. Egypt also feared that a peace settlement between Israel and Abdullah would give the latter Arab Palestine, help him to proceed with Greater Syria, and end up by upsetting the balance in the Arab world in favour of the Hashemites. An Egyptian press campaign conducted with the utmost virulence discredited his policy of compromise with Israel and accused him of betraying the Arab cause. The influential Cairo daily, *Al-Misri*, reported a friendly exchange of letters between Israel's foreign minister, Moshe Sharett, and King Abdullah, ending in a call for Jordan's expulsion from the Arab League: 'The time has come for the Arab League to cut off relations with Transjordan, a country that has betrayed Islam and Arab unity and the Arab cause. The time has come to sever this decayed member from the body of the Arab world, to bury it and to heap dung on it.'[3]

Official Egyptian support for Hajj Amin al-Husayni was directed less against Israel than against Jordan, with the aim of influencing the approaching Jordanian elections. Egyptian encouragement and support were extended not just to the mufti himself but to Abdullah's Jordanian and Palestinian opponents, and particularly to defectors like Abdullah al-Tall and Muhammad Fahmi Hachem.

The Israelis were aware of Cairo's behind-the-scenes activities to discredit Abdullah and block the path of compromise but they kept out of this family quarrel. Ben-Gurion summarized in his diary a report he received from Reuven Shiloah: 'The League is organizing war against Abdullah. They are organizing gangs in Transjordan. Egypt is strengthening the mufti. They wanted Hawari to help the mufti and he

---

[2] *New York Herald Tribune*, 27 Mar 1950; *La Bourse Egyptienne*, 15 Apr. 1950.
[3] *Al-Misri*, 19 Mar. 1950.

refused. The "king" is in need of money.'[4] It is not clear from this entry whether Abdullah himself had asked for money, whether Shiloah thought he needed money, or whether Ben-Gurion planned to do anything about it. But putting the word 'king' in inverted commas betrayed a snide and grudging attitude on the part of the Israeli leader towards an ally who was displaying undeniable courage in defence of an unpopular policy.

The war of words against Abdullah reached its climax during the twelfth ordinary session of the Arab League Council in Cairo, which lasted from March 25 to April 13. In this session Jordan was placed in the dock and two main charges were pressed against her: annexation of Arab Palestine without the consent of the League and breaking the Arab front by negotiating separately with Israel. The first charge was underscored by the invitation extended to three members of the phantom 'Gaza government' to attend the League's deliberations. As in the October 1949 session, the All-Palestine government was used by Egypt to challenge Abdullah's claim to Arab Palestine. The second charge was underscored by the resolution of the Council, passed unanimously on April 1, that no member of the Arab League may negotiate a separate peace treaty with Israel or any military, political, or economic agreement, and any state that did so would be considered to have forfeited her membership.[5]

Some mystification was caused by the Jordanian vote in favour of this resolution since it was known that negotiations had been going on between Jordan and Israel which seemed to promise accord between the two countries. King Abdullah's *volte-face* was probably due to the fact that elections in his country were due to take place in ten days' time, when he also planned to announce the incorporation into Jordan of Arab Palestine. It was therefore scarcely the moment to exacerbate Arab feelings and to provoke an open rupture with the League. Defiance on both charges would have provoked such a rupture, leading to Jordan's expulsion from the League. Abdullah apparently yielded on negotiations with Israel, the better to make his stand on annexation.

In retrospect, some Israelis considered that the compromise reached between Abdullah and the League was at their expense. Yaacov Shimoni, one of the Foreign Ministry's most perceptive Arab experts, was not surprised by Abdullah's *volte-face*; on the contrary, he thought that this diplomatic puzzle can be explained very simply:

Abdullah did a trade-off which was unfortunate for us but legitimate from the

[4] Ben-Gurion's diary, 29 Mar. 1950.
[5] Muhammad Khalil, *The Arab States and the Arab League*, 2 vols. (Beirut: Khayats, 1962), ii 165 f.

point of view of the dirty game called international politics. The Arabs threatened him with expulsion from the League because he was making the final preparations for annexation and because they heard that he was going to sign a peace agreement with Israel. He said to them: 'let us do a deal—I shall forego a peace treaty with Israel if you accept my annexation. I shall also present the annexation in a way that would make it easier for you to live with by saying that it is only a temporary measure until a permanent solution is found to the Palestine problem.' In other words, he sold the idea of a peace agreement with Israel in exchange for an Arab acceptance of his annexation of the West Bank. He calculated, he weighed the pros and cons and found that the second thing was more useful to him than the first.[6]

This solution to the diplomatic puzzle is generally convincing, but it is unduly harsh in implying that Abdullah abandoned the idea of peace with Israel altogether. A more likely explanation is that Abdullah intended to wait until after the elections were over and Greater Jordan had become a fact before resuming the quest for a peace treaty with Israel. To Gerald Drew, the recently appointed American minister to Amman, Abdullah said quite plainly that after the elections he planned to resume the negotiations with Israel, to inform the Arab League, and to call on the other Arab states to follow the same course. If all persisted in their opposition, he was fully prepared to face expulsion from the League for which he displayed ill-concealed contempt. Abdullah emphasized the important role he hoped the new Parliament due to convene on May 1 would play in furthering the negotiations with Israel.[7]

Abdullah projected the same supreme self-confidence and optimism when explaining his plan to the Israelis. A secret messenger was sent from Amman bearing a letter written in Turkish which said that 'the old man' had kept his word, and that he was standing upright in the face of the attacks on him from inside and outside Jordan. The Israelis were told not to worry if they read that he had made his peace with the Arab League because the League's resolution only committed a government that was about to resign anyway. Even if he had to leave the League, he would not go back on his word. The British and the Americans were giving him encouragement and promising to stand by him if he got into economic difficulties.

The Israelis also deciphered a cable from the Iraqi minister in Amman which reported Abdullah as saying that there was no comparison between his position and that of the others; he had a long border with Israel and 700,000 refugees. If a conflict broke out, would the Arab states come to his aid? He was not afraid of the publication of the documents about which Egypt's newspapers were making such a

---

[6] Interview with Yaacov Shimoni.　　　[7] *FRUS 1950*, v. 836 f.

fuss. He had not contacted the enemy until after the armistice and he was not in a hurry to make peace. The new parliament would settle this matter. To all his allies—American, Israeli, and Iraqi—Abdullah thus gave the same explanation for the Jordanian representative's surprising vote in favour of the League's resolution.[8] If Abdullah was double-crossing anyone, it was not the Israelis but his rivals in the Arab League.

Abdullah seized at a proposal made by the Palestine Conciliation Commission aimed at ending the impasse in its work in order to give a measure of legitimacy to bilateral negotiations with Israel and in order to fend off the menace of reprisals from his Arab rivals. The proposal was for a series of committees with representatives from the parties and from the PCC, thereby meeting the Israeli desire for direct negotiations and the Arab desire for mediation by the PCC. Abdullah seemed to think that this procedure would cover him against any charges of violating the Arab League's resolution against separate negotiations with Israel. He therefore cordially welcomed the PCC delegation which arrived in Amman on April 9 and evinced great enthusiasm for its plan of mediation between the Arab states and Israel. On the following day, however, in complete contradiction of the king's position, the leading ministers insisted that Jordan could only resume negotiations with Israel if Egypt took the lead. Israel was highly critical of the PCC's new proposal and only relented when it became clear that there would be advantages to Abdullah in utilizing the UN machinery. But by this time it had also become clear that the opposition to separate negotiations with Israel was simply too great inside and outside Jordan to be deflected by the polite fiction of the UN mediation.[9]

The union

To complete the annexation of Arab Palestine was now Jordan's most urgent task. On April 11 general elections were held for the new Parliament to represent both banks of the kingdom. The electorate was more than doubled by giving all the Palestinians, including the refugees, the right to vote, and the numbers of seats in the Chamber of Deputies was increased from 20 to 40 to make room for 20 Palestinians. One hundred and twenty candidates stood for election on a personal, non-party programme. Of the 20 East Bank deputies, 7 were elected unopposed, whereas on the West Bank all the seats were contested, reflecting a higher level of political consciousness. With the police and the Arab Legion in the background, the elections were conducted fairly

[8] Ben-Gurion's diary, 3 Apr. 1950.   [9] *FRUS 1950*, v. 825–7, 832–6, 849–51.

and firmly, with only minor disturbances in Jerusalem, Nablus, and Hebron.

Among the new West Bank deputies there were former followers of the mufti who had crossed over into Abdullah's camp, like Kamal Arikat who had commanded the Palestinian Arab paramilitary organization, al-Futuwa, and Anwar Nuseiba who had been the secretary of the Gaza government. But they were greatly outnumbered by vehement critics of Abdullah, prominent among whom were Abdullah Nawas, a Christian from Jerusalem and a leader of the Baath party, and Abdullah Rimawi from Ramallah, another leader of the left-wing movement and the editor of its newspaper, *Al-Baath*. In the Senate there were only eight Palestinians and twelve Transjordanians, with Tawfiq Abul Huda appointed by the king as president and Sulayman Tuqan elected as his deputy. But the mood of the Palestinians emerged clearly enough during the campaign and was faithfully reflected in the new Chamber of Deputies: union with Transjordan was acceptable, peace with Israel was not.[10]

Said al-Mufti was asked to form and hold the balance in a new Cabinet consisting of five Transjordanians and five Palestinians. For the task of holding the balance he was well equipped both by virtue of being the leader of the Circassian community and of being fearless and independent. Muhammad Shureiki became foreign minister, Fawzi el-Mulki remained as defence minister, and Falah Madadha as minister of the interior. Thus despite the pretence at equal representation, all the key portfolios in the new Cabinet were given to East Bankers.

While the elections were taking place in Jordan, the Arab League continued its deliberations in Cairo. On April 13 the Council confirmed its earlier resolution to expel any members that reached a separate agreement with Israel. With Jordan abstaining, the Council also reaffirmed its resolution of 12 April 1948 which provided that the entry of the Arab armies into Palestine for the purpose of saving it should be viewed as a temporary measure free of any characteristics of occupation or partition of Palestine, and that following its liberation it should be handed to its owners so that they might rule it as they pleased. Satisfied that they had Abdullah on the run as far as negotiations with Israel were concerned, the Arab League leaders in an unusual display of collective restraint, decided not to press him too hard, at least for the time being, on the question of annexation. With Iraq acting as the mediator, a compromise formula was reached to recognize Jordan's *de facto* administration but to refuse *de jure* recognition to her annexation of Arab Palestine. Tawfiq al-Suweidi, the prime minister of Iraq and chairman of the current council session, joined in the general con-

[10] Dearden, *Jordan*, 83 f.; *Hamizrah Hehadash* 1/4 (1950), 301–5.

demnation of Jordan for her dealings with Israel but then added: 'King Abdullah knows that there is no objection to his annexing Arab parts of Palestine, but the Arab population must be consulted first.' The council did not provide for sanctions, as it did on the question of a separate accord with Israel, and merely declared that if annexation took place, a special meeting of the council would be called to consider appropriate action.[11]

Immediately after the council adjourned, the Egyptian foreign minister declined on behalf of the Arab states the PCC's invitation to participate in joint committees until Israel had accepted the UN resolution on the refugees. Israel interpreted this reply as evidence of the anti-peace tendencies of the Arab League and a justification for pursuing its efforts for a bilateral accord with Jordan. At a meeting with the American delegation to the PCC, Gideon Rafael read from a letter which he said came from Abdullah in which the king stated that he wanted to restart negotiations after the annexation of East Palestine had been proclaimed and that the discussions in Geneva under the auspices of the PCC should be used simply as a cover for the real talks in Palestine. Rafael also revealed that it had been made clear to Abdullah that Israel would look favourably on the annexation of eastern Palestine only within the context of a final peace settlement or a non-aggression pact.[12]

Interestingly, Ben-Gurion's worry was not that the Arab states would reject the PCC's proposal but that they would agree to sit with Israel in joint committees and thereby block the possibility of separate talks with Jordan. The danger would be all the greater if Britain and America backed the Arab League. To forestall this 'danger' of direct negotiations with the Arabs—which Israeli propaganda always presented as the only way of resolving the Arab–Israeli dispute—the Foreign Ministry asked Ben-Gurion to meet Abdullah in person, arguing that the king would be hard put to refuse since he himself had requested such a meeting. Ben-Gurion, however, remained non-committal, although all the reports reaching him stressed the improbability that Egypt would take the lead in breaking the taboo on negotiations with Israel.

Major-General Riley, the American head of UNTSO, told Ben-Gurion that he had despaired of the possibility of converting the

<hr/>

[11] Khalil, *The Arab States and the Arab League*, ii. 166 f.; Benjamin Shwadran, 'Jordan Annexes Arab Palestine', *Middle Eastern Affairs* 1/4 (1950), 99–111; Musa and Madi, *The History of Jordan in the Twentieth Century*, 583; Amin Abdullah Mahmoud, 'King Abdullah and Palestine: An Historical Study of His Role in the Palestine Problem from the Creation of Transjordan to the Annexation of the West Bank, 1921–1950', Ph.D. thesis (Washington, DC: Georgetown University, 1972), 179 f.

[12] *FRUS 1950*, v. 858 f., 867 f.

armistice agreement between Egypt and Israel into a peace agreement. The Egyptian army commanders, feeling vulnerable to Israeli attacks, wanted peace but did not dare express this view before King Farouk. The king and foreign minister were for war, and the ailing prime minister, Nahas Pasha, was under their influence and that of the mufti. The men of peace in Egypt did not have the courage of their convictions. It was better therefore, according to Riley, to complete the negotiations with Abdullah because though it would cause some tension at the beginning, in the long run it would impel Egypt to make peace with Israel.[13]

Abdullah renewed the secret contact with Israel despite the threat of expulsion from the Arab League. On April 21 he sent Abdel Ghani al-Karmi to meet Moshe Sasson in the latter's house in Jerusalem. Sasson junior explained to Karmi the Israeli attitude to the annexation of the West Bank and then read out to him the text of the Israeli government's decision:

This is a unilateral act which in no way binds Israel. We are bound to the Hashemite Kingdom of Jordan by the armistice agreement and it is our firm intention to abide strictly by it. But this agreement does not empower the Government of Jordan to do what it has done. This agreement does not contain a final political settlement and no final settlement is possible without negotiations and the conclusion of peace between the two sides. It must be clear therefore that the Government of Israel does not recognize the annexation and the status of the Arab areas west of the Jordan remains an open question as far as Israel is concerned.

After reading the text, Moshe Sasson asked his visitor to inform King Abdullah that the Israeli government would be ready to review her attitude to the annexation if an agreement was signed between her and Jordan. Sasson added that at his next meeting with the King, Reuven Shiloah would amplify and clarify Israel's official position.[14]

On April 24 the new Parliament convened for the first time for the avowed purpose of confirming the union between Jordan and Arab Palestine. In a skilful speech from the throne, Abdullah defended the union and repudiated the accusations of the Arab League: 'My Government considers that the resolution of the Arab League Political Committee, passed on 12 April 1948, no longer stands valid as the Arab states have agreed to the permanent armistice and have followed this with the acceptance of the partition resolution of the United Nations Organization, in contravention of the aforementioned resolution of the Political Committee.' As a sop to his critics and in order to place himself on the right side of the Arab League's resolution of 13 April 1950,

[13] Ben-Gurion's diary, 18 Apr. 1950; Biran to Sharett, 16 Apr, 1950, 2447/6, ISA.
[14] Moshe Sasson. Meeting with Hayogev [Abdel Ghani al-Karmi], 24 Apr. 1950, 2453/3, ISA.

Abdullah added that the union would not prejudice the final settlement which would establish Arab rights in Palestine but, on the contrary, would serve to 'strengthen the defence of a united people and its just cause'.[15]

The same day both houses of Parliament, the Chamber of Deputies and the Senate, in a joint session, adopted the following resolution:

In the expression of the people's faith in the efforts spent by His Majesty, Abdullah, towards attainment of natural aspirations and basing itself on the right of self-determination and on the existing *de facto* position between Jordan and Palestine and their national, natural, and geographic unity and their common interests and living space, Parliament, which represents both sides of the Jordan, resolves this day and declares:

First, its support for complete unity between the two sides of the Jordan and their union into one state, which is the Hashemite Kingdom of Jordan, at whose head reigns King Abdullah Ibn El Hussein, on a basis of constitutional representative government and equality of the rights and duties of all citizens.

Second, its reaffirmation of its intent to preserve the full Arab rights in Palestine, to defend those rights by all lawful means in the exercise of its natural rights but without prejudicing the final settlement of Palestine's just case within the sphere of national aspirations, inter-Arab co-operation, and international justice.[16]

That Abdullah did not plan to renege on his promises to Israel once Greater Jordan had materialized is evident from the fact that only a day after the historic session at which the Parliament passed the Decree of Unification he received Reuven Shiloah in Amman without even waiting for the storm to subside. Elaborate precautions were taken to prevent the new government from finding out about this meeting which was held in the house of the king's confidant, Muhammad al-Zubeiti. The king was cheerful and optimistic. He was confident that his people would support peace with Israel and that his present government was stronger than the last one and would co-operate in executing his policy. The king reaffirmed his loyalty to the previously agreed statement of principles. A reference to compensation for the refugees was the only sign Shiloah could discern that the king might increase his demands. What Abdullah said was that he did not want a single refugee to return to Israel; he wanted them all to stay but he wanted Israel to accelerate the payment of compensation to the refugees who opted not to return. Nor was Abdullah afraid of actions by the Arab League, and if sanctions were imposed on Jordan he would leave the League. His hope was that if sanctions were imposed, Israel would extend aid to him. For

[15] Jordan, *Al Jarida al-Rasmiyya* (Official Gazette), 2 June 1949.
[16] Ibid. The speech from the throne, the decree on the unification and the replies of the Senate and the Chamber of Deputies also appear in full in Abdullah, *My Memoirs Completed*, 13–20.

his part Abdullah promised to take all possible steps to ensure that an agreement was reached in the near future, with the negotiators sitting continuously for several days to iron out all the difficulties and to complete a paper which would then be submitted to the PCC.[17]

What Abdullah seriously misjudged was the strength of the internal opposition to his peace policy and the effect which the storm in the Arab League had on the readiness of his ministers to carry out this policy. He only took Kirkbride into his confidence several days later, to ask him to inform Said al-Mufti and find out whether he would agree to the resumption of talks. In effect, Abdullah was asking the British minister to serve as a mediator between himself and the Jordanian government. The prime minister replied that all the members of his Cabinet would be opposed and asked Kirkbride to prevail on the king not to press for the resumption of the talks. Kirkbride was reluctant to assume responsibility for the postponement of the talks though he estimated that no more than five or six members of Parliament would support peace negotiations at that time and that the Cabinet would resign if the king forced its hand. To the American minister Kirkbride confided that this was the first time that the king had held out on him and that he probably realized that he was acting hastily. Recalling that the negotiations in March had failed primarily because of Abdullah's impetuous demand for speedy action, Kirkbride commented that the king had got himself into a bad hole and that he was going to have difficulty in extricating himself.[18]

Britain and the Jordanian–Israeli negotiations

Although the Foreign Office consistently backed Abdullah's plan to annex Arab Palestine and although it did not rate the Arab League very highly, it saw no reason to provoke another storm in the immediate aftermath of the union. It was also thought that official British recognition of the union would strengthen Jordan's position *vis-à-vis* the Arab League and in any eventual peace negotiations with Israel.[19] Accordingly, on April 27, the minister of state of the Foreign Office, Kenneth Younger, announced in the House of Commons that the British government accorded formal recognition to the union and declared that the Anglo–Transjordanian Treaty of 1948 would apply to all the territory included in the union, with the exception of Jerusalem. Simultaneously, the British government accorded *de jure* recognition to the State of Israel and announced that it had no intention of requesting

[17] Ben-Gurion's diary, 26 Apr. 1950; *FRUS 1950*, v. 877.
[18] Kirkbride to FO, 4 May 1950, FO 371/82178, PRO; *FRUS 1950*, v. 880.
[19] *FRUS 1950*, v. 859 f.

the establishment of military bases in the area of Palestine now united to the Kingdom of Jordan.[20] Israeli protest about the extension of the treaty to the West Bank was met with the reply that *de jure* recognition was accorded to the union and to Israel simultaneously in the hope of creating the most favourable conditions for reaching a final settlement between Israel and Jordan.[21]

Such assurances were not enough to dispel Israeli suspicions that Britain did not favour a separate peace between Jordan and Israel and was interfering with Abdullah's efforts to reach peace with Israel. As the months went by and the sporadic contacts with Abdullah failed to yield a definitive accord, the Israelis' suspicions hardened, their disappointment increased and a tendency developed to blame Britain for the lack of progress. Allegations that Britain had sabotaged the promising quest for a Jordanian–Israeli peace in 1950 were given wide currency by Zionist officials and commentators. Typical was the interview given by Elias Sasson to an Israeli journalist:

Today I can say that we came to a complete accord. The only thing that kept us from reaching a peace agreement was British interference. I remember how Abdullah once said to me: 'Elias, my friend, I must stop negotiating a peace settlement with you. Our friends, the British, have told me to stop. They think the time hasn't come yet. They think we should wait a while. Only the British are to blame, only the British.'[22]

The reality was too complex to admit of such a simple and one-dimensional explanation. It is true that Abdullah rarely took an important step without consulting the British; it is true that they did not press him to conclude a fully-fledged peace agreement with Israel and it is true that the Foreign Office was not well disposed towards Israel. Nevertheless, it is not true to say that Britain alone blocked the road to peace. Britain wanted peace but not at any price. This was the crux of the Foreign Office position as explained by Geoffrey Furlonge, the head of the Eastern Department, to Sir Knox Helm, the fervently pro-Israeli Minister in Tel-Aviv:

As regards our attitude towards a final settlement between Israel and her Arab neighbours, I think this is best expressed by saying that we should like to see peace but not at any price. In other words we feel that the Israelis, by playing on the weakness of the United Nations, have got away with so much more than

---

[20] Statement by Minister of State, Kenneth Younger, in the House of Commons, 27 Apr. 1950, Hansard, vol. 474, no. 35.

[21] Interview, British Minister with Director General, 27 Apr. 1950, 2412/26, ISA.

[22] Raphael Bashan, 'Meeting with Eliahu Sasson', *Maariv*, 13 Oct. 1964, English translation in the papers of Dan Kurzman, box 10, file 51, Mugar Memorial Library, Boston University. This account of British policy contained all the simplifications and distortions against which Sasson warned his colleagues at the time. See, for example, Sasson to Divon, 18 May 1950, 2382/1, and Sasson to Eytan, 27 May 1950, 2382/1, ISA.

they are entitled to that any settlement between them and Jordan at least could only be equitable if it involved them in appreciable concessions, particularly in Jerusalem and the Negeb.[23]

Furlonge, who was usually a very reserved character, once told an Israeli diplomat that he strongly resented what he felt was deliberate misrepresentation of British policy in certain Israeli quarters. If they were not hindering Abdullah, were they encouraging him, asked the Israeli. In reply Furlonge gave a masterly exposition of British policy:

The answer is no on both counts. It is generally believed that Abdullah can't blow his nose without asking for our permission. It is quite true that on some things he can't but in this particular instance we have adopted a hands-off policy right from the beginning. We have known of the intermittent contacts over the past few months. We have not, I assure you, discouraged them. On the other hand, we have not pressed Abdullah to make peace with you. Abdullah is now a constitutional monarch and his Government is dependent on the support of an electorate of whom a good half could conceivably be opposed to a settlement with you. It is true that he got overwhelming support for the union, but that does not mean that he would get the same support for peace with you. If we pressed him, he might end up without a Cabinet and with most of his country against him. This would not bring peace. It would also not do us any good, or Abdullah any good, or you any good.[24]

There was one other consideration that accounted for the Foreign Office reluctance to move from the position of sympathetic neutrality to one of active support for Abdullah's policy: the economic consequences of exerting pressure on Jordan. Furlonge, who was to succeed Kirkbride as Britain's minister in Amman, explained that in the light of their often repeated desire to see the Arab states reach a settlement with Israel, they could hardly refuse to help Jordan if she reached such a settlement and became subjected to an Arab economic blockade as a result. In her already weakened economic situation, which Furlonge did not think would be significantly improved by peace with Israel, Jordan would find it difficult to survive without direct British assistance. Nevertheless, concluded Furlonge, they could hardly discourage Abdullah from settling with Israel if he could.[25]

---

[23] Furlonge to Knox, 19 Mar. 1950, quoted by Jon Kimche in a letter to *The Times*, 8 Feb. 1983. Furlonge's letter is cited by Mr Kimche as an example of Britain's 'rather naive and transparent way of torpedoing any hope of a Jordanian–Israeli peace'.

[24] M. R. Kidron to Michael S. Comay, Interview with Furlonge, 16 May 1950, 2412/26, ISA.

[25] Minute by Furlonge, 31 May 1950, FO 371/82178, PRO; Mordechai Gazit, 'The Isolation of King Abdullah in His Struggle for a Settlement with Israel, 1949–1951' (Heb.), *Gesher* 113/2 (1986), 124–33. Gazit is an Israeli diplomat who served in London in the early 1950s and, like the present author, concluded from a study of the British and American documents that the Israeli doubts about Abdullah's commitment to peace and Israeli charges against British diplomacy are equally unjustified.

One of the problems which exacerbated the tension between Tel Aviv and London was that King Abdullah was not above using his dependence on Britain as an excuse for his inability to proceed as fast as his Israeli friends would have liked him to. Kirkbride, who was wise to Abdullah's little ploys of exploiting a tactical advantage when he saw one, specifically requested that Britain should not be saddled with the responsibility for the limitations of the king's freedom of action. Yet at one meeting in early May, Abdullah told the Israelis that the British had advised him to go slow on the negotiations but that he was determined to proceed despite this advice.[26] What Abdullah did not realize was that the British knew much more about his contacts with the Israelis than he chose to tell Kirkbride because Reuven Shiloah regularly reported to Sir Knox Helm on progress or lack of it. It is also possible that the British embassy had an informer with access to Shiloah's files, or so it would appear from the fact that it obtained a copy of the Anglo–Transjordanian Treaty, underlined and annotated in Shiloah's handwriting. This document, incidentally, was received with great interest by the Ministry of Defence, for it formed the basis of Israel's formal protest to Britain over the extension of the treaty and it also revealed that the Israelis knew of a British plan to establish land communication between Jordan and Egypt so that the former might be better able to defend herself in time of war.[27]

Even when all these factors are taken into consideration, it is difficult to avoid the conclusion that the Israeli portrayal of the British role in the negotiations was self-serving and to some extent involved deliberate misrepresentation. This was conceded by Gershon Avner, head of the West European Department at the Foreign Ministry during the period under consideration:

After the attempt to make peace with Abdullah failed, we put the blame on the British, just as we had done with the Lausanne conference. Mutual brain-washing is a very deep process in Israel and it even engulfs people with political understanding. Ben-Gurion was the first to cast the blame on the British and this idea spread like fire. We were absolved of the responsibility. It was a good propaganda ploy and we exploited it to the full.[28]

For Ben-Gurion himself British responsibility for the lack of movement on the peace front was not just a convenient propaganda ploy but a deeply held conviction, a doctrinal assumption, that was not suscep-tible to modification. Sir Knox Helm tried hard to persuade him that a change had taken place in British policy, that Britain wanted peace in

[26] Tel Aviv to FO, 10 May 1950, FO 371/82178, PRO.
[27] Yoseph Pinklestone, *Maariv*, 9 Jan. 1981, reviewing the British documents for 1950 released under the thirty-year rule.
[28] Interview with Gershon Avner.

the Middle East and Jewish–Arab cooperation, that British influence was being brought to bear on the recalcitrant Jordanian government, and that after Jordan would come Egypt's turn. But Ben-Gurion clung to his view that there had been no change in the attitude of the Foreign Office and that the continuation of the conflict between Egypt and Israel served British interests as perceived by the Foreign Office.[29]

Britain received little credit for the Tripartite Declaration she issued on 25 May 1950, together with America and France, with the aim of preventing the development of an arms race between the Arab states and Israel, promising to take joint action against any violation of the existing borders and promoting peace and stability in the Middle East. The Foreign Office specifically intended the declaration to secure Jordan's border against Israeli or Syrian attack and indeed suggested timing the declaration with the announcement of the formal union to deter any internal or external opposition to the union. Apart from its contribution to security and stability, the declaration was also expected to serve as a stimulus to peace, and above all to a Jordanian–Israeli peace agreement. Yet King Abdullah was dissatisfied with the declaration because it supported the existing frontiers in the Middle East, while he still entertained the hope that one day he might induce the British government to let him march the Arab Legion into Syria.[30] Ben-Gurion, on the other hand, saw some value in the guarantee of the existing borders against change by force, but he remained convinced that no real change had taken place in Bevin's attitude to Israel and he regarded the declaration as giving licence for arms sales to the Arabs and for withholding arms from Israel.[31]

British hopes that the Tripartite Declaration would help to promote a Jordanian–Israeli agreement were quickly dispelled. No progress was made in the summer of 1950 despite all the efforts of King Abdullah and Reuven Shiloah, who staked his personal reputation on being able to bring about a settlement with Jordan. Abdullah was in a quandary. The Council of Ministers ignored his hints about the desirability of getting an understanding with Israel and he suspected that the majority in Parliament were with the ministers in this matter. On the other hand he wanted to keep the Israelis tagging along until circumstances changed. He continued therefore to stage these meetings and to urge complete secrecy on all and sundry. So long as he did not ask the ministers to participate, they did not object to these contacts.

On June 6 Abdullah met Reuven Shiloah in the house of Abdel Ghani al-Karmi in east Jerusalem. Great care was taken to keep the

[29] Ben-Gurion's diary, 30 June 1950.
[30] Ilan Pappé, 'British Policy Towards the Middle East, 1948–1951', 343–5.
[31] Ben-Gurion's diary, 28 and 30 May 1950.

meeting secret but the ministers got to hear about it. Abdullah's version of the meeting was that he tried to ascertain what further concessions the Israelis would be prepared to make and that they kept referring him back to the principles they had agreed in February while making vague hints about possible adjustments in favour of Jordan. He also announced his intention to appoint a new delegation to the Special Committee and to charge it with working out various proposals which could then be presented to the Palestine Conciliation Commission. Shiloah had no doubt about Abdullah's desire for agreement, but the king appeared less confident than ever before and Shiloah concluded that he needed British encouragement and support. Kirkbride, however, pointed out that if either he or Abdullah put pressure on Prime Minister Said al-Mufti the latter would resign, and Abdullah would have great difficulty in forming another Council ready to negotiate with Israel unless they were convinced in advance that Israel would make concessions which would enable them to meet the criticism of the Arab world.[32]

Sir Knox Helm took a less pessimistic view of the situation, believing that outside help was necessary to get things moving. The time had come, he argued, for British diplomats to be more positive and if not to act as brokers, at least to be usefully active behind the scenes and to persuade Jordanian politicians to get on with it. Jordan had much to gain from a settlement. If Egypt got in first, Jordan would lose a lot of her attraction. On this ground also, Helm thought, the Jordanians would be well advised not to waste any more time but to 'set about gathering the rose buds even though they are not without their thorns'.[33]

Helm's letter on the resumption of negotiations between Jordan and Israel gave Kirkbride an opportunity to review the situation from his end. He prefaced his remarks by saying that no one was more anxious for a settlement between Jordan and Israel than he himself, and that this attitude was largely selfish because peace would remove half of his official worries and change the general atmosphere of constant strain which left little zest for the simpler pleasures of life which were available in Jordan. Kirkbride did not wish to abuse his personal position in Amman by trying in vain to persuade the Jordanian ministers to follow a course repugnant to them. The principal reasons for their reluctance to enter into further direct negotiations were four: (a) the resentment at the brutal methods used by the Israelis on the frontier; (b) the belief that the Israelis, in spite of vague promises, were not prepared to make territorial adjustments in favour of Jordan or to

---

[32] Helm to FO, 16 Jun. 1950, and Kirkbride to FO, 20 Jun. 1950, FO 371/82178, PRO.
[33] Helm to Furlonge, 3 July 1950, FO 371/82178, PRO.

pay substantial compensation for seized Arab property; (*c*) growing doubts as to the readiness of the Israelis to abide loyally by any bargain that might be struck; (*d*) the belief that economic stress would compel Israel to be more forthcoming. Where the Englishman's sympathy lay was all too evident from his portrayal of Abdullah's position:

His desire for a settlement with Israel is also basically selfish and not really due to far-sighted statesmanship. He is obsessed with the idea of recovering his fatherland, the Hejaz, towards which a settlement with Israel is the first step. The next would be the creation of Greater Syria and, then, the final showdown with the Saudis. The fact that there is really no chance of his dream being realized does not diminish the importance of its effect on all his actions and thoughts.

(His Ministers, who also understand the King's motive, accuse him, in addition, of expecting to receive a large sum of money from the Israelis when peace is concluded. I can find no evidence in support of this belief and it may well be based on nothing more than the assumption that Jews always bribe.)

It is in this that lies the explanation of the King's readiness, during the preliminary talks, to give away the Wailing Wall and access to the north end of the Dead Sea, etc., without securing any adequate return.

The King, therefore, will bless any settlement, however favourable it may be to the other side, of which he can secure acceptance by his Ministers, Parliament and the inhabitants. Public opinion, elsewhere in the Arab world, carries little weight with him.

Fortunately or unfortunately, according to the point of view, he is no longer able to act independently in such matters.

Kirkbride did recommend an alternative to direct negotiations which he thought would be acceptable to both the king and his ministers, and that was co-operation with the Palestine Conciliation Commission if the latter could be persuaded to move to Jerusalem. Finally, Kirkbride suggested that an attempt might be made to convince the Israelis that the methods used by their troops to control the frontier were increasing the difficulty of finding Arabs who would participate in negotiations for a settlement.[34] Both suggestions were adopted by the Foreign Office.

The king persisted in his efforts to convince the Council of Ministers that the majority of the inhabitants of the West Bank were anxious for a settlement with Israel. He assured them that everyone he spoke to was in favour of peace; the Ministers retorted, as respectfully as possible, that everyone they spoke to seemed to be against any settlement with the Jews. To find out the facts regarding public opinion on this issue, the prime minister and the minister of foreign affairs were delegated to make a tour of the West Bank. The tour took place towards the end of July and agents of the Palace were sent over to whip up support for

---

[34] Kirkbride to Furlonge, 14 July 1950, FO 371/82179, PRO.

King Abdullah. The investigating commission similarly set about proving the government's thesis concerning Palestinian opposition to peace. Although the ministers were on a fact-finding mission, they let it be known in advance what facts they wished to find. The result was a general condemnation of a separate peace and a grudging mandate to the Jordanian government to contact the Palestine Conciliation Commission.[35]

The king was so angry he nearly had an attack of apoplexy. Yet he could not fail to be impressed by the weight of public opinion against direct negotiations between Jordan and Israel or by the determination of the politicians not to undertake so unpopular a task. Anger moved him to try to sabotage co-operation between the Council of Ministers and the PCC when the latter returned to Jerusalem to resume its work. Kirkbride therefore intervened, as tactfully as possible, to ask the king not to place obstacles in the way of this attempt of his ministers to come to terms with Israel. The king agreed to this request with good grace though he doubted the commission's ability to secure as favourable terms from Israel as he could have done.[36]

The Israeli contention that Britain failed to encourage Jordan to negotiate in the summer of 1950 is thus largely without substance. It was not opposition to a separate agreement between Jordan and Israel or fear of repercussions in the Arab League that accounted for British caution. The consideration which weighed most, according to the head of the Eastern Department, was quite simply that undue pressure on the Jordan government would have precipitated its resignation and no alternative government was likely to be more amenable. To the Israeli Legation in London Furlonge explained that Britain must reserve the right to run her foreign policy in her own way and that Israel's own attitude in the matter had not been altogether helpful. Furlonge did not hold the Israelis solely responsible for the lack of progress in the negotiations with the Arab states, but since it was the Israelis who kept criticizing Britain for this lack of progress, he thought it should be made clear to them that before indulging in these criticisms, they should examine whether their own conduct was wholly without blame.[37]

Diplomatic deadlock and military escalation

Israel certainly bore a share of the responsibility for the progressive deterioration in the relations between herself and Jordan that was to

[35] Kirkbride to Younger, 29 July 1950, FO 371/82179, PRO.
[36] Kirkbride to Bevin, 2 Aug. 1950, FO 371/82179, PRO.
[37] Furlonge to J. E. Chadwick (Tel Aviv), 30 August 1950, FO 371/82179, PRO.

culminate in an armed clash in the last month of 1950. Public opinion was not well disposed towards Jordan, seeing it as a British protectorate and King Abdullah as a British puppet. Support for a compromise with Jordan involving Israeli concessions would have therefore been difficult to mobilize even if the will had been there. The opposition parties, on the other hand, found it quite easy to stir up public opinion against the Jordanian annexation of the West Bank.

The Knesset held a special debate at which the opposition parties of the left and the right, for different ideological reasons, denounced the annexation and repudiated Jordan's claim to any territory west of the Jordan. The Communists and the left-wing Mapam opposed the extension of British influence and the alienation of Russia. They demanded that a protest be submitted to the Security Council. The right-wing parties, Herut and the General Zionists, claimed that the Jewish people had a historic right to all of Palestine. Herut's leader, Menachem Begin, proclaimed that the severance of the historic homeland would not be recognized by a future Israeli government. (Twenty-seven years later, Begin's government declared Judaea and Samaria to be an inalienable part of the Land of Israel and as such not subject to negotiation with Jordan). In 1950, however, only Nathan Yellin-Friedman, a former leader of the Stern Gang, called for sending the army to fight the British and Abdullah. All in all, however, Ben-Gurion was so appalled by the ignorance and irresponsibility of the speakers that he declined to participate in the debate.[38]

It was left to the foreign minister to defend the government's policy and to reiterate that the government did not recognize the annexation or the application of the Anglo-Transjordanian Treaty to the area that was being annexed. In their relations with Jordan, said Sharett, four options presented themselves: (a) maintenance of the status quo established by the armistice agreement with Jordan; (b) the possibility of creating an independent Arab state on 'the eastern part of western Palestine'; (c) the possibility of a war of conquest on their part; (d) and the annexation of the West Bank by Jordan. Sharett personally would have preferred the status quo based on the armistice demarcation lines, had that status quo not begun to wobble, not simply as a consequence of Jordan's expansionist tendencies but also under the influence of Egypt, of the mufti and of the entire Arab League. The option that came to the fore was therefore the establishment of an independent Arab state within the borders set by the UN partition resolution of November 1947. This option received a further push forward from the UN resolution on the internationalization of Jerusalem. Under these circumstances, concluded Sharett, Israel's foreign policy could not

[38] Ben-Gurion's diary, 3 May 1950.

remain passive. Hence the striving to reach a peace agreement with Jordan.[39]

Within the government there was a general consensus in favour of a peace settlement with Jordan based on the 1949 armistice lines. Inability to attain peace on this basis left the Israeli leaders with a feeling of frustration. Whereas they knew where they stood and what they wanted, the Jordanians, as one British diplomat put it, could not 'talk turkey' without deviating from the high principles of the Arab League, and no one in Jordan, except for the king, was willing to be a deviationist. 'And then, "talking turkey" means pretty hard bargaining in which the Israelis are going to give away very little: peace, when it comes, must in their view be virtually on the basis of the *status quo*.'[40]

Israel's leaders had hoped that the elections to the Jordanian Parliament would give the king general support for his peace policy. The reality was that Abdullah stood alone and lacked the power to push forward his policy of peace with Israel. In the annexation of the West Bank the British and his ministers were with him; in relation to Israel he remained in splendid isolation. Those in Israel who thought that the union of Arab Palestine and Jordan would embitter relations with Israel began to raise their heads again. Diplomatic deadlock bred frustration, and frustration manifested itself in a more belligerent mood, in growing pressure from the military for direct action, and in the surfacing of expansionist ideas. Whereas Israel's diplomats continued to quest for peaceful solutions, the military wanted it to be recognized that the diplomats had tried and failed and should therefore take a back seat and that they themselves should be given a free hand to solve Israel's problems in their own way.

A distinction was made by IDF planners from very early on between basic security and current security. 'Basic security' was the long-term security of the state at the strategic level against the threat of all-out war, or the 'second round' as it was then called. 'Current security' was the short-term security in the border areas against infiltration, minor incursions, and low-level forms of violence. Israel's fundamental dilemma was that current security in the border areas required a large number of troops as border guards, lightly armed and trained for police duties, whereas basic security against large-scale attacks required field units with heavy weapons and battle training. The army did not have sufficient manpower for both. There was a Border Police but it was only a few thousand strong and could only guard the most sensitive parts of the armistice lines. In 1950, unable to protect every kilometre of the armistice lines, the IDF adopted a more active strategy of retaliation.

[39] *Divrei Haknesset* (Proceedings of the Knesset), 3 May 1950.
[40] John Chadwick (Tel Aviv) to Furlonge, 12 Sept. 1950, FO 371/82179, PRO.

Reprisal raids first against villages and later against Arab police stations and army units were seen as the only means of deterring Arab governments from allowing or encouraging incursions into Israeli territory.[41]

The armistice lines in central Palestine—long, winding, passing through inhabited areas, and with large concentrations of refugees near them—were the most difficult to guard. Many of the infiltrators across this line, which was not marked on the ground, were of an innocent kind: civilians who wanted to return to their homes or look for a lost member of their family, or retrieve money and belongings they had left behind, or harvest their crops and pick the fruit from their orchards. Only a minority were real predators who crossed the border to kill, smuggle, and rob the usurpers.

The Israeli public was full of righteous indignation and quite oblivious to the fact that most of the infiltrators were refugees who had been brutally driven out of their homes and now wanted to rebuild their shattered lives. The Israeli government, yielding to pressure from the public and the military, inaugurated the policy of direct reprisals. Wrongly it assumed, or at least it claimed, that the Jordanian authorities condoned and even encouraged these clandestine border crossings. In fact the Jordanian authorities did their best to discourage infiltration and curb border incidents. They did this not out of love for the Israelis but because they could not afford the risk of the resumption of war and because they could not count on any help from their Arab allies. Moreover, they suspected that their worst enemies, the mufti, Egypt, Syria, and Ibn Saud, encouraged infiltration in the hope of embroiling Jordan with Israel. Glubb was to claim that these enemies wanted to destroy Jordan even if Israel were to be the instrument of her destruction.

Israel was aware of these facts, but she also wanted to destroy Jordan. For if Jordan were to collapse, Israel could hope to advance her frontier to the Jordan river or beyond. Consequently the Israeli government did not concern herself with the debate as to whether the Jordan government was organizing or preventing infiltration. If the infiltrations came from Jordan soil, then the reprisals would be directed against Jordan.[42]

The desire to advance Israel's frontier to the Jordan was nowhere as universal as Glubb implies, but he was right to suggest that unrest along the border encouraged Israeli expansionism. This was particularly true of Moshe Dayan, now a major-general and commander of the southern front. Dayan became acutely dissatisfied not only with the

[41]   Edward Luttwak and Dan Horowitz, *The Israeli Army* (London: Allen Lane, 1975), 105 f.
[42]   Glubb, *A Soldier with the Arabs*, 250 f.

situation along Israel's armistice lines but with the armistice lines themselves, especially the one with Jordan that he himself had helped to negotiate. In the General Staff Dayan emerged as a leading hawk and an advocate of the policy of hard-hitting military reprisals. At this stage he did not have a clear political conception to guide his thinking but simply believed that if Israel threw down the gauntlet to the Arabs and gave repeated demonstrations of her military power, they would stop harassing her. Gradually, Dayan developed the theory that the War of Independence was not yet over and that several further large-scale operations were required to bring it to a more favourable conclusion. Various proposals were floated by Dayan for the capture of the Gaza Strip, Mount Hebron, and the West Bank, all designed to stem the tide of infiltration, to round off Israel's borders, and to assert her military dominance in such a crushing manner that the Arabs would give up any hope of a second round. Instead of Israel being threatened with a second round, Dayan wanted Israel to threaten the Arabs and to constantly escalate the level of violence so as to demonstrate her superiority and to create the conditions for territorial expansion.[43]

A conference of Israel's ambassadors held in Tel Aviv in the third week of July provided the setting for one of the earliest confrontations between the moderates and the hard-liners on relations with the Arabs. Moshe Sharett concentrated in his address on the need for peace and normal relations with their neighbours. He thought it would be easier to reach a settlement with each Arab country separately than with all of them together. Although it was better to start with Egypt because she was the leader and because the differences with her were not fundamental, Jordan was first in line. Sharett underlined that peace with Jordan was not just an end in itself but, given Jordan's reasonable position on the refugee question, an important precedent for a peace settlement that did not involve the return of the refugees. Jordan's opposition to the internationalization of Jerusalem was a further reason for negotiating with her first.

Major-General Dayan, who followed the foreign minister, questioned the value of formal peace agreements with the Arab countries. Only Jordan had a concrete interest in peace, he pointed out, because she stood to receive compensation. The other Arab states were not compelled by any practical reasons to make peace with Israel; on the contrary, their prestige would be harmed by making peace. From Israel's point of view, claimed Dayan, it was more important to penetrate the region economically, to become part of the Middle East economy than to achieve formal peace.

[43] Interview with Meir Pail.

Dayan went on to expound his view that the first round of fighting in the process of establishing Israel as an independent state was not over yet because Israel herself had not defined the final extent of her borders. He called for a decision on the grounds that if they were satisfied with their borders, time was on their side but if they wanted to extend them, then time would work against them. For his part, Dayan was for seizing the opportunities that had been opened up by the Second World War. In 1948, he recalled, the fear of a clash with the British had prevented them from moving eastward to the Jordan. Dayan suggested that that fear had been misplaced and that it was not too late to rectify the mistake. In short, Dayan was insinuating that instead of negotiating a formal peace agreement with Jordan and paying a price for it, Israel should simply capture all the territory up to the Jordan River. He even considered that Israel should aim to keep the Arab world divided and adopt a permanent policy of resistance to the creation of blocs in the Arab world. The only qualification he added was that if the creation of such blocs gave Israel any opening to charge her borders, then the opportunity should not be missed.

The famous black patch worn by Dayan on his left eye served to underline the piratical nature of the policy proposed by the young officer. His controversial and far-reaching proposal called for a reply, and the reply was given by Moshe Sharett:

The state of Israel will not get embroiled in military adventurism by deliberately taking the initiative to capture territories and expand. Israel would not do that both because we cannot afford to be accused by the world of aggression and because we cannot, for security and social reasons, absorb into our midst a substantial Arab population. However, if the Arabs, whether out of stupidity or wickedness, create a situation which would permit Israel to extend her borders without a frontal attack on the concepts of justice and decency that are accepted among nations and without having to harm an Arab population, it would be necessary to consider the matter. The War of Independence was also conducted on the basis of these cautious principles and we did not diverge from them except when it became extremely vital. We cannot sacrifice Jewish fighters, nor can we harm others in an arbitrary fashion merely in order to satisfy the appetite for expansion.[44]

Ben-Gurion did not participate in this session but in his subsequent address to the conference he expressed his conviction that power took precedence over persuasion in getting the other side to accept Israel's position. The emergence of the state of Israel, he said, was accompanied by three problems—borders, refugees, and Jerusalem— and not one of them had been solved or could be solved by the power of

[44] The Conference of Ambassadors, 17–23 July 1950, Third Session: 'Israel and the Arab World', 36–9, 112/18, ISA.

persuasion. In any attempt to solve them, deeds were more important than words, even if they aroused the hostility of the outside world. Israel's foreign policy was described by the prime minister as 'nothing but an auxiliary instrument of secondary importance' in contrast to the foreign policy of 'existing and static states'. He conceded that in politics there was no absolute instrument; everything was relative, including power and diplomacy. 'But we are still in the period of establishing the state, and the establishment of the state comes before everything else, and hence the creation of facts is accompanied by persuasion but is not subordinate to persuasion and its consequences.'[45]

The management of armistice affairs by the young state provides one of the best examples of the way in which this general philosophy was translated into action. Ben-Gurion perceived control over armistice affairs as an extension of Israel's struggle for security and as such the prerogative of the army and the Ministry of Defence. Sharett considered that the Mixed Armistice Commissions with Egypt, Jordan, and Syria were Israel's only regular avenue of contact with her neighbours and therefore a vital aspect of her foreign relations that ought to be under the control of the Foreign Ministry.[46] Control over armistice affairs was eventually vested in the Defence Ministry and the IDF, and army officers were appointed as Israel's delegates to the MACs.

The consequences for Israel's relations with her neighbours were not altogether felicitous, to judge from a letter sent by Elias Sasson to Moshe Sharett in July 1951:

One of the gravest errors . . . is subjecting the mixed armistice commissions to the control of the army. You will agree with me that the commissions are the principal channel for our contacts with the Arabs, a channel which is, in effect, diplomatic rather than military. During the three years of their existence, these commissions, by their approach to the issues and their mode of elucidating matters, have managed to convince the Arabs that Israel is extremist, wily, and heavy-handed, as well as harbouring evil intentions and far-reaching objectives. Every Arab, however moderate and realistic, now regards us with mistrust, if not fear. None of us, Israel's representative in West or East, would undertake the post of staff officer for the mixed armistice commissions with the confidence he could feel in undertaking various responsible tasks in the country to which he is accredited. By contrast, the military men undertake the post willingly, without hesitation or second thoughts, relying exclusively upon their one and only tool: force. Had we entrusted the Rhodes talks entirely to military men, I am convinced that we would not, to this day, have achieved the signing of the armistice agreements. Is this the way to induce the Arabs 'to bow their heads to the decree of destiny and come to

---

[45] Ben-Gurion's diary, 22 July 1950.
[46] Brecher, *The Foreign Policy System of Israel*, 399–401.

terms with us'? We are all of us sensible of the full extent and tension of hatred for Israel, and thirst for revenge, which permeate the Arab Middle East, but no proper attempt is made to consider whether our own behaviour does not on occasion pour oil on the flames.[47]

Rejection of some constructive Jordanian proposals for checking infiltration had indeed poured oil on the flames of Arab hatred for Israel. Glubb Pasha was of the opinion that border incidents arising out of infiltration should be handled by the local police on both sides rather than by the military. He noted that in the Jenin and Tulkarem areas, where the police controlled the border, incidents rarely arose, so in June 1950 he offered to extend this system to the south. But the Israelis refused.[48]

King Abdullah shared the views of his chief of staff. He once asked the Israelis to withdraw their army from the frontier and to replace it with a national guard. He pointed out that the border area was populated by civilians, and when they crossed the border, for whatever reason, the army opened fire; a national guard, he said, was better suited to maintain law and order. The Israeli reply was reported to have been that no one had the right to tell them how to protect their own border.[49]

As the chances of some sort of agreement with Jordan faded away, the Israeli policy on the common frontier became more aggressive and often provocative. Israel turned to a policy of exacting every advantage in their dealings with the Jordanian authorities unless the latter showed themselves more willing to co-operate. It was widely suspected that this stiffer policy was a form of pressure calculated to force Jordan to agree to Israel's terms for a settlement. Dayan said as much to an officer at the UN Secretariat in Jerusalem.[50] Reuven Shiloah also admitted that in the absence of the restraining influence of peace negotiations he could no longer successfully urge on his colleagues leniency in border matters, hence the tightening of controls and 'possible occasional violations of correct procedure'.[51] Officers in UNTSO were shocked by Israel's conduct, though General Riley, the American officer who headed it, was extremely careful not to criticize or antagonize the Israelis. Colonel de Ridder, Riley's Belgian deputy, was more outspoken. He once told the Israeli delegate to the MAC that 'The Jordanians cause trouble through ignorance, but you Israelis are dishonest and do it deliberately', and spoke in a similar vein to the Israeli government.[52]

[47] Sasson to Sharett, 18 July 1951, 2410/9, ISA.
[48] Glubb, *A Soldier with the Arabs*, 251 f.; *FRUS 1950*, v. 945 f.
[49] Interview with Mordechai Gazit.   [50] Franks to FO, 25 Jun. 1950, FO 371/82204, PRO.
[51] *FRUS 1950*, v. 944 f.   [52] Dow to Furlonge, 4 Dec. 1950, FO 371/82211, PRO.

A major flare-up occurred at the end of August when Israeli troops crossed the River Jordan to cultivate a plot at Naharayim, near the confluence of the Yarmuk River, which on the Rhodes map was shown on the Israeli side of the armistice line. The reaction in Jordan was violent, and a resort to force to expel the intruders was only avoided with difficulty. King Abdullah had indeed surrendered this area during the secret talks with the Israelis at Shuneh at the time of the Rhodes negotiations but he did not feel confident enough to own up publicly to the secret stipulations. The Israelis, knowing that they were technically in the right, offered to discuss the matter in the MAC but the Jordanian foreign minister, Muhammad Shureiki, submitted a complaint to the Security Council, accusing Israel of military aggression and of forging the Rhodes map in order to cover up their aggression. When the Security Council rejected the complaint, Shureiki turned to Baghdad for military assistance to repel the aggression and appealed to the United States, Britain, and France for action against the aggressors in accordance with the Tripartite Declaration of 25 May 1950. The Western powers counselled moderation and in the end Jordan withdrew the complaint from the Security Council and retracted the charge about the forgery of the map.[53]

Israel's special relations with Abdullah were of little value in handling this particular crisis. On the contrary, viewing these relations as the private affair of the king made the ministers more extreme and more ready to co-operate with the Arab League. It was a vicious circle. As the king became less useful to the Israelis, they offered him fewer inducements for a settlement, and in the absence of a generous peace offer from Israel his authority at home was further undermined.

Meeting Abdullah half-way

The British secretary of state for air asked Ben-Gurion during a visit to Israel in late September whether his government still accepted the Heads of Agreement initialled with Abdullah's representatives in February of that year. He replied that they did, except that they were not now prepared to agree to a corridor between Jordan and the Mediterranean. Henderson then told Ben-Gurion that King Abdullah had said to him that he was prepared to meet the government of Israel half-way. Ben-Gurion replied: 'we are prepared to do the same', and continued that King Abdullah was an honest and sincere man with whom they would have no difficulty in arriving at a settlement of outstanding differences. He very much doubted, however, whether

[53] *Jordan: Annual Review for 1950*, 13 Jan. 1951, FO 371/91788, PRO; Jordan–Israel 1950, n.d., 2453/3, ISA; Abidi, *Jordan: A Political Study*, 71 f.

Abdullah retained his former authority over his government. Ben-Gurion also revealed that a meeting with the king was due to take place shortly and expressed the hope that the British government would help to bring about a settlement.[54]

On Walter Eytan fell the task of going to Amman on October 1 to smooth the king's ruffled feathers. Ben-Gurion briefed him on the discussion with Henderson and gave him clear instructions: if the king proposed the renewal of the old agreement on the principles of a territorial settlement, he was to agree but without any corridor. Eytan thought that the king would offer to fire his foreign minister in return for an Israeli withdrawal from Naharayim. Ben-Gurion replied that this was an internal matter that did not concern them; what they should insist on was observance of Article 8 of the armistice agreement on free access to Mount Scopus and the places of worship in the Old City, and if the king proposed to observe Article 8 in return for an Israeli withdrawal from Naharayim it should be a matter for negotiation.[55]

The king professed to Eytan that he was still keen on a peaceful understanding with Israel but that his Cabinet, especially the prime minister and the foreign minister 'sang Egypt's tunes' and made things difficult for him. The Naharayim storm had been started in his absence and was being exploited against him personally and as a result his position was being weakened. He himself had never seen the map showing the Yarmuk River 'concession' and was extremely shocked to see Colonel Jundi's signature affixed to it. As a 'personal favour' the king asked Eytan to return the occupied zone, and Eytan replied that some such step might be considered within the framework of a general settlement, but first of all Article 8 had to be honoured; that was the key to future relations because if commitments were not kept, there was no point in entering into agreements.

Abdullah swore that so long as he was alive Jordan would not attack Israel provided the Jews did not attack first. He did not mention Article 8 specifically but he did mention the Special Committee and said that it should not be taken seriously as he himself had instructed his representatives on this committee to go slow and refrain from entering into serious negotiations as long as the present Council of Ministers was in power. The king's plan was to dismiss the council and appoint a new one that would be more amenable to his wishes. When this was accomplished, he would be ready to resume negotiations with Israel where they had been broken off and possibly conclude a five year non-aggression pact or 'something similar'.

---

[54] Ben-Gurion's diary, 28 Sept. 1950; Michael Lay (Air Ministry) to R. E. Barclay (FO), 4 Oct. 1950, FO 371/82179, PRO.
[55] Ben-Gurion's diary, 1 Oct. 1950.

At this point Eytan suggested that if further negotiations were to take place their form should change, and that instead of hit-or-miss clandestine meetings at the dead of night preceded by 'large indigestible dinners', a more businesslike procedure be adopted with regular meetings attended by duly authorized representatives. The king said this made sense and that with the new Council of Ministers in place some such regularity might be instituted. He added that he was preparing to send a delegation to the General Assembly's meeting at Lake Success with instructions to diverge from the general Arab line on two matters: Jerusalem and the refugees. Eytan left with the impression that the king was indeed ready to reach an agreement with Israel but first he had to reach an agreement with his own official family.[56]

The visit was followed by another trial of strength between the king and his ministers on the subject of improving relations with Israel. The king sent for the prime minister and demanded that the council should make direct contact with the Israelis. Said al-Mufti made it clear that he was not prepared to accede to the king's wishes and tendered his resignation. But Abdullah failed to find anyone to replace him and had to ask Said Pasha to remain in office.[57] Muhammad Shureiki was replaced as foreign minister by a Palestinian, Ruhi Abdul Hadi, who issued a statement to say that Jordan would not enter into negotiations with Israel and that her policy would be in line with that of the Arab League. The number of Palestinians in the reshuffled Council of Ministers rose from five to six. This element, as the Israelis realized, further eroded the king's authority and with it the prospects for a settlement.[58]

The other Arab states launched a propaganda campaign against Israel while the dispute in Naharayim was being considered by the Security Council. Egypt, which had hitherto used the MAC to settle local border affrays without fuss, protested to the Security Council about the expulsion from southern Israel of some 4,000 bedouins, and the transfer of the inhabitants of Majdal to the Gaza Strip. The backing given to these complaints by other Arab governments convinced the Israelis that a concerted attack was being launched on them in preparation for the General Assembly, and they in turn complained to the Security Council of the refusal of Egypt and Jordan to carry out the terms of the armistice. The council's examination of these complaints in October seemed generally to uphold the Israeli case and the

[56] Ibid. 2 Oct. 1950; Helm to FO, 7 Oct. 1950, FO 371/82179, PRO; *FRUS 1950*, v.1020 f.
[57] Kirkbride to FO, 4 Oct. 1950, FO 371/82179, PRO.
[58] Sasson to Sharett, 8 Sept. 1950, 2441/3; Gershon Avner's brief on the Situation at Transjordan, 19 Oct. 1950, 92.02/163/4, ISA.

resolution adopted called on all parties to settle their differences through the armistice machinery.[59]

At this point another major crisis erupted, culminating in an armed clash between the Arab Legion and the IDF. The Jordanian government discovered that the road built through Wadi Araba a year previously by the Israelis passed for a short distance through Jordanian territory, and at the end of November an Arab Legion detachment was sent to block the road. This action was taken without the king being consulted or even informed beforehand.

The Israelis took a very grave view of this incident. Ben-Gurion was on holiday in Greece and the chief of staff, General Yadin, went before the cabinet to insist that the Jordanian troops be ejected, by force if necessary, even if it led to war. He also requested permission to mobilize sufficient forces in preparation for the possibility of war.[60] After several hours of deliberations, the only decision reached by the Cabinet was to send Maj.-Gen. Mordechai Makleff, the chief of operations, to Athens to get Ben-Gurion's advice. As soon as Ben-Gurion saw Makleff he said 'you must throw them out of there'. At Makleff's request he wrote a letter to his Cabinet colleagues telling them that had he been there he would have proposed to take action and not to hesitate. Ben-Gurion made some disparaging remarks to the young officer about the moderates and the appeasers in the Cabinet, and especially about Sharett, whose leadership of the doves he resented and whose pompous and long-winded lectures he could not abide. Makleff took Ben-Gurion's letter to an emergency meeting of the Cabinet at which the mood suddenly became militant, and within an hour a decision was reached to instruct the IDF to take action to remove the Jordanian roadblock at kilometre 78 of the Beersheba–Eliat road.[61]

The Israeli force that was sent to kilometre 78 under the command of Major-General Dayan failed to dislodge the Arab Legion detachment, in spite of superiority in numbers and armaments. An exchange of fire took place on December 3 but there were no casualties. After the skirmish, the Arab Legion obeyed the order of the United Nations observers to fall back and permit the resumption of traffic along the road. The Israelis not only declined to accept UN orders but flagrantly patrolled the bypass with the apparent object of provoking the Legion forces to open fire. An inquiry by the Mixed Armistice Commission revealed that the road did pass through Jordanian territory, and in March 1951 this stretch of the road, from kilometre 74 to kilometre 78,

[59] *Israel: Annual Report for 1950*, 21 Jan. 1951, FO 371/91705, PRO.

[60] Interview with Gen. Yigael Yadin.

[61] Interview with Mordechai Makleff, fifth meeting, 16 Dec. 1975, Oral History Project, the Leonard Davis Institute of International Relations, the Hebrew University of Jerusalem.

was handed over to Jordan after the completion of a parallel road on the Israeli side of the border.[62]

The Wadi Araba incident finally brought about the resignation of Said al-Mufti and the appointment of a new government headed by Samir Rifai. On taking office, Rifai stated in Parliament and in public that he was not prepared to conclude a peace with Israel independently of the other Arab states. In private he added that he would nevertheless be prepared to do all he could, within the scope of the Rhodes agreement, to remove the causes of friction.[63]

The Wadi Araba incident cast a long shadow over the relations between Israel and the king. Abdullah had reached the end of his patience with the Israelis and the former goodwill was no longer manifest. To the American minister in Amman, he complained that every time he was close to a settlement, the Israelis spoilt everything by some act of aggression. He was very bitter about an Israeli plane circling his palace on December 3 which he considered a personal insult. He indicated his awareness of the Anglo-American interest in peace between the two countries and reiterated his devotion to that objective, but went so far as to threaten, if Israeli aggression continued, to revert to the tactics he learnt during the Arab Revolt and organize sabotage and terrorism within Israel. This threat was not taken seriously but it showed that at least for the time being the Israelis had lost their one sincere friend in the whole Arab world.[64]

The Israelis were not sensible of the effect that their own behaviour was having on relations with Jordan. Occasionally, they still tried to put the blame on Britain and succeeded at least in persuading Sir Knox Helm that Britain had not done as much as she could to steer the Arabs towards a settlement. Sir Geoffrey Furlonge firmly rebutted the innuendo that the Foreign Office or Kirkbride had been putting the brake on Abdullah. The brake was there, he observed, but it was applied by the Jordanian ministers who in turn were influenced as much by the actions of the Israelis as by their fears of eventual action by the other Arab states against Jordan if she made a settlement. For its part the British government was prepared publicly to approve a Jordan–Israeli settlement, in order to encourage Jordan to resist Arab League pressure or coercion for having made a settlement with Israel but, as Furlonge pointed out, the effective assistance they could give Jordan if she were, for example, blockaded by the Arab League, might be somewhat limited.[65]

[62] Jordan: Annual Review for 1950, 13 Jan. 1951, FO 371/91788, PRO; Dayan, Milestones, 100 f.

[63] Jordan: Annual Review for 1950, 13 Jan. 1950, FO 371/91788, PRO.

[64] FRUS 1950, v. 1069 f.

[65] Knox to Wright, 7 Oct. 1950; minute by Furlonge, 20 Oct. 1950, and Furlonge to Helm, 26 Oct. 1950, FO 371/82179, PRO.

Kirkbride was appreciative of the backing he was getting from his superiors in the Foreign Office. 'You will realize', he wrote to Furlonge, 'that we are in the throes of a revolution here. What has happened hitherto are just first skirmishes in a major battle for power between the Legislature, stuffed with politically-minded Palestinians, and the Executive, which consists of King Abdullah and his Ministers.' As for his own famous influence, Kirkbride noted that when those whom he could influence lost their power to guide events, he too lost potency. He had not worked with the Palestinians before, and their tendency was to react negatively to all British suggestions. Yet Kirkbride cautioned against extreme measures by Britain to get her way. Specifically, if the Arab Legion subsidy was withheld, he predicted that Jordan would crash economically and political chaos would inevitably follow economic chaos. 'The alternatives will then be to abandon the place to ultimate division between the neighbouring states, or to commence, at great expense and trouble, to try and reconstruct the edifice which we built during the twenty-six years of the British mandate.'[66]

Another major concern for Kirkbride was the effect that Israel's increasingly rough treatment of border incidents was having on the British position in Jordan. He thought that Israel's aggressive policy was based on their belief that the best way to treat the Arabs was to terrorize them. This theory had often been urged on him when he was district commissioner for Galilee during the Arab Rebellion in the late 1930s. In any case, the result of Israel's policy in the second half of 1950 was to inflame public opinion, to poison the atmosphere, to make armed clashes like the one in Wadi Araba more likely, and to make any agreement or working arrangement between the two countries virtually impossible. Advice to refer disputes to the Mixed Armistice Commission and to the United Nations observers came to be regarded in Jordan as, at best, a bad joke, since every matter referred by Jordan was either hushed up and allowed to die or the Israelis were allowed to get away with whatever they were after at the moment. The effect on the Jordanians was to produce a feeling of annoyance and frustration directed as much against the British as against the Israelis. People stood up in Parliament and said that Jordan would never get justice unless she resorted to force, and newspaper articles were making the same point. If anyone asked why force was not used, the usual reply was that Glubb or Kirkbride prevented it. At the height of the storm over Naharayim, for example, one speaker demanded that Glubb should be court-martialled and that Kirkbride's recall should be asked for.

Unless this growing anti-British feeling was checked, warned Kirkbride, it would reach dangerous proportions. The only way of stopping

---

[66] Kirkbride to Furlonge, Personal and Confidential, 30 Nov. 1950, FO 371/82716, PRO.

the rot was a demonstration that Israel could not disregard and defy everybody and always get away with it. How or by whom this should be done was beyond Kirkbride's province, but he feared that unless it was done the British position in Jordan would be undermined and he himself would be discredited personally to a degree which would reduce his value to His Majesty's government to vanishing point.[67]

Thus, as 1950 drew to a close, the policymakers in Britain, Jordan, and Israel were forced to recognize that the prospects of a peaceful settlement had all but vanished. Progress made in the earlier part of the year had not just been arrested, actual deterioration had set in. The whole trend towards a settlement had been reversed. Diplomatic deadlock led to military escalation, and military escalation further undercut the efforts to reach a peaceful settlement. While the trend was unmistakable, responsibility for it was a matter of dispute. The British blamed the Israelis; the Israelis blamed the British and the Arab League; King Abdullah blamed the Israelis; Glubb Pasha apportioned a share of the blame to the Arab League and the lion's share to the Israelis.

'The King's attempted negotiations with Israel failed, for two reasons', wrote Glubb.

The first was the intense agitation raised by the other members of the Arab League, which frightened the government, though not the King. The second reason was that the Israelis, though apparently desirous of peace, wanted it only on their own terms. They were not prepared to make adequate concessions. King Abdullah realized that, if he were to make peace, he would have to be able to show substantial advantages therefrom. With Israel unprepared to make concessions, there was little inducement to defy the other Arab countries.[68]

Sir Knox Helm, who usually took it upon himself to explain Israel to his colleagues, went even further than Glubb in his critique of Israel. 'Her greatest disability', he wrote, 'remains the most disagreeable features of the Jewish character, with an inability to realize that obtaining the last farthing does not necessarily mean the best bargain, that in an imperfect world unrelieved seriousness is not a virtue and, perhaps above all, that strength is not always displayed through force.'[69]

[67] Kirkbride to Furlonge, 5 Dec. 1950, FO 371/82716, PRO.

[68] Glubb, *A Soldier with the Arabs*, 258.

[69] Helm's despatch dated 17 Jan. 1951, quoted in Louis, *The British Empire in the Middle East*, 620.

19

VIOLENT FINALE

The economic approach to peace

The year 1951 was ill-starred for Jordan. It was marked by political turmoil, acute economic crisis, continuing isolation within the Arab world, and persistent tensions on the border with Israel, with occasional outcroppings of violence. Most unsettling of all was the internal struggle for power and the Palestinian challenge to the king's authority, culminating in his murder in July. As Sir Alec Kirkbride noted in his annual report on the Hashemite Kingdom of Jordan for 1951: 'The transformation of the tribal patriarchy of Transjordan into the pseudo-democracy of Jordan complete with the nationalistic ideologies of the modern Arab state which began with the union of Transjordan with Arab Palestine in April 1950, was continued in 1951. The assassination of King Abdullah in July was the most outstanding event in this process.'[1]

Economically the state of the country deteriorated further, making it less viable rather than more viable than it had been before the union. From a total population of a little under a million and a half, approximately one-third was the indigenous population of Transjordan, one-third was made up of the inhabitants of the West Bank, and one-third was made up of refugees who lived mainly on the West Bank. The total number of Palestinians was in excess of 900,000, compared with around 450,000 Transjordanians. Although the Palestinians outnumbered the Transjordanians by two to one, political and economic power was largely concentrated in the hands of the Transjordanians, and this was a source of friction and conflict between the two banks.[2]

The policy of the Hashemite regime was to counter any feeling of a distinct Palestinian national identity and to facilitate the integration of the Palestinians into the normal life of the country.[3] Throughout the year the refugees continued to demand compensation for their losses and the right to return to their homes in Palestine. There was active

---

[1] *Annual Report on the Hashemite Kingdom of Jordan for 1951*, FO 371/98856, PRO.

[2] Naim Sofer, 'The Absorption of the West Bank into the Jordanian Kingdom' (Heb.) *Hamizrah Hehadash*, 3/23 (1955), 189–96.

[3] Plascov, *The Palestinian Refugees in Jordan*, chs. 2, 3.

opposition from West Bank politicians to any policy which could possibly be construed to mean a renunciation of the right to return home. Nevertheless, there was reason to believe that the payment of compensation would cause a large reduction in the volume of demand for repatriation, and it was privately admitted by the more well-to-do refugees that they only wished to return home in order to personally supervise the sale of their property in Israel after which they would return to settle down in Jordan.

The funds brought to the country by the refugees slowly ran down, while the cost of maintaining them, even with United Nations help, continued to mount. A poor cereal harvest, resulting from extremely low rainfall, added to the general economic plight. Unemployment in the kingdom, including the refugees, reached 475,000. At the same time Jordan's sterling reserves were rapidly running down, leaving very little capital for development schemes. Various efforts were made by the government to develop some of the country's meagre natural resources and to improve her economic position but, despite the assistance of foreign experts, the chances of any real achievement were frittered away by equivocation, intrigue, and the lack of a clear policy. The road to economic viability was long and full of pitfalls.[4]

Ravaged by war, cut off from its natural markets, flooded with refugees, and wracked by unemployment, the West Bank faced especially severe problems. Economic pressure rekindled King Abdullah's interest in normalizing relations with Israel. A settlement with Israel, he hoped, would open up a large market for his kingdom's agricultural produce, provide capital in the form of compensation for the refugees, help to improve general economic conditions, and open up new development possibilities and assistance from the United Nations and the United States.

Some of the more imaginative Israeli officials recognized that assistance towards the economic development of Jordan held out the best hope for the future. But the official policy remained unimaginative and short-sighted, refusing to make any concessions to Jordan unless there was a corresponding gain. All the constructive ideas came not from the top but from the officials directly involved in the conduct of relations with Jordan.

Foremost among these was Reuven Shiloah. Initially, there was tremendous enthusiasm at the Foreign Ministry for a settlement with Abdullah but with the growing scepticism, and especially after Elias Sasson took up his post in Ankara, maintaining the contact with Abdullah came to be seen as Shiloah's private affair.[5] Because

---

[4] *Annual Report on the Hashemite Kingdom of Jordan for 1951*, FO 371/98856, PRO.
[5] Interview with Walter Eytan.

Shiloah's Arabic was somewhat less than perfect and because of the importance that Abdullah was known to attach to the personal element in diplomacy, Sharett appointed Moshe Sasson, the son of Elias Sasson, as an assistant to Shiloah for the last phase of the negotiations. There was thus an element of continuity on the Israeli side.[6]

Moshe Sasson accompanied Shiloah to the last four or five meetings with Abdullah and wrote a report on each of them and about the frequent meetings he had with Abdel Ghani al-Karmi, code-named by the Israelis 'Hayogev', who now served as Abdullah's principal emissary. In all the meetings with Abdullah, whether they were discussing Israel, Jordan, the Palestinians, or the British, one royal quality always stood out—pragmatism. It was this quality that Abdullah now determinedly tried to apply to the resolution of the Arab–Israeli conflict. He sought to make peace with Israel as a result of a cold and sober calculation of the Jordanian national interest.

Because of the family connection, Moshe Sasson enjoyed greater freedom than a junior diplomat would normally allow himself in the presence of a monarch. Once, standing on the stairs of Abdullah's palace in Amman, Sasson said he wanted to ask two questions which were difficult and possibly discourteous. 'Ask, my son', said Abdullah in a friendly, paternal voice. 'Why do you want peace with Israel?' asked Sasson. Without a moment's hesitation Abdullah replied: 'I want peace not because I have become a Zionist or care for Israel's welfare, but because it is in the interest of my people. I am convinced that if we do not make peace with you, there will be another war, and another war, and another war, and another war, and we would lose. Hence it is the supreme interest of the Arab nation to make peace with you.'

The young Israeli was sufficiently impressed with this answer to forego his second question but Abdullah gently encouraged him by clasping his hand and stroking it until he posed his second question: 'If you want peace for the sake of your people, why do you run ahead of the people? Why don't you wait for the Palestinians to come to you and ask you to make peace so that you will be seen to be acting in response to their wishes and public appeals?' Abdullah gave a benign smile but no answer. It was left to Samir Rifai to take the novice to a corner and explain that as an absolute ruler, King Abdullah saw it as his duty to decide what was best for his people without having to ask for their opinion or to receive their support for what he considered to be the right policy.[7]

Encouraged by these replies to his questions, Moshe Sasson concluded that Jordan remained the Arab country most likely to be first to

[6] Interview with Moshe Sasson.   [7] İbid.

conclude a peace agreement with Israel. This assumption was widely held in the Foreign Ministry despite the recent setbacks. First to challenge it was Elias Sasson who conceded in a letter from Ankara that Jordan was the Arab country most inclined towards peace with Israel but added that it was also the Arab country with the greatest demands, demands to which Israel could not possibly agree. Furthermore, in Jordan Israel depended on one man, a foreigner of advancing years, a man with courage and goodwill, but lacking the independence and freedom to direct matters. This man was King Abdullah. Three questions presented themselves: what if Abdullah did not survive until the signature of a peace agreement? What if his British allies ordered him to stop in the middle of the negotiations? What if he could not find a prime minister who would be prepared to sully his own reputation and stay with him to the end? So long as no satisfactory answers were available to these three questions, Elias Sasson considered it premature to speak of Jordan as the Arab country with which a settlement could be reached before all the others.[8]

Reuven Shiloah was of the opinion that with Samir Rifai in power, a new opportunity presented itself for making a strong bid for an Israeli–Jordanian settlement. Assuming an all-round settlement with all the Arab states was for all practical purposes ruled out, Jordan had to be the bridgehead. Since spectacular Israeli concessions to win over public opinion, like giving back Lydda and Ramleh, were also out of the question, Shiloah thought of a development plan geared to increasing prosperity and absorbing some of the refugees which would have popular appeal and the support of a few influential personalities in Jordan. Such a plan had to show that economic development required first finance and second a steady market. That was where Israel would come in, for compensation would make a contribution to the finance, and Israel would provide the market. In other words, what Shiloah had in mind was to sell the idea of a settlement with Israel as part of a scheme with very particular attraction for Jordan.[9]

Shiloah was disappointed to find only the king and his personal physician when he arrived at the palace in Shuneh on 12 December 1950. Abdullah expressed his pleasure at having Samir Rifai as prime minister again and assured the visitor that Samir knew about the meeting and could not attend only because he was detained in Parliament. The atmosphere was eminently cordial but nothing concrete was discussed. Abdullah intimated that he hoped to be ready for more serious talks in about a fortnight when Samir would participate. So the meeting represented no more than the renewal of personal

[8] E. Sasson to R. Shiloah and M. Sasson, 25 Jan. 1951, 2408/13, ISA.
[9] Helm to Furlonge, 11 Dec. 1950, FO 371/82179, PRO.

contact between two imaginative and venturesome individuals with responsibility for Jordanian–Israeli relations. Shiloah always had a soft spot for the king and he was obviously flattered when the latter made a point of calling him 'Aziz' (my dear).[10]

Another proposal for a fresh approach to Jordan was made by Yehoshafat Harkabi, now a Lieutenant-Colonel and IDF staff officer for armistice affairs. Harkabi suggested that Jordan be offered free port facilities at Haifa, without waiting for a peace settlement, to import and export goods. He noted that the port facilities at Aqaba were primitive while the use of Lebanese and Syrian ports was costly and troublesome, and that the Rifai government would be able to present such an arrangement as a great achievement. He also noted that since swallowing up Arab Palestine, Jordan had been in the throes of a sociological change that tended to make her much more similar to the other Arab states. The end result of this process, unless something was done to halt it, would be Jordan's adoption of the Arab League line and the reinforcement of the Arab boycott against Israel. 'Our interest requires support for the enlightened absolutism of the king against the strident democratic nationalism that prevails in the other Arab states. Therefore, if by allowing the passage of goods to Jordan through our territory we can strengthen the King's position, we ought to do it.' Samir Rifai's government could turn out to be the last twitch of the king's influence, and its failure would open the way to the elements that were sold on the Arab League.

From such an arrangement Israel could only gain, especially in terms of Jordanian economic dependence, concluded Harkabi.

It seems to me that if we propose it to Jordan tactfully, without asking for an immediate return and without presenting it as a peace settlement, Jordan would accept this arrangement very gladly. For us this would be the first breach in the Arab boycott, the driving of a permanent wedge between Jordan and the Arab world and the binding of her to us. Even if Jordan rejects this proposal, we would be able to point to it before the Western powers as an altruistic proposal on our part whose sole aim was to consolidate the stability of this part of the world.

Although this proposal involved little or no cost, and although the potential advantages for Israel were clearly underlined, Harkabi's superiors did not endorse the proposal, saying it was a matter for the Foreign Ministry.[11]

The foreign minister was always ready to examine ideas for peace in stages, or as he called it 'retail peace' rather than 'wholesale peace'.

---

[10] Helm to FO, 13 Dec. 1950, FO 371/82211, PRO; *FRUS 1950*, v. 1075 f.
[11] Yehoshafat Harkabi to the Deputy Chief of Staff, 26 Dec. 1950, 2408/13, ISA; interview with Yehoshafat Harkabi.

But, like a retailer, he insisted on reciprocity and on a limit to unconditional advances from Israel. Free port facilities in Haifa went beyond the limit of what he considered a reasonable advance. He regarded this as a major card in Israel's hand to entice Jordan into a settlement and feared that if Israel surrendered it, Jordan would cease to have an incentive to meet Israel half-way. In short, he was prepared to offer Jordan free port facilities at Haifa in exchange for the renewal of normal trading relations between the two countries; he was not prepared to offer these facilities if Jordan was to support the Arab economic boycott of Israel.[12]

In the first weeks of 1951 attention turned to the question of compensation. Israel had to decide whether to offer round sums to the governments and institutions responsible for the resettlement of the refugees and thus gain some credit in the eyes of the mass of the refugees or to give compensation on an individual basis to win over a smaller group of the wealthier refugees.[13]

Abba Eban, Israel's ambassador to the United States, took the lead in suggesting an élitist approach to the refugee problem. On the basis of his own experience of co-operation with Ahmad Tuqan, Jordan's delegate to the General Assembly, Eban challenged the assumption that the desire for a settlement was felt only by the Hashemite king while all the other political groups recoiled from the very idea of a Jordanian–Israeli settlement. Eban went on to suggest that if compensation was paid to members of the Jordanian government and Parliament, their attitude to Israel would change dramatically. Arab politicians were said by Eban to look at political matters from a personal angle and to place their individual interest above the general interest. Hence his confidence that if the Israelis cast their bread upon the water, they would not be the losers.[14]

Walter Eytan did not doubt that Arab politicians were self-seeking and indifferent to the fate of the poor, but he objected to Eban's proposal both on moral grounds as contrary to their own concept of social justice and on practical grounds as unlikely to solve the basic problems in Israeli–Jordanian relations.[15] Enquiries by Moshe Sasson revealed that only a minority of the members of the Jordanian government and Parliament had property in Israel. While not denying that Eban's proposal could have some positive effects, he pointed out that passive acceptance of the idea of peace with Israel in some Jordanian political circles was not the same as readiness to fight for this cause.[16] It

[12] Circular from the Director-General of the Foreign Ministry, 22 Oct. 1952, 2453/3, ISA.
[13] A. Biran to Eytan, 9 Jan. 1951, 2441/4, ISA.
[14] Eban to Eytan, 10 Jan. 1951, 2408/13, ISA.
[15] Eytan to Eban, 26 Jan. 1951, 2408/13, ISA.
[16] M. Sasson to Eban, 4 Feb. 1951, 2408/13, ISA.

was not until several months later that the Israeli government took a secret decision to 'release an appreciable part of the accounts frozen in Israeli banks in favour of account holders living in Jordan'.[17]

In the meantime it was decided, and officially announced by Sharett in the Knesset on 23 January, 1951, to pay only collective compensation to the Arabs of Palestine. This statement, according to Karmi, came as a serious blow to the supporters of a settlement with Israel. One Jordanian minister was quoted as saying that Sharett's statement had been made in order to compel the Jordanian government to break off contact with Israel. Those ministers who favoured a settlement with Israel saw individual compensation as the chief benefit of such a settlement and saw no point in continuing the talks so long as Israel adhered to the principle of collective compensation. A delegation of the property-owning refugees who had made representations to the government in favour of a settlement with Israel now said it would not continue to support a settlement in view of the new Israeli stand.[18] King Abdullah considered Sharett's statement as a disservice both to Israel and to Jordan and asked Karmi for urgent clarifications of Israel's thinking on the subject.[19]

Israel's thinking was rather murky. Its aim was to get the best of both worlds at the lowest possible cost to herself. Her official policy was to pay only collective compensation as part of a peace settlement, but she was prepared to give special consideration to the claims of those who wielded political influence in order to demonstrate that those who acted in line with Israel's interests could expect a reward and in order to create divisions in the Arab camp. In her propaganda Israel emphasized that time was not on the side of the Arabs and that the longer they delayed making peace, the less they would get.[20] This point was also made by Sharett in response to King Abdullah's request for clarifications. His statement in the Knesset, said Sharett, reflected the official policy of the Israeli government, but the offer of compensation was liable to be withdrawn, like any other offer, unless it met with a positive response from the other side. In other words, the Arabs should not assume that an offer made by Israel at a particular time would be open for ever. Sharett added that he hoped that this explanation would satisfy King Abdullah and help him to move things forward towards a settlement.[21]

The truth of the matter was that Israel gave Abdullah little solid help

[17] E. Sasson to Divon, 15 May 1951, 2453/3, ISA.
[18] M. Sasson to Sharett, 31 Jan. 1951, Talk with Hayogev, 27 Jan. 1951, 2408/13, ISA.
[19] King Abdullah to Abdel Ghani al-Karmi, 28 Jan. 1951, copy in 2408/13, ISA.
[20] Minute by M. Sasson and S. Divon, 27 Jan. 1951, 2408/13, ISA.
[21] Sharett to Karmi, 11 Feb. 1951, 2453/3, ISA.

in moving things towards a settlement. Although the orthodox approach of keeping everything for the final peace bargaining had been tried for two and a half years and had been unsuccessful, there was strong resistance to any attempt to replace it with what in American diplomatic jargon was called the 'tissue-knitting' approach to peace. A cultural gulf had developed between Israel and the Arabs. Whereas under the mandate there had been a brisk traffic in ideas between Arabs and Jews, Israelis were now unconcerned by Arab thoughts and feelings. The tendency in blockaded Israel was to ignore the existence of the Arab world except as something menacing and encircling. It was extremely difficult to explain to the Israeli public why Israel should undertake courses of action favourable to the Arabs. The leaders failed to bring home to the Israeli people the importance of their geographic and ethnic surroundings. The difference, as Eban remarked to an American diplomat who urged the 'tissue-knitting' approach, was that Ben-Gurion 'hardly knows there is an Arab world—Sharett does know'. Eban himself saw the reasoning behind the functional approach but felt that it called for a special breed of Israeli—a 'super Israeli' who would accept the principle of unorthodox and magnanimous acts in the face of Arab League boasts of plots for his destruction.[22] In short, the mood in Israel was not conducive to unilateral concessions or gestures of conciliation. On the contrary, as Samir Rifai discovered soon after his return to power, the Israeli policymakers were more orthodox than ever in their approach, seeking to trade off each little concession for some reciprocal advantage.

Samir Rifai and Israel

Samir Rifai was chosen to succeed Said al-Mufti largely because of his moderate and reasonable attitude to Israel. To maximize his freedom of action in foreign policy, Samir formed a stable and moderate government, thereby increasing Abdullah's expectations of rapid progress towards a settlement with Israel. Yet public opinion, inflamed by Israel's aggressive behaviour on the border, could not be ignored. Samir's reputation was too precious to waste on a settlement that could make him look like a traitor and that was sure to be denounced as a sellout by the opposition in Jordan and in the Arab world. He realized that his country needed to come to terms with Israel but the personal sacrifice he was called upon to make seemed too great. He therefore tried to find a middle way that would give the king some satisfaction

---

[22] *FRUS 1951*, vol. v, *The Near East and Africa* (Washington: United States Government Printing Office, 1982), 777–9.

without however jeopardizing his own reputation and standing as a national leader.

Implementation of the armistice agreement was the key to Samir's policy. The king kept pressing for a general settlement with Israel. Previous governments, on the other hand, had done little to ensure the implementation of the armistice agreement, so Samir's policy was to accept the obligation to implement fully the armistice agreement, and in particular Article 8, if he could count on a co-operative and conciliatory attitude from Israel. His aim was to squeeze all the advantages he could from this agreement and to give Israel the minimum to which she was entitled. To the king local arrangements reached in this way could be presented as stepping stones towards a final settlement; to the public as real gains from the negotiations with Israel; and to Israel as the fulfilment of Jordan's obligations under the Rhodes agreement.[23]

Neither King Abdullah nor the Israelis were satisfied with this policy. The king took the initiative by writing a letter to Ben-Gurion to suggest the renewal of talks and promising, if the Naharayim and Wadi Araba disputes could be settled, to implement Article 8 of the armistice agreement as a first step towards peace. Ben-Gurion and his advisers were worried that Article 8 would not be implemented even if they withdrew from Naharayim, so they accepted Shiloah's suggestion that an agreement on all the outstanding problems should be reached but that the decision on Naharayim could be published first and the decision on Mount Scopus later. Shiloah went to a meeting with Samir Rifai at Shuneh on 12 January 1951. Rifai suggested a re-examination of the Rhodes agreement as a basis for extended co-operation, and Shiloah was content to follow this approach. Elias Sasson, on the other hand, warned that Israel's consent to re-examine the Rhodes agreement could only be interpreted by the Arabs as a sign of weakness and that it would create a dangerous precedent. Samir was asking for Israeli concessions in return for a full implementation of the Rhodes agreement. What he held out as a *de facto* state of peace, Sasson regarded as a trap and he accordingly recommended that armistice matters be left to the Mixed Armistice Commission and that high-level meetings be reserved for negotiating a peace settlement.[24]

By this time, however, Ben-Gurion had come to question not just the feasibility but also the desirability of a political settlement with Jordan. His hostility to Britain ran so deep that he was reluctant to do anything

[23] Memorandum by Moshe Sasson on Samir Rifai's policy towards Israel, Feb. 1951, 2408/13, ISA.

[24] Ben-Gurion's diary, 3 Jan. 1951; E. Sasson to M. Sasson, 25 Jan. 1951, and E. Sasson to R. Shiloah, 25 Jan. 1951, 2408/13, ISA.

that would strengthen Britain's position. To Moshe Sharett he revealed that he had grave doubts as to whether a settlement with Jordan was desirable at all.[25] To Reuven Shiloah, who came to consult before a meeting with Abdullah on February 13, Ben-Gurion gave no less than seven reasons for his doubts. First, Jordan was not a natural or stable political entity but a regime based on one man who could die any minute and who was entirely dependent on Britain. Second, a political settlement with Jordan was liable to get in the way of a settlement with Egypt. Third, an accord with Abdullah without peace with Egypt could not lift the siege that Israel faced in the continents of Asia, Africa, and Europe. Iraq would continue to block Israel's path to the east, Syria to the north, and Egypt to the south. Fourth, such an accord would reinforce Britain's hold over the surrounding area. The fifth reason was presented in the form of a question: 'Do we have an interest in committing ourselves to such ridiculous borders?' Sixth, an accord with Egypt would settle Israel's relations with the entire Arab and Islamic world, open the door to the south as well as the north, and yield important economic links. Finally, Egypt was a natural and stable country and, objectively speaking, there was no conflict between her and Israel.[26]

Abdullah's commitment to a settlement with Israel appears all the more remarkable against the background of Israeli prevarication. A day after Reuven Shiloah's visit, he summoned his ministers and handed Samir Rifai an Israeli memorandum which he asked him to read out. Samir stalled, so Abdullah explained that the memorandum dealt with infiltration across the border and that it showed that there were two sides to every coin. He then reviewed the danger of a world war and warned that if war broke out Israel would not be able to pay compensation to the Arabs of Palestine, while the Western Powers would be too preoccupied with rearmament to pay any attention to Arab demands. If Jordan was not ready to conclude peace, at the very least she had to sign a non-aggression pact and any minister who had reservations about the king's policy was free to go. Before bringing the meeting to an end, Abdullah also reminded the prime minister of his undertaking to submit a paper on all the problems connected with the armistice.

Abdel Ghani Karmi, who reported to Moshe Sasson on the new governmental crisis in Amman, also expressed the fear that the governmental crisis in Israel would bring down Ben-Gurion, Sharett, Shiloah, and the rest of Jordan's friends in the ruling party and elevate to power Herut and the religious parties who would want to capture all the territory at least as far as the Jordan River. An immediate

[25] Ben-Gurion's diary, 7 Feb. 1951.   [26] Ibid. 13 Feb. 1951.

agreement with Israel, thought Karmi, would bolster the position of Mapai, and this was also the advice he gave to his king.[27]

Under pressure from the king, Rifai met Shiloah again on February 23. Abdullah did not appear at all, while Dr Sati and Abdel Ghani Karmi joined the negotiators only for dinner. No definite conclusions were reached, except for a general understanding that at this stage the discussions should be confined to the implementation and development of the armistice agreement, and for a mutual undertaking for each side to submit its proposals on this basis.[28] In due course the two of them met again and Rifai submitted his proposals in writing. Shiloah did not submit counter-proposals but contented himself with certain negative reactions on the spot.

By the end of March the matter had progressed, or rather retrogressed, a stage further. Through Karmi, Israel's official reaction to the Jordanian proposals and a set of counter-proposals were conveyed to the king. The king was in general prepared to go along with the Israeli proposals and asked Karmi to inform Rifai. Rifai reacted strongly. He refused to agree to the suggestions regarding Naharayim, Tulkarem, and Mount Scopus, accused the Israelis of trying to squeeze all possible advantage out of a settlement without being willing to make any concessions, and demanded that Shiloah give him a formal reply in writing.

King Abdullah was so angered by Rifai's attitude that he started to look for an alternative and more amenable prime minister. According to Karmi's report, Kirkbride encouraged him in this direction on the grounds that Rifai was clearly not prepared to risk his influence and standing by making an agreement with Israel which would be unpopular in Jordan and in Arab circles generally. The king thus again confronted the internal difficulties which had faced him before Rifai took office, now aggravated by the failure to make any real advance towards a settlement with Israel during Rifai's premiership.[29]

Shiloah sent Israel's formal reply to Rifai on April 16. It suggested that initially items outside the scope of the armistice agreement be excluded from the talks. It affirmed Israel's willingness to hand over Naharayim provided a prior understanding was reached on all outstanding details connected with the armistice. Israel rejected Jordan's suggestion that Article 6 be extended to villages east of the demarcation line in the sector formerly held by the Iraqis but offered compensation to the landowners on the Israeli side who had chosen to move to Jordan.

[27] Moshe Sasson, 'A Meeting with Hayogev, 17 Feb. 1951', 2408/13, ISA.
[28] Moshe Sasson, 'Meeting with Samir Rifai, 23 Feb. 1951', 2408/13, ISA.
[29] Comay to Elath, 3 Apr. 1951, 2408/13, ISA; *FRUS 1951*, v. 601–4, 647–9.

Israel also accepted in principle free movement on the Latrun–Jerusalem road and the operation of the Latrun pumping station to be achieved by the division of no-man's land and suggested that the details be worked out by the military. But she expressed amazement at the suggestion that Mount Scopus be treated as Jordanian territory since the area had been held by Israeli forces prior to the military agreement on 7 July 1948. The entire Mount Scopus area, said the note, 'is and must remain Israel territory'.[30]

The dispatch of this inflexible note was followed by another conference between Shiloah and King Abdullah. When Shiloah enquired whether the king wished to have Samir present, Abdullah replied that he preferred to speak to him alone since he was displeased with both Samir and Shiloah over the exchange of correspondence. He deplored the raising of the question of sovereignty over Mount Scopus and Israel's undiplomatic rejoinder and wondered whether both governments might withdraw their communications. Shiloah replied that it would be difficult but not impossible. He also mentioned that Israel might be prepared to release some of the blocked bank accounts in order to create a more favourable atmosphere. The king showed a lively interest in this prospect and said he thought it would serve a useful purpose. Shiloah's general impression, however, was that though Abdullah meant well and had good ideas, he had become a 'wishful thinker', lacking the power to implement the ideas that were his alone.[31]

Monnet Davis, the new American ambassador to Israel, told Shiloah very frankly after being shown the correspondence with Jordan that he thought ground had been lost rather than gained. Davis suggested that more attention should be paid to the motives behind the Arab position as a prelude to a sustained Israeli effort to change the Arab attitude. He expressed the belief that the Israelis with their intelligence and determination could accomplish more if they considered the matter important enough. He cited as factors contributing to the lack of progress the unnecessarily provocative language in the correspondence, the generally rough handling of border incidents, and the apparent lack of any concerted effort to create better feelings. Shiloah agreed that imagination was needed to avoid phraseology that could embarrass the other side and took in good part the expression of views he had invited.[32]

Samir Rifai replied to the Israeli communication on April 30. In essence he stated that

1. Jordan agreed with Israel that first the armistice agreement had to

---

[30] *FRUS 1951*, v. 647–9.   [31] Ibid. 656 f.   [32] Ibid. 658.

be implemented fully and only then consideration might be given to other matters.

2. Jordan considered that Articles 6 and 8 had thus far not been implemented and that steps should be taken to rectify this state of affairs.

3. There appeared to be a basic difference of interpretation between Jordan and Israel on the meaning of these articles and especially on the meaning of Article 8 regarding the institutions on Mount Scopus.

4. Since the interpretation of an agreement was a legal matter, Jordan believed that an international tribunal should be asked to adjudicate.

5. Israel was invited to refer the dispute to the International Court of Justice or to submit alternative proposals for the settlement of the dispute by a competent judicial authority. (For the full text of the Jordanian note see Appendix 5.)

The king had sought to dissuade Samir from sending this reply, saying that the Israelis had promised to pay Jordan 'a lot of money'. Samir took the stand that hitherto the Israeli concessions had been limited to the offer to evacuate Naharayim and to release some blocked accounts. These were both due to Jordan as a matter of right and justice and could not therefore be considered as Israeli favours.[33]

Karmi related to Moshe Sasson that the king had spent a whole hour with the Council of Ministers when Samir's reply was being considered but had failed to persuade Samir to modify his reply and walked out of the meeting in anger. Only strong royal pressure had induced Samir to add the final sentence inviting Israel to suggest an alternative judicial procedure for settling the dispute. Karmi also conveyed the following verbal message from the king to Shiloah: 'I stand by everything to which we agreed at our last meeting and remind you of your promise not to send your reply to Samir Pasha Rifai before you meet with me. The prime minister's trip to Egypt will give us a very good opportunity for a meeting.'

Samir was displeased with the king's attempts to maintain independent contact with the Israelis behind his back and with the role played by Karmi in these contacts. He asked Karmi to sign the official communication on his behalf so that he himself, as an Arab head of government, would be spared the embarrassment. He also insisted that Karmi sign not with his initials (S.R.) but with the initials of his post of prime minister (P.M.). In Karmi's opinion the note was typical of Samir's basic approach to negotiations with Israel which was to play

---

[33] Ibid. 660 f.; Jordan Comments on the Note Dated 16 April 1951, 2408/13, ISA.

for time and prolong his stay in power. To this end nothing was better calculated than an appeal to the International Court of Justice.[34]

Israel did not agree to refer the dispute to the International Court of Justice. She was not sure of the legal basis for her claim to sovereignty over Mount Scopus and feared that agreement to international arbitration would weaken her position and vindicate the Jordanian position. She also declined to suggest an alternative procedure for arbitration. Abdullah had another visit from Shiloah on May 11, while his prime minister was out of the country, and Mount Scopus was discussed without any concrete result. This appears to have been the last meeting between the king and the Israeli envoy.[35] Relations between the two countries thus reached a dead-end at the official level. There was no meeting of minds, and no real negotiations took place. When he assumed power, Samir Rifai had counted on a co-operative and conciliatory attitude from Israel, and when this was not forthcoming he dug his heels in. King Abdullah, on the other hand, was anxious to move forward to a settlement with Israel but was increasingly isolated and powerless in his quest for peace.

Moshe Sasson described this process as 'the sinking of King Abdullah's regime'. He and his colleagues in the Middle East Department recognized that the effective challenge mounted by the Palestinians to Abdullah's absolute rule changed the internal balance of power within the enlarged kingdom in a way that was detrimental to the prospects of peace. The internal changes and their implications for Israel were clearly noted in a position paper written by Moshe Sasson in January 1951:

Since the annexation of the Arab parts of Palestine to Transjordan and since the initialling of the agreement, we have been witnessing a process of decline in Abdullah's real power on the one hand and the rise of opposition and anti-Israeli groups on the other. This process limits the prospects of peace with Transjordan and narrows the possibility of interim arrangements. Over the last year we have witnessed a parallel process of reduction in the Jordanian demands from Israel on the one hand and a diminution in the aims of the negotiations on the other (peace–non-aggression–interim arrangements–revision of the Rhodes agreement). The conclusion that must be drawn is that our traditional support for the Jordanian royal court and fight against the opposition circles will not take us towards the desired target. We have to look for a new approach and new methods.[36]

There was very little that was new, however, in Israel's approach to

---

[34] M. Sasson to R. Shiloah, 2 May 1951, 2408/13, ISA.

[35] Kirkbride to FO, 12 May 1951, and Tel Aviv to FO, 15 May 1951, FO 371/91364, PRO.

[36] Middle East Department to the Foreign Minister, 'Israeli–Arab Relations', 18 Jan. 1951, 2410/9, ISA.

Jordan during the premiership of Samir Rifai. The meetings between the king and the prime minister and Shiloah continued intermittently until the king's death but the efforts were switched away from a general peace settlement to extended co-operation under the Rhodes agreement. Even in working towards this modest goal, the two sides made very little progress. The positive results of these efforts were confined to a settlement of the frontier dispute in Wadi Araba and an agreement to establish liaison between the commanders along the frontiers so that border incidents and infiltration could be dealt with in a more co-operative fashion. Further accord was prevented by the dispute over sovereignty in Mount Scopus. In June Jordan protested to the secretary-general of the United Nations and to the three powers who had guaranteed the status quo in the Middle East against Israeli interference with the waters of the River Jordan. After this, relations between the two countries worsened steadily and the death of the king ended the era of personal diplomacy.[37]

Abdullah's visit to Turkey towards the end of May rekindled Elias Sasson's interest and faith in personal diplomacy. There was a great deal he wanted to say to his old friend and he was also anxious to hear the 'oral doctrine' from the lips of the king himself. But the Foreign Ministry failed to make the necessary arrangements with Karmi and the meeting did not take place. Sasson's disappointment only increased on hearing that the Palestine Conciliation Commission had reached the conclusion that the armistice agreements had exhausted their usefulness and were in danger of collapsing under the weight of border disputes. Sasson read in the independent Israeli daily *Haaretz* that American, French, and British diplomats blamed Israel for the failure to attain peace because she had no constructive Arab policy since the end of the war except for firmness, which was no substitute for a policy. From his distant vantage point in Ankara, it seemed to Sasson that there was a good deal of truth in this observation.[38]

Moshe Sharett hotly denied this. When Western diplomats spoke of the absence of a constructive policy on Israel's part as the reason for the failure to achieve peace, wrote Sharett to Sasson, what they meant was that Israel was not prepared to make the concessions which in their view would make peace possible. This was nothing new. During the mandate the lack of Jewish–Arab agreement was variously attributed to the Jewish refusal to limit immigration, to the policy of building an exclusively Jewish economy, to the resistance to a Legislative Council with an Arab majority, and so on. Now the State of Israel was being accused of blocking peace by her refusal to allow refugees to return, by

[37] *Annual Report on the Hashemite Kingdom of Jordan for 1951*, FO 371/98856, PRO.
[38] E. Sasson to S. Divon, 25 May 1951, 2410/9, ISA.

her refusal to give up certain territories, and by her very denunciation of the refusal of the Arab states to make peace. 'I am not impressed by these arguments', concluded Sharett. 'And what good would it do me if I were impressed.'[39]

Britain and the defence of the Middle East

From Whitehall issued forth not just the old criticism of Israel for her lack of a constructive policy but also new ideas for the defence of the Middle East. The trend in British policy had been to move away from support for Egypt to consolidation of her position in Jordan and from trying to unite the Arabs through the Arab League to support for the Hashemite bloc against its rivals. At the same time, and as part of the same trend, Britain came to appreciate the need for an understanding and closer co-operation with Israel.[40] Following the outbreak of the Korean war in June 1950 the British began to search for new Middle East military bases which would be closer to the scene of operations in the event of a Russian attack through Iran and Greece and at the same time make possible a reduction of the forces in the Suez Canal zone. Turkey and Iran were considered as well as the Gaza area as a subsidiary base which would provide a link between the Mediterranean and the Red Sea at Aqaba.

Richard Crossman, the left-wing member of Parliament well known for his pro-Israeli leanings, revealed to the Israelis that the British General Staff were interested in bases in the Negev and in enlarging the Aqaba base to accommodate some of the troops from the canal zone.[41] Crossman sounded out Ben-Gurion about facilities for Britain in Haifa and the possibility of a military pact between Britain and Israel, but Ben-Gurion refused to comment on proposals that did not reach Israel through official channels.[42]

Support for closer military links between Britain and Israel also came from an unexpected quarter: Sir Thomas Rapp, the new head of the British Middle East Office in Cairo. Rapp visited Israel and Jordan towards the end of 1950 and was greatly impressed with what he saw in Israel and worried by what he saw in Jordan. The king was old and weak, he reported, time was not working in favour of a settlement, and Britain should force the pace.[43] This suggestion did not go down well with the Eastern Department. Sir Geoffrey Furlonge replied that the

---

[39] Sharett to E. Sasson, 3 June 1951, 2382/1, ISA.
[40] Rafael to Shiloah, 28 Dec. 1950, 2403/12, ISA.
[41] Comay to Elath, 9 Jan. 1951, 2403/12, ISA.
[42] Ben-Gurion's diary, 26 Dec. 1950 and 4 Jan. 1951.
[43] Rapp to Furlonge, 15 Dec. 1950, FO 371/82178, PRO.

idea of applying pressure in Jordan was under constant review but it was felt that the Arabs could only be led, not driven, and it would therefore be a mistake to try to force the pace.[44]

During a visit to Israel in February 1951, Furlonge's assessment was that the time was not propitious for a general settlement. The Arabs were genuinely frightened of Israel and convinced of her aggressive intentions, and this was a source of difficulty for Britain in her dealings with certain Arab states. Not many people in London appreciated that there was a powerful emotional urge towards Arab unity, felt even in a country like Jordan. Even if this urge did not enable the Arabs to combine effectively, it still operated negatively in deterring individuals and governments from acting against general Arab opinion. Furlonge himself knew the Middle East in minute detail, especially the Levant where he had served for twelve years. From experience he knew that the Arabs did not act so much on logic as by instinct and emotion. On matters of major importance to them they could become as stubborn as mules, and no mere appeal to their material self-interest could then move them. It was a mistake, therefore, in Furlonge's view, to think that the Arabs invariably had their price.[45]

While the climate was not propitious for a general Arab–Israeli settlement, Israel's strategic value continued to rise in British eyes with the rise in international tension. Increasingly hefty hints were dropped in high places about Britain's interest in strategic co-operation with Israel. In mid-January, Sir William Strang, the under-secretary of state for foreign affairs, invited Eliahu Elath, the Israeli ambassador, to a 'private talk' at the Travellers Club in Pall Mall and then proceeded to tell him that Ernest Bevin knew and approved of the meeting. General Sir Brian Robertson, the commander-in-chief of the British Middle East Land Forces, was going to make contact with the Israeli General Staff, and Strang wished to discuss the political background. Strang said that in the event of a Soviet attack, the Middle East would be a vital area because it was a source of oil and a shield for Africa, and because the Suez Canal was the lifeline of the British Commonwealth. The facilities Britain enjoyed in Egypt, Iraq, Jordan, and Turkey were inadequate, hence the desire to involve Israel in Britain's defence plans, either on a regional basis or on a bilateral basis. Strang mentioned two specific ideas: (a) Israeli agreement to a British base in Gaza with a corridor to Jordan and (b) bases in Israel. 'The pact', added Strang, 'would of course be on the basis of complete equality.'

Elath flew to Israel to report on this conversation to a meeting

---

[44] Furlonge to Rapp, 15 Jan. 1951, FO 371/82178, and minute by Furlonge, 20 Jan. 1951, FO 371/91364, PRO.

[45] M. S. Comay, 'Report on Furlonge's Visit', Feb. 1951, 2403/12, ISA.

convened by Ben-Gurion to discuss Robertson's forthcoming visit. Ben-Gurion, still suffering from acute Anglophobia, raised a host of objections to this latest British overture. Despite the promise of complete equality, he was convinced that the British wanted to return to Palestine and launched into a tirade against them.

Why should we give them a toehold? Their policy in the Near East is without change, despite the change in public opinion and in some of the members of the government. Not Cripps or Morrison or Bevan direct foreign policy—but Bevin, and it is a policy of hostility: support for the League whose only activity is war against Israel, supplying arms to Egypt which the Egyptians at any rate intend for war not against Russia but against Israel.

With America, on the other hand, Ben-Gurion was prepared to discuss anything because she was giving Israel aid and because American protection of the Near East would mean protection of Israel as well. The latest British proposal was dismissed as an arrangement between Britain and Egypt at the expense of Israel's independence and well-being. Giving bases to Britain would identify Israel as an enemy of Russia, and Russia could retaliate by stopping the emigration of Russian Jews to Israel. It would also 'deliver us into the hands of the Arabs. Now we can expel the Legion when it takes the law into its own hands at kilometre 78; if the British were here, we would not be able to, and they would rule over us. This is an insulting suggestion. What are they offering us? Why did they not ask themselves why Israel should do it?' Ben-Gurion's suspicion of Britain had evidently not abated in the two years that had elapsed since the end of the war. He charged that Britain did not really want peace between Israel and the Arabs and spoke disparagingly about the Arab Legion as a British army and about Abdullah as a British old-age pensioner.[46]

Ben-Gurion's suspicion of British motives surfaced again when General Robertson arrived in Israel to look around the country, inspect military bases, and hold talks with senior members of the IDF General Staff. At one of these talks Ben-Gurion asked about British plans in the event of war with Russia, and the general replied that Russia would probably attack in a southerly direction towards Iraq and the British forces would move north from their bases in Egypt through Israel, Jordan, and Iraq. 'Do you think we are a British colony?' interjected Ben-Gurion angrily, 'Or do you think we are a country like Jordan which you rule? Israel is a small but independent country. Before you decide to turn it into a passageway for your armies, you must come and talk to us.' The British general was taken aback and after a tense pause said 'I am sorry. I am a soldier. This is a political question.' Before the

---

[46] Ben-Gurion's diary, 27 Jan. 1951.

general could recover his poise, the prime minister sprung another surprise. 'It is possible to establish different relations between Israel and Britain', he said. 'Why don't we join the British Commonwealth? You have more in common with us than with Ceylon. We could create a new network of relations between us, like the one between you and New Zealand.'[47]

Robertson reported on his conversations to Herbert Morrison who had taken over as foreign secretary from the ailing Bevin in early March. One of Morrison's first acts as foreign secretary was to write to Ben-Gurion to welcome the suggestion he had made to Robertson and to propose military co-operation as the first step in a gradual process of transforming the relations between the two countries. Ben-Gurion remained cagey, both because he preferred co-operation with America and because he believed that as long as there was no peace between Israel and her neighbours, Britain was unlikely to abandon her pro-Arab stand in order to enter into an alliance with Israel.[48]

Just when Ben-Gurion was denying the possibility of change, Britain's Middle East experts were reviewing their country's options in relation to the Arabs and Israel. The debate was sparked off by a long despatch from Sir Hugh Dow, the consul-general in Jerusalem, proposing that Britain remove the emphasis she had traditionally placed on Egypt as the most important country strategically in the Middle East and base her planning for the area on Jordan. A settlement between Jordan and Israel was presented by Dow as the only secure foundation for lasting peace in the Middle East.

Neither Israel nor the Arabs are going to be much use to us while they remain at daggers drawn with each other. It ought to be a cardinal point of our policy to heal the breach between them, and it is submitted that the best hope of doing this quickly is to concentrate on Israel and Jordan even if this means for a time some deterioration in our relations with other Arab states. Among the Arab states, Jordan is the only one that regards us, in spite of the troubles which they feel we have involved them in, with real friendliness. Jordan is also the only one likely to be of any military use. It is the one whose borders march for the most part with Israel, and although it is on Jordan that has fallen almost the whole burden of the war with Israel, it is only Jordan's ruler who, in spite of setbacks and opposition, shows any disposition to make peace with Israel, and to realise that long term interests dictate the resumption of friendly relations between the two states. We should therefore concentrate the help, military or economic, that we can give to Jordan. If we do that, and let both Jordan and the other Arab states and Israel clearly understand that we mean to stick by Jordan and help her if she is attacked, we should do more to encourage Arab unity than we can do in any other way. If we make Jordan strong and confident of our continuing help, the other Asian Arab states, with

---

[47] Bar-Zohar, *Ben-Gurion*, ii. 904.   [48] Ibid. 905 f.

perhaps the exception of Saudi Arabia, will tend to group themselves round her. We can then leave Saudi Arabia to the United States, and Egypt to herself to attempt to realize her dreams of African hegemony.

Such a change in Britain's policy towards the Arabs implied a complementary change in her policy towards Israel and, in particular, a firmer attitude over peace negotiations. Israel was in a better position to make concessions as gestures of strength than the Arabs. The trouble, according to Dow, was that

the Israelis see their position of strength as one rather enabling them to extort additional concessions than to grant them, and American policy encourages them in this. It is extraordinary that a nation, thinking itself at the beginning of a long career of growing influence, should be so shortsighted. With Israel, an over-anxiety to exploit every tactical advantage is combined with, perhaps indeed is responsible for, a strange impercipience on questions of strategy. Israel's long term interests demand a friendly Jordan, supported by a friendly Great Power, on her borders: without this she runs the danger that all the Arab states will take advantage of a Russian war, to combine to sweep her into the sea. Israel has the knowledge that Jordan is the only one of the Arab states, which although she has suffered most, is prepared to make peace with her. Yet instead of making generous gestures, by her intransigent attitude and unreasonable demands, she is piling up more and more Arab enmity. We should not let the ability with which Israel argues her case in the international forum blind us to the fact that, in her relations with the Arabs, though her lips drop oil, her hand still holds the whip.[49]

In the Foreign Office it was thought that this despatch was tinged with strong anti-Israel and anti-Egyptian feelings and that it reflected Richard Crossman's view that Britain should put all her eggs in the Jordanian basket.[50] Furlonge informed Dow that they did not share his conclusions and restated the case for the existing policy. There could be no two opinions, he said, about the desirability of an early settlement between Israel and her neighbours and he also agreed that a beginning could best be made between Israel and Jordan. Recent developments suggested that both sides were anxious for improved relations, and it was right for Britain to encourage them but she had to be careful not to force the pace because

[h]owever much King Abdullah may want an accommodation, he does not seem to control his Government and subjects as he did in the past, and we imagine that he cannot afford to disregard the hostility which a premature settlement with Israel would arouse both among his own people and in the other Arab states. Similarly the Israel Government, however anxious for a

[49] Dow to Bevin, 3 Mar. 1951, FO 371/91184, PRO.
[50] Minute by H. A. Dudgeon, 16 Mar. 1951, FO 371/91184, PRO.

settlement with Jordan, could hardly buy one at the price of concessions which Israel public opinion would regard as a surrender.

While recognizing that an Arab–Israeli settlement would greatly assist in planning Middle East defence, the Foreign Office did not consider it a prerequisite. Indeed, it acted on the assumption that such a settlement could not be made in time and accordingly concentrated on attempts to reach bilateral arrangements with each of the countries concerned. The results of General Robertson's visits to various Middle East capitals were considered encouraging in the majority of cases.

One last reason was given by Furlonge for the reluctance to force the pace in trying to reach an Israeli–Jordanian settlement, or to put all Britain's eggs in the Jordan basket. It was probably the most crucial reason: 'So long as the Middle East as a whole is threatened with Russian aggression we cannot afford to disregard the susceptibilities of any of the component countries. It is true that this involves dispersing our activities over a wide field, but in all the circumstances that seems to be the lesser of the evils.'[51]

Dow conceded that he had put his case somewhat too trenchantly and that in saying they should concentrate on Jordan he did not mean to imply that they should abandon the other Arab states. His point was rather that by showing that they were firmly behind Jordan they would do more to encourage unity among the Arab states than by more diffusion of effort. Continuing Furlonge's own metaphor, he stated that the difficulty was that they had so many baskets and so few eggs to put them in.[52]

Other heads of missions joined in this great debate on war and peace in the Middle East. Sir Ralph Stevenson argued from Cairo that Britain's main strategic objective in the Middle East was to strengthen her position in Egypt and to endeavour to maintain her bases there after 1956 when her treaty with Egypt was due to expire. He touched on the necessity for peace between Israel and the Arab states and suggested that a prior agreement between Britain and Egypt would improve the prospects of peace.[53]

Sir Knox Helm countered with the argument that if Britain gave priority to reaching an agreement with Egypt, it would be difficult to establish mutual confidence with the Israelis whose great fear was that Britain should suddenly abandon their interests for the sake of the Arabs as they claimed she had done in the past. The prospect of the Arab League being torn apart by a split between the Hashemites and the rest did not worry him unduly. His worry was that by being the first

---

[51] Furlonge to Dow, 2 Apr. 1951, FO 371/91184, PRO.
[52] Dow to Furlonge, 13 Apr. 1951, FO 371/91184, PRO.
[53] Stevenson to Bevin, 6 Mar. 1951, FO 371/91184, PRO.

to make peace with Israel, Egypt would secure the bulk of the concessions that Israel would be prepared to make to obtain a settlement. Jordan would then lose her trump card in her dealings with Israel. Helm therefore still maintained that Britain's interest required that Jordan should be the first Arab state to make peace with Israel: 'She is our friend, she needs peace with Israel, King Abdullah and his present Prime Minister want to make it, and I think we should try to ensure that she rather than Egypt gets the pickings.'

Helm also believed that it was in Britain's power to bring about a Jordanian–Israeli settlement. He realized that Abdullah and Samir were afraid of the Arab League and that there was opposition within Jordan itself. Nevertheless, he felt that both would weigh less at Amman if Britain were to actively support King Abdullah in a policy of peace with Israel and let this be known to the other Arab states.[54]

Helm returned to the charge that Britain was not doing enough to moderate the Arabs and prepare the way for peace. He had a conversation with Shiloah towards the end of June. Shiloah seemed to feel the pinch of isolation and spoke in a pessimistic vein about the future. Helm found much food for thought in his remarks. One facet was the danger that those Israelis, like Shiloah, who had been working for peace with the Arabs would throw in their hand and let the wild men have their way. Another facet was the critique of the role played by Britain in the Arab world. Like Shiloah, Helm felt that Britain had been prodigal with pious advice when incidents happened or appeared about to happen but did little positive in the periods between. She did much less than she could have done to foster a peace mentality among the Arabs and this was all the more regrettable after the advance made with the Tripartite Declaration.[55]

There was one quality that Sir Knox Helm and Elias Sasson had in common and that was the capacity to confront honestly and critically the shortcomings exhibited by their own side. Sasson conceded that there was much truth in the charge that Israel was to blame for the failure to attain peace because she had no constructive Arab policy. Helm conceded that Britain had not acted as positively as she might have done to prepare the way for peace. Only King Abdullah's commitment and dedication to the cause of peace were beyond question. If there was any criticism of Abdullah, and there was no shortage of Arab critics, it was that he showed himself to be overzealous in his pursuit of peace with Israel.

---

[54] Helm to Bowker, 23 Mar. 1951, FO 371/91184, PRO.
[55] Id., 23 June 1951, FO 371/91368, PRO.

The murder of King Abdullah

In the last weeks of his life Abdullah was a lonely and disappointed man and may have even had a premonition of his approaching end. Three weeks before his death he invited an American officer of the Palestine Conciliation Commission named Fisher to his palace in Amman. Abdel Ghani Karmi acted as interpreter. After discussing certain specific aspects of Jordanian–Israeli relations, Abdullah asked Fisher to stay and talk to him about what he called 'a most personal and confidential problem which is breaking my heart'. This problem was that of peace with Israel. 'I am an old man', said Abdullah. 'I know that my power is limited; I know that I am hated by my own son . . . I also know that my own people distrust me because of my peace efforts. But despite all that, I know that I could get peace settled if I only had some encouragement and could get any reasonable concessions from Israel.'

Fisher pointed out to the 69-year-old monarch that it was unlikely that any Israeli government on the eve of general elections would be prepared to make concessions it had refused eighteen months previously. Abdullah agreed, but still wanted to raise the matter again after the elections if these should result in the establishment of a 'stable and sane Jewish government'. Fisher than asked what in the king's opinion would be the reaction of the Arab League and of his own government to such a move. The king declared that he and his government were prepared to defy the Arab League but 'we cannot defy my own people'. He said his own people distrusted him because they suspected him of wanting to make peace without any concessions by Israel. He emphasized that this was an obstacle which he could not overcome. 'Please understand', he said, 'that despite the Arab League I would have the support of my own people and the tacit support at least of the British if I could justify a peace by pointing to concessions made by the Jews. But without any concessions from them I am defeated before I even start.'

Elaborating on the concessions that might be required by Jordan, the king spoke of territorial adjustments in the Triangle or elsewhere and of a corridor to the Gaza Strip which would become Jordanian territory. Concerning the refugees he said he realized that wholesale repatriation or even complete compensation was impossible. But he expressed his conviction that the bitterness could be alleviated if the propertied refugees were permitted to go to Israel for a limited period to settle their affairs and if such refugees could get at least the income from their property, even if not the property itself. This and a partial release of the blocked accounts would make it possible for many to re-establish themselves elsewhere and to forget their bitterness.

The king ended the interview by saying 'Please help me. I can do it if I can get some help and encouragement. But I am an old man. I have not much time left and I don't want to die of a broken heart.' Fisher had had frequent opportunities for informal discussions with the king in the past but had not seen him for several months prior to this meeting and was struck by the fact that the latter had aged greatly and that his appeal both at the beginning and at the end of this confidential interview was almost an imploring one.[56]

It was not a broken heart that killed Abdullah but a bullet in the head. On Friday, 20 July 1951, he went to pray at the Al-Aksa Mosque in the Old City of Jerusalem, accompanied by his grandson, Husayn, and an Arab Legion bodyguard. They entered the vast courtyard surrounding the Muslim Holy Places just before twelve. First Abdullah visited the tomb of his father and then proceeded to the entrance of the Great Mosque where the Koran was being recited to about two thousand worshippers. As he stepped across the threshold, the old shaikh of the mosque, a venerable ecclesiastic with a long white beard, came forward to kiss his hand. The king's guard fell back and as they did so, a young man stepped out from behind the massive door of the Mosque, pressed a pistol to the king's ear and fired a solitary shot which killed him instantly. The king fell forward and his turban rolled away across the marble pavement. The murderer continued to fire left and right but was swiftly done to death by the frenzied royal bodyguard.[57]

The atmosphere in Jordan had reeked of murder and violence ever since the assassination of Riad al-Sulh, the former prime minister of Lebanon, a week earlier. Reports of plots against Abdullah's life added to the anxieties of the Jordanian authorities and led them to step up security precautions. Sir Alec Kirkbride begged the king not to go to Jerusalem but to pray at the mosque in Amman instead where he would be amidst his own people but came up against Abdullah's fatalism. He smiled and recited an old Arabic proverb, 'Until my day comes nobody can harm me: when the day comes nobody can guard me.'[58] The American minister, who had called on the king on the morning of his departure to urge him to refrain from visiting Jerusalem where disloyal elements were said to be plotting and agitating, met with a similarly fatalistic response.[59]

Nasir al-Din Nashashibi has hinted at British involvement in the murder of King Abdullah. Nashashibi, as his name indicates, is a Palestinian from the Nashashibi family. At the time of the murder he was personal secretary to King Abdullah and director of the Royal

[56] *FRUS 1951*, v. 735–7.   [57] Glubb, *A Soldier with the Arabs*, 276 f.
[58] Kirkbride, *From the Wings*, 131 f.
[59] Musa and Madi, *The History of Jordan in the Twentieth Century*, 552.

Broadcasting Corporation. Various statements are alleged by Nashashibi to have been made by the king in private shortly before his death about his hatred of the British, his refusal to forget how they had humiliated his father, their determination to keep Jordan small and dependent, and the proximity of the British minister's residence to the palace as a constant reminder of British occupation of the country.[60] But the theory that Britain was in some way implicated in the plot against Abdullah is completely without substance. Machinery for detecting crime and political intrigue scarcely existed in Jordan and there was no forewarning of the murder. Kirkbride had no specific information about a plot against the king but only a general feeling that stricter security arrangements and greater vigilance were needed to protect the king against his many enemies at a time of rising tension.

The real question is why, despite the pleas of Kirkbride and the American minister, Abdullah insisted on going to Jerusalem for noon prayers on Friday. Nashashibi's explanation is that the king regarded al-Sulh's assassination as being directed against the security and stability of the kingdom, and that by going to Jerusalem he wanted to demonstrate that he was not afraid and that he was still in charge of the entire kingdom, including the West Bank.[61]

There was one other reason for the king's determination to go to Jerusalem which only a handful of people knew about at the time and which has remained a closely guarded secret: the king had arranged to meet Reuven Shiloah and Moshe Sasson in the house of Abdel Ghani Karmi in Jerusalem on Saturday, July 21.[62] The contact with Israel was thus maintained, in face of all the opposition and the hazards involved, literally until the king's dying day.

Yet it would be erroneous to conclude that King Abdullah was assassinated just because of his contacts with the Israelis and because of his well-known desire to make peace with them. The real background to the murder was the long-standing rivalry between Abdullah and the Husaynis. It is true that his opponents were opposed to a settlement with Israel, but this was not their sole reason for instigating his murder. Political assassinations in the Arab world were common and they did not necessarily spring from conflict of opinion on the subject of relations with Israel.[63]

What made the assassination of King Abdullah all the more base and vile was that it was not only an act of political fanaticism but also the work of mercenaries trading on the Egyptian and Saudi interest in King Abdullah's death. Six of the eight accused were apprehended, tried by a special court, and hanged. All were either common criminals or former

---

[60] Nashashibi, *Who Killed King Abdullah?* 33–41.   [61] Ibid. 24.
[62] Interview with Moshe Sasson.   [63] Ibid.

terrorists and adherents of Hajj Amin al-Husayni. The murderer himself was a tailor's apprentice from Jerusalem with a criminal record and a member of the mufti's radical paramilitary organization Al-Jihad al-Muqqadas or Holy War. The chief instigator was Abdullah al-Tall who was not in the dock but at large in Cairo because the Egyptian authorities refused to extradite him. Tall's principal accomplice and the man who organized the assassination was Dr Musa al-Husayni, a relative of the mufti. Two other members of the powerful Husayni family were implicated in the conspiracy, one of them a member of the Arab Higher Committee that in 1948 had formed the All-Palestine government in Gaza. The Arab Higher Committee, however, dissociated itself from the murder after it had been committed by issuing a statement that neither the committee nor its president, Hajj Amin al-Husayni, were in any way responsible for or connected with the assassination of King Abdullah.[64]

Indeed, the assassination of King Abdullah was not part of a broad Palestinian bid to capture power in Jordan or to reverse Jordanian foreign policy. The conspirators did not propose to renew the war against Israel. Some of them were moved by the dream of an independent, resurgent, Arab Palestine, and by the fear of further Jewish advances at the cost of the Palestinian Arabs which the British-controlled Arab Legion might be either unable or unwilling to prevent. It was significant that all the conspirators, except Abdullah al-Tall, were Palestinian Arabs who belonged to the mufti's camp. But although all the signs seemed to point to the shadowy figure of the mufti, no evidence was discovered of his direct complicity in the murder.

Many of the findings of the commission of inquiry into the events surrounding King Abdullah's death were revealed to Moshe Sasson by Ahmad Bey al-Khalil, the governor of Arab Jerusalem and Jordan's delegate to the Mixed Armistice Commission. According to this account, the murderer had accomplices who helped him to plan the crime, supplied him with the revolver, and paid him for his deed. Dr Musa al-Husayni, head of the group in Jerusalem who was personally responsible for planning, financing, and executing the crime, confessed that he was in contact with Abdullah al-Tall who had instigated the murder from Cairo, and there was documentary evidence bearing this out. Husayni justified his action by saying that in his view and that of Abdullah al-Tall, King Abdullah was responsible for the Arab defeat in the war against the Jews; he was a traitor who served the interests of the British; and the peace that he was on the point of making with Israel

---

[64] Werner Ernest Goldner, 'The Role of Abdullah Ibn Husain, King of Jordan, in Arab Politics, 1914–1951', Ph.D. thesis (Stanford, 1954), 304–7.

would have removed any chance of realizing the aspirations of the Palestinians.

It emerged that a sum of £P 60,000 or £P 70,000 had been placed at al-Tall's disposal to finance the assassination. Most of this sum was taken by al-Tall for himself, some of it was given to Dr Musa al-Husayni, and a small fraction was spent on the murder itself. Although no evidence had emerged to suggest personal intervention by the mufti, the investigators were convinced that Husayni and al-Tall had only carried out an idea that came from higher up, and it was assumed that the mufti, King Ibn Saud, and Egypt had all played a part in instigating and financing the murder.[65]

Abdullah's death evoked very different reactions from various individuals, groups, and countries. The majority of the inhabitants of Arab Jerusalem barely concealed their joy at the murder of Abdullah— 'the dog who sold Palestine to the Zionists'. The mufti's name was on everybody's lips. Most people liked Prince Talal, Abdullah's heir, because of his patriotic views and because he had shown courage in standing up to his father and to Glubb. It was believed that he would co-operate with the mufti in the struggle to liberate the whole of Palestine. Nayef, the younger brother and son of a Turkish woman, was regarded as no better than the father.[66]

News of the death of the leader of the Hashemite bloc was also received with glee in the non-Hashemite Arab countries and provoked a frenetic spate of inter-Arab intrigues, dynastic rivalries, and jockeying for power. Nuri al-Said launched his bid for union between Jordan and Iraq under the Iraqi crown at Abdullah's funeral. He backed the pretensions of Nayef against the legitimate heir Talal, who was undergoing psychiatric treatment in Switzerland, and he sided with Tawfiq Abul Huda against Samir Rifai, who had tendered his resignation a few days after the murder. The Egyptian Legation in Amman started agitating for the independence of Arab Palestine under a mandate from the Arab League, while the Saudi legation pressed for partition of the whole kingdom, the northern part going to Syria and the southern part to Saudi Arabia.[67]

In British official circles there was genuine regret at the death of a loyal friend, a desire to preserve the integrity of the kingdom, and a fear that Palestinian influence would make Jordan more nationalistic and pull her away from the Western camp. Prime Minister Attlee told the House of Commons that 'Great Britain has lost a trusted friend and

---

[65] Information for Israeli Missions Abroad, no. 335, In the Kingdom of Jordan, 13 Aug. 1951, 2408/11, ISA.

[66] Research Department, Foreign Ministry. Information on Events in Jordan, 2 Aug. 1951, 2408/11, ISA.

[67] *FRUS 1951*, v. 993 f.

ally. His was no fair weather loyalty. He stood by us in all circumstances and came unhesitatingly to our aid when it seemed that we had little to rely upon except our own faith in our survival.' Winston Churchill recalled with pride the part he had played in appointing Abdullah as amir of Transjordan and described him as 'a skilled and consistent worker for the peace and prosperity of that part of the world and for the interests and honour of the Arab peoples wherever they may be'.[68]

The question of Jordan's viability without Abdullah was raised in an acute form since it was the most artificial of the post-First World War experiments in state-building. Some British officials were apprehensive that the scaffolding of the Jordan state might crack and advocated a union with Iraq. Kirkbride argued that union would never work and challenged the proposition that Jordan on her own would be viable neither economically nor politically. No one underestimated the gravity of the crisis for, in the words of Sir John Troutbeck:

The principal prop has been eliminated. The sudden removal of King Abdullah upon whom we placed so great a reliance for our whole policy in the Arab world is surely bound to have serious repercussions. . . . It is not merely 'one Arab ruler' who has been eliminated but the man who held his country together almost single-handed and was at the same time our staunchest supporter in the whole area.[69]

In official Israeli circles the reaction to Abdullah's assassination was one of profound shock and concern for the future. Abdullah's assassination was generally considered a serious blow to Israel since he was seen as the closest thing to a friend of Israel among the Arab leaders. No one felt the blow more acutely than Elias Sasson; he described Abdullah's disappearance from the political scene as a grave loss to Jordan, to the Arab world, to the Western world, and to Israel. As he wrote to his superiors,

King Abdullah was the only Arab statesman who showed an understanding for our national renewal, a sincere desire to come to a settlement with us, and a realistic attitude to most of our demands and arguments. It is also a fact that King Abdullah, despite being an Arab nationalist and a Muslim zealot, knew how to look with an open and penetrating eye on events and on the progress of the world in different spheres and to adapt his private life and the life of his country. He also served as the trumpet announcing these changes to the members of his nation and religion wherever they might be, in a pleasant, moderate, and logical tone. We as well as some of the Arabs and foreigners are going to feel for a long time to come his absence, and to regret more than a little his removal from our midst.[70]

---

[68] Hansard, 23 July 1951.   [69] Louis, *The British Empire in the Middle East*, 628–31.
[70] E. Sasson to W. Eytan, 21 July 1951, 2408/11, ISA.

Moshe Sasson gave a sober analysis of the likely consequences of the removal for Israel. 'The murder of Abdullah', wrote Sasson junior, 'brought to a tragic end the process that we called "the sinking of Abdullah's regime".' Sasson did not wish to speculate on the question of which would have been preferable—the slow death of a regime that was full of genuine desires and faint hopes for peace with Israel, or the sudden end that wrenched Israel back from the world of mutual desires to the world of mutual capabilities and possibilities. What Sasson saw very clearly was that with Abdullah's death the political centre of gravity would shift further away from the royal court to the government and the House of Representatives. In the Arab arena Sasson predicted that the removal of the head of the house of Hashem and the strengthening of the Egyptian bloc in the Arab League would lead to greater co-operation, if not actual union, between the two Hashemite countries.

In the new Jordanian and inter-Arab constellation it would no longer be possible, thought Sasson, to continue with an approach which was based on the declared desire for peace but evaded the concrete problems that called for a solution, like the refugee problem. Progress towards a settlement would depend on Israel's ability to find real solutions to the fundamental problems in her relations with the country with which she shared the longest of her borders.[71]

In political circles the reaction to Abdullah's death was much less measured. The crisis and the possibility that Jordan would be incorporated into Iraq revived the Revisionist Zionists' claim to the whole of western Palestine. The crisis also whetted David Ben-Gurion's appetite for expansion—not altogether surprisingly since when it came to dealing with the Arabs, he had more in common with Zeev Jabotinsky and Menachem Begin than he did with the moderates inside his own party. Until 1951 he accepted the territorial status quo or at any rate did nothing deliberately to disturb it. Abdullah's death marked a turning point in his thinking. He concluded that peace with the Arabs could not be attained by negotiation; they would have to be deterred, coerced, and intimidated. In addition, he no longer saw any compelling reason why Israel should not extend her borders to the Jordan to give herself more land and strategic depth, and to rectify the mistake of late 1948 which he had termed a cause for weeping for generations.

Thus, on hearing the news of Abdullah's assassination, Ben-Gurion's attitude changed with dramatic suddenness. The chief of staff was ill, so Ben-Gurion summoned his deputy, Gen. Mordechai Makleff, early in the morning of July 21 and asked what trained and

---

[71] Information to Israeli Missions Abroad, no. 335, 'In the Kingdom of Jordan', 13 Aug. 1951, 2408/11, ISA.

armed forces could be despatched to capture the territory up to the Jordan in the event of Abdullah's legacy being annexed by Iraq. Makleff replied that they had three brigades and five battalions, and that at four days' notice they could mobilize seven or eight brigades, field artillery, and two air force squadrons. He added that this force would be sufficient to capture the territory, and that they had adequate reserves for protecting their borders with Syria and Egypt.

Not content with the contingency plan to capture the West Bank, Ben-Gurion began to consider the possibility of seizing the entire Sinai Peninsula, all the way up to the Suez Canal. Later in the day he had a visit from Benjamin Akzin, a former secretary to Zeev Jabotinsky and a professor of political science at the Hebrew University of Jerusalem. Akzin gave Ben-Gurion the idea of an approach to Britain to suggest the expulsion of the Egyptians from Sinai to make way for British bases there and to turn the Suez Canal into an international waterway. At the same time it could be suggested to Britain that Israel's border should be the Jordan, while Britain took Transjordan. Alternatively, a partition along these lines could be proposed to Syria. Before leaving, Akzin invited the prime minister to lecture at the university on the nature of statecraft or to give the comments of a modern statesman on Plato's classic treatise, *The Republic*.[72] Comments on Machiavelli's *The Prince* would have been more in keeping with the theme of the preceding conversation between the political theorist and the statesman.

The more Ben-Gurion thought about the idea of capturing Sinai with the help of the British the more he liked it, especially since the Sinai Peninsula, unlike the West Bank, was not densely populated with Arabs. Two days later he presented the idea to Moshe Sharett and Reuven Shiloah. Sharett suggested that they serve notice on Britain and America that a change in the status quo would raise grave questions. Ben-Gurion replied that the status quo had already been changed: Nayef was not Abdullah or even his rightful heir, and the Arab League supported Talal's claim to succeed Abdullah. Instead, he said,

First of all we must talk to Britain, because Britain needs us now in the Middle East. The trouble is that Morrison is a fox and is not to be trusted. Nor does he grasp the affairs of the Arab world. The ground should be tested in a conversation with Churchill—he has vision and he knows the Arab world and us. It should be explained to him that we must reach the Jordan, and possibly Suez too, and turn the canal into an international canal. America is squeezing England out of Iran and is liable to do the same in the Arab countries, and there is a common interest with the English.

If Churchill was receptive, Herbert Morrison could be approached

---

[72] Ben-Gurion's diary, 21 July 1951.

later. Ben-Gurion thought it would be better if the approach to Churchill came not from Israel but from an English Jew. Shiloah suggested Isaiah Berlin, the eminent Oxford philosopher and admirer of Churchill, and it was decided to invite Berlin to go to Israel immediately to be briefed for this delicate mission.[73]

But Isaiah Berlin was unable to go to Israel and Shiloah was sent to London instead. He spoke to a number of people but their reaction to Ben-Gurion's plan was less than enthusiastic. 'In the Foreign Office', reported Shiloah, 'no appreciable change has taken place yet, they do not hate us as much as they used to, but there is a desire to appease the Arabs. In army circles the attitude is better . . . they are angry with Egypt, they know that the Arabs are of no military value, they talk about Turkey and Israel in one breath, but it has not come yet to a fundamental change of attitude.'[74] Ben-Gurion had to abandon the idea of Sinai until five years later, and the capture of both Sinai and the West Bank was left to Ben-Gurion's successors sixteen years later.

The fatal shot at the entrance to the Great Mosque thus had a definite impact on the association between the ruler of Transjordan and the Zionist movement that had endured, despite all the strains and stresses, for thirty years. The fear that Abdullah's death would precipitate a violent change in Jordan's attitude to Israel turned out to be misplaced. Talal did not harbour in his heart the same deep yearning for peace with Israel as his father had, but his government, headed by Tawfiq Abul Huda, was careful to observe the armistice agreement. The new government made it clear that it would abandon Abdullah's efforts to realize the Greater Syria scheme and that it would not continue his policy of seeking a bilateral settlement with Israel.[75] But it had no wish to renew the war against Israel or to prepare actively for the second round. Thus the special relationship between the Hashemites and the Zionists survived the death of its most dedicated proponent, though not entirely intact.

[73] Ben-Gurion's diary, 23 July 1951.
[74] Ben-Gurion's diary, 1 and 18 Aug. 1951; Bar-Zohar, *Ben-Gurion*, ii. 907 f.
[75] *FRUS 1951*, v. 990 f.

20

CONCLUSIONS

The relations between Abdullah Ibn Husayn and the Zionist movement occupy a special place in the long and troubled history of
Palestine. Two national movements competed for possession of
Palestine during the first half of the twentieth century: the Palestinian
national movement led by Hajj Amin al-Husayni and the Jewish
national movement led by Chaim Weizmann and later David Ben-
Gurion. Whereas all the other Arab states sided with the Palestine
Arabs in their conflict with Jews, Abdullah pursued a policy of
collaboration with the enemy. The Jewish aim in relation to the rulers
of all the surrounding Arab countries was to obtain their support for the
Zionist enterprise or at least to deny their support to the Palestine
Arabs. The general Arab consensus was for keeping Palestine in Arab
hands and for resisting Jewish intrusion into the country.

Agreement to a Jewish national home in Palestine, always a euphemism for a Jewish state, would have thus constituted a serious deviation
from the general Arab consensus. For Arab rulers the price for such
deviation was therefore extremely high and likely to lead to loss of
power, while the rewards they could expect were extremely meagre.
The one exception was Abdullah Ibn Husayn. For him the price of co-
operation with the Zionist movement was tolerable—at any rate it was
a price he was prepared to pay—while the rewards were extremely
high, or so they seemed to him. The upshot was that the salient feature
of the relations between the Zionist movement and the other Arabs was
conflict, whereas the salient feature of the relations between the Zionist
movement and Abdullah was co-operation. It was this co-operation
that, more than any other factor, eventually determined the fate of
Palestine.

The political relationship between Transjordan and the Zionist
movement was special in more ways than one. It was a relationship
based on one man—Abdullah. It is no accident that the subtitle of this
book speaks not of Transjordan and the Zionist movement but of King
Abdullah and the Zionist movement. For it was not the amirate of
Transjordan or the Hashemite Kingdom of Jordan but the ruler of this
kingdom who alone was responsible for the formulation and conduct of
policy towards the Jewish community in Palestine and later the State of

Israel. Other individuals and institutions, like the government and Parliament, were involved, but usually either as servants and emissaries of the king or as a pressure group working against him. The policy itself always originated with the king, who as far as possible also kept the actual conduct of relations in his own hands. There was thus an assymetry between the two sides: on the Jordanian side policy was made by an absolute ruler; on the Israeli side there was a more democratic and institutionalized process of decision-making involving a government with collective responsibility and a modern civilian and military bureaucracy charged with the conduct of policy on a day-to-day basis.

The Jewish leaders, for their part, were acutely aware that in their relations with their neighbour to the east they depended almost entirely on one individual and they regretted that it proved impossible to develop normal state-to-state relations even after both countries had attained formal independence. But for the most part they accepted this exclusive link with the royal court as an unfortunate fact of life. Typical of this attitude was a comment made by Ben-Gurion in a consultation on Arab policy held after the Egyptian revolution of July 1952. 'We did have one man' recalled Ben-Gurion, 'about whom we knew that he wanted peace with Israel, and we tried to negotiate with him, but the British interfered, until a bullet came and put an end to business. With the removal of the Abdullah factor, the whole matter was finished.'[1]

Throughout Abdullah's political career, he remained the decisive factor if not the only one in the making of Jordan's foreign policy in general and in her policy towards the Jewish community in Palestine in particular. Four fundamental factors shaped Abdullah's attitude towards the Zionist movement. First and foremost was his political ambition. There was a huge disproportion between the dream nursed by the Hashemites during the First World War, of forming and leading an independent Arab empire, and the settlement foisted on the Middle East by the Great Powers following the dissolution of the Ottoman Empire. No other Hashemite felt more thwarted and frustrated than Abdullah. The amirate of Transjordan was a very poor consolation for the failure to realize his far-reaching political aspirations. In the apt words of a contemporary, he was a falcon trapped in a canary's cage. No sooner installed as the amir of Transjordan than he began the struggle to break out of the cage and to enlarge his territories and his political power base. His aim was a Greater Syria that would include Transjordan, Syria, Lebanon, and Palestine under his leadership. He worked towards this end consistently and indefatigably through a

---

[1] Israel and the Arab States, a consultation in the Prime Minister's office, 1 Oct. 1952, 2446/7, ISA.

network of agents and sympathizers in all the countries concerned but his efforts were not crowned with success. In the aftermath of the Second World War he lowered his sights to a merger between Transjordan and Palestine under his crown. Palestine was his last hope of turning his impoverished and peripheral desert kingdom into an entity of real weight in regional politics. He yearned for the possession of the whole of Palestine and offered the Jews autonomy within a united kingdom; when they turned down his offer he lowered his sights further still to the annexation of only the Arab part of Palestine.

The second factor that influenced Abdullah's attitude to the Zionist movement was his estrangement from his Arab environment. Although Abdullah had been in the vanguard of the struggle for Arab independence as one of the commanders of the Arab Revolt, he had progressively alienated the Arab nationalists by his subservience to Britain, and the rest by his schemes for territorial expansion and regional hegemony. His most immediate enemy was Hajj Amin al-Husayni for though they shared a conservative social, political, and religious outlook, each one of them wanted to be the ruler of Palestine. King Abdul Aziz Ibn Saud, who had expelled the Hashemites from Saudi Arabia, was a sworn enemy of Abdullah, and the dynastic rivalry between them was deepened by Abdullah's well-known dream of reconquering the ancestral kingdom of the Hijaz. King Farouk of Egypt was in direct competition with Abdullah for leadership of the Arab world, while Syria and Lebanon regarded the Greater Syria scheme as a threat not just to the status quo in the Arab world but to their own independence. One of the few things that united the Arabs, with the partial exception of the Iraqis, was in fact their fear of and contempt for Abdullah.

A third factor that impinged on Abdullah's relations with Zionists as well as fellow Arabs was the British connection. Britain established the amirate of Transjordan as part of the Sharifian policy devised by Churchill after the First World War and she continued to exercise a controlling influence long after the grant of formal independence in 1946. For Abdullah the British connection was both a source of strength and a major constraint. Without the financial subsidy from the British Exchequer and the British contribution in personnel, equipment, and training to the Arab Legion, his kingdom would have scarcely been viable. But this very dependence on Britain also meant that Abdullah had to defer to British advice. It seriously curtailed his freedom of action on matters of real importance, like Greater Syria and Palestine.

Finally, Abdullah's general attitude to the Jews had some influence on his political relationship with the Zionist movement. Through co-operation with the Jews, Abdullah hoped to reduce his dependence on Britain and to strengthen his position *vis-à-vis* his numerous Arab opponents. Like other Arab leaders, Abdullah regarded Zionism as a powerful international force with financial resources, propaganda skills, and diplomatic leverage that the Arabs could not hope to match. Unlike other Arab leaders, he had no compunction about using the resources of Zionism to further his own ends. He was not infected by the visceral hatred of Jews and Zionism that were so common among the Arabs. On the contrary, his attitude was open-minded, flexible, and pragmatic. To him the Jews, with their energy, scientific knowledge, and organizational skills, represented a positive force for progress. He greatly admired their achievements in building for themselves a national home and saw no reason why their skills and energy could not be harnessed to the development of his own country. There was one other important motive for Abdullah's openness to the Jews: he hoped to obtain the financial assistance of which he personally as well as his country were in dire need. It was in the hope of boosting his income and in order to procure Jewish capital and Jewish skills for the development of his country that Abdullah offered to lease his land to the Jewish Agency in the early 1930s.

The heads of the Jewish Agency, for their part, were not slow to recognize the value of Abdullah's friendship in breaking through the wall of Arab hostility and gaining legitimacy for their programme. Although the negotiations for Jewish settlement on the amir's lands in Transjordan were aborted by Palestinian and British opposition, the Jewish Agency continued to pay for the option on the lease in what amounted to a covert financial subsidy to lubricate the relations with the amir and his aides. The officials of the Jewish Agency were very diligent in cultivating the friendship of the amir and his entourage and from this source they also obtained valuable information about Transjordan, about Arab politics, and about British policy in the Middle East. Yet the amount of money actually given by the Jewish Agency to the impecunious but prodigal amir was trifling. It was canary feed and totally out of proportion with the risk that Abdullah had to assume in exposing himself to the charge of selling out Palestine for Jewish money and favours.

Despite the limitations of his position, despite his dependence on Britain, and despite his unpopularity in the Arab world, Abdullah was a very welcome and important ally to the Jewish Agency. There were several reasons for this. First of all there was Abdullah's political realism that enabled him to see the correlation of forces between the Zionist movement and its opponents much more clearly than the other Arab leaders and made him more amenable to compromise. In particular he realized that the power of the Jewish community was increasing during the 1930s and 1940s while that of the Palestinian community was waning and that consequently he himself could achieve more by co-operating with the Jewish community than by fighting it. Secondly, there was the geographic proximity of Transjordan to the main centres of Arab population in Nablus, Jerusalem, and Hebron. Thirdly, the Arab Legion was superior to all the other Arab armies in terms of discipline, training, equipment, and combat ability. It was not all that small either by Middle Eastern standards and it was much more conveniently positioned for gaining control over the strategically vital hill country of western Palestine. Neutralizing the Arab Legion was a major aim of Zionist diplomacy and it assumed an even greater importance when the struggle for Palestine began in earnest following the announcement of the British decision to surrender the mandate.

As one international inquiry followed another in rapid succession, and as one plan after another fell by the wayside, the friendly relations between the Jewish Agency and Abdullah developed into a political and strategic partnership. The Jewish Agency had achieved a breakthrough in Egypt but the fall from power of Ismail Sidqi in 1946 put an end to the hope of Egyptian support for the partition of Palestine and marked the beginning of the Abdullah era in Zionist diplomacy. At two meetings in August 1946 Elias Sasson prepared the ground for closer co-operation and on the second occasion he handed over £5,000 in cash, which Abbdullah mistakenly assumed would be followed by further and larger payments.

A few days before the United Nations pronounced its verdict in favour of the partition of Palestine into separate Jewish and Arab states, Abdullah had his first meeting with Golda Meir. This meeting, at which a firm agreement was reached on another kind of partition, under which the Arab part of Palestine was earmarked for annexation by Transjordan, was the point of maximum understanding between the two sides about the future of Palestine. From this point on Abdullah concentrated his efforts on preparing the ground for the occupation of western Palestine by the Arab Legion, on gaining Arab approval for such a move, and on persuading the British to back his plan.

Success in getting Britain's agreement to the occupation of central Palestine by the Arab Legion was finally achieved at the meeting between Prime Minister Tawfiq Abul Huda and Ernest Bevin in February 1948. Britain never really believed that partition would work and repeatedly stated that she would not help to enforce any plan that was not acceptable to both sides. But nor did Britain welcome the prospect of an undignified Arab scramble for Palestine. The most promising solution, indeed the only one, was that Abdullah should annex the residue of Palestine after the establishment of a Jewish state, and that the facilities enjoyed by Britain under the treaty with Transjordan should extend to the new territories. Britain was careful not to get involved in active collusion with Abdullah in frustrating the United Nations partition scheme and gave only implicit agreement to Abdullah's plan. The point of the agreement was not to prevent the birth of a Palestinian state, since by that time it was clear that the Palestinian leaders were not prepared to set up a state in part of Palestine, but to prevent the Jews from occupying the whole of Palestine. One thing is clear in any case and that is that Britain had no intention of preventing the birth of a Jewish state. Thus Bevin, who is usually portrayed in Zionist accounts of this period as the great ogre who unleashed the Arab armies to strangle the Jewish state at birth, emerges from the documents as the guardian angel of the infant state. It was not encouragement to do battle that Bevin conveyed to Abdullah through his prime minister but a clear warning not to cross the borders of the Jewish state as laid down in the United Nations partition plan.

At this stage the British expected and encouraged a 'clean' partition of Palestine between their protégé and the Jews. This was also the preference of the parties to the active collusion. Ben-Gurion assumed that the Yishuv did not have sufficient military power at its disposal to conquer the whole of Palestine and strongly preferred Abdullah as a neighbour to the uncompromising Palestinian Arab leadership. Abdullah also expected an orderly and peaceful partition of Palestine with the Jews, and this was not an unrealistic expectation on his part since the other Arab states were opposed at this time to intervention by their regular armies.

What changed the situation radically was the disintegration of the Palestinian community and the eclipse of its military forces. Divided internally, betrayed by their leaders and let down by the Arab League, the Arabs of Palestine lost the unofficial war which was provoked by the passage of the UN partition resolution. After successfully waging guerrilla warfare in the first stage of this war, they fell into disarray and suffered a series of military defeats that helped to set in train the mass exodus of the civilian population from Palestine. The Jews meanwhile recovered from their initial setbacks and embarked on a vigorous military offensive which looked likely to sweep them well beyond the borders laid down by the United Nations. Riding the wave of military successes, the Jews neglected to maintain their contact with Abdullah and were definitely unwilling to settle for less than the territory allocated to them by the United Nations.

Abdullah was alarmed by the Deir Yassin massacre, by the growing flood of Arab refugees arriving in Jordan, and by the desperate appeals for protection from the Arabs who were holding on in the face of intense Jewish military pressure. He was also caught up in the whirlwind of Arab pressures to commit his army to the fight against the Jews. Abdullah's public denunciation of the Jews became so bellicose that they suspected him of reneging on the promises he had made to Golda Meir in November 1947. A last-minute effort was made to restore Abdullah to the path of co-operation by sending Mrs Meir to Amman three days before the expiry of the British mandate and the proclamation of the State of Israel. But by this time it was too late to reverse the trend for intervention in Palestine by the regular armies of the Arab states, with the Hashemite armies at their head.

Abdullah's aim remained the same; it was circumstances that had changed since his previous meeting with Mrs Meir. He still wanted to occupy only the part of Palestine that was contiguous with his territory; he still regarded the Palestinian national movement and its leaders as the principal obstacle to the realization of his plan; and he had no intention of getting side-tracked into a full-scale war against the Jews that could only benefit his Palestinian rivals.

Abdullah also realized that the other Arab rulers had decided on the invasion of Palestine not only because of the danger of a Jewish state but because they were opposed to his own plan and feared that the annexation of Palestine would embolden him to try to realize his older ambition of Greater Syria and of Hashemite hegemony in the Arab world. This is why he insisted on being given overall command of the invading armies and immediately used, or rather abused, this position to wreck the invasion plan that had been prepared by the Arab League's military experts.

Of all the Arab participants in the 1948 war, only Abdullah had clearly thought out goals that did not overstep the means at his disposal and a flexible strategy for overcoming the numerous obstacles that stood in his way. By the end of the first week of fighting he had secured his basic objective of occupying central Palestine. He was careful not to trespass on the territory of the Jewish state. After the invasion, the Arab Legion was deployed in defensive positions in the purely Arab areas adjacent to the Jordan. The only major clash between the Arab Legion and the Israeli army occurred in Jerusalem, outside the territory officially recognized as part of the Jewish state, where the Jews had been the aggressors. Despite this clash, the general strategic picture was characterized by limited objectives and mutual restraint on the part of the Jordanian and the Israeli war leaders.

During the ten days' fighting in July both leaders signalled by their behaviour that they still wished to abide by the strategic accord that had momentarily been unhinged by the resort to war. The collapse of the ramshackle Arab coalition during this period restored Abdullah's diplomatic freedom of action, and a month later direct contact with the Israelis was resumed. Through this secret channel Abdullah cunningly arranged to remain neutral when Israel attacked the Egyptian army in the south towards the end of 1948 and this channel was used again to secure the withdrawal of the Iraqi army from the West Bank early in the following year.

During the armistice negotiations the Israelis exerted strong pressure on Abdullah to cede some of the territory previously held by the Iraqis, yet they were careful not to cross the threshold between coercive diplomacy and the actual resort to force. Tough bargaining took place but in the end the Israelis obtained the areas that were of vital strategic importance to them without breaking the unwritten rules of the game. By stopping short of a challenge to Abdullah's principal gain from the war—the possession of central Palestine—they made it easier for him to yield on matters of secondary importance.

In the final reckoning the Palestine Arabs were the principal losers in the 1948 war, while the Israelis and Abdullah were the principal beneficiaries. Collusion across the Jordan had yielded tangible rewards. Both sides emerged from the war in better shape and with greater assets than they had at the outbreak of the war. The Israelis had not only consolidated their independence but also enlarged the boundaries of their state. Abdullah had won additional land and population that went some way towards fulfilling his ambition of a Greater Transjordan. Abdullah's achievements seem all the greater when his position is compared with that of the other Arab states and that of the Palestinian leadership at the end of the war.

The end of the war brought no respite from the endemic inter-Arab rivalries that were in large measure responsible for the Palestine catastrophe; indeed, they intensified in the aftermath of the war. Unable to close ranks in face of the bittter consequences of defeat, the Arabs indulged in mutual recriminations and a search for scapegoats that further weakened their position in the diplomatic negotiations that followed the war. Abdullah was singled out for the most vituperative attacks because he had accepted partition, because he was willing to trade on Palestinian rights, and because he was widely suspected of conspiring with the enemy against his fellow Arabs. Though he had done well out of the war, Abdullah was thus doomed to spend the closing years of his reign in bitter conflict with his fellow Arabs.

Undeterred by Arab opposition, Abdullah embarked on negotiations with Israel. These negotiations reached a climax in February 1950 with the initialling of a peace treaty by the authorized representatives of the two sides, but by this time his isolation was so complete that he was unable to prevail on his own government to ratify the treaty. A further complicating factor was the annexation of Arab Palestine which was enshrined in the Act of Union in April 1950. Only Britain and Pakistan recognized the Union. The Arab League was resolutely opposed to it and now condemned him for the annexation of Arab Palestine as well as his negotiations with Israel. With his customary realism, Abdullah estimated that he could not simultaneously defy the Arab League on both issues. So he agreed to suspend the negotiations with Israel in order to secure the League's tacit consent to the annexation of Arab Palestine.

Although Abdullah's long-term plan was to resume negotiations with Israel after consolidating his hold over the new territories, his relations with Israel gradually lost their momentum and their vitality. This was reflected in the lowering of the objective which the negotiations, once resumed, were designed to achieve. Not full peace but a non-aggression pact was the object of the negotiations in the second half of 1950. When this proved unattainable the aim was lowered yet again to full implementation of the Rhodes armistice agreement, but even this modest aim had not been achieved by the time of the king's death.

Two principal factors were responsible for the failure of the post-war negotiations: Israel's strength and Abdullah's weakness. Israel's resounding military victory in the first full-scale confrontation with all the surrounding Arab states lessened her interest in accommodation and compromise. So confident was the fledgling Jewish state in her military superiority over the Arabs that her willingness to make concessions for the sake of a settlement of the conflict was seriously curtailed. The armistice agreements were thought to meet Israel's essential need for recognition, security, and legitimacy. Consequently, Israel adopted a tough stance, offering little by way of concessions to the Arabs and insisting that peace be based substantially on the territorial status quo and without repatriation of the Arab refugees. Such a stance compounded by hypocrisy and double-dealing, was bound to have a negative effect on the negotiations with Abdullah. It confirmed the general Arab belief in Israeli intransigence and made it difficult for Abdullah to sustain his line of argument that the right way to deal with Israel was by negotiation rather than confrontation. He was sincere beyond question in his offer of peace and he deserved a less cavalier treatment than he got. The risks he took upon himself and the courage he displayed in swimming against the current made the treatment he received from the Israeli leaders all the more astonishing. There was always a tendency among them to underrate and belittle Abdullah, but as their power and self-confidence increased, so did their disregard for him, a revealing example of which was Ben-Gurion's refusal to meet him face to face.

Another contributory factor in the failure to achieve peace between Israel and Jordan was what the Israelis themselves termed the sinking of Abdullah's regime. By extending his dominion to include western Palestine, Abdullah himself helped to unleash forces that ended up by eroding his previously absolute personal rule. In the new political constellation following the merger, he could no longer lay down the law in the arbitrary fashion to which he was accustomed but had to take account of public opinion, of the feelings of his Palestinian subjects, of Parliament, and above all of the growing opposition among his own ministers to his policy of peace with Israel. His commitment to peace was unaffected by the new setting but his ability to give practical expression to this commitment was seriously diminished.

For his desire to make peace with Israel, Abdullah paid with his life. But he left behind him a legacy of moderation and realism that continued to govern Jordanian foreign policy during the brief inter-regnum of his son Talal and the much longer reign of his grandson Husayn. It was no accident that Jordan stayed out of the Suez War in 1956, the War of Attrition in 1969–70, the October War of 1973, and the Lebanon War of 1982. It was a peculiar concatenation of circumstances that forced King Husayn against his better judgement to throw in his lot with the other Arabs in June 1967, and the penalty he had to pay for this was the loss to Israel of the West Bank of the Hashemite Kingdom of Jordan which his grandfather had secured in the 1948 war.

Israel's foreign policy, too, has shown a not-so-secret bias in favour of the Hashemite monarchs of Jordan. After the shock of King Abdullah's death, and after its hopes that the Egyptian Revolution of 1952 would pave the way to peace were dashed, the Hashemite orientation gradually reasserted itself in Israel's foreign policy. In June 1967 Israel went to war not with an expansionist design to conquer the West Bank but in self-defence. Even as the war was being waged, both sides hoped for early reconciliation. After the war the Israelis contacted King Husayn to explore the possibilities of a settlement. The ruling Labour Party adhered to a 'Jordanian option' which signified preference for a peace settlement with Jordan based on a territorial compromise to a settlement with the Palestinians of the West Bank, whose claim to an independent state of their own was now rejected with the same vehemence with which the Palestinians had rejected the Jewish claim to statehood before 1948. King Husayn accepted the invitation to hold parleys behind the veil of secrecy and over the next ten years he had frequent meetings with senior Israelis, including Abba Eban, Moshe Dayan, Yigal Allon, Yitzhak Rabin, and Shimon Peres. With Golda

Meir, King Husayn allegedly met ten times when she was prime minister—five times as often as his grandfather. At these meetings King Husayn told the Israelis that he was prepared to have normal, peaceful relations with them provided they restored all the territory they had captured from Jordan in the course of the June War. He rejected the Allon Plan for keeping strategic points on the West Bank in Israeli hands while returning the heavily populated areas to Jordan.[2] With the Likud ministers headed by Menachem Begin who rose to power in 1977 there was no basis even for a dialogue, for they regarded Jordan as a Palestinian state and insisted on keeping the whole of the West Bank as an integral part of the Land of Israel.

The early contacts between the amir of Transjordan and the Jewish Agency can thus be seen to have given birth to a unique and fascinating bilateral relationship revolving around the problem of Palestine. This complex and many-sided relationship has been punctuated by endless ups and downs, by crises and misunderstandings, by discord as well as collaboration. Yet, for good or ill, it has been and is likely to remain a critical if not the critical factor in determining the fate of Palestine. The collusion across the Jordan that gave rise to the partition of Palestine between the Hashemites and the Zionists in 1948 has become a more or less permanent feature of the rugged political landscape of the Middle East.

[2] Dan Raviv and Yossi Melman, 'Hussein's Secret Peace Path', *Observer*, 10 May 1987.

APPENDIX 1

Agreement Between the Hashimite Jordan Kingdom and the State of Israel, 23 March 1949

The undersigned duly authorised by their respective Governments have reached the following agreement:

1. Israel agrees to the taking over by the Arab Legion of the Iraqi front.

2. The demarcation line between the armed forces of the parties to this agreement shall be as marked on the map annexed hereto.

3. Establishment of the line described in Article 2 shall be effected in accordance with the following timetable:

   (*a*) In the area west of the road from Baqa to Jaljulia and from there to the east of Kafr Qasim: within five weeks of the signature of the General Armistice Agreement now being negotiated at Rhodes between Israel and the Hashimite Jordan Kingdom.

   (*b*) In the area of Wadi Ara north of the line from Baqa to Zububa: within seven weeks of the signature of the General Armistice Agreement now being negotiated at Rhodes between Israel and the Hashimite Jordan Kingdom.

   (*c*) In all other areas: within fifteen weeks of the signature of the General Armistice Agreement now being negotiated at Rhodes between Israel and the Hashimite Jordan Kingdom.

4. Israel, for its part, has made similar changes for the benefit of the Hashimite Jordan Kingdom in other areas.

5. The Hashimite Jordan Kingdom agrees that the substitution of Iraqi troops by the Arab Legion in the sectors at present held by the former shall not take place until after the signing of the General Armistice Agreement now under negotiation at Rhodes. The Hashimite Jordan Kingdom guarantees for all Iraqi forces in Palestine and agrees that their numbers shall be included in any formula governing the reduction of forces provided for in the General Armistice Agreement now being negotiated at Rhodes as if they were forces of the Arab Legion.

6. It is agreed between the Parties that the armistice demarcation line to be inserted in the General Armistice Agreement now under negotiation at Rhodes shall be based on the positions held on the date of the cease-fire agreement concluded at Rhodes as certified by the observers of the United Nations Truce Supervision Organisation. The General Armistice Agreement concluded at Rhodes shall provide that the armistice demarcation line shall be subject to local rectifications which have been or may be agreed upon by the

parties hereto, such rectifications having the same force and effect as if they had been incorporated in full in the General Armistice Agreement.

7. The parties hereby agree that the General Armistice Agreement now under negotiation at Rhodes shall contain provisions for its revision by mutual consent at any time, and therefore that immediately after the signature of the General Armistice Agreement the present Agreement shall take effect as if it were a revision to the General Armistice Agreement.

8. In the case of villages affected by the terms of this agreement, their inhabitants shall be entitled to their full rights of residence, property and freedom. If such villagers decide to leave, they shall be entitled to take with them their livestock and other movable property and to receive without delay full compensation for their land which they leave behind.

9. Israel will pay to the Hashimite Jordan Kingdom the cost of building twenty kilometres of first-class road in compensation for the road between Tulkarem and Qalqiliya.

10. The Parties to this agreement shall establish a mixed commission which shall peg out the demarcation line provided for in Article 2 above. This commission shall consist of not less than two representatives of each Party and of a chairman appointed by the United Nations Chief of Staff.

11. This Agreement shall not be published except with the consent of both Parties, nor shall it in any way prejudice an ultimate political settlement between the Parties.

12. This Agreement is subject to ratification by the Prime Minister of the Hashimite Jordan Kingdom, such ratification to be communicated to the Government of Israel in writing not later than 30th March 1949. Failing such notification, this Agreement shall be null and void, and of no force or effect.

In faith whereof the undersigned representatives of the High Contracting Parties have signed hereunder.

Done at Shuneh, on the twenty-third day of March one thousand nine hundred and forty-nine.

For the Hashimite Jordan Kingdom
Falah el-Madadha
Hussein Siraj

For the State of Israel
Walter Eytan
Yigael Yadin
Moshe Dayan

APPENDIX 2

Agreement Between the Hashimite Jordan Kingdom and the State of Israel, 31 March 1949

1. It is agreed between the undersigned, duly authorized by their respective Governments, that the Agreement between the Hashimite Jordan Kingdom and the State of Israel of 23rd March 1949 shall be amended as follows:

(a) Article 4 is hereby amended to read as follows:
'Israel, for its part, has made similar changes for the benefit of the Hashimite Jordan Kingdom in the Hebron area, as delineated in blue ink on the map annexed hereto.'

(b) Article 7 is hereby deleted.

(c) Article 8 is hereby amended by the inclusion of the following provisions after the first sentence:
'Neither Israeli nor Transjordan forces shall enter or be stationed in such villages, in which local Arab police shall be organised for internal security purposes.'

(d) Article 11 is hereby amended to read as follows:
'This Agreement shall not in any way prejudice an ultimate political settlement between the Parties.'

(e) Article 12 is hereby deleted.

2. The present Agreement and the Agreement of 23rd March 1949 as amended by the present Agreement are to be interpreted and executed as instructions binding upon the Delegations of the State of Israel and the Hashimite Jordan Kingdom now negotiating a General Armistice Agreement at Rhodes, and their provisions are to be incorporated into the General Armistice Agreement as a condition of its signature by the representatives of the Parties.

3. The present Agreement and the Agreement of 23rd March 1949 shall be considered void upon the signature of the General Armistice Agreement referred to in paragraph 2 above, and their existence as documents will not be made public by either Party.

In faith whereof the undersigned representatives of the High Contracting Parties have signed hereunder on the thirtieth day of March one thousand nine hundred and forty-nine.

For the Hashimite Jordan Kingdom
Fawzi Mulki
A. Sudki el-Jundi

For the State of Israel
Walter Eytan
Yigael Yadin
Reuven Shiloah

APPENDIX 3

Israeli–Jordanian General Armistice Agreement, 3 April 1949

Preamble

The Parties to the present Agreement,

Responding to the Security Council resolution of 16 November 1948, calling upon them, as a further provisional measure under Article 40 of the Charter of the United Nations and in order to facilitate the transition from the present truce to permanent peace in Palestine, to negotiate an armistice;

Having decided to enter into negotiations under United Nations Chairmanship concerning the implementation of the Security Council resolution of 16 November 1948; and having appointed representatives empowered to negotiate and conclude an Armistice Agreement;

The undersigned representatives of their respective Governments, having exchanged their full powers found to be in good and proper form, have agreed upon the following provisions:

ARTICLE I

With a view to promoting the return of permanent peace in Palestine and in recognition of the importance in this regard of mutual assurances concerning the future military operations of the Parties, the following principles which shall be fully observed by both Parties during the armistice, are hereby affirmed:

1. The injunction of the Security Council against resort to military force in the settlement of the Palestine question shall henceforth be scrupulously respected by both Parties.

2. No aggressive action by the armed forces—land, sea or air—of either Party shall be undertaken, planned, or threatened against the people or the armed forces of the other; it being understood that the use of the term 'planned' in this context has no bearing on normal staff planning as generally practiced in military organisations.

3. The right of each Party to its security and freedom from fear of attack by the armed forces of the other shall be fully respected.

4. The establishment of an armistice between the armed forces of the two Parties is accepted as an indispensable step toward the liquidation of armed conflict and the restoration of peace in Palestine.

ARTICLE II

With a specific view to the implementation of the resolution of the Security Council of 16 November 1948, the following principles and purposes are affirmed:

1. The principle that no military or political advantage should be gained under the truce ordered by the Security Council is recognised.

2. It is also recognised that no provision of this Agreement shall in any way prejudice the rights, claims and positions of either Party hereto in the ultimate peaceful settlement of the Palestine question, the provisions of this Agreement being dictated exclusively by military considerations.

ARTICLE III

1. In pursuance of the foregoing principles and of the resolution of the Security Council of 16 November 1948, a general armistice between the armed forces of the two Parties—land, sea and air—is hereby established.

2. No element of the land, sea or air military or para-military forces of either Party, including non-regular forces, shall commit any warlike or hostile act against the military or para-military forces of the other Party, or against civilians in territory under the control of that Party; or shall advance beyond or pass over for any purpose whatsoever the Armistice Demarcation Lines set forth in Articles V and VI of this Agreement; or enter into or pass through the air space of the other Party.

3. No warlike act or act of hostility shall be conducted from territory controlled by one of the Parties to this Agreement against the other Party.

ARTICLE IV

1. The lines described in Articles V and VI of this Agreement shall be designated as the Armistice Demarcation Lines and are delineated in pursuance of the purpose and intent of the resolution of the Security Council of 16 November 1948.

2. The basic purpose of the Armistice Demarcation Lines is to delineate the lines beyond which the armed forces of the respective Parties shall not move.

3. Rules and regulations of the armed forces of the Parties, which prohibit civilians from crossing the fighting lines or entering the area between the lines, shall remain in effect after the signing of this Agreement with application to the Armistice Demarcation Lines defined in Articles V and VI.

ARTICLE V

1. The Armistice Demarcation Lines for all sectors other than the sector now held by Iraqi forces, shall be as delineated on the maps in Annex I to this Agreement, and shall be defined as follows:

(a) In the sector Kh Deir Arab (MR 1510–1574) to the northern terminus of the lines defined in the 30 November 1948 Cease-Fire Agreement for the Jerusalem area, the Armistice Demarcation Lines shall follow the Truce Lines as certified by the United Nations Truce Supervision Organisation.

(b) In the Jerusalem Sector, the Armistice Demarcation Lines shall correspond to the lines defined in the 30 November 1948 Cease-Fire Agreement for the Jerusalem area.

(c) In the Hebron–Dead Sea sector, the Armistice Demarcation Line shall be as delineated on Map 1 and marked (B) in Annex I to this Agreement.

(d) In the sector from a point on the Dead Sea (MR 1925–0958) to the southernmost tip of Palestine, the Armistice Demarcation Line shall be determined by existing military positions as surveyed in March 1949 by United Nations Observers, and shall run from north to south as delineated on Map 1 in Annex I to this Agreement.

ARTICLE VI

1. It is agreed that the forces of the Hashemite Jordan Kingdom shall replace the forces of Iraq in the sector now held by the latter forces, the intention of the Governnment of Iraq in this regard having been communicated to the Acting Mediator in the message of 20 March from the Foreign Minister of Iraq authorising the Delegation of the Hashemite Jordan Kingdom to negotiate for the Iraqi forces and stating that those forces would be withdrawn.

2. The Armistice Demarcation Line for the sector now held by Iraqi forces shall be as delineated on Map 1 in Annex I to this Agreement and marked (A).

3. The Armistice Demarcation Line provided for paragraph 2 of this Article shall be established in stages as follows, pending which the existing military lines may be maintained:

(a) In the area west of the road from Baqa to Jaljulia and thence to the east of Kafr Qasim: within five weeks of the date on which this Armistice Agreement is signed.

(b) In the area of Wadi Ara north of the line from Baqa to Zubeiba: within seven weeks of the date on which this Armistice Agreement is signed.

(c) In all other areas of the Iraqi sector: within fifteen weeks of the date on which this Armistice Agreement is signed.

4. The Armistice Demarcation Line in the Hebron–Dead Sea sector, referred to in paragraph c of Article V of this Agreement and marked (B) on Map 1 in Annex I, which involves substantial deviation from the existing military lines in favour of the forces of the Hashemite Jordan Kingdom, is designed to offset the modifications of the existing military lines in the Iraqi sector set forth in paragraph 3 of this Article.

5. In compensation for the road acquired between Tulkarem and Qalquiliya, the Government of Israel agrees to pay to the Government of the Hashemite Jordan Kingdom the cost of constructing twenty kilometres of first-class new road.

6. Wherever villages may be affected by the establishment of the Armistice Demarcation Line provided for in paragraph 2 of this Article, the inhabitants of such villages shall be entitled to maintain, and shall be protected in their full rights of residence, property and freedom. In the event any of the inhabitants should decide to leave their villages, they shall be entitled to take with them their livestock and other movable property, and to receive without delay full compensation for the land which they have left. It shall be prohibited for Israeli forces to enter or to be stationed in such villages, in which locally recruited Arab police shall be organised and stationed for internal security purposes.

7. The Hashemite Jordan Kingdom accepts responsibility for all Iraqi forces in Palestine.

8. The provisions of this Article shall not be interpreted as prejudicing, in any sense, an ultimate political settlement between the Parties to this Agreement.

9. The Armistice Demarcation Lines defined in Articles V and VI of this Agreement are agreed upon by the Parties without prejudice to future territorial settlements or boundary lines or to claims of either Party relating thereto.

10. Except where otherwise provided, the Armistice Demarcation Lines shall be established, including such withdrawal of forces as may be necessary for this purpose, within ten days from the date on which this Agreement is signed.

11. The Armistice Demarcation Lines defined in this Article and in Article V shall be subject to such rectifications as may be agreed upon by the Parties to this Agreement, and all such rectifications shall have the same force and effect as if they had been incorporated in full in this General Armistice Agreement.

ARTICLE VII

1. The military forces of the Parties to this Agreement shall be limited to defensive forces only in the areas extending ten kilometres from each side of the Armistice Demarcation Lines, except where geographical considerations make this impractical, as at the southernmost tip of Palestine and the coastal strip. Defensive forces permissible in each sector shall be as defined in Annex II to this Agreement. In the sector now held by Iraqi forces, calculations in the reduction of forces shall include the number of Iraqi forces in this sector.

2. Reduction of forces to defensive strength in accordance with the preceding paragraph shall be completed within ten days of the establishment of the Armistice Demarcation Lines defined in this Agreement. In the same way the removal of mines from mined roads and areas evacuated by either Party, and the transmission of plans showing the location of such minefields to the other Party shall be completed within the same period.

3. The strength of the forces which may be maintained by the Parties on each side of the Armistice Demarcation Lines shall be subject to periodical review with a view toward further reduction of such forces by mutual agreement of the Parties.

ARTICLE VIII

1. A Special Committee, composed of two representatives of each Party designated by the respective Governments, shall be established for the purpose of formulating agreed plans and arrangements designed to enlarge the scope of this Agreement and to effect improvements in its application.

2. The Special Committee shall be organised immediately following the coming into effect of this Agreement and shall direct its attention to the formulation of agreed plans and arrangements for such matters as either Party may submit to it, which, in any case, shall include the following, on which agreement in principle already exists: free movement of traffic on vital roads, including the Bethlehem and Latrun–Jerusalem roads; resumption of the normal functioning of the cultural and humanitarian institutions on Mount Scopus and free access thereto; free access to the Holy Places and cultural institutions and use of the cemetery on the Mount of Olives; resumption of operation of the Latrun pumping station; provision of electricity for the Old City; and resumption of operation of the railroad to Jerusalem.

3. The Special Committee shall have exclusive competence over such matters as may be referred to it. Agreed plans and arrangements formulated by it may provide for the exercise of supervisory functions by the Mixed Armistice Commission established in Article XI.

ARTICLE IX

Agreements reached between the Parties subsequent to the signing of this Armistice Agreement relating to such matters as further reduction of forces as contemplated in paragraph 3 of Article VII, future adjustments of the Armistice Demarcation Lines, and plans and arrangements formulated by the Special Committee established in Article VIII, shall have the same force and effect as the provisions of this Agreement and shall be equally binding upon the Parties.

ARTICLE X

An exchange of prisoners of war having been effected by special arrangement between the Parties prior to the signing of this Agreement, no further arrangements on this matter are required except that the Mixed Armistice Commission shall undertake to re-examine whether there may be any prisoners of war belonging to either Party which were not included in the previous exchange. In the event that prisoners of war shall be found to exist the Mixed Armistice Commission shall arrange for an early exchange of such prisoners. The Parties to this Agreement undertake to afford full co-operation to the Mixed Armistice Commission in its discharge of this responsibility.

ARTICLE XI

1. The executions of the provisions of this Agreement, with the exception of such matters as fall within the exclusive competence of the Special Committee

established in Article VIII, shall be supervised by a Mixed Armistice Commission composed of five members, of whom each Party to this Agreement shall designate two, and whose Chairman shall be the United Nations Chief of Staff of the Truce Supervision Organisation or a senior officer from the Observer personnel of that Organisation designated by him following consultation with both Parties to this Agreement.

2. The Mixed Armistice Commission shall maintain its headquarters at Jerusalem and shall hold its meetings at such places and at such times as it may deem necessary for the effective conduct of its work.

3. The Mixed Armistice Commission shall be convened in its first meeting by the United Nations Chief of Staff of the Truce Supervision Organisation not later than one week following the signing of this Agreement.

4. Decisions of Mixed Armistice Commission, to the extent possible, shall be based on the principle of unanimity. In the absence of unanimity, decisions shall be taken by majority vote of the members of the Commission present and voting.

5. The Mixed Armistice Commission shall formulate its own rules of procedure. Meetings shall be held only after due notice to the members by the Chairman. The quorum for its meetings shall be a majority of its members.

6. The Commission shall be empowered to employ Observers, who may be from among the military organisations of the Parties or from the military personnel of the United Nations Truce Supervision Organisation, or from both, in such numbers as may be considered essential to the performance of its functions. In the event United Nations Observers should be so employed, they shall remain under the command of the United Nations Chief of Staff of the Truce Supervision Organisation. Assignments of a general or special nature given to United Nations Observers attached to the Mixed Armistice Commission shall be subject to approval by the United Nations Chief of Staff or his designated representative on the Commission, whichever is serving as Chairman.

7. Claims or complaints presented by either Party relating to the application of this Agreement shall be referred immediately to the Mixed Armistice Commission through its Chairman. The Commission shall take such action on all such claims or complaints by means of its observation and investigation machinery as it may deem appropriate, with a view to equitable and mutually satisfactory settlement.

8. Where interpretation of the meaning of a particular provision of this Agreement, other than the Preamble and Articles I and II, is at issue, the Commission's interpretation shall prevail. The Commission, in its discretion and as the need arises, may from time to time recommend to the Parties modifications in the provisions of this Agreement.

9. The Mixed Armistice Commission shall submit to both Parties reports on its activities as frequently as it may consider necessary. A copy of each such report shall be presented to the Secretary-General of the United Nations for transmission to the appropriate organ or agency of the United Nations.

10. Members of the Commission and its Observers shall be accorded such freedom of movement and access in the area covered by this Agreement as the

Commission may determine to be necessary, provided that when such decisions of the Commission are reached by a majority vote United Nations Observers only shall be employed.

11. The expenses of the Commission, other than those relating to United Nations Observers, shall be apportioned in equal shares between the two Parties to this Agreement.

ARTICLE XII

1. The present Agreement is not subject to ratification and shall come into force immediately upon being signed.

2. This Agreement, having been negotiated and concluded in pursuance of the resolution of the Security Council of 16 November 1948 calling for the establishment of an armistice in order to eliminate the threat to the peace in Palestine and to facilitate the transition from the present truce to permanent peace in Palestine, shall remain in force until a peaceful settlement between the Parties is achieved, except as provided in paragraph 3 of this Article.

3. The Parties to this Agreement may, by mutual consent, revise this Agreement or any of its provisions, or may suspend its application, other than Articles I and III, at any time. In the absence of mutual agreement and after this Agreement has been in effect for one year from the date of its signing, either of the Parties may call upon the Secretary-General of the United Nations to convoke a conference of representatives of the two Parties for the purpose of reviewing, revising, or suspending any of the provisions of this Agreement other than Articles I and III. Participation in such conference shall be obligatory upon the Parties.

4. If the conference provided for in paragraph 3 of this Article does not result in an agreed solution of a point in dispute, either Party may bring the matter before the Security Council of the United Nations for the relief sought on the grounds that this Agreement has been concluded in pursuance of Security Council action toward the end of achieving peace in Palestine.

5. This Agreement is signed in quintuplicate, of which one copy shall be retained by each Party, two copies communicated to the Secretary-General of the United Nations for transmission to the Security Council and to the Conciliation Commission on Palestine, and one copy to the United Nations Acting Mediator on Palestine.

DONE at Rhodes, Island of Rhodes, Greece, on the third of April nineteen forty-nine in the presence of the United Nations Acting Mediator on Palestine and the United Nations Chief of Staff of the Truce Supervision Organisation.

For and on behalf of the Government of the Hashemite Jordan Kingdom	*For and on behalf of the Government of Israel*
A. Sudki El-jundi	Reuven Shiloah
Mohammed Mowaita	Moshe Dayan Sgan Alouf

APPENDIX 4

Treaty of Amity and Non-aggression Between the State of Israel and the Hashemite Jordan Kingdom, March 1950

WHEREAS on the third day of April, 1949, the Contracting Parties signed at Rhodes a General Armistice Agreement to remain in force until a peaceful settlement between the Parties is achieved,

AND WHEREAS the Parties now desire, in order to promote normal relations and as a further step toward a peaceful settlement, to reinforce the said General Armistice Agreement and extend the scope of mutual accord between them,

HAVE THEREFORE agreed to conclude the following Agreement of Amity and Non-Aggression and have accordingly appointed as their Plenipotentiaries

The State of Israel . . . .
The Hashemite Jordan Kingdom . . . .

who, after presentation of their full powers, found in good and due form, have agreed on the following provisions.

ARTICLE I

1. Each of the Contracting Parties undertakes not to resort to war or acts of armed violence or other acts of aggression or hostility against the other, or to invade territories under the control of the other, or to permit any territory under its control to serve as a base or to be used for passage for armed attack by a third party on the other.

2. If, on any occasion, there should arise between the Contracting Parties differences of opinion which they are unable to settle between themselves, they undertake to have recourse to the conciliatory and arbitral procedures offered under international law for the settlement thereof, or such other means of pacific settlement as shall be agreed upon by the Parties.

ARTICLE II

For the duration of this Agreement the Armistice Demarcation Line described in the said General Armistice Agreement shall remain in force subject to any modifications agreed to by both Parties in accordance with the terms of the said General Armistice Agreement. In order to reduce possible friction, the Contracting Parties agree to eliminate the various areas of 'no-man's land' the continued existence of which they consider undesirable.

ARTICLE III

The Contracting Parties are agreed upon the necessity for taking joint steps in order to protect the Holy Places of all faiths in Jerusalem and to ensure freedom of access thereto and freedom of worship without threat to the adherents of all faiths. A joint Declaration by the Contracting Parties in this regard is contained in Annex I to the present Agreement. The Contracting Parties further agree to offer requisite assurances to the United Nations regarding the inviolability of the Holy Places and the observance of the said Declaration.

ARTICLE IV

1. The Contracting Parties are agreed upon the desirability of establishing economic and commercial relations between them.

2. For the implementation of this Article economic and commercial accords shall be concluded between the Parties. Trade Delegates shall be exchanged between them not later than three months from the coming into force of this Agreement. They shall negotiate these economic and commercial accords and be responsible for their effective observance.

ARTICLE V

The Contracting Parties are agreed that all necessary steps shall be taken to ensure the resumption of the normal functioning of the cultural and humanitarian institutions on Mount Scopus and the use of the cemetery on the Mount of Olives and free access thereto, as well as the free movement of traffic on the Bethlehem–Jerusalem road, in accordance with Article VIII of the said General Armistice Agreement.

ARTICLE VI

1. Having regard to the purposes of this Agreement and in order to implement its provisions and to formulate the basis for a final peaceful settlement, the Contracting Parties hereby establish a Mixed Commission to be known as the Israel–Jordan Commission.

2. The Israel–Jordan Commission shall *inter alia*:

   (*a*) Examine all territorial problems outstanding between the Contracting Parties.

   (*b*) Consider and elaborate plans for the determination of rights to financial recompense and the assessment and payment thereof in respect of immovable property in Jerusalem which was abandoned by its owners as a consequence of the armed conflict.

   (*c*) Examine ways and means for the settlement of the just claims for compensation of persons permanently resident in the territory of either of the Contracting Parties for property abandoned by them in the territory of the other Contracting Party. The commission may consider the feasibility, in suitable cases, of the owners of such property in person, or by their duly authorised agents, being admitted to the territory of the other Party for the purpose of settling such claims. Should this not be found practicable, the Commission itself shall prepare plans for the final settlement of these claims.

(d) Devote its attention to the question of the establishment of a free zone in the Port of Haifa for the Hashemite Jordan Kingdom for commercial purposes.

(e) Examine measures for the full resumption of operations by the Palestine Electric Corporation and by the Palestine Potash Company Limited.

(f) Generally supervise the proper execution of the Present Agreement.

ARTICLE VII

1. The Commission established pursuant to Article VI hereof shall be composed of . . . representatives of each Party designated by the respective Governments.

2. This Commission has the power to appoint such sub-commissions as it deems necessary in order to make possible the expeditious completion of its task.

3. The Contracting Parties shall immediately nominate their representatives to the Commission, which shall hold its first meeting not later than seven days from the coming into force of this Agreement. Subsequent meetings shall take place upon the first and fifteenth days of each month thereafter, unless such dates fall on a Friday or on a Saturday, in which event the meeting will be postponed for not more than two days.

4. The Commission's headquarters shall be at Jerusalem.

5. The Commission and its sub-commissions shall establish their own rules of procedure.

6. Members of the Commission and of sub-commissions shall, while on the territory of the other Contracting Party, be granted the appropriate privileges and immunities.

ARTICLE VIII

The Contracting Parties agree that the Mixed Armistice Commission set up in accordance with the said General Armistice Agreement shall have no powers or functions in relation to the execution of this Agreement.

ARTICLE IX

This agreement shall enter into force immediately upon signature, and shall remain in force for a period of five years or for so long as the General Armistice

Agreement signed at Rhodes on 3 April, 1949, is in force, whichever period shall be the shorter.

ARTICLE X

A copy of this Agreement shall be communicated to the Secretary General of the United Nations for transmission to the appropriate organs of the United Nations.

ARTICLE XI

Nothing in the present agreement is intended to, or shall in any way, prejudice the rights and obligations which devolve, or may devolve, upon either of the Contracting Parties under the Charter of the United Nations.

IN FAITH WHEREOF the Plenipotentiaries of the Contracting Parties have signed the present Agreement and have hereunto affixed their seals.

Done in duplicate in the Hebrew, Arabic and English languages, all authentic, this . . . day of March, 1950, corresponding to the . . . day of Adar in the year 5710 since the creation of the world, and the . . . day of Jumada-l-ula in the year 1369 of the Hijra.

For the State of Israel   *For the Hashemite Jordan Kingdom*

Annex One

Joint declaration concerning the Holy Places, religious buildings and sites in Jerusalem

The Governments of Israel and of the Hashemite Jordan Kingdom,

CONSCIOUS of their responsibilities concerning the protection and preservation of the sanctuaries in Jerusalem of the three great religions;

SOLEMNLY UNDERTAKE by the provisions of the present Declaration to guarantee the protection and preservation of and free access to the Holy Places, religious buildings and sites of Jerusalem.

ARTICLE I

The free exercise of all forms of worship shall be guaranteed and ensured in accordance with the Declaration of Human Rights of 10 December, 1948, the Declaration of Independence of Israel and the Constitution of the Hashemite Jordan Kingdom.

ARTICLE II

The Holy Places, religious buildings and sites which were regarded as Holy Places, religious buildings and sites on 14 May 1948, shall be preserved and their sacred character protected. No act of a nature to profane that sacred character shall be permitted.

ARTICLE III

The rights in force on 14 May 1948 with regard to the Holy Places, religious buildings and sites shall remain in force.

The Governments of the Hashemite Jordan Kingdom and Israel undertake in particular to assure the safety of ministers of religion, those officiating in religious services and the members of religious orders and institutions, to allow them to exercise their ministries without hindrance; and to facilitate their communications both inside and outside the country in connexion with the performance of their religious duties and functions.

ARTICLE IV

The Governments of the Hashemite Jordan Kingdom and Israel undertake to guarantee freedom of access to the Holy Places, religious buildings and sites situated in the territory placed under their authority by the final peaceful settlement between them, or, pending that settlement, in the territory at present occupied by them under armistice agreements; and, pursuant to this undertaking, will guarantee right of entry and of transit to ministers of religion, pilgrims and visitors without distinction as to nationality or faith, subject only to considerations of national security, all the above in conformity with the *status quo* prior to 14 May 1948.

ARTICLE V

No form of taxation shall be levied in respect of any Holy Place, religious building or site which was exempt from such taxation on 14 May 1948.

No change in the incidence of any form of taxation shall be made which would either discriminate between the owners and occupiers of Holy Places, religious buildings and sites, or would place such owners and occupiers in a position less favourable in relation to the general incidence of that form of taxation than existed on 14 May 1948.

APPENDIX 5

Jordan's Comments on the Israeli Note of 16 April
1951

1. Regret that a little delay has taken place in this reply to the Note dated 16th April, 1951, from Mr. (R. Sh.) due to certain pre-occupations.

2. In reference to Para 1 of the above Note, it is fully agreed that under existing circumstances the best procedure to be adopted in the joint efforts to settle some of the outstanding problems between Jordan and Israel would be that the two parties would confine themselves, in the first instance, to the full implementation of the provisions of the General Armistice Agreement. It is also agreed that after the implementation of any Articles of that Agreement, which either party claims have not been properly put into effect, or which have not been implemented so far, it may be then possible to proceed with a wider discussion.

3. In adoption of the above principle, agreed to by both sides, it is the view of the Jordan Government that the scope of the present discussions should now be reduced to the application of Articles VI and VIII of the General Armistice Agreement.

4. In connection with these two Articles, the Jordan Government observes that the Israeli contention expressed in Paras. 3 & 5 of the Note under reference, constitutes a fundamental difference to the Jordan contention in the manner of understanding as well as in the *meaning* of the provisions of the said two Articles. This basic dispute appears to a far greater extent in the Israeli interpretation of the specific provisions relating to the Mount Scopus Institutions in Article VIII.

It is, therefore, considered that any attempt to reach agreement on these questions by the continuance of the present discussions, before the legal dispute, which appears to exist in the understanding of the two parties as to the correct meaning of the reference to these matters in Article VIII and Article VI, is decided one way or another, would serve no useful purpose, nor would it bring about any conclusive results.

In order to realise the mutual earnest desire of both sides to settle these questions in the right manner, and because the points at issue, particularly with regard to the reference to the institutions on Mount Scopus in Article VIII, are entirely *legal* ones, it becomes obviously essential that these points should be decided by a competent judicial tribunal. In the opinion of the Jordan Government, the International Court of Justice seems the proper Tribunal for such decision. Consequently, it is proposed that if early agreement on such legal procedure were reached by the two parties, their true desire to settle the points at issue would thus be more progressively achieved.

The Israeli Government is cordially invited to agree to this proposal, or to suggest, for consideration by the Jordan Government any alternative proposals they may wish to make for the settlement of the disputed legal points by a competent judicial authority.

30th April, 1951 (P.M.)

BIBLIOGRAPHY

ARCHIVES

Archive of the History of the Haganah, Tel Aviv
Ben-Gurion Archive, Sde Boker
Central Zionist Archives, Jerusalem
Israel State Archives, Jerusalem
Labour Party Archive, Beit Berl, Kfar Saba
National Archives, Washington, DC
Public Record Office, London

PRIVATE PAPERS

Arthur Creech Jones, Rhodes House, Oxford
Clark M. Clifford, Harry S. Truman Library, Independence, Missouri
Sir Alan Cunningham, Middle East Centre, St Antony's College, Oxford
Col. Desmond Goldie (privately held), Wallingford
Sir Henry Gurney, Middle East Centre, St Antony's College, Oxford
Dan Kurzman, Mugar Memorial Library, Boston University, Boston
James G. McDonald, Columbia University, New York
Elizabeth Monroe, Middle East Centre, St Antony's College, Oxford
Dean Rusk, National Archives, Washington DC

SELECT LIST OF PERSONS INTERVIEWED

Interviewee	Principal posts, 1947–1951	Date
AVIDAR, YOSEPH	Major-General, deputy commander of the Haganah; IDF, OC Northern Front	11 Aug. 1982
AVNER, GERSHON	Head of Western Europe Department, Foreign Ministry	27, 29 June, 4, 14 July 1982, 6 Sept. 1983
BAR-ON, MORDECHAI	Major, IDF, Southern Front	25 June 1986
CARMEL, MOSHE	Major-General, IDF, OC Northern Front	1 Sept. 1983
DANIN EZRA	Haganah intelligence service; Foreign Ministry	3 May, 15 Aug. 1982
DASKAL, AVRAHAM	Manager of the Palestine Electric Corporation, Naharayim	18 Sept. 1983
EYTAN, WALTER	Director-General, Foreign Ministry	28 Apr., 18 May 1982
GAZIT, MORDECHAI	Foreign Ministry	22 Aug. 1982, 2 Sept. 1983

GOLDIE, DESMOND	Colonel, Arab Legion, OC 1st Brigade	15 Sept., 12 Nov. 1985
HAREL, ISSER	Head of the Mossad	13 Aug. 1982
HARKABI, YEHOSHAFAT	Lieutenant-Colonel, liaison officer between IDF and Foreign Ministry; IDF staff officer for armistice affairs	11 June, 12, 17 Aug. 1982
AL-JUBURI, SALIH SAIB	Lieutenant-General, chief of staff, Iraqi army	12 Sept. 1986
KHALIDI, RASHID	Professor, nephew of Husayn Fakhri Khalidi, the secretary of the Arab Higher Committee	18 Nov. 1986
MARDAM-BEY, SALMA	Daughter of Syrian prime minister, Jamil Mardam	14 July 1986
NUSEIBA, ANWAR	Secretary of All-Palestine government, Gaza	18 July 1982
PAIL, MEIR	Colonel, IDF, Southern Front	9 June 1982
PALMON, YEHOSHUA	Haganah intelligence service; adviser on Arab affairs to the prime minister	31 May, 14 June, 18 Aug. 1982, 26 Sept. 1983
RAFAEL, GIDEON	Foreign Ministry	17, 27 May 1982, 28 Sept. 1983
SASSON, MOSHE	Middle East Department, Foreign Ministry	8 Sept. 1982, 23 Sept. 1983
SHAMIR, SHLOMO	Major-General, IDF, OC 7th Brigade	3 Aug. 1986
SHAREF, ZEEV	Secretary to the provisional government of Israel	24 May 1982
SHILOAH, BETTY	Foreign Ministry (wife of Reuven Shiloah)	18 Aug. 1982
SHIMONI, YAACOV	Deputy head, Middle East Department, Foreign Ministry	26 Aug. 1982, 26, 29 Sept. 1983
YADIN, YIGAEL	Major-General, chief of operations, chief of staff, IDF	19 Aug. 1982, 30 Aug. 1983

WORKS CITED

ABDULLAH, King of Transjordan, *Memoirs*, ed. Philip R. Graves (London: Jonathan Cape, 1950).
———— *My Memoirs Completed: 'Al Takmilah'* (London: Longman, 1978).
ABIDI, Aqil Hyder Hasan, *Jordan: A Political Study, 1948–1957* (London: Asia Publishing House, 1965).
EL-AREF, Aref, *The Disaster* (Arab.), 6 vols. (Beirut and Sidon: al-Maktaba al-Asriya, 1956–60).
ARLOZOROFF, Chaim, *Jerusalem Diary* (Heb.) (Tel Aviv: Mapai, 1949).

DE AZCARATE, Pablo, *Mission in Palestine 1948–1952* (Washington, DC: The Middle East Institute, 1966).

BAR-JOSEPH, Uri, 'The Relations Between Israel and Transjordan, November 1947–April 1949' (Heb.), MA thesis (Jerusalem, 1982).

BAR-ZOHAR, Michael, *Ben-Gurion: A Political Biography* (Heb.), 3 vols. (Tel Aviv: Am Oved, 1977).

BEGIN, Menachem, *The Revolt*, rev. edn. (New York: Dell, 1977).

BEN-GURION, David, *Letters to Paula* (London: Vallentine, Mitchell, 1971).

—— *Israel: A Personal History* (Tel Aviv: Sabra Books, 1972).

—— *My Talks with Arab Leaders* (Jerusalem: Keter Books, 1972).

—— *Memoirs* (Heb.), vol. iii, 1936, (Tel Aviv: Am Oved, 1973).

—— *Memoirs* (Heb.), vol. iv, 1937, (Tel Aviv: Am Oved, 1974).

—— *When Israel Fought in Battle* (Heb.) (Tel Aviv: Am Oved, 1975).

—— *War Diary: The War of Independence, 1948–1949* (Heb.), 3 vols., Gershon Rivlin and Elhanan Orren, eds. (Tel Aviv: Ministry of Defence, 1982).

BER, Israel, *Israel's Security: Yesterday, Today, Tomorrow* (Heb.) (Tel Aviv: Amikam, 1966).

BERNADOTTE, Folke, *To Jerusalem* (London: Hodder and Stoughton, 1951).

BIALER, Uri, 'David Ben-Gurion and Moshe Sharett: The Shaping of Two Political Conceptions in the Israeli–Arab Conflict' (Heb.), *Medina ve-Memshal* 1/2 (1971), 71–84.

BILBY, Kenneth W., *New Star in the Near East* (New York: Doubleday, 1951).

BRECHER, Michael, *The Foreign Policy System of Israel: Setting, Images, Process* (Oxford University Press, 1972).

BULLOCK, Alan, *Ernest Bevin: Foreign Secretary, 1945–1951* (London: Heinemann, 1983).

CAPLAN, Neil, *Futile Diplomacy*, vol. ii, *Arab–Zionist Negotiations and the End of the Mandate* (London: Frank Cass, 1986).

COHEN, Aharon, *Israel and the Arab World* (Boston: Beacon Press, 1970).

COHEN, Amnon, *Political Parties in the West Bank under the Jordanian Regime, 1949–1967* (Ithaca: Cornell University Press, 1982).

COHEN, Michael J., *Palestine and the Great Powers, 1945–1948* (Princeton University Press, 1982).

COHEN, Yeroham, *By Light and in Darkness* (Heb.) (Tel Aviv: Amikam, 1969).

COLLINS, Larry, and LAPIERRE, Dominique, *O Jerusalem* (New York: Pocket Books, 1972).

CONDIT, Kenneth W., *The History of the Joint Chiefs of Staff*, vol. ii, *1947–1949* (Washington, DC: Historical Division, Joint Secretariat, Joint Chiefs of Staff, 1976). Record Group 218, Records of the Joint Chiefs of Staff, The National Archives, Washington, DC.

COPELAND, Miles, *The Game of Nations* (London: Weidenfeld and Nicolson, 1969).

DANN, Uriel, *Studies in the History of Transjordan, 1920–1949: The Making of a State* (Boulder: Westview Press, 1984).

DAYAN, Moshe, *Story of My Life* (London: Weidenfeld and Nicolson, 1976).

—— *Milestones: An Autobiography* (Heb.) (Jerusalem: Edanim Publishers, 1976).

DEARDEN, Ann, *Jordan* (London: Robert Hale, 1958).

DOTHAN, Shmuel, *The Struggle for Eretz-Israel* (Heb.) (Tel Aviv: Ministry of Defence, 1981).

DUGDALE, Blanche, *Baffy: The Diaries of Blanche Dugdale, 1936–1947*, ed. N. A. Rose (London: Vallentine, Mitchell, 1973).

EBAN, Abba, *An Autobiography* (London: Weidenfeld and Nicolson, 1977).

EL-EDROOS, Syed Ali, *The Hashemite Arab Army, 1908–1979* (Amman: The Publishing Committee, 1980).

ELAM, Yigal, *Haganah: The Zionist Way to Power* (Heb.) (Tel Aviv: Zmora, Bitan, Modan, 1979).

ELIACHAR, Elie, 'An Attempt at Settlement in Transjordan', *New Outlook* 18/5 (1975), 71–5.

EYTAN, Walter, *The First Ten Years: A Diplomatic History of Israel* (London: Weidenfeld and Nicolson, 1958).

—— 'Three Nights at Shuneh', *Midstream* (Nov. 1980), 52–6.

FADDAH, Mohammad Ibrahim, *The Middle East in Transition: A Study of Jordan's Foreign Policy* (London: Asia Publishing House, 1974).

FLAPAN, Simha, *Zionism and the Palestinians* (London: Croom Helm, 1979).

FORSYTHE, David P., *United Nations Peacemaking: The Conciliation Commission for Palestine* (Baltimore: Johns Hopkins University Press, 1972).

FRIEDMAN, Isaiah, 'The Palestine Partition Plan of the Royal Commission, 1937, and the British–Zionist–Arab Triangle' (Heb.), in *Studies in Partition Plans, 1937–1947* (Sde Boker: The Ben-Gurion Institute, 1984), 9–20.

GABBAY, Rony E., *A Political Study of the Arab–Jewish Conflict: The Arab Refugee Problem* (Geneva: Librarie E. Droz, 1959).

GARCIA-GRANADOS, Jorge, *The Birth of Israel: The Drama as I Saw It* (New York: Alfred A. Knopf, 1948).

GAZIT, Mordechai, 'The Isolation of King Abdullah in his Struggle for a Settlement with Israel, 1949–1951' (Heb.), *Gesher* 113/2 (1986), 124–33.

GELBER, Yoav, 'The Negotiations Between the Jewish Agency and Transjordan, 1946–1948', *Studies in Zionism* 6/1 (1985), 53–83.

GLUBB, Sir John Bagot, *A Soldier with the Arabs* (London: Hodder and Stoughton, 1957).

——*The Changing Scenes of Life: An Autobiography* (London: Quartet Books, 1983).

GOLDMANN, Nahum, *The Autobiography of Nahum Goldmann: Sixty Years of Jewish Life* (New York: Holt, Rinehart and Winston, 1969).

GOLDNER, Werner Ernest, 'The Role of Abdullah Ibn Husain, King of Jordan, in Arab Politics, 1914–1951', Ph.D. thesis (Stanford, 1954).

AL-HASHIMI, Taha, *The Memoirs of Taha al-Hashimi, 1942–1955*, vol. ii, *Syria, Iraq, Palestine* (Arab) (Beirut: Dar al-Talia 1978).

AL-HAWARI, Muhammad Nimer, *The Secret of the Catastrophe* (Arab.) (Nazareth, 1955).

HIRST, David, *The Gun and the Olive Branch: The Roots of Violence in the Middle East* (London: Faber and Faber, 1977).

HOROWITZ, David, *In the Service of an Emergent State* (Heb.) (Tel Aviv: Schocken, 1951).

HUREWITZ, J. C., *The Struggle for Palestine* (New York: Schocken Books, 1976).

AL-HUSAYNI, Muhammad Amin, *Facts About the Palestine Question* (Arab.) (Cairo: Dar al-Kitab al-Arabi, 1956).

IRAQ, *Report of the Parliamentary Committee of Inquiry on the Palestine Problem* (Arab.) (Baghdad: The Government Press, 1949).

ISRAEL DEFENCE FORCES, *History of the War of Independence* (Heb.) (IDF History Branch: Maarahot, 1959).

ISRAEL STATE ARCHIVES, *Provisional State Council: Protocols, 18 April–13 May 1948* (Heb.) (Jerusalem, 1978).

———— *Documents on the Foreign Policy of Israel (DFPI)* (Jerusalem), vol. i, *14 May–30 September 1948* (1981); vol. ii, *October 1948–April 1949* (1984); vol. iii, *Armistice Negotiations with the Arab States, December 1948–July 1949* (1983); vol. iv, *May–December 1949* (1986).

———— and CENTRAL ZIONIST ARCHIVES, *Political and Diplomatic Documents, December 1947–May 1948* (Jerusalem, 1979).

JOHN, Robert, and HADAWI, Sami, *The Palestine Diary*, vol. i, *1914–1945*, vol. ii, *1945–1948* (Beirut: The Palestine Research Center, 1970).

JORDAN, Ministry of Foreign Affairs, *The Jordan White Book on Greater Syria* (Arab.) (Amman, 1947).

AL-JUBURI, Salih Saib, *The Palestine Misfortune and its Political and Military Secrets* (Arab.) (Beirut: Dar al-Kutub, 1970).

KAZZIHA, Walid, 'The Political Evolution of Transjordan', *Middle Eastern Studies* 15/2 (1979), 239–58.

KEDOURIE, Elie, *In the Anglo-Arab Labyrinth: The McMahon–Husayn Correspondence and Its Interpretations 1914–1939* (Cambridge University Press, 1976).

KHALIDI, Walid, ed., *From Haven to Conquest: Readings in Zionism and the Palestine Problem until 1948* (Beirut: Institute of Palestine Studies, 1971).

———— 'The Arab Perspective', in Louis and Stookey, eds., *The End of the Palestine Mandate* (London: I. B. Tauris, 1986).

KHALIL, Muhammad, *The Arab States and the Arab League*, 2 vols. (Beirut: Khayats, 1962).

KHOURI, Fred J., *The Arab-Israeli Dilemma*, 2nd edn. (New York: Syracuse University Press, 1976).

KIMCHE, Jon, *Seven Fallen Pillars* (London: Secker and Warburg, 1950).

———— and David, *Both Sides of the Hill* (London: Secker and Warburg, 1960).

KIRKBRIDE, Alec Seath, *A Crackle of Thorns* (London: John Murray, 1956).

———— *From The Wings: Amman Memoirs 1947–1951* (London: Frank Cass, 1976).

KISCH, F. H., *Palestine Diary* (London: Victor Gollancz, 1938).

KUBBAH, Muhammad Mahdi, *Memoirs* (Arab.) (Beirut: Dar al-Talia, 1965).

KURZMAN, Dan, *Genesis 1948: The First Arab–Israeli War* (London: Vallentine, Mitchell, 1972).

LAWRENCE, T. E., *Seven Pillars of Wisdom* (London: Jonathan Cape, 1935).

LEVIN, Harry, *Jerusalem Embattled* (London: Vicor Gollancz, 1950).

Louis, Wm. Roger, *The British Empire in the Middle East, 1945–1951: Arab Nationalism, The United States, and Postwar Imperialism* (Oxford: Clarendon Press, 1984).

——— 'British Imperialism and the End of the Palestine Mandate' in Louis and Stookey (eds.) (1986).

——— and Stookey, Robert W., eds., *The End of the Palestine Mandate* (London: I. B. Tauris, 1986).

Lucas, Noah, *The Modern History of Israel* (London: Weidenfeld and Nicolson, 1974).

Lunt, James, *Glubb Pasha: A Biography* (London: Harvill Press, 1984).

Luttwak, Edward, and Horowitz, Dan, *The Israeli Army* (London: Allen Lane, 1975).

McDonald, James G., *My Mission in Israel, 1948–1951* (New York: Simon and Schuster, 1951).

McGhee, George, *Envoy to the Middle World: Adventures in Diplomacy* (New York: Harper and Row, 1983).

Mahmoud, Amin Abdullah, 'King Abdullah and Palestine: An Historical Study of His Role in the Palestine Problem from the Creation of Transjordan to the Annexation of the West Bank, 1921–1950', Ph.D. thesis (Washington, DC: Georgetown University, 1972).

al-Majali, Haza, *My Memoirs* (Arab.) (Beirut: Dar al Ilm lil-Malayin, 1960).

Marlowe, John, *The Seat of Pilate: An Account of the Palestine Mandate* (London: The Cresset Press, 1959).

Meir, Golda, *My Life* (London: Weidenfeld and Nicolson, 1975).

Monroe, Elizabeth, 'Mr Bevin's "Arab Policy"', St Antony's Papers, no. 2, *Middle Eastern Affairs*, ed. Albert Hourani (London: Chatto and Windus, 1961), 9–48.

——— *Britain's Moment in the Middle East, 1914–1971* (London: Chatto and Windus, 1981).

Morgan, Kenneth O., *Labour in Power, 1945–1951* (Oxford: Clarendon Press, 1984).

Morris, Benny, 'The Crystallization of Israeli Policy Against a Return of the Arab Refugees, April–December 1948', *Studies in Zionism* 6/1 (1985).

Morris, James, The Hashemite Kings (London: Faber and Faber, 1959).

Muhafaza, Ali, *Jordanian–British Relations, 1921–1951* (Arab.) (Beirut: Dar al-Nahar, 1973).

Musa, Sulayman, and al-Madi, Munib, *The History of Jordan in the Twentieth Century* (Arab.) (Amman, 1959).

Nachmani, Amikam, 'Middle East Listening Post: Eliyahu Sasson and the Israeli Legation in Turkey, 1949–1952', *Studies in Zionism* 6/2 (1985), 263–85.

Nakdimon, Shlomo, *Altalena* (Heb.) (Jerusalem: Edanim, 1978).

Narkiss, Uzi, *The Liberation of Jerusalem* (Heb.) (Tel Aviv: Am Oved, 1977).

Nashashibi, Nasir al-Din, *Who Killed King Abdullah?* (Arab.) (Kuwait: Manshurat al-Anba, 1980).

Nasser, Gamal Abdul, 'Memoirs of the First Palestine War', trans. and annot. Walid Khalidi, *Journal of Palestine Studies* 2/2 (1973), 3–32.

NEUMANN, Emanuel, *In the Arena: An Autobiographical Memoir* (New York: Herzl Press, 1976).

NEVO, Joseph, *Abdullah and the Arabs of Palestine* (Heb.) (Tel Aviv: Shiloah Institute, 1975).

—— 'Abdullah and the Arabs of Palestine', *Wiener Library Bulletin*, 31/45–6 (1984), 51–62.

NIMRI, Kamal T., 'Abdullah Ibn al-Hussain: A Study in Political Leadership', Ph.D. thesis (London, 1977).

NOVOMEYSKY, M. A., *Given to Salt: The Struggle for the Dead Sea Concession* (London: Max Parrish, 1958).

O'BALLANCE, Edgar, *The Arab–Israeli War, 1948* (London: Faber and Faber, 1956).

OVENDALE, Ritchie, *The English-Speaking Alliance: Britain, the United States, the Dominions and the Cold War, 1945–1951* (London: Allen and Unwin, 1985).

PAIL, Meir, 'The Problem of Arab Sovereignty in Palestine, 1947–1949' (Heb.), *Zionism* 3 (1973), 439–89.

—— 'The Zionist–Israeli Strategy on the Jerusalem Question in the War of Independence' (Heb.), *Chapters in the History of Jeruselem in Modern Times* (Jerusalem: Yad Ben Zvi, 1976).

—— 'Political Constraints on Military Moves' (Heb.), *Davar* 30 Apr. 1979.

PAPPÉ, Ilan, 'British Foreign Policy Towards the Middle East, 1948–1951: Britain and the Arab–Israeli Conflict', D.Phil. thesis (Oxford, 1984).

—— 'Moshe Sharett, David Ben-Gurion and the "Palestinian Option", 1948–1956', *Studies in Zionism* 7/1 (1987), 77–96.

PERETZ, Don, *Israel and the Palestine Arabs* (Washington, DC: The Middle East Institute, 1958).

PLASCOV, Avi, *The Palestinian Refugees in Jordan, 1948–1957* (London: Frank Cass, 1981).

PORATH, Yehoshua, *The Emergence of the Palestine-Arab National Movement*, vol. i, *1918–1929* (London: Frank Cass, 1974).

—— *The Palestine-Arab National Movement*, vol. ii, *1929–1939: From Riots to Rebellion* (London: Frank Cass, 1977).

—— *In Search of Arab Unity, 1930–1945* (London: Frank Cass, 1986).

AL-QAWUQJI, Fawzi, 'Memoirs, 1948', pt. ii, *Journal of Palestine Studies* 2/1 (1972), 3–33.

ROSE, N. A., *The Gentile Zionists: A Study in Anglo-Zionist Diplomacy, 1929–1939* (London: Frank Cass, 1973).

RUBIN, Barry, *The Arab States and the Palestine Conflict* (New York: Syracuse University Press, 1981).

AL-RUSAN, Mahmud, *Battles of Bab el-Wad and Latrun* (Arab.) (n.p.: 1950).

SAFRAN, Nadav, *From War to War: The Arab–Israeli Confrontation, 1948–1967* (Indianapolis: Pegasus, 1969).

SASSON, Eliahu, *On the Road to Peace* (Heb.) (Tel Aviv: Am Oved, 1978).

SCHUEFTAN, Dan, *A Jordanian Option* (Heb.) (Yad Tabcnkin: Hakibbutz Hameuhad, 1986).

SEALE, Patrick, *The Struggle for Syria* (London: Oxford University Press, 1965).

SEGEV, Tom, *1949: The First Israelis* (Heb.) (Jerusalem: Domino Press, 1984).

SELLA, Avraham, *From Contacts to Negotiations: The Relations of the Jewish Agency and the State of Israel with King Abdullah, 1946–1950* (Heb.) (Tel Aviv: Shiloah Institute, 1986).

SHALTIEL, David, *Jerusalem 1948* (Heb.) (Tel Aviv: Ministry of Defence, 1981).

SHAREF, Zeev, *Three Days* (London: W. H. Allen, 1962).

SHARETT, Moshe, *At the Gate of the Nations, 1946–1949* (Heb.) (Tel Aviv: Am Oved, 1958).

———— *Political Diary* (Heb.) 5 vols. (Tel Aviv: Am Oved), vol. i, *1936*, (1968); vol. ii, *1937*, (1971); vol. iii, *1938*, (1972); vol. iv, *1939*, (1974); vol. v, *1940–2*, (1979).

AL-SHARIF, Kamil Ismail, *The Muslim Brotherhood in the Palestine War* (Arab.) (Cairo: Dar al-Kitab al-Arabi, 1951).

SHEFFER, Gabriel, 'Resolution *vs.* Management of the Middle East Conflict: A Re-examination of the Confrontation Between Moshe Sharett and David Ben-Gurion', *Jerusalem Papers on Peace Problems*, no. 32 (Jerusalem: The Magness Press, 1980).

SHIMONI, Yaacov, 'The Arabs and the Approaching War with Israel, 1945–1948' (Heb.) *Hamizrah Hehadash* 47/3 (1962), 191–211.

SHLAIM, Avi, *The United States and the Berlin Blockade, 1948–1949: A Study in Crisis Decision-Making* (Berkeley: University of California Press, 1983).

———— 'Britain, the Berlin Blockade and the Cold War', *International Affairs* 60/1 (1983–4), 1–14.

———— 'Conflicting Approaches to Israel's Relations with the Arabs: Ben-Gurion and Sharett, 1953–1956', *The Middle East Journal* 37/2 (1983), 180–201.

———— 'Husni Zaim and the Plan to Resettle Palestinian Refugees in Syria', *Journal of Palestine Studies* 15/4 (1986), 68–80.

———— Peter Jones, Keith Sainsbury, *British Foreign Secretaries Since 1945* (Newton Abbot: David and Charles, 1977).

SHWADRAN, Benjamin, 'Jordan Annexes Arab Palestine', *Middle Eastern Affairs* 1/4 (1950), 99–111.

———— *Jordan: A State of Tension* (New York: Council for Middle Eastern Affairs Press, 1959).

SOFER, Naim, 'The Absorption of the West Bank into the Jordanian Kingdom' (Heb.), *Hamizrah Hehadash* 3/23 (1955), 189–96.

STEIN, Kenneth W., *The Land Question in Palestine, 1917–1939* (Chapel Hill: North Carolina University Press, 1984).

SUSSER, Asher, *Between Jordan and Palestine: A Political Biography of Wasfi al-Tall* (Heb.) (Tel Aviv: Hakibbutz Hameuhad, 1983).

AL-TALL, Abdullah, *The Palestine Tragedy* (Arab.) (Cairo: Dar al-Qalam, 1959).

TEVETH, Shabtai, *Ben-Gurion and the Palestinian Arabs: From Peace to War* (New York: Oxford University Press, 1985).

TOUVAL, Saadia, *The Peace Brokers: Mediators in the Arab–Israeli Conflict, 1948–1979* (Princeton University Press, 1982).

UNITED STATES, Department of State, *Foreign Relations of the United States (FRUS)* (Washington, DC: Government Printing Office), *1948*, vol. v (1976); *1949*, vol. vi (1977); *1950*, vol. v (1978); *1951*, vol. v (1982).

VATIKIOTIS, P. J., *Politics and the Military in Jordan: A Study of the Arab Legion, 1921–1957* (London: Frank Cass, 1967).

WEISGAL, Meyer, ed., *Chaim Weizmann: Statesman, Scientist, Builder of the Jewish Commonwealth* (New York: Dial Press, 1944).

WEIZMANN, Chaim, *Trial and Error* (London: Hamish Hamilton, 1949).

WILSON, Mary Christina, 'King Abdullah of Jordan: A Political Biography', D.Phil. thesis (Oxford, 1984).

INDEX

Note: 'Abdullah, Amir of Transjordan' is abbreviated to 'Abd.'; 'Britain/British' to 'Br.'; 'Israel/Israeli/Israelis' to 'Isr.'; 'Jordan' to 'Jor.'; 'Palestine' to 'P.'; 'Transjordan' to 'Tr.'; and 'Zionist movement/Zionist' to 'Zion.'

Index compiled by Peva Keane

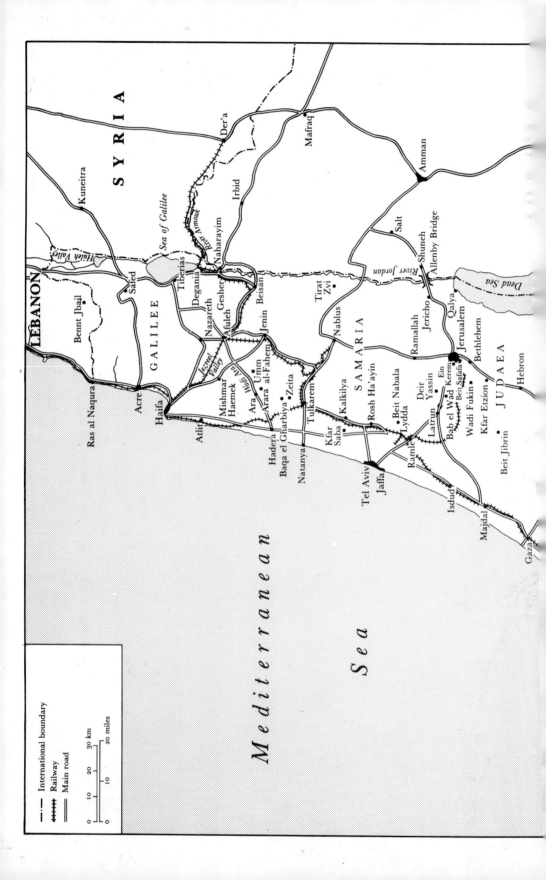